# Contemporary Systems Thinking

*Series Editor:*
Robert L. Flood
Maastricht School of Management
The Netherlands

More information about this series at http://www.springer.com/series/5807

Janet McIntyre-Mills · Norma Romm
Yvonne Corcoran-Nantes
Editors

# Balancing Individualism and Collectivism

## Social and Environmental Justice

Springer

*Editors*
Janet McIntyre-Mills
School of Social and Policy Studies
Flinders University
Adelaide, SA
Australia

Yvonne Corcoran-Nantes
Discipline of Women's Studies, College of Humanities, Arts and Social Sciences
Flinders University
Adelaide, SA
Australia

Norma Romm
Department of Adult Basic Education
University of South Africa
Pretoria
South Africa

ISSN 1568-2846
Contemporary Systems Thinking
ISBN 978-3-319-58013-5 ISBN 978-3-319-58014-2 (eBook)
DOI 10.1007/978-3-319-58014-2

Library of Congress Control Number: 2017939322



Printed on acid-free paper

This Springer imprint is published by Springer Nature
The registered company is Springer International Publishing AG
The registered company address is: Gewerbestrasse 11, 6330 Cham, Switzerland

*We hope that the contributions will provide ideas for exploring ways to live better lives through enhancing ethical policy making and praxis to address social, economic and environmental justice as a priority.*
*The designs of policy responses and the terms of reference need to appreciate that human beings are interconnected living systems reliant and dependent on ecological systems in which we are a strand, but which we can shape in ways that are positive or negative.*

# Foreword

**Reynaldo Treviño-Cisneros**

## Ethics and the Anthropocene

## Introduction

The Anthropocene denotes the time period in which the global effects of human activity on the atmospheric, geologic, hydrologic, biospheric and other earth system processes is both apparent and measurable. For Crutzen (2006, 13–18) this represents a new geological epoch. Governing the Anthropocene therefore, may have the following implications: conducting the evolution of planet Earth through human intervention in interactive, properly creative ways over its components: flora, fauna and inanimate things, in order to produce harmony among them, and to secure sustainability of conditions adequate for supporting and expanding biodiversity, intelligent life and the prolonged wellbeing of all living species.

This perspective presupposes that human responsibility is inherent to making good decisions and that a complementary processing of thought and action to maintain attitudes of discernment and commitment is essential. Thus, for it to be executed, this governance requires continuous reflection with respect to achieved knowledge; development of pertinent rewarding skills; design of alternatives for action and foresight into their likely consequences. This would be achieved from a reasonable human standpoint which takes into account an explicit consideration of the values inspiring the successive steps of the transformation of reality. In other words, this process requires the application of both individual and collective learning.

Interconnections will naturally exist. But these connections need to be analyzed for positive or negative contributions. Nonetheless, a focal point of interest stands in trying to insert *positive feed forward* by selecting inputs for the whole Earth system and for the cross-fertilization of its subsystems. Each subsystem has to operate in order to produce what Earth, as a whole, living entity, needs to maintain itself, to enrich its beauty, and to stir up emergent properties useful to its components that can ultimately materialize into coherent states of splendour.

Is destruction a necessary step to attain what *governing the Anthropocene* truly implies? We would naturally wish that we could keep evolution on a developing path where the decay and loss of components could be considered natural, or at least accepted as proportionate transitions necessary to reach superior states of being. We also need hope to maintain experimentation in development. Thus, we need to know what a superior state of being means, or at least have some appreciation of our developing state as being better or improved when compared to past states of being, i.e., that 'good properties' should have developed in our planet Earth through the passing of time.

## Going Deeper

'Anthropocene' is the widely accepted term for the last millennia of the Holocene era of the evolution of the universe, beginning after the rise of agriculture as the lifestyle model in human communities that replaced hunting and gathering for survival. This transformation to produce the daily necessary nurturing goods for groups of men, women and children, initiated a revolutionary change in the Earth's landscape that continues to this day. A dedication to agricultural activities was a less dangerous organization of collective daily activities than hunting and gathering. It eliminated the separation of men from women and children during hunting activities and almost permanently secured the provision of food and better conditions for physical and biological reproduction. Since then, the human race has put in motion many relevant processes that can be observed and measured, which in turn have induced a remarkable change in the configuration of our planet.

In terms of demography, there has been an exponential increase in human population all over the world, close to 7.25 billion dwellers in 2015, wherein most are concentrated in cities creating a large scale demand for the use of natural resources and of services within the urban environment. Many rural areas remain with a few poor people who suffer from scarce access to goods and services to facilitate their lives and render them better conditions for living. Migration from farms to more populated centres leaves behind the value of considering Earth a natural environment that offered humans many opportunities to appreciate the grandeur of our Common Home, and it erodes the sense of cohesion and interdependence with our environment. Accelerated depletion of the necessary resources for living, such as fresh water, fertile soil and forests, and the human abuse of unclean sources of energy have induced a likely irreversible process of climate change that is greatly affecting our milieu.

In addition, climate change is triggering floods; droughts; the impossibility of the seas to absorb the carbon dioxide produced by the use of fossil fuels for industry and transportation; the disappearance of the arctic ice, gigantic beds with noxious liberation of methane and other gases; the rising up of sea levels that might extinguish insular countries; more harmful meteorological events all over the world such as storms and tornados, and the elevation of the average temperature of the planet past limits that might become irreversible.

The specialization and integration of knowledge by humans has increased, but the former is overwhelming the latter. The need to complement both has resulted in humans having a sense of a totality going in the right or wrong direction many times along evolution. Nowadays, it seems that philosophy with its parts: the theory of knowledge, anthropology, cosmology, ethics, and the prevalence of transcendental thought (the comprehension of the origin of all that exists) over the comprehension of mere isolated phenomena have unfortunately lost attraction to our minds. The segmented studies of abstract and natural sciences and their framing outside the humanist disciplines: history, art, psychology, economy, sociology, communication and politics, have allowed the achievement of very useful and important human skills by individuals and societies. They generate awe every day through communication and marketing, and already include genetic transformations through biotechnology as well as the manipulation of physical materials at nano-scale dimension in order to attain better conditions of life for the human race. Nonetheless, many of these goals arrived with a set of side effects. We have forgotten the vast inequalities in human rights appropriation. We have abided by the sense of commitment with the future generations and their environment. We have unlearned past and present lessons to help us avoid massive harm and ruination in the future. We are now expecting technology to solve what the lack of foresight has unfortunately brought. We left equity as an implicit unsolvable problematic. Human beings do not ponder what a Common Rule of Law could do for the benefit of the Earth as a whole. Respect for diversity, as necessary as it may be, does not mean that people of different cultures cannot recognize how all living beings want to be treated.

Cooperation among human beings of different countries and social groupings within them is just beginning—but with ample backlash—to induce changes within each culture and to spread beyond different cultures. The creation of nation-states, as preferred political entities for groups of populations inside certain delimited territories, introduced the sense of values connected to traditions, place of origin, beliefs, language, art and ordinary habits of people, to convey an idea of appurtenance within a manageable set of variables. However, it has also overemphasized the value of diversity by introducing competitiveness in the development process of countries. The *standard of living* substituted the *art of living*. We began to think that we needed all the goods and services enjoyed by the powerful people on Earth. A misunderstanding of the particular mission of every human being dissolved the longing for communion with Earth and all that exists. Nevertheless, the ideas of complementation and interdependence began to change what was apparently settled. We are relational beings, not isolated units. We know that love is a vehement desire for every one of us. Thus, cooperation should become our next goal in terms of evolution. If we understand and promote cooperation, then a different dissipative social structure will be evident sooner than we can imagine.

## Proposals Derived From the Ethics Implied in Governing the Anthropocene

By now, we understand that the last part of the Holocene era has been characterized by a massive intervention of human beings over the components (or subsystems) of our planet. These transformations have influenced life on Earth in different, radical ways. Some interventions, such as world wars, agropecuarian, mining and industrial production, as well as the territorial concentration-dispersion pattern of living species induced by humans have notably affected the supporting life systems of the Earth: fresh water, available energy, quantity of reserves of natural non-renewable resources, forest and sea ecological subsystems, causing great damage to humans, animals and plants. We have directly experienced the loss of some valuable species among its fauna. Research has confirmed that other species of fauna and flora are endangered or in peril of extinction. The sustainability of Earth needs urgent attention if we are to understand that the following generations have the right to receive our planet in similar conditions to those we have enjoyed during our life span, if not better.

Because of our actions through human history, the configuration of Earth has transformed in positive and negative ways. We need to discern between both carefully. We need to eliminate harmful interventions and promote positive ones. This is the 'ethos' of mankind. We must praise and honour it. Awareness and responsibility, both at the individual and collective levels, are inextricably required.

In 2013, Bethania Arango Hisijara and I, with the kind editorial help of Kenneth C. Bausch of the Institute for 21st Century Agoras, published the first volume of the monograph series, *A Social Systems Approach to Global Problems.*[1] In this monograph, we developed an articulated strategy to cope with the 15 monumental global challenges postulated in 2010 by Millennium Project researchers Jerome C. Glenn, Theodore J. Gordon, and Elizabeth Florescu.[2] These researchers have led a Delphi study since 1996 that included the participation of more than 3000 people around the world. Every year, this survey has been updated and the number of people who have participated in it has increased. Taking this study and combining it with the 49 Continuous Critical Problems conceptualized in 1970 by the great planner Hasan Ozbekhan in his paper *The Predicament of Mankind* presented to the Club of Rome,[3] Bethania and I, with the aid of CognisCcope II™ software, mapped a vision of the actions to solve that set of problems, which unfortunately, still remain. We assert that this articulated set of actions constitute a global strategy that could work to solve the global problematic. However, we also felt compelled to search the point of view of diverse local, national and international groups of stakeholders, who would also be interested in discussing the whole issue and arrive at their own conclusions. To that end, we recommend for future works the use of the methodology of Structured Dialogic Design (Christakis and Bausch 2006[4]; Christakis and Flanagan 2013[5]), because we consider that this methodology can be used successfully to manifest each group's own vision and to make the contents of possible new insights explicit.

Elaborating further on the proposals arising from our research, we can approach the extraordinary complexity of *governing the Anthropocene*. Among a set of 60 actions, Bethania and I identified 20 as driving factors to secure the global democratic organization of a wide array of human activities. Incorporating democracy as an omnipresent trait of collective life is the best human way to cope with local, regional, national and global problematic, in spite of the many difficulties implied by the different degrees of comprehension of reality.

In the following paragraphs, I will present a proposal: We need to establish a common global value system that incorporates the following guiding principles:

- Global sustainable development
- Equity
- Peace
- Wellbeing
- Gender equality
- Mutual respect for cultural differences, and
- Harmony

The above statement is comprehensive and involves the necessary care for preserving our planet from dysfunctionality or destruction of its life-supporting ecosystems.

Since several of these guiding principles can seem very abstract in nature, let us clarify one of them, harmony, as it could eventually encompass all the others. Harmony, refers to human relationships that praise permanent trust; solidarity in cases of disaster; love for complementarity; permanent inclination to eradicate poverty and sickness; tuning in with continuous improvement of life conditions; enriched beauty of human settlements; an always higher state of conviviality; respect and honour for beings other than human; continued cultural development; preservation of the hereditary treasures of the past, and, recapitulating, sensibility to the signs of the times. A good metaphor for 'harmony' as a development goal is the beautiful emission of glorious music played by a symphonic orchestra that replenishes the ears and heart of its listeners. In order for that to happen, multiple factors have to come together in mutually enhancing ways: energy of the musicians, multiple individual efforts, numerous rehearsals, beautiful and original composition scores, the synchronization of many different players and their instruments, a magisterial conduction as a service for modulation and excellence, enthusiasm, everyone's best effort during the concert, and the arousal of sighs from the public. The unity of these elements in one single presentation is a fine expression of 'harmony'. We should find their correspondence in what we mean by 'sustainable development'.

Since the creation of the Club of Rome in approximately 1970, the need for a holistic conceptualization of the world's problematic took form in the minds of scientists and planners first, and later in those of many people. Some of the people involved tried to design strategies that could overcome the challenges presented to humankind in a collective yet systematic way. Our planet Earth began to be conceptualized as a web of intrinsically interrelated facts along its pattern of evolution.

Were those facts completely separate from each other? Were those facts connecting each other in such a way that anything occurring in one corner of the planet exerted a measurable influence over the rest of the facts involved in ulterior stages of evolution? Could a fact or group of facts influencing Earth enter in action irreversibly, and bring it to an unstable and degrading form of existence? Are humans responsible for contributing to the harmony or to the ruination of Earth? Thinking of today's global conditions, which of the consequences would be the most likely to occur? How can we become responsible for Earth's sustainability as a whole?

From time to time, these questions have entered the minds and hearts of social leaders and members of society, particularly when they joined to cooperate with many others in order to change what they had perceived, understood or judged as wrong or unfair towards future progenies about the actual state of affairs.

This ethical manifesto has been an attempt to offer proposals to address those questions, for the benefit of Earth as a whole entangled Web, which is in the ongoing movement. To *govern the Anthropocene,* we offer what we believe are impartial, honest and applicable answers generated by an ever-increasing number of communities that can finally make a difference in re-directing Earth's evolution to its most harmonious path of development.

## References

Christakis AN, Bausch KC (2006) How people harness their collective wisdom and power to construct the future in co-laboratories of democracy. Information Age Publishing Inc., USA

Crutzen PJ (2006) The anthropocene. In: Ehlers E, Thomas K (eds) Earth system science in the Anthropocene. Springer, Berlin Heidelberg

Flanagan T and Christakis AN (2010) The talking point: creating an environment for exploring complex meaning. Information Age Publishing Inc., USA

Glenn J, Gordon T, Florescu E (2010) State of the future. The Millennium Project, USA

Ozbekhan H (1970) The predicament of mankind. 19 Oct 2010, http://sunsite.utk.edu/FINS/loversofdemocracy/Predicament.PTI.pdf

Papa Franciscus. Carta encíclica Laudato si'. Sobre el cuidado de la casa común. Junio 2015

Treviño-Cisneros R, Arango-Hisijara B (2013) Strategic articulation of actions to cope with the huge challenges of our world today: a platform for reflection. Volume One of the Institute for twenty first century Agoras Monograph Series, A Social Systems Approach to Global Problems, edited by Kenneth C. Bausch, pp 121, 123

**Reynaldo Treviño-Cisneros** received a B.S. degree in Chemical Engineering and Management from ITESM, campus Monterrey, and a M.S. degree in Systems and Planning from Universidad Iberoamericana, campus Mexico, D. F. He has been interested in philosophy and epistemology since 1968, and made an original contribution to General Systems Theory in 1984 through his post-graduate dissertation. He has been considered a qualified Interactive Management practitioner for six years. He is now focusing his work in regional development, and in strategic planning.

# Acknowledgements

Our thanks to Jennifer Wilby for permission to publish the papers that were presented in the Special Integration Group 'Balancing Individualism and Collectivism' as part of the 59th Annual Meeting of the International Society for the Systems Sciences Conference, entitled: 'Governing the Anthropocene' in Berlin, 2015.

Our thanks to these contributors and to the many other colleagues and graduates who have contributed to this volume which aims to share original ideas and or critical review essays on ways to govern the Anthropocene and to live in ways that are egalitarian and non-Anthropocentric.

## Acknowledgements of Visual Materials

Unless otherwise specified all the diagrams and photographs are created by the authors of each chapter. In chapter 4 some of the diagrams have been created by Rudolf Wirawan in some instances he has drawn on figures in Wikipedia commons, unless otherwise cited. In Chap. 5 the artists are cited by Veronica McKay are Samantha van Riet: Figures 1, 2, 3, 4, 5, 7, 9, 12, 15, 16 and Tasia Rosser: Figures 6, 8, 10, 11, 13, 14.

# Contents

# Editors and Contributors

## About the Editors

**Dr. Janet McIntyre-Mills** (DLitt et Phil, Sociology) is Associate Professor in the School of Social and Policy Studies at Flinders University, Adjunct Professor at the University of Indonesia and Islamic National University in Indonesia, and Honorary Professor at the University of South Africa. Her research focuses on systemic representation, accountability and re-generation applied to social and environmental justice concerns such as health, housing and social inclusion and the mitigation and adaptation to climate change. She addresses complex needs by exploring the meanings and 'what if' questions with diverse stakeholders.

Her recent books include 'From Wall Street to Wellbeing: Joining up the dots through Participatory Democracy and Governance to Mitigate the Causes and Adapt to the Effects of Climate Change'. ISBN 978-1-4899-7465-5 and 'Systemic ethics and Non-anthropocentric Stewardship: Implications for Trans disciplinarity and Cosmopolitan politics', ISBN 978-3-519-07655-3.

**Dr. Norma Romm** (DLitt et Phil, Sociology) is Research Professor in the Department of Adult Basic Education and Youth Development, the University of South Africa. She is the author of The Methodologies of Positivism and Marxism (Macmillan, 1991), Accountability in Social Research (Springer, 2001), New Racism (Springer, 2010), People's Education in Theoretical Perspective (with V. McKay, Longman, 1992), Diversity Management (with R. Flood, Wiley, 1996), and Assessment of the Impact of HIV and AIDS in the Informal Economy of Zambia (with V. McKay, ILO, 2008). She has co-edited two books—Social Theory (with M. Sarakinsky, Heinemann, 1994) and Critical Systems Thinking (with R. Flood, Plenum, 1996). She has published more than 95 research articles on the contribution of research to social development, the way in which research can be practised accountably, Indigenous ways of knowing and living, and the facilitation of adult learning. She has worked on a range of projects aimed at increasing equity for organizations such as the ILO, ADEA, IOM, and UNESCO.

**Dr. Yvonne Corcoran-Nantes** (PhD, Sociology) is widely known in the field of gender studies, regularly being interviewed on gender and political issues by the media in Australia and overseas. She has worked with women in such diverse locations as Central Asia, Mongolia, Indonesia, East Timor and Brazil in many research and development projects to improve the rights and status of women in their respective countries. At the present time she is undertaking research on women ex-combatants in contemporary Vietnam. While Dr. Corcoran-Nantes currently teaches in the areas of international studies and women's studies, her main research interests are: Gender and International Politics, Gender and International Development and Women and Armed Conflict. Dr. Corcoran-Nantes is Head of Women's Studies and Associate Professor in the School of Social and Policy Studies at Flinders University.

## Contributors

**Francis A. Akena** University of South Africa, Pretoria, South Africa

**Eshantha Ariyadasa** Flinders University, Adelaide, Australia

**Clare Buswell** Flinders University, Bedford Park, Australia

**Thea Bygojordet Sveen** European University Institute, Florence, Italy

**Alexander N. Christakis** Institute for 21st Century Agoras, Heraklion, Crete, Greece

**Claudia Coral** Humboldt University of Berlin, Berlin, Germany

**Yvonne Corcoran-Nantes** Flinders University, Bedford Park, Adelaide, SA, Australia

**Jeff Foote** Institute of Environmental Science and Research, Christchurch, New Zealand; School of Health Sciences, University of Canterbury, Christchurch, New Zealand

**Mervin Gascon** Flinders University, Adelaide, Australia

**Susan Goff** Murray-Darling Basin Authority, Canberra, Australia

**Novieta Hardeani Sari** Department of Communication Science, Faculty of Social and Politics Science, Universitas Nasional, South Jakarta, Indonesia

**Maria Hepi** Institute of Environmental Science and Research, Christchurch, New Zealand

**Maria Kakoulaki** Institute for 21st Century Agoras, Heraklion, Crete, Greece

**Stanley Machuki** Flinders University, Bedford Park, SA, Australia; UN Habitat, Nairobi, Kenya

**Janet McIntyre-Mills** School of Social and Policy Studies, Flinders University, Adelaide, SA, Australia

**Veronica McKay** University of South Africa, Pretoria, South Africa

**Helen Jaqueline McLaren** Public Administration Department, Universitas Padjadjaran, Bandung, West Java, Indonesia; Flinders University, Adelaide, Australia

**Juliane Mendelsohn** Freie Universität, Berlin, Germany

**Keith Miller** School of Social and Policy Studies, Flinders University, Adelaide, Australia

**Rachel Outhred** Oxford Policy Management, Oxford, UK

**Kofi P. Quan-Baffour** University of South Africa, Pretoria, South Africa

**Marara Rogers-Koroheke** Hokianga Health Enterprise Trust, Rawene, New Zealand

**Norma R. A. Romm** University of South Africa, Pretoria, South Africa

**Snigdha Roy** Flinders University, Adelaide, SA, Australia

**Bambang Shergi Laksmono** University of Indonesia, Depok, Indonesia

**Jackwin Simbolon** Flinders University, Adelaide, Australia

**Hone Taimona** Hokianga Health Enterprise Trust, Rawene, New Zealand

**Ida Widianingsih** Public Administration Department, Universitas Padjadjaran, Bandung, West Java, Indonesia; Flinders University, Adelaide, Australia

**Rudolf Wirawan** Wirasoft Pty Ltd, Sydney, Australia; IDN-NSW, Eveleigh, NSW, Australia; IDN-Global and Oceania, Eveleigh, NSW, Australia; Indonesian Research Consortium, Depok, Indonesia

# Audio Visual Links

https://archive.org/details/VN860553 (Reconsidering Boundaries and What Constitutes Knowledge)
https://archive.org/download/pathway_DEMO_1 (Pathways to Wellbeing)
https://ia801606.us.archive.org/20/items/pathway_DEMO_1/pathway_DEMO_1.mp4
https://archive.org/details/VN860546 (Ethics and Design)
https://archive.org/details/VN860542 (Topics)
https://archive.org/search.php?query=subject%3A%22critical+systemic+thinking+and+practice%22 (Critical Systemic Thinking and Practice)
https://archive.org/details/VN860537/VN860535.MP3 (Governance Across Boundaries)
https://archive.org/details/VN860540 (Designing a Response too Address an Area of Concern)
https://archive.org/details/VN860555 (Wicked Problems)
https://archive.org/details/VN860538 (Non Anthropocentric Approaches)
https://archive.org/details/VN860534/VN860533.MP3 (Social and Environmental Justice)
https://archive.org/details/KeithMillerAudio1464245981160526003 (See Chapter)
https://archive.org/details/ShortTalkForUNISAOnReschAsResisVN860390 (Research as Resistance Janet McIntyre)
https://archive.org/details/eshanta
https://archive.org/details/Riswanda
https://archive.org/details/veronica2016
https://archive.org/details/KofiPartA20165
https://archive.org/details/Kofi24
https://archive.org/details/NormaRommAndFrancisAkena
https://archive.org/details/MervinreindigenisationOfAgrVN860392
https://archive.org/details/Jackwin3MT (Jackwin Simbolon on Water Management in One of the Driest Regions in Indonesia)
https://archive.org/details/VN860455_201609
https://archive.org/search.php?query=subject%3A%22Indigenous+policy+transformation%22 (Indigenous Policy Transformation)

https://www.youtube.com/watch?v=SKwXw6hFpAA (Dialogue Beyond Borders Documentary [New Edition]) by Maria Kakoulaki
https://www.youtube.com/channel/UC4tdtblZTjb0qCwqdC79v8Q (Maria Kakoulaki)

# Prologue

## Balancing Individualism and Collectivism: Towards Non-anthropocentric Stewardship Rights and Responsibilities

The volumes in the series comprise: (1) *Balancing Individualism and Collectivism* and (2) *Planetary Passport: Towards Representation, Accountability and Re-Generation.* They address the paradox raised by Wadsworth (2010: xvii) that 'we want change—and yet we do not want [to] change'. Democracy and governance need to be open to diverse views but democratic governance also needs to provide a public education role where people think about the consequences of their social, economic and environmental choices and the implications for this generation within nations and regions.

The links across Systems Thinking, Participatory Action Research and Mixed Methods are well established by Wadsworth in the *Systemic Practice and Action Research Journal* and by Robert Flood in the *Action Research Handbook* as well as in the *Consciousness Journal*. By definition systems thinking is transdisciplinary and spans a range of variables and addresses interrelated concerns. Working in participatory design teams makes sense and so the papers sit well together.

Contributors of this volume add to our understanding by working across cultural studies, women's studies, development studies, biology, physics and environmental studies. The scope of the volume is rethinking boundaries, interconnections, relationships, flows, the nature of consciousness, identity, anthropocentric, and non-anthropocentric knowing. We address ways to learn from a changing environment and how to translate decision-making into praxis at multiple levels applied to multiple forms of intervention.

The challenge is to develop new approaches to address needs comprising many interrelated variables that are perceived differently by different stakeholders with different life chances and different capabilities. Significantly we seek to establish whether participatory democracy enables participants to consider the consequences of socio-economic decisions for long-term sustainable wellbeing versus short term acceptable coping strategies (McIntyre-Mills et al. 2014) and thus to ascertain if it supports the will to manage the consumption of resources carefully—as opposed to denying or brushing aside the role we could play or the voluntary changes we can make as individuals and as conscientious ecological citizens (Dobson 2006, 2007).

Balancing individualism and collectivism addresses the social and environmental justice challenge to live sustainably and well by:

- Considering the consequences of our social, economic and environmental policy and governance decisions for this generation and the next.
- Testing out ways to improve representation, accountability and re-generation. It addresses the need to take into account the ethical implications of policy and governance decisions in the short, medium and long terms based on testing out the implications for self, other and the environment. The work of West Churchman on a Design of Inquiring Systems provides an approach to balancing individual rights and responsibilities with collective rights and responsibilities by working through questions that consider the implications of policy decisions by means of 'what if' scenarios that take into account the perceptions, values and narratives of diverse stakeholders (irrespective of socio-demographic and cultural characteristics). A policy decision that supports social and environmental justice is informed by the axiom that we can be free and diverse to the extent that our choices do not undermine the rights of others and the environment in this generation and the next. Papers that explore complex social and environmental justice issues at a local, national and international level are discussed. Expanded Pragmatism dedicated to sustainable social and environmental justice is more important than ever.

In the wake of the elections in UK, Europe, and USA people have demonstrated the depth of their dissatisfaction that Rorty (1999) summed up in 'Achieving Our Country'. He stressed that 'something will crack' as follows:

"The non suburban electorate will decide that the system has failed and start looking around for a strongman to vote for—someone willing to assure them that, once he is elected, the smug bureaucrats, tricky lawyers, overpaid bond salesmen, and postmodernist professors will no longer be calling the shots."

Rorty said 'nobody can predict' what such a strongman would do in office, but painted a bleak picture for minorities and liberal causes. "One thing that is very likely to happen is that the gains made in the past forty years by black and brown Americans, and by homosexuals, will be wiped out," he wrote. "Jocular contempt for women will come back into fashion." (Rorty 1999: 87–91 and cited by Helmore 2016).[1]

People in Western democracies have voted for national identity and prioritizing local jobs. The so-called 'deplorables' whom Hilary Clinton stereotyped in the

[1]Helmore, E. 2016 https://www.theguardian.com/us-news/2016/nov/19/donald-trump-us-election-prediction-richard-rorty.

bitter presidential election of 2016 as 'racist, sexist, xenophobic, Islamophobic' and inward looking have gained a voice in the UK and in the USA. The fact that Rorty predicted this makes it all the more important to take note that cultural leftism expressed in policies that do not make a difference in the run-down inner city areas makes it all the more important to demonstrate transformation through practical interventions that provide the basis for learning what works why and how. Dewey's pragmatism and agency remain important ways forward to develop agency for the future of democracy. Rorty criticizes the lack of agency in academia.

The volumes in this series propose agency for both social and environmental justice through practical interventions. The focus of this volume is on the need to take into account the views of those who feel left out as demonstrated by the extent to which recent polling resulted in the British Exit (Brexit) from the European Union because people feel left behind by the global economy.

The same trend has resulted in the election of Donald Trump[2] in the United States. Some would argue that democracy has failed because it has allowed a small majority to say 'no' to business as usual. Those who are forgotten within the boundaries of the nation state have spoken out, but the problem is deeper than the lack of representation within nations. It includes the lack of representation of people within regional areas that are facing social, economic and environmental conflict, disaster and upheavals that translate into the challenge to survive. Human beings have diverse values, but they have in common the need for food, energy and water security.

The divisions caused by elitist globalized economic decisions needs to be redressed through job creation that focuses on protecting social and environmental justice. People who are left out because they do not have skills or who are excluded need to be enabled to create opportunities. As Pauli (2016) stresses 'There is no unemployment in ecosystems'. The next point is that ecosystems do not stop at the boundary of the nation state. The divisive us/them or containerist thinking will not help to meet the needs of the excluded. What is needed is a re-framing of society and economics based on integrating a respect for the environment and living systems of which we are a strand.

---

[2]O'Sullivan, J. 2016 'Identity politics crosses the floor as the invisible people find their voice' *Weekend Australian*, 12–13 November, pg. 17: "... Patriotism and popular democracy are reborn with the rise of Trump and Britain's Brexit vote....But when David Blankenhorn set out to find out why people supported Trump in a tour of the American south he discovered that his supporters... liked his candour...They were the invisible victims of the policies of social interventionism and control driven by identity politics—the politics of race, gender and class—that the US government has progressively imposed in the post-Reagan era. Most obviously, they are not members of the 'protected' groups that benefit from affirmative action...They are the people who feel themselves to be the people who sustain this structure of controls and social benefits with their work and taxes without benefiting proportionately from it...As this identity regime spreads from bureaucratic arrangements across much of employment, academic and public life to political rhetoric, some people feel left out...In all these cases this aggressive identity politics sets group against group and divides traditional social groups from those organized by the states along quasi ethnic lines...The Trump campaign, Brexit...and the refugee row in Europe have signaled the rebirth of patriotism and popular democracy against progressive global governance and its forced transformation of societies...".

This is the focus of the second volume which develops a form of participatory democracy and governance links to Sustainable Community Development through triple bottom line accounting to help people to identify sources of abundance in terms of what they have, what they need, what they are prepared to add or discard from their lives, turning points for the better and worse and barriers. The software generates EXCEL sheets with weightings (McIntyre-Mills et al. 2014). I see the potential for this to be also linked to a decision-making and design tool with co-operatives as it is a form of inclusive triple bottom line representation, accounting and accountability see http://wirasoftfoundation.org/en_GB/web/smartenergy/plenary-presentation.

The volumes extend the work conducted in several workshops with academics, students and practitioners in Indonesia and South Africa as well as the work of the Special Integration Group: 'Balancing Individualism and Collectivism' that I have chaired since 2006 for International Systems Sciences conference and papers delivered at the conference 'Governing the Anthropocene' (McIntyre-Mills 2015). This last session was co-chaired at my request by Prof. Norma Romm.

The challenge for governing the Anthropocene is one of moving away from disciplinary and functional differentiation, in order to achieve transdisciplinary knowledge spanning biological, psychological, social, cultural, spiritual, political, scientific, economic and environmental dimensions to support living ethically in ways that redress the worst aspects of modernisation (Berger and Luckmann 1966). Thus the threefold aims are to:

- Deepen our understanding of how people perceive local climate challenges and experiences (Hulme 2009, 2010; Nazarea 2006; Satre 1976; Vaske and Kobrin 2001) through multispecies ethnography (Raikhel 2010) and an adapted version of Soft Systems Mapping (Checkland and Scholes 1991).
- Explore the social influences (Berger 1974), customs and behaviours (Hogget 2010) that potentially shape attitudes and emotions towards consumption with a particular focus on discourses about rights and responsibilities.
- Investigate the dimensions of face-to-face and digital public engagement that could encourage people to explore ways to live simply and well through caring for diverse others (Donaldson and Kymlicka 2011).

To sum up these volumes explore:

- A priori norms for ecological citizenship at the local level and
- A posteriori performance measures for ecological citizenship.
- New ways to protect future generations through remembering our heritage, re-connecting to others (including sentient beings) and re-generating the gendered ecological.
- Alternative forms of praxis inspired by leaders such as Wangari Maathi, Vandana Shiva, Dorothy Bird Rose and Donna Haraway as a way to preserve a sense of our connection with the earth and waters on which we depend.
- Ways to decolonialize knowledge formation in public policy

- The case for an alternative approach to governance and democracy that takes into account a range of local people's perspectives.

Drawing on and adapting Hofstede et al. (2010) this research extends the approach to consider the consequences of different cultural values for governing the Anthropocene. The approach is to work with diverse people who have experience of living in urban, suburban and regional areas and to explore the way in which they think in qualitative terms food. Unlike Hofstede's research, a qualitative approach is used to explore perceptions. The volumes aim to explore the extent to which people understand the implications of their choices. Wangari Maathi founded the Green Movement and stresses that the simple act of planting trees in Kenya could make a difference through mobilizing people to take action and to make a small difference. She calls this 'the humming bird approach', because these actions (although small in themselves) can make a collective change. Besides it is better to make a small contribution than to do nothing. In taking action we can inspire others to join us. In her Nobel Peace prize speech she invites us all to think about the sort of environment we want for the future, one in which children can play safely in water and in which they can watch tadpoles grow. The magic of being shown how a tadpole grows into a frog is one I associate with my childhood, playing in a river bed. My grandfather showed me how they change as an introduction to the notion of the sacred and the way we are all part of a process of transformation.

Vandana Shiva's work provides another source of inspiration through reminding us that we are all seeds for change and that we are reliant on water, earth and seeds for our survival. Whilst the work of Deborah Rose Bird on multispecies ethnography suggests a way to help us think about non-anthropocentricism, 'caring for country' and then working towards what consciousness of trans species interconnections means for governance and democracy in the future. Donna Haraway's understanding of hybridity provides a starting point for this discussion in volume two.

Perhaps one of the most insightful contributions to the book was made from the margins when discussing with Prof. Veronica Mckay the process of developing and teaching children at school in South Africa. Veronica discusses the hidden and explicit curriculum of her workbooks that construct a model for human interaction in the new South Africa that is non-racist and non-anthropocentric in a society that respects gender, age and diverse species of life. The workbooks provide interactive exercises linked with a curriculum and classroom guides for teachers. The engagement with the hidden curriculum was discussed spanning human rights (gender, race, class, culture, language) as well as the rights of sentient beings and the environment. In conversation with Veronica about the books Romm and I commented on the quality of the books which would bring joy to a classroom and that the notion of sentient beings was extended through a sense of solidarity with all forms of life including plants that were depicted in the workbooks with scientific accuracy but which also included a sense of 'play' and perhaps 'hyperrealism' through depicting non-human life communicating positively with human beings. The energy of positive relationships plays out in how we relate to others and the reverence we show for all forms of life by acknowledging our interdependency and the importance of respect and compassion for all life forms.

The work of Maathi Wangari, for example, features in an exercise to illustrate how planting trees can be a means to empower women and to protect the environment. Her attention to detail is illustrated in the way in which relationships across cultures, species and the ecosystem are featured in daily lessons on living well and living ethically. The chapter is also linked to a podcast in which she is interviewed by the editor during a visit to South Africa in December. Veronica explains the process of developing the workbooks in a team that worked according to the principles of participatory action research. All the participants were encouraged to voice their ideas and the workbooks are tested in the classrooms and modified in response to the suggestions made by team members in collaboration with teachers and learners.

The conversations about the papers are extended by means of audio and visual links by some contributors to an internet archive so that some of the material can be explored through other media. The hope is that by demonstrating what is possible, it will inspire more people to live differently and that it will lead to policy and governance changes.

Firstly, Reynaldo Treviño-Cisneros explains the concept of the Anthropocene and makes a plea for using dialogue to establish harmony across interest groups. Then Norma Romm discusses the notion of the Anthropocene critically and makes a plea for restoring a sense of connection with others and the environment through caring. She explains the implications for current societies in a paper delivered at the International Systems Sciences Conference in Berlin (2015).

Janet McIntyre-Mills chapters propose an alternative approach to democracy and governance on the notion of a Planetary Passport to support a Global Covenant and Earth Democracy. Janet discusses the need for education to foster the protection of diversity. Science, Democracy, Agriculture and Ethics thrive on the testing out of ideas, while the paper also makes a case that social systems need to foster freedom and diversity to the extent that it does not undermine the rights of others in this generation or the next. The stewardship approach to ethical policy and governance praxis is developed in this chapter and in her second chapter she stresses that binary oppositions based on subject/object, male/female/water/earthanimal/human, planet/economics play out as part of the modernization agenda.

If we are to set aside the so-called 'Monocultures of the Mind' (Shiva 2012a,b) we need to 'Make Peace' with ourselves, others and the earth. The need to protect seed diversity from industrial farming is Shiva's mission because corporatized farming has become part of the problem. She has taken on Monsanto in legal proceedings because the so-called 'Terminator seeds' from Monsanto replace biodiverse plants because they do not self-generate and are reliant on costly farming processes. She stresses that avoiding these threats to food security requires understanding that the linear assembly line approach to farming or making a living is unsustainable.

Diversity in nature is as important as it is in society: in a kindergarten or university classroom or an industry board room. The a priori capabilities to enable participation in a life worth living has been detailed as an ethical priority for all sentient beings by Nussbaum (2006, 2011). Thus the democratic minimum requires the capability to protect a decent quality of life and the environment on which we depend. The violence of silencing women and children in domestic situations can also be seen as a synecdoche of the sort of violence shown towards natural diversity. If we weed out and exterminate difference we become increasingly vulnerable to change. In agriculture seeds that survive through generations of testing need to be protected. This has been echoed by Indigenous voices and is now core to facilitate policy transformation through enabling the voiceless including all marginalized peoples, in particular women and children, to engage in expressing their rights while exercising a duty of care to protect other sentient beings and the environment on which we all depend.

Patriarchal science and society have played a role in silencing protest. The rights of animals to a life free of pain has been stressed by Singer who discusses the a posteriori consequences of unethical living. As a utilitarian, he argues that extending solidarity to others makes sense because it fosters the wellbeing of all[3]. These chapters explore perceptions on whether people understand that growth in the size of the ecological footprint of cities, growth in the size of species loss, growth in the size of the gap between rich and poor (as a result of the greed of a few at the expense of the majority in this generation and the next) is unsustainable. Some of the best examples of structuralist agendas are constitutions that give rights to the marginalized and to nature. The Ecuadorian constitution makes some steps in this direction, but could be criticized for the lack of implementation of the norms enshrined in the constitution.

Some of the best examples of *voluntarism* include encouraging people to become more politically active in transforming what is valued through 'being the change'. The issues of the day are summed up as follows:

- Growing gap between rich and poor (in particular those who are displaced)
- The growing rise in the size of ecological footprints of some at the expense of the majority
- The growth in unsustainable food choices and the growth of displaced people
- The need for a new narrative in the sense used by Jacob Von Uexkoll, new architecture for participatory governance and participatory democracy and a new sense of relationship with nature and other animals.

The options can be summed up as follows: We can emphasize structuralist interventions through constitutions that give rights to nature and develop policy to protect all sentient beings as suggested by Nussbaum (2011) and to protect habitat for wild and liminal animals as suggested in Zoopolis (Donaldson and Kymlicka 2011). We can encourage voluntarist approaches through educating people to become engaged citizens through scaling up the potential of ecological citizens to participate in decision-making (as suggested by the Aarhus Convention, see Florini

[3]http://www.pambazuka.net/en/category.php/features/96307.

2003) and the right to justice in post national regions governed by a Global Covenant (Held 2004).

Eshanta Ariyadasa discusses his Ph.D. research on ways to enhance the public education of children in Sri Lanka as part of his research on the governance of children's homes. In Sri Lanka the number of orphans as a result of war, natural disasters and the migrant work of women has necessitated measures to protect them. His practical action research program supported by an Endeavour Award Scholarship involves the evaluation of children's homes and it draws on his experience as the founder of one of these homes. The action learning program with young people includes recycling, organic gardening and bee keeping as a way to live healthy sustainable lives. His focus is on ways to ensure that the UN rights of the child are upheld in deed not merely as words to guide the policies governing children. The idealistic capabilities approach of Nussbaum forms the basis for developing a priori guidelines in line with the UN goals and they provide a basis for developing indicators for wellbeing. A video podcast on his research is also linked with this chapter.

Yvonne Corcoran-Nantes and Clare Buswell discuss the importance of gender and nonviolence as it relates to governing the Anthropocene and this theme is continued by Gascon, Widianingsih and McLaren. The work of Donna Haraway on gendered violence provides a source of inspiration for the volumes in this series. Her work on the way thinking shapes design is vital for transformation. We are the boundaries, she reminds us. Transformation of the Anthropocene to more sustainable ways of life require us to 'be the change'.

Keith Miller and Susan Goff explore land and culture and how loss of land and culture affects the wellbeing of Aboriginal Australians, whilst Jeff Foote together with Maria Hepi, Marara Rogers-Koroheke and Hone Taimona discuss Maori community wellbeing and living systems. Kofi Quan Bouffour explains the systemic importance of land and the implications of loos in Ghana. The themes of land loss are also taken up by Clare Buswell and Yvonne Corcoran-Nantes who explain the precarious lives of women who often depend on access to the land through marriage. Although the majority of the world's farmers are women they do not own the land. When they are divorced, widowed, suffer illness in the family or take on mortgages to engage in mechanized corporatized farming they run the risk of land loss which severely impacts on the subsistence and survival strategies of women and their communities.

The process of losing land in Mindanao, Philippines is described in a chapter by Mervin Gascon. Mervin is undertaking his Ph.D. research on the most vulnerable in Mindanao, namely women and children who have lost or on the verge of losing land. Simbolon underlines that Indonesia provides constitutional support for the right to water security for all and the implications of corruption on public health. Akena makes a case for communal land ownership to protect food security in Africa, whilst Quan Baffour takes up the theme of public education and land management.

The message that runs as a leit motif through this collected volume is that resistance and resilience depends on cultural transformation and modelling alternative ways of being the change. We are indeed the boundaries and it is up to us to be the agents of transformation towards non-anthropocentricism.

Alexander Christakis with Maria Kakoulaki considers the importance of participatory democracy and governance with reference to agriculture in Cyprus. This case study on managing diversity is particularly relevant as Cyprus is closer to Syria than it is to the EU wherein it is an uneasy member state.

This special edition ends by discussing the awareness of natural inclusion developed by the biologist, Alan Rayner who sums up our interrelatedness through explaining how definitive thinking, whether divisive or unifying, is constructed from abstract presuppositions that overlook the intrinsic flux and spatial receptivity that are vital to the existence of all forms of life. His work uses mixed methods of visual and verbal communication, including art and poetry, to describe, illustrate and account for the diversity across all scales of life from microbes to mammals and from moss cushions to forests. A favourite poem and painting, entitled 'The Hole in the Mole', emphasizes the attentive receptivity essential to sustainable ways of living, and how this influences natural energetic flows and formations.

Like Shiva, his message is that we are dependent on the earth, and this dependency necessarily entails both generative and degenerative processes. It takes all kinds to make and sustain the vibrancy of life on Earth, including hedgehogs and earthworms.

This first volume builds on previous publications cited in the chapters below and develops a case for non–anthropocentrism through both structuralist and voluntarist approaches to 'being the change'.

To sum up, the focus of the two volumes is knowing our place in the universe and recognizing our hybridity. It makes the case that current architectures for governance and democracy are part of the problem.

Adelaide, Australia — Janet McIntyre-Mills

## References


Berger P, Luckmann (1966) The social construction of reality. Penguin, London

Berger PL (1974) Homeless mind: modernization and consciousness. Penguin, London

Checkland P, Scholes J (1991) Soft systems methodology in action. Wiley, London

Donaldson S, Kymlicka W (2011) Zoopolis: a political theory of animal rights. Oxford University Press, Oxford

Dobson A, Eckersley R (2006) Political theory and the ecological challenge. Cambridge University Press, 10 Aug 2006—Political Science

Dobson A (2007) Environmental citizenship: towards sustainable development. Sust Dev 15: 276–285 (www.interscience.wiley.com). Doi: 10.1002/sd.344

Dobson A (2012) Listening: the new democratic deficit. Polit. Sci. 60:843–859. doi: 10.1111/j.1467-9248.2012.00944.x

Held D (2004) Global covenant: the social democratic alternative to the Washington Consensus. Polity

Hoggett P (2010) Politics, identity and emotion. Paradigm, Boulder

Hofstede G, Hofstede GJ, Minkov M (2010) Cultures and organisations: software of the mind: intercultural co-operation and its importance for survival. McGraw Hill, New York
Hulme M (2009) Why we disagree about climate change. Cambridge University Press
Hulme M (2010) Cosmopolitan climates. Hybridity, foresight and meaning. *Theor Cult Soc* 27(2–3):267–276
Florini A (2003) The coming democracy. Island Press, Washington DC
McIntyre-Mills J with Devries D, Binchai N (2014) Wall Street to wellbeing: joining up the dots through participatory democracy and governance to mitigate the causes and adapt to the effects of climate change. Springer, New York
McIntyre-Mills J (2014) Systemic ethics and non-anthropocentric stewardship: implications for transdisciplinarity and cosmopolitan politics. Springer, New York
McIntyre-Mills J (2015) Governing the Anthropocene through balancing individualism and collectivism, 59th Annual International Systems Sciences, Berlin Conference, 2–7th August, Published http://journals.isss.org/index.php/proceedings59th
Nazarea V (2006) Local knowledge and memory in biodiversity conservation. Ann Rev Anthropol 36: 317–335
Nussbaum M (2011) Creating capabilities: the human development approach. The Belknap Press of Harvard University Press, London.Chapter 2: The Central Capabilities
Nussbaum M (2006) Frontiers of justice. Harvard University Press, London
Pauli G (2010) The Blue economy: Report to the Club of Rome. Paradigm Publications. New Mexico
Rorty R (1999) Achieving our country: The William E. Massey Sr. lectures in the history of American civilization. Harvard University Press
Rivière D (2015) Thirsty Elephant—India's Water Security Challenges: a test for regional relations over the next decade. Colonel Daniel Rivière, CD, PMP, September 2015
Sartre J (1976) Critique of dialectical reason. New Left Review, London
Shiva V (2002) Water wars: privatization, pollution and profit. Pluto Press, London
Shiva V (2011) Earth Democracy. Portland University. http://www.youtube.com/watch?v=UOfM7QD7-kk/
Shiva V (1989) Staying Alive: women, ecology and survival in India. Zed Books, London
Shiva V (2012a) Making peace with the earth. Fernwood Publishing, Winipeg
Shiva V (2012b) Monocultures of the mind: perspectives on biodiversity and biotechnology. Third World Network. Penang
Singer P (2002) One world: the ethics of globalisation. Text Publishers, Melbourne
Vaske J, Kobrin K (2001) Place attachment and environmentally responsible behavior. J Environ Education 32(4) 16–21
Wadsworth Y (2010) Building in research and evaluation. Human inquiry for living systems. Allen and Unwin, Sydney

# Chapter 1
# Foregrounding Critical Systemic and Indigenous Ways of Collective Knowing Toward (Re)Directing the Anthropocene

**Norma R.A. Romm**

**Abstract** This paper begins with the understanding that the global commons is under threat. In the light hereof, I consider why it is important to appreciate Indigenous styles of collectively oriented knowing, where selves are understood as "selves-in-relation" to one another and to all living and nonliving things, as part of the web of life. I suggest that often accounts of the Anthropocene (as proposed by various authors postulating this concept) do not accentuate how the forcefulness of human impact on the world (by virtue of humans manipulating and extracting resources) can be regarded as rooted in Western-oriented supposedly rational styles of knowing and calculating, which to date have been historically dominant. This approach to knowing and being-in-the-world is ill equipped to incorporate a conception of our existing as humans *in relation to others*, including to all that exists. Indigenous thinking as expounded by various Indigenous authors across the globe (which I define as I proceed with the paper) starts with the premise of connectivity of life forces, and therefore with the assumption that we, as humans, *are called upon to play a responsible role in our caring for each other and for the earth.* Working in terms of the notion of care does not mean that we are less rational, but on the contrary that we recognize that our existence is contingent on our supporting, and being supported by others (including nonliving entities). This in turn implies an attitude of respecting how "individual" well-being is a function of the well-being of the whole. Based on these considerations, I propound in the paper that planetary stewardship *should not be envisaged as applicable only now that we have entered the epoch named by some as the Anthropocene*, where the human power to manipulate the environment has become a global geological force in its own right. Instead, we need to question the way in which this power has hitherto been used, and the (dominant) worldview that enabled the use of such power as a manipulative enterprise. Such questioning allows us to *reconsider the values in terms of which the Anthropocene can be approached,* by taking on board—and indeed foregrounding—Indigenous views, and bases, of stewardship. The paper concludes

N.R.A. Romm (✉)
University of South Africa, Pretoria, South Africa
e-mail: norma.romm@gmail.com



J. McIntyre-Mills et al. (eds.), *Balancing Individualism and Collectivism*, Contemporary Systems Thinking, DOI 10.1007/978-3-319-58014-2_1

with some considerations of how diverse knowledge systems can be brought into communication/integrated towards enhanced ecosystem governance.

## Introduction: Conceptualizing the Anthropocene

Steffen et al. (2011a, p. 842) define the onset of the Anthropocene in terms of the scale of the human imprint on the global environment which now, they argue, "rivals some of the great forces of Nature in its impact on the functioning of the Earth's system." Otherwise put, the term Anthropocene suggests that "humankind has become a global geological force in its own right" (2011a, p. 843). Looking historically at the human–environment relationship, they state that prior to the Anthropocene, indeed over the last millions of years, humans and their ancestors have "modified natural ecosystems to gain advantage in gathering vegetable food sources they required or in aiding the hunt for animals they hunted"—but they were never able to fully transform the ecosystems around them. They indicate that certain pre-industrial events are sometimes cited as already heralding the beginning of the Anthropocene, but for them, it was the Industrial Revolution, with its origins in Great Britain in the 1700s, or the thermo-industrial revolution of nineteenth century Western civilization [that] "marked the end of agriculture as the most dominant human activity and set the species on a far different trajectory from the one established during most of the Holocene [the prior epoch of more stable human–environment relations] (2011a, p. 848).

Steffen et al. indicate furthermore that after World War II the human enterprise (and imprint on the global environment) switched gears, creating a dramatic change such that the 1945–2000 era can aptly be called the "Great Acceleration". They surmise that the quest for renewed economic growth is what "drove the final collapse of the remaining pre-industrial European institutions" (2011a, p. 850). They explain how the post-world war economic system, led by the USA, was built around neo-liberal economic principles stressing "open trade and capital flows". They note that "the post-World War II economy integrated rapidly, with growth rates reaching their highest values ever in the 1950–1973 period" (p. 850). They explain that:

> Partnerships among government, industry and academia became common, further driving innovation and growth. More and more public goods were converted into commodities and placed into the market economy, and the growth imperative rapidly became a core societal value that drove both the socio-economic and the political spheres (2011a, p. 850).

But they point out that "environmental problems received little attention during much of the Great Acceleration" (2011a, p. 850). Indeed "emerging global environmental problems were largely ignored" (Steffen et al. 2011a, p. 852).

In setting out their account of the onset of the Anthropocene, they point to the skewed distribution across countries of impact on the environment to date, noting that "the poorest countries … have contributed less than 1% of the cumulative CO2 emissions since the beginning of the Industrial Revolution" (Steffen et al. 2011a, p. 853). However, recent data suggests "dramatic changes over the past decade: For 2004, the emissions from developing countries had grown to over 40% of the world total" (2011a, p. 853). Nonetheless, they add that "about 25% of the growth in emissions over the last decade from developing countries was owing to the increase of international trade in goods and services produced in these developing countries *but consumed in the developed world"* (2011a, p. 854, my italics). They also add that it is clear that resource constraints will prevent developing countries (other than China and India) from following the growth trajectory of the more advanced economies (2011a, p. 854).

From Steffen et al.'s (2011a) account of the Anthropocene we can see that for them it seems as if—during what they call the "Great Acceleration" period—there has been a general consensus throughout the globe that economic growth needed to be accomplished, including at the cost of environmental damage. The environment was seen as exploitable/manipulable for the benefit of human advantage (as indeed they postulate also occurred throughout human history, but to a lesser extent). *They do not refer to differences in worldviews,* where, for instance, certain Indigenous patterns of behavior and lifestyle mitigated against this exploitative understanding of humans in relation to nature.

It is also noteworthy that although Steffen et al. point to the skewed benefits which accrued to different countries, they do not highlight the dominant/imperialist influence of Western-styled views on so-called core societal values that "drove both the socio-economic and the political spheres" (Steffen et al. 2011a, p. 850). *They assume that these "core values" (as they call them) were more or less shared across the globe*. Or rather, they leave in abeyance the question of who subscribed to these "core values". The imperialist consequences of the quest for unlimited growth as built into the political agenda of the rich countries (at the expense of underdeveloped ones) does not feature in their account, where they focus mainly on what they call "open trade and capital flows" (2011a, p. 850) instead of on the way in which (underdeveloped) countries were colonized and resources extracted for the benefit of the wealthy. It can, therefore, be argued that they are not sufficiently critical in reflecting upon how the growth agenda rode roughshod over other human values, such as care for people and for the environment.

When Steffen and a range of other authors (Steffen et al. 2011b) consider the question of how planetary stewardship may now be instated as an alternative to the unlimited growth agenda, they note that at present a human development index (HDI) has been devised to measure development in human terms (p. 749). Furthermore, recognizing that material wealth is not the sole (or best) indicator of wellbeing, they point out (2011b, p. 749) that deficiencies can be located even in this index in that it fails to incorporate "cultural or psychological dimensions or security considerations" (as also highlighted by Wilkinson and Pickett 2010). And they note (p. 750) that global aggregates of increase in wealth "mask the ways in which the distribution of wealth and the impacts of ecosystem service decline are skewed, between nations and within them, a factor that may have a strong bearing on well-being". (Here again they cite Wilkinson and Pickett 2010). But I suggest in this paper that they do not fully appreciate the alternative values that need to be brought to bear, and that have indeed been suggested by various Indigenous and Indigenous-oriented authors writing about sustainable development (cf. Barnand and Van Paassen 2013; Bawden 2011; Bullard 2002; Cannella and Manuelito 2008; Chilisa 2012; Christakis and Bausch 2006; Cisneros and Hisijara 2013; Harris and Wasilewski 2004; McIntyre-Mills 2002, 2008, 2014a, b; Murove 2005; Romm 2014, Ross and Pickering 2002; Smith 2011).

It should be noted that I use the word "Indigenous-oriented" in this paper to apply to authors who do not necessarily have an Indigenous background in a country by birth, but who *sympathize with the values and worldviews as espoused in Indigenous traditions*, and who enter "Indigeneity" in this way. Some of these authors/practitioners become recognized by Indigenous people, and become what Christakis calls honorary members of the community (cf. Romm's reference to this 2010, p. 12). Lowan-Trudeau also suggests that through "mutually respectful engagement" non-Indigenous people can be "welcomed into Indigenous communities, further expanding opportunities for intercultural and eventually transcultural experiences and creations grounded in a … sense of collective connection" (2014, p. 360). McIntyre-Mills offers another discussion of ways of applying Yeperenye dreaming to heal divides between Indigenous and non-Indigenous thought systems as part of a process of "pooling human knowledge" and finding solutions to the "shared future of humanity as we know it and the planet as we know it" (2003, p. 327).

In the light hereof, I suggest, as do, for instance Harris and Wasilewski (2004) that one of the problems with imperialism—to which Steffan et al. allude when they speak about a USA-led liberal economic (indeed capitalist) system (2011a, p. 850)—is that *alternative value systems (and attendant worldviews/cultural orientations and understandings of the economy) became voiceless in the dominant drive for increasing material wealth at all costs*. In addition, when they suggest that the time has come in the current context for "the transformation from resource exploitation towards stewardship of the Earth System" (2011b, p. 746), they seem to forget that many Indigenous authors have postulated the idea of stewardship as built into Indigenous knowledge systems. This is not only *now* required, now that the Earth is no longer able to carry the costs of human exploitation, but can be seen as value-based—based on values of always caring for that which is around us (other humans and living and nonliving things). In the next section, I point to certain authors contributions in considering our stewardship role, which can be seen to be somewhat at variance with (and critical of) Steffen and colleague's concentration on the need only now (now that we have reached the epoch of the Anthropocene) to recognize the importance of stewardship, as they imply in their article "from global change to planetary stewardship" (Steffen et al. 2011b, p. 746). But first I unpack further some of their assumptions.

## Some Assertions (of Those Defining the Anthropocene) that Can Be Reviewed

Steffen et al. (implicitly) reiterate their assertion that certain core values prevailed post-World War II when they indicate that Diamond (2005) proposes that "societies collapse if core values become dysfunctional as the external world changes and they are unable to recognize emerging problems" (2011b, p. 751). They cite Diamond and others as referring to societies becoming locked into obsolete values, hindering the "transition to new values" (p. 751). In this context they suggest that:

> A core value of post-World War II contemporary society is ever-increasing material wealth generated by a growth-oriented economy based on neoliberal economic principles and assumptions … a value that has driven the Great Acceleration but that climate change and other global changes are calling into question (Steffen et al. 2011b, p. 751).

What is missing from this account of "contemporary society", I suggest, is a consideration of *alternative values that have been propounded within other cultural frameworks* (other than the neoliberal tradition), but which became sidelined/silenced via dominant discourses. Also, what is missing in this account is not only that *climate change* is calling into question these values, but that these values had been called into question prior to the "Great Acceleration" as they name it, within many Indigenous knowledge systems operating in terms of alternative "core values".

In their article entitled *Indigeneity, an Alternative Worldview* (2004), Harris—founder of the organization called Americans for Indian Opportunity (AIO)—and Wasilewski (2004) explain what they take to be a value cluster that can be associated with Indigeneity across the globe. In outlining these values, Harris and Wasilewski identify four R's, which they see as part of the cultural heritage offered by "Indigenous societies", although they admit that there is still scope for strengthening of these processes:

**Relationship** is to be understood in the

> profound sense that we human beings are related, not only to each other, but to all things, animals, plants, rocks—in fact, to the very stuff the stars are made of. This relationship is a kinship relationship …. We thus live in a family that includes all creation (Harris and Wasilewski 2004, p. 492).

**Responsibility** means that we feel obligated to

> care for all of our relatives. Our relatives include everything in our ecological niche, animals and plants, as well as humans, even the stones, since everything that exists is alive (Harris and Wasilewski 2004, pp. 492–493).

**Reciprocity** implies that

> once we have encountered another, we are in relationship with them….. At any given moment the exchanges going on in a relationship may be uneven. The Indigenous idea of reciprocity is based on very long relational dynamics (Harris and Wasilewski 2004, p. 493).

**Redistribution** is rooted in a

> sharing obligation. Its primary purpose is to balance and rebalance relationships. Comanche society, for example … had many, many ways of redistributing material and social goods …. The point is not to acquire things. The point is to give them away. Generosity is the most highly valued human quality …. This obligation means sharing, not only material wealth, but information, time, talent and energy, one's total self (Harris and Wasilewski 2004, p. 493).

Smith (1999), writing from a Maori perspective, also refers to these values and notes that they are related to a worldview that emphasizes connectedness, which she sees as a common thread running through Indigenous styles of thinking albeit that there is still clearly diversity within meanings, and interpretations, of Indigeneity. She suggests that a common thread that Indigenous authors stress, is the "importance of making connections and *affirming connectedness*…. Connectedness positions individuals in sets of relationships with other people and with the environment" (1999, p. 148, my italics). And Kovach (2009) suggests that the term "self-in-relation" (a translation of the Cree word *nisitohtamowin*" (2009, p. 27) aptly captures the essence of the spirit of Indigenous styles of knowing and being in the world, where, she notes, it is understood that selves cannot and should not be considered as separated from their connections with other living and nonliving entities. Lowan-Trudeau summarizes that "inherent in most Indigenous worldviews is recognition of the inherent value, spirit, and interconnectedness of all people, living creatures, and bioregions" (2014, p. 356).

Cannella and Manuelito, for their part, indicate how an Indigenous-oriented feminist-based environmentalism "offers unique epistemologies that assume interconnections between human and nonhuman life and nonlife". They see such a feminism as rooted in an ethic of care, while encouraging engagement in "theorizing and construction of knowledge that avoid dualistic, rationalist individualism" (2008, p. 53). In other words, once individualism is avoided and it is recognized that "reason" goes hand in hand with emotion (caring) then the foundation is laid for forms of action that are not based on manipulation either of people or of the environment.

Christakis (2014, p. 18) indicates how in his conversations with La Donna Harris (founder of AIO) she expressed implications of Indigenous ways of knowing in terms of an orientation to developing mutual visions, rather than an orientation to "win" over and above others (or the natural environment). He cites Harris as follows:

> Who is winning becomes unimportant. What becomes important is the effectiveness of the entire group. This collective success by way of individual participation is an ancient traditional value, and it enables us to see the collective reality. …. This is what attracted us at AIO to structured dialogue [a way of designing dialogue developed by Christakis and others, aided by computer software] … because it enables people from totally different backgrounds carrying totally different histories to see collective realities as they emerge in an ever dynamic present Harris, as cited in Christakis (2014, p. 18).

Based on this kind of thinking, Harris and Wasilewski express concern that the course taken by globalization dominated by "power and profit" from the start threatened the potential for positive relationships, where people could more collectively define the trajectory of history, while also caring for Mother Earth (2004, p. 489). They contend that:

> As we look at the world around us, we have to recognize that existing systems based on Western models of governance are not working. The imposition model continues to cause great pain. We need to establish respectful, caring relationships of responsibility with each other [and with Mother Earth] (2004, p. 499).

They go on to indicate that the problem with the system that became established/imposed (based on "free market principles") was "devoid of care". As they state: "the economic system does not care if any of these communities [at local, regional or national level], or if the Earth itself, exists into the future" (Harris and Wasilewski 2004, p. 499).

From this unease, evidently the "core values" identified by Steffen et al. of "ever-increasing material wealth" would not be subscribed to by Indigenous-oriented authors and/or ecofeminists who see that this growth trajectory as ill-fated from the start.

Steffen et al. assert that:

> We are the first generation with widespread knowledge of how our activities influence the Earth System, and thus the first generation with the power and the responsibility to change our relationship with the planet. Responsible stewardship entails emulating nature in terms of resource use and waste transformation and recycling, and the transformation of agricultural, energy and transport systems (2011b, p 757).

Again, this assertion of Steffen et al. *seems to erode the contributions that Harris and others associate with a more ancient wisdom (and not only with "this generation")*, where concerns with the way in which humans relate to "the planet" were (often) written into cultural traditions. Nonetheless, Harris and other Indigenous thinkers would agree with Steffen et al. that at this historical conjunction, as Steffen et al. put it, "an effective architecture of a governance system for planetary stewardship is likely to be polycentric and multi-level rather than centralized and hierarchical" (2011b, p. 757). And they would agree that it "needs to be achieved quickly" (as put by Steffen et al. 2011b, p. 757). For this to happen, though, these Indigenous authors suggest that *ways of appreciating what Indigenous knowledge systems have to offer, need to be (quickly) developed too.*

## An Alternative Understanding of Neoliberal Economics: A View from Africa

The trajectory taken when neoliberal economic principles became worldwide applied (led by the USA, as Steffen et al. 2011a, p. 850, note) was not the only possible one that could have been taken. To support this point, I refer primarily to

Murove's African-centered analysis of the consequences of this global imposition and how it rested on a specific view of economics that was not universally shared. This is not to say that Murove's analysis of what Indigenous African worldviews offer is uncontestable or that all those espousing an African humanism would agree with his analysis. But I am using his work in the context of this paper because he connects African humanism very clearly with also caring for "Mother Earth". He refers favorably to the Stoic philosophy of the Church Father Gregory of Nazinzen, as cited in Hengel (1986), and sees connections between this and African worldviews. He notes that Gregory of Nazinzen interprets two major phases in (economic) history:

> The first phase was characterized by harmonious existence between humanity and nature, whereby humanity was under the tutelage of nature. In this primordial state, nature was seen as a relative to live with instead of subduing. The second phase in the history of this evolution became that of avarice-driven private ownership of property. This phase was a precipitation of social and environmental discord and humanity's ultimate vulnerability (2005, p. 24).

From Murove's understanding of the "first phase", where nature is seen as a *relative*, we can see that this concurs with Harris and Wasilewski's account of the family on earth, where we are all relatives (2004, p. 492). And the notion that relatives should live in harmonious relationships (as expressed by Harris and Wasilewski) is likewise shared by Murove. Like Harris and Wasilewski, Murove laments the stage of "evolution" driven by avarice, which went hand in hand with social as well as environmental discord.

Murove refers to the African concept of *Ubuntu* (translated as "I am because we are") and relates this to the Shona concept of *Ukama*. He explains that *Ukama* means:

> being related and interrelated, whereby human well-being and the well-being of everything that exists is understood in terms of interrelatedness. Relationality is seen as indispensable to the well-being of everything (2005, p. 151).

Now he argues that according to both Ubuntu and Ukama, human identity is not only restricted to fellow human beings, but includes the whole of life:

> What it means to be human is not only restricted to human society but also to the natural world. .. .. In Ukama, "a person can only be a person in, with and through not just other people but in, with and through the natural environment (Murove 1999, p. 1; Prozesky 2001 p. 4; Murove 2005, p. 151).

Murove does not interpret African humanism as implying that the natural environment becomes marginalized in status in the scheme of things (relative to humans), but on the contrary as implying *that our humanity rests upon our connectedness with nature*. (This makes provision for Midgley's (1996) suggestion that a critical systemic approach need not imply that ecological concerns are undervalued in the quest for human emancipation. Smith adopts a similar approach in regard to the concerns of critical systemic thinking with "the simultaneous improvement of human well-being and ecosystem health" (2011, p. 1)).

Murove suggests that in contrast to Cartesian conceptions of human rationality (as linked to individual identity), “the individual’s identity is something communal or is an identity that ceases to be meaningful outside the realm of communion with others in society as well as with all realities that constitute existence” (2005, p. 154). Based on this view of “human nature”, Murove offers a critique of economic structures premised on the idea of humans as essentially selfish. He argues, following Polanyi (1968), that, as he puts it,

> self-interest or greed did not have a universal applicability in all economic relations, rather, it was an evolutionary antecedent of early modernity in western society. Polanyi went a step further to argue that in many non-western societies, selfishness was rather externally induced, especially during the era of colonialism (2005, p.72).

Murove treats Polanyi as suggesting, by implication, that

> in societies where people have an inherent tendency to care for each other, economic relations based on competitive greed could not have existed. It follows that economic relations that were based on greed or selfishness were actually invented in the same way that they were invented in the western societies during the era of early modernity (Murove 2005, p. 72).

Murove proposes that the liberating effect of this analysis is that we can understand “the free market idea as an historical social creation, or a phenomenon that was consciously brought into existence by philosophers and economists” (2005, p. 73). This implies that it is capable of being altered and indeed that its alteration is not out of line with “human nature” (seen from an Indigenous perspective). Furthermore, the quest to care for all that exists—including for all living and nonliving things—can also be seen as consistent with our human potentialities, as humans. McIntyre-Mills supports and extends this argument when she notes in her book on *Systemic Ethics* that “transdisciplinary research diverges from the limited calculations of economics and is instead rooted in notions of what wellbeing actually means for cultural change” (2014a, p. 28).

Also addressing the question of how the natural world outside of human existence became seen in calculative terms, Masemula (2013) expresses, with reference to Cajete (2000), how “Western paradigmatic views of science are largely about measurement using Western mathematics” (2013, p. 125). He notes how Cajete criticizes the imposed mathematization of nature wherein “mathematics has … been superimposed on nature like a grid and then examined within that framework” (p. 125). A consequence of this mathematization is that other ways of comprehending, and engaging with, nature become excluded.

In addition, Masemula cites Gingras’s (2001) critique of the way in which Newtonian mechanics distilled knowledge “into science and non-science [with the latter being devalued], while the mathematization of physics further distilled the knowledge of nature that had been the domain of philosophers” (2013, p. 126). He refers to Gingras’s account of the negative consequences of the mathematization of our knowledge of nature:

- **Socially**, the use of mathematics in explaining nature "excluded actors from legitimately participating in discourses on natural philosophy". (It was thus elitist in essence, rather than inviting collective considerations around our relationship to nature).
- **Epistemologically**, the use of mathematics in dynamics had the effect of "replacing explanations by calculations". (Indigenous-oriented understandings of the natural world, as expressed in non-mathematized language, were thus quashed).
- **Ontologically**, "by its ever more abstract treatment of phenomena", it allowed scientists to assume an emotional distance from the realm of nature—with, as we have seen, deleterious consequences for possibilities of developing a caring relationship (Masemula 2013, p. 126).

What I wish to show with reference to these authors' work, is that there is clearly a need for humans to appreciate *diverse perspectives*, rather than primarily credentializing Western-oriented approaches to knowing and to living, which then become imposed (either physically or symbolically). McIntyre-Mills (2014c) expresses a similar sentiment as follows:

> Significant research needs to contribute to developing insight and foresight. It needs to strive to foster and manage diverse forms of knowledge, including verbal, visual, physical, musical mathematical, introspective and interpersonal (2014c, p. 8).

Only in this way, McIntyre-Mills argues, can we hope to "address complex socio-environmental challenges" (2014, p. 8). Of course, as many Indigenous authors themselves recognize, the (re)credentializing of Indigenous knowledge systems and styles of knowing does not imply that all "knowledge" (and ways of acting) as proffered within Indigenous systems has to be accepted. Rather, the point is to be open to a dialogical engagement with a variety of ways of knowing, appreciating what Indigeneity has to offer, but not assuming that it is all-knowing (cf. Romm 2014). Goduka clarifies this stance:

> There is historical and contemporary evidence that Indigenous peoples have committed environmental "sins" through over-grazing, over-hunting, over-cultivation of the land and sometimes over-reliance on their knowledge without wanting to draw on and integrate other ways of knowing (2012, p. 14).

Goduka calls for an openness of spirit which allows Indigenous Knowledge (IK) to be a *dynamic system* of knowledge production, which can accommodate alternative visions (and approaches to knowing).

In the next Section, I turn to two examples of attempts to indeed foster diverse approaches to knowing, in the context of ecosystem governance. The first example is of a case in South Africa; the second refers to an Intergovernmental Science-Policy Platform on Biodiversity and Ecosystem services.

## Synthesizing Modern Science and Indigenous Knowledge Systems: Some Examples

The first example that I discuss in this section is a case offered by Kaschula Twine and Scholes (2005) of coppice harvesting of fuelwood species on a South African Common.

### *A Community-Based Approach to Sustainable Coppice Harvesting (South Africa)*

Kaschula et al. (2005) explain their approach to research, based on utilizing scientific and indigenous knowledge in a community-based natural resource management project in South Africa. They indicate that the research was set up as a cooperative relationship between "local" (Indigenous) and "scientific" ways of knowing. The project was aimed at dealing with coppice harvesting of fuelwood species towards engendering a community-based natural resource management process. The project took into consideration the Indigenous concern with recognizing that "Indigenous cosmologies … treat plant, animal, and human interactions as a single spiritual, moral, and regenerative system". The research sought to "incorporate these cosmological traits into management policy" (2005, p. 388).

As far as the research process is concerned, this meant that the researchers tried to move towards processing "a complex collection of biological and social data with a view to implementing sustainable, locally-administered, resource management practice" (Kaschula et al. 2005, p. 392). This in turn meant respecting that there are a variety of ways of approaching the question of how to encompass local understandings of tree vegetative regeneration. Apart from collecting "biological data" (and interpreting it via the use of variable analysis) they also were concerned with investigating how communities make use of, and manage their own natural resources. The researchers were keen to consider the comparison between the "subjective" accounts of participants (in regard to tree regeneration) with the supposedly more "objective" scientific information gained by isolating identified variables.

They comment as follows:

> Where as scientific knowledge is inferred from the isolation and quantification of single variables, Indigenous knowledge tends to focus more on the bigger picture, bracketing plant responses into general trends and "rules of thumb" rather than specific categories (2005, p. 410).

Furthermore, the Indigenous way of approaching the issues was, in the researchers' view, more systemic, in that it required understanding and operating "at the broadest systems-level scale" to encompass multiple levels—including social and political and not just biological levels (Kaschula et al. 2005, p. 410).

Ultimately, according to Kaschula et al.'s account, the researchers, with participants, worked to unite but not deny the differences between these different approaches, so that a community-based natural resource management system which gave credence to both could become developed. This was by admitting that the scientifically isolated variables could be seen as part of a web of interrelated variables (which themselves were seen as in effect not isolatable from other variables), and by taking this interconnectedness into account in the communal development of a workable way of knowing in this context.

The next example to which I turn is one that reports on efforts to develop functional mechanisms in an international forum for "legitimate, transparent and constructive ways of creating synergies across knowledge systems" (Tengo et al. 2014, p. 579).

## *An Intergovernmental Science-Policy Platform on Biodiversity and Ecosystem Services (IPBES)*

Tengo et al. (2014) refer to the recently established Intergovernmental Science-Policy Platform on Biodiversity and Ecosystem Services (IPBES), which they see as an initiative aimed at specifically providing for "indigenous and local knowledge and its contribution to the conservation and sustainable use of biodiversity and ecosystems" in its operational principles and as part of its evaluation of processes (IPBES 2012; 2013a, b). They note that in the context of the IPBES, where "power inequities and epistemological differences between diverse knowledge systems are brought to the fore" it is important that the participants recognize that there are various ways in which one can treat the differences in outlook as offered in different knowing systems (2014, p. 582). They refer to three options that can be differentiated:

- integration of knowledge;
- parallel approaches to developing synergies across knowledge systems; and
- co-production of knowledge.

They also note that these terms (integration, parallelism, and co-production) may be used differently by different scholars, but they argue that the tendency within an "integrative" approach, is for the credentializing of local/Indigenous knowledge *only when it can be brought into alignment with methods for scientific validation* (as in laboratory trials). In contrast to this, a parallel approach tries to assign *equal status* to different ways of knowing, viewing each as "legitimate in its own right" (legitimated by invoking different criteria of validation in each case)—2014, p. 582). However, they suggest that the encouragement of this parallel approach *may not necessarily lead to people's learning* across the different knowing systems. Finally, they refer to what they consider to be a preferable approach to working with different styles of knowing (and conceptions of its validation), namely, "the *co-production of knowledge*" (2014, p. 582, my italics). This involves people engaging in dialogue with one another, and collaborating in deciding how to develop synergies across the knowledge systems. (This can be argued to be the approach encouraged by Kaschula et al. in the example discussed above, where the idea was to develop a workable way forward through using the research to bring together the different knowing systems). What is important to focus upon in this third approach is the quality of the interaction among knowledge systems, so that none of them comes to dominate the other by claiming a better way of being able to address the issues under consideration. To this effect Tengo et al. note that cross-cultural workshops, where participants are made aware of different ways of developing and validating "knowing" and can talk across their perspectives so as to learn from one another, were established by IPBES (2014, p. 582).

Tengo et al. note that the challenge of validation has been a continuing problem for the social sciences, but that historically in practice "an overly narrow understanding of what constitutes valid scientific practice" has prevailed. This has, for instance, "led to the detrimental exclusion of knowledge produced by local scientific practices from official forest management and forest policy in the US" (2014, p. 583). In the context of interaction between (Western) science and other knowledge systems, this has meant "a failure to capture the claims and perspectives of other knowledge holders … and undermined the participation of different groups in decision making" (2014, p. 583). They argue that there are a myriad of contexts in which this failure to capture/accommodate alternative knowing systems has led to deleterious consequences (in terms of human–environment interactions). They thus plead for an approach (which they offer in the paper) for "stressing the importance of grounding collaboration on an equal starting point", with a view to developing synergistic understanding "across knowledge systems" (2014, pp. 583–584).

Tengo et al. indicate that in the intersubjective approach that they espouse, validation becomes organized in terms of what Kvale (2002) calls "communicative validity", in which, as they note, "the validity of knowledge claims is tested in a dialogue with informants and peers" (2014, p. 884). What is also important, one may add, is that—as Mugadza (2015) suggests—the quest for truth or falsity becomes sidestepped here as the aim is rather to define, with others, what "could be" in terms of designing our relationship with the world. Mugadza states that it "this logic that informs design" (2015, p. 3). This focus on looking at the web of life as *in the process of becoming based on how we see and act in it* ties in with Kvale's (2002) elucidation of a pragmatic conception of validity: this is arguably an extension of the notion of communicative validity, in that action options are co-created as people mutually define (and imagine) options for what is possible—see Romm's discussion on this (2015a, b).

Returning to Tengo et al.'s exposition, they indicate that it is the communicative notion of validation (as proposed by authors such as Kvale) that was generated and nurtured in the cross-cultural workshop referred to earlier. What is important, they suggest, is to "embed an ongoing cross-cultural practice across the world" (2014, p. 584). Here they echo the plea expressed by, for example, Harris and Wasilewski

(2004) and Goduka (2012), for an open dialogical space as the only way of fruitfully being able to connect diverse knowledge systems for "enhanced ecosystem governance" (2014, p. 579). Tengo et al. see the IPBES as having made important steps in this direction, which can be strengthened and carried over to other policy-making arenas.

What all these authors as cited in this section underscore is that the drive toward what McIntyre-Mills calls "expanding markets based on extracting profit from workers and the environment" (2014a, p. 10) *has to be questioned by invoking alternative ways of envisaging the world and our place in it.* This also means that in the development of processes for enhanced ecosystems governance we have to be mindful, as McIntyre-Mills reminds us, that "the environment is primary and that designs need to ensure that they protect the web of life, rather than pitting profit versus the planet systemic ethics" (2014a, p. 10). To take this on board in effect means foregrounding what many Indigenous and Indigenous-oriented authors have repeatedly stressed, that we cannot but orient to taking seriously our stewardship responsibilities to care for "mother earth" (and all our relatives on earth).

## Conclusion

As stated by Owuor (2007), the word *Indigenous* has often been used to refer to "specific groups of people defined by ancestral territories, collective cultural configurations and historical locations" (2007, p. 22). Goduka notes, though, that this does not imply a static view either of Indigeneity or of the "knowledge" that becomes created in Indigenous communities. Indeed Goduka suggests that IK "evolves in situ and is dynamic and creative, constantly growing and adapting to meet new conditions" (2012, p. 3). She suggests that we consider IK as "cultural knowledge in its broadest sense", that is, in the sense that it "is embedded in a dynamic system in which spirituality, kinship, local politics and other factors are tied together and influence one another" (2012, p. 3). This understanding of IK focuses on its being rooted in a particular community or culture, but does not preclude communication across cultural heritages, insofar as the intention is to "experience the world as a whole, recognizing the inherent rights of other people and beings and living accordingly" (as Lowan-Trudeau puts it 2014, p. 356).

In this paper, I have argued that what is problematic is when Indigenous understandings of the connectedness of all living and nonliving things is ignored in the quest for what Harris and Wasileski (2004) call "power and profit". I have focused on drawing out aspects of Indigeneity (as expressed by various authors) that imply an orientation of caring for others and for "Nature". I have not tried to deal with the question of whether all Indigenous communities would subscribe to this orientation to the same extent. In the context of Africa, as Quan-Baffour and Romm point out (2015), African humanism is itself in a process of re-invention as Africans continually 'read, challenge, [and] rewrite their discourses' (Mudimbe 1988, p. xi, as cited in Quan-Baffour and Romm 2015). As Goduka also states,

Indigeneity and what it implies in practice, is neither clear-cut nor fixed, but is a dynamic system of knowledge-production (2012). What I suggest is that the features of Indigeneity relating to "connectivity" or "selves-in-relation" can make place for what Lowan-Trudeau calls a "third space between Western and Indigenous ecological approaches" (2014, p. 354). Because the Indigenous worldviews as explicated in this paper embody a deep (emotion- and value-based) appreciation of the connectedness of the web of life (as also understood within versions of critical systemic thinking), I have proposed that we need to foreground Indigenous—and Indigenous-oriented—ways of understanding our stewardship responsibilities, while working collaboratively towards (re)directing the Anthropocene in the current era.

## References

Barnand C, Van Paassen A (2013) Equity power games, and legitimacy: dilemmas of participatory natural resource management. Ecol Soc 18(2):21–31

Bawden RJ (2011) Epistemic aspects of social ecological conflict. In: Wright D, Camden-Pratt C, Hill S (eds) Social ecology: applying ecological understanding to our lives and our planet. Hawthorne Press, Stroud

Bullard R (2002) Poverty, pollution and environmental racism: strategies for building healthy and sustainable communities. Environmental justice resource center, clark Atlanta University. (Retrieved at: http://www.ejrc.cau.edu/PovpolEj.html.45)

Cajete G (2000) Native science: native laws of interdependence. Clear Light, New Mexico

Cannella GS, Manuelito KD (2008) Feminisms from unthought locations: indigenous worldviews, marginalized feminisms, and revisioning an anticolonial social science. In: Denzin NK, Lincoln YS, Smith LT (eds) Handbook of critical and indigenous methodologies. Sage, London

Chilisa B (2012) Indigenous research methodologies. Sage, London

Christakis AN, Bausch KC (2006) Co-laboratories of democracy: how people harness their collective wisdom and power to construct the future. Information Age Publishing, Greenwich

Christakis AN (2014) An epic learning journey: from the club of rome to dialogic design science & demosophia. In: Metcalf GS (ed) Social systems and design. Springer, New York

Cisneros RT, Hisijara BA (2013) A social systems approach to global problems. Institute for 21st century agoras, createspace Independent Publishing Platform

Diamond J (2005) Collapse: how societies choose to fail or succeed. Viking, New York

Gingras Y (2001) What did mathematics do to physics? History Sci 39:383–416

Goduka N (2012) Re-discovering indigenous knowledge—Ulwazi Lwemveli for strengthening sustainable livelihood opportunities within rural contexts in the eastern cape province. Indilinga Afr J Ind Knowl Syst 11(1):1–19

Harris L-D, Wasilewski J (2004) Indigeneity, an alternative worldview. Syst Res Behav Sci 21:489–503

Hengel M (1986) Earliest christianity: containing acts and the history of earliest christianity: property and riches in the early church. SCM Press Ltd, London

Intergovernmental Science-Policy Platform on Biodiversity and Ecosystem Services (IPBES) (2012) Report on meeting to determine modalities and institutional arrangements for an intergovernmental science-policy platform on biodiversity and ecosystem services, UNEP/IPBES.MI2/9. Bonn, Germany

IPBES (2013a) Report on plenary of the intergovernmental science-policy platform on biodiversity and ecosystem services IPBES/2/17. Bonn, Germany

IPBES (2013b) Consideration of initial elements: recognizing indigenous and local knowledge and building synergies with science IPBES/1/INF/5. Bonn, Germany

Kaschula SA, Twine WE, Scholes MC (2005) Coppice harvesting of fuelwood species on a south african common: utilizing scientific and indigenous knowledge in community based natural resource management. Human Ecol 33(3):387–418

Kvale S (2002) The social construction of validity. In: Denzin NK, Lincoln YS (eds) The qualitative inquiry reader. Sage, Newbury Park, CA

Lowan-Trudeau G (2014) Considering ecological métissage: to blend or not to blend? J Exp Educ 37(4):351–366

Masemula MB (2013) Integration of modern science and indigenous knowledge systems: towards a coexistence of the two systems of knowing in the South African curriculum. Masters thesis, University of South Africa

McIntyre-Mills JJ (2002) Critical systemic praxis for social and environmental justice. Syst Pract Action Res 15(1):3–35

McIntyre-Mills JJ (2003) Yeperenye dreaming in conceptual, geographical, and cyberspace. Syst Pract Action Res 16(5):309–338

McIntyre-Mills JJ (2008) Systemic ethics: social, economic and environmental implications of eating our yellow cake in South Australia. Syst Res Behav Sci 25:225–248

McIntyre-Mills JJ (2014a) Systemic ethics and non-anthropocentric stewardship. Springer, New York

McIntyre-Mills JJ (2014b) Transformation from wall street to wellbeing. Springer, New York

McIntyre-Mills JJ (2014c) Reconsidering boundaries. Sociopedia, International Sociological Association

Midgley G (1996) What is this thing called CST? In: Flood RL, Romm NRA (eds) Critical systems thinking: current research and practice. Plenum, New York

Mudimbe VY (1988) The invention of africa: gnosis, philosophy, and the order of knowledge. Indiana University Press, Bloomington

Mugadza G (2015) Systems thinking and design thinking: complementary approaches? Syst Think World J Reflect Action 4:1–7. (http://stwj.systemswiki.org)

Murove MF (1999) The shona concept of ukama and the process philosophical concept of relatedness, with special reference to the ethical implications of the contemporary neo-liberal economic practices. Masters thesis, University of Natal

Murove MF (2005) The theory of self-interest in modern economic discourse: a critical study in the light of african humanism and process philosophical anthropology. Doctoral thesis, University of South Africa

Owuor JA (2007) Integrating African indigenous knowledge in Kenya's formal education system: the potential for sustainable development. J Contemp Issues Educ 2(2):21–37

Polanyi K (1968) The great transformation: the political and economic origins of our time. Renehart and Company Inc, New York

Prozesky MH (2001) Well-Fed animals and starving babies: environmental and developmental challenges in process and african perspectives. In: Murove MF (ed) African ethics: an anthology of comparative and applied ethics. University of KwaZulu-Natal Press, Scottsville

Quan-Baffour PK, Romm NRA (2015) Ubuntu-inspired training of adult literacy teachers as a route to generating "community" enterprises. J Lit Res 46(4):455–474

Romm NRA (2010) New racism: revisiting researcher accountabilities. Springer, New York

Romm NRA (2014) Indigenous ways of knowing and possibilities for re-envisaging globalization: implications for human ecology. J Human Ecol 48(1):123–133

Romm NRA (2015a) Reviewing the transformative paradigm: a critical systemic and relational (indigenous) lens. Syst Pract Action Res 28:411–427

Romm NRA (2015b) Reflections on the epistemological grounding of structured dialogical design. Paper prepared for presentation at the 2015 international conference on the science of dialogic design Cyprus University of Technology, 4–8 May

Ross A, Pickering K (2002) The politics of reintegrating australian aboriginal and american indian indigenous knowledge into resource management: the dynamics of resource appropriation and cultural revival. Human Ecol 30(2):187–214

Smith LT (1999) Decolonizing methodologies: research and indigenous peoples. Zed books, New York

Smith T (2011) Using critical systems thinking to foster an integrated approach to sustainability: a proposal for development practitioners. Environ Dev Sustain 13:1–17

Steffen W, Grinevald J, Crutzen P, McNeill J (2011a) The anthropocene: conceptual and historical perspectives. Philos Trans Royal Soc 369:842–867

Steffen W, Persson A, Deutsch L, Zalasiewicz J, Williams M, Richardson K, Crumley C, Crutzen P, Folke C, Gordon L, Molina M, Ramanathan V, Rockstrom J, Scheffer M, Schellnhuber HJ, Svedin U (2011b) The anthropocene: from global change to planetary stewardship. Ambio 40:739–761

Tengo M, Brondizio ES, Elmqvist T, Malmer P, Spierenburg M (2014) Connecting diverse knowledge systems for enhanced ecosystem governance: the multiple evidence base approach. Ambio 43:579–591

Wilkinson R, Pickett K (2010) The spirit level: why equality is better for everyone. Penguin, London

## Author Biography

**Norma Romm** (DLitt et Phil Sociology) is a research professor in the Department of Adult Basic Education and Youth Development, University of South Africa. She is the author of The Methodologies of Positivism and Marxism (Macmillan, 1991), Accountability in Social Research (Springer, 2001), New Racism (Springer, 2010), People's Education in Theoretical Perspective (with V. McKay, Longman, 1992), Diversity Management (with R. Flood, Wiley, 1996), and Assessment of the Impact of HIV and AIDS in the Informal Economy of Zambia (with V. McKay, ILO, 2008). She has co-edited two books—Social Theory (with M. Sarakinsky, Heinemann, 1994) and Critical Systems Thinking (with R. Flood, Plenum, 1996). She has published more than 95 research articles on the contribution of research to social development, the way in which research can be practised accountably, Indigenous ways of knowing and living, and the facilitation of adult learning. She has worked on a range of projects aimed at increasing equity for organisations such as the ILO, ADEA, IOM, and UNESCO.

# Chapter 2
# Risks, Crisis and the European Union Law: Implications and Parallels for Addressing Financial, Energy Security and Environmental Catastrophe

**Juliane Mendelsohn and Thea Bygojordet Sveen**

**Abstract** This paper compares crisis narratives and descriptions of the Anthropocene to the institutional and substantive changes that have been brought on the way by the creation of the Banking and Energy Union in the EU. From the aims alone, it becomes clear that both the Banking and the Energy Union were born out of the political desire to make each of the systems more robust, but that the visions themselves fall short of significant substantive change or a reinvention of the system. Whilst the explanation of this is almost entirely political, some of the reasons also have to do with the functioning and the mechanisms of the law. The law, in particular public law, stands and falls with formal legal principles, has a particular difficulty dealing with, defining and coming up with solutions for risk whilst staying true to formal principles such as certainty and proportionality. Risk detection requires the introduction of new procedures and agencies (institutions). The mitigation of risks requires a multicontexual and multipolar balancing of rights and interests. Both proceduralism and a complex act of balancing can guarantee the integrity of law and its methodology, but they do not bring about substantive change. This paper sees a third method of risk mitigation in the creation of new institutions (such as the Energy Union, but also the United Nation or NATO). This is perceived as the creation of something that is larger than the threat it addresses ('super structures'), but substantively ends up enforcing little more than the "lowest common denominator". This paper, therefore, suggests abandoning such methodological approaches and changing the principles on which the EU and the law of the common market is based instead. It proposes a "first best" and a "second best" solution. The first is the introduction of new and prevalent aims and principles and

J. Mendelsohn (✉)
Freie Universität, Berlin, Germany
e-mail: jkmendelsohn@gmail.com

T. Bygojordet Sveen
European University Institute, Florence, Italy
e-mail: thea.bygojordet@gmail.com



J. McIntyre-Mills et al. (eds.), *Balancing Individualism and Collectivism*,
Contemporary Systems Thinking, DOI 10.1007/978-3-319-58014-2_2

an actual change of the economic system. The second (though more likely solution) proposes a mere extension of the goals of the European union, which results in a careful act of balance between more sustainability and the development of the liberal common market project.

## Introduction: Notions of Catastrophe and Crisis Narratives

> Justice herself, famed for fair Dealing,
> By Blindness had not lost her Feeling;
> Her Left Hand, which the Scales should hold,
> Had often drops', bribed with Gold.
>
> **Mandeville**

In the past couple of years, crisis narratives of both climate change and financial instability have become embedded in our unconscious as types of "known unknowns". Regarding climate change, we are forced to assume that rising levels of CO2 emissions will ultimately intoxicate and impoverish European citizens and will wipe up thousands of persons in regions of the world that are more susceptible to drought or rising seas. Financial capitalism, on the other hand, has reached a point of instability where with each new crisis massive amounts of wealth are eradicated and that doctrines such as 'too big to fail' mean that profits are almost entirely privatized by the few, whilst risks are almost entirely socialized ("Inequality" (Piketty 2013) or "snowball inequality" (Markovits 2015)). The effects of climate change and post-capitalism have been described as follows by various authors:

> We know that if we continue on our path of allowing emissions to rise year after year, climate change will change everything about our world. Major cities will very likely drown, ancient cultures will be swallowed by the seas, and there is a very high chance that our children will spend a great deal of their lives fleeing and recovering from vicious storms and extreme droughts (Klein 2014, p. 4).
>
> As with the end of feudalism 500 years ago, capitalism's replacement by post-capitalism will be accelerated by external shocks and shaped by the emergence of a new kind of human being. And it has started (Manson 2015).
>
> Living with this kind of cognitive dissonance is simple part of being alien in this jarring moment in history, when a crisis we have been studiously ignoring is hitting us in the face – and yet we are doubling down on the stuff that is causing the crisis in the first place (Klein 2014, p. 72).

The process of financialization that led to the crisis we are living in now is distinct from all other phases of financialization historically recorded in the twentieth century. Classical financial crises were situated at a precise moment of the economic cycle, particularly at the end of the cycle, in conjunction with a fall of profit margins as a result of capitalist competition on an international scale, in addition to social forces under- mining geopolitical equilibrium in the international division of labor. Typical twentieth-century financialization thus represented an attempt, somewhat "parasitic" and "desperate," to recover what capital could no longer get in the real economy in financial markets (Marazzi 2010, p. 26).

Though there is still hope, descriptions of the Anthropocene—which has either already begun or lies in the near future—are not far removed from the above descriptions. The notion of the Anthropocene suggests that "humankind has become a global geological force in its own right" (Steffen et al. 2011a, p. 843). Life and the law in the Anthropocene seems to run under the assumption that from this point forward:

> no government, whether in an over-consuming or under-consuming region, rich or poor, has enough money or personnel to restore communities disrupted by climate change events to their condition before the tragedy. It will not be possible to rebuild everywhere to restore what was.

From the perspective of legal scholarship the Anthropocence assumes irreversability and that every dimension of life is different from times past. Under the premises of the Anthropocene, legal theorists, therefore, adopt an approach to law and policy that is fundamentally new and transformative:

> When law has integrity, it is because it reflects profound social norms, shared in a society; law can also be instrumental, a tool of authority. As humans learn to cope with the disruptions occasioned by a changing climate, the need to strengthen communities around fundamental norms will be a determinant to human well-being (Robinson 2014).

The description of the Anthropocene and crisis narratives have undeniable commonalities and both suggest that it is necessary to fundamentally change the system and the norms on which it is based and to abandon the idea that the system can be "fixed" and that crisis is either temporary or managable.

We would like to use these notions and suggestions as 'guiding stars' in order to analyse and critique the actual legal and political changes that have been made and the new institutions that have been put in place in order pose the fundamental question, whether we have done enough or whether the change are in fact more form than they are content.

In the aftermath of a banking crisis and the evermore daunting likelihood of an energy and environmental crisis, the EU has created two institutions: the Banking Union and the Energy Union as means and vehicle as solutions to the financial energy security and climate change crisis (tri-crisis) and to make European market more sustainable in future.

The Banking Union consists of three pillars: the single rulebook for regulatory oversight of banks; the single supervisory mechanism, for supervising Europe's largest banks, and the single resolution system for resolving failing banks in future. The Banking Union aims to:

- ensure banks are robust and able to withstand crisis
- prevent situations where taxpayers' money is used to save failing banks
- reduce market fragmentation by harmonising the financial sector rules
- strengthen financial stability in the euro area and the EU as a whole.

Though EU energy law is more developed and integrated than banking law and there are several references to actual legal notions which may be more adequately operationalized, in order to reach the aims set forth. The Energy Union, therefore, consists of the following five mutually reinforcing and closely interrelated dimensions which are designed to bring greater energy security, sustainability and competitiveness (Energy Union 2015, 4):

- Energy security, solidarity and trust;
- A fully integrated European energy market;
- Energy efficiency contributing to moderation of demand;
- Decarbonising the economy, and
- Research, Innovation and Competitiveness.

From the aims alone, it becomes clear that both the Banking and the Energy Union were born out of the political desire and capital to end crisis and make each of the systems more sustainable and robust but that the visions themselves fall short of a reinvention or overhaul of the system. This is either due to an unwillingness or an impossibility fix or reinvent the system whilst still clinging to old beliefs and paradigms.

Whilst the reasons for this are almost entirely political, some of the reasons also have to do with the functioning and the mechanisms of the law. As Robinson (2014) puts it: „The discipline of the law is deeply implicated in the systems that have caused the end to the Holocene, and at once is central also to the reforms needed to cope with the emerging Anthropocene.“As we shall see in the next section, the way the law classically deals with risks and catastrophe does not necessarily help to overcome our "cognitive dissonance" (Klein 2014).

## Risks and the Response of the Law

The necessity to calculate future risks, to seek insurance or find other means of dealing with the uncertainties of our daily lives have almost become all-encompassing. This has been adequately described by Ulrich Beck as life in a "global risk society" in which "the category of risk consumes and transforms everything". The constant fear or unconscious knowledge of large threats and future personal or global catastrophe has made our daily lives and states of mind one of an almost tangible psychosis. To Ulrich Beck "risk is not the same as catastrophe, but the anticipation of the future catastrophe in the presence. As a result, risk leads a dubious, insidious, would-be, fictitious, allusive existence: it is existent and non-existent, present and absent, doubtful and real" (Beck 2009, p. 1).

Currently, we experience what could be termed as a risk-taking paradox. A society, evermore prone to risk is founded on paradigms deemed impossible to change. Risk taking in the short-term seems to be uncoupled with the need for a long-term commitment to change the marked-based system. Aware of the difficulties to change our current path the remedies proposed do not question the very structure that led to the legitimisation and everyday risk taking in the first place. This short sighted, risk-taking society is being led by institutions both blind to but also responsible for their possible elimination or reduction.

The law, in particular public law that stands and falls with formal legal principles, has a particular difficulty dealing with, defining and coming up with solutions for risk, whilst staying true to formal principles such as certainty and proportionality. It is inherently impractical and at times seemingly impossible to formulate normative rules or conclude a proportionate act of balancing different rights and interests in face of uncertainty: "while law itself is a complex, multi-layered phenomenon, it famously trades in binaries, taxonomies and other conceptual reductionisms. This—it is increasingly clear—is a deep-seated orientation ill-suited to the complexity of rapidly mutating, polycontextural, densely interwoven contemporary predicaments" (Grear 2015).

Notions and different degrees of "threat" and "danger“, ranging from an imminent threat to an apparent danger, are most common to public administrative, police and international law. Compared with notions of threat and danger, notions of risk and the necessity to regulate risks and hazards, pose a challenge to the law, as they are even less tangible and shrouded in uncertainty. Theories, definition and suggestions on the regulations of risks first surfaced when environmental challenges and nuclear, pharmaceutical and hazards relating to the materials of certain goods become evermore prominent. The law had to address these risks needed in a manner that was still proportionate with regards to the holders of property rights and rights of occupation. The law therefore developed methods to first detect these risks and hazards and then to mitigate them in a proportionate manner. Risk detection and the creation of an awareness of future risk requires the introduction of new procedures and agencies (institutions). The mitigation of risks requires a multicontexual and multipolar balancing of rights and interests (DiFabio 1994; Lepsius 1995; Ladeur 2004).

Both proceduralism and a complex multipolar balancing of interest can guarantee the integrity of law and its methodology, but they do not bring about substantive change or lead to the avoidance of catastrophe in the most effective manner. By example, it seems plausible to ban the production of nuclear energy or to break up big banks, but both can only be achieved by a transformation of the economic system rather than by an act of balancing currently existing rights and interest. On the other hand, as risks become evermore present and all-encompassing Cass Sunstein (2013) rightly points to the excessive movement towards partnerlization and limitations governments can easily and readily impose on the rights and freedoms of their citizens in time of crisis or catastrophe. Citizens no longer understand the basis and the assumptions on which government action is based and the nature of the events they aim to avoid.

A third way to curb risks, which we identify and is most striking on an international and EU level, is by the creation of super institutions, such as the NATO, the UN, the Basel Committee, the World Economic Forum, the IMF, the World Bank and most recently the Banking and Energy Union. We assume that the success of these institutions is a product of the belief that they are simply larger than the problems they address. The size of the institutions and the competences conferred onto them do not however, automatically lead to equally large substantial change. Not only the choice of wrong instruments (most recently the IMF's stern position on austerity), but almost always an insufficient degree of action are born out of the necessity to make political compromise. The current state of the Banking and Energy Union is constituent with these fears.

## The Aims and Content of the Banking and Energy Union

### *Aims and Content of the Banking Union*

The Banking Union to date consists of three pillars: the so-called "single rule book" to harmonize the regulatory requirements posed to all banks in all member states; the single supervisory mechanisms, which means that Europe's largest banks (so-called Significant Financial Institutions or "SIFIs") are now regulated by the ECB and the single resolutions mechanism: the attempt to create a resolution scheme and a functioning bankruptcy law for banks.

The single rule book consist of: (a) the Requirements Directive IV (CRD IV; Directive 2013/36/EU of 26 June 2013; Regulation (EU) No 575/2013 of 26 June 2013) which implements the Basel III capital requirements for banks; (b) the Deposit Guarantee Scheme Directive (DGSD; Directive 2014/49/EU of 16 April 2014) which regulates deposit insurance in case of a bank's inability to pay its debts; and (c) Bank Recovery and Resolution Directive (BRRD; Directive 2014/59/EU of 15 May 2014), which establishes a framework for the recovery and resolution of credit institutions and investment firms found to be in danger of failing. The single resolutions mechanism is the creation of uniform rules and a uniform procedure for the resolution of credit institutions and certain investment firms. The single supervisory mechanisms (SSM) is a new institutions that is part of the European Central Bank and has been monitoring the stability of Europe's largest banks since November 2014, after the release and review of hundreds of stress-tests.

As was the general critique of 'super intuitions' above, the creation of a large institution does not necessarily raise the bar in terms of material requirements significantly. Since the financial crisis of 2008, we know that banks hold too little capital/are too indebted and take too many risks. Since low capital creates incentives for risk taking, the solution to reducing the fragility of financial sector is obvious and simple. The implementation of the Basel III requirements in the "single rule book" undeniably causes banks to hold more capital than they did before the crisis and the regulation of different types of banking risks, in particular systemic risks, is much more nuanced and no longer places all of its faith on the internal risk management and risk assessment of financial institutions. Capital requirements are, however, still low, meaning that the way banks do business has not changed since the crisis, everyone has just become more aware of the inherent risks. The inherent paradoxes as well as the incentives to enter into extensive risk transformation, maturity transformations and risk diversification are also still present. The regulations try to hamper these effects by creating options for counter cyclical and systemic risk buffers as well as a so-called leverage ratio of 3%. To date we are not certain whether we are any better at predicting a crisis than before, making buffers an invalidated instrument.

The alternative to capital requirements is the introduction of an even simpler and basically the inverse instrument: a leverage ratio. A leverage ratio expresses the proportion of equity to debt or places a cap on the amount of debt a financial institution can hold. Many economists have suggested introducing a leverage ratio of 15–30% and making it the central mechanism of risk regulation (Admati and Hellwig 2013). Both legally and economically/empirically, it is impossible to determine the exact leverage ratio required to make the system less volatile since "more is always better". It is, however, clear that the currently debated leverage ratio of 3% is nothing but a mere act of symbolism.

Whilst one of the main goals of the banking union is to safely resolve or restructure insolvent banks in future and to sever banking debt or a banking crisis from a sovereign debt crisis, the mechanisms the resolution scheme relies on are far from functional. One of the inherent flaws is leaving it up to banks to write up "testaments" for their future resolution and restructuring. The perverse incentives and room for regulatory capture already trump the belief that such a complex endeavor could be pulled off in future. The EU, however, also currently lacks the means to save or even to restructure banks. The resolution fund will be set up over the next couple of years. Until it is in place, funds from the ESM may be used to recapitalize banks, but even these are not sufficient to recapitalise a medium sized banks at present (Mendelsohn 2014; Hellwig 2014).

Lastly, whether a central bank is the correct institution to regulate large financial institutions is almost secondary to the fact that all of these institutions are still "systemic", they are all either still too big or too complex to fail and this does not only pose a threat to financial stability to also causes them to act the way they do and take the risks they take.

## *Aims and Content of the Energy Union*

According to Energy Union Strategy (Communication 2015), which calls for "full implementation and strict enforcement of existing energy and related legislation", a fundamental transformation of Europe's energy system is required (Energy Union 2015, p. 1). However, the primary goal of this Energy Union is "to give EU consumers—households and businesses—secure, sustainable, competitive and affordable energy". This falls short of being a statement to end climate change or to end our reliance of fossil fuels and to radically reduces emissions in the near future.

Rather it seems that the Energy Union we have created to date is still merely many declarations of intent.

Agencies within the European Union have increasingly gained powers by means of delegation from the other institutions in order to cope with technical details and specific questions. Notably, the Agency for Cooperation of Energy Regulators (ACER), which previously only assisted and coordinated national regulators but has had very limited decision-making rights, requires new powers and independence "in order to carry out regulatory functions at the European level to enable it to effectively oversee the development of the internal energy market and the related market rules as well as to deal with all cross-border issues necessary to create a seamless internal market" (Energy Union 2015, p. 9). If the existing complexity of the legal framework requires several agencies in order to make it operational, it is more than legitimate to ask whether or not a simplification of its very nature or rather a more structural change is a needed.

As previously described, the Energy Union strategy has five mutually reinforcing and closely interrelated dimensions designed to bring greater energy security, sustainability and competitiveness. These are energy security, solidarity and trust; a fully integrated European energy market; energy efficiency contributing to moderation of demand; de-carbonizing the economy, and research, innovation and competitiveness (Energy Union 2015, p. 4). A timetable for revision of the most important legal texts has been annexed to the Energy Union communication and aims to address all five dimensions.

The measures listed within the timetable are both of legal and political nature. The legislative proposals are listed in detail and the time-frame has been set, giving a coherent roadmap to the Energy Union in practical terms. It is noteworthy that the first and most important priority of the Energy Union is of a legal nature. Whilst the Rule of law should and will always be one of the hallmarks, virtues and principles of European integration, it is questionable whether the statement that "the Commission will use all instruments to ensure that Member States fully implement energy legislation … and it will strictly enforce the Treaty's competition rules" will actually lead to the outcome envisaged if the current framework is not substantially modified. Simply adding more percentages to the existing targets or revising existing legislation does not overcome our inability to think on the basis of alternative parameters different from the internal market paradigm. In order to reach other objectives than a functioning internal market, massive derogations are needed. However, these derogations are the ones that may enhance environmental protection, give member states leverage to correct market failures and drive the European integration project in a less market-driven orientation.

It is also currently still questionable whether all these revisions of existing and new legal instruments will coexist in a harmonious way and whether future conflicts between them will be solved without questioning the current status of EU law and the competences conferred to the Union. The potential conflict is further emphasized in the strategy itself which states that: "(r) enewable energy is a no-regrets option but there have been concerns about the costs and impact on the functioning of the internal market" (Energy Union 2015). It is in particular in the cases related to the promotion of renewable energy sources that the conflict with the internal market has called for creative derogations to the general rule. The Energy Union as such demands increased amounts of public intervention contrary to the internal market logic. Much has been done in the name of a main predominant environmental purpose in order to avoid a competence creep on the energy policy side where member states are still sovereign (Sveen 2014), but this approach needs to be clarified in order to establish legal certainty and clarify the boundaries of EU action within its renewable energies policies.

Alongside consumer issues and responses to climate change, the Energy Union was also established as a response to the European energy security crisis in connection with Russia′s annexation of the Crimean peninsula. The Energy Union thus builds on the European Energy Security Strategy which called on policy makers at national and EU level to make clear to citizens the choices involved in reducing the dependency on particular fuels, energy suppliers and routes (Energy Union 2015, p. 4). This was indeed one of the most important backgrounds for the creation of an Energy Union, the catalyst of a larger European project. As the energy security debate confines itself to rectify immediate risks and avoid these in the long-term, the creation of the Energy Union construct demands a broader, more holistic vision of EU energy policy in general.

## Options for Regulating Future Catastrophe in Two Tiers

As the descriptions of the banking and energy union have shown, and a comparison with the literature on the Anthropocene highlights, we have managed to create super structures and many new institutions, but without significant substantive change. This is not only reflective of an inability to formulate new rules and laws and but also an inability to think of our future devoid of these risks and working according to different principles. The promised transformation in both the energy and banking sector does not explicitly seek to rectify the core aspects the crisis but stand as a mere change in appearances.

Looking at the Anthropocene, Steffen et al. state that “societies collapse if core values become dysfunctional as the external world changes and they are unable to recognize emerging problems” (2011b, p. 751). Today the European Union, is faced with this threat. “Europe is suddenly not seen as an icon of success but as an emblem of austerity, thus in terms of its promise of prosperity, failure. If success breeds legitimacy, failure, even wrongly allocated, leads to the opposite” (Weiler 2012, p. 831). It seems evermore likely that we will either continue to wrongly assume that this experiment was and will never be more than an internal market or that we will soon be faced with complete disillusion of the entire integration process.

> When tackled by legal theorists the Anthropocene trope suggests that 'humanity' stands freshly united in a new negative human universality predicated upon common vulnerability in the face of climate crisis.

According to Chakrabarty:

> Here the overarching Anthropocene sense of a new, universal humanity bearing responsibilities towards the planet also carries the promise of a more eco-responsive normativity – a normativity reflected in biocultural rights discourse – but it remains critical to counterbalance this 'new' Anthropocene 'human commonality' with the fact that human universals remain stubbornly marked by histories, presents and future histories of profound hierarchical inequality.

Skeptics of financial capitalism and climate change realists have long suggested that only a complete revision of our systems and their mechanisms can prevent catastrophe. In this context material changes to radically reform the financial sector or to end man made climate change require the establishment of new legal doctrines and principles. This is our "first best solution".

As a second-best solutions we propose is development of the legal principles of environmental protection and financial stability. Alongside other principle, careful acts of balancing would mean that these goals are constantly taken into consideration on an EU level. Certainly in the field of environmental protection these necessary treaty or EU constitutional law changes are already well on their way.

## Complete Reinvention of the System and its Principles

The calls for new principles are a new economic and legal system: a "fair economy" (Finketscher et al. 2013) or the introductions of "regenerative capitalism" are by no means mainstream or present in everyday political life, but are becoming ever-more frequent. Alongside people like Naomi Klein capturing the climate debate and Thomas Piketty bringing equality back on the agenda, the capital institute has recently put for a white paper that proposes a "Regenerative (economic) hypothesis":

> The purpose of a Regenerative Economy is to promote and sustain human prosperity and well-being in an economy of permanence. A new generation of legal principles can come to be applied to give deeper meaning to both sustainability and environmental rights across all nations. The fact that environmental rights are being acknowledged and embraced independently, in different places, is evidence that they share common roots in human instincts and cultural values about human relations with nature.

If we believe that Anthropocene scenarios are real and already present and we also believe that the instability and destructiveness of the financial sector posses an imminent threat to the overall wealth and equality of our societies, we need to change the fundamental assumptions on which our economic systems are based and the goals they are meant to serve. Translated into law and legal theory, this is nothing more than the introduction of new principles and the transposition of rules to make sure that these principles are optimized.

This notion of the principles of law is borrowed from Ronald Dworkin's and the German legal theorist Robert Alexy's respective theories of legal principles. Dworkin distinguishes principles from rules, as the two most important types of legal norms. Principles are legal considerations that lack the all-or-nothing applicability of legal rules (Dworkin 1977, p. 24). Rules are considered rigid norms that are formulated in manner, which does not allow balancing or optimization, but means, that are either to be applied—or not applied. According to Alexy, if a rule cannot be applied and there it is not possible to formulate legal exemption, then it is invalid and needs to be eliminated from the legal system. Since principles are no-rigid statements of intent, resolving the conflict between two principles is more complex than rules. Principle statements such as 'no man may profit from his own wrong' cannot always be enforced, but are always valid. According to Robert Alexy principles are statements of law that need to be fulfilled to the highest degree possible at any given point in time. When two or more principles come into conflict, they do not cancel each other out, but require balancing and the optimization of each principle: "wherever legal principles exist, the duty to optimise their normative impact follows" (Alexy 2003, p. 135).

According to Alexy and many of his critics (Poscher 2012), this first requires the balancing of the conflicting principles: "the greater the degree of non-satisfaction of, or detriment to, one principle, the greater must be the importance of satisfying the other." (Alexy 2002, p. 47). In most cases, the second step follows from the fact that the result of this balancing will be the partial or complete prioritization/precedence of one principle over another, but only for a specific case or in a specific circumstance. Here, Alexy proposes defining the exact conditions and requirements that need to be fulfilled, in order to give one principle priority. Hereby "the circumstances under which one principle take once principle takes precedence over another constitute the conditions of a rule which has the same legal consequences as the principle taking precedence" (Alexy 2002, p. 47).

Climate change needs to be stopped, the Anthropocene dealt with and "finance needs to go back to being an instrument directed towards improved wealth creation and development" (Lastra and Wood 2009, p. 531–550). In each of these cases, principles such as **sustainability, longevity, cooperation, distribution and equality** come to mind. All of these principles are described and envisioned by Robinson (2014). These principles need to be poised directly against and override the principle of wealth maximization and the acceptance that profit can be achieved without any consideration for others or the environment. These 'new principles' would therefore be given precedence/priority and a new legal and economic system would need be created by means of rules that optimize the fulfilment of these principles. In the Anthropocene context and based on the same theories, Paloniitty (2015) suggests the need to formalize the weighing of competing legislative values and objectives—arguing that the formalization of such balancing should become the judicial norm. Her hope is that this kind of interpretive, adjudicative methodology will allow judicial decision-making better to respond to the complexity of the issues involved in the deterioration of ecosystems and bring about a "paradigmatic shift".

The degree of threat or the sheer necessity to change to rethink or change the system, as was to some degree the case with the Deal New or the rise of the social market economy after of the banking crisis of 1929, does not in itself overcome the massive political and legal hurdles that challenge to systemic change in Europe as well as in the member states. Whilst the member states constantly guard their sovereignty and own interests, the European Union is deeply settled in the idea that it is primarily a trade union and a "common market". The lack of a European government and the inability to set its own agendas and policies, make it impossible for the European Union to re-envision its own future in times of crisis.

Though many have suggested that the 'ever closer union' is moving towards being more than a common market, this "more" is not yet tangible.

> For some Maastricht was finally the ushering forth of 'real' European integration. No longer merely a marketplace, but veritable economic and monetary union, the upgrading of the European Parliament, human rights and the environment in the Treaty expresses verbs with the expectation of more to come (…). For others, Maastricht was a shill game, smoke and mirrors: a half-baked monetary union, an ever-yawning democracy deficit with the power to shift the EU not match by veritable accountability and citizens impact, a vacuous concept of citizenship, with no duties and empty rights and an abandonment of the original and humane concept of Community for the hackneyed Union … (Weiler 2012, p. 826.)

Principles such as distribution and sustainability bear no relation to a mere trade union or the further integration of a common market. They would require that the aims and the identity of the European Union are reinvented and probably necessitate a change that is more radical and more transformative than the failed attempts at constitutionalism or the mere integration of the European Charta of Human Rights—an elevation of rights and norms that all member states had already agreed upon.

In reference to the legitimacy crisis Weiler states that: "This is an interesting time to be reflecting on the European construct. Europe is at a nadir which one cannot remember for many decades and which, various brave and pompous or self-serving statements notwithstanding, the Treaty of Lisbon has not been able to redress. The surface manifestations of crisis are with us every day on the front pages: the Euro crisis being the most current. Beneath this surface, at the structural level, lurk more profound and long-term signs of enduring challenge and dysfunction and malaise". Beyond reflecting on the structure and content of the European Union, it is also an (interesting) time to reflect on the eradicating and dehumanizing effects of financial capitalism and a time to realize that the threats of climate change are very real. According to Steffen et al.:

> We are the first generation with widespread knowledge of how our activities influence the Earth System, and thus the first generation with the power and the responsibility to change our relationship with the planet. Responsible stewardship entails emulating nature in terms

of resource use and waste transformation and recycling, and the transformation of agricultural, energy and transport systems (2011b, p. 757).

It is therefore time to reinvent both the structure and the principles of the European Union and to go in search of its possible future identity. In the past, such changes and the abandonment of old ideas and structures have been brought about remarkable and crass political "events" (Badiou 2012), such as the French Revolution regarding our notion of freedom and World War II regarding the spirit still transported by the *Schuman Declaration*. For many reasons, it is unlikely that the daunting financial or climate catastrophe will be such a transformative "event" in the very near future. Certainly not on a European level: "Globalized capitalism exploits people locally. Despite the hopes of left internationalization and liberal cosmopolitanism, effective politics still takes place at home" (Douzinas 2013). Both the undemocratic structures in Europe as well as the complexity of the issues at hand make it difficult convey a sense of broader public agency and make the currently existing structures evermore implicated in capture and the interest of firms who profit from the status quo.

## Inclusion of New Goals and Introduction of a Careful Act of Balancing

The second-best solutions propose the integration of new principles into the current system or rather activating the legal principles within the treaty itself. These would not override currently dominant aims such as the development of a competitive common market, but would be weighted and balanced against them carefully. Legally this can be done by means of the expansion of the goals of the European Union and by the introduction of so-called integration clauses where important principles are described.

The goals of the EU have already been expanded to include environmental protection. Art. 3(3) TEU now states that "the Union shall establish an internal market. It shall work for the sustainable development of Europe based on balanced economic growth and price stability, a highly competitive social market economy, aiming at full employment and social progress, and a high level of protection and improvement of the quality of the environment. It shall promote scientific and technological advance". Within this lies the complexity of balancing all existing aims of European integration. However, Art. 11 TEU (the environmental integration clause) now demands that:

> environmental protection requirements must be integrated into the definition and implementation of the Union's policies and activities, in particular with a view to promoting sustainable development". Such integration clauses "participate in a common project, namely ensuring that the actions of the Union are guided by a quality-of-life project … these values are, indeed, a counterweight to the project of an essentially economic nature "(De Sadeleer 2014, p. 25).

The legal status of the environmental integration clause is debatable and faces several challenges (De Sadeleer 2014, p. 21). Some argue that they are mere statements of intent and "void of any legal significance" (De Sadeleer 2014, p. 25–26). However, making more explicit use of the environmental integration clause or rather "taking it seriously"(Sjåfjell and Wiesbrock 2015) may trigger a gentle however precise change of the current market-based system without changing its core. This exercise combined with a horizontal reading of the treaties (meaning that all aims and goals are considered equal) places principles and values other than the common market in the forefront of European integration. This holistic approach that requires decision-makers to take into account not only the full range of interests affected by their decisions could rescue the current market-based logic which is not able to respond adequately to the risks faced.

As explained by Johnston and Van der Marel (2013 p. 189):

> [t]he preservation and improvement of the environment is, together with the functioning of the internal market, one of the two aims of Article 194 TFEU. This means that a derogating measure which does not achieve a higher level of environmental protection is contrary to both of the objectives of Article 194 TFEU, since by definition a derogating measure will also be an obstacle to the functioning of the internal market

The *sui generis* nature of EU law, which is sometimes perceives as a weakness could then turn out to be its very strength. Notably, the focus on a teleological interpretation of the treaties causes a "focus on the overreaching objectives and a dynamic interpretation of legal requirements to flow from them" (Sjåfjell and Wiesbrock 2015, p. 71). Hence the "codification of the principle of sustainable development entails all-encompassing legal duty to integrate environmental protection requirements in the policies and activities of the Union" (Sjåfjell and Wiesbrock 2015, p. 52).

More is left to be seen but the principles outlined in the integration clause needs to be more explicitly operationalized by the Court of Justice. If climate change and environmental protection are to be made more operational within the legal framework, there is a need to explicitly describe how the environmental integration clause is ordered with regards to other priorities. A clarification on the way in which it operates with regards to other primary laws—the market freedoms and competition rules—is also necessary in order to avoid confusion and enhance legal certainty. The Treaties contain tools and they all need to be activated by a thorough evaluation and interpretation by the European Court of Justice.

With regards to the banking sector, further goals such as financial stability, social welfare, sustainable development and the equal distribution of wealth and opportunities, could also be included without changing the competences or current constitutional structure of the EU. Elevating both financial stability as well as environmental protection to this level, may lead to the sought-after transformation sought for. It is not merely a change in appearances but a credible alternative in order to make the changes necessary without rewriting the European constitutional framework.

It is also perhaps time to reconsider, that European political integration may bear fruits beyond the physical transportation of the energy itself. Locking together European countries by way of infrastructure and the smart-grid discourse is not enough. The "finalisation of the internal energy market-paradigm"—one of the main aims of the energy union—requires Member states to work together politically and not only economically. The Banking and Energy Union should go hand in hand with a revision of the aims of the European Union as such, firmly allowing the right remedies to be sought and thereby avoiding the application of the market-based approach where the internal market in all its forms and shapes may solve the existential crisis the Union is facing. Europe cannot be made according to a single plan as was set out by the Schumann Declaration itself. Even if the Treaty of Lisbon and the political integration prior to it made the Union "more than an internal market", much is still left to be done in order to create the structures and legal remedies necessary in order to face the challenges of our time. Mens sana in corpore sano should be a guiding principle also in this case. According to Weiler, the Milwardian rescue of the nation state is now reversed. Rather, "the pendulum has swung and in the present crisis it will be the nation state rescue of the European Union" (Weiler 2012, p. 827). This can only be done by allowing the integration clauses to work by conferring the competence necessary to the EU level. This is a matter left up to the Member States and is indeed not merely a question of technicality. It is rather a question of what sort of political integration Europe should be and what kind of values the European Union should protect.

## Conclusion

In the aftermath of the financial crisis and in the face of climate catastrophe, the European Union created both a Banking and an Energy Union. These super institutions can be seen as significant moves towards greater coordination and serve the realization of goals such as stability and sustainability. These are important and noble goals, but the essential question is whether the substantive changes they offer are sufficient. Questions of sufficiency and degree, which are as difficult to capture with the language and methodology of the law, as notions of risks and catastrophe, are posed by comparing crisis narratives and literature on the Anthropocene with the content and aims of the respective unions. Literature on the Anthropocene describe a fundamental change and paradigm-shift, that suggest the necessity to abandon status quo assumptions about social life and envision a life based on principles such as sustainability, longevity, cooperation, distribution and equality. What needs to be abandoned is the complete reliance on the mechanisms of the market as the primary force regulating societal system. Albeit politically unlikely, we suggest that this can be done by a complete reinvention of the system and the principles on which it is based. Our second-best solution requires the extension of the principles and aims of the European Union. This too would require reinventing the function and the identity of the European Union itself and truly envisioning a

Europe that is more than merely a market. In this spirit, and particular regarding the continuation of trying to solve remarkable crisis solely with mind-numbing market-related tools such as bad banks, new types instruments and expansive emissions trading systems: There are not only true or false solutions, there are also false questions (Zizek 2006).

Communication from the Commission to the European Parliament, the Council, the European Economic and Social Committee, the Committee of the Regions and the European Investment Bank: A Framework Strategy for a Resilient Energy Union with a Forward-Looking Climate Change Policy COM (2015) 80 final Brussels 25.2.2015; Communication from the Commission to the European Parliament and the Council: European Energy Security Strategy COM (2014) 330 final, Brusse 28.5.2014.

## References

Admati A, Hellwig M (2013) The banker's new clothes: what's wrong with banking and what to do about it. Princeton University Press, New Jersey

Alexy R (2002) A theory of constitutional rights (trans: Rivers J, 2012). Oxford University Press, Oxford

Alexy R (2003) Fundamental right, balancing, and rationality. Ratio Juris 16(2):131–140

Badiou A (2012) Ethics: an understanding of evil verso, London

Beck U (1986) Risikogesellschaft. Auf dem Weg in eine andere Moderne Nomos Baden-Baden

Beck U (2009) Critical theory of world risk society: a cosmopolitan vision. Constellations 16(1): 3–22

Chakrabarty D (2009) The climate of history: four theses. Crit Inq 35:197–222

DiFabio U (1994) Risikoentscheidungen im Rechtsstaat: Zum Wandel der Dogmatik im öffentlichen Recht, insbesondere am Beispiel der Arzneimittelüberwachung Mohr Siebeck Heidelberg

Douzinas C (2013) Philosophy and resistance in the crisis, Greece and the future of Europe. Wiley, London

Dworkin R (1977) Taking rights seriously. Harvard University Press, Harvard

Finkestscher W, Hacker P, Podzsun R (2013) FairEconomy, crisis, culture, competition and the role of the law. Springer, Berlin

Fullerton J (2015) Regenerative capitalism, how universal principles and patterns will shape our new economy

Johnston A, Van der Marel E (2013) Ad Lucem? Interpreting the new EU Energy Provision, and in particular the meaning of article 194 (2) TFEU. Eur Energy Environ Law Rev 22:181–199

Klein N (2014) This changes everything, capitalism vs. the climate. Simon and Schuster, New York

Ladeur K-H (2004) Das Umweltrecht in der Wissensgesellschaft. Von der Gefahrenabwehr zum Risikomanagement, 1995. Duncker & Humblot, Berlin, p 15

Lastra RM, Wood G (2009) The causes of 2007–09 nature, causes and reactions. J Int Econ Law 13(3):531–550

Lepsius KR (1995) Risikosteuerung durchVerwaltungsrecht. Ermöglichung oder Begrenzung von Innovationen? VVDStRL 63(2004):264

Manson P (2015) The end of capitalism has begun. The Guardian (Online 17.7.2015)

Marazzi C (2010) The violence of financial capitalism. Semiotext(e), Los Angeles

Paloniitty T (2015) Taking aims seriously: how legal ecology affects judicial decision-making. J Hum Rights Environ 6(1):55–74
Poscher R (2012) The principle theory: how many theories and what is their merit? In: Klatt M (ed) Institutionalizing reason. Perspectives on the legal philosophy of Robert Alexy. Oxford University Press
Robinson NA (2014) Fundamental principles of law for the anthropocene? Environ Policy Law 44 (1–2)
Sjåfjell B, Wiesbrock A (2015) The greening of European business under EU law: taking article 11 TFEU seriously. Routledge, London
Steffen W, Grinevald J, Crutzen P, McNeill J (2011a) The anthropocene: conceptual and historical perspectives. Philos Trans Royal Soc 369:842–867
Steffen W, Persson A, Deutsch L, Zalasiewicz J, Williams M, Richardson K, Crumley C, Crutzen P, Folke C, Gordon L, Molina M, Ramanathan V, Rockstrom J, Scheffer M, Schellnhuber HJ, Svedin U (2011b) The anthropocene: from global change to planetary stewardship. Ambio 40:739–761
Sunstein C (2013) The storrs lectures: behavioural economics and paternalism. The Yale Law Journal 122(79):1826–1898
Weiler JHH (2012) In the face of crisis: input legitimacy, output legitimacy and the political messianism of European integration. J Eur Integr 34(7):825–841

## Author Biographies

**Juliane Mendelsohn** grew up in South Africa and studied law at the Free University of Berlin and the University of Connecticut School of Law. Mendelsohn has written her legal doctoral dissertation on ‘Systemic Risk and Too Big to Fail’ in the banking sector. She has presented at numerous legal conferences. In her free time she enjoys writing (The European Magazine, Critical Legal Thinking, The New York Times Room for Debate), philosophy and is a Worlds Universities Debating Championships Finalist (Manila 2012).

**Thea Bygojordet Sveen** is a researcher at the European University Institute (EUI). Her current PhD research interests evolve around the principle of solidarity within the European Union legal system.Sveen has international experience from the European Commission and the Council of Europe. She has been leading an international research project in European Renewable Energy Law at the University of Oslo and worked at the Ecole Nationale d′Administration (ENA) Gutenberg Chair in cooperation with the University College of London (UCL). Sveen holds a double degree in European Union Law and European Studies from Science Po Strasbourg and at the Free University of Berlin.

# Chapter 3
# Pathways to Wellbeing—Low Carbon Challenge to Live Virtuously and Well: Participatory Design and Education on Mitigation, Adaptation, Governance and Accountability

**Janet McIntyre-Mills, Rudolf Wirawan, Bambang Shergi Laksmono, Ida Widianingsih and Novieta Hardeani Sari**

**Abstract** The impact of climate change has been underestimated and the way in which built capital is valued at the expense of social and environmental capital has resulted in development and urbanization processes that threaten food, energy and water security. These issues were discussed and raised at a previous conference on sustainability hosted with Universitas Nasional in 2015, Jakarta where I presented a plenary paper. This issue was also addressed by delegates from the West Java

J. McIntyre-Mills (✉)
Flinders University, Adelaide, Australia
e-mail: janet.mcintyre@flinders.edu.au

R. Wirawan
Wirasoft Pty Ltd, Sydney, Australia
e-mail: rwirawan@gmail.com

R. Wirawan
IDN-NSW, Eveleigh, NSW, Australia

R. Wirawan
IDN-Global and Oceania, Eveleigh, NSW, Australia

R. Wirawan
Indonesian Research Consortium, Depok, Indonesia

I. Widianingsih
Public Administration Department, Universitas Padjadjaran, Sumedang Regency, Indonesia
e-mail: ida.widianingsih@unpad.ac.id

N. Hardeani Sari
Department of Communication Science, Faculty of Social and Politics Science, Universitas Nasional, South Jakarta, Indonesia
e-mail: novietahs@gmail.com

B. Shergi Laksmono
University of Indonesia, Depok, Indonesia
e-mail: bshergi@yahoo.com

 
J. McIntyre-Mills et al. (eds.), *Balancing Individualism and Collectivism*,
Contemporary Systems Thinking, DOI 10.1007/978-3-319-58014-2_3

Provincial Government who attended a 10-day leadership workshop at Flinders University. Workshops at the Ministry of Finance, Ministry of Religion and Ministry of Social Affairs in 2013 and 2014 and workshops with members of the Indonesian Research Consortium in 2016 have resulted in establishing the basis for this research. This research is in several stages and this is stage one in Indonesia. The objective is to develop a way to enhance the management of carbon footprints by participants. This chapter discusses the following: • Design and preparation for a participatory action research project based on engagement with staff at Universitas Nasionale, Padjadjaran, Indonesian State Islamic University and West Java Provincial Council and Wirasoft, Sydney. • Processes to date that have involved developing a research consortium with universities and Wirasoft. The participatory process supports the design of a Participatory Action Research Programme to be implemented in three stages across Depok (a highly urbanized area with a diverse population), Jatinangor (an area that is becoming increasingly suburban) and Cianjur (a food production area). The fourfold aim of this PAR research in public policy and administration is to: • **Develop and pilot processes for public education and engagement** to address the rights and responsibilities of ecological citizens through participatory public education. The approach to the research will be to pilot the engagement software and to test the understanding that people have of social, economic and environmental challenges before and after using the software. • **Work with people** to find local solutions and to explore what works, why and how and what does not work why and how. It will do so by exploring the following hypothesis: The greater the level of public participation (a) the greater the understanding of UN Development Goals, (b) the greater the personal application of the goals. • **Address the low carbon challenge** by finding ways to regenerate the way we live in cities and to be mindful that the United Nations Sustainability Development Goals do not go far enough to prevent food, energy and water insecurity in unliveable environments. It addresses and considers food, energy and water security by enabling people to engage in local governance at the local level. • **Extend** the previously funded research by the Local Government Association, entitled: "Decision Making Software to address mitigation and adaptation to climate change" (Ethics Protocol 5262) (The research was conducted from 2010 and completed in 2012 and the results were published in 2014 in the form of two Springer volumes. The results of the de-identified data have been published by Systems Research and Behavioural Science and by Springer. McIntyre-Mills, J. 2012a "Anthropocentricism and wellbeing: a way out of the lobster pot?" Syst. Research and Behavioural Science. Published online in Wiley Online Library. (wileyonlinelibrary.com) DOI:10.1002/sres.2131 (A ranking ABDC Australian Business Deans Council Journal Quality List). McIntyre-Mills, J and de Vries, D. 2012b. "Transformation from Wall Street to Well-being" Syst. Research and Behavioural Science First published online: 10 OCT 2012 DOI: 10.1002/sres.2133 (A ranking ABDC Australian Business Deans Council Journal Quality List). McIntyre-Mills, J. with De Vries and Binchai, N. 2014, "From Wall Street to

Wellbeing" Springer, New York, 253 pp. ISBN 978-1-4899-7465-5). McIntyre-Mills, J. 2014b, "Systemic Ethics and non-anthropocentric stewardship" Springer, New York, 270 pp.). Thus the research will: • Deepen our understanding of how people perceive local climate challenges and experiences. • Explore the social influences habits and a range of behaviours that potentially shape consumption. • Test the kinds of face-to-face and digital public engagement that could encourage people to explore ways to live simply and well. The research is low risk and the data will be collected by Assoc. Prof Janet McIntyre and co-researchers. The research will be conducted through focus groups, interviews hosted via the participating organizations and a web-based survey.

## Introduction: Ethics and the Anthropocene: Hybridity Versus Extinction: Implications for Policy and Public Administration

This morning I woke up to hear the news that 330 million (almost a quarter of India's population)[1] are affected by drought. The media has drawn attention to this and now an NGO has filed a petition asking the top court to order the Prime Minister Narendra Modi's government to step up relief to the hardest hit areas. Similarly Southern Africa is experiencing the worst drought in 35 years and Lamble (2016) reports that this is affecting school attendance in Malawi and Zambia and that whereas the World Food Programme warned that 16 million were food insecure this has been raised to 31.6 million by the Southern Africa Food and Nutrition Security Working Group. Mozambique, Zimbabwe and Malawi face food insecurity as a result of El Nino weather events. Women in Africa spend 85% of their time collecting water. This amounts to approximately 40 billion hours of work.[2] This is time that could be spent in education or other forms of employment. In South Africa, food insecurity grows in rapidly urbanizing areas that become so-called 'food deserts' for some. In both Southern Africa and India, many of the urban and rural poor are the most affected. As the urban poor become increasingly food insecure bin picking in the suburbs of Western Cape coastal villagers or surviving by scavenging on the Mumbai dump become short-term survival strategies. Usually the urban rich feed off the surplus value extracted from the labour of the working poor and the destitute feed off the rubbish dumps in Mumbai. But now the situation has changed because attention to the health impact of the 'trash mountain' (Lakshmi 2016) is a focus of attention because the fires and fumes impact on the lives of others in the city. Now the so-called professional 'weekend warriors' load pictures of the dump on social media and draw attention to how the fires (that are caused by the decomposing

---

[1]https://www.google.com.au/search?q=population+of+india%3F&ie=UTF-8&oe=UTF-8&hl=en&client=safari.

[2]http://www.ipsnews.net/2012/08/women-spend-40-billion-hours-collecting-water/.

rubbish) are causing respiratory illnesses—along with many other infectious diseases for those living on or nearby the dump. Politically, the interests of the very poor are receiving attention as the dump affects the lives of others. Ironically the dump is the only form of food security they have.

My work in Australia is relevant to South Africa and Indonesia where I hold adjunct roles. Food insecurity has an increasing human and economic cost to Indonesia (in the region of 5 billion is lost annually) as a result of malnutrition from lack of food or poor diets (Word Food Programme 2016).

Participatory democracy and governance is needed for a growing population so that policies take into account the so-called requisite variety principle (Ashby 1956) that suggests that people who are going to be affected by the policy decisions ought to be represented when the policy content is shaped.

Currently, the quality of life of the majority in this generation and the next is compromised, according to Joseph Stiglitz (previous Chief Economist of the World Bank).

High carbon emissions impact on anthropocentric climate change. The approach assumes that lowering carbon emissions will enhance human security in terms. A growing population with expectations of a better life style is often cited as the main reasons for the challenges we face today of rising carbon emissions. The size of urban footprints needs to be managed in growing cities where the gap between rich and poor is increasing in cities in Africa, Indonesia and India, for example. Urbanization per se may or may not be problematic depending on the way in which wellbeing stocks are protected. This is a concept developed by Stiglitz et al. (2011: 15) based on a multidimensional measure of wellbeing spanning: "1. Material living standards (income, consumption and wealth), 2. Health, 3. Education, 4. Personal activities including work, 5. Political voice and governance, 6. Social connections and relationships, 7. Environment (present and future conditions), 8. Insecurity, of an economy as well as a physical nature."

| Regeneration of the environment, greater rural–urban balance and sustaining this balance | |
|---|---|
| Social changes—growing populations and increased urbanization | Wellbeing stocks need to be developed |
| Economic approaches that focus on growth in debt and growth in profit | The pursuit of profit at the expense of people and the environment is a central problem for democracy and governance |
| Environmental approaches that focus on profit for some at the expense of others and the environment | Habitat for living systems needs to be the focus for new forms of transparent governance based on positive sanctions that reward the protection, promotion and regeneration of wellbeing stocks. Negative sanctions by organizations for social and environmental justice need to protect living systems and prevent complicit exploitation of people and the planet by big business |

The exploitation of sentient beings (workers and animals) and the environment for profit is no longer sustainable. The notion of planetary passport developed in this paper is drawn from "*Planetary Passport: Representation, Accountability and Sustainability*". The notion of a planetary passport is a heuristic device to argue for protecting this generation of life and the next through rethinking rights and responsibilities in terms of governing our human footprints and protecting habitat. Habitat refers to the living spaces for human beings and other living systems which we share and on which we are mutually dependent in overlapping biospheres. Some scholars (Christakis and Flanagan, 2010; Dryzek 2010) argue that a lack of cultural understanding about our interlinked and entangled lives affects human rights insofar as it shapes access to water, energy and food security. The systemic focus of the book is on being mindful of the need to design policy that supports living systems. We, the people, need to ensure that the requisite variety of habitat is protected to support living systems. The challenges are to address planetary issues. Thus when framing research it is important to realize that the wellbeing of individual citizens cannot be protected unless the global commons is protected.

The starting point for this paper based on previous research begins where *Wall Street to Wellbeing* (McIntyre-Mills et al. 2014) and *Systemic Ethics* (McIntyre-Mills 2014a) ends, namely that the addiction[3] of the powerful to consume luxury goods is at the expense of future generations of life. The way in which diverse people understand the implications of urbanization, loss of territory, loss of species and the implications for living systems of which we are a strand (Bird Rose 1996, 2005; Atkinson 2002; Shiva 1988, 2005, 2007) needs to be addressed.

Achieving the demographic transition to low population growth is vital today through public education to provide numeracy, literacy and opportunities for women so that they are able to have more control over their own lives. Personal agency is enhanced as educated women will strive to choose the number of children and to become part of the paid workforce and part of the democratic and governance processes so that they can make policy and shape the politics for transformation.

[3]The desire of the rich to consume and the desire of the majority of the poor to leave the ghetto are expressed through emulating the rich. Socio-demographic research shows that debt and bankruptcy in developed nations—such as the USA and nations within the EU—are driven by advertising, easy credit and the desire to 'keep up appearances' by emulating the standards of the very rich (Frank, 2007, Wilkinson and Pickett, 2009). Making and invoking treaties and conventions that control commodification need to be a priority and need to be ongoing if justice is to be maintained. The approach could be buttressed through federations supported by, for example, the Lisbon Treaty (Horvath and Odor, 2010) which requires that social, economic and environmental legal considerations be met. Unfortunately, the structural and process mechanisms of the EU are not able to manage the distribution of power or funding (Rhodes, 1997). Clearly if the EU is to survive it needs to be supported by a means to balance individual and national interests with the collective good of the union. More and more members of the union are disenchanted for a number of reasons.

A point emphasized by Martha Nussbaum (2011) and Amartya Sen (2000) in their work on human development and human capabilities. This research adapts the Human Development approach and builds on the need to enhance capabilities for women (Crocker 1995). This is one aspect of the challenges facing the planet. The other is to enable people to voice their concerns and to be heard.

The point I want to make is that the size of urban footprints needs to be managed through encouraging low carbon living and minimizing the size of the ecological footprint. The chapter summarizes research detailed in volume 2 proposes a way to enable this to occur.

Urbanization per se may or may not be problematic depending on the way in which wellbeing stocks are protected. The purpose of this book is to explain the need to develop the capability to appreciate wellbeing stocks through public education linked with a so-called planetary passport—which provides a way to enhance awareness on ways to manage social, economic and environmental resources for current and future generations of life and the importance of ensuring that when 65–75% of the population are urbanized (as is the case in South Africa and Indonesia, for example, where I also work) that the balance between rural and urban areas is protected.

So we need to think about how to do different kinds of governance and democracy to promote food, energy and water security through minimizing the size of the urban footprint. What I have suggested is a way to manage the wellbeing stocks locally through enhancing human development capabilities in terms of:

- Public education to 'join up the dots' so that people are aware of the implications of their social, economic and environmental decisions.
- Representation of local people (particularly the marginalized and the dispossessed) and accountability in terms of the fair use and distribution of resources.
- Sustainability and in terms of the way resources are used.
- Governance needs to be based on a new architecture to support people and the planet by reframing what accountability means, the policy tools that are used to support it, the role of government, the style and the goals of government as detailed below. The starting point for the planetary passport idea is to adapt the five areas of priority highlighted by Archibugi as:
- Control over the use of resources and equitable sharing enforced through both positive and negative sanctions
- Acceptance of cultural diversity by ensuring internal sovereignty based on constitutional rules that enable freedom and diversity to the extent that the freedom and diversity of others is not undermined. External sovereignty is "replaced by global constitutionalism"(Archibugi, in Wallace and Brown 2010: 321);

- Strengthening the self-determination of people based on participatory democracy and the 'absence of domination' over other states based on a notion that each nation state can be free and diverse to the extent that freedom and diversity does not undermine the rights of others by mis-using resources that need to be shared with others;
- Monitoring internal affairs, based on a form of monitory democracy and governance;
- Participatory management of the global commons as the fabric of life.

This paper discusses a particular case study that is in the process of being developed with members of the Indonesian Consortium which:

- **Proposes a different approach** to the way in which we live our lives in terms of our consumption of energy resources, fresh water, transport and meat consumption and the implications for wellbeing and sustainable living (Pretty 2013; Pauli 2010).
- **Develops** a new stewardship to protect the planet based on understanding that what we do to others and the planet we do to ourselves.
- **Explores perceptions** on whether people understand that growth in the size of the ecological footprint of cities, growth in the size of species loss, growth in the size of the gap between rich and poor (as a result of the greed of a few at the expense of the majority in this generation and the next) is unsustainable. The stigmatization and victimization of 'the other' needs to be addressed through re-conceptualizing the law on sovereignty (Donaldson and Kymlicka 2011:173, McIntyre-Mills and De Vries 2011).

The scope of the research is on rethinking relationships at multiple levels and the implications for ethical living. It discusses ways in which to move from competition, towards cooperation and an appreciation of both space for diversity and our interconnectedness.[4] My area of concern is: what combinations of social, cultural, political, economic and environmental factors make a difference to wellbeing and our capability to adapt to climate change at the local level and mitigate its effects by scaling up local interventions? The premise is that the UN Sustainable Development Goals do not go far enough and that cultural and economic transformation is vital. We will try to learn more about diverse ways of knowing (Cruz et al. 2009) that could support effective environmental management by taking into consideration: 1) Non-anthropocentric knowing drawing on the environment as well as knowing through all our senses—including empathy and intuition, 2) Respect for 'know how' developed through empirical trial and error, 3) Creativity

[4]As Fiona Stanley said in her 11th Annual Hawke Oration in 2008: the challenges faced by Aboriginal Australians in terms of housing, health and social inclusion are issues that will be felt by many as climate change deepens the impact on social, economic and environmental challenges (McIntyre-Mills, 2011, 2014b). All life will be threatened.

in maintaining sustainable relationships with the land, 4) Respect for spiritual awareness, the wisdom of experience as well as the social and natural sciences, 5) Artistic expression of feelings, perceptions and emotions, 6) Caring for future generations of life, 7) 'Phronesis' or Aristotelian wisdom to match the right knowledge in context.

Testing out ideas requires preserving freedom, space for doubt, diversity and disagreement to the extent that diversity does not undermine the right to freedoms of others. An open approach to design and to research could be extended through acknowledging the praxis knowledge associated with reading the environment and living systems of which we are part.

Research needs to span consciousness, cultural studies and systemic praxis to link the notion of relationships between humans and the land as a source of wellbeing and the broader societal need for environmental protection and effective ecosystem management. The following Design of Inquiring Systems Approach provides guideline for designing a public education response. They are based on Ulrich (1983, 1994, see: http://wulrich.com/csh.html).

## Working Across Boundaries Through Co-creating a Community of Practice to Address the Low Carbon Challenge to Mitigate the Causes of Climate Change and to Protect Human Security

Developing a greater number of connections enhances consciousness (Greenfield, 2000, 2003, 2008). My research to date tests the extent to which mindfulness based on enhancing the capability of people to think about our thinking could help us to create closer bonds with others based on the realization that we are interdependent and thus that we need to bridge differences. The string theory workshop hosted by Louis Kauffman[5] (2002, 2016) provided a metaphor for a deep understanding of dependency and the need for co-determination of our shared future (see also McIntyre-Mills 2008). The Mobius Band was used in these publications to demonstrate our interconnectedness has been used as a metaphor for my ongoing research.

We are interconnected—we can address differences through 'loyalty' and 'voice', but exit—as described by the development economist Albert Hirschman—is no longer viable because the problems are planetary. The level of analysis needs to be extended by working on transdisciplinary capacity to address the convergent challenges (social, economic and environmental) that do not allow exit from the problem which is in global. Similarly, we need to understand that space ship earth is

[5]46th Annual Meeting of the International Society for the System Sciences at Shanghai, People's Republic of China, August 2-6, 2002.

the new 'ark of the covenant'—planet earth and not the ark of 'us versus them'. Thus the clash of cultures (Huntington's 1996) thesis is problematic.

The notion of a continuous flow of consciousness is as relevant to education as it is to community development. Thinking matters when it manifests in our relationships with others and the environment. Inclusive stewardship or exclusive profiteering helps to enhance representation and accountability through exploring ideas and engaging in dialogue.

It is a priority for regional neighbours to protect their shared biosphere. We are the boundaries and we can recognize our dependency on the land and that some of the results of our attempts at development are the monsters of our own creation. In this sense, I also draw on Hannah Arendt's core notion of the 'banality of evil' to reframe the way in which we do democracy and governance that needs to nudge people to make the right choices. New architectures for democracy and governance need to be piloted to support regeneration (rather than merely sustainability) because the current system is so deeply problematic that it requires our *being the change in our daily lives*.[6]

The many people who are moving across Europe have been treated with varying degrees of welcome.

According to Evans Pritchard, the Nuer understood that they needed to unite against a common enemy so they set aside their differences. Whereas in the past concerns were at the level of the organization or nation state, they are now at a post national, regional level.

## Water Flows: A Synecdoche for Planetary Democracy and Distributive Governance

Water management as a synecdoche for new architectures and processes for governance and democracy has implications of building *stocks for the future* (Stiglitz et al. 2010) and reframing not only economics but our relationships.

[6]This book is based on the idea that democracy and governance needs to be reframed through better representation, accounting and accountability. This involves valuing the human and natural resources and relationships appropriately and appreciating the opportunity costs that are created by not doing the right thing and not monitoring the distribution of resources fairly and equitably. This requires a transformation in our thinking, decision-making and practice to ensure a liveable future for this generation and the next. Accelerated climate change will adversely affect wellbeing and sustainability (Flannery, 2005; Singer, 2002; Stiglitz et al. 2010) if we continue to consume at current rates (Davies and World Institute 2008). The impact has been underestimated (Lovelock 2009; Rockström et al. 2009) by the Intergovernmental Panel (IPPC) on Climate Change (2001) and the Stern Review on the Economics of Climate Change (2007). The IPPC concluded that the goal of reducing the carbon footprint should be 387 parts per million of carbon, but Rockström et al. (2009) have argued that it should be lower at 350 parts per million.

The complexity of the use of flows, also needs to take into account community interests or values that are central to a sense of wellbeing (Shiva 2002: 80).

Hence the need to critically analyse the work by Stiglitz. Raising the educational capabilities of marginalized women would be a step in the right direction and not disempowering them through multinational companies. Women farmers and nurturers have developed knowledge over millennia that has been swept aside as seeds are patented. Trade-related intellectual property rights have to be contested by empowering networks of local people to hold corporations and their political supporters to account.

Shiva stresses the importance of enhancing the strategic needs of women, not just their basic needs and giving women a voice in decisions at the domestic level, community level as well as a strong voice in the public and private sectors. Ann Florini has stressed in a series of books the importance of empowering people from below.

Polly Higgins also suggests that a new planetary law should be passed to protect the viability of the planet and that current systems of law are inadequate to protect people and the planet.[7] Stiglitz has made the same point in relation to economics, whilst the need to reframe boundaries across a range of disciplines has made similar points as I stressed in a recent entry in Sociopedia called: 'Reconsidering boundaries' (McIntyre-Mills 2014b). Whilst the proposal was made by Higgins and others to the UN, Bolivia has succeeded in leading the way by passing a law to recognize the need to protect the earth. This could help to ensure that elected leaders remain more connected to the people they are supposed to represent.

So the future lies in participatory democracy and more direct interventions. What is needed is a greater emphasis on core principles and engagement with the people through discursive forms of democracy. When we look into the eyes of the displaced, surely we can feel empathy for their plight?[8]

---

[7]See https://www.youtube.com/watch?v=QPUmN88htCo and Earth democracy http://m.youtube.com/watch?v=Bq0lrbznsjc. http://www.theguardian.com/world/2015/may/31/the-heat-and-the-death-toll-are-rising-in-india-is-this-a-glimpse-of-earths-future.

[8]Silencing and distancing of those who seek asylum raises many long term issues for social justice. The implications of silencing and ignoring 'the other' at the organizational level or interorganizational national and post national level can be gleaned by considering the implications at an interpersonal level. A precedent for such an approach is the work on the 'Authoritarian Personality' by Theodor Adorno written as a reflection on the Second World War. The notion that fascism is associated with a particular kind of personality associated with particular types of interpersonal relations already exists. Perhaps another step can be taken when considering the implications of silencing and ignoring non-citizens? I make this link in my forthcoming book towards a: "Planetary passport" (McIntyre-Mills 2017 forthcoming). The implications of silencing and distancing at the international relations level can be gleaned by considering the implications at an interpersonal level of distancing and the prevention of bonding. The Image of the Mother's Eye: Autism and Early Narcissistic Injury. The studies of autism also show that bonding between mothers and children can be enhanced through gazing deeply into a child's eyes, Maxson J. McDowell, Ph.D.,http://cogprints.org/2593/1/eye22fixed_by_cogprints.html.

## Human Development Based on the Capabilities Approach and the Max Neef's Human Sustainability Index

Human development needs to be fostered through the capabilities approach to address poverty and carbon emissions by using the Max-Neef Human Sustainability Index (1991) applied to valuing, measuring and managing environmental and human assets. The index that supports the engagement process to help people think about their wellbeing is called the Being, having, doing and interacting Index (McIntyre-Mills with Binchai 2013). It enables people to think about the implications of what we have, what we need, what we are prepared to add or discard from our lives and the turning points for the better or worse.

These indicators are assessed by the interactive, web-based 'Pathways to Wellbeing' that acts as a Resilience Score card which could be linked with a Planetary Passport to become a basis for demonstrating ecological citizenship. The research explores whether engagement in thinking through 'if then scenarios' could aid discursive dialogue within communities of practice to support post materialism and wellbeing. The community approach to water governance underpins this planetary passport to protect the global commons. The laws for water management highlight the challenges, but also the way forward for water management. I will discuss the four theories of water rights raised by Shiva (2002: 77):

> The first law is the **Harmon Doctrine** which **protects the sovereignty of states** and is derived from British private property law. Sharing of water for downstream users is only moderated by the suggestion that good neighbourliness is preferable.
>
> The second approach is the **natural water flow** theory based on protecting the rights of up and down stream riparian users. The re-introduction of the hydro-electric power agenda on dams is relevant. The implications of the World Banks attitudes towards linking with market partners to provide water is increasingly problematic as the commons is threatened by the increased emphasis on the economic bottomland that creates scarcity and a market for selling water.
>
> The third is the **Helsinki principle** based on the equitable apportionment of water, but as Shiva (2002: 78) stresses: 'equitable utility is defined as the maximum benefit accruing to all the riparian states, in light of their differing economic and social needs. **Community of interest is closely related to the Helsinki Rules on the Uses of the Waters** of International Rivers, "Each basin state is entitled, within its territory, to a reasonable and equitable share in the beneficial uses of the waters of an international drainage basin." (Shiva 2002: 79).

This reasonable and equitable distribution needs to be based on what we have, what we need, what we are prepared to add or discard, turning points for the better and worse (in terms of food, energy and water security).

### *Demographic Transition Through Enhancing Capabilities and Empowering the Strategic Rights of Women*

The aim of the Human Development Capabilities Approach is to empower the marginalized (particularly women) to have a public voice. The more women are able to demonstrate personal and interpersonal agency in their lives the more likely they are able to lower the birth rate and move towards achieving a demographic transition. As we can see from the diagram below the India population pyramid has an expanding type:

Population under 15, between 15 and 64 and population which is over 65 year old.

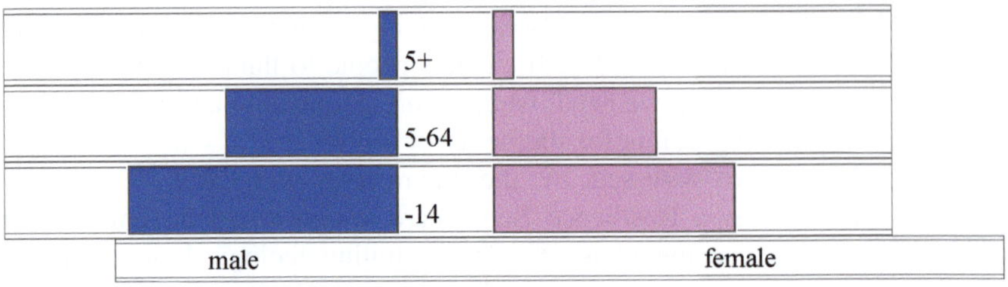


Source[9]: The estimation data for section 'India age structure' is based on the latest demographic and social statistics by United Nations Statistics Division. http://countrymeters.info/en/India

This type of pyramid is common for developing countries with high birth and death rates. Relatively short life expectancy, as well as low level of education and poor health care also describe such kind of population age distribution model. In India, the villagers are receiving water delivered by trains (ABC news 1st May 2016). "More than 350 million Indians live in cities and that will probably rise to 650 million by 2020" (Lakshmi 2016).

The government is responding to the effects of the crisis through some attempts at adapting to the effects such as working at night, remaining hydrated, indoors and covering up. Another response to the growing temperature rises is the ban on cooking during the day.[10]

According to the Guardian 29/04/2016:

> "The country reels from severe water shortages as desperately poor farmers suffer crop losses.... A senior government lawyer, PS Narasimah, told the supreme court that a quarter of the country's population, spread across 10 states, had been hit by drought after two consecutive years of weak monsoons....the government has released funds to affected regions, where a shortage of rainfall had forced the rationing of drinking water to some communities...villagers walk long distances to find water after their wells have dried up...".

---

[9]Note: The pyramid provided is not corresponding to data given above because the age groups have different number of years.

[10]http://www.theguardian.com/world/2016/apr/30/daytime-cooking-ban-in-india-as-heatwave-claims-300-lives.

This is not a one-off event, for example, in May last year a similar scenario unfolded as reported below:

> "In only 10 days, the death toll is reported to have reached around 1,800, a 20-year high. The brunt of the burden has fallen on the southern state of Andhra Pradesh, where 1,300 people have died, the highest loss of life due to heat the state has known, according to officials. By comparison, 447 people in the state died from the heat last year. The blistering temperatures may, mercifully, be about to break, as there are signs that the longed-for monsoon may be arriving in the form of showers and thunderstorms in the south. But as temperatures neared 50C in recent weeks, leave for doctors has been cancelled and the government has issued warnings for people to stay indoors and stay hydrated. For many, though, that isn't an option. The greatest loss of life has been among the elderly and the poor, in particular day labourers who have little alternative but to risk their lives in the heat for fear of losing their livelihoods" (De Lange 2015).[11]

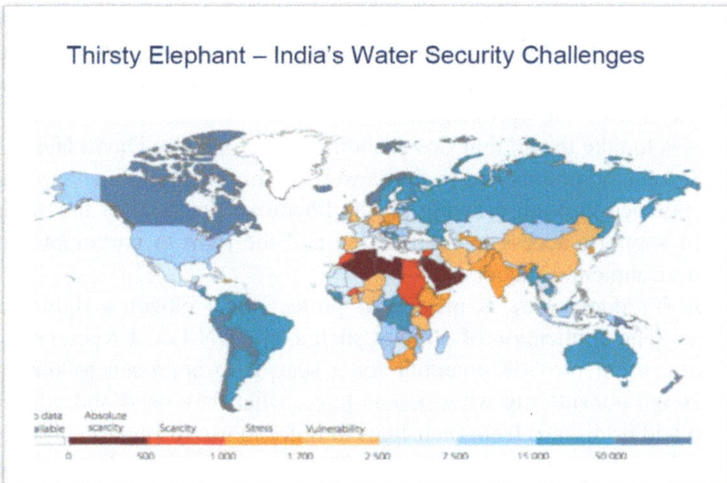


Source: Rivière, D. (2015). Thirsty Elephant—India's Water Security Challenges: A test for regional relations over the next decade. Report by Colonel Daniel Rivière, CD, PMP, September 2015.

As we can see the map above shows how water insecurity poses a post national threat to international security if water is not shared within and beyond national boundaries in a careful manner that is representative, accountable and sustainable in terms of delivering social and environmental justice.

[11]http://www.theguardian.com/world/2015/may/31/the-heat-and-the-death-toll-are-rising-in-india-is-this-a-glimpse-of-earths-future.

This has been detailed in volume two: "Hunger and Thirst: towards a Planetary Passport". It makes a case for developing a new architecture for governance and democracy to protect both people and the planet through promoting social and environmental justice for all through promoting and enabling accountability for low carbon living'. Designing public education requires enabling participants to address representation, accountability, sustainability and regeneration. The planetary passport is a way to encourage 'if then thinking'. It draws on the work of C. West Churchman's (1979) Design of inquiring systems approach based on questioning the boundaries of inclusion and exclusion and it examines the so-called 'enemies within' (religion, mortality, politics and aesthetics) by considering the consequences of our choices for ourselves, others and the environment.[12] The purpose is to help people to question their choices and to rethink what we value by appreciating our dependency on living systems of which we are a strand. It helps to address a core issue such as food, water and energy security and to demonstrate that it is a systemic issue that poses both challenges and opportunities. The book uses the analogy of flows by building on the work of Vandana Shiva, who is an eco-feminist, trained as a physicist and winner of the Sydney Peace Prize. It also builds on the work of Joseph Stiglitz.

The idea is to take the Global Covenant idea developed by David Held (2004) to protect the global commons and to find a way for this cosmopolitan approach to be applied in practice through drawing on the liberative potential of the Aarhus convention that supports access to information and the right to participate and to be heard on environmental matters.

Participatory democracy is needed to protect local citizen's rights to a safe environment. The application of policies such as the UN Local Agenda 21 and the Aarhus Convention provide potential for a scaled up approach to managing resources through considering what people have, what they need and what they are prepared to add or discard from their lives in order to use resources carefully and to feed forward resources for future sharing. This works along the lines of the veil of ignorance approach underpinning the social contact but it is expanded to the entire human population on the planet.

As we do not know where the next disaster will be located within the region, human security and hospitality is extended across the region. Resources are managed carefully so that resource rich areas share with those in need. Stocks are not stored and used within contained areas or interest groups. They are shared according to a system of accountability that measures resources in terms of a planetary passport and score card. This has implications for complex decision-making within and across regions.

[12]It is based on questioning boundaries of inclusion and exclusion, it examines the so-called 'enemies within' (religion, mortality, politics and aesthetics) and it considers the consequences of our choices.

People who are displaced need to be able to track and link with other people in their local area. The software could provide a means to do this by enabling displaced people to continue to link with people in their geographical space and with those with whom they connect beyond their immediate community. In other worlds, it provides a means of tracking resource use and networks of people.

The sticking point is that weak cosmopolitanism argues for equality of all human beings without realizing that recognition of human rights requires securing the basic conditions for life.

Today the understanding of carbon-based cultures and economies is relevant to climate change. So the starting point is a recognition that economically wellbeing needs to be the outcome of economic choices—not merely productivity.[13] So how can we address the issue of rights and responsibilities at a local level?

Could this be the basis for scaling up management of our Social, Economic and Environmental choices at a regional level?

Florini (2003) suggests the potential of the Aarhus convention. I have combined this with the policy potential of the UN Local Agenda 21 and other policies detailed below, such as Paris Development Agenda and the UN development goals. Thus the participatory action research aims to: address the challenge posed by the Earth Charter: "Everyone shares responsibility for the present and future wellbeing of the human family and the larger living world." (cited by Hayden in Wallace and Brown 2010: 368).

The challenge is to move beyond the rhetoric of cosmopolitan citizenship and to address both justice and sovereignty. The nation state needs to be held to account by an Earth Charter that is supported by overlapping regional institutions (supported by inclusive regional research institutions, policies, the rule of law including parliaments and courts). Co-determination in regions needs to be based on a new architecture for governance, democracy and ethics. Communities of practice within learning communities are needed to support public education and dialogue to develop mindfulness. These aspects are discussed in these volumes. The design is sketched in 'Wall Street to Wellbeing' and 'Systemic Ethics' and is extended in a forthcoming volume, entitled 'Planetary Passport'. West Churchman's critical and systemic Meta approach to working with, rather than within the boundaries of a single paradigm inspires my work. I draw on several approaches that locate Nussbaum's 10 Central Capabilities—relevant to all sentient beings

[13]These public interests include environmental considerations. Today the decision to for example to use energy selfishly and excessively has implications for other communities who may be more affected by extreme weather events as a result of our choices. For example, we may choose to drive an SUV when it is unnecessary or when it is possible to walk to meet our friends. We may use water excessively for forms of agriculture that will have a downstream risk to other communities needs to be governed by laws that protect the common good. Furthermore, complex decisions need to be informed by those who will be affected by the decisions Ashby's rule of Requisite Variety (1956) to establish ways to enhance representation, accountability and engagement.

(Nussbaum 2011: 33–34)[14]—within the ethical literature, in order to address life, health and ability to live a life worth living.

---

[14]Source: Nussbaum, M. C., 2011. Creating Capabilities: The Human Development Approach. London: Harvard University Press.

1. Life. Being able to the end of a human life of normal length; not dying prematurely, or before one's life is so reduced as to be not worth living.
2. Bodily health. Being able to have good health, including reproductive health; to be adequately nourished; to have adequate shelter.
3. Bodily integrity. Being able to move freely from place to place; to be secure against violent assault, including sexual assault and domestic violence; having opportunities for sexual satisfaction and for choice in matters of reproduction.
4. Senses, imagination and thought. Being able to use the senses, to imagine, think and reason—and to do these things in a 'truly human' way, a way informed and cultivated by an adequate education, including, but by no means limited to, literacy and basic mathematical and scientific training. Being able to use imagination and thought in connection with experiencing and producing works and events of one's own choice, religious, literary, musical and so forth. Being able to use one's mind in ways protected by guarantees of freedom of expression with respect to both political and artistic speech, and freedom of religious exercise. Being able to have pleasurable experiences, and to avoid non-beneficial pain.
5. Emotions. Being able to have attachments to things and people outside ourselves; to love those who love and care for us, to grieve at their absence; in general, to love to grieve, to experience longing, gratitude and justified anger. Not having one's emotional development blighted by fear and anxiety. (Supporting this capability means supporting forms of human association that can be shown to be crucial in their development).
6. Practical reason. Being able to form a conception of the good and to engage in critical reflection about the planning of one's life. (This entails protection for the liberty of conscience and religious observance).
7. Affiliation.

    (A) Being able to live with and toward others, to recognize and show concern for other human beings, to engage in various forms of social interaction; to be able to imagine the situation of another. (Protecting this capability means protecting institutions that constitute and nourish such forms of affiliation, and also protecting the freedom of assembly and political speech.)

    (B) Having the social bases of self-respect and non-humiliation; being able to be treated as a dignified being whose worth is equal to that of others. This entails provisions of non-discrimination on the basis of race, sex, sexual orientation, religion, caste, ethnicity and national origin.

8. Other species. Being able to live with concern for and in relation to animals, plants and the world of nature.
9. Play. Being able to laugh, to play, to enjoy recreational activities.
10. Control over one's environment.

    (A) Political. Being able to participate effectively in political choices that govern one's life; having the right of political participation, protection of free speech and association.

    (B) Material. Being able to hold property (both land and movable goods); having the right to seek employment on an equal basis with others; having freedom from unwanted search and seizure. In work, being able to work as a human being, exercising practical reason and entering into meaningful relationships of mutual recognition with other workers.

| Haraway and Singer on a posteriori approaches | Arendt and Butler on interconnectedness | Deborah Bird Rose, Vandana Shiva |
|---|---|---|
| Haraway shows that we are already Cyborgs with connections to enhance capabilities and animal connections to sustain life through medical research. Haraway's work criticizes privileging the human. Both Singer and Nussbaum also strive to avoid speciesism but their ethical stance differs. | Hannah Arendt's core notion of the banality of evil to acknowledge that everyday choices contribute to creating monstrous systems. | Life is based on a continuum of connections across past, present and future.<br>We depend on the earth and we return to it<br>The seed is a synecdoche of life and cannot be commodified<br>Water is another example of why we need to protect the land and water through a transformation in the way we live and relate to one another. Not merely through measuring things in a different way/ |

The work of Hannah Arendt has also helped to shape my thinking about the question: how should we live? Her notion of the 'banality of evil' is particularly relevant as we need to consider the broad context and the structures that lead people to make unethical choices at a personal, interpersonal and planetary level. The values that shape our current social and economic choices are the root cause of a way of life that benefits a minority at the expense of the majority in this generation and the next.[15]

The most powerless and voiceless are those who do not have the vote. They are young people, children, asylum seekers, the disabled, sentient beings who are commodified and traded and of course the planet which has no rights at all. So the focus needs to be on the inadequacies of the nation state and the social contract.

I am also inspired by the work of Haraway, because she stresses that women must not be subject to the design of others, they need to be designers of their own future. It is for this reason that we have worked on technology for monitory democracy and governance to try to give a voice to people and to empower them at the local level.

---

[15]Currently, my practical concern that there are more refugees and asylum seekers now than ever before and the current form of democracy and governance does not work. I strive to focus on the need to work with many forms of knowledge and across conceptual and spatial boundaries to address the big issues of the day, namely peace, gender mainstreaming and social, economic and environmental security within increasingly densely populated cities that need to respond to increasing poverty and climate change. This has implications for the quality of life from a human, non-anthropocentric and environmental perspective. We need education that enables co-determination of our future and that protects both human and environmental wellbeing. Her notion of the 'banality of evil' is particularly relevant as we need to consider the broad context and the structures that lead people to make unethical choices at a personal, interpersonal and planetary level. The banality of evil evident in media coverage spanning values, freedom of movement and violence expressed in the language of religion or politics.

| | Ancient Public Administration | Traditional Public Administration | New Public Management | New Public Governance | New architectures for people and the planet |
|---|---|---|---|---|---|
| Accountable to | Subjects | Voters | Customers | Citizens | Living systems |
| Policy tool | Minimal | Direct | Contracting out | Co-production | Co-determination |
| Role of government | Rule | Row | Steer | Facilitate | Steward |
| Style | Royal | Post Autocratic Bureaucratic | Post Bureaucratic Competitive | Collaborative | Post national cosmopolitanism |
| Accountability | Leader | Hierarchy | Market | Network | People and habitat |
| Goal | Loyalty | Law | Results/performance | Relationships | Protection |

Source: Column 6 is added to a diagram adapted from Zeger Van der Wal, Flinders Symposium, April, 2016

New local forms of engagement and governance (Held 2004) are needed to protect residents against environmental hazards and the subsequent economic and social consequences. Major challenges in local communities include the need to achieve or maintain: (a) access to safe housing (including energy and water), appropriate education and employment; within (b) livable cities[16]; that are in turn supported by (c) sustainable regions.

## *Multilevel Engagement Through Mindfulness and Critical Systemic Praxis*

Ulrich poses 12 boundary questions. He stresses that they should be asked in terms of: "what is the case now?" (Describes the current situation by using the DIS) and "what ought to be the case?" (Making judgments informed by ethical considerations). The questions drawn from Ulrich, Werner and Reynolds, Martin (2010) are as follows: (Table 3.1)

The groups of questions cover sources of motivation, control, knowledge and legitimacy Ulrich uses questioning to unfold the implications of particular approaches: 1. How do we know what to do? 2. What is the best approach in this context and why, who says so?

Participants need to work with many forms of knowledge and across conceptual and spatial boundaries to address the big issues of the day, namely poverty and climate change within increasingly densely populated cities. Critical Systems

[16]Opportunities exist to include creating a better balance between rural and urban areas and greening cities (Dryzek, 1999, 2000, 2010) through the creation of urban agriculture in open spaces, on top of, attached to and within buildings.

**Table 3.1** The boundary categories and questions of CSH (Adapted from Ulrich 1996. p. 44)

| Source of influence | Boundary judgements informing a system of interest (S) | | | |
|---|---|---|---|---|
| | Social roles (Stakeholders) | Specific concerns (Stakes) | Key problems (Stakeholding issues) | |
| Sources of motivation | 1. *Beneficiary* Who ought to be/is the intended beneficiary of the system(S)? | 2. *Purpose* What ought to be/is the purpose of S? | 3. *Measure of improvement* What ought to be/is S's measure of success | **The involved** |
| Sources of control | 4. *Decision-maker* Who ought to be/is in control of the conditions of success of S? | 5. *Resources* What conditions of success ought to/be are under the control of S? | 6. *Decision environment* What conditions of success ought to be/are outside the control of the decision-maker? | |
| Source of knowledge | 7. *Expert* who ought to be/is providing revelent knowledge and skill for S? | 8. *Expert* What ought to be/are *revelent new knowledge and skill for S?* | 9. *Guatantor* What ought to be/are regarded as assurance of successful implementation? | |
| Sources of legitimacy | 10. *Witness* Who ought to be/is representing the interests of those negatively affected by but not involved with S? | 11. *Emancipation* what ought to be/are the opportunities for the interests of those negatively affected to have expression and freedom from the worldview of S? | 12. *Worldview* What space ought to be/is available for reconciling differing worldviews regarding S among those involved and affected? | **The affected** |

*Source* Ulrich, Werner and Reynolds, Martin (2010), Chap. 6.p. 245

thinking and if-then questions (heuristics) can help to address these concerns in learning organizations and learning communities to create bridges across diversity.

When people are affected by the shared health concerns associated with food or water contamination they can strengthen bonds of friendship through enabling people to feel that they have a voice and a right to a voice. Participation in vertical democracy through elections (whilst important need to be extended to include other forms of participation). Discursive discussion and direct votes on policy ideas could help to foster connections and a shared ideology for a sustainable socially and environmentally just future.

## *Policy Context and Options for Social Democracy*

The liberative potential of the Aarhus convention to enable local people to have access to information and the right to speak out and to be heard on environmental issues provide a means to scale up the principle of subsidiarity. If this is combined with a revised Triple Bottom Line Approach that develops social, economic and environmental wellbeing indicators—to ensure quality of life within and across national boundaries, then policy could move closer towards addressing social and environmental justice for current and future generations of life.

Specifically the research responds to the policy context,[17] in order to achieve better forms of distributive governance adapted from Murray et al. (2007) Tuvalu test and Local Agenda, triple bottom line accounting (Elkington 1992, 1997):

- United Nations Local Agenda 21 and variants that strive to scale up triple bottom line accountability—not only at a local level—but also networks of local organizations internationally that could effectively extend the approach.
- Section 2(a) of the Aarhus convention stresses that local residents "accept that with the right to own manage and use natural resources comes the duty to prevent environmental harm and to protect the rights of people".
- Section 9(a) of the Aarhus convention addresses the guarantee to "the right to potable water, clean air, food security, uncontaminated soil, shelter, and safe sanitation, allocating the national and international resources required."
- "Section 10(a) of the Aarhus convention addresses the promotion the equitable distribution of wealth within nations and among nations."
- Section 13(a) of the Aarhus convention upholds "the right of everyone to receive clear and timely information on environmental matters and all development plans and activities which are likely to affect them or in which they have an interest."
- "Section 13(b) of the Aarhus convention supports local, regional and global civil society, and promote the meaningful participation of all interested individuals and organizations in decision making." (cited by Hayden in Wallace Brown and Held 2010: 369)

To draw on and extend Hayden (cited by Hayden in Wallace Brown and Held 2010: 369):

> "these clauses together with the UN Declaration of Human Rights, The UN Sustainable Development Goals and the Paris Development Agenda goals that stress the need to harmonize the interests of all the development participants (2006) as well as the Earth Charter (in particular—4a) recognizes that the freedom and rights of each generation is qualified by the needs of future generations. Hyden stresses that clause 6c. "ensures that decision-making addresses the cumulative, long term, indirect, long distance, and global

[17]Anthropocentrism and humanism need to move towards respect for Biodiversity (Nagoya Summit in Japan in 2010).The purpose of this research paper is not to rehearse the same arguments about rights and responsibilities – these are taken as a given. This paper is also not about 'what is the case' or 'what ought to be the case'. Instead it takes it as given that social injustice and inequality exists and that the disappearance of biodiversity will make a difference to the ecosystemic web of life and to human wellbeing. The loss of insects, such as bees along with greed and hubris will impact on food security—just as it will jeopardize seed security. Instead this research is located in the domain of how to develop a new architecture in response to Dahl's (1967) pessimism about extending the scale of democracy and governance.

consequences of human activities". Furthermore, the Millennium Goals cannot be met unless these are addressed".

The decisions taken at local level on how we live have an impact on the way others live. So when personal decisions are made to use food,[18] energy or water resources it has public implications for others as well as the environment. Thus the research enables the development of a personal score card to manage social, economic and environmental decisions. Triple Bottom Line Accounting and accountability is applied through United Nations Local Agenda 21 at the local level. This is a macro policy that has been applied by Local Governments in Australia and elsewhere. The aim is to extend the research to other locations. The challenge is to develop indicators that are meaningful for residents, who need to understand the links across personal choices and the implications these could have for adapting to climate change and mitigating the worst affects.

Furthermore it provides the means to achieve scoring personal choices to enable people to consider what they have, what they need to achieve wellbeing, what changes they are prepared to take through adding actions or adding changes in their attitudes towards others or the environment and through discarding certain taken for granted ideas.

## Piloting a Way to do Things Differently by Translating the Theory and Policy into Practice

### *Transformative Research for Regeneration*

The current team comprises Assoc. Prof Janet McIntyre (Social and Policy Studies) and Pak Rudolf Wirawan (Wirasoft, CEO, leader of Indonesian diaspora, Australia). Ida Widianingsih Assoc Prof at Padjadjaran University and Ibu Novieta Hardini, lecturer at Universitas National with the support of Prof Banbang of University of Indonesia. The research[19] is based on:

- *Being* supported by an MOU between West Java and South Australian government.
- *Doing* collaborative research as PhD supervisor and collaborating with staff at the University of Indonesia, Universitas National, Universitas Padjadjaran,

[18]According to the Word Food Programme (2016), malnutrition is a problem in Indonesia as many become under nourished as a result of food insecurity or obese as a result of changing diets in increasingly urbanized contexts. The cost to the economy is in the region of 5 billion annually.

[19]McIntyre will be assisted by Novieta Hardeani Sari, Lecturer and Research Fellow in Universitas Nasional Jakarta, Indonesia and Dr Ida Widiansingh (Flinders PhD) to facilitate the research in Indonesia across the three case study areas detailed below. Universitas Nasional students will test the prototype first then the first case study will commence. Participants will be invited by administrators at the following organizations: Universitas Nasional, Padjadjaran, the Ministry of Education and Ministry of Religion and through the West Java Provincial Council.

National Islamic University, West Java and the SA Local Government Association (in particular in Alice Springs and Adelaide).

- *Facilitating* workshops, e.g. Ministry of Religion, Finance and Social Affairs in Indonesia, two invited workshops for the Chief Ministers Policy Unit in Canberra in 2009 and numerous local government workshops in South Australia and research on behalf of the Attorney General's Dept. on resilience, research on behalf of the ARC and local government on wellbeing.
- *Facilitating* a leadership workshop at Flinders University together with delegates from West Java Provincial Government on the public education training and leadership. This was in line with the Paris Development Agenda (1997) that underlines the notion that development should be based on collaborative principles. The participants in this workshop stressed the importance of the need to develop leadership opportunities for women and young people. The challenges they face in West Java are associated with the impact of urbanization as people face congested cities, lowering living standards and high risks for women and children who are unable to express their strategic rights to a voice within households, communities local government and national level organizations.

| Participant Type/Group | Population Pool | Numbers to be approached | Expected/Required No. |
|---|---|---|---|
| Pilot | 40 post grads The participants include staff and students who will be recruited via the research office through a general letter sent to all students and not directly via class room contexts | 40 | 30 |
| Focus groups | The first will be held in Jakarta with a population of 1.898.537. It has a low unemployment rate of 2.4%. It will be conducted in they urbanized area of Depok City at the University of Indonesia | Purposive judgmental sampling | 60 a purposive sample spanning three focus groups as follows FG1 public sector (20), FG2 private sector (20) and FG3 (20) NGOs |
| Interview | As above | Purposive judgmental sampling | 10 |

(continued)

(continued)

| Participant Type/Group | Population Pool | Numbers to be approached | Expected/Required No. |
|---|---|---|---|
| Focus groups | The second will be held in Jatinangor, a suburban area that is becoming increasingly affected by loss of land as urban sprawl extends, with a population of 4407. The poverty rate is 11.85% with an unemployment rate of 6.5% | Purposive network sample of participants at the local government level will be invited through the Ministry of Education and Ministry of Religion and through the West Java Provincial Council 10 in depth interviews | 50 a purposive sample spanning three focus groups as follows FG1 public sector (20), FG2 private sector (20) and FG3 (20) NGOs |
| Interview | As above | Purposive judgmental sampling | 10 |
| FGD | **A third case study** will be held with residents from Cianjur, a food production area with a population of 570.991 and an unemployment rate of 11.43% and a poverty rate of 5.63 | | 60 a purposive sample spanning three focus groups as follows FG1 public sector (20), FG2 private sector (20) and FG3 (20) NGOs |
| Interview | As above | Purposive judgmental sampling | 10 |

To what extent can we extend solidarity to others? Other sources of inspiration are drawn from a sabbatical in South Africa, Indonesia, England and Japan during 2013 that are discussed in more detail in "Hunger and Thirst: towards a planetary passport". Once the pilot has been completed we will then use the data collection tool to explore: (a) awareness of scarcity and sensible use of scarce resources as keys to sustainability; (b) how living more simply promotes sustainability and can minimize inequality; and (c) views on consumption-related ethical decision-making. We will also examine how participatory democracy and public education translate theories about living sustainably into personal practice.

The focus groups with the public, private and volunteer sectors will deepen this understanding of public knowledge and it will assess to what extent people have a greater understanding after using the software. Then we will ask participants to use the software online via a digital portal and to invite others to do so as well. We will assess the questions about social, built and environmental capital before and after using the 'if then scenarios' spanning business as usual, making small changes and living virtuously and well.

The FGD will begin with viewing publicly available material in the form of videos by Costnaza[20] Natural capital, Built capital, Social capital. http://blogs.worldwatch.org/sustainabilitypossible/state-of-the-world-2013/Please watch the following video explaining the implications of the size of our carbon footprint. and Vandana Shiva[21] as well as a basic introduction to the nature of the Anthropocene.[22] The focus group participants will be asked to consider the following questions:

- What do you think are the implications for the Public/Private/NGO sector?
- What are the challenges for food, energy and water security in Jakarta and more regional areas as the city grows in size?
- Please give examples of food security challenges
- Please give examples of energy security challenges
- Please give examples of water security challenges
- Please discuss the implications of changes and challenges posed by urbanization for Natural capital, Built capital and Social capital
- What do I have in my life that could help me to live ethically and well? For example: I have the following things in my life—understanding of human rights, respect for biodiversity, fear for the future/hope for the future, a confidence, lack of confidence, loss of home due to natural or other disaster, no family/community support, responsibility to care for others and very high levels of stress.
- *My own story is*: ——————————
- What do I need in my life to help me live ethically and well? For example: I need in my life—a home, a sense of safety, a place near public transport and hope for the future. My own story is: ————
- What am I prepared to do to change my life by adding new ideas or actions? For example I will add to my life—more community supports from a range of services and/or more community engagement to lobby for resources, more connection to nature My own story is:—————————-
- What am I prepared to do to change my life by discarding some preconceptions or harmful habits? For example
- *I will discard* from my life—a sense of hopelessness, a sense of entitlement, excessive consumption. My own story is: ——————————
- What can I learn by thinking about what has changed in my personal life, my family, community and environment? Self-reflection on the turning points for the better or worse—hope that consumption can be replaced with greater sense

[20]Notes for the Public/NGO/Private sector. Please watch the following video by Robert Costanza as a precursor for our discussions on.

[21]Vananda Shiva Growth = Poverty Published on Nov 10, 2013http://sydneyoperahouse.com/ideas Ideas at the House: http://www.youtube.com/ideasatthehousehttps://www.youtube.com/watch?v=7M3WJQbnHKc.

[22]Anthropocene- magnitude of human footprint – implications for new forms of governance. https://www.linkedin.com/grp/post/6973569-6044442047962697729 http://www.ageoftransition.org/#!transformation/c6fi.

of attachment to others and the environment. My own story is: ————————————————————————

- *What can I learn by considering the barriers* that currently exist and thinking about what could be done to transform society and our relationship to the environment?
- *My own story is:*————————————————————

## *How the Engagement Process Works*

- Personal stories based on addressing the question "how should we live in order to achieve wellbeing" reveal patterns
- Patterns of adaptation to effects and mitigation of causes provide residents and service providers the opportunity to explore pathways to wellbeing
- The software lets residents build on other people's experiences
- The software summarizes personal experiences and perceptions for service providers.

The following dimensions of the passport are extracted from the user guide published as part of the Springer book 'From Wall Street to Wellbeing' with De Vries and Binchai[23]: **Wellbeing** is (a) **Achieved by** making time to connect with people and place; a sense of community. (b) Enhanced through access to sustainable public and private infrastructure for housing such as affordable transport, safe cycle paths and accessible public transport. (c) **Agencies/facilitators of wellbeing** include; willingness to use & reuse resources carefully; give up greed & waste; sense of community & respect others. (d) **Constraints** to achieving wellbeing include: **lack of time & money; sense of hopelessness; inappropriate infrastructure**. (e) **Related to/closeness of fit; a sense of community and belonging; connection with native; family friends; beautiful streetscapes; few cars.**

The passport is based on the following logic:

- Individuals address personal wellbeing in terms of social, economic and environmental factors that impact on food, energy and water security. Those with heavy footprints who consider only their own wellbeing at the expense of others will be required to self-contract to make social, economic and environmental adjustments.
- This user-centric evidence-based approach addresses the social, economic and environmental overlaps in Venn Diagrams to create pathways to move from

[23]This information was provided to local government to help them to plan and deliver services to residents. The administrators are able to access summarized data in spreadsheets. Axial themes according to Max Neef (1991) resonate with the axial themes identified in McIntyre-Mills et al. (2008, 2011, 2014).

(a) business, (b) making small steps towards, (c) living harmoniously in ways that enhance wellbeing.

- The individual, neighbourhood, community and regional post national biosphere comprises a series of overlapping spirals that are interconnected. The carbon footprint of each person is considered as an individual weighting made up of (a) what they have in their lives, (b) what they need, (c) what they are prepared to add or discard, d) the turning points for the better and worse, (e) the barriers and services they are prepared to contribute to as well as (f) the services they need. (g) A drop down list of post-coded socio-economic and environmental wellbeing services is provided.
- Spreadsheets of the domains for each individual, organization and region span boundaries to protect the individual and the common good through creating shared pathways that provide sustainable futures through regenerating relationships that span living systems.
- Thus it reframes democracy, governance and economics based on the synecdoche of water ripples and water spirals.

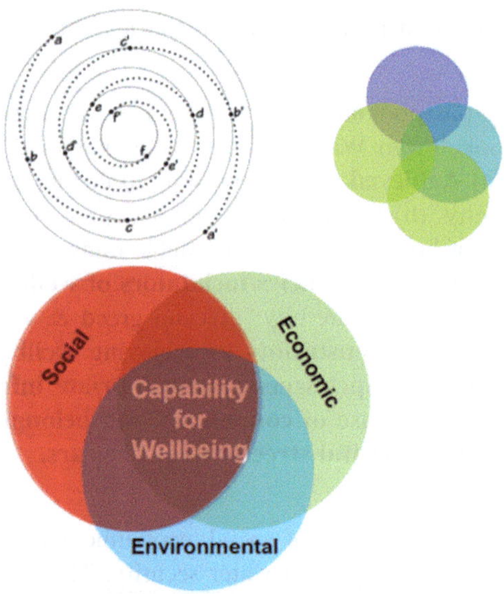


The pathway address for local government is
http://wirasoft.com/pathways-to-wellbeing/
User name = test
Password = test

**Data collection system**

- People rank what they have in their lives to support wellbeing and what they need to make their lives better in terms of quality of life and wellbeing. This requires building "stocks for the future" and developing links with one another and the environment.

- Accountability rests on showing the links across excessive consumption, unfair distribution and harm (Saul et al. 2012: 167).
- The planetary changes associated with increased risk of drought, famine, floods, fire and tornados are becoming more pervasive. These are not one-off events. They are a way of life that poses a human (not merely a national security).
- The software collects people's responses and perceptions to the following considerations:
- *I have* the following things in my life
- *I need* in my life
- *I will add* to my life
- *I will discard* from my life
- Plus, self-reflection on:
- *The turning points*—for better or worse
- *Consideration of the barriers*—for self and society

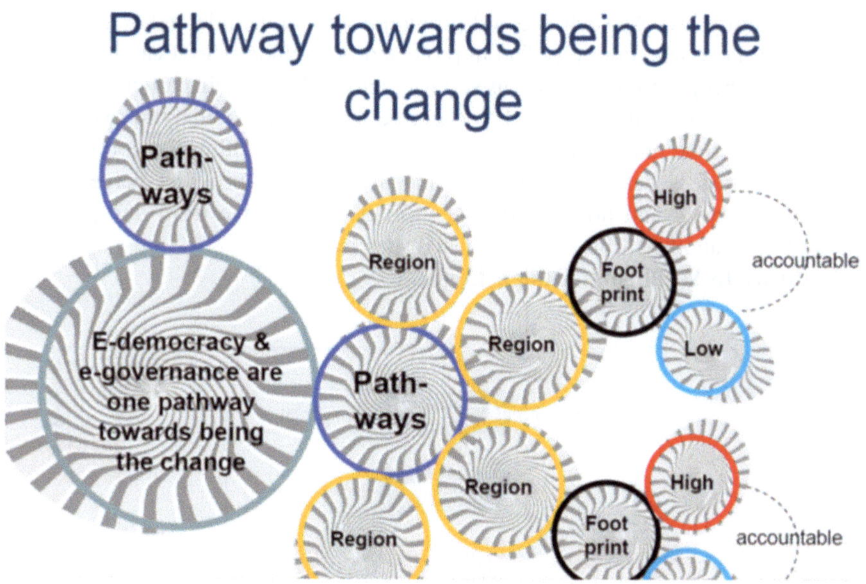


## Pathways To Wellbeing: the reconsideration of our democratic rights and responsibilities

The objective of the Pathways to Wellbeing software is to assist the reconsideration of our democratic rights and responsibilities by using participatory engagement aimed to match services to needs—within limits—so that local communities make the best decisions that minimize social, economic and environmental risks and that shape "policy from below" by enabling people to engage in a process of thinking about what material and non-material resources they have to support wellbeing; what they are prepared to discard; and then to consider what they personally consider to be the social, economic and environmental turning points for better or worse.

They are also asked to consider the barriers that experience in achieving wellbeing. All their decisions are based on their own perceptions about material and non-material facets of their life. The software updates as they add their new ideas and these help to inform others who see only the list of de-identified social, economic and environmental factors and the particular local resources that are available to assist them to move from (a) business as usual to (b) making small changes and (c) sustainable wellbeing.

The spreadsheets have the purpose of showing cross tabulations across the domains that are linked with socio-demographics. Thus age, gender are cross tabulated with haves, needs, what people are prepared to change, etc. This part of the software is the section that develops the "Being, doing, having and interacting" index which acts as a Human Development Index to build capabilities in own life and community life. As such it could provide a way to include and engage young people and those who currently feel unprotected or excluded. So it can be used as a way to help people by matching up services and skills to their particular needs.

The data can be mined or 'read' by service users and providers to explore own progress over time and the progress of groups of people within the community or region. Progress is defined in terms of the user and the provider perceptions of "what works, why and how" to enable individuals to move from one point in a continuum to another. The software design has evolved.

**Pathway to Wellbeing: Design Logic**

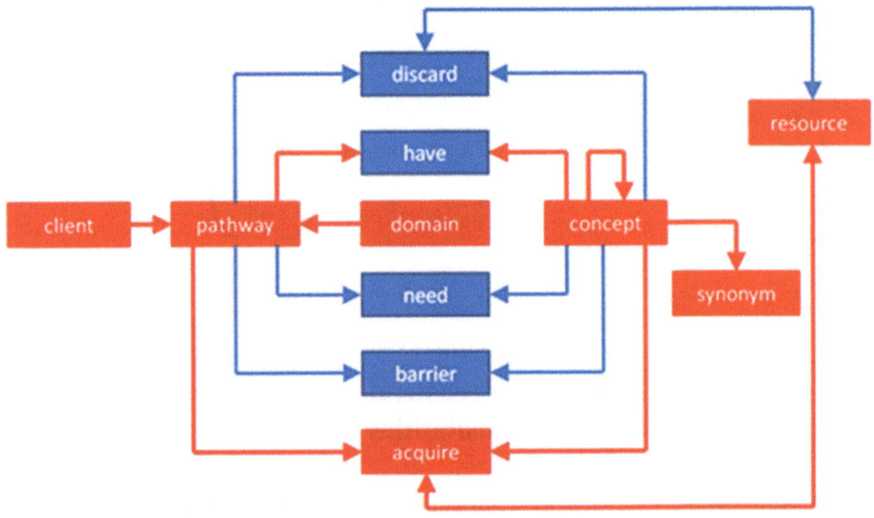

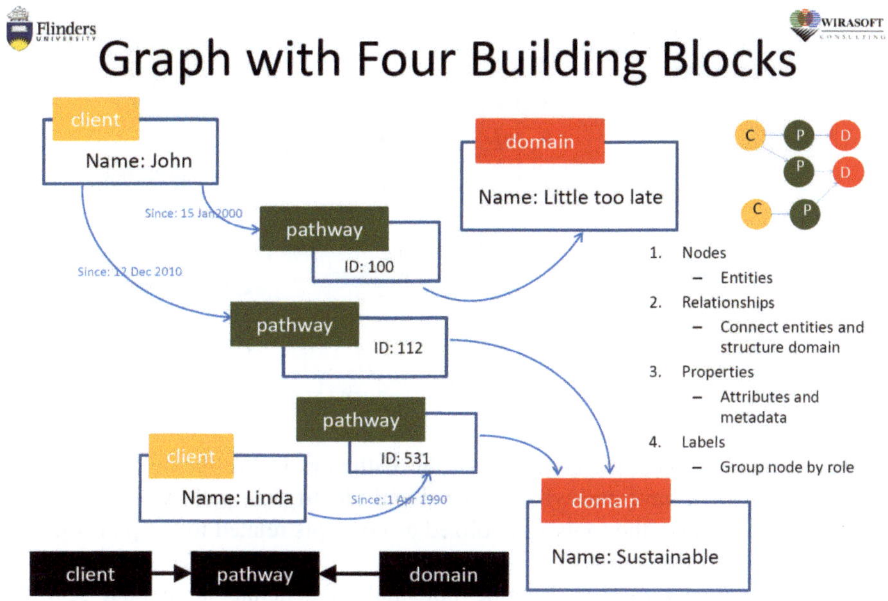
Flinders UNIVERSITY
WIRASOFT CONSULTING
Graph with Four Building Blocks
client
Name: John
Since: 15 Jan 2000
Since: 12 Dec 2010
pathway
ID: 100
pathway
ID: 112
pathway
ID: 531
domain
Name: Little too late
client
Name: Linda
Since: 1 Apr 1990
domain
Name: Sustainable
client
pathway
domain
C P D
P D
C P
1. Nodes
– Entities
2. Relationships
– Connect entities and structure domain
3. Properties
– Attributes and metadata
4. Labels
– Group node by role

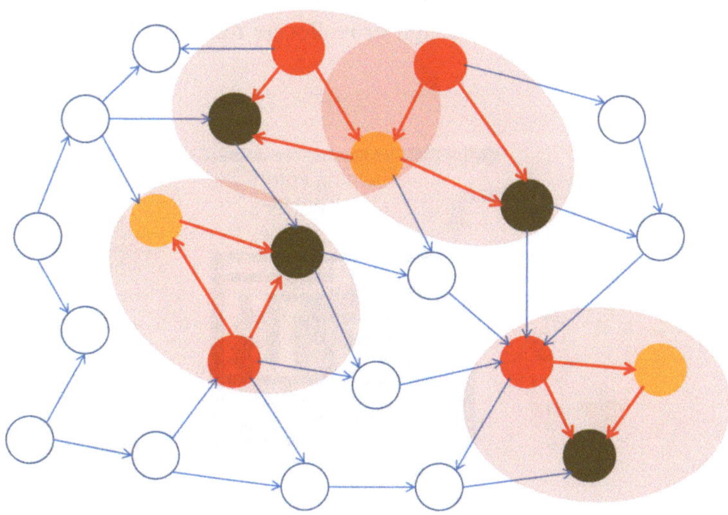

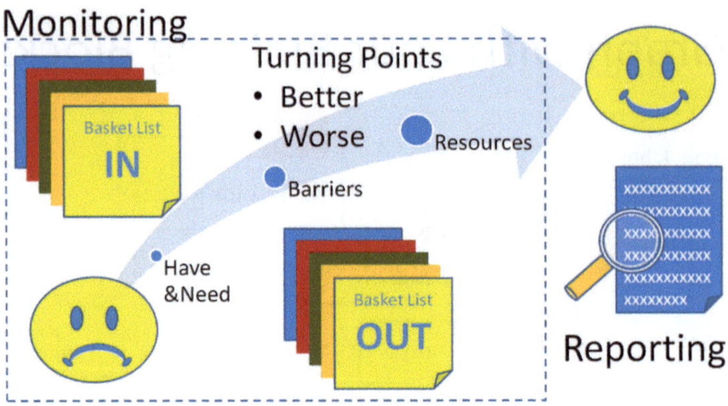


The diagram depicts the core idea of the Pathways to Wellbeing software. We start with what we have and what we need and identify the path we would like to pursue. Then we take the tools symbolized as concepts related to the path we have selected and start the journey.

This engagement process has the potential to generate large data sets that indicate patterns of success or failure as a result of following certain paths, which can be used as a guide for other people so that they do not need to reinvent the wheel or make the same mistakes that others have made. The data collected in a survey could be used to help redesign or reallocate resources to match services to needs.

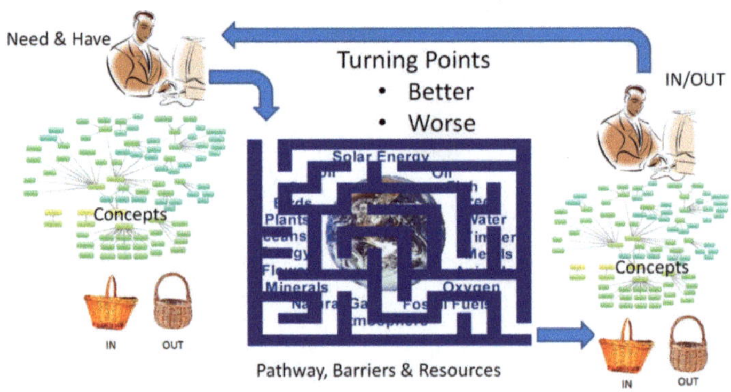


The software has been designed as an iterative process, so people can continue to enhance their journey or path by taking another turning point or simply by choosing a different path, so their goal can be designed in a step-by-step manner as depicted in the diagram on the left.

On the way out from the maze the service users and providers begin to appreciate that changes need to be made, in terms of the decisions that are made every day about food, energy, water the design of infrastructure or transport systems. The evaluation of the level of importance of multiple and a simultaneously important issue is important by reflecting on one's life in terms of different scenarios and the consequences of these choices, for example:

- I have the following things in my life—understanding of human rights, respect for biodiversity, fear for the future/hope for the future, a confidence or lack of confidence, loss of home due to natural or other disaster, no family/community support, responsibility to care for others and very high levels of stress.
- I need in my life—a home, a sense of safety, a place near public transport and hope for the future.
- I will add to my life—more community support from a range of services and/or more community engagement to lobby for resources, more connection to nature
- I will discard from my life—a sense of hopelessness, a sense of entitlement, excessive consumption
- Self-reflection on the turning points for better or worse—hope that consumption can be replaced with greater sense of attachment to others and the environment
- Consideration of the barriers that currently exist and consideration of what could be carried out to transform society and our relationship to the environment

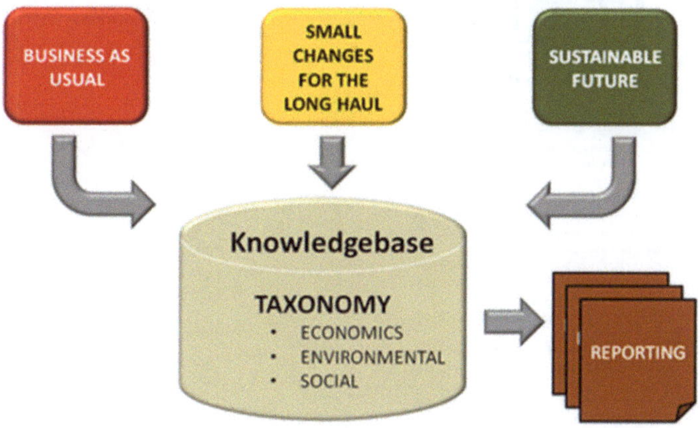


The next stage of the research seeks to establish whether participatory democracy enables participants to consider the consequences of socio-economic decisions for long-term sustainable wellbeing versus short term liveability and coping strategies (McIntyre-Mills et al. 2014) and hence ascertain if it supports the will to manage the consumption of human resources carefully—as opposed to denying the voluntary changes we can make as ecological citizens (Dobson, 2003). The research aims to make a contribution through showing a) how to engage participants, b) translate qualitative data and values into weightings that c) can be used to shape policy in pragmatic ways that address the complex social, economic and environmental consequences of decisions. The research will explore the axiological ethical dimensions of food consumption and food security, transdisciplinary views on food, energy and water, epistemological ways to address subject–object dualism and ways to enhance praxis (through testing a new architecture for participatory democracy and governance to enable enhanced mindfulness of consumption and the implications for, risk resilience, the stewardship of biodiversity and wellbeing as detailed below:

## *Matching Up Services and Skills to Needs*

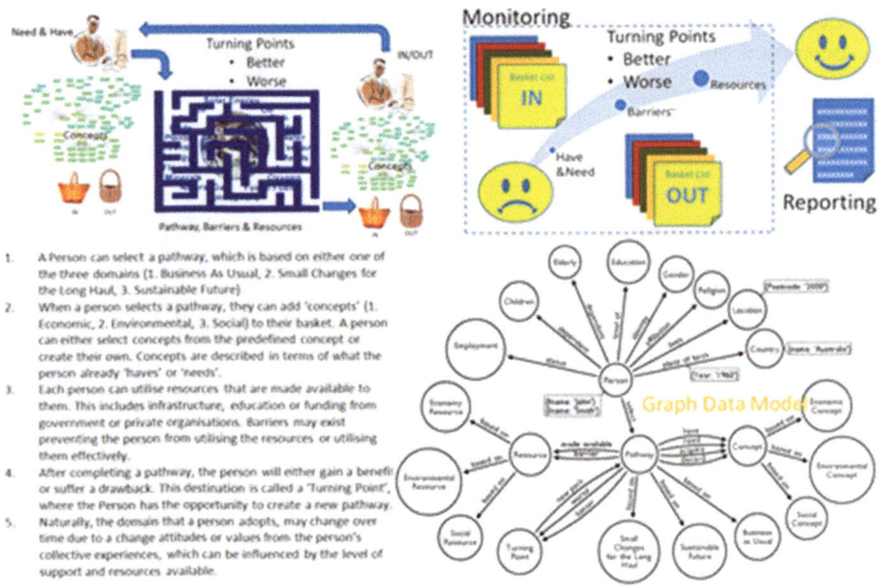


Drop down menus already prompt people to think in terms of what they have, what they need, what prepared to add or discard, turning points for the better and worse and barriers to enable the participants to address some of the 17 Sustainable Development Goals. Although each person cannot hope to address all the goals they can think about what they are able to achieve towards meeting these shared goals as part of their planetary passport approach to sustainable living. The engagement process will address ways that participants could strive to meet each of the 17 goals at the individual, personal and interpersonal level. The spreadsheets have the purpose of showing cross tabulations across the domains that are linked with socio-demographics. So age, gender are cross tabulated with haves, needs, what people are prepared to change etc. The next phase develops the "Being, doing, having and interacting" index (Max Neef, 1991) to address capabilities to meet sustainable and regenerative living at a personal and community level. It is a way to engage young people and those who are currently excluded (see McIntyre-Mills, Roddick and De Vries, 2014 that draws on the report for South Australian Local Government Association and further interpretation of the ideas in McIntyre-Mills 2014b). So it can be used as a way to help people by matching up services and skills to needs. The data can be mined or 'read' by service users and providers to explore own progress over time and the progress of groups of people within the community or region. Progress is defined in terms of the user and the provider perceptions of "what works, why and how" to enable individuals to move from one point in a continuum to another. The passport is developed as follows:

- Individuals address personal wellbeing in terms of social, economic and environmental factors that impact on food, energy and water security. Those with heavy footprints who consider only their own wellbeing at the expense of others will be required to self-contract to make social, economic and environmental adjustments.
- This user-centric evidence-based approach addresses the social, economic and environmental overlaps in Venn Diagrams to create pathways to move from (a) business, (b) making small steps towards (c) living harmoniously in ways that enhance wellbeing.
- The individual, neighbourhood, community and regional biosphere comprises a series of overlapping spirals that are interconnected. The carbon footprint of each person is considered as an individual weighting made up of (a) what they have in their lives, (b) what they need, (c) what they are prepared to add or discard, (d) the turning points for the better and worse, (e) the barriers and services they are prepared to contribute to as well as (f) the services they need. (g) A drop down list of post-coded socio-economic and environmental wellbeing services is provided.
- Spreadsheets of the domains for each individual, organization and region span boundaries to protect the individual and the common good through creating shared pathways that provide sustainable futures through regenerating relationships that span living systems. Thus it reframes democracy, governance and economics based on the synecdoche of water ripples and water spirals.

**2. Application Domain Scenarios**

To facilitate the "if-then" scenarios to enable people to consider the consequences of one choice versus another, there domain scenarios have been defined as a) Sustainable Scenario (Best case), Small changes for the "Long Haul", and c) Business as usual Worse case). As depicted in the diagram above, there are three concepts defined as taxonomy, such as economics, environmental and social.

For example in environmental terms we can think in terms of buying less, living simply and engaging in community education or volunteering and in terms of environmental dimensions it could include shared spaces, shared assets, big playgrounds, volunteering, sharing skills, cheaper renewable transport, and so on. In terms of social taxononomy it could include providing more public transport, shared spaces safe for children, encouraging accessible, affordable public transport, growing food, sharing skills and car-pooling as well as volunteering through community groups. These examples demonstrate integrated design that could help achieve social, economic and environmental transformation.

All information will be stored in a knowledgebase database, so it can be used to product report using different criteria or parameters.

### 2.1 Sustainable Future

In this scenario, we think that we live in an environment that can support this generation and the next. Housing is affordable and made of sustainable materials. We have faced up to the convergent social, economic and environmental challenges, and we are resilient because we live in clusters of homes. We share rain tanks and solar grids that are subsidized by local governments. Poor local governments and rich local governments form twinning arrangements to support each other. No one in our community is homeless because those who are ill or unable to work are assisted in community housing where they make a contribution in many different ways to public projects spanning home construction, food production, repairs, art projects and recycling materials.

### 2.2 Small Changes For The Long Haul

In this scenario, people make slow annual progress towards goals which they meet for the benefit of their children and grandchildren. But they do not move quite fast enough.

People of all ages and from all walks of life who are able to 'join up the dots' could help to motivate cultural transformation towards a better future. They are motivated by concerns for others and the environment and are becoming increasingly less selfish and more concerned about the common good. They empathize with others. Local governments and non-government organizations take the initiative. We hold workshops to demonstrate how people can make a difference.

We listen to the people and help local groups to respond to local challenges. Together, we undertake model projects that demonstrate how it will be possible to live differently.

### 2.3 Business as Usual

In this domain scenario, we continue to believe in economic arguments that ignore the social and environmental dimension, and we continue to think that our way of life is sustainable and are not prepared to manage the risks of climate change by changing our way of life. We blame the increasing risk of drought, bush fires and floods on 'one-off' unrelated events or deny that climate change can mean rising temperatures in some areas and plummeting temperatures in others as melting ice affects the ocean currents. The sea is used as a dumping ground, and it no longer helps regulate our climate. More and more of us suffer from viruses and food poisoning. Animals are diseased. Most of our rivers are polluted, and many have dried up. We fight over the last of energy and natural resources.

**3. Reporting**

The aim of the report is to identify a range of issues need to be addressed, such as in the environmental as well as issues in social that need to be addressed.

The collected data can be analysed in spreadsheet and by means of word queries to cross-tabulate concepts. The extent to which demographic variables (age, gender, level of education, place of birth, home language, religious affiliation, type of occupation or employment status) make a difference to the following:

- which scenario they identify with,
- what they perceive they need to add to their lives to make a difference to mitigating or adapting to climate change,
- what they perceive they need to discard from their lives to make a difference to mitigating or adapting to climate change,
- what they perceive are the turning points for the better or worse,
- what the barriers are and
- what services make a difference?

Telling a story and thinking about what we have and what we need and what we are prepared to add or discard from life are part of stepping into another conceptual space and thinking about the way we see the world.

## References

Atkinson J (2002) Trauma trails. Recreating song lines. Spinefex, London

Ashby WR (1956) An introduction to cybernetics. Chapman and Hall, London

Crocker D (1995) Functioning and capability: the foundations of Sen's and Nussbaum's development ethic, Part 2. In: Nussbaum M, Glover J (eds) Women, culture and development: a study of human capabilities. Clarendon Press, Oxford

Held D (2004) Global covenant: the social democratic alternative to the Washington Consensus. Polity

Lakshmi R (2016) Battle to move Mumbai's trash mountain. The Guardian 29/04

Lovelock J (2009) The vanishing face of Gaia: a final warning: enjoy it while you can. Allen Lane

Max-Neef M (1991) human scale development. Apex, London

McIntyre-Mills J, Bausch K, Christakis A, De Vries (2008) How can we break the mould? Democracy, semiotics and regional governance. Syst Res Behav Sci 25:305–321

McIntyre-Mills J (2012a) Anthropocentricism and wellbeing: a way out of the lobster pot?' Syst Res Behav Sci (Published online in Wiley Online Library. (wileyonlinelibrary.com)). doi:10.1002/sres.2131

McIntyre-Mills J, de Vries D (2012b) Transformation from Wall street to well-being. Syst Res Behav Sci (First published online: 10 Oct 2012). doi:10.1002/sres.2133

McIntyre-Mills J, Binchai N (2013) Being, having, doing and interacting: towards ethical democracy, governance and stewardship. In: Proceedings of the 57th annual meeting of the ISSS HaiPhong, Vietnam, 2013

McIntyre-Mills J (2014a) Systemic ethics. Springer Encyclopedia of Food Ethics ISBN 978-94-007-0928-7, doi: 10.1007/978-94-007-6167-4_342-6 # Springer Science + Business Media Dordrecht
McIntyre-Mills J (2014b) Systemic ethics and non-anthropocentric stewardship: implications for transdisciplinarity and cosmopolitan politics. Springer, New York
McIntyre-Mills J, De Vries D, Binchai N (2014) Wall Street to Wellbeing: joining up the dots through participatory democracy and governance to mitigate the causes and adapt to the effects of climate change. Springer, New York
OECD (2006) The Paris declaration on aid effectiveness: Five principles for smart aid
Pauli G (2010) The blue economy: report to the Club of Rome. Paradigm Publications, New Mexico
Rockström J, Steffen W, Noone K (2009) A safe operating space for humanity. Nature 461:472–475
Rivière D (2015) Thirsty Elephant—India's water security challenges: a test for regional relations over the next decade. Colonel Daniel Rivière, CD, PMP, 2015
Rose DB (1996) Nourishing terrains: Australian aboriginal views of landscape and wilderness. Australian Heritage Commission, Canberra, ACT, BCIN Number: 236409
Rose DB (2005) Dislocating the frontier. http://epress.anu.edu.au/dtf/html/frames.php see http://epress.anu.edu.au
Saul B, Sherwood S, McAdam J, Stephens T, Slezak J (2012) Climate change and Australia: warming to the global challenge. The Federation Press, Sydney
Sen A (2000) Development as freedom. Knopf, New York
Shiva V (2002) Water wars: privatization, pollution and profit. Pluto Press, London
Singer P (2002) One world: the ethics of globalisation. Text Publishers, Melbourne
Ulrich W (1983) Critical heuristics of social planning: a new approach to practical philosophy. Wiley, New York
Ulrich W, Reynolds M (2010) Critical systems heuristics. In: Reynolds M, Holwell S (eds) Systems approaches to managing change: a practical guide. Springer, London, pp 243–292
World Food Programme (2016) https://www.wfp.org/stories/10-facts-about-malnutrition-Indonesia. Accessed 15 May 2016

## Author Biographies

**Dr. Janet McIntyre-Mills** is an Associate Professor in the School of Social and Policy Studies at Flinders University, Adjunct Professor at the University of Indonesia and Islamic National University in Indonesia, and Honorary Professor at the University of South Africa. Her research focuses on systemic representation, accountability and re-generation applied to social and environmental justice concerns such as health, housing and social inclusion and the mitigation and adaptation to climate change. She addresses complex needs by exploring the meanings and 'what if' questions with diverse stakeholders.

Her recent books include 'From Wall Street to Wellbeing: Joining up the dots through Participatory Democracy and Governance to Mitigate the Causes and Adapt to the Effects of Climate Change'. ISBN 978-1-4899-7465-5 and 'Systemic ethics and Non-anthropocentric Stewardship: Implications for Trans disciplinarity and Cosmopolitan politics', ISBN 978-3-519-07655-3.

**Rudolf Wirawan** is the founder of Wirasoft Pty Ltd in Sydney, Australia. Previously, Rudolf worked with companies such as IBM, WANG and Nixdorf Computers. Wirasoft offers services ranging from consulting, training, to the development of enterprise-scale applications. Enterprise applications are used in global companies across industries such as banking, telecommunications, insurance, mining, etc. They help deliver information in a timely manner to optimise business operations and can also provide pathways to generating future investment.

**Professor Bambang S Laksmono** is a social scientist based at the University of Indonesia. He has published widely and has acted in senior roles such as the held the role of Dean and Head of Department (bshergi@yahoo.com).

**Dr. Ida Widianingsih** is Head of Department and Associate Professor in the Faculty of Social and Political Sciences, Universitas Padjadjaran (Unpad), Indonesia. She is a PhD graduate of Flinders University. Her focus is on participatory approaches to development and translating the theory of development into practice.

**Novieta Hardeani Sari** is based in the School of Graduate Studies at Universitas Nasional. Her focus is communication studies applied to sustainable living and she is able to draw on her engineering skills when working in an interdisciplinary manner across cultures.

# Chapter 4
# Governing the Anthropocene: Through Balancing Individualism and Collectivism as a Way to Manage Our Ecological Footprint

**Janet McIntyre-Mills and Rudolf Wirawan**

**Abstract** The current way of life is unsustainable (Papadimitriou in The coming 'tsunami of debt'. The Guardian.com, Sunday 15 June 2014 17.58 BST 2014) and in a bid to maintain the status quo—profit is extracted from people and the environment. The challenge of scaling up efforts to engage people in an alternative form of democracy and governance is that currently the response to social, economic and environmental challenges is that internationally politics is being shaped by so-called realist politics (Beardsworth in Cosmopolitanism and international relations theory. Polity, Cambridge 2011) based on (a) competition for resources, (b) the notion that profit and loss, win and lose is contained/carried by 'the other' and (c) Huntington's 'clash of cultures' thesis rather than an understanding of our interlinked, co-created and co-determined *fate*.

## Introduction

According to Vandana Shiva (2013): "Growth = poverty".[1] Growth in the size of the population and cities, growth in the size of the gap between rich and poor as a result of the greed of a few at the expense of the majority in this generation and the next is unsustainable. Unrestrained urban planning is leading to problems associ-

---

[1]https://www.youtube.com/watch?v=o2o_QQTYc7I Festival of Dangerous ideas, 2013. Also see Shiva and Barlow (2011) on the need for a new narrative of Earth Democracy and Governance (http://www.democracynow.org/2011/4/22/earth_day_special_Vandana_Shiva_and Maude Barlow.

---

J. McIntyre-Mills (✉)
School of Social and Policy Studies, Flinders University, Adelaide, Australia
e-mail: janet.mcintyre@flinders.edu.au

R. Wirawan
Wirasoft, Sydney, Australia
e-mail: rwirawan@gmail.com



J. McIntyre-Mills et al. (eds.), *Balancing Individualism and Collectivism*,
Contemporary Systems Thinking, DOI 10.1007/978-3-319-58014-2_4

ated with congestion in cities, lowing living standards and high risks for women and children who are unable to express their strategic rights within households, communities and local government. The issues of the day are summed up as follows:

- The growing gap between rich and poor.[2]
- The growing rise in over reach of the ecological footprints of the Global North.
- The growth in unsustainable food choices.
- The growth in displacement of people.[3]
- The need for a new narrative (see Jakob Von Uexkoll) on a new architecture[4] for participatory governance and participatory democracy and a new sense of relationship with nature and other animals.

The program of research on which this paper is based is that democracy and governance needs to be reframed through better accounting and accountability. This involves valuing human and natural resources and relationships appropriately and monitoring them fairly and equitably. This requires a transformation in our thinking, decision-making and practice to ensure a liveable future for this generation and the next.

> Hybridity and our connection with the land are understood by Aboriginal Australians. We read our past in the landscape and we create its future through our choices (McIntyre-Mills 2014a, b, 10).

The paper aims to address ways to balance individual and collective interests.

> No complex system can be managed effectively without clear goals and appropriate mechanisms for achieving them. In managing the earth we are faced with a nested hierarchy of goals that span a wide range of time and space scales. In any rational system of management, global ecological health and sustainability should be 'higher goals' than local, short-term national economic growth or private interests. Economic growth can only be supported as a policy goal in this context to the extent that it is consistent with long-term global sustainability… (Costanza et al. 2015: 175)

---

[2]As stressed elsewhere (see McIntyre-Mills 2011) rising living costs led to food riots and the so-called Arab Spring, culminating in the Occupy Wall Street Movement.

[3]Magnay, J 2016, 'Berlin's push to swap failed asylum seekers', Jan 30–31. *The Weekend Australian*, pp. 12 The Port of Calais could become a symbol of inhumanity and the breakdown of the nation state system where no formal services are provided to those trying to leave France en route to the UK. But the violence attributed to recent asylum seekers in Paris and Cologne has resulted in efforts to support Syrians in neighbouring countries and to return illegal migrants to Turkish camps: "In exchange, the EU would accept up to 250,000 documented asylum seekers a year from Turkish camps" Europe's approach to Asylum seekers needs some consistency based on a priori norms and a posteriori measures of service delivery. These need to be put into place to protect displaced people and to ensure that indicators for humane responses are applied consistently.

[4]http://www.worldfuturecouncil.org/838.html.

The Anthropocentric changes at a planetary level require a new form of governance for 'Planetary Stewardship' (Steffen et al. 2011). In order to protect the ecological web of life of which humanity is a strand—we need to do more than 'build stocks for the future'; we need to achieve a quantum leap towards recognizing our interdependency and our role as stewards or destroyers. The choice is ours. It is a value-based choice. But it is also rational. By thinking carefully about the consequences of our choices we can arrive at a sense of the sacred. Expanding pragmatism is based on a deep understanding of the consequences for current and future generations of life.

## Theory and Key Concepts

The notion of ecological footprint has been shaped largely by theorists who work across disciplines. The term ecological footprint or carbon footprint can be traced back to the thinking of Chief Seattle[5] "Every part of the earth is sacred… the earth is our mother…the rivers are our brothers, they quench our thirst. Crystal Lameman, Beaver Lake, Cree nation (2015) says of the Tar sands exploitation in Canada, we ought to extract resources only up to the level necessary for agriculture and that the land is not owned by any one.[6] Gro Brundtland a medical practitioner realized that personal health could only be secured by peace and human security through protecting 'Our Common Future' (Brundtland Report 1987). This landmark report helped to lay the groundwork for an appreciation of the limits of growth and was the basis of the sustainable development movement.

But the work of Howard and Elizabeth Odum (1996) on modelling for all scales showed that we needed to think differently about the use of energy resources. Also the work of Meadows and Randers (1992) in 'Beyond the Limits' set the basis for the Club of Rome approach on the use of natural resources to support an unsustainable way of life at the expense of future generations.

The problem with the modelling used by some of the members of the so-called Club of Rome group was—according to Christakis (McIntyre-Mills 2006) inadequate because it was top-down and did not engage people in considering the 'if then scenarios' associated with peak oil and heavy carbon footprints.

The work of cybernetics (Von Foerster 1995) and social cybernetics is important in understanding the role of people in shaping the environment, in particular the notion that all living creatures are better off when others and the environment—on which we depend—are better off. The first mention of climate change in sociology is by Constance Lever Tracey (Pidgeon and Fischhoff 2011). The link between the policy choices that human beings make and capitalist economics (based on profit)

---

[5]http://www.halcyon.com/arborhts/chiefsea.html

[6]Klein N (2015) http://www.theguardian.com/environment/2015/mar/08/how-will-everything-change-underclimate-change

needs to be understood if the notion of human ecological footprint is to be understood. The idea that surplus value can be extracted from the labour of human beings and realized as profit when the value-added items that have been processed have been sold.

The idea that profit is sustainable has been critiqued by Stiglitz et al. in 'Mis-measuring our lives'. He makes a case for providing a value for natural and social assets. He calls this recognition of aspects previously regarded as so—called externalities, 'wellbeing stocks' for future generations. These ideas have been criticized as they give a price to nature and thus commodify it. Monbiot (2014) stresses the importance of mobilizing for change. People need to be able to voice their values and shape the indicators of well-being that matter to them. Whilst I agree that the market is the problem, it could change if the power to frame it is given to people and not to CEOs. Without a shift in power, decisions will continue to be made in the interest of the top 10% of the population, Monbiot (2014) concludes by arguing:

> If we surrender to the financial agenda and say, 'This market-led neoliberalism thing is the way forward,' then we shift social values. Environmentalists are among the last lines of defense against the gradual societal shift towards extrinsic values. If we don't stand up and say, "We do not share those values, our values are intrinsic values. We care about people. We care about the natural world. We are embedded in our communities and the people around us and we want to protect them, not just ourselves. We are not going to be selfish. This isn't about money", who else is going to do it?

The challenge is to:

- Face up to our interconnectedness
- Understand that human futures are interconnected with the environment on which we depend.

This requires the capability to hold in mind many variables and not to think in terms of 'us/them' expressed in terms of tribes, organizations and nation states. Spaceship Earth is the concept developed by Kenneth Boulding in his policy plea that we achieve transcendence. There is no such thing as an externality according to his thesis that we are part of space ship earth.

Nussbaum (2006) argues for social justice and for capabilities for human beings and other sentient beings. De Waal makes a case for co-operation based on empathy and reciprocity as one of the bases of animal nature along with the capacity for compete. Both aspects are important for evolution.

In times of crisis—Albert Hirschman (1970) suggested three options—loyalty, voice or exit. Although it was possible for him to apply all three options to great acclaim in his life time—to exit totalitarian states and to demonstrate alternative ways of doing things, times have changed. His work could be characterized as striving to reveal 'in the small new ways of seeing the whole' (Adelman 2013, 9). He contributed to re-framing the way in which areas of concern were perceived. But the challenges we face today cannot be addressed by working within the boundaries of a nation state or leaving a nation state that has become totalitarian, because issues are now at a planetary scale.

The work of Hannah Arendt (1963, 1972) emphasizes both potential and risks. It holds resonance today, because she talks about the banality of evil which seems perhaps even more relevant today than it did when she wrote about Eichmann's trial. As a Jew, she stressed that the man Eichmann was part of a monstrous system that appeared quite banal as it was widespread and part of a culture and a bureaucracy that was taken for granted.

Today we need to be thinking critically about taken for granted structures. We need to take the liberative potential of small-scale projects (as suggested by Hirschman) and try to think of their potential as a way to do things differently. Hannah Arendt stressed the banality of evil and the need to consider the broad context and the structures that lead people to make unethical choices.

The work of Stuart Hall (1992, 1997; Hall and Du Gay 1996), a cultural theorist discussed the diversity within the modern state and stressed the need to consider the way resources are distributed and consumed within nation states by asking: What is the social, cultural, economic and environmental context? Who gets What, When, Why and So what? His contribution to praxis is important as he stressed that the notion of national identity today requires a long narrative response to explain each of our origins. Where we live, where our parents live, what they did for a living and where they came from and why. When we think of cultural identity we also think of food, hospitality and fostering friendships through sharing.

Where our food comes from is now a global concern and we also need to think of our responsibility when consuming cheap food that is supplied by food chains that make a profit as a result of the lack of rights of the food producers, for example.

Robert Costanza in 'An introduction to ecological economics' (2015) stresses that the magnitude of the anthropocentric human footprint has implications for new forms of governance:

> Satisfaction of basic human needs requires a balance among social, built, human and natural capital (and time). Policy and culture help to allocate the four types of capital defined earlier as a means for providing these opportunities. One institution that helps build social capital is a strong democracy…. where all citizens are free (and expected) to participate in all political decisions affecting the community. Interactive discussion plays an important role…preferences and opinions are not fixed and hence can be changed/shifted through a deliberative process. The process of deliberative democracy involves 1. Sharing of information and policy options among a set group of individuals, 2) the process of deliberation among the group, and 3) the socialization and dissemination of the results of this process (Held and Hervey 2009; Herbrick and Isham 2010) (Costanza et al. 2015: 294–295).

## Extending the Critique of Social Contract Approaches

Is the social contract adequate to protect the environment and interests of citizens who are young, disabled or members of other species? Furthermore the social contract is not extended to non-citizens and more and more people are displaced and outside the protection of the nation state.

Giddens (2009) in 'the Politics of Climate Change' warns that localized efforts, whilst important for prefiguring change are insufficient to hold the market to account, unless they are applied regionally and internationally. The signing of the United Nations Declaration of Human Rights has not lead to detailed covenants or the means to implement the noble ideas:

> After adopting the Universal Declaration they argued intensely over the highly controversial and emotionally charged question of whether this proclamation imposed international legal commitments or not. The complicating problem of international politics in the United Nations itself became particularly serious. The United Nations and its allies in the Cold War increasingly came to fear the organization was falling under the radical influences of Communists interested in threatening the status quo by destroying colonial empires… This East West confrontation soon affected nearly everything that the United Nations attempted, including what has been called the 'The Deep Freeze" for international human rights (Paul 2003: 236).

We envisage that the Low Carbon footprint approach could be used to identify sources of social, economic and environmental well-being in line with creating so-called 'wellbeing stocks' (Stiglitz et al. 2010) based on a design and creativity approach that supports the so-called 'blue economy' (Pauli 2010) based on sources of abundance identified through social, economic and environmental engagement that considers what each participant in a co-operative could contribute to achieving the Sustainable Development Goals.

It takes triple bottom line accounting to the next level and makes it possible to give credit and accreditation to infrastructure and transport systems that are part of a co-operative network.

Enabling the transformation of identity through governance and public education is the challenge for ethical systemic governance. The election of conservative governments in the UK and the USA reflect the concerns of an electorate who fear globalization and the impact it will have on their quality of life.

Roberts (2015) previously stressed that the notion of 'clash of civilisations' just helps the terrorists'. Huntington's (1996) 'clash of culture' thesis is understood as part of a self-fulfilling narrative. The problem with Huntington's clash of civilisations thesis is that it assumes cultures are static. Furthermore, Western culture is assumed to be the touchstone of civilization without considering the exploitation it has wreaked in social, economic and environmental terms. Huntington's thesis describes 'what is the case' without making suggestions as to how the clash narrative could be redressed through political and policy interventions through identifying sources of abundance in a design approach. It adopts a realist approach to politics and a formalist approach to economics. It assumes that the identities of opposing groups are inevitably locked in conflict. As an explanatory paradigm it is in line with Mary Douglas' notion of sacred and profane. Those who share the same paradigm or our own cultural narrative and those who do not share our cultural narrative are regarded as profane. Critical Systems thinking (or critical heuristics) draws on the work of Kenneth Boulding (1956) on transformational evolution based on a recognition that human beings can make conscious decisions as to how they wish to live in ways that support so-called 'wellbeing stocks' (Stiglitz et al. 2010). Instead of assuming 'business as usual' can produce a liveable future for all, we suggest that knowledge systems that appreciate the essential values of life could help to transform society and current attitudes towards consumption supported by formalist, capitalist economics. The Blue Economy approach of Gunter Pauli (2010) outlines more than a 100 ways to create opportunities through environmental thinking that does not privilege the environment at the expense of people, instead his approach is to find ways to enable the unemployed to benefit through working on environmental challenges, his motto is: 'There is no unemployment in eco-systems' (Gunter Pauli 2010).[7] He stresses the need to provide integrated opportunities through design that taps into the abundant talent and environmental opportunities that can be found and to ensure that the designs protect both people and habitat. A critical systemic approach that could ensure that people come up with solutions that do not create binary oppositions between people and the environment. It is unnecessary to argue that for people to flourish the environment must suffer.

This research adapts the Blue Economy approach by drawing on the work of West Churchman and his student Werner Ulrich and others such as Jackson (2000), Midgley (2000), Flood and Romm (1996), McIntyre-Mills (2003) who argue that social systems can be transformed are not closed they are open and can be re-defined or reframed.

People tend to feel connected to those who share the same culture, values and language and disconnected or 'less connected' to those defined as 'other'. This is in part the result of the so-called social contract—a product of social democracy—being extended only to those within the boundaries of the nation state. And even then being limited to those who can prove that they are entitled to support by virtue of being (a) citizens 'in good standing' or (b) 'in need' who qualify in terms of reference points that are becoming increasingly residualist as resources become scarce.

[7]https://www.speakersassociates.com/speaker/gunter-pauli.

## Re-Design: Curating Stewardship Praxis

How can we 'curate the conditions for a thrivable planet' (International Systems Sciences 2013) by transforming democracy and governance? Consumption and happiness is now a focus of attention, because the consumption of more resources has not resulted in greater happiness. Instead people with more time and more social capital are found to lead healthier happier lives (Wilkinson and Pickett 2009).

The ways forward are fourfold:

- Extend the social contract through new forms of communications for discursive democracy (Dryzek 1999, 2000, 2005, 2010) and inclusive governance within and beyond the nation states to include regional post national constellations.
- Declare a priori global covenant, norms, ideals and laws to protect the planet through constitutions like Bolivia and Ecuador and ensure that these declarations are more than window dressing. This can be achieved through more engagement by civil society in monitoring the way in which resources are valued as well as the way in which they are used, exchanged or redistributed. Systemic relationships are relevant to the understanding of ecological footprints as is the development of an understanding of our inter dependency and that we evolved through our ability to co-operate, not only our ability to compete with others or to exploit others and the environment (De Waal 2006, 2009).
- Transform a posteriori performance accounting and accountability from below (Hill 2015) through new measures that protect rights and that ensure that being socially and environmentally responsible is protected in terms of a new set of indicators, spanning doing work that supports living systems, having a social and environmental conscience (demonstrated in terms of the choices and decisions we make daily) to protect the social and environmental fabric of life and—thus protecting our ecological footprint. Global policy needs to address food, energy and water security. Policy requires balancing individual and collective interests. This requires addressing the wider regional biosphere. Wilkinson and Pickett (2009) argue that after a certain point, more consumption does not lead to more happiness. Thus, increased consumption based on increased economic growth does not make people happier—in fact it poses 'existential risks'. 'More equal societies almost always do better' socially, economically and environmentally.

Public education to protect the global commons and the public good through transforming the curriculum through formal and informal means to enhance the capacity for transformation through teaching people to value living systems through protecting water, food and renewable forms of energy. These basic, systemic needs are best protected through valuing so-called 'cultural flows'. The approach strives to avoid the dangers of the commodification approach in "mis-measuring our lives" made by Stiglitz et al. (2010) and instead makes a plea for changing the way in which some human beings live (at the expense of others and future generations of life) based on a recognition that the 'personal is indeed political'.

Let us start with the IPCC formula that addresses the implications of polarizing people versus the planet. IPCC formula E (Emissions) = Population × Consumption per person × Energy Efficiency × Energy Emissions. Existential Risk has implications for representation, accountability and sustainability. Consumption is very unequal and the gaps between rich and poor become wider and wider.

Accountability rests on showing the links across excessive consumption, unfair distribution and harm (Saul et al. 2012: 167). The root cause of consumption is power without responsibility—so whoever comes to power needs to be held to account through mechanisms to develop social, economic and environmental indicators that secure the well-being stocks for the future. The 'price of inequality'—national and global has escalated. Minority greed at the expense of the majority and future generations of life who face hunger, thirst, disease, displacement without access across open borders and death.

This suggests that the privileged lives of some could lead to 'existential risk' for all forms of life on the planet (Bostrom 2011).

> The IPCC estimates that between 1.1 and 3.2 billion people could experience water scarcity by 2080…..Around 655 million people in Asia lack safe drinking water, while 1.9 billion lack access to basic sanitation…." (Saul et al.: 204).

The IPCC formula suggests that the privileged lives of some could lead to existential risk for people and the planet (Bostrom 2011). This has implications for the way we live and the need to change our way of life through living sustainably. Representation, accountability and sustainability challenges need to be met through addressing consumption choices that are currently very unequal. The gaps between rich and poor, the powerful and the powerless have become wider and wider.

Each of the concepts will defined in turn. I refer to the recent Sydney Peace Prize Winners Vandana Shiva (2010,[8]) and Julian Burnside (2014,[9]) and Noam Chomsky (2011,[10]) as indicative of some of the key social and environmental justice concerns:

- Global panoptican—the surveillance approach that has been revealed by the Guardian through the work of Greg Snowden and Julian Assange (2012)[11]
- Penal states—the incarceration of asylum seekers because of the containerist approach to social justice in nation states—(Julian Burnside 2014)
- Disappearing states—the rising sea levels destroying some nation states (see the work of Vandana Shiva, a scientist, feminist and environmentalist on commodification, capitalism, climate change and the implications for rising sea levels.

---

[8]http://sydneypeacefoundation.org.au/peace-prize-recipients/2010-dr-vandana-shiva/

[9]http://sydneypeacefoundation.org.au/?s=justice+julian+burnside

[10]http://sydneypeacefoundation.org.au/peace-with-justice-noam-chomsky-in-australia/

[11]http://sydneypeacefoundation.org.au/?s=Julian+assange&submit.x=-696&submit.y=-246&submit=Go

Complex challenges such as poverty, climate change and terrorism comprise many, interrelated variables that are perceived differently by those who hold different values. Religion, morality, politics and aesthetics are the values that make us human. They enable us to co-operate and to compete. They are what Churchman calls, the so-called the 'enemies within'. The notion of wicked problems is his concept (albeit popularized by Rittell and Webber). The notion of taming is not a critical heuristics concept. It is oppressive and it assumes power over others and including non-sentients and nature!

Critical heuristics when applied to thinking through 'if then' policy scenarios is a precursor for decision making. This does require 'drawing a line'. But who draws it, what is included and excluded, where it is drawn and how it is drawn matters. Ethically, we need to consider many ways of knowing before making a decision. This is different from the language of 'taming wicked problems' or governing from above. It is about stewardship based on appreciating many dimensions and many ways of knowing. We need to think of the logical coherence of an argument, the empirical data and norms to protect the planetary on which we depend (Table 1).

The greatest challenges are the consequences of inaction that will potentially pose an existential risk to humanity. These challenges include representation of the increasingly diverse populations within nation states along with accountability to ensure that resources (e.g. water, food, and energy) are used fairly, equitably and sustainably in local and regional biospheres. The 'price of inequality'—national and global has escalated. The global figure for displaced people passed 50 million for first time since the Second World War, according to the United Nations High Commissioner and by 2050 it could be 150 million (Rusbridger 2015, 13).

**Table 1** Architecture for cosmopolitan democracy and governance of ecological footprints in overlapping domains?

| | Structure | Process | Action |
|---|---|---|---|
| Micro-level individuals | Aarhus convention (1998) | Questions raised and posed to local government by individuals | Local government, NGOS and individuals |
| Meso states and regions | Aarhus convention linked to Global Covenant | On line monitory democracy and governance to address state/market/civil society concern | Networking NGOs and INGOS to address representation and accountability |
| Macro cosmopolitan governance | Legal structures to support the global covenant, Aarhus convention and biospheres convention | International criminal court United Nations | Global action to pass laws to protect social and environmental justice in overlapping biospheres |

*Source* Adapted from Archibugi (in Wallace Brown and Held 2010: 322 cited in McIntyre-Mills et al. 2014: 93–95) and McIntyre-Mills (2014a, b: 7) in Reconsidering boundaries, Sociopedia

And yet the needs of the displaced are not addressed through the current architectures of democracy, governance and education. Surely it is time to reframe the social contract and to support public education to enable people to join up the dots?

We need a new narrative of Earth Democracy. According to Evans Pritchard, the Nuer understood that they need to unite against a common enemy so they set aside their differences. We need to understand the arc as planet earth—not 'the other'. We are interconnected—we can no longer address differences through loyalty, voice and exit as described by the development economist Albert Hirschman, because whereas in the past concerns were at the level of the organization or nation state, they are now at a post-national global level.

The level of analysis needs to be extended to address the convergent challenges (social, economic and environmental) that do not allow exit from the problem which is global.

Hannah Arendt's work on the banality of evil provides the other side of the coin. We are all vulnerable to evil and we are all dependent on one another to do the 'right thing'. Recognition of our vulnerability needs to underpin our working towards being resilient.

The links across actor network theory, socio cybernetics and the debate by Habermas (1984; Bausch 2006 cites Habermas 1989) and Luhmann (1995) on the nature of reality (Bausch 2001). Habermas stresses that human beings can shape systems through their constructing constitutions and laws. Luhman stresses that we are part of the system along with other non-human agents. Habermas and Luhman both shifted ground from their extreme positions as a result of their ongoing dialogue and agree broadly that human beings shape the environment and are in turn shaped by it. Relationships are systemic.

'Knowing our place through recognizing our hybridity and interconnectedness' is an extension of this argument with an emphasis on food security as a way out of the current social, economic and environmental crisis.

Dialectical engagement to address alternative arguments needs to be based on considering the consequences of decisions for human and environmental well-being. Discursive engagement enables people to test out ideas and to enhance their capacity to think critically and to join up the policy dots. It also enhances their capabilities to engage in the policy and politics as to who gets what, when why, how and to what effect.

The three approaches to economics are (according to Polanyi 2001); reciprocity, redistribution and exchange. At face value reciprocity (give and take) may appear egalitarian as does the notion of redistribution, whilst exchange may appear to be most formal. How these concepts are interpreted matters when considering the current social, economic and environmental crisis. Narratives can be seen as formal (modernist), informed by political economy critiques or substantive (based entirely on the perspectives of people's own lived experiences). All these lenses provide a dimension of the situation. The problem with the realist clash paradigm is that although it describes the situation it can hasten the movement towards conflict. This is the self-fulfilling prophecy argument, to which I subscribe.

An alternative future needs to be modelled and co-determined by with and for people of good will. This is the cosmopolitan agenda. It is not naïve. It can be argued to be logical and scientific if we consider the work of Buckminster Fuller on Space Ship earth and Kenneth Boulding's work on domains of knowledge and evolution from inorganic to organic life to living systems comprising human systems that can consciously evolve in directions that they can shape with a sense of purpose.

The evolutionary direction is shaped by values. Hence, the justification for co-determining and co-creating the direction of policy and politics (McIntyre-Mills 2014a, b):

- For those who argue for more state intervention, the state has all the answers to welfare and environmental concerns
- For those who argue that the market provides the answers, more economic freedom is advocated
- For those who argue that the state is inadequate to protect human rights and democracy and accountability a case is made for openness to ideas and freedom of information. Transparency and monitoring from below is needed.

A responsive approach requires a multilevel response to areas of concern and the right response in context. The nation state cannot control the global market which impacts on the welfare of all its citizens, let alone be left to determine what constitutes social and environmental justice. The argument developed is that a new 'post national constellation' (Habermas 2001) approach to social democracy is needed. The zero sum approach to law in the so-called 'national interest' has prevailed in undermining human rights and the environment. The zero sum approach is based on the idea that my gain must be at your expense. It is based on the idea that life can be compartmentalized. Losses and gains are not understood as being systemically interconnected. To have any hope of buttressing well-being and the global commons we need to find ways to identify with the future of the planet, rather than the rights of the powerful to make the law to protect their own interests.

Pilots to prefigure change that provide examples of learning how to do governance differently are necessary, in order to maintain or reduce the size of our ecological footprint.

For example: Murray's notion of a Tuvalu test for decision making provided inspiration for the development of a new architecture for democracy and governance developed, tested and discussed (McIntyre-Mills et al. 2014). The approach is about enabling people to voice their intrinsic values and to shape agendas 'from below' as detailed in 'Transformation from Wall Street to Wellbeing' and its companion volume 'Systemic Ethics for non-anthropocentricism'. These works discuss the testing of a pilot project to develop raft of systemic well-being indicators to address the notion of well-being stocks and being the change globally. We test the principal of subsidiarity and Ashby's rule and strive to implement Murray's notion of a Tuvalu test for decision-making. Murray is a physicist who argues that decisions made in one country affect the life chances of people in other parts of the world. The Tuvulu test refers to rising sea levels. Thus rising sea levels in Tuvalu or in Samoa, for example are a result of the choices made in other developed nation states within the region. Hence the so-called Tuvalu test for decision which asks us to think about the consequences of our thinking. The second volume emphasizes that political and economic systems are constructions that can be reframed by moving beyond the recognition of well-being stocks systems to take into account cultural flows. Water and seeds can be seen as a synecdoche of a new economics and perhaps a new constitution that recognizes the role of human beings as stewards is not merely about neoliberal markets shaping and commodifying nature (Monbiot 2014). Monbiot critiques the thesis raised in works such as 'Six Capitals: the revolution capital has to have or can accountants save the world?' see http://www.monbiot.com/2014/07/24/the-pricing-of-everything.

Thus praxis (McIntyre-Mills et al. 2014 and McIntyre-Mills 2014a, b) takes as its starting point the issue of commodification and suggests not merely a new form of performance accountability but also a transforming what we value and how we live. Ways to reduce the size of our ecological footprint through alternative forms of governance and democracy has been demonstrated with Global Agoras team. The governance of the footprint 'from below' through subsidiarity—means that decisions need to be made at the lowest level possible and that freedom and diversity should be fostered—with the caveat that these decisions should not undermine the rights of others or future generations of life. Governance is necessary to maintain the balance across individual and collective interests. The current architectures for democracy, economics and governance are fatally flawed and that the time to reframe it is long overdue. Our responsibility as global stewards is to ensure that we protect living systems for this generation and the next. The planetary passport detailed in volume 2 of this series suggests a way to operationalize the axiom, that we can be free and diverse to the extent that we do not undermine the rights of others in this generation and the next. Each participant is encouraged to think through what they have in material and nonmaterial terms and what they actually need in order to live well. They are asked to think what they are prepared to do to translate thinking into practice through maximizing turning points for the better and through minimizing turning points for the worse through overcoming practical praxis barriers. Each participant is asked to reflect on what they are prepared to add or discard from their lives in order to live in ways that protect multiple species. Then the next step is to document these steps which form a contract to minimize the size of their ecological foot print. Each de-identified participant's thoughts and actions form part of a growing map that informs and inspires other residents and service providers. A directory of services is provided to assist sustainable living in each participating region by post code. An introduction to the research is provided by means of a series of podcasts in which she explains the research whilst visiting colleagues at the University of South Africa. She raises the question in these podcasts about the implications of increased migration to cities in Indonesia and South Africa where 75 and 80% of the population will be based by 2050. With this trajectory the prospect of 'food deserts' in urban jungles poses a very real threat. South Africa needs to encourage the best and brightest to remain in rural areas through being awarded prestigious scholarships to agricultural institutes in rural areas. Just as Turok (2012) set up a mathematics and science academy to foster the next Albert Einstein in urban South Africa we need to set up rural science academies to foster the next Vandana Shiva or Kenneth Boulding in rural South Africa to foster ways to balance individual and collective needs.

How democratic is democracy if it does not foster food and human security? Liberal democracies are increasingly criticized for not representing the interests of diverse citizens, engaging stakeholders in dialogue, building a shared sense of identity, whilst enabling individual diversity, capability and freedom to the extent that the diversity, capability and freedom *of others* is not undermined. The current difficulties in addressing representation, accountability and sustainability are theoretical, methodological and value based and it has implications for the size of our ecological footprint. The privileged lives of some are at the expense of the majority and at the expense of future generations of life.

The issue is that the nation state is no longer able to address the challenges that span national boundaries because poverty and climate change do not respect political boundaries. Critiques need to avoid reifying systems, rather than addressing the potential to enhance representation, accountability and sustainability through re-framing the architectures of democracy and governance.

## Pan Optican: Surveillance 'From Above' Needs To Be Balanced By Surveillance 'From Below' To Enable Systemic Governance For Stewardship

Surveillance 'from below' and above is needed to protect food, energy and water security by protecting the non-renewables and by ensuring that local people can live lives that are worth living and are capable of achieving quality of life (Nussbaum 2006) by holding elites to account and ensuring that they do indeed have a 'a voice'. The phrase: 'Drain the swamp' used by Trump to mobile the working classes, underemployed and unprotected unemployed gained support simply because the angriest decided that they wanted to be heard. The rise of increasingly xenophobic, nationalist responses it indicative that more and more of the marginalized including the working classes and middle classes feel 'unprotected' by policy makers and politicians.[12] The mistake made by the angry voters, however. is that the challenges of poverty and climate change are faced by people in many nation states and that co-operative approaches are needed, rather than a zero sum

[12]Noonan 2016. Trump and the rise of the unprotected'. *Wall Street Journal* Feb 25.

approach of us versus them. They are right to suggest that global capitalism and global markets are not serving the interests of the majority, but the transformation requires finding ways to enhance social and environmental rights not to lapse into containerist approaches summed up as 'building walls'.

So how can we address the issue of rights and responsibilities at a global level? Could local engagement provide the basis for scaling up management of our Social, Economic and Environmental choices at a regional level?

It would be ideal to be able to protect planetary citizens in ways that respect rights and responsibilities within local communities and in ways that are protected through international law that protects the rights of minorities. But to enable the implementation of social and environmental justice we need a new form of governance and a new form of democracy that enables participation and monitoring. But we also need free accessible ways to ensure that transparency does not become a vehicle for the panopticon authoritarian state.

It is insufficient to argue for global covenants in overlapping regions. We need:

- A movement that ensures we live differently and that we value sustainable living and the rights of Indigenous peoples and Indigenous habitat.
- Overlapping republican rights not a Penal state supported by global panoptic on
- Power of the state through judiciary, police and army to subjugate and incarcerate.
- Power of surveillance the challenge is to avoid surveillance from above without monitoring from below.

Six principles of sustainable governance underpin the Costanza R. et al. (2007) these principles are: responsibility (individual and collective), scale matching (at multiple levels), precaution rather than narrow minded profit, adaptive management based on integrating as much social, economic and environmental information as possible, full cost allocation based on considering the inter connected dimensions of social and environmental considerations and markets should be adjusted and participation based on engagement using discursive dialogue. Previously the work of Ulrich Beck (1992) discussed the so-called 'boomerang affect' of poverty and pollution, but he did not explain the implications for climate change or the ecological footprint.

Governance and democracy have to deal with three options pertaining to truth (McIntyre-Mills 2000, Crowder 2003): (a) One truth responses defended by grand narratives or conflict, (b) No truth (postmodernist) approached defended by relativism, (c) Mediated (harmonized) responses based on stewardship. Beck (2009: 96) stresses the need for sub politics 'from above' and 'below'. How to achieve this is the goal of current research on balancing individual and collective needs. The focus is on the local, so that the poor will not be silenced and so that local wisdom can be drawn upon. This enables creative responsive transformation and the emergence of new relationships.

All genuine threats have become global threats. The situation of every nation, every people, every religion, every class and every individual is also the result and cause of the human situation. The key point is that henceforth concern about the whole has become a task. It is not optional but the human condition (Beck 2009: 19)

This remains a challenge although the world has become more nationalistic in the wake of Britain's exit from the European Union (Brexit), the conservative reactions to immigration in Europe and the election of Donald Trump by people who feel that their needs are being neglected.

The objective of the Pathways to Wellbeing software is to assist the reconsideration of our democratic rights and responsibilities by using participatory engagement aimed to match services to needs - within limits - so that local communities make the best decisions that minimize social, economic and environmental risks and that shape "policy from below" by enabling people to engage in a process of thinking about what material and non-material resources they have to support well-being; what they are prepared to discard; and then to consider what they personally consider to be the social, economic and environmental turning points for better or worse

## The Updated Database Design

The choices individuals make in terms of 'HAVES', 'NEEDS' and what these individuals are prepared to 'ACQUIRE' or 'DISCARD' from their life can be expressed in an Entity Relationship Diagram (ERD). These are depicted in the "Have and Need—Concepts" ERD and the "Discard & Acquire Resources, Pathways and Concepts" ERD in the following subsections.

### *Haves and Needs—Concepts*

The following ERD shows that a client can have one or more pathways, which is based on a domain, which can either be (a) business as usual (b) making small changes for the long haul or (c) sustainable well-being.

Each pathway can be associated with one or more HAVES and NEEDS in terms of the CONCEPTS that each individual identifies with.

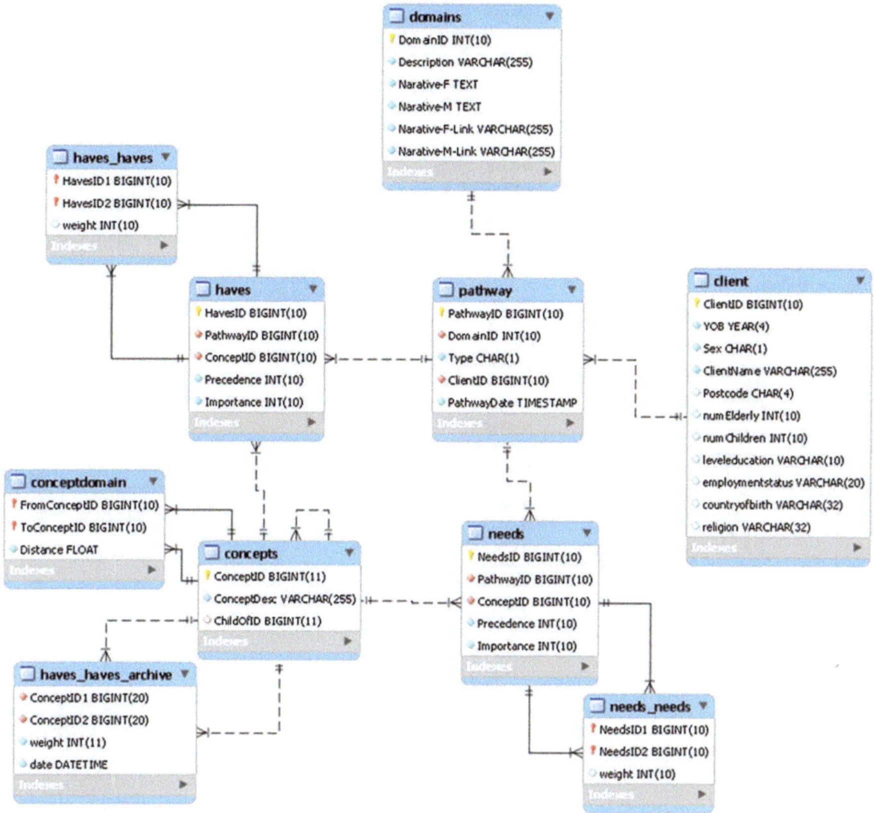


## *Discard and Acquire*

Each PATHWAY can also have one or more BARRIERS associated with it. In response to BARRIERS experienced in the pathway, one may rethink their strategy in life. Individuals if given the opportunity can ACQUIRE RESOURCES or select a new PATHWAY. Individuals will also acquire or discard CONCEPTS depending on the HAVES and NEEDS that they have already identified as described earlier, which can change as they experience different everyday situations.

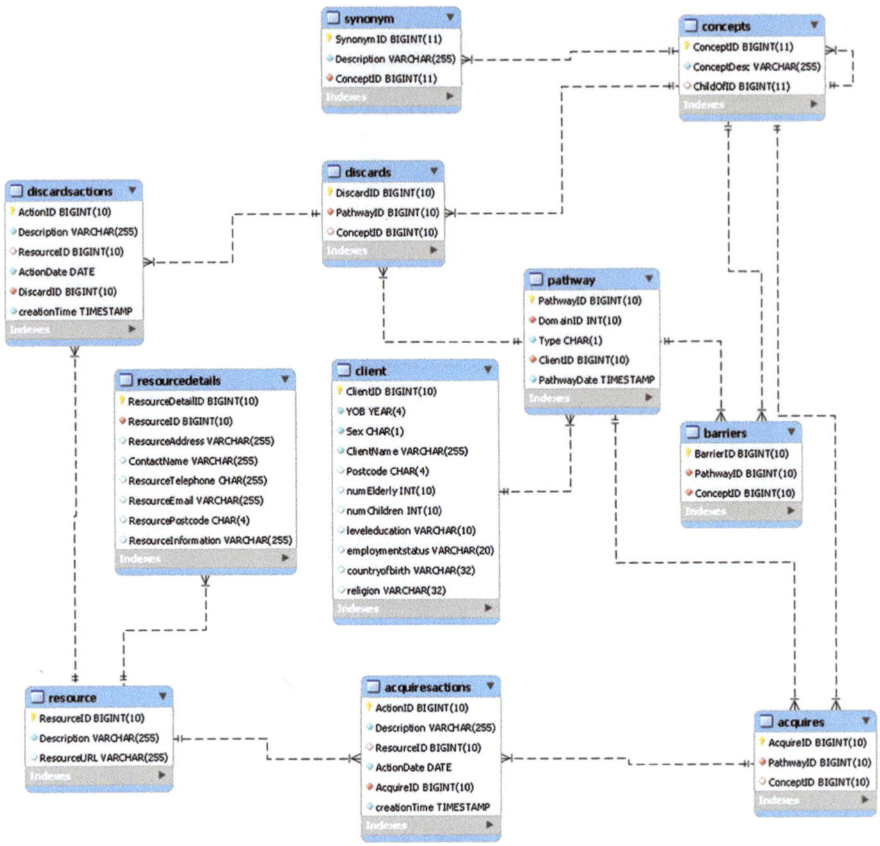


## The Updated Pathways to Well-being Architecture

The pathways to well-being is based on the Google Web Toolkit (GWT) framework, which is based on open source technologies and allows developers to build sophisticated browser-based applications using Java technology.

The diagram below shows the key components of the current state architecture, which involves a development mode and a production mode.

The development mode uses servlets (written in Java), which reside on a servlet container (Tomcat). These servlets support AJAX to make websites dynamic and interactive.

GWT facilitates the translation of these servlets into pure Java Script, which can run in production on a HTTP server using PHP to make dynamic calls to the database.

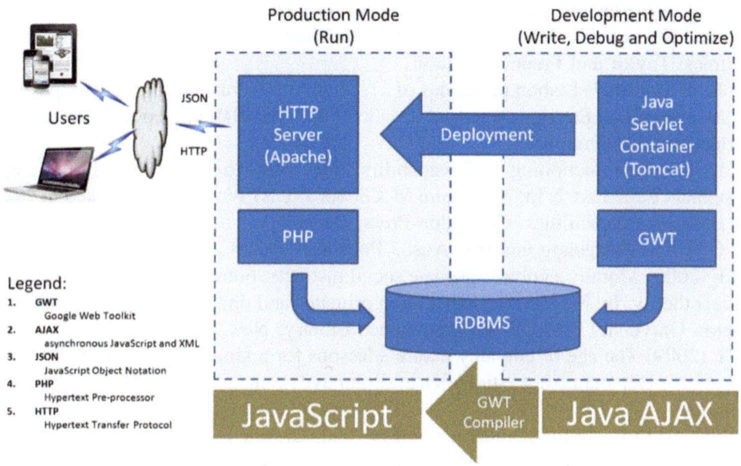


## References


Aarhus Convention (1998) On access to information. Public participation and access to justice in environmental matters, Denmark, 25 June. http://aarhusclearinghouse.unece.org/resources.cfm?c=1000069

Adelman J (2013) Worldly philosopher: The odyssey of albert O. Hirschman, Princeton University Press, Princeton

Archibugi D (2008) The architecture of cosmopolitan democracy. In: The global commonwealth of citizens: towards cosmopolitan democracy. Princeton University Press, New Jersey and also Archibugi D (2010) The architecture of cosmopolitan democracy. In: Brown GW, Held D (eds) Cosmopolitan reader. Polity Press, Cambridge

Arendt H (1963) Eichmann in Jerusalem: a report on the banality of evil. Viking Press, New York

Arendt H (1972) Crises of the Republic. Harcourt Brace, Orlando (First published in 1969)

Article Stable. http://www.jstor.org/stable/3072534. doi:10.2307/3072534

Bausch K (2006) Be your enemy: the contributions of west churchman to doing better governance and international relations. In: McIntyre-Mills J (ed) Rescuing the enlightenment from itself: critical and systemic implications for democracy. C. West churchman series, vol 1. Springer, New York

Beardsworth R (2011) Cosmopolitanism and international relations theory. Polity, Cambridge

Beck U (1992) Risk society towards a new modernity. Sage, London

Beck U (2009) World at risk. Polity, Cambridge

Borradori G (2003) Philosophy in a time of terror. Dialogues with Habermas and Derrida. University of Chicago Press, Chicago

Bostrom N (2011) Existential risk prevention as the most important task for humanity. Faculty of Philosophy & Oxford Martin School University of Oxford. http://www.existential-risk.org

Boulding K (1956) General systems theory—the skeleton of science. Manage Sci 2:197–208
Brundtland G (1987). http://www.worldinbalance.net/agreements/1987-brundtland.html. The report "Our Common Future"
Clark JL (1985) Thus spoke chief seattle the story of an undocumented speech: prologue quarterly of the national archives. 17(1):58–65
Costanza R, Cumberland J, Daly H, Goodland R, Norgaard R, Kubiszewski I, Franco C (2015) Examples of policies, instruments and institutions. In: An introduction to ecological economics. Taylor and Francis, London
Costanza R. et al. (2007) Lisbon principles of sustainable governance. In: Encyclopaedia of earth. Ed. C. J. Cleveland. Environmental information coalition, National council for science and the environment, Washington D.C
Crocker D (1995) Functioning and capability: the foundations of Sen's and Nussbaum's development ethic Part 2. In: Nussbaum M, Glover J (eds) Women, culture and development: a study of human capabilities. Clarendon Press, Oxford
Crowder G (2003) Hedgehog and fox. Aust J Polit Sci 38(2):333–377
De Waal F (2006) Morally evolved: primate social instincts, human morality, and the rise and fall of veneer theory. In: Macedo S, Ober J (eds) primates and philosophers: how morality evolved. Princeton University Press, Princeton Science Library, New Jersey
De Waal F (2009) The age of empathy nature's lessons for a kinder society. Harmony, New York
Dryzek J (1999) Democratising rationality in discursive democracy. Cambridge University Press, Cambridge
Dryzek J (2000) Deliberative democracy and beyond. Oxford University Press, New York
Dryzek J (2005) The politics of the earth. Environmental discourses, 2nd edn. Oxford University Press, New York, pp 156–157
Dryzek J (2010) Green democracy, Cunningham Lecture Series, ANU, Occasional Paper
Flood R, Romm N (1996) Diversity management: triple loop learning. Wiley, Chichester
Giddens A (2009) The politics of climate change. Polity, Cambridge
Greg S, Julian A (2012) http://sydneypeacefoundation.org.au/?s=Julian+assange&submit.x=-696&submit.y=-246&submit=Go
Habermas J (1984) The Theory of communicative action: Reason and the rationalization of society. Beacon, Boston
Habermas J (1989) The structured transformation of the public sphere. Polity Press, Cambridge
Habermas J (2001) The postnational constellation. Political essays. Polity, Cambridge
Hall S (1992) Our mongrel selves. In: New statesman and society
Hall S (1997) Representation: cultural representations and signifying practices. SAGE Publications Ltd presentation, London
Hall S, Du Gay P (1996) Cultural Identity. Sage, London
Hill D (2015) 'Is bolivia quietly planning to frack' mother earth? The guardian weekly, 6 Mar 2015
Hirschman AO (1970) Exit, voice, and loyalty: responses to decline in firms, organizations, and states. Harvard University press, Cambridge
Jackson M (2000) Systems approaches to management. Kluwer, London
Julian B (2014) http://sydneypeacefoundation.org.au/peaceprize-recipients/2014-julian-burnside-ao-qc/
Lameman C (2015) The Guardian, 'Keep it in the ground'https://www.theguardian.com/environment/keep-it-inthe-ground-blog/2015/apr/08/life-above-alberta-tar-sands-why-were-taking-government-to-court
Luhmann N (1995) Social systems (trans: John Bednarz Jr, with Dirk Baecker)
Magnay J (2016) 'Berlin's push to swap failed asylum seekers', Jan 30–31. The Weekend Australian, pp 12
Monbiot G (2013) 'Money just makes the rich suffer'. Guardian Weekly, May 13 pg. 9
Monbiot G (2014) The pricing of everything. http://www.monbiot.com/2014/07/24/the-pricing-of-everything

Midgley G (2000) Systemic intervention: philosophy, methodology, and practice. Kluwer, New York
McIntyre-Mills J (2014a) Reconsidering boundaries. In: Sociopedia, international sociological association. doi:10.1177/2056846014102
McIntyre-Mills J (2014b) Systemic ethics and non-anthropocentric stewardship: Implications for transdisciplinarity and cosmopolitan politics. Springer, New York
McIntyre-Mills J, De Vries D, Binchai N (2014) Wall Street to Wellbeing: Joining up the dots through participatory democracy and governance to mitigate the causes and adapt to the effects of climate change. Springer, New York
McIntyre-Mills J, De Vries D (2011) Identity, democracy and Sustainability. Emergence, ISCE, USA, Litchfield pp–380
McIntyre-Mills J (2006) Systemic governance and accountability: working and re-working the conceptual and spatial boundaries of international relations and governance. Volume 3 of the 'C. West Churchman and Related Works Series'. Springer, London
McIntyre-Mills J (2003) Critical systemic praxis. For social and environmental justice: participatory policy design for a global age. The contemporary systems series kluwer, UK, London.
McIntyre-Mills J (2000) Global Citizenship and Social Movements: creating transcultural webs of meaning for the new millennium. The Netherlands, Harwood
Meadows D, Randers J (1992) Beyond the Limits. Global collapse of a sustainable future. Earthscan Publications, London
Noonan P (2016) Trump and the rise of the unprotected. Wall Street Journal Feb 25th
Nussbaum M (2006) Frontiers of justice. Harvard University Press, London
Odum HT, Odum E (1996) Environmental accounting: energy and environmental decision making. Wiley, New York
Papadimitriou D (2014) The coming 'tsunami of debt'. The Guardian.com, Sunday 15 June 2014 17.58 BST
Pauli G (2010) The blue economy: report to the club of Rome. Paradigm Publications, New Mexico
Paul GL (2003) The evolution of international human rights: visions seen
Pidgeon N, Fischhoff B (2011) The role of social and decision sciences in communicating uncertain climate risks. http://www.nature.com/nclimate/journal/v1/n1/full/nclimate1080.html
Polanyi K (2001) The great transformation. The political and economic origins of our time. Beacon Press, Boston
Roberts D (2015) No war with Islam, Obama says, but conflicts continue. The guardian, 27 Feb 2015
Rusbridger A (2015) Why we are putting the climate threat to earth front and centre. The guardian weekly, 13 Mar 2015
Saul B, Sherwood S, McAdam J, Stephens T, Slezak J (2012) Climate change and Australia: warming to the global challenge, The Federation Press, Sydney
Shiva V (2012) 'Monocultures of the mind: perspectives on biodiversity and biotechnology'. Third World Network, Penang
Shiva V (2012) 'Making peace with the earth'. Fernwood Publishing, Winipeg
Shiva V, Barlow M (2011) On the need for a new narrative of Earth Democracy and Governance. http://www.democracynow.org/2011/4/22/earth_day_special_Vandana_Shiva
Stiglitz J, Sen A, Fitoussi JP (2010) Mis-measuring our lives: why the GDP doesn't add up. The New Press, New York
Steffen W, Grinevald J, Crutzen P, McNeill J (2011) The Anthropocene: conceptual and historical perspectives. Phil. Trans. R. Soc. A 69:842–867. doi: 10.1098/rsta.2010.0327
Turok N (2012) The universe within Allen and Unwin. Based on the CBC massy lectures
United Nations Economic and Social Development Local Agenda 21 1992
Vandana S (2013) Festival of Dangerous ideas. https://www.youtube.com/watch?v=o2o_QQTYc7I

Von Foerster H (1995) Cybernetics of cybernetics. Future systems, 2nd edn. Inc, Minneapolis
Wilkinson R, Pickett K (2009) The spirit level. Why more equal societies almost always do better. Allen Lane, London

## Author Biographies

**Dr. Janet McIntyre-Mills** is an Associate Professor in the School of Social and Policy Studies at Flinders University, Adjunct Professor at the University of Indonesia and Islamic National University in Indonesia, and Honorary Professor at the University of South Africa. Her research focuses on systemic representation, accountability and re-generation applied to social and environmental justice concerns such as health, housing and social inclusion and the mitigation and adaptation to climate change. She addresses complex needs by exploring the meanings and 'what if' questions with diverse stakeholders. Her recent books include 'From Wall Street to Wellbeing: Joining up the dots through Participatory Democracy and Governance to Mitigate the Causes and Adapt to the Effects of Climate Change'. ISBN 978-1-4899-7465-5 and 'Systemic ethics and Non-anthropocentric Stewardship: Implications for Trans disciplinarity and Cosmopolitan politics', ISBN 978-3-519-07655-3.

**Rudolf Wirawan** is the founder of Wirasoft Pty Ltd in Sydney, Australia. Previously, Rudolf worked with companies such as IBM, WANG and Nixdorf Computers. Wirasoft offers services ranging from consulting, training, to the development of enterprise-scale applications. Enterprise applications are used in global companies across industries such as banking, telecommunications, insurance, mining, etc. They help deliver information in a timely manner to optimise business operations and can also provide pathways to generating future investment.

# Chapter 5
# Introducing a Parallel Curriculum to Enhance Social and Environmental Awareness in South African School Workbooks

**Veronica McKay**

**Abstract** This chapter focuses on the ways in which educational and curriculum reforms in post-apartheid South Africa have attempted to tackle the national problem of poor learner achievement in literacy and language through the development of school workbooks which provide one lesson per day to support teaching and learning. In addition to addressing the pedagogical and curricula challenges, the developers of the workbooks strove to extend the pedagogy by infusing it with ethical values of social and environmental justice so as to form a parallel curriculum. The chapter location considers the teaching of values from an Ubuntu perspective, which is predicated on communal relationships and extends to include relationships in the animal and eco-environment. The chapter includes various pictorial codes from the materials to illustrate the issues raised. The legacy of apartheid left severe backlogs in education in general, and specifically with regard to literacy and language - necessitating curriculum support for learners in all public schools. In addition to addressing the pedagogical and curricula challenges, the post-apartheid project of social integration made it imperative for the designers of the workbooks to extend the pedagogy so as to infuse ethical values of social and environmental justice. While the books aimed to teach the overt curriculum (language and literacy), they were designed in such a way to ensure that the covert curriculum supported the values of democracy, Ubuntu, inclusivity (race, class, gender, ability and both urban and rural identity). In addition, the overt and covert messages strove to explore the children's relationship with the planet and the animal- and eco-environment—striving at all times to ensure these sophisticated concepts were accessible to a target population of children aged from 4–13 years.

V. McKay (✉)
University of South Africa, Pretoria, South Africa
e-mail: mckayvi@gmail.com



J. McIntyre-Mills et al. (eds.), *Balancing Individualism and Collectivism*,
Contemporary Systems Thinking, DOI 10.1007/978-3-319-58014-2_5

## Introduction

The legacy of apartheid left severe backlogs in South African schooling in general, and in the essential areas of literacy and language teaching in particular, which necessitated large-scale curriculum support for approximately 9 million children as part of South Africa's post-apartheid educational reforms.

Concern about poor learner performance, a lack of educational resources such as textbooks, and the impact of poorly trained teachers gave rise to a Presidential injunction requiring the Department of Basic Education to develop and deliver resources, specifically workbooks that would provide direct support to teachers in classrooms by means of a lesson a day to improve performance in the critical areas of literacy and language. This mass-scale intervention took advantage of economies of scale to ensure that every child received their quota of workbooks—something that, historically, has never occurred. This was in line with the country's aims to accelerate progress towards the United Nations goal of *Education for All* and the endeavours to ensure access to quality education.

Despite the strives made to universalise education in post-apartheid, South Africa was still left with the legacy of poor learner performance—a problem especially acute among learners in rural areas, where the problems of weak literacy and numeracy abilities were cumulative across the curriculum, with learners often leaving school with low levels of literacy and numeracy.

The poor outcomes of schooling were evident in mathematics and language learning assessments: In particular, poor results in standardised tests such as the PIRLS and TIMMS[1] as well as the continental SACMEQ and the National Annual Assessments all signalled the need for more *structured* intervention. Moreover it was recognised that learners in schools lacked resources and learner support materials—with learners needing to share textbooks with one or more learners (Chetty and Moloi 2010; Taylor 2009; Howie et al. 2008; Spaull 2011a, b, c; 2013a, b; DBE 2011a). Teachers often tried to remedy the situation by using photocopied or homemade worksheets—a solution that was time-consuming, expensive and understandably challenging (McKay 2013, p. 13).

Learners' poor performance was identified as a major concern by the Presidency and was listed as a priority in government's Plan of Action (DBE 2011b). A presidential injunction required the South African Department of Basic Education (DBE) to develop and provide resources—specifically workbooks—that would assist learners to improve their performance in the critical areas of literacy and numeracy from Grade R to Grade 9 (McKay 2012). JET (2009) provides a nuanced

[1]Although it is recognised that the PIRLS and TIMMs are Northern oriented assessments, increasing the likelihood that South Africans would perform poorly, children also performed poorly on the continental SACMEQ and the South African National Annual Assessments.

analysis of the problem, concluding that the scope, depth and frequency of appropriate curriculum coverage, assessment, homework and pacing was lacking in the schooling system. It was revealed that learners' exercise books often contained only one or two extended written activities, suggesting low levels of learning and teaching. To counter this, the workbooks developed and distributed by the DBE aimed to provide regular practice. The books are also intended to facilitate monitoring since most of the written work is done in the workbook and learners fill in their answers in the spaces provided making it possible for teachers (and subject advisors) to see at a glance, whether learners are completing the prescribed written activities.

The development of the South African school workbooks therefore aimed to address the problems of poor learner performance by:

- providing easy-to-use, sequenced worksheets packaged into workbooks aligned to the curriculum
- ensuring that schools that lacked learning resources and/or photocopying facilities would be supported through the provision of worksheets
- providing a variety of activities to reinforce literacy/language/numeracy skills
- introducing learners to the language and concepts required to understand and learn their other school subjects
- assisting teachers to focus, in a targeted manner, on the skills that learners should be acquiring in each grade as outlined in the curriculum
- helping teachers to monitor learners' performance in key activities, and prepare learners for the formats used in various standardised assessments (DBE Submission for Workbooks 2010; McKay 2012, 2013).

## Part 1: A Proposed Solution for Improving Learning Outcomes and Embedding Positive Values

Outhred et al. (2014 p. 60) point out that the role of learner and teacher support material in optimal teaching and learning is often cited as critical, and textbooks are frequently used as a way of bridging systemic learning deficits. They refer to the importance of well-designed[2] instructional materials, specifically when curriculum changes are introduced or when teachers lack the necessary teaching skills. Outhred et al. (2014) cite Sampa (2008), who stresses the need for well-designed instructional materials to strengthen learners' and teachers' interaction with the curriculum, and who argues that when teaching needs strengthening, such materials offer an opportunity to reinforce and supplement teaching and learning.

[2]It is important to note that because of the large quantities of paper that would be used to print the books, it was decided to print on acid-free paper using vegetable-based ink which would not pollute the environment and which made recycling possible.

In South Africa, the development and delivery of school workbooks and other learner support materials as part of the workbook project were regarded as critical interventions aimed at addressing school book shortages necessary towards equalising education.

The large-scale production by the state utilised specialists in materials development, children's artwork, graphic design and languages to develop the workbooks. The state's free provision of 8 workbooks per child per year resulted in the bulk production of books (250 million books[2] were delivered to schools during the period 2011–2017), which provided an opportunity to take advantage of economies of scale reducing the cost to the state, thus providing a strong cost-benefit ratio (Outhred et al. 2014). The large-scale intervention also provided the opportunity to convey messages about human rights and environmental sustainability nationwide.

The workbook intervention was critical because, despite government doubling its expenditure on learner and teacher support materials in the period 2008–2012, textbook provision fell short of ensuring one textbook per child per subject. The problem was more acute for learners in low quintile schools (schools in low socio-economic areas), who were in resource-poor homes and schools.

## *The Importance of Textbooks*

Much research has been conducted on the importance of textbooks in supporting the curriculum. City et al (2009) state that for any real improvement in learning to be achieved, the instructional core—which comprises teachers' knowledge and skills as well as their content knowledge, and the role of the learner in the instructional process—needs to be improved. They thus emphasise the important relationship between the teacher, the learner and the content and learner and teacher support material (textbooks and workbooks) as being fundamental to the instructional core. " The instructional core refers to "the relationship between the teacher, the student and the content—not the qualities of any one of them by themselves—that determines the nature of instructional practice". They point out that "the instructional task is the actual work that students are asked to do in the process of instruction—not what teachers think they are asking students to do, or what the official curriculum says that the students are asked to do, but what they are actually asked to do" (City et al 2009, pp. 22–23).

Workbook development team explored the role workbooks (and textbooks) might play in improving the instructional core. Accordingly, the workbooks were conceptualised with a view to supporting teachers with what they should ask learners to do. The workbooks were therefore designed to fulfil the roles of both textbooks and workbooks or structured collections of worksheets. While they include some instruction, explanation and extensive reading text, they also guide the learner–teacher engagement with regard to the content, encouraging discussion and "doing". As a *hybrid* between textbook and workbook[4], the workbooks were designed to ensure curriculum coverage by providing instruction and activities for each fortnightly division specified in the curriculum, thus forming a comprehensive study programme for the year. Each section is set out systematically, providing expositions of concepts, definitions of the terms and symbols of the topic in question, and a number of practice exercises. Each workbook provides spaces in which learners are able to write their answers, thus scaffolding the type and the amount of text learners write (so as to address the problem of insufficient written text referred to above).

In the process of design, we as developers remained cognisant of the fact that the workbooks would be immensely influential in conveying social norms and values, and of their pervasiveness, given that they would be delivered to every child, in every public school, in every grade from Grade R to Grade 9, in each of the 11 official South African languages. It was also recognised that school books act as de facto curriculum, especially in times of curriculum change. It was therefore essential that the workbook development team explored the parallel role that the workbooks might play in reinforcing values and attitudes, so as to ensure that all the messages in the books—both overt and implicit—conveyed the positive values of cultural diversity and inclusivity. They needed to portray positive representations of race, gender, socioeconomic status, urban and rural localities, disability and the relationship between humans and the eco-environment. It was also necessary to imbue the books with the values and principles that are entrenched in the South African Constitution.

## *The Parallel Curriculum*

The subsequent section of this chapter provides a case study of the efforts made by the DBE to provide workbooks as one of the interventions aimed at addressing poor learner performance. The paper focuses on the rationale underlying the conceptualisation of the workbooks—specifically on how, through this intervention, the developers aimed to infuse values education, both through the overt curriculum and via the covert curriculum, which is often referred to as the "hidden curriculum".

In traditional Marxist literature, the hidden curriculum is perceived negatively due to its transmission of certain class or gender messages which are generally aimed at reproducing and perpetuating existing social relations. The study by Bowles and Gintis (1976), entitled "Schooling in capitalist America", pointed out that, from a Marxist perspective, public schooling is designed to prepare pupils for their destiny in the working class through perpetuating patterns of domination and subordination hidden in the broad curriculum and practices of the school. While some authors focused on resistance to these messages, others argued that children often unwittingly colluded with the reproductive outcomes (Apple 1979, 1982; Willis 1977).

McKay and Romm (1992, p. 64) point to the racial element of this reproduction in South Africa—a legacy feature which still underlies the inequality of the present post-apartheid system of education. Çubukçu (2012) explains that the various activities of a hidden curriculum, such as social, cultural, free-time and sporting activities; the celebration of special days; and school extramural activities can be considered strong value-gaining tools to help learners understand and internalise character or citizenship values. This chapter focuses on how the hidden curriculum was "specifically designed" in school workbooks to bring about a new consciousness and to convey positive values of inclusivity, care and respect for others in tandem with teaching the official curriculum. McKay (2016) refers to this as a "parallel curriculum".

Hence, while the books overtly aimed to teach the content of the official curriculum (language and literacy), they were designed in such a way as to ensure that the covert (or hidden) curriculum supported the values of democracy, social and environmental justice, as well as ethical conduct and inclusiveness in terms of race, class, gender and ability. They also strove to raise awareness of the need for humanised societies, regardless of residential location (whether rural or urban). McKay (2016) refers specifically to the importance of the "parallel" curriculum being developed in tandem with the overt, official curriculum, and the need to make artists, designers and all the members of the materials development team aware of its importance. In addition, both the overt and the parallel messages endeavoured to support the children's relationship with the planet, with other species, and with the eco-environment—striving at all times to ensure that sophisticated concepts and values of sustainability and human rights were accessible to a target population of children in the 4–13 year age band.

It is recognised that, in Marxist terms, the covert or hidden curriculum usually carries with it negative connotations. However, in the case of the workbooks, the development team chose to manipulate aspects of the material often constituting the hidden curriculum to ensure that the parallel curriculum supported the positive values of the South African Constitution.

## *Ubuntu as an Underlying Philosophy*

The African context of the workbooks necessitated the materials being underpinned by the African philosophy of Ubuntu. This forms a contrast with Western individualism in its recognition of the collective and of connectedness by privileging the I/we relationship; the concepts "I am us", "I am because we are", and "We are because I am" form the foundation of the Ubuntu philosophy (Chilisa 2009, p. 407). As South African Desmond Tutu explains: "My humanity is bound up in yours, for we can only be human together".

Letseka (2000, p. 179) identifies the "notion of *botho* or *buntu* (humanism) as pervasive and fundamental to African socio-ethical thought, illuminating the communal rootedness and interdependence of persons, and highlighting the importance of human relationships as an important measure of human wellbeing or human flourishing in traditional African life".

In relation to the notion of communal interdependence, Chilisa (2009, p. 407) speaks of brotherhood, sisterhood, and community togetherness and contrasts this with individualistic Eurocentric view of Descartes "I think, therefore, I am" (Chilisa 2009, p. 407).

Oviawe (2016, p. 5) elaborates by explaining how Ubuntu embraces the ecosystem: it is a more human-centred, holistic worldview that recognises the interdependencies within the ecosystem of people, planet and place. As she formulates it (2016, p. 9):

> Communities are networks of relationships both biological and social that exist within a given ecosystem. It is clear that humans and nature are intertwined and have a relationship of reciprocity whereby one depends on the other to survive. Indeed, the collective ethos is not limited to human communities only but rather they are connected to their environment. … [Ubuntu] provides a roadmap for viewing the world in a more holistic and ecologically sound manner, revealing the processes behind the connections and patterns that crystallise seemingly separate parts into a unified whole.

The development of the workbooks therefore drew on the humanist values of Ubuntu, and strove to infuse an approach to education of a more inclusive society intertwined with the ecosystem. While we endeavoured to infuse these values into the formal, overt curriculum, we also attempted to ensure this by remaining aware at all times of the hidden or parallel curriculum.

## *Positive Values*

In developing the parallel curriculum, we took our inspiration from the South African Constitution, the social justice agenda of the Millennium Development Goals (MDG) and the recent Sustainable Development Goals (SDG). SDG Goal (The essential precursor to all 16 other SDGs) sets the target, through SDG 4.7, of ensuring that by 2030, all learners acquire the knowledge and skills needed to promote sustainable development, including, among others, sustainable production and consumption, sustainable lifestyles, human rights, gender equality, a culture of peace and non-violence, global citizenship and an appreciation of cultural diversity.

Clearly, if education is to respond to these goals, it is necessary to ensure that education inculcates positive values that transcend content knowledge and promote:

- human rights
- gender equality
- a culture of peace and non-violence
- global citizenship
- an appreciation of cultural diversity
- peaceful societies
- inclusive societies
- justice for all
- sustainable lifestyles
- environmental and eco-stewardship.

## *Promoting Sustainable Development Through Education*

Education has a critical role to play in promoting sustainable development and improving people's capacity to address environmental and developmental issues (Agenda 21, 1992, article 36.4). How to extend the workbooks to go beyond the teaching of reading, writing and mathematics, so as to focus on the values of social justice, inclusiveness and environmental stewardship, was a challenge that the development team needed to explore.

McKay (2016), the author of this paper[5], who was the coordinator of the workbook development project, explains the approach taken in conceptualising the workbooks so as to ensure a synergy between the overt curriculum of language (or mathematics) teaching and the parallel curriculum, by infusing ethical values of inclusion and environmental morality and social justice whilst assisting (often poorly trained) teachers to mediate both the official and the parallel curriculum.

## *Democratising the Curriculum: A Constructivist Approach*

In line with the importance attached to the negotiated curriculum in the South African context (McKay and Romm 1992), the workbook development process sought the participation of teachers, subject advisors and children with regard to content, design, curriculum alignment and embedded messages.[3]

As part of advancing the agenda for democracy in South Africa, and specifically in education, the development of the workbooks was seen as a discursive process through which the voices of teachers, learners and officials informed the various iterations of materials and their use in school classrooms. While the actual

---

[3]I am writing this case study as the coordinator of the school workbook initiative, which I initiated while I was seconded from my university to the Ministry of Basic Education. I took on the task both as a sociologist and as an educator. The critical review process engendered much debate and decision-making around, for example, traditional and non-traditional gender roles, rural versus urban living, the importance of debunking racial and gender stereotypes, and ways of validating South Africa's diverse cultures in order to develop a series of learner support materials by South Africans for South African learners across the country and across cultures. This form of participatory practice was made possible because this was a government project and we were therefore able to draw large samples of teachers, subject advisors and children into the consultative process. The process was essential in order to explore not only curriculum matters but also the way in which so-called Western and indigenous understandings of education would be dealt with. In the subsequent discussion, some of the issues of contention will be elaborated on to show how the process unfolded, resulting in a package of more than 400 titles of learner support materials delivered to approximately 9 million children each year. These materials constitute one of the few large-scale interventions by government, which arose from engagement with various stakeholders, the books having being improved over 5 editions, based on the reception of the materials by teachers and learners country-wide.

curriculum upon which the materials were based had been negotiated, the workbooks and graded readers were pre-prepared and piloted in classrooms, and thereafter subjected to stakeholder engagement to further democratise and contextualise all the materials in all the languages.

Various processes were followed. Teachers and subject advisors were invited to national and provincial meetings aimed at reviewing the materials to ensure a fit between the newly developed curriculum and the assessment policy, and to interrogate the values and messages conveyed by the materials. The various editions of the workbooks were also revised as the emerging official curricula were being adjusted, refined and translated shaped by the feedback from practitioners.

Pre-development surveys and interviews were carried out with teachers and learners to establish what features they considered important in school books, interviews were conducted with children and teachers, and workshops were held to enable teachers and subject advisors to participate in reviewing the various editions of the workbooks and other support materials. In addition, workshops with teachers and subject advisors were held across the country, and inputs and recommendations were considered for subsequent editions of the materials across the grades and across the 11 official languages.

## *Language as Inclusivity*

Selecting the languages that materials are developed in, and the care that is afforded to languages, is usually a "hidden curriculum" matter. Therefore language issues were taken seriously as one of the vehicles of inclusiveness in the development of the workbooks.

The workbook package was conceptualised in accordance with the spirit of the Constitution of the Republic of South Africa (Act 106 of 1996, Sect. 6), which seeks to enhance the status and development of the indigenous official languages, namely Sepedi, Sesotho, Setswana, siSwati, Tshivenda, Xitsonga, Afrikaans, English, isiNdebele, isiXhosa and isiZulu. The Constitution requires national and provincial government to take practical measures to elevate the status of these languages, and to monitor their use in order to ensure that they enjoy parity of esteem and are treated equitably. In terms of the African value system of Ubuntu, this implies the restoration of social justice for those whose languages were historically denigrated (Brock-Utne 2016, p. 34):

> The Pan South African Language Board (PanSALB), which was established in terms of the Constitution, is required to create conditions for the development of the 11 official languages, to promote and ensure respect for all languages, promote multilingualism, and safeguard the language rights of the groups concerned.

This is manifested in government's additive bilingualism/multilingualism policy (whereby each person should learn a language or languages in addition to his or her home language), has been articulated in the Language-in-Education Policy and has given rise to the decision to develop mother-tongue or home-language workbooks across the 11 official languages (McKay 2012).

Literature on the importance of learning through the mother tongue (e.g. Alidou et al. 2006), propound that children learn better when they are taught through a language they know well. If a child begins learning in his or her first language, he or she is more likely to succeed academically and is, in fact, better equipped to learn additional languages than children who begin learning in a second (or foreign) language, and who will, at least initially, find learning that much harder.

While much of the discussion on language policies and the use of the mother tongue are based on the importance of language for learning, Brock-Utne (2016) draws on an Ubuntu perspective arguing for the use of (African) mother-tongue instruction as the basis of inclusiveness. Arguing that countries of the global South are disadvantaged and less likely to institute educational practices suited to their unique sociocultural, socio-economic and geopolitical realities as long as these continue to be borrowed from northern systems. Moreover, she points out that the inclusion of mother-tongue instruction to achieve effective and equitable education is critical in enhancing parental support of children's learning; communication between children's home and their school thus bridging the gap between home and school/society.

The South African workbooks were intended to contribute to inclusiveness and parity of esteem, as all 11 official languages are treated equitably. The pedagogical advantages of this are well documented, for example by Cummins (2000), MacDonald (1990, 1991) and Alidou et al. (2006) argue that learning in the mother tongue is what enables children to build on knowledge they already have, and to develop the more advanced concepts and knowledge that they need to continue learning in their mother tongue as the conduit for transferring learning to their second language. The workbook project therefore gave equal attention to all the languages, not only to ensure that the pedagogical and cognitive advantages of mother-tongue learning would be benefited from, but also in order to ensure the language rights of all learners were met.

## *Exploring the Content and Messages*

The Department of Educations (2005) report on *Values, Human Rights in the Curriculum,* outlines how positive values should be infused across the education system and notes that:

> Human rights claim their roots as being simply in the humanness persons "contain", which cannot be separated from their being. Whilst some values may be specific to a culture or a religion, there are those that many would consider 'universal'. Amongst these are the values that form the cornerstone of our own democracy: dignity, equality, justice and freedom (DOE 2005, p. 5).

This chapter will now focus on how the issue of values was treated by way of the official and parallel curriculum. The subsequent discussion includes various examples from the workbook material, both pictorial and textual, to illustrate the issues raised and the positive messaging of the "hidden" or parallel curriculum.

## Part 2: Diversity, Culture and Inclusiveness in the Workbooks

In the development of the national workbooks, attempts were made to ensure that the parallel curriculum responded to the diversity of needs of the national target of learners. The development team drew on the values enshrined in the South African Constitution and also in the MDG/SDG agenda—especially on the values of education for social inclusiveness.

Biraimah (2016, p. 53) defines inclusive schooling as the reorganisation of school practices to ensure that schooling is responsive to the diverse needs of learners. She refers specifically to those at risk of being marginalised, such as "orphans, poor children, displaced children, children with special needs and those suffering from HIV/AIDS". She stresses the importance of all learners having "equitable access to the same broad-based national basic education curriculum, and equal chances to complete the cycle and achieve core learning". The South African workbooks were developed to provide curriculum support especially for learners in low quintile schools (in poor communities), where curriculum support was needed to contribute to equalising education.

In utilising the role of the parallel curriculum, much attention was focused on the illustrations or tasks in the workbooks or reading books that require learners to engage through identifying their responses or feelings or expressing their thoughts about scenarios or perspectives. The illustrations provided opportunities to explore prejudices and concerns and reflect on diversity and civic and moral responsibility, especially in relation to equity, diversity, inclusiveness and eco-stewardship.

### *Benchmarking Our Practice*

To properly fulfil our responsibility to design national learner materials, we examined and analysed all commercial materials available in South Africa. Indeed, we learned many lessons (regarding both the good and the bad) from our review of the overt and hidden curricula of materials available in South African schools.

> Our review of the materials produced by commercial publishers, we found that "the values being communicated [in many of the commercial packages] were not consistent with the Constitution. … There are pictures of children being caned, of gender violence, and of strange acts of violence such as a boy chopping a live donkey (SAIDE 2011, p. 23).

In contrast to the commercially published materials, the national school workbooks aimed to uphold the values of the South African Constitution, which implied avoiding and even condemning any form of violence. We believe that we have achieved this goal, as almost all the teachers surveyed across a representative sample of 500 schools believed that the books teach positive values, fewer than 3% not acknowledging their role in this regard.

## *Culturally Diverse Curriculum Content*

The books aimed to portray the South African "rainbow nation", and we made a concerted effort to be culturally inclusive, basing racial composition proportions used in the artwork on demographics. Biraimah (2016, p. 53) points out that, because textbooks (and by implication workbooks) act as a proxy for curriculum, they need to reflect inclusiveness and equity. She argues that, in practice, topics and characters should reflect a cross-section of the population. She further believes that culturally inclusive practices are critical to diverse learner retention and must be responsive to ethnicity, urban/rural location, gender and socio-economic class. In this regard, education needs to embrace and validate diversity, if it is to be culturally responsive and transformative. As Biraimah (2016, p. 46) puts it:

> Culturally responsive instruction insists that all learners will achieve greater educational outcomes when instruction includes and reflects their own cultural experiences. This means that current discontinuities between school culture and the learner's home culture and community are critically implicated in low achievement, particularly with regard to marginalised students. Conversely, it is anticipated that when their school's culture and curriculum and their teachers' pedagogy are built upon their own cultural and linguistic strengths, marginalised students' achievement will skyrocket.

Cultural context was also taken seriously in the national school workbooks, and we undertook to present a range of social and cultural contexts for the national target of children to whom the books were distributed. While we recognised that the vast majority of the learners were living in poverty, we consciously chose not to portray only impoverished circumstances. After much stakeholder consultation it was agreed that the materials would be aspirational rather than lock learners in their present realities. We recognised that approximately 50% of the South African population was urban—we did not want to limit learners' knowledge to only their present contexts—whilst at the same wishing to enhance the perceptions of rural dwelling. The books therefore provide a good urban and rural mix, showing trains, cranes, planes and tractors, whilst taking into account that the larger portion of the targeted learners were living in poverty.

Rather than focusing on the stereotypical deficiencies of the poor, the books often subtly, tacitly and inclusively depict poverty as a complex problem and include references to school feeding programmes (see, for example, Fig. 5.1) and to state-provided health care while recognising and valuing the resilience of children living in poverty.

Lazar et al. (2012, p. 19) point out that poverty is one of the most powerful factors preventing children from achieving the learning outcomes. Children from poor households have less access to reading material and are unlikely to have parents who can help them with their homework: In the South African context, the high adult illiteracy rates negatively affect parents' ability to assist with their children's homework.

According to Lazar et al. (2012, p. 20), children from poor households and communities are further disadvantaged because they are not exposed to travel or experiences that take them beyond their homes and communities and broaden their knowledge base. And often, poor children attend schools that are resource-poor and are hence unable to compensate for these deficiencies. The workbooks have endeavoured to compensate for these limitations and generally present lessons that take children into expanded contexts. We specifically designed lessons about school tours to the city, to a rain forest, a farm, a game park, the beach and the village, and so forth. In more than one book, children go camping (see, for example, Fig. 5.2) to give the expanded experience of being in natural settings.

The lessons have been designed to entertain and to give learners exposure to people and places beyond their own life circumstances. This has meant that the workbooks expose learners to ships and dolphins and the planets. We wanted learners to imagine an alternative future.

The books are aspirational, offering far more than the materials provided by the apartheid government, which were developed specifically for black children and intended to limit their vistas to their homeland and rural poverty[6]. Hence, while affirming the cultural contexts of the all learners, we recognised that we needed to expand their vistas. Letseka (2016, p. 50) sums this up as an acknowledgement of

**Fig. 5.1** Children in a school feeding lunch queue. These feeding schemes usually target poor children. We attempt to 'normalise' feeding by depicting an atmosphere of care and a multicultural group. Note the 'sentinel dog' participating as an active member of the group

**Fig. 5.2** Exposing city children to nature

our "communally inclined selves and personhood with a recognition of world citizenship".

In practice, affirming contexts meant that we depicted a mud or shack dwelling in an affirming way, for example by including trees, flowers, butterflies and goats, and by including both black and white characters in the same illustration. We attempted to de-stigmatise low socio-economic status or "ruralness".

However, the multicultural materials often gave rise to debate and contestation. In one of the teacher workshops, it was found that some teachers objected to the inclusion of white characters in traditionally African settings. This gave rise to negotiations and discussions among teachers and subject advisors from across the African language groups, during which questions such as whether indeed whites could be poor or rural, whether they should be depicted in an African language book, and whether black rural children might ever encounter white children at some stage of their lives, and if not why not, were hotly debated. At times we had lively conversations with teachers who opposed the inclusion of white or Indian people, or who felt that rural learners did not need to know about modern transport. The larger group of teachers (from all 11 language groups) eventually reached consensus, agreeing that the multiracial pictures were appropriate.

**Fig. 5.3** Depicting South Africa's cultural mosaic

In another teacher workshop a teacher objected to a lesson on dolphins and one on trains, because their province was not only largely rural but also landlocked. As she put it, "we don't have trains and we don't have dolphins in our part of the world". This led to a robust discussion. In this case it was agreed by the group that children would, in the course of their lives, encounter a train, and that we should not deprive children of at least knowing about dolphins as part of their own general literacy.

It was interesting to note that race and location did not emerge as issues in our surveys with children, and that a large proportion of teachers surveyed in a study by the University of South Africa confirmed that the workbooks contributed to the nurturing of good values.

Based on the views expressed by Biraimah (2016), we believed in the workbook development process, holding that the role of "Ubuntu-style" pedagogy was to ensure that education remained inclusive and acted as an equaliser in school classrooms by affirming cultural diversity without silencing the aspirations of learners or locking them into their present contexts as did apartheid.

**Fig. 5.4** The multicultural characters featured across the series

Rather, as Biraimah (2016) suggests, we recognised, through the characters in the books, "the resilience of children who thrive under extremely challenging circumstances so that low-income or rural families are portrayed as robust and worthy, rather than as laden with deficits".[4]

As mentioned above, in considering social contexts as vital for education, the workbook team reviewed existing commercial textbooks used in schools. This was necessary in helping the team to define its own approach, which was distinctly African and specifically South African. We consciously avoided what SAIDE (2011) refers to as the "homeland mentality", which was then common in the commercial textbooks used in schools. As SAIDE (2011, p. 13) points out:

> Some of the African language packages are caught in the "homeland" mentality of the past, where the reader is positioned as rural and ethnically singular. In the Sesotho readers, only the Basotho culture (from Lesotho, not even South Africa) is shown. In one of the Tshivenda readers, there is a picture of a battle axe, a relic of the past which will be entirely unfamiliar to contemporary Venda children. Even where there is reference to rural as well

[4]During apartheid black South Africans were legally considered to be citizens of "homeland" reservations and were restricted to these areas. The apartheid legislation prohibited their migration to the rest of the country, under the pass law regulations.

**Fig. 5.5** Children and families actively participate in ensuring their household food security

as urban life, the references in many of the packages tend to be mono-cultural. The increasingly multicultural and multinational reality of South Africa is not embraced.

The workbooks aimed to overcome this by developing characters depicting the cross-section of the South African cultural mosaic across urban and rural areas. As Outhred (2014, p. 64) confirms:

> The workbooks provide illustrations or tasks requiring learners to engage through identifying their responses, feelings or express their thoughts about scenarios or perspectives. The aim is to provide opportunities to explore prejudices and concerns and reflect on diversity and civic and moral responsibility. Illustrations include grade appropriate pictures, maps, photos, drawings et cetera of items and objects.

## *Racial Diversity*

The books feature racially and culturally mixed groups of children to validate diversity (see, for example, Fig. 5.3). The same basic children characters run through the series, and the group grows as new characters are needed. The main characters are Bongi, Jabu, Ann, Sam and Mandu, and ever present is a dog named Ben, who participated in all their activities (see Fig. 5.4 and others). The names of these characters are obviously "versioned" for use across the 11 languages.

We consciously presented our characters to correspond with former President Nelson Mandela's vision of the South African "rainbow nation" (indeed producing the books under the imprint *Rainbow Workbooks*), and we ensured that both white and black characters live in and visit both rural and urban areas, the suburbs and township areas and that they spend time in natural settings.

**Fig. 5.6** Gender neutral household chores

The energy of the positive relationships between the characters manifests in how they relate to one another and the respect they show for all forms of life by acknowledging their interdependency.

## *Environment*

The books show children of all races engaged in environmental activities, water purification, clean-ups, vegetable gardening and poultry farming, thus affirming the value of caring for the environment (Fig. 5.5).

While much of the focus of the books is on environmental issues, one of the Grade 4 books includes the childhood story of Wangari Maathi, who founded the green movement, and stresses that the simple act of planting trees in Kenya could make a difference through mobilising people to take action. This led to the safeguarding of an environment in which children can play safely and watch tadpoles grow.

**Fig. 5.7** Girls playing games and sports that are traditionally considered to be male sports. Note the intercultural nature of the players

## *Gender*

Gender equality features strongly in the materials, in which boys and men are shown caring for children or working in the kitchen (Figs. 5.6 and 5.7) and girls playing sports, including soccer and cricket, which are usually considered boys' sports.

Girls (as well as boys) are depicted as achievers and winners, and both boys and girls are shown climbing trees or cycling on open roads (see Fig. 5.8).

Given the legacy of apartheid in South Africa, it was important to affirm the status of black women as leaders or as professionals, particularly in a culture in which black women have generally been depicted as cleaners or labourers or in professions considered "women's" professions. We therefore ensured that a number of the illustrations in the workbooks show women in what is traditionally considered "male" professions—for example as doctors and police officers (see Figs. 5.9 and 5.10).

**Fig. 5.8** Girls engaged in outdoor adventures

**Fig. 5.9** Black female doctor in a profession traditionally considered male domain. Note also the interculturality of the visitors

**Fig. 5.10** Woman in an occupation traditionally considered to be a male domain. Note the situation of care

Disability has also been portrayed across the series by featuring adults and children in wheelchairs (see, for example, Fig. 5.11).

The same characters—a young girl in a wheelchair, a bespectacled boy and a disabled teacher—were incorporated across all the workbooks. The artwork throughout the series shows clearly how learners are exposed to multicultural situations that are inclusive of age and ability with the dog and cat participating too.

## *Sentient Beings*

Without exception, the workbooks portray the characters as kind towards animals. There are, for example, stories about children finding and helping stray animals, and adopting a caring attitude towards animals is a recurring theme.

The books also highlight the rights of other sentient beings. It is shown that animals are sentient in that they experience both positive and negative sensations

**Fig. 5.11** Depicting gender, racial and disability inclusivity

and emotions, including pain and distress but also happiness. We have an in-book dog who appears (and sings) at school concerts, on the school bus (see Fig. 5.12), in the children's homes (Fig. 5.4), on school tours), at weddings and parties (Fig. 5.13), and so on. The dog usually expresses the "mood" of the story. He laughs and wags his tail when the children are happy, he is sad when the mood of the story dictates this, and he acts as a counsellor and a role model.

The introduction of the dog led to a certain amount of contention, however. Many teachers argued that that it did not fit in with their particular culture, and argued that, "In our culture we do not allow dogs into the house", or "We do not have animals in our schools", "We do not let them into our homes". In our negotiations with teachers, we asked whether the children enjoyed seeing the dog in their books, and whether the dog helped to teach them how to care for animals. In negotiating with teachers, we occasionally had to offer to remove the dog from the books of a particular language or cultural group, however, in each instance, teachers subsequently agreed to allow the dog to remain.

**Fig. 5.12** The ever-present dog waiting to board the school bus

## *Rights and Responsibilities*

The language books and graded readers presented many opportunities to embed positive values within the text. All the comprehension reading texts deliberately seek to nurture positive values. We included stories about:

- Boys who felt guilt after telling an untruth to their grandmother denying that they had left her garden gate open, resulting in goats destroying her vegetable garden. The boys then make amends by fixing the lock on her gate and planting a new crop of vegetables.
- Children considering stealing a bird's eggs from its nest. After serious deliberation, they do the right thing by leaving the eggs in place. There is jubilation as the story ends with little chick taking its first flight.
- A child sharing her lunch with another child who did not have lunch.
- Girls assisting a cat that was trapped on a barbed wire fence.
- Children helping the elderly or younger children.

In terms of child safety, we included phone numbers for organisations that deal with child abuse, numbers to report bullying and information about ways of dealing with personal and social conflict. We also provided information about safety in and around the home, and about road safety. In each book, we also included a child-friendly version of children's rights and responsibilities, which illustrates the responsibility associated with each of the rights.

**Fig. 5.13** The dog and cat attending a party

## *Going Beyond*

We hope that, through the provision of the national school workbooks, we have enabled children to be inspired by the humanistic vision, which we have shown to be based on respect for life and human dignity. We believe that we are teaching them, one lesson at a time, to value cultural diversity, equality and human rights, and to be committed to a shared responsibility for ensuring a sustainable future.

In other words, we believe the books are the first step towards education for a global common good.

## References

Alidou H, Aliou B, Brock-Utne B, SatinaDiallo Y, Heugh K, Ekkehard Wolff H (2006) Optimizing learning and education in Africa–the language factor: a stock-taking research on mother tongue and Bilingual Education in Sub-Saharan Africa. Association for the Development of Education in Africa

Apple MW (1979) Ideology and curriculum. Routledge and Kegan Paul, London

Apple MW (1982) Education and power. Routledge and Kegan Paul, London

Aronowitz S, Giroux H (1986) Education under siege: the conservative, liberal and radical debate over schooling. Routledge and Kegan Paul, London

Biraimah KL (2016) Moving beyond a destructive past to a decolonised and inclusive future: the role of Ubuntu-style Education in providing culturally relevant pedagogy for namibia. Int Rev Educ 62: 45–62.
DOI 10.1007/s11159-016-9541-1

Bowles S, Gintis H (1976) Schooling in capitalist America. Routledge and Kegan Paul, London

Brock-Utne B (2016) The ubuntu paradigm in curriculum work, language of instruction and assessment. Int Rev Educ 62:29–44. doi:10.1007/s11159-016-9540-2

Chetty M, Moloi Q (2010). The SACMEQ III Project in South Africa: a study of the conditions of Schooling and the quality of education. Department of Basic Education, Paris/Pretoria

Chilisa B (2009) Indigenous African-centered ethics: contesting and complementing dominant models. In: Mertens DM, Ginsberg PE (eds) The handbook of social research ethics. Sage, London, pp 407–426

City EA, Elmore RF, Fiarman SE, Teitel L (2009) Instructional rounds in education. Harvard Education Press

Çubukçu Z (2012) The effect of hidden curriculum on character education process of primary School students. Educ Sci Theory Pract 12(2): Spring. (Supplementary special issue.)

Cummins J (2000) Language, Power and Pedagogy: Bilingual children in the crossfire. Multilingual matters, Clevedon

Department of Basic Education (2010) Proposal for the development of the workbooks: internal document. Department of Basic Education, Pretoria

Department of Basic Education (2011a) Report on the annual national assessments of 2011. Department of Basic Education, Pretoria

Department of Basic Education (2011b) Action plan 2014: towards the realisation of Schooling 2025. Department of Basic Education, Pretoria

Department of Basic Education (2012) Workbook training manual. Department of Basic Education, Pretoria

Department of Education (2005) Report on Values, Human Rights in the Curriculum. Department of Education, Pretoria

Howie S, Venter E, Van Staden S, Zimmerman L, Long C, Du Toit C (2008) PIRLS 2006 summary report: South African Children's reading literacy achievement. Centre for Evaluation and Assessment, Pretoria

Joint Education Trust (JET) (2011) National school effectiveness study-synthesis report. JET Education Services, Johannesburg

Lazar A, Edwards A, Thompson M (2012) Bridging literacy and equity: the essential guide to social equity teaching. Teachers College Press, New York

Letseka M (2000) African Philosophy and Educational Discourse. In: Higgs P, Vakalisa NCG, Mda TV, Assie-Lumumba NT (eds) African voices in education. Juta, Cape Town, pp 179–193

Letseka M (2016) The amalgamation of traditional African values and liberal democratic values in South Africa: Implications for conceptions of education. Unpublished thesis submitted for the degree of Doctor of Education. University of South Africa, Pretoria

Macdonald C (1990) Threshold project. HSRC Pretoria

Macdonald C (1991) Eager to talk and learn and think. Cape Town, Maskew Miller Longman

McKay V (2012) The development of the SouthAfrican School workbooks. AusAID Education Resource Facility, Canberra

McKay V (2013) Improving the quality of learning and teaching: strengthening curriculum implementation from 2010 and beyond. Department of Basic Education, Pretoria. http://www.education.gov.za/Portals/0/Documents/Publications/Curriculum%20News%202013.pdf?ver=2015-03-20-114054-043. Accessed 16 June 2016

McKay V (2016) The workbooks: recorded interview. https://archive.org/details/veronica2016. (Accessed)

McKay VI, Romm NRA (1992) People's education in theoretical perspective. Maskew Miller Longman, Cape Town

Outhred R, Nuga Deliwe C, Stubberfield C, Beavis A, Wilkinson J, Murphy M (2014) Towards quality as an equity imperative: workbook development, supply, utilisation and quality in the Republic of South Africa. In: Zhng H, Chan PWK, Boyle C (eds) Equality in education: fairness and inclusion. Sense Publishers, Rotterdam

Oviawe OJ (2016) How to rediscover the Ubuntu paradigm in education. Inter Rev Educ 62:1–10. doi:10.1007/s11159-016-9541-1

Sampa F (2008) Keynote address. Report on the Foundation Phase Conference, Makapane, Limpopo. 30 September – 1 October 2008. UNICEF/DBE

South African Institute for Distance Education (SAIDE) (2011) Expert review of foundation phase literacy resource packages for the evaluation of the Gauteng primary literacy strategy SAIDE, Johanneburg. (Draft.)

Spaull N (2011a) A preliminary analysis of SACMEQ III South Africa. Stellenbosch. (Economic Working Papers.)

Spaull N (2011b) Primary School Performance in Botswana, Mozambique, Namibia and South Africa. Southern and Eastern African Consortium for Monitoring Educational Quality (SACMEQ), Paris

Spaull N (2011c) Primary School performance in Botswana, Mozambique, Namibia and South Africa: a comparative analysis of SACMEQ III. Paris. (SACMEQ Working Papers, Working Paper no. 8.)

Spaull N (2013a) Poverty and privilege: Primary School inequality in South Africa. Int J Educ Dev 33:436–447

Spaull N (2013b). South Africa's education crisis: the quality of education in South Africa 1994–2011. (Report Commissioned by the Centre for Development Enterprise.)

Unesco (2015) Rethinking education: towards a global common good? Unesco, Paris

United Nations (2015) Sustainable development knowledge platform: open working group proposal for sustainable development goals. https://sustainabledevelopment.un.org/sdgsproposal.html. Accessed 20 July 2015

University of South Africa (2014) Making Schools better: a study in five Provinces of South Africa-Eastern Cape, Free State, KwaZulu Natal, Limpopo and Mpumalanga. UNISA, Pretoria. (Report compiled by the 5000 schools community engagement project.)

Willis P (1977) Learning to labour. Saxon House, Farmborough

## Author Biography

**Dr. Veronica McKay** is Professor and Executive Dean of the College of Education, University of South Africa where she is responsible for the implementation of programmes for initial and continuous teacher development, from preschool to post-schooling, including adult and community education. Her research areas include education, adult learning and literacy, second language teaching, gender, HIV and the broad field of development. Prof McKay spent a period seconded from the university to the South African Ministry of Education where was appointed as the Chief Executive Officer of the South African National Literacy Campaign aimed at enliterating 4,7 million adults. She was also appointed as a coordinator and author of the South African School Workbook development project - a project which has delivered 250 million books to school children. Prof McKay has broad national and international experience, serving on two South African Ministerial Committees and having conducted research for the ILO, UNESCO, EU, ADEA, DFID and GIZ. She is a UNESCO Fellow and currently serves as a member of the South African National UNESO Commission.

# Chapter 6
# Decision-Making Towards a Fully Realised Equity Agenda in Sustainable Development: The Case of Sustainable Development Education and the Education-Related Sustainable Development Goal

**Rachel Outhred**

**Abstract** There is wide scientific consensus that global warming is taking place due to the emission of greenhouse gases and it is predicted that developing countries will both suffer the economic impacts to a greater extent and will likely be less able to adapt to changes (McGuigan et al. in Assessing impacts in developing countries and the initiatives of the international community. The Overseas Development Institute, London 2002: 3). There is growing recognition that a global response is required, with '*real change and real action*' (McGuigan et al. 2002, pp. 30–31), yet the international, national and local responses required to address climate change and poverty are not straightforward as the question of how to simultaneously reduce the impact of human life on the earth and mitigate the effects of this impact on the world's poorest people is a wicked policy problem. While it is widely recognised that an increased engagement across stakeholder groups is required to address climate change and poverty, currently no framework for conceptualising how to manage diverse worldviews across stakeholder groups to both frame the problem and devise solutions has been forthcoming.

## Introduction

This chapter uses the case of sustainability education in the pursuit of the education-related SDG to highlight the intrinsically wicked problems policy-makers face in addressing climate change and poverty. Social, economic and environmental priorities are often perceived differently by different stakeholders, due to the fluid nature of sustainability definitions, intellectual traditions in international develop-

R. Outhred (✉)
Oxford Policy Management, Oxford, UK
e-mail: rachelouthred@hotmail.com



J. McIntyre-Mills et al. (eds.), *Balancing Individualism and Collectivism*,
Contemporary Systems Thinking, DOI 10.1007/978-3-319-58014-2_6

ment which place traditional knowledge at odds with sustainable development goals and the history of unequal participation in development processes.

This contribution reviews the conceptualisation of 'education quality' as depicted by different stakeholders, examines the history of epistemological concerns in education and highlights the political, technical and ideological aspects of monitoring sustainability knowledge globally. The chapter argues that current approaches should be reframed within a multilevel framework (following Flood and Romm 2000) and decision-makers should reflect on the judgements of multiple stakeholders, against locally generated criteria. The contribution argues that this can be undertaken through an expanded counter-hegemonic curriculum project and a widely informed validation programme to respond to difference, life chances, consensus and equity within the context of defining, measuring and monitoring sustainability education for the coming 15 years.

There is wide scientific consensus that global warming is taking place due to the emission of greenhouse gases. The Intergovernmental Panel on Climate Change Working Groups (IPCC) has predicted an average global temperature increase of 1–3.5 °C over the coming one hundred years (International Panel on Climate Change Working Group 2001). The concerns regarding climate change centre around how this will affect extreme weather events and increases in precipitation changes in differential ways across regions. It is predicted that due to these differential effects, developing countries will both suffer the economic impacts to a greater extent and will likely be less able to adapt to changes (McGuigan et al. 2002: 3). The IPCC report that the incidence of natural disasters including droughts and floods, agricultural production, fisheries and marine life, water resource availability, industry and human health will likely increase wealth gaps between the developed and the developing world and the already poor and marginalised populations within developing countries will be most affected by climate change (McGuigan et al. 2002: 3).

There is growing recognition that a global response is required, with '*real change and real action*' regarding: (1) the level of consumerism and resource use in the developed world (Drexhage and Murphy 2010, p. 2), (2) national level planning to reduce greenhouse gas emissions in low, middle and high income countries and (3) the provision of resources to support the adaptation, resilience and protection of the poor and marginalised populations within developing countries (McGuigan et al. 2002, p. 30–31).

The international, national and local responses required to address climate change and poverty evidence the scale at which we are '*implicated in each other's lives*' (Flood and Romm 2000, p. 3) and the way we live should not cause harm to others (Nussbaum 2007, p. 296). However, how to ensure we do not cause harm to each other and the next generation of life is not straightforward. In order to successfully address the problem of climate change and the unequal threats it poses to different groups of global citizens, the international community needs to draw on diverse models and methodologies to both frame the problem and devise solutions (Flood and Romm 2000). The question of how to simultaneously reduce the impact of human life on the earth and mitigate the effects of this impact on the world's poorest people is a wicked policy problem.

Wicked problems occur when a purely scientific-rational approach cannot be applied because the problem itself cannot be definitively defined due to a variety of different perspectives being held by stakeholders. In social policy a wicked problem is faced when:

- the solution depends on how the problem is framed and vice versa;
- stakeholders have radically different world views and different frames for understanding the problem;
- the resources needed to solve the problem change over time; and
- the problem is never solved definitively (Stolterman 2008).

Following Flood and Romm, this chapter argues that in framing problems and devising pathways to solutions, diverse ways of thinking and doing must be managed if the international community is to pursue *equity-focused* sustainable development. This chapter uses the case of sustainable development education and the Sustainable Development Goals (SDGs) as a case study to highlight the complexities of developing responses to wicked problems within the context of a globalised world. The chapter argues that current approaches should be reframed within a multilevel framework (following Flood and Romm 2000) and decision-makers should reflect on the judgements of multiple stakeholders, against locally generated criteria.

There is currently ample evidence that wide engagement across stakeholder groups is required in order to both frame the problem of climate change and poverty and devise solutions. The Overseas Development Initiative's (ODI) assessment of the major initiatives being undertaken with respect to climate change through Overseas Development Assistance (ODA) points to the need to expand current activities to include more divergent stakeholder groups (McGuigan et al. 2002, p. 28). McGuigan et al. note that the current approaches to climate change taken by bilateral and multilateral donors fails to fully acknowledge the interdependence of the environment and the people who live within it, stating:

> To effectively address the enormous problems of climate change and poverty, bilateral and multilateral donors needs to broaden their view of both the problem and suitable solutions. Rather than perceiving it as solely an environmental problem that requires national level planning and the reduction of GHGs, donors must address vulnerability and the importance of adaptation, resilience and protection. (McGuigan et al. 2002, p. 30–31).

Similarly, Drexhage and Murphy (2010, p. 2) point out that *'there is a huge gap between the multilateral processes, with their broad goals and policies; and national action, which reflects domestic political and economic realities'*. McGuigan et al. note that while working with governments is important, for adaptation to be effective capacity building and training is also required at the community level (McGuigan et al. 2002, p. 28). Abeygunawardena et al. (2002) also argue for a stronger link between the national and local levels in order to address climate change and poverty, proposing improved governance, the mainstreaming of national strategies for sustainable development into multiple ministries and the empowerment of communities to participate in assessments as a way to ensure both national and institutional level approaches with 'bottom-up' approaches.

In addition to improving international, regional, national and local stakeholder engagement, better engagement between economically developed countries and developing countries is widely recognised as necessary to address sustainable development. The UN background paper on sustainable development notes that:

> without change and real action to address levels of consumerism and resource use in developed countries, one can hardly expect a receptive audience among developing countries when attempts are made to direct attention to their economic development practices. More sustainable development pathways are needed in both developed and developing countries; which require a level of dialogue, cooperation and, most importantly, trust that simply is not reflected in today's multilateral institutions or regimes (Drexhage and Murphy 2010, p. 2).

However, while it is widely recognised that an increased engagement across stakeholder groups is required to address climate change and poverty, currently no framework for conceptualising how to manage diverse worldviews across stakeholder groups has been forthcoming.

## Conceptualising Sustainable Development and Poverty

The recently published controversial Bill Leak cartoon depicting starving Indians attempting to eat UN supplied solar panels with mango chutney (The Telegraph 14 December 2015) highlights the stark contrast in perceptions regarding how the immediate and future needs for life on this planet should be prioritised. These priorities are perceived differently by different stakeholders with different life chances and capabilities. The image was the cartoonist's response to the first universal climate deal signed in Paris in December 2015. The cartoon also highlighted the differences in perspectives within the development sector regarding how to allocate finite resources. These different stakeholders prioritise social, economic and environmental needs differently, highlighting the difficulties faced by the international community in implementing sustainable development over the past 20 years.

The concept of sustainable development first gained political traction in the development community at the World's First Earth Summit in Rio in 1992, following the 1987 report published by the World Commission on Environment and Development. The definition of sustainable development was stated as *'Development that meets the needs of the present without compromising the ability of future generations to meet their own needs'* (Bruntland 1987). Since then this basic definition has been expanded and extended by various stakeholders. The Forum for the Future defines sustainable development as a dynamic process which enables people to realise their potential and improve their quality of life while protecting and enhancing the earth's life support systems (HEC Global Learning Centre 2016). The Real-World Coalition argued in 1996 that sustainable development means preserving essential ecosytems functions, the integration of economic and environmental policy and the dual policy foci of improvements in the overall quality of life, not just income growth, the equal distribution of resources and wide participation in decision-making

(Real World Coalition 1996). The Dorset Education for Sustainability Network argued that sustainable development concepts must be integrated into everything that we do (Dorset Education for Sustainability Network) and the Learning for a Sustainable Future Teacher Centre states that a healthy environment, economic prosperity and social justice must be pursued simultaneously to ensure the well-being and quality of life for present and future generations (HEC Global Learning Centre 2016). Drexhage and Murphy state that it is broadly accepted that sustainable development requires consideration of the three ‘pillars’ of sustainable development: economic development, social equity and environmental protection (Drexhage and Murphy 2010). However, while it is clear that sustainable development incorporates the welfare of future generations and that the social, economic and environmental worlds both effect each other and are affected by each other, it is unclear how to conceptualise the immediate priorities across the ‘pillars’ of sustainable development or how finite resources should be allocated to address the needs of the world’s poor and future generations. Against the backdrop of international development discourse, perhaps it is unsurprising that despite over 20 years of political traction in the concept of sustainable development, there remains no universally accepted definition (HEC Global Learning Centre 2016).

Despite the international development era now spanning almost 70 years (Esteva 1992), there remains no universally accepted definition of development itself. Rather, previous theories of international development, nestled within the thinking of high modernity (Scott 1999), provide problematic notions of development that stand at odds with conceptualisations of sustainable development. Modernisation theory’s false traditional/modern continuum places traditional knowledge and ways of knowing at odds with sustainable development goals. Within this worldview traditional indigenous ways of knowing are constructed as the antithesis to development (Pigg 1996, p. 161) and given a lower status than other knowledges (Magni 2016).

In order to highlight the difficulties of both conceptualising and addressing climate change and the unequal threats it poses to different groups, this chapter explores the role of education in achieving the SDGs, an international shift in conceptualising equity, the impact of previous notions of development and proposes strategies to address the wicked problem. The chapter does this using the case of sustainability education within the context of pursuing and monitoring progress towards the education-related SDG.

## The Case of Sustainability Education and the Education-Related SDG

One of the chief mechanisms proposed to address the wicked problem of implementing sustainable development is through sustainability education. The nexus between education and other development outcomes has been widely acknowledged. The provision of (formal and informal) quality education was identified at the 2015 World Education Forum as one of the key mechanisms by which we can end poverty, improve nutrition, move towards sustainable forms of agriculture, promote safe drinking water, reduce child mortality, empower girls and women, improve sanitation management systems and practices, promote sustainable energy sources and protect the earth's natural resources for future generations (World Education Forum 2015). In addition, within the next generation of the development goals the education-related SDG specifically states that by 2030 all learners should acquire the knowledge and skills needed to promote sustainable development and sustainable lifestyles (amongst other knowledge and skills including those needed to promote human rights, gender equality, promotion of a culture of peace and non-violence, global citizenship and appreciation of cultural diversity and of culture's contribution to sustainable development) (World Education Forum 2015).

In agreeing to implement a global agenda where all learners are taught the knowledge and skills required to promote sustainable development and sustainable lifestyles, it is implied that agreeing on these knowledge and skills is possible. However, despite the education-related SDG receiving wide acknowledgment as a worthy and respectable agenda, what children should know and be able to do as a result of schooling is contested and conceptualised differently by different groups.

## Reconceptualising Equity in Education

As we approach the beginning of a new generation of development goals, the international community has reflected on the achievements made during the Millennium Development Goal (MDG) period. During this time the number of out-of-school children decreased by 43 million and the net enrolment of children in developing regions went from 83% to 91% (UN 2015). The focus on access to schooling as an equity imperative can be traced back through multiple declarations, legislation and conventions. The 1917 US National Child Labour Committee Report aimed to safeguard American children from loss of education, overwork or neglect (National Child Labour Committee 1917: 3), the Universal Declaration of Human Rights affirmed in 1948 that elementary education was to be made available to all children (Education For All Monitoring Report 2005) and the 1989 Convention on the Rights of the Child recognised the *right* of children to be protected from work that threatens their education (Article 32). However, these national and international laws, treaties and declarations remained silent regarding the *quality* of education to be provided (EFA 2005). Quite early on in the MDG period practitioners, policy-makers and researchers began to question the usefulness of increases in education enrolment as the main education-related goal within a global framework aimed at fighting poverty within its many dimensions. The Dakar Framework for Action was the first international agreement declaring that access to *quality* education was the right of every child, however the Framework's expanded definition of quality set out the desirable characteristics of learners, learning processes, content and systems (EFA 2005) but did not outline what children should know and be able to do after the completion of a quality primary school education.

In moving from the education-related MDG to the education-related SDG, the international community moved from being primarily focused on distributive social justice concerns in education to content related social justice concerns. As the global community begins to implement this equity shift, the difficulties in implementing a global social justice agenda that relies on more than crude counts of learners in school come to the fore.

## Global Learning and Curricular Justice

What children should know and be able to do as a result of schooling is contested within and across local, regional, national and international settings. Underpinning these different perspectives are both different epistemological views and differing levels of engagement and participation in the sociological processes that have shaped the organisation and selection of knowledge included in the school curricular.

Epistemological issues have '*always enjoyed a central place… in philosophical thinking about education*' (Siegel 2006). The fundamental epistemic aim of education is perceived differently by different stakeholders with different life chances and capabilities. The nature of knowledge, the criteria and justification of truth and sources of knowledge to justify belief differ across groups. It is now widely recognised in the scientific world that pure objectivity in the pursuit of knowledge does not exist. Freedman states, '*The ideal of a "detached" observer has been thoroughly trounced, feminists have pointed out that individuals are socially situated in a particular ethnic, historical, social and political context*' (Freedman 2009). Connell argues that scientific knowledge is produced in a highly organised social process, evidenced by the range of research communities and institutions and communication networks that are the social milieu required for knowledge to be produced. These institutions and networks are both located within social structures and are shaped by them (Connell 1993, p. 30–31).

In addition to epistemological concerns regarding how knowledge itself is constructed, the sociological processes that shape the organisation and selection of knowledge for inclusion in the school curriculum also reflect historical and present day inequalities, valuing the priorities and views of particular stakeholders over others. As Connell (1993, p. 31) articulates:

> Once produced, knowledge still has to be selected or compiled to make a curriculum. This is not done in heaven by a committee of epistemological angels… Rather, historical research has traced the creation of school 'subjects' like geography by inquiries, syllabus committees, academic entrepreneurs, and bureaucrats.

Critical theorists argue that these processes value some forms of knowledge over other forms of knowledge, reflecting the wider distribution of social power (UNESCO 2005). In response, some critical approaches to education claim that an oppositional and separate curriculum needs to be developed, over which the poor and/or marginalised have control. However, such approaches leaves the hegemonic curriculum intact as it supports an outcome that sees the perspective of the 'other' not included in the hegemonic viewpoint (Connell 1992, p. 53). In addition, oppositional curriculum approaches deny poor children access to mainstream knowledge that is often privileged within society, further embedding their positions of lower life chances (Zipin 2013). Rather, counter-hegemonic strategies seek to work with disadvantaged groups to reorganise the curriculum in ways that give priority to the perspectives of the 'other' (UNESCO 2005), yet still gives disadvantaged students *'systematic access to programs which will equip them with economic and political understanding so that they can act individually or together to improve their circumstances'* (Connell 1992, p. 54).

Currently, the knowledge and skills learners need to live sustainable lives is necessarily described in broad terms and referenced within definitions of education quality. For UNICEF, a quality education includes several components, one of which is '*content that is reflected in relevant curricula and materials for the acquisition of basic skills, especially in the areas of literacy, numeracy and skills for life, and knowledge in such areas of gender, health, nutrition, HIV/AIDS prevention and peace'* (United Nations Children's Fund 2000). UNICEF's description of the content required to deliver *quality* schooling references the need to consider national goals for education, national and local values and references possibilities of incorporating local knowledge into traditional subject areas (United Nations Children's Fund 2000, p. 11–13). However, consideration of how to balance or prioritise divergent views across stakeholder groups is not specified. Similarly, UNESCO's concept of quality education is built on four pillars (United Nations Educational 2013); Learning to know (that learners build their own knowledge daily, combining indigenous and 'external' elements), Learning to do (focusing on the practical application of what is learned), Learning to live together (addressing the critical skills for a life free from discrimination, where all have equal opportunity to develop themselves, their families and their communities) and Learning to be (emphasising the skills needed for individuals to develop their full potential). For UNESCO, learning is affected at the level of the learner and at the level of the learning system, whereby policies, legislation and resource distribution is implemented and enacted and learning outcomes are measured (UNESCO 2005, p. 30).

These broad descriptions of what learners should know and be able to do as a result of education reflect the differing epistemological perspectives, differing levels of engagement and participation in the sociological processes that shape knowledge creation and selection and the differing knowledge needs of learners across the globe. The difficulties in recognising diverse educational needs across local, regional, national and international landscapes has gained ample international consensus and are well documented in the UNESCO Education for All Global Monitoring Report 2005. However, this diversity is challenged in the face of the development sector drive to robustly measure and monitor changes in education quality globally. How to define, measure and monitor learning is a challenge that spans technical, political and ideological domains and without managing diversity within a framework that can hold multiple worldviews, the challenge threatens to undermine a fully realised socially-just approach to education over the next 15 years.

## *Measuring and Monitoring Progress*

The UNESCO Institute for Statistics (UIS), the official source of internationally comparable education data, has been given the challenging mandate to coordinate the production of indicators to monitor the new global education goal and targets. UIS established a Learning Metrics Taskforce (LMTF), made up of representatives of national and regional governments, Education for All convening agencies, regional political bodies, civil society and donor agencies. These stakeholders engaged in an 18-month global consultation process to build consensus around the measuring and monitoring of learning globally (United Nations Educational 2013, p. 11). The first product of the consultation resulted in a global framework of learning domains. The LMTF report *Toward Universal Learning: What Every Child Should Learn* states that the framework is intended for the purpose of identifying areas in which to measure learning outcomes (through learning assessments) and is not intended to inform policymaking, curriculum or instruction.

While clear agreement on the precise methodologies and parameters of the global monitoring framework are yet to be agreed (EFA GMR team, UNESCO Headquarters), architects of the new framework are likely to face the same limitations present in the current LMTF Global Learning Framework, with respect to sustainability education. The terms of reference for the development of measures for the knowledge and skills needed to promote sustainable lifestyles deny the differing epistemological perspectives, differing levels of engagement and participation in the sociological processes that shape knowledge creation and selection, and the differing knowledge needs of learners across the globe.

The establishment of a global learning framework within a context where the complexities of defining education quality globally are well documented, speaks to the difficulties of navigating the technical, political and ideological aspects of pursing and monitoring the SDGs. Politically, changes against the SDGs need to be monitored in order to advocate for national policies that support their realisation and to inform national and donor budgets that allocate resources towards the most marginalised. This is essential to ensure the accountability of stakeholders against their espoused values and goals. Technically, in order to monitor changes regarding learners' knowledge on sustainable development and sustainable lifestyles, the constructs need to be defined before they can be measured. Yet ideologically, epistemological and equity concerns come to the fore when the parameters of such definitions are decided at a global level. These political, technical and ideological aspects are interlinked and interdependent. For example, the three measurement standards required for test credibility are reliability, validity and fairness, however each of these standards are themselves '*value-laden concepts*' (Messick 1988).

Reliability refers to the extent to which an assessment tool produces stable and consistent results. Reliability is a measurement standard required for test credibility as consistent and stable results are central in order to use data for its proposed purpose. The key question of validity is '*can this test support the decisions based on it?*' Without reliability, the validity standard cannot be met, however validity is broader than reliability as it is concerned with the meaning and consequences of measurement. Traditionally validity has been majorly concerned with score meaning —in that score meaning does not differ across groups. This past conceptualisation viewed validity as residing in the test through content validity (adequate coverage), criterion validity (similar instrument) and face validity (looks appropriate) (Roever 2016). Construct validity is important within the context of the education-related SDGs as cultural and environmental differences in testing groups should not introduce score differences on tests. For example, if a group of learners are not familiar with pandas and polar bears, their responses to an item asking them to count how many pandas appear in a painting featuring pandas and polar bears may reflect their knowledge of these animals, rather than their proficiency in counting (introducing construct irrelevance). However, current conceptualisations of validity are concerned not only with the validation of a test, but validation of both construct (what does the test claim to measure?) and decisions (are test scores useful for supporting the decisions that they are informing?). This current conceptualisation sees that:

> what is to be validated is not the test or observation device per se but rather the inferences derived from test scores or other indicator inferences about score meaning or interpretation and about the implications for action that the interpretation entails (Messick 1988, p. 3).

Within the context of measuring sustainability knowledge, such justifications regarding the use of scores on assessments to inform high-stakes decisions (national budgeting, donor funding and programme implementation), are imperative. Yet, the validation decisions required to determine such justifications are themselves, informed by social values (Messick 1988).

## Managing Diversity

Diversity management is about… '*...people managing the increasing diversity of issues they confront by increasing the diversity of types of model, methodology and theory available to do the job.*' (Flood and Romm 2000). Diversity is important as the international community moves to a broader conception of equity and justice in relation to the education-related SDG because without consideration for diversity the defined knowledge needs of learners will be narrowed, to the detriment of all.

Flood and Romm argue that in order to answer the question of how diversity and emancipation can be designed within one scheme of thought, contemporary social theory has four main styles of responses. These include pragmatism, isolationism, imperialism and complementarism (Flood and Romm 2000, p. 3–4). Pragmatic approaches do not require the interventionist to reflect on an underlying theory or the methodology of model and rather, is reliant on a trial and error approach. Within this context a pragmatic approach could include the introduction of separate or oppositional curriculums globally, with no underlying theory regarding how to support teaching and learning in the areas of individual and national resource use, the reduction of greenhouse gas emissions and strategies to support the adaptation, resilience and protection of the poor and marginalised populations in developing countries. Connell (1993, p. 35) argues that '*Any curriculum must make a selection from possible knowledges and possible methods; and there is no general guarantee of the correctness of that selection'*. At first glance this may appear to be an argument for a pluralist response to curriculum development, yet Connell warns against seeing the basis of curriculum as an arbitrary cultural content as no production or selection of knowledge is neutral (Connell 1993, p. 35).

Isolationism refers to adherence to one theory on how affairs can be managed. Isolationist approaches limit people's choices, and the promotion of one way of doing things inevitably involves devaluing other ways. While the introduction of a Global Learning Framework to define what every child should learn through sustainability education might be considered an isolationist approach, the authors of 'What Every Child Should Learn' clearly state that the framework is not intended for use for policymaking, curriculum or instruction (United Nations Educational 2013). However, in an attempt to manage diversity and navigate the complex epistemological landscape surrounding the education-related SDG, the report's claim fails to account for the well-established role of assessment in shaping the curriculum in both western schooling systems (Connell 1993, p. 32) and within developing country contexts (Allen and Outhred 2016). In this way, relying on a global framework on what all global learners should know in relation to sustainable development and sustainable lifestyles to inform high-stakes decisions verges towards an imperialist approach. Imperialism is much like isolationism, however when incongruities in the preferred theory appear, recognition is given to other theories in order to respond to the problem (Flood and Romm 2000, p. 5). Yet, within the imperialist framework, the recognition given to other theories is always viewed through the lens of the imperialist's arguments. Ironically within this example a global learning framework regarding sustainability education edges towards imperialism due to the attempt to acknowledge diversity. This is because specifying the knowledge requirements of all global learners to live sustainable lifestyles is an approach that is fundamentally constrained, as it is unable to hold multiple worldviews.

Within a Complementarist approach, interventionists can act within various worldviews. This can be achieved when choices are made using locally generated criteria, informed by wider considerations involving multiple stakeholders (Flood and Romm 2000, p. 7). Being informed by wider considerations is important in differentiating Complementarist approaches to participatory approaches. Edwards argues that poor people must be included in order for programmes to remain relevant, stating, '*we cannot be relevant to people unless we understand their problems, but we cannot understand these problems unless people tell us about them*' (Edwards 1993, p. 79). Edwards argues that in order to increase the control which poor people have in decision-making, they must be participants in the development process. While participation is important, participation alone does not ensure an increased ability for those most vulnerable to adapt to the effects of climate change as adaptation and protection knowledge must be widely informed. The knowledge learners need to live sustainable lives reside both across the traditional subjects of the hegemonic curriculum and within the knowledge systems of the marginalised. For example, recent research suggests that the loss of traditional indigenous knowledge poses a risk to the ability of indigenous populations to adapt to the effects of climate change (Magni 2016), still other forms of adaptation rely on recent knowledge and technologies, including advanced materials science and remote satellite sensing (UNFCC 2006).

A Complementarist approach avoids both cultural relativism and fundamentalism by drawing on multiple stakeholders with diverse worldviews to inform decision-making. A mediated and harmonised approach to truth (McIntyre 2000) avoids relativism and fundamentalism because *'background assumptions are often invisible and only with the contrasting values of another interest group do our particular value commitments come to light'* (Freedman 2009, 47–48). In the case of sustainability education, a mediated truth can be pursued through a counter-hegemonic curriculum development process and monitoring validation processes, using locally generated criteria which is widely informed by multiple stakeholder perspectives (development practitioners, policymakers, researchers, scientists, teachers, parents and learners).

Traditionally, counter-hegemonic curriculum projects have focussed on reorganising the curriculum through the participation of the marginalised to enable poor or disadvantaged learners to improve their success in education and improve their life chances (Zipin 2013). However, in order to increase the life chances of the world's poorest populations, there is a need to expand counter-hegemonic strategies beyond the classrooms of the marginalised. For example, sustainability knowledge can only turn to action when both 'advantaged' and 'less advantaged' learners (and other stakeholders) capacities are increased to reconsider their roles and responsibilities towards society and the future generations of life on this planet (For McIntyre-Mills 2006). Therefore, an expanded counter-hegemonic curriculum project engaging both the advantaged and disadvantaged would allow for multiple worldviews in both framing the problem of climate change and poverty and devising pathways to solutions. Locally generated criteria in this case, asks '*what do learners within this context need to know to live a sustainable life?*' and a widely informed process asks *'Are the decisions regarding what learners need to know to live a sustainable life based on a harmonised approach to truth (rather than fundamentalism or relativism)?'*

A counter-hegemonic curriculum project does not resolve the political, technical and ideological aspects inherent in monitoring sustainability knowledge globally. Developing reliability in measures of learning outcomes is technically complex, yet achievable. However assessing if tests (1) have adequate coverage of sustainability knowledge (content validity), (2) will produce similar results as a similar instrument (criterion validity) and (3) have items that look appropriate (face validity) across a variety of contexts and cultures cannot be achieved by one stakeholder alone. Similarily, assessing if the inferences derived from such test scores are justified (decision validity), is informed by social values and therefore, must be informed by diverse social value perspectives. Consequently, in order to pursue a harmonised approach to truth, engagement with multiple stakeholders who hold differing worldviews is required.

Kane (2013) builds on Cronbach's (1989) earlier work in presenting the role of argument in test validation. Kane discussed validation as the process of developing both an interpretive argument and a validation argument regarding the validity of assessment programmes and their utilisation for decision-making. The *'interpretive argument specifies the proposed interpretations and uses of test results by laying out a network of inferences and assumptions leading from the observed performances to the conclusion and decisions based on the performances*' (Kane 2013, p. 23). The validation argument then brings together evidence and logical analysis to evaluate the claims of the interpretive argument. These two types of argument are then brought together in a systematic analysis of the uses, interpretations and claims and form a comprehensive validation programme for a test (Linn 2009).

A comprehensive validation programme traces each step from test conceptualisation to test use (Kane 2013), making judgements concerning: the extent to which what is being measured is represented in the items, the kind of data generated by the test, the scoring of learner responses, the sample of observations and the set of items used, the test's prediction of real-world performance and if the test is useful for decision-making and has beneficial consequences (Roever 2016). Figure 6.1 represents each of the steps from test conceptualisation to test use and the validation processes leading from one test stage to the next (domain description, scoring, generalisation, explanation, extrapolation and utilisation). Collectively, the validation stages seek political, technical and ideological judgements regarding the extent to which the test results can justifiably be used for decision-making purposes.

Figure from Purpura (2011, p. 738), based on Kane (2013).

Shepard summarises the validity argument's key questions as *'what does the testing practice claim to do? What are the arguments for and against the intended aims of the test?* and *'What does the test do in the system other than what it claims?*' (Linn 2009).

The validation of a programme aimed at monitoring the extent to which learners possess the knowledge required to promote sustainable development and live sustainable lifestyles, can only be undertaken using judgements made against locally generated criteria. This is particularly important in making utilisation judgements. Utilisation judgements consider if the score meanings of the tests have been made clear to stakeholders, if test uses are clearly defined and if the test

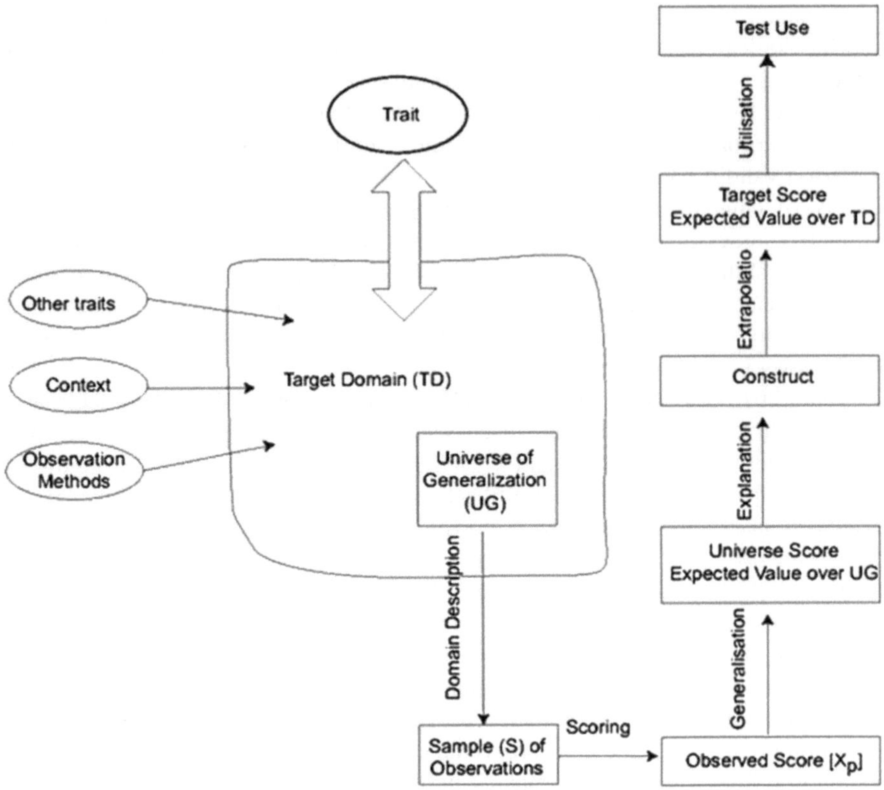


**Fig. 6.1** An Argument-based approach to test validation

generates positive or negative washback (e.g. does the test influence teaching and learning and in what ways?) (Roever 2016).

It is proposed that if a global assessment is developed to measure sustainability knowledge, a comprehensive validation programme be undertaken to engage diverse stakeholder groups across testing contexts. Decision-makers utilising such test scores to inform decision-making in various contexts should then also reflect on the extent to which the assessment can justifiably inform specific decisions.

## Framing Problems and Devising Solutions to Climate Change and Poverty Within a Framework Underpinned by Complementarianism

The case of sustainability education and the pursuit of the SDGs highlights the intrinsically wicked problems policy-makers face in addressing climate change and poverty. *'Real change and real action'* (Drexhage and Murphy 2010) are required as responses across international, national and local levels in order to ensure we do not cause harm to each other or the next generation of life. However, social, economic and environmental priorities are often perceived differently by different stakeholders. This is due to the fluid nature of sustainability definitions, intellectual traditions in international development which place traditional knowledge at odds with sustainable development goals and the history of unequal participation in the development process. In the case of sustainability education, a content related approach to social justice highlights epistemological and sociological concerns of devising a global learning framework. These concerns come to the fore when the history of knowledge development and selection is reviewed. The difficulties in recognising diverse educational needs across diverse contexts has been well recognised within the international development community (UNESCO 2005), however the political need to monitor changes in learning to inform decision-making threatens to undermine the SDG equity agenda, if processes are not undertaken with wide engagement against locally generated criteria (Following Flood and Romm 2000). As we approach the next generation of development goals, the world community has reflected on the achievements made during the Millennium Development Goal (MDG) period. While advances were made in increasing access to education practitioners, policymakers and researchers began to question the usefulness of increases in education enrolment as the main education-related goal and shifted to a focus on quality. UNESCO UIS has recently established a Global Alliance for Learning to work with stakeholders to ensure that quality data are used to track progress to improve the learning outcomes of all children. However, how to define, measure and monitor learning is a challenge that spans technical, political and ideological domains. What children should know and be able to do as a result of schooling is perceived differently by different stakeholders with different life chances and capabilities. The recently published controversial Bill Leak cartoon, depicting starving Indians attempting to eat solar panels with mango chutney, highlights this stark contrast (The Telegraph 14 December 2015). This contribution highlights the complexities of defining 'educational quality' across diverse settings and examines the history of epistemological concerns in education. The contribution proposes a framework for thinking about difference, life chances, consensus and equity within the context of defining, measuring and monitoring the education-related SDG for the coming 15 years.

## References

Abeygunawardena P, Vyas Y, Knill P, Foy T, Harrold M, Steele P, Sperling F (2002) Poverty and climate change: reducing the vulnerability of the poor through adaptation

Allen R, Outhred R (2016) Strengthening Examinations and Assessment in Uganda: a Roadmap. Oxford: Oxford Policy Management. http://www.heart-resources.org/wp-content/uploads/2016/06/Inception-Report-Strengthening-Assessment-and-Examinations-in-Uganda.pdf

Appadurai A (2004) The capacity to aspire: culture and the terms of recognition. In: Rao V, Walton M (eds) Culture and public action. Standford University Press, Standford

Bruntland (1987) Our Common Future. World Commission on Environment and Development
Connell RW (1992) Citizenship, Social Justice and Curriculum. International studies in sociology of education 2(2):133–146
Connell RW (1993) Schools and social justice. Temple University Press, Philadelphia
Cronbach LJ (1989) Construct validation after thirty years. In: Linn RE (ed) Intelligence: measurement, theory, and public policy. University of Illinois Press, Urbana, pp 147–171
Dorset Education for Sustainability Network. (n.d.) Education for Sustainability. http://www.dorset-lea.org.uk/efsn/pages/efsnet.htm
Drexhage J, Murphy D (2010) Sustainable development: from Brundtland to Rio 2012. United Nations, New York
Edwards (1993) How Relevant is Development Studies? In: Schuurman, beyond the impasse: new directions in development theory. Zed Books, London
EFA GMR team, UNESCO Headquarters. (n.d.). Concept note for a 2016 report on 'Education, Sustainability and the Post-2015 Development Agenda'. UNESCO, Paris: http://www.unesco.org/new/fileadmin/MULTIMEDIA/HQ/ED/GMR/images/2014/2016_Concept_Note_rev2.pdf. Accessed 9 Aug 2016
Esteva G (1992) Development. In: Sachs W (ed) The development dictionary–a guide to knowledge as power. Zed Books, London
Flood R, Romm N (2000) Diversity management. triple loop learning. Wiley Publishing, Chichester
Freedman (2009) Diversity and the fate of objectivity. Soc Epistemology, 23(1), 45–56
Guijt, S, Chambers (1998) The myth of community: gender issues in participatory development. Intermediate Technology Publications, London
Harma J (2015) Private schooling and development: an Overview. In: Counihan C, Dixon P, Humble S (eds) Handbook of international development and education
HEC Global Learning Centre (2016) What is sustainability? London.. http://www.globalfootprints.org/sustainability
Hobbs J (2006) Rights-based development. In: Kochendorfer-Lucius G, Pleskovic B Equity and development. The World Bank, pp 165–171
International Panel on Climate Change Working Group (2001) Climate change 2001: impacts, adaptation, and vulnerability
Kane M (2013) The argument-based approach to validation. Sch Psychol Rev, 42(4)
Linn R (2009) The concept of validity in the context of NCLB. In: Lissitz RW The concept of validity. revisions, new directions, and applications. Information Age Publishing, Charlotte, pp 195–112
Magni G (2016) Promoting indigenous knowledge within the sustainable development agenda. Global education monitoring report world education blog. Paris. https://gemreportunesco.wordpress.com/2016/08/09/promoting-indigenous-knowledge-within-the-sustainable-development-agenda/. Accessed 9 Aug 2016
McGuigan C, Regynolds R, Wiedmer D (2002) Assessing impacts in developing countries and the initiatives of the international community. The Overseas Development Institute, London
McIntyre J (2000) Global citizenship and social movements: creating transcultural webs of meaning for the millennium. Harwood, The Netherlands
McIntyre-Mills J (2006) Systemic governance and accountability. Working and re-working the conceptual and spatial boundaries series: C. West Churchman's Legacy and Related Works
Meade A (2015). Australian newspaper cartoon depicting Indians eating solar panels attached as racist. The Guardian, Delhi. https://www.theguardian.com/environment/2015/dec/14/australian-newspaper-cartoon-depicting-indians-eating-solar-panels-attacked-racist. Accessed 14 Dec 2015
Messick S (1988) consequences of test interpretation and use: the fusion of validity and values in psychological assessment. Educational Testing Service, New Jersey
Nussbaum M (2007) Frontiers of justice: disability, nationality, species membership. The Belknap Press of Harvard University Press, Cambridge
Outhred R (ed) (2012) Reconceptualising inclusion in higher education. Int J Inclusive Educ, 16(9)

Pigg S (1996) The credible and the credulous: the question of "villagers' beliefs" in Nepal. Cultural Anthropol, pp 160–161
Purpura JE (2011) Quantitative research methods in assessment and testing. In: Chapelle C, Hinkel E, Validation in language assessment. Handbook of research in second language teaching and learning, pp 731–751. Lawrence Erlbaum Associates
Purpura JE (2016) Second and foreign language assessment. Mod Lang J, 190–208
Real World Coalition (1996) The politics of the real world. Earthscan, London
Roever C (2016) Validity in language testing. The University of Melbourne, Melbourne, Australia
Rostow WW (1960) The stages of economic growth: a non-communist manifesto. Cambridge University Press, Cambridge
Schech S, Haggis J (2000) Culture and development: a critical reader. Wiley-Blackwell, Padstow
Scott JC (1999) Seeing like a state: how certain schemes to improve the human condition have failed. Yale University Press, New Haven, CT
Siegel H (2006) Philosophy of Education, Epistemological issues. The encyclopaedia of philosophy. http://www.encyclopedia.com/article-1G2-3446801560/philosophy-education-epistemological-issues.html. Accessed 31 July 2016
Stolterman E (2008) The nature of design practice and implication for interaction design research. Int J Desig 2:55–65
UNESCO (2005) UNESCO Education for All Global Monitoring Report. Understanding Quality. UNESCO, Paris
UNESCO (2012) Education for All. UNESCO, Paris
UNFCC (2006) Technologies for Adaptation to Climate Change. UNON Publishing Services, Bonn
United Nations Children's Fund (2000) Defining Education Quality. UNICEF, New York
United Nations Educational, Scientific and Cultural Organisation (2013) Institute of statistics and centre for universal education at brookings. Toward universal learning. What every child should learn. UNESCO, Paris
United Nations Educational, Scientific and Cultural Organization (2013) Toward universal learning. recommendations from the learning metrics task force. Centre for Universal Education at Brookings, Paris
World Education Forum (2015) Incheon Declaration: education 2030: towards inclusive and equitable quality education and lifelong learning for all. UNESCO
Zipin L (2013) Engaging middle years learners by making their communities curricular: a funds of knowledge approach. Curriculum Perspect 33(2):1–12

## Author Biography

**Dr. Rachel Outhred** is Education Metrics Lead and Senior Consultant at Oxford Policy Management. Dr Outhred's recent work focuses on the monitoring and evaluation of large-scale education programmes in low and middle income countries, including Nigeria, Tanzania, Pakistan, Uganda, Lesotho, South Africa, Zimbabwe and Sierra Leone. Rachel Outhred works with national examinations and assessment bodies to establish systems to monitor learning outcomes and develop policy and programme recommendations to improve learning. She is widely published in the areas of education quality as an equity imperative.

[illegible]

# Chapter 7
# Educating and Empowering Children for Governing the Anthropocene: A Case Study of Children's Homes in Sri Lanka

**Eshantha Ariyadasa**

**Abstract** Educating children and young people on how to care for the environment is the focus of this paper. Today's children will encounter the adverse effects of global population growth and subsequent pollution by adults at the expense of the environment. Thus it is important to draw children's attention to carbon footprints and climatic changes. Through participation they will have opportunities to learn more about the implications of the way we choose to live our lives in the short, medium and long terms. Children learn about their rights and responsibilities by being given the opportunity to express their ideas and to translate policy into practice through small scale interventions that make a difference to this generation and succeeding ones. Such interventions can include lessons on recycling, use and re-use of resources, composting, organic and ethical farming, water and energy conservation techniques and much more. The essence of this paper has been extracted from my Participatory Action Research (PAR) on the life chances of children and young people in institutional care in Sri Lanka. This PAR largely employs qualitative investigations to manipulate the information collected during the study in order to assess and evaluate the findings. During the PAR, it was identified that some children's homes have initiated a few enhanced ecosystem governance practices that redress problems associated with the worst aspects of industrialisation. These practices promote the harmonious coexistence of humanity and nature and have adopted the concerns of critical systemic thinking with consequent improvement of human well-being and ecosystem health. The potential of these homes to provide education for these vulnerable children by improving their ability to deliver stewardship responsibilities towards the environment should never be underestimated.

E. Ariyadasa (✉)
Flinders University, Adelaide, Australia
e-mail: nevikaeshantha@gmail.com



J. McIntyre-Mills et al. (eds.), *Balancing Individualism and Collectivism*, Contemporary Systems Thinking, DOI 10.1007/978-3-319-58014-2_7

## Introduction

This paper first discusses the environmental problems caused by human activities in the Anthropocene epoch. Following this, the relationship between environmental impacts and the institutional care of children is highlighted. It emphasises the significance of educating and empowering children for governing the Anthropocene by unfolding three examples of good governance practices exercised by children's homes that showcase how diverse knowledge systems can be included in the discussion of enhanced eco-system governance. The lessons learnt from these case studies confirm that there is enormous potential for these homes to provide education for institutionalised children to improve their ability to deliver stewardship of the environment.

## Environmental Problems Caused by Human Activities in the Anthropocene Epoch

Looking historically at the human–environment relationship, (2011) state that prior to the Anthropocene,[1] i.e. during the Holocene,[2] humans and their ancestors modified the natural ecosystem to gain advantage in gathering plant food sources they required or in hunting for animals, but they did not transform the ecosystem around them on a large scale. They indicate that it was the industrial revolution, with its origins in Great Britain in the 1700s, that marked the end of agriculture as the most dominant human activity and set the species on a far different trajectory from the one established during most of the Holocene.

According to Steffen et al. (2011a, b) the era after the World War II (from 1945 to 2000) can be aptly referred to as the "Great Acceleration". They point out that environmental problems received little attention during much of the Great Acceleration; indeed emerging global environmental problems were largely ignored. During this period there was a general global consensus that economic growth needed to be accomplished at all costs, including at the cost of environmental damage. The environment was viewed as open for exploitation and manipulation for the benefit of human advantage. Some prominent examples of the dire consequences of environmental manipulation include the recent landslides in the hill country of Sri Lanka as a result of tea plantations, hydroelectric power

[1]The word Anthropocene fell into common usage after Paul Crutzen, an atmospheric chemist, and the late biologist Eugene Stoemer, used the term in the Global Change Newsletter in May 2000. The word joins the Greek word 'anthropos', for human, to the suffix 'cene', meaning new or recent, to suggest an epoch defined by recent human activity (Source: http://www.theguardian.com/science/2014/oct/16/).

[2]Holocene: The prior epoch of more stable human-environment relations (Source: Romm 2015, p. 2).

projects and construction of reservoirs. Investigations carried out by National Building Research Organisation indicate that haphazard and unplanned land use, inappropriate construction methods and wanton human intervention have led to an increase in landslide susceptibility (cited in Bandara 2015). Sugawara (2013) lists; excavation, filling, tunnelling, as some of the factors which may cause instability. Construction of reservoirs for the purpose of generating hydroelectricity and agriculture purposes has also been identified as a triggering factor for landslides.

The human–elephant conflict in Sri Lanka is also an adverse effect of the Anthropocene epoch. Deforestation for human settlement, construction of reservoirs and slash-and-burn agriculture has lessened the fallow cropland for the elephant to roam around. Thus, elephants enter villages because, having lost much of their wilderness habitat, they compete with human communities for land and food. Elephant incursions have increased over the past five years. These massive animals eat crops, trample fields, smash into houses and sometimes attack people they perceive as a threat (Dissanayake 2015).

## Environmental Impacts and Institutional Care of Children

Children are more susceptible to becoming victims of adults' adverse actions against the environment. The more we harm the environment, the more we produce demand for children's homes to care for children because adults are unable to care for them. This may be the result of either parental death due to anthropogenically instigated disaster, or because removal or destruction of the natural resources of Sri Lanka dictates that parents can no longer support their families. Thus there is an urgent need to identify strategies to eliminate actions which harm the environment in order to decrease the demand for institutional care of children. Romm (2015, p. 4) emphasises that "the earth is no longer able to carry the cost of human exploitation", whilst Steffen et al. (2011a, b, p. 746) assert that "the twenty-first century provides an essential context for the transformation from resource exploitation towards stewardship of the earth system". The author's findings through PAR 2012[3] have demonstrated that in the North Central Province (NCP) and the Central Province (CP) nearly 50%; North Western Province (NWP) and Eastern Province (EP) over 30% of children supported by children's homes[4] are there because they are victims of adverse environmental impacts. Owing to tsunami, floods, cyclones, landslides, droughts and elephant attacks, children become orphaned and families become homeless. As a result, children are institutionalised in children's homes as a measure to address their need for housing,

[3]The author of this article conducted the field study throughout Sri Lanka in 2012 as part of PhD research using PAR and critical systemic praxis undertaken at Flinders University of South Australia (referred to as 'PAR 2012').

[4]Children's homes: Institutional care settings for orphaned, abandoned and destitute children that are provided by Non-Government Organisations (DPCCS, 2010).

food and other basic human rights issues (source: Provincial DPCCS commissioners' interviews, PAR 2012). This group of children, as a result of poor environmental management, become a potential tool to better nurture the stewardship of the earth in this Anthropocene epoch.

Ariyadasa (2013) states that natural disasters, civil war and poverty have made institutional (rather than parental) care an inevitable measure to protect children's well-being and safe guard their rights. In present day circumstances, the advantages of the prevalence of children's homes outweigh their disadvantages, because the government alone cannot address the issues of children's rights and needs when large numbers of children become orphaned or destitute due to unexpected environmental problems. For instance; according to International Development Law Organization (2007), in Sri Lanka, an estimated 5,500 children lost one or both parents to the tsunami that struck in December 2004. Thus, in a Sri Lankan context, environmental impacts have been a catalyst for the creation and the growth of many children's homes, away from the need created by other causes such as poverty, parents' migration for work abroad and domestic violence (Ariyadasa 2015a, b). The tsunami was a natural phenomenon, but the incident provides an example of the need to deal with the effects on children of catastrophic events, anthropogenic or otherwise.

Wide media coverage was given in the local and foreign media on the devastating landslides in Haldumulla–Koslanda areas in Sri Lanka (Fig. 7.1). It was reported that around 250 people including children were buried alive with another 150 still unaccounted for (Jayawardena 2014). Jayawardena states that this is the worst natural disaster since the tsunami in 2004 that killed over 38,000 people along

**Fig. 7.1** About 140 houses were engulfed by the disaster, some houses have been buried in 30ft (9 m) of mud [*Source* (BBC 2014)]

the coastal belt of Sri Lanka. I challenge Jayawardena's description of the Koslanda landslide as a *natural* disaster when there is ample evidence pointing to it being the result of human activities in the area over the last few centuries. This mudslide, triggered by monsoon rains, buried around 140 workers' houses at a tea plantation in central Sri Lanka. (Mallawarachi 2014) states that children who had left for school in the morning returned to find that their homes and families had disappeared without a trace. The BBC confirms Mallawarachchi's statement, quoting local Member of Parliament Udith Lokubandara; "Many parents had returned home after leaving their children at school when the landslip happened. It is a very sorry situation because there are many children who have become orphans" (BBC 2014).

Dissanayake (2015) asserts that the long-running conflict between humans and wild elephants in rural Sri Lanka is intensifying, with the number of reported attacks increasing in the past five years. According to the Department of Wildlife Conservation, the number of attacks causing property damage rose from fewer than 700 in 2008 to nearly 2,000 in 2010 and nearly 3,200 in 2012. Bruno (2015) asserts that elephants kill over 150 humans annually. The conflict is deadly to the elephants as well (Fig. 7.2). Between 2005 and 2010, people have killed 1,154 elephants, an average of nearly 200 a year (cited in Dissanayake 2015). These figures justify the statements of policy makers and policy officers of PAR 2012. One provisional commissioner states that "Children's homes in my province recently have started having more orphaned and destitute children than any other period due to human–elephant conflict. Some of these children have lost their breadwinners owing to

**Fig. 7.2** A crowd gathers around a dead elephant in Sri Lanka, possibly killed in retaliation for raiding crops (Courtesy the Sri Lanka Wildlife Conservation Society) [*Source* (Bruno 2015)]

elephant attacks and some have become homeless and destitute due to devastation attacks to their houses and crops by elephant herds".

Sri Lanka experienced civil war for more than 25 years from 1983. Northern and Eastern Sri Lanka were the main battlefields of a conflict between the rebel group known as the Tamil Tigers and the Sri Lankan army that produced many thousands of orphaned and destitute children (Ariyadasa and McIntyre-Mills 2014a). The conflict, which is said to be the longest running war in South Asia, came to an end in 2009 but the consequences of this war have impacted on all children in Sri Lanka. Children who have lost one or both parents, as well as homeless and destitute children were directly institutionalised in children's homes. War Child (2014) asserts that the long-lasting war has had an enormous impact on children.

When fighting ended in May 2009, families that had abandoned villages in the Northern and Eastern Provinces returned. However, the end of the armed conflict contributed to the rise in human–elephant conflict. According to the Department of Wildlife, the war affected areas had been dominated by elephants, and when humans reclaimed the land, this created issues. The human–elephant conflicts started to intensify in these areas around 2011. Now that most abandoned villages have been re-inhabited, the situation is stabilising. Many families in villages vulnerable to attack have stopped cultivating family vegetable plots because they draw elephants close to the homes. People live in fear of the havoc that elephant herds would cause in the village (Dissanayake, 2015). Thus, people undergo life threats directly and indirectly owing to elephant attacks. A person can be severely injured or killed by an elephant which is the direct threat to their lives. The damage that elephants cause to property and/or crops that impact the livelihood of people is the indirect threat. This envisages that the demand for institutional care has been increased as a result of human–elephant conflict in Sri Lanka. These examples demonstrate that the environmental problems and the institutional care of children have a significant relationship.

## Children's Involvement for Governing the Anthropocene: Three Case Studies from Children's Homes in Sri Lanka

Romm's declaration (2015, p. 1) "that we, as humans, are called upon to play a reasonable role in our caring for each other and for the earth" is applicable for the field of institutional care of children. If NGOs are to promote the care and protection of children deprived of parental care in its "true" meaning and not for any other hidden agendas[5] , they are obliged to care for the earth too. For they cannot achieve the former in any long term sense without catering for the latter, i.e. to care

[5]Some provincial commissioners of DPCCSs revealed that some NGOs have hidden agendas such as financial gain and religious conversion in lieu of the "true" meaning of their manifestation, i.e. care and protection for children.

and protect children well, the earth should also be cared for and protected well. The number of institutionalised children and the government and non-government bodies involved in the management of these children's homes is quite substantial. Thus, managing children's homes is a significant Anthropocene assignment. Looking after the children's social, cultural, educational, physical and emotional development is the major aim of children's homes. Whilst there are a number of studies that have researched these aspects of children's homes, literature on the environmental context is lacking. This paper fills this gap and identifies three genuine exercises for 'governing the Anthropocene' by managers' of children's homes in Sri Lanka.

## *Case Study-1: Governing the Anthropocene—Integration of Renewable Resources*

As the principal researcher of the PAR 2012 entitled "Life chances of children and young people in institutional care in Sri Lanka" (Ariyadasa 2013), the author visited thirty children's homes. During the field study he witnessed that every children's home manages a garden of their own to produce vegetables and fruit. With few exceptions, however, un-healthiness, untidiness, lack of maintenance and attention were common features of most gardens visited. In contrast to the optimistic approach and outlook of the most productive and successful gardens, the unsuccessful gardens had many reasons for their failure. This case study reveals the story of the most successful home. This home caters for the needs of twenty young vulnerable children and has been mindful of its governance challenges in social, cultural, economic and environmental aspects. The manager of this children's home expressed the opinion that the day he could feed all children under his care with food that was not exposed to agrochemicals would be the day that he could be considered as the children's true carer. His full statement when author posed the question "What are the strategies that you have taken to enhance the life chances of children under your care?" was as follows:

"I am well aware that most of the vegetables, grains and fruit that we purchase from markets to feed our children are exposed to range of poisons from their birth to harvest and storage until sales. The artificial fertilisers, pesticides and agro-chemicals that are utilised for preserving food during storage, lead us towards unforeseeable illnesses. The most affected are the children. By consuming these foods their un-matured organs start deteriorating day by day. Therefore, I am hesitant to feed children under my care with poisoned foods. In actual fact, if I am not hesitant to do so, in its true meaning I am not a true carer. That is why I started running an organic farm in our children's home premises. Now it provides around one third of the provisions that are required for children's meals. I will be a real father on the day I can supply 100% of organic food to these children. I am driven by the possibility of thriving organic farming and eco-friendly projects for enhancing the life chances of children".

In achieving these objectives the management of this home strategically manages and integrates the renewable resources. This in turn makes a positive contribution towards creating an eco-friendly society while simultaneously responding to its own governance challenges. This children's home consists of a series of interconnected eco-systems (Fig. 7.5). They produce bio-gas energy using human and animal waste along with the home's kitchen food scraps. The bio gas then runs through the kitchen first, supplying energy for cooking meals for the inhabitants of the home. The remainder runs through the vocational training centre (VTC), supplying gas for boiling herb containers. The VTC produces garments using clothes dyed with varying colours soaked in boiled herbs. The manager says;

> Dying clothes using herbs is a pure and natural process, free from use of artificial chemicals of any kind. Then the leftovers from the VTC are directed to the organic farming field directly, the waste water is used for watering the organic farm and the herb waste is used in the compost yard. The effluent from the bio-gas tank is effectively utilised for producing compost and for the home's worm farm. The cattle shed houses three cattle and provide sufficient dairy products for the residents. The waste water from the kitchen and the toilets runs to a field that grows grass for the cattle. The waste from the cattle shed is in turn used to enhance the biogas and compost production. All vegetables and the fruit from the garden are fully organic and have assured residents' food safety. In addition to the vegetable garden, the home has built a productive plant nursery and herb garden. The beehives positioned in three places around the premises contribute not only to the supply of honey for the home but the bees also pollinate the trees in and around the premises.

The manager also identified the strengths, weaknesses, opportunities and threats to their eco-system health. His organic farm is surrounded by paddy fields and coconut plantations. People spray excessive amounts of pesticides to protect the paddy from insects. According to the manager, these insects attack the vegetable garden which is free from pesticides. However, they have been able to protect most of their harvest using indigenous eco-friendly methods. Systemic characteristics of this project have also been helpful to address the challenges of their own eco-system. The VTC uses the parts of the Neem tree called colloquially *kohomba* (*Azadirachta indica*) tree which is famed in the country and indeed throughout South East Asia for its medicinal/antiseptic and insecticidal properties. *Kohomba* seeds, leaves and bark are used to dye clothes at the VTC and the boiled leftovers are used in the organic farm. The waste water that comes out as a result of boiled *kohomba* tree parts are sprayed on vegetable plants as it is a natural insecticide. Ruk Rakaganno (2006) asserts that some insects have been found to starve rather than to eat plants treated with *kohomba* oil.

The tradition of 'Dane' or alms giving brings many donors to this children's home (Ariyadasa 2015a). During their presence at the home, the donors receive the opportunity to visit the VTC, organic farm and to view all other eco-systems maintained in this home. Visitors purchase the produce of the VTC, plants from the nursery and the organic products such as honey, vegetables and compost. The knowledge and the experience that they earn while roaming around the cattle shed, beehives, organic farm, plant nursery, herb garden, worm farm, compost yard and bio-gas unit enables the spread of eco-system governance practices into society. Hundreds of school children in the region who have visited this home learn and experience its practices, demonstrating the popularity that this project has gained over the recent years.

The combination of different ecosystems and their coexistence have systemically balanced the children's home environment. The VTC contributes employment and has empowered three disadvantaged women and continues to provide vocational training for numerous institutionalised children. The organic garden and herb farm employ two labourers and a traditional agricultural inspector. The opportunity for children to spend their leisure time helping with the gardening activities contributes to building their capacities and capabilities in many fields. These include biological dyeing techniques, organic farming, worm farming, compost production, plant nursery marketing, bee keeping and dairy farming (Fig. 7.3). The dynamics of the eco-systems governed by this particular children's home can be described in a systemic manner (Fig. 7.4). It demonstrates how systems and sub systems can share their values to contribute to a common goal. The children grow up immersed in an environment that values the ecosystems health which contributes immensely to each child developing a greater understanding of the significance of environmental protection and stewardship.

This project characterises the harmonious existence between humanity and nature. The management sees nature as a relative which reflects the notion that relatives should live in harmonious relationships (Harris and Wasilewski, 2004 cited in Romm, 2015). It makes provision for the suggestion that a critical systemic

**Fig. 7.3** Illustration to interpret the systemic intervention for governing the Anthropocene through integration of renewable, reusable and recyclable resources (*Source* PAR 2012)

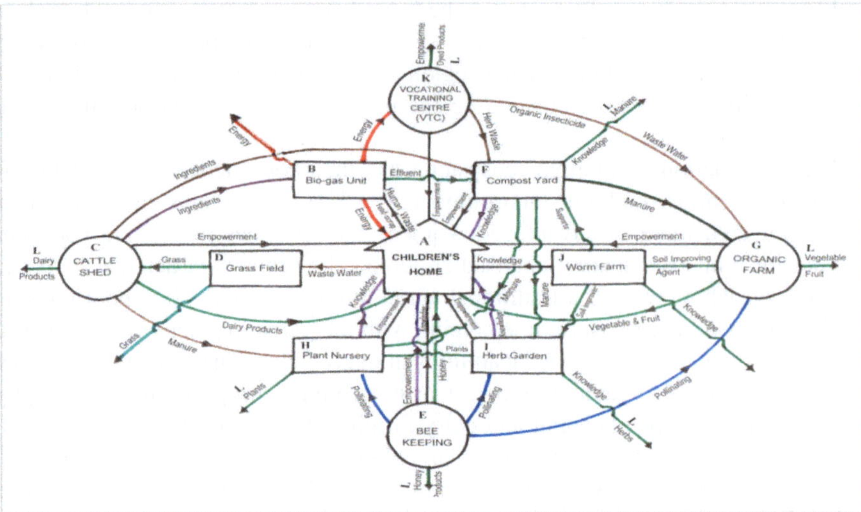


**Fig. 7.4** Systemic diagram to represent the eco-system dynamics of case study-1 (Fig. 7.5): A combination of different ecosystems and their interactions have systemically balanced the children's home environment and its management

approach need not imply that ecological concerns are undervalued in the quest for human emancipation (Midgley, 1996). Smith (2011, p. 1) adopts a similar approach with regard to the concerns of critical systemic thinking with a description of "the simultaneous improvement of human well-being and ecosystem health" (2011, p. 1 cited in Romm 2015). This management team has designed their project to maintain their own natural resources. While managing the children's home which is their primary objective, the managers have introduced processes for enhanced ecosystem governance. As McIntyre-Mills (2014, p. 10) reminds us "the environment is primary and that designs need to ensure that they protect the web of life, rather than pitting profit versus the planet systemic ethics".

Wanigasuriya et al. (2011) assert that chronic kidney disease (CKD), of uncertain aetiology, in the NCP mainly affects males from poor socio-economic backgrounds who are involved in paddy farming raising the possibility of agro-chemical exposure as a cause for this disease. Thus, the systemic strategies that this home practices can be further studied to address the increasing trend in mortality and morbidity due to CKD mainly in the NCP of Sri Lanka. The case study-1 can be identified as praxis that paves the ways of understanding our environmental stewardship responsibilities for governing the Anthropocene.

## *Case Study-2: Governing the Anthropocene—The Lunch Packet Concept—Reject, Renew, Reduce, Reuse, Recycle (5R)*

The industrial revolution has influenced people to travel away from their homes for work or schooling during the day time. Thus, it is generally expected that they have their lunch at the work place or at school. The lunch routine and context could understandably be different for each individual. One could have lunch at the work place canteen or in a restaurant near the work place. In the Sri Lankan context, however, it is typical to have a pre-prepared lunch that one takes from home. The most customary lunch consists of rice and curry served on a thin polythene paper (referred to as 'lunch sheet') and wrapped using a sheet of newspaper and packed in a polythene bag (referred to as 'shopping bag').

After the lunch is eaten, several kinds of waste material are generally disposed of into the environment. They are; shopping bag, newspaper sheet, lunch sheet and the food left overs. Managing the waste that has been generated by the lunch packet can be regarded as an Anthropocene assignment, because it is an outcome of the Anthropocene epoch. The significance of this typical lunch packet and its relationship to waste management is reflected in both empirical findings and secondary data of PAR 2012 conducted by the author. The following case study provides strategies of how to overcome environmental problems that result from lunch packet use. This particular children's home has placed four bins for the disposal of waste (Fig. 7.5). The bins are for specific categories of waste; polythene/plastic, paper/cardboard, waste food materials and lunch sheets. The manager explained the reasoning behind this:

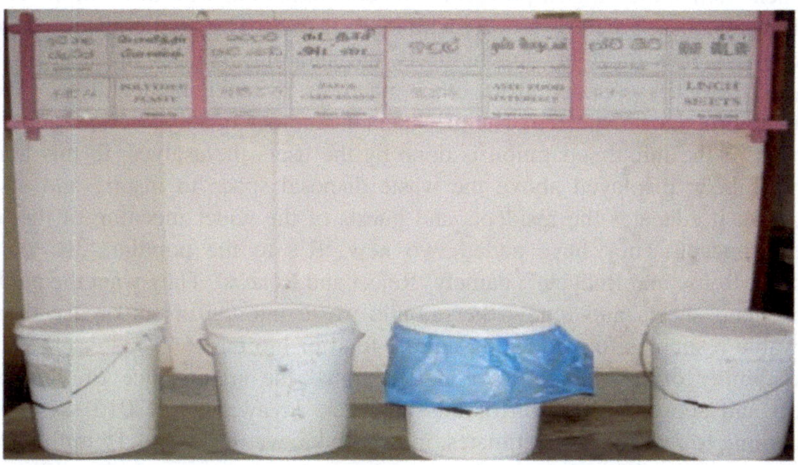

**Fig. 7.5** Lunch packet concept: segregated disposal (*Source* PAR 2012)

"The most common form of excess rubbish at any workplace or school is the waste as a result of lunch packets. When one has eaten his lunch, he rolls the left overs using the lunch sheet and then wraps it using the sheet of newspaper. Then he puts it into the polythene bag and throws it into the garbage bin provided, or throws it into a space where garbage had already being stacked. This is the beginning of many disasters. The stray dogs and cats steal them and mostly end up consuming the food leftovers along with the very thin lunch sheet. When this waste is taken to an open garbage disposal premise away from human vicinity, it becomes the meals of crows, cows and any other animal varying from hedgehog to an elephant. The big animals who can only smell the food but unable to unwrap it, eat it along with the lunch sheet and/or the shopping bags. Anyone can understand the consequences to their health. Not only that, the rain collects the waste and takes it to drains and has become the major cause of recent floods in urban areas. These garbage collection centres have become major fly breeding beds and the sources for various diseases. Thus, I have built the lunch packet concept for disposing of garbage systemically that gives many solutions to these environmental dilemmas".

This manager convinces us that the rubbish disposed in accordance with the "Lunch packet concept" represents the majority of waste disposed by a family or an institution. Shopping bags represent clean polythene/plastic-based materials that can be reused or recycled. Newspaper sheets represent clean paper/cardboard-based materials that can also be reused or recycled. Leftovers from the lunch represent organic materials that can be used as a renewable resource to feed animals or to produce compost and bio gas. Unfortunately the lunch sheets are contaminated by oil and food materials. This type of waste represents materials that cannot be reused or recycled.

According to Yatawara (2014) a considerable portion of the post-consumer plastic consists of lunch sheets and shopping bags. In recycling these plastic and polythene items, the biggest problem is its contamination with dirt—in the case of lunch sheets, these are thrown away with leftover food. This contamination needs to be removed, thus recycling lunch sheets and shopping bags is not an easy task. They have to be separated from other materials if an efficient and an effective recycling process is expected. The mechanism becomes much easier and more cost effective, if the initial separation is done by the users themselves. In this home a flyer has been displayed above the waste disposal space to inspire and instruct (Fig. 7.6). It educates the residents and guests of the wider meaning of the lunch packet concept. They have added two new 'R's to the popular '3R' concept "Reduce, Reuse and Recycle": namely 'Reject and Renew'. They want the public to reject lunch sheets and renew the organic waste into fertilisers or use them as renewable resources for producing animal food or bio gas.

A number of researchers have demonstrated the significance of the timely, critical and appropriate action of this manager. Jayawardane (2015) asserts that "According to recent study estimates, in Sri Lanka, we dispose of 15 million lunch sheets a day; 20 million shopping bags are dumped each day, nearly 20 million food containers such as yoghurt cups are disposed of in addition to many other plastic products. Only a fraction of this is recycled, and a greater percentage ends up in

**Fig. 7.6** Let's dispose our waste into the correct bin (*Source* PAR 2012)

landfill or other natural ecosystems (such as water bodies and wetlands) causing serious environmental issues.

Plastic and polythene account for approximately 6% of the municipal solid waste composition in Sri Lanka" (Fig. 7.7). Yatawara (2014) states that every time someone goes shopping they bring home several polythene bags which are not recycled or reused. Around six to seven food packaging bags are discarded each day by a family. When multiplied by approximately 4.2 million families in this country, this represents a significant waste stream.

Dr. Priyan Perera, Senior Lecturer in the Department of Forestry and Environmental Science, University of Sri Jayawardenepura asserts:

> Irresponsible disposal of plastics and polythene degrades aesthetic beauty and environmental quality. Plastic and polythene that is improperly dumped can impede water-flow in drainage channels, and provides breeding places for disease vectors such as mosquitoes. Open burning of Plastic and polythene contributes to atmospheric pollution and may cause serious health problems. Many plastics and polythene ends up in aquatic environments such as inland water bodies and oceans. Some reports indicate that over 80% of ocean debris is in fact plastic. Plastic degrades due to solar radiation (photo-degradation) and oxidation into smaller particles, eventually forming plastic dust. They can pollute deep ocean sediments and then enter food chains (Jayawardane 2015).

**Fig. 7.7** In the western province alone, 60–70% of the waste is perishable waste and another 15–20% is recyclable waste. Improper waste disposal, a colossal loss to the country [*Source* (Yatawara 2014)]

Plastic was invented during the latter part of the 19th century, and large scale manufacturing and applications took place only after the 1st World War. So, it is technically possible to live in a world without plastic or polythene, and our own history can provide such evidence. Before lunch sheets were introduced, people used to pack their lunches using eco-friendly materials such as banana or water lily leaves and betel nut leaf stems. In rural areas, even in the present day, banana leaves are used in lieu of umbrellas for protection from rain. Thus the majority of families had identified the significance of growing banana trees in their gardens, in addition to its benefit as a fruit provider. In the present day context, urban life, with minimal space for gardening, has undermined the use of these eco-friendly materials. Furthermore, the convenience, low-cost and multi-purpose characteristics of polythene have substituted and marginalised the use of once common organic materials for household purposes.

When adopting the lunch packet concept as the garbage disposal mechanism, it convinces individuals to consider that lunch sheets should be rejected or reduced as it pollutes the environment in many ways. It also focuses attention on the importance of the separation of waste as an outcome of lunch packets in particular and all other waste in general to maximise their reusability, recyclability and renewability.

## *Case Study-3: Governing the Anthropocene—Learning by Doing*

One particular children's home runs a club activity called "Green-birds". According to the manager, he attempts to enhance children's life chances and build their capacities whilst engaged in environment conservation projects. He explains their major green-bird activity as follows:

We have divided our children in the home into three groups. Once a fortnight, each carer takes one group to a nearby town or a temple where many people gather. Then we start collecting all sorts of litter that the public have thrown away. It does not take long to fill our bags. We come across many materials. Temple premises are full of polythene bags. Devotees bring fresh flowers and after offering them, bags are thrown to a corner of the temple premises. We sort them out and collect them into our rubbish bags. At viewpoints, PET[6] bottles, polythene bags, empty confectionery boxes and leftovers from lunch packets are often encountered. Our intention is not just to collect as much rubbish as possible, but to enhance our children's awareness of the immense environmental impact from this waste. Most of all, when children collect rubbish, the people around them can learn from the children's action and may reconsider throwing litter around, and of course regret previous littering. Some people join us and help us with our deeds. I have also found this a better way for our children to interact with the general public. The public have a general consciousness that institutionalised children are vulnerable and helpless and that it is public's duty to support children's homes. When we have initiated this kind of social work, people admire the children's action which naturally empowers them to build their morale and confidence.

The manager's words are indicative of a children's home which presents a good example of educating children for governing the Anthropocene. He has provided children with "Green-bird" T shirts, gloves and tongs for use when they are engaged in collecting rubbish (Fig. 7.8). The manager has also extended the project to include participation from other local school children outside his children's home. His intention is to promote the Green-bird project nationally around Sri Lanka to protect the environment from discarded rubbish and educate and change the public's unacceptable habit of excessive littering. His activity in his own words is; "example is better than precept". He ends his narrative saying "I am pretty sure that in future we will have number of environmentalists produced from our children's home".

After every rubbish pickup, Green-birds gather around their picked rubbish bags and have a discussion over refreshment. It gives an opportunity for the participants

[6]Poly-Ethylene Terephthalate.

**Fig. 7.8** Collecting rubbish at a temple by green-birds (*Source* PAR 2012)

to express their feelings and attitudes about their participation. A comment book provides them with further space to express their thoughts. Of many hundreds valuable comments, the following three from participants are provided to emphasise the significance of the green-bird activity whilst educating children:

> I have not taken much effort to throw litter into a garbage bin earlier. For example, throwing a toffee paper, bus ticket or a grocery bill into the environment was a very general habit of mine. I am convinced that the litter which I collected today was the result of many individuals whom might have the same habit as mine. If every one of us had refrained from littering everywhere we need not have collected rubbish today. The environment would have been free from litter and a pleasant place for everyone.

> The places that have been most visited by people are the most affected by rubbish. Of course in many places either the garbage bins had not been placed or were overflowing. Loads of litter has been stacked everywhere with no proper covers to protect them from being exposed to the environment. It is a pity to witness how people have destroyed the beautiful places at the expense of their attractiveness. If they do not find a proper waste disposal mechanism around, mindfulness to take back their own litter with them, would have kept the environment clean without harming its beauty.

> I am proud to be a green-bird

## Strategies for Maintaining the Human–Environment Friendly Relations in the Anthropocene

Constructing reservoirs for hydroelectricity and agricultural purposes, tunnelling for roads and railways for transportation, filling and excavation for building roads, deforestation for tea plantations and agriculture are human activities that continue in the Anthropocene epoch. Although these said human activities are supposed to enhance human well-being and the standard of living, sometimes the opposite happens. This paper reveals that these human activities have been the major causes for many environmental problems including landslides and human–elephant conflicts. Thus, it is time to learn from past experience to avoid future depredation. This paper emphasises the importance of a thorough consideration of environmental impacts and the consequent adverse effects to the human lives prior to the implementation of any project that might hinder the environmental equilibrium. The significance of ethical conduct in accordance with Environmental Impact Reports and the importance of listening to the voice of the public have been discussed as strategies to maintain the human–environment friendly relations in the Anthropocene epoch.

## Lessons Learnt from the Case Studies

The first case study shows that our existence is contingent on our supporting, and being supported by, others (including non-living entities). It also teaches us to limit our use of fertilisers and pesticides which have the potential for environmental harm. It introduces alternative measures on how to protect crops from agrochemicals that eradicate endangered herbs at the expense of commercially driven food production. Strategies for avoiding and banning chemically driven food production and reducing carbon footprints through systemically integrating interdependent renewable resources are the lessons learnt from this children's home. According to the manager of this home, he has initiated the organic farming with the principal intention of maintaining the good health and longevity of the children. It is interesting to note that the central focus on organic farming has become the hub of many capacity building initiatives that are linked with central capabilities including; safety, education, standard of living, productive valued activities, quality social interactions, recreation and play (Ariyadasa and McIntyre-Mills 2014a; Canoy et al. 2010; Nussbaum 2011). Furthermore, the eco-system governance practices of this home have paved many paths in empowering children for diverse occupations such as organic, dairy and worm farmers; bee keepers; plant nursery marketing; compost and bio-gas producers; herbal medicine practitioners; environmentalists; and agricultural inspectors. The vocational training atmosphere is consistent with the

Guidelines[7] for the Alternative care of Children (United Nations 2010) and the General Standards[8] for Promoting the Quality of Services of Voluntary Children's Homes (DPCCS 1991).

The second case study builds capacities in resource management for institutionalised children in particular and the public in general. It involves lessons on recycling use and re-use of resources. The lunch packet concept has conceptualised a practical solution for the issue of waste management in Sri Lanka. It also addresses many issues related to environmental impacts, health hazards, and social and economic crises due to improper waste disposal mechanisms. Furthermore, it prompts the urgent need to develop alternatives to lunch sheets and encourages us to at least use a lunch box made of reusable material that can be recycled after a reasonable time. The manager showed the author the records of three high school students who had researched this lunch packet concept for their final year assessments. According to the manager, two schools have initiated schemes to implement waste disposal mechanisms in accordance with the lunch packet concept. It indicates the significance of this concept for wider application throughout the country.

The third case study shows that volunteering to clean up the cities empowers the citizens' attitudes to maintain an eco-friendly environment by eradicating the habit of the careless disposal of litter. Furthermore, the generous gesture of this children's home to involve other school children and public in their green-bird activities demonstrates their willingness to campaign for public awareness of a clean environment. It not only helps to keep the environment clean, but keeps a harmonious relationship between the children's home and the external world through a worthy cause. The discussion after every rubbish pickup helps participants to reflect on their activity and provides an incentive to take home the message of their good deeds. The certificates that the manager awards for green-bird participants, are a manifestation of the manager's enthusiasm to mould children to become leaders, guiding society towards a clean and healthy environment.

One of the greatest concerns that has been underscored in many of the research reports written on institutionalised children, and which impedes upon their experiencing competence, is the lack of opportunities to acquire social skills required for adult life (Dunn et al. 2005; Mann 2001; Save the Children 2005; Tolfree 1995). Jayasooriyya (2008, p. 30) state that "Many of the children expressed fear about society outside the children's institution and were worried about their inability to deal with it once they left the institution". However, the most prominent characteristic of the three examples of good governance practices discussed in this paper is the ability for institutionalised children to interact with wider society and environment. Thus, during their institutionalisation, they acquire the courage and confidence that they need to deal with societies outside the high walls and the

[7] UN Guideline 134 and 135.

[8] General Standards 5.22 and 5.23.

locked gates of children's homes when they are re-integrated.[9] All three projects educate and empower children, young people and also the adults about how to care for the environment. Mindfulness of eco-friendliness, global warming and climatic changes are the underlying features of the tacit endeavour of these management teams. These practices characterise the harmonious existence between humanity and nature and have adopted the concerns of critical systemic thinking with the simultaneous improvement of human well-being and ecosystem health.

## Conclusion

A small group of thoughtful committed citizens can change the world. Indeed it's the only thing that ever has (Margaret Mead).

Crutzen (2002) cited by Smith and Zeder (2013) assert "A daunting task lies ahead for scientists and engineers to guide society towards environmentally sustainable management during the Anthropocene". There is an ongoing debate on reckless and abuse conduct in children's homes. Children's homes that build capacities and enhance the capabilities of institutionalised children on environmental affairs were found to be rare. However, the three case studies that have been discussed in this paper showcase the endeavours of a few individuals who have guided their children's homes and their societies towards environmental sustainability by implementing projects on eco-systems and environmental protection. The ethos of these people is summed up by the words of Margaret Mead, who stated that "A small group of thoughtful committed citizens can change the world. Indeed it's the only thing that ever has" (cited in Seneviratne 2006).

The most important aspect of these projects is that these managers have incorporated institutionalised children in their projects with the intention of empowering them to be the future governors of the Anthropocene. They have pioneered a change in the attitudes of the general public which once held that children in institutional care are helpless and hopeless (Ariyadasa 2015a). While educating children on the consequences of the human activities in the Anthropocene epoch, these managers attempt to ensure that the mistakes made by earlier generations are not repeated by the current ones. Children learn about their rights and responsibilities by being given the opportunity to express their ideas and to translate policy into practice through small scale interventions that make a difference to this generation and the next.

These explicit examples are exemplary exercises for governing the Anthropocene. They provide intellectual materials to other homes and similar institutions for inventing their own strategies when governing their institutions with

[9]Re-integration: In this PAR *re-integration* is referred to as 'a child's reunification with family/natural birth environment, socialisation with society/community or other permanent care solutions such as local/foreign adoption'. Source: (Ariyadasa and McIntyre-Mills 2014b).

the mind-set that we all belong to a single biosphere[10] which includes "not only the biota, but all of their relationships – the web or network of life, the life community" (Caddy 2014).

Be the change you want to see in the world (Mahatma Gandhi).

**Acknowledgements** This research is funded by the Australian Government's Endeavour Scholarships and Fellowships. The structure, ideas and philosophies presented in this paper draw on research under the supervision of Associate Professor Janet McIntyre, Dr Helen McLaren and Dr Leonie Solomons. Insights and feedback offered by Mr. James Turner Alvey, Dr Chandani Panditaratne and Dr Greg Collings were invaluable. The author would like to acknowledge their contributions.

## References

Ariyadasa E (2013) Life chances of children and young people in institutional care in Sri Lanka: acritical review of policy and governance with reference to case studies. Paper presented at the ISSS—2013, Vietnam, Haiphong

Ariyadasa E (2015a) Poverty and perception: driving Sri Lankan children's homes at multiple levels. Paper presented at the KDU international research conference—2014, Colombo, Sri Lanka

Ariyadasa E (2015b) With mother away, they need a place they can call home: a practical solution to restrict children's institutionalisation due to mothers' migration for work overseas. The Sunday Times

Ariyadasa E, McIntyre-Mills J (2014a) Quality of life of Sri Lankan children: participatory action research to address the governance issues of voluntary children's homes. Syst Pract Action Res 9339:1–26. doi:10.1007/s11213-014-9339-7

Ariyadasa E, McIntyre-Mills J (2014b) A systemic governance approach to an effective re-integration process for the institutionalized children in Sri Lanka: application of critical systems heuristics. Syst Pract Action Res 9338:1–23. doi:10.1007/s11213-014-9338-8

Bandara RMS (2015) Landslides in Sri Lanka. Vidurava 22(2):9–13

BBC (2014) Sri Lanka landslide: '100 feared dead'. http://www.bbc.com/news/world-asia-29813981

Bruno D (2015) In Sri Lanka, elephants and humans struggle to live in close quarters. http://www.citylab.com/politics/2015/03/. Accessed 4 June 2015

Caddy JT (2014) Morning earth. http://www.morning-earth.org/. Accessed 3 June 2015

Canoy M, Lerais F, Schokkaert E (2010) Applying the capability approach to policy-making: the impact assessment of the EU-proposal on organ donation. J Socio-Econ 39(3):391–399. doi:10.1016/j.socec.2009.11.002

Crutzen PJ (2002) Geology of mankind. Nature:415

Dissanayake C (2015) Legally protected, proliferating and losing habitat, elephants step up deadly struggle with Sri Lankan villagers. http://www.indiagazette.com/index.php/sid/232312107. Accessed 2 June 2015

DPCCS (1991) General standards for promoting the quality of services in voluntary children's homes S3/Gen/15, Colombo, Sri Lanka

[10]The biosphere is the part of the Earth, including air, land, surface rocks, and water, within which life occurs, and which biotic processes in turn alter or transform. The geologist who in 1875 coined the word biosphere, Eduard Suess, defined it as "the place on Earth's surface where life dwells" (Source: http://www.morning-earth.org/).

DPCCS (2010) Statistical Report—2010. Department of Probation and Child Care Services, Colombo, Sri Lanka, pp 1–45
Dunn A, Jareg E, Webb D (2005) A last resort: the growing concern about children in residential care. International Save the Children Alliance, UK
Harris LD, Wasilewski J (2004) Indigeneity, an alternative worldview. Syst Res Behav Sci 21:489–503. doi:10.1002/sres.631
International Development Law Organization (2007) Guidebook on the rights of the child in Sri Lanka (Ranasinghe H, ed). Printall Int
Jayasooriyya C (2008) Rehabilitation, care and protection of children in contact with the law: is institutionalization the best option? http://www.academia.edu/
Jayawardane I (2015, March 19). Plastic perils: reduce, re-use and recycle. Daily News
Jayawardena D (2014, 5 Nov) Analysis on devastating landslides in Haldumulla–Koslanda areas. Daily Mirror. https://shar.es/1r4Xpd
Mallawarachi B (Producer) (2014) Deadly landslide at Sri Lanka tea plantation triggered by monsoon rains. http://www.thestar.com/news/world/2014/10/29/deadly_landslide_at_sri_lanka_tea_plantation_triggered_by_monsoon_rains.html
Mann G (2001) Network of supports: a literature review of care issues for separated children: save the children, Sweden
McIntyre-Mills JJ (2014) Systemic ethics and non-anthropocentric Stewardship. Springer, New York
Midgley G (1996) What is this thing called CST? In: Flood RL, Romm NRA (eds) Critical systems thinking: current research and practice. Plenum, New York
Nussbaum MC (2011) Creating capabilities: the human development approach: Harvard University Press
Romm NRA (2015) Foregrounding critical systemic and indigenous ways of collective knowing towards (re)directing the Anthropocene (unpublished). In: Conference paper to be presented at the ISSS 2015, Berlin, Germany
Ruk R (2006, 5 Feb) Shady tree of medicinal fame. Sunday Times. http://www.sundaytimes.lk/060205/plus/8.html
Save the Children (2005) Home truths: children rights in institutional care in Sri Lanka. Save the Children, Colombo, Sri Lanka
Seneviratne M (ed) (2006) CSEC the crime against children: commercial sexual exploitation of children. First Impressions, Colombo, Sri Lanka
Smith BD, Zeder MA (2013) The onset of the Anthropocene. Anthropocene 4:8–13. doi:http://dx.doi.org/10.1016/j.ancene.2013.05.001
Smith T (2011) Using critical systems thinking to foster an integrated approach to sustainability: a proposal for development practitioners. Environ Dev Sustain 13:1–17
Steffen W, Grinevald J, Crutzen P, McNeill J (2011) The Anthropocene: conceptual and historical perspectives. Philos Trans R Soc A 369:842–867. doi:10.1098/rsta.2010.0327
Steffen W, Persson Å, Deutsch L, Zalasiewicz J, Williams M, Richardson K, Svedin U (2011) The Anthropocene: from global change to planetary Stewardship. Ambio 40(7):739–761. doi:10.1007/s13280-011-0185-x
Sugawara J (2013) Landslides in tea plantation fields in Shizuoka, Japan. [Reviewed under GEOMATE publication policies]. Int J GEOMATE 4(1):495–500
Tolfree D (1995) Roofs and roots the care of separated children in the developing world: Ashgate Publishing Limited, England
United Nations (2010) Guidelines for the alternative care of children A/RES/64/142. United Nations General Assembly, New York, pp 1–23
Wanigasuriya KP, Peiris-John RJ, Wickremasinghe R (2011) Chronic kidney disease of unknown aetiology in Sri Lanka: is cadmium a likely cause? BMC Nephrol 12(32). doi:10.1186/1471-2369-12-32

War Child (2014) Where we work: Sri Lanka. http://www.warchildholland.org/sri-lanka. 10 May 2014

Yatawara D (2014, 23 Nov) Improper waste disposal, a colossal loss to the country. Sunday Observer. http://www.sundayobserver.lk/2014/11/23/fea06.asp

## Author Biography

**Dr. Eshantha Ariyadasa** completed his PhD studies at Flinders University, Adelaide, Australia. Dr. Ariyadasa through his research highlights the significance of the leadership and the stewardship of policy makers and service providers in building the capacities of institutionalized children to support an eco-friendly planet. Eshantha Ariyadasa pioneered the Sputnik International Organization to promote world peace through languages, sports and cultural education. He is the founder of the Sputnik Girls' Children's Home in Sri Lanka. The paper (published in this volume) was presented at the 59th Annual Meeting of the International Society for the Systems Sciences in Berlin, 2015 for which he received the Margaret Mead Memorial Award. He has published five journal articles and one newspaper article, and has contributed to the existing literature.

# Chapter 8
# Gender, Climate Change, and Sustainable Development in Bangladesh

**Yvonne Corcoran-Nantes and Snigdha Roy**

**Abstract** Climate change has become one of the most important global development issues in the current global political context. The impact of a changing climate is witnessed daily across nations north and south as a result of industrialization, greenhouse gas emissions, deforestation, fossil fuel burning, and other human activities (Mignaquy, Gender perspectives on climate change, 2014: 3). It impedes basic human livelihoods to the extent that the lack of food, shelter, energy, water and problems in access to education and health impedes sustainable development. Climate change triggers other environmental problems affecting both food security and human security such as: flooding, storms, drought, desertification, deforestation, sea level rises, the melting of glaciers, increased soil salinity, and decreased availability of fresh water (Dankelman et al. Gender, climate change and human security: lessons from Bangladesh, Ghana and Senegal, ELIAMEP:WEDO, 1–71, 2008: 5). It is also a global threat to ensure sustainable international development. In the strategies for survival and sustainability, women hold a central role nowhere more so than in the global south where communities of the working poor struggle to meet basic needs and where climate change exacerbates existing constraints to sustainable development. This study will explore the gender-specific implications of climate change. Although climate change impacts globally, its impact is not equal everywhere due to geographical location, socioeconomic conditions, political will, poverty, and race and gender inequality. Consequently our case study Bangladesh is illustrative of the intersectionality of experience, needs and outcomes that need to be negotiated on the road to a global environmentally sustainable future

The Paris Climate Change Conference held by the United Nations in November 2015 represented a further attempt to have the majority of countries worldwide prepared and willing to meet the climate change challenge. Under the Paris

Y. Corcoran-Nantes (✉) · S. Roy
Flinders University, Adelaide, SA, Australia
e-mail: Yvonne.Corcoran-Nantes@flinders.edu.au

S. Roy
e-mail: snigdharoy77@gmail.com

 
J. McIntyre-Mills et al. (eds.), *Balancing Individualism and Collectivism*,
Contemporary Systems Thinking, DOI 10.1007/978-3-319-58014-2_8

Agreement, just under 200 countries agreed to take action to curtail greenhouse gas emissions in order to ameliorate, if not reverse, the long-term effects of climate change. In the broad scheme of climate change effects, the impact of perennial flooding, storms, drought, desertification, deforestation, sea level rise, glacial erosion, increased soil salinity, and decreased availability of fresh water is global (Dankelman et al. 2008: 5). It is predicted that in the next 20–30 years climate change will gradually turn arable land into desert threatening world food security, creating demographic change and rising global energy demands (Wisner et al. 2007: 2). For the developing countries of the global south the consequences run far deeper, it hampers basic human livelihoods to the extent that the lack of food, shelter, energy, water, and problems in access to education and health impedes sustainable development. Thus climate change is now recognized as a major human security issue impoverishing the most economically compromised populations of which women form the majority. The nexus between women, the environment and human security in many developing countries is underwritten by women's role as the principal food producers. Sustainable development relies not merely on global climate change policy but in the recognition that addressing social inequalities, most especially gender inequality, is pivotal to its success (Stern 2006: 6).

It is generally recognized that poor and marginalized people are the most vulnerable to the negative impacts of climate change and that women constitute 70% of this group. Climate change economists, argue that it is this social group that has limited access to the resources and information to adapt to changing climate patterns and are less likely to be invited to participate in decision-making on climate change policy (Demetriades and Esplen 2008: 24). Consequently this chapter will explore the gender-specific implications of climate change using Bangladesh as a case study.

In Bangladesh, women play a vital role in agriculture, water management, reforestation, energy management and sustaining biodiversity yet gender mainstreaming has not been integrated into agriculture, natural resource management and climate related strategies and action plans. Moreover, Bangladeshi women also play a crucial role in climate change mitigation strategies despite the lack of gender inclusive climate change policy and practice. As the principal agriculturalists and food producers women should play an integral and substantive role in both policy making and the formulation of development strategy. The patriarchal social system of Bangladesh, poverty and the gender division of labor contributes to positioning women behind men with respect to priority access to education, information, and resources, environmental, economic and social activities which, as a consequence, impedes sustainable development.

This chapter contributes to a deeper understanding of the differentiated impacts of climate change on women, female initiated adaptation strategies and provides a critique of the traditional form of policy which excludes women's experience and knowledges from its formulation. This chapter will examine how social constraints, the gender division of labor; unequal power relations and poverty disproportionately impact on women due to climate change and compromise the introduction of a sustainable development program in Bangladesh.

## Gender and Climate Change in Bangladesh

The principal cause of global inequality is the unequal distribution of power and resources. Of the world's total poor, 70% are women whose livelihoods,[1] either directly or indirectly, are dependent on natural resources, subsistence agriculture, and informal sectors, which are threatened due to climate change (Resurreccion 2013: 39; Lambrou and Piana 2006: 13; Dankelman et al. 2008: 14). Moreover, nowhere do women have equal access to resources as compared to men; of the world's total land less than 2% is owned by women and of the world's total income only 10% is received by women (WEDO 2015; Frisby et al. 2009: 14). Thus women are not able to make independent decisions in adapting to changing climate patterns in the same way as men due to a lack of access and/or control over resources. As a result, the impact of climate change is not gender neutral because climate change adversely affects women's livelihood (Resurrección 2013: 39; Lambrou and Piana 2006: 13; UNFCC 2014) (Fig. 8.1).

Thus, the vulnerability of women is strongly correlated with poverty and women's dependency on the environment for their livelihoods which as we can see in the table above, disasters and conflict further exacerbate the already precarious situation of women. Perennial flooding and typhoons in Bangladesh have shaped the course of strategies for action against climate change and women's participation in that.

Eco-feminists argue that women are closer to nature than men and that 'nature is the primary topic of political conservation' (Sandilands 2008: 308). Eco-feminist, Vandana Shiva argues that rural women are vital contributors to life and the rightful conservers of nature (Shiva 1995). Furthermore, women have a greater predisposition to care for nature than men not least because their survival strategies as the principal food producers depend on it (Sandilands 2008: 307). Shiva describes this by saying that 'from seed to table the food chain is gendered' whereby over 50% of the world's food is produced by women and in developing countries women produce and process 60–80% of all food production (Shiva 2009: 19). Women are the principal gatherers of water, food, fodder, and fuel which are threatened due to deforestation and intensive monoculture and yet they are poorly represented in conservation projects (Resurección 2013: 35). Accordingly, women are more likely to perform effectively and efficiently in natural resource management by preserving biodiversity, reducing greenhouse gas emission, and increasing food production than men and this helps to reduce vulnerability owing to climate change. The relationship between women and nature also influences economic, social, and environmental relations. The failure to incorporate women's knowledge in natural resource management has led to monoculture, health hazards, environmental degradation, and the use of agro-chemicals, as well as a decrease in biodiversity,

---

[1]This statement does not subscribe to the feminization of poverty thesis but specifically recognize that in these circumstances women form the majority of those adversely affected by climate change events.

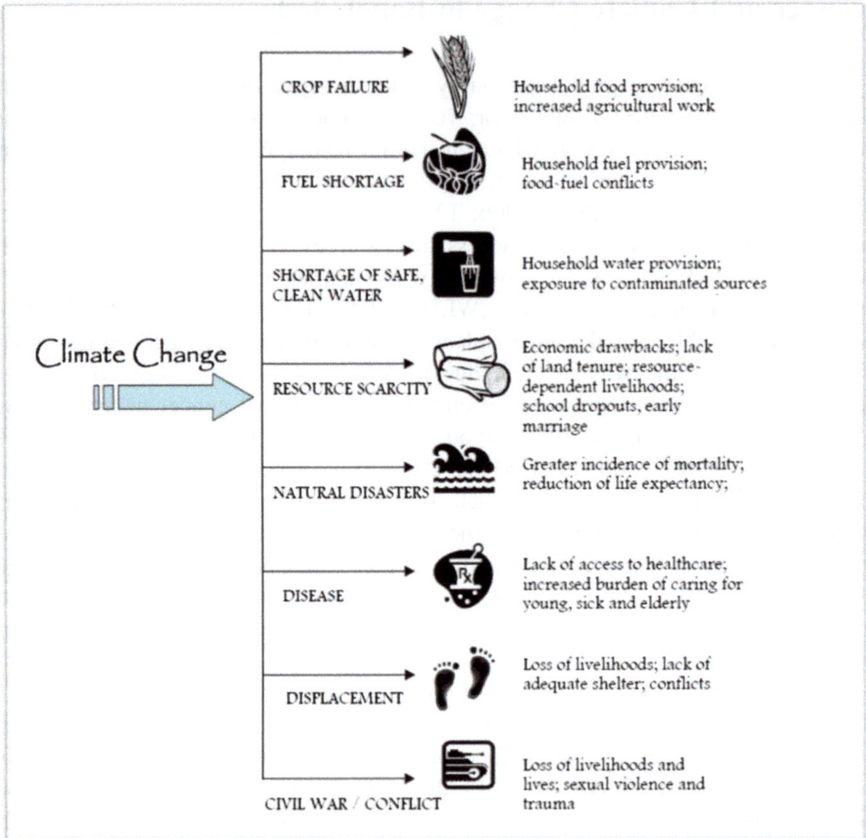


**Fig. 8.1** Showing the impacts of climate change on human security and vulnerability on women (reproduced from WEDO 2008)

all of which could become threats to achieving sustainable development with changing climate patterns (Gaard 2015: 23–26). Thus, the incorporation of eco-feminist theory and the considerations imbued within it is central to the larger context of climate change and political decision-making.

Bangladesh is a country that is most vulnerable to climate change. Bangladesh has experienced higher mean temperatures over the last three decades and it is predicted that the annual mean temperature will increase by 1 °C, 1.4 °C, and 2.4 °C by the years 2030, 2050, and 2100 respectively (Amin et al. 2015: 899). In the third IPCC assessment, they predicted that the average global sea level rise will be 9–88 cm by 2100 whereas, in Bangladesh it is assumed to be 30–100 cm (Agarwal et al. 2003: 15). Floods and cyclones perennially affect Bangladesh whereby almost one-third of the land is flooded every summer (Cannon 2002: 45). Floodplains now account for almost 80% of total land area in Bangladesh in a political economy in which two-thirds of the population depend on agriculture (Ayers et al. 2014: 298).

The impact of climate change and 'natural' disasters impact most severely on women and such vulnerability 'is not innate; rather it is a result of inequities produced through gendered social roles, discrimination, and poverty' (Gaard 2015: 23).

In 2002, Cannon's study of women's nutritional status showed that poverty is a key factor for coping with the effects of a climate hazard; in Bangladesh, women are more calorie-deficient and more susceptible to disease than men (2002: 48). For example, annual flooding in Bangladesh has led to an increase in some water borne diseases such as malaria, cholera, and diarrhea, which affects women more than men because women are more likely to be nutritionally disadvantaged and thus more vulnerable to disease (Dankelman et al. 2008: 19). Moreover, cultural and social constraints such as responsibility for children and their style of clothing can negatively affect their capacity to respond swiftly when disaster strikes (Cannon 2002: 48; Dankelman et al. 2008: 7). Consequently, more women than men die during natural disasters, for example, in the 1991 cyclone and flood disaster in Bangladesh 90% of the victims were women (Cannon 2002: 49). The causes are multiple: forewarning information was not sent to women, who were largely confined in their homes; women are not trained swimmers; women's care-giving responsibilities meant that women trying to escape the floods were often holding infants and towing elder family members, while husbands escaped alone (Gaard 2015: 23). Furthermore, the loss of a home and other property and goods as well as the risk of sexual assault may lead to women's forced relocation and further socioeconomic insecurity (Dankelman et al. 2008: 18).

Within a culturally circumscribed gender division of labor inside the family, women spend less time in paid work and experience reduced mobility due to unpaid productive work carried out in the home such as child care and domestic duties. It is the latter that is most affected in the aftermath of extreme climate events whereby the time spent undertaking tasks such as fetching water and foraging for fuel can lead to women traveling up to 5–6 km each day to complete these tasks (Women Watch 2014: 4; Dankelman et al. 2008: 10). In some areas daughters may be called upon to assist their mothers in such difficult times which can lead to more young girls dropping out of school as subsistence tasks take priority over education (Dankelman et al. 2008: 10; UNDP 2015). Moreover, the physical stress of collecting of water from distant locations, in the period of the floods for pregnant women has contributed to unusually high rates of premature births, miscarriage and stillbirth annually (Dankelman et al. 2008: 19 and UNDP 2015). Consequently, women have less access to education, training programs, income generating activities, social activities, and other decision-making activities because climate change events have led to increased unpaid household activities, which affects any initiatives to reduce gender inequality and empower women (Dankelman et al. 2008: 10; UNDP 2015).

Coastal areas are more affected by natural disasters such as cyclones, storms, and floods. In Bangladesh, 30% of the land mass is coastal zone, but very few shelters exist in the coastal regions and those that do exist are only able to accommodate 27% of the total coastal population (Huq et al. 2004: 35; Rasul and Chowdhury 2010: 11). Additionally, the cyclone shelters are not woman friendly as the lack of privacy and sanitation present human security risks in the form of risk of sexual assault and health hazards for women. Thus women become more vulnerable when they seek shelter during disasters (Sharmin and Islam 2013: 6). As a result many women send other family members to a cyclone shelter but prefer not to go due to a lack of security which places them at risk (CCC 2009: 33).

## Gender and Climate Change Adaption Strategies in Bangladesh

Within much contemporary development discourse there is a nuanced analysis which, by presenting women as victims of poverty and climate change fails to recognize that women have agency, and use it to ameliorate or combat the effects of climate change. Women, as primary agriculturalists, located in rural areas in Bangladesh are consistently faced with a range of challenges emanating from environmental issues and climate change events. Resourcefulness, strategic actions and the formulation of local solutions to agrarian problems is the signature of rural women farmers in their struggle to maintain family subsistence levels and resource local markets. This is recognized in the United Nations Framework Convention on Climate Change (UNFCC 2014) wherein Bangladeshi women are identified as undertaking a pivotal role in climate change mitigation by initiating different strategies to combat climate hazards.

A study on climate change and gender undertaken by the Ministry of Environment and Forestry in Bangladesh revealed that rural women are able to reduce food scarcity due to climate hazards in many different ways. Post disaster the vulnerability of entire communities becomes apparent:

Disaster damages livestock (i.e., cows, goats, and buffaloes), poultry (i.e., chickens, ducks), fisheries, trees, crops (i.e., rice, wheat, nuts, chilies, and lentils), seeds and animal fodder. During and after disasters, the lack of fodder for livestock and poultry results in reduced milk and meat production (Islam 2010, 2011: 154).

Thus, women engage in a wide range of activities to ameliorate the impact of flood, cyclone, and storms by preparing and storing dry food, fuel, fodder, seeds, and medicine while utilizing portable mud stoves when critical situations arise from climate events (Ministry of Environment and Forests nd:3; Rahman 2013: 80). Female traditional knowledge of food production and their understanding of the need to protect biodiversity lead to the development of creative adaptive strategies to challenge changing climate patterns (CCC 2009: 31). Most especially, women have adapted to climate change by transforming food production. For instance, during and after flooding when the cultivation of food crops such as rice is untenable women will produce other local vegetables which are flood tolerant to ensure food security for their family and community (Dankelman et al. 2008: 56). Similarly, women have also taken to planting multipurpose trees on the roadside to provide fruits and vegetables for the community and to increase or maintain their income by selling surplus produce (UNFCC 2014). Roadside plantation not only helps to reduce environmental degradation and maintain biodiversity but also helps build a strong community-based approach to sustainable development through supporting biodiversity.

Sometimes by changing the family diet, women are able ensure food security. In coastal areas, women preserve fish by drying it, which provides the protein needs for their family during times of food scarcity due to climate change events and this provides a further source of income for those who sell the surplus. Using their traditional knowledge and skills, women will also further develop 'homestead gardening' expanding the cultivation of herbs, fruits, and vegetables to every available space including rooftops. Thus, women are able to deal with periods of food scarcity for both their family and community (Islam 2010, 2011: 155–6). In the southern region of Bangladesh, women are able to adapt to flooding by establishing floating home gardens using local weeds called hyacinths. They prepare floating mats on which they spread soil, manure, and rotting hyacinths in this way they are able to cultivate different types of food crops through periods of flooding (Akhter et al. 2010: 21, UNDP 2010: 13). In this way, women are able to meet the subsistence needs of both family and community members as well as generating income from surplus produce (Dankelman et al. 2008: 56).

The fourth assessment report of the Intergovernmental Panel on Climate Change (IPCC) reported that 'women play a central role in the provision, management and safeguarding of water' (IPCC 2007: 83). To address fresh water scarcity, for example, Bangladeshi women increase the height of deep tube wells so that they will not be inundated by contaminated flood water (Dankelman et al. 2008: 9). In the southern region of Bangladesh, women build dams to preserve fresh water which also helps to reduce scarcity and increased salinity (UNFCC 2014). Both examples demonstrate that women also play a central role in water management strategies which helps to reduce the negative impacts of climate change events. Clearly, Bangladeshi women have an essential engagement in agriculture, fisheries, and livestock pursuits as well as a pivotal role in food production. In Bangladesh, more than 50% of the agricultural labor force is female but they are not well paid and as family labor they remain unpaid (FAO 2011). Although the United Nations Conference on Population and the Environment recognized the significance of women's role in natural resource management and identified them as the energy managers of the household. Yet women continue to be side-lined by policy makers, researchers, and development planners with respect to having input in the decision making process (Denton 2002: 12; Dankelman 2002: 25). In 2011 the Food and Agricultural Organization stated that if women had equal access and control over resources in the same way as men then almost 100 million people could be lifted out of poverty. Moreover, to fight against poverty and to ensure sustainable development, women's participation and empowerment should be guaranteed in environmental conservation and food production (Wanjiru 2012: 6).

When it is noted that Bangladeshi women play a vital role in food production through maintaining biodiversity and adaption strategies they are not treated equally in community politics where policies are formulated on the assumption that men's and women's needs are the same rather than intrinsically different and gender specific (PRB: 2012). In the process of policy formulation women's knowledge and experiences are disregarded in the absence of gender mainstreaming and this makes women more vulnerable (Demetriades and Esplen 2008: 26). For example, in Charlands, one of the flood prone areas of Bangladesh, women play a vital role in land management by using their traditional knowledge and practices of environmental management. However, their contributions are not yet recognized in policy development (Dankelman 2002: 25). Thus, women's experiences are currently ignored in policy formulation regarding climate change mitigation despite their success in engaging in gender-specific strategies and practices to ameliorate the more damaging aspects of climate events. Some of the examples already cited here clearly indicate that state and non-state institutions have much to learn and knowledge to gain from women's critical role and practice in combating the effects of climate change.

Concomitantly, in Bangladesh few community-based approaches deal with or recognize women regarding climate change issues and the sustainable use of natural resources. For example, community-based deep tube wells play a crucial role as the means by which women can gather safe drinking water. Even though the Department of Public Health and Engineering (DPHE) have taken some steps to increase the number of deep tube wells in rural areas it has not been sufficient to meet the needs of vulnerable communities and therefore, many women still have to travel considerable distances to collect safe drinking water (CCC 2009: 73). One of the community-based programs, the Comprehensive Disaster Management Program, underscores community development but while gender-specific issues are mentioned they are not given due consideration in the disaster action plan. As Islam points out.

Gender concerns are clearly addressed within the documentation of this new policy. But, often gender issues vanish from the discussion list at the community level. Even when they are discussed, some key issues are seldom mentioned while there are certain sets of women's concerns that are easily recognized and included in the disaster action plan (2010/11: 151–2).

Insufficient research has been undertaken that critically analyses gender sensitive issues related to climate change in Bangladesh. In addition, there is not yet sufficient research to consider the long-term effects of how any adaptation strategies impede sustainable development. For example, over the last 15 years salinity has increased in the southwestern regions of Bangladesh due to climate change and in that period shrimp farming has become a major industry in the fisheries sector increasing production by 20% annually. Shrimp cultivation is now defined as a serious threat to local ecosystems, livelihoods and agricultural productivity, as more land is dedicated to shrimp farming (Swapan and Gavin 2011: 46). Most people in those particular areas are dependent on natural resources such as honey, fuel wood, and fish which are diminishing due to the focus on shrimp cultivation (Swapan and Gavin 2011: 47). Women dedicate a large proportion of their time to harvesting the shrimp and the prolonged periods in saline water is having deleterious effects on women' reproductive health as the numbers of women suffering from gynecological problems arising from the collection of shrimp from saline water increases (The Asia Foundation 2012: 45) Despite this, there is no single policy that deals with salinity, natural resource management, and the impact of these changes on both women's health and livelihoods in coastal areas.

## Gender and Climate Related Policies in Bangladesh

Bangladesh has taken some steps to reduce the negative impacts of climate change by developing responses although gender equity is not assured which currently impedes sustainable development programs. The National Women's Development Policy was formulated in 2011, to support women farmers by providing the necessary resources such as, loans, fertilizers, seeds, and a farmers ID card to adapt to changing climate patterns (MoEF 2013: 39). However, the policy did not focus on gender-specific risks associated with climate change (The Asia Foundation 2012: 45). In Bangladesh, the National Agricultural Policy (NAP) was formulated in 2010, which recognizes women's vulnerability without any reference to their pivotal contribution to agricultural productivity and role in ensuring food security. (MoEF 2013:20). The NAP claims to empower women by increasing their participation in agricultural productivity, marketing strategies, and income generating opportunities. It also states that it will allocate a specific agricultural budget for women but does not include gender-specific extension services such as women-friendly technology transfers, control over their own income and women's needs within extension services (MoEF 2013: 40). Moreover, there is no proposal in the gender action plan to collaborate with nongovernment organizations working on women and climate change programs which would both enhance and inform the knowledges applied to the realization and the broad implementation of NAP (MoEF 2013: 42) (Fig. 8.2).

Basically, there are two major climate change policies and strategies existing in Bangladesh. One is the National Adaptation Program of Action (NAPA) and the other is the Bangladesh Climate Change Strategy and Action Plan (BCCSAP). Bangladesh is one of the countries which has established a National Adaptation Program of Action (NAPA) based on the UNFCC of 2005 (Ayers et al. 2014: 44; Dankelman et al. 2008: 59). NAPA has devised 15 projects in Bangladesh, to meet 'urgent and immediate' climate change mitigation needs yet women are not recognized as major stakeholders in any of these adaptation strategy initiatives (Ayers et al. 2014: 46; Dankelman et al. 2008: 59). UNFPA has been a foremost critic of these projects in which the absence of women as active contributors to both the formulation and implementation of climate change mitigated responses lacks foresight and impacts negatively on the efficacy of the projects (2009). Moreover, by disregarding women in one of the principal climate change policies of Bangladesh who are the main stakeholders in the process of climate change mitigation fails to address the disproportionate impact of climate change on women.

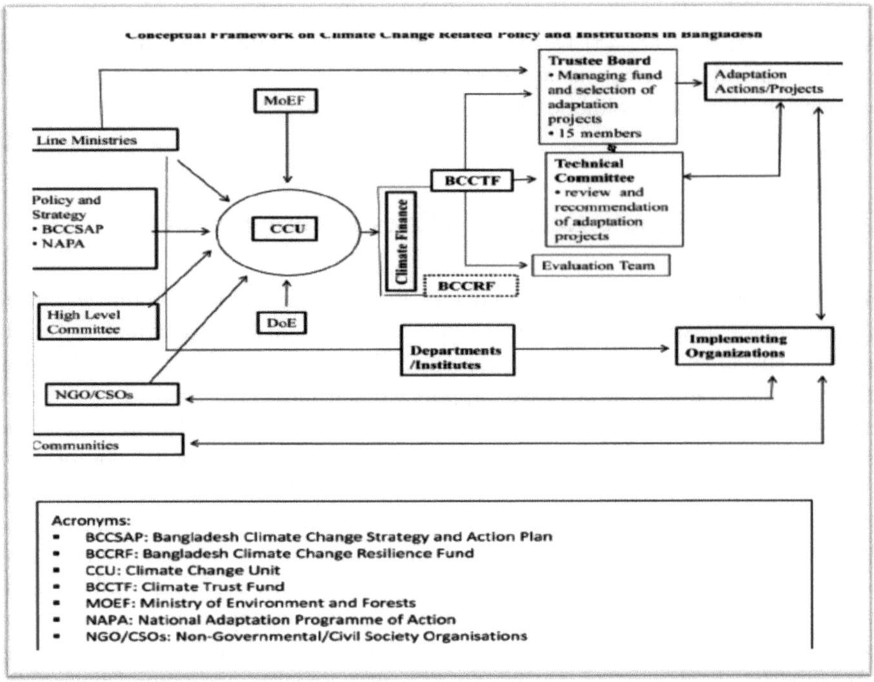


**Fig. 8.2** Conceptual framework on climate change-related policy and institutions in Bangladesh (reproduced from Ayers et al. 2014, p. 300)

Concomitantly, although NAPA recognizes women as the most vulnerable social group in the process of climate change there is, as yet, little statistical evidence revealing the extent of gender inequality with respect to education, health care, and property ownership which might guide the focus of any proposed gender-specific economic support from government to adjust to changing climate patterns. WEDO while commending Bangladesh for NAPA as the first policy document of its kind there are few if any commendations for the failure to integrate women:

Although it contains brief references to gender and women, the NAPA does not include women as stakeholders or actors in proposed adaptation actions. In developing the NAPA, 'indigenous women' were noted as consultants, but no details are provided as to the ratio of male to female participants, and no women's rights or gender-equality organizations or gender experts are mentioned as contributors. Women are repeatedly referred to as one of the most vulnerable groups, yet no statistical or factual evidence is provided on gender-differentiated income levels, occupations, or demographics. Particularly striking is the omission of women in discussing the public health situation of the country (i.e., no mention of gender-differentiated access to health care, differences in life expectancy or breakdown of government expenditures by gender). The NAPA presents women as victims of climate impacts; women are not considered active participants in adaptation to those impacts (Dankelman et al. 2008: 59).

The upshot is that NAPA fails to ensure gender inclusive policy formulation and gender mainstreaming in its climate change mitigation strategies. As WEDO quite rightly notes the proclivity for portraying women, as victims rather than protagonists in the challenge to climate change events and the development of climate change mitigation strategies limits the possibilities for action and broad-ranging transformative outcomes within the communities perennially affected by devastating climate events.

Bangladesh was also one of the first countries to develop a Climate Change Strategy and Action Plan (BCCSAP) in 2010 (Mallick and Rahman 2010: 35). Climate change issues are dealt with in BCCSAP through vulnerability and capability perspectives (Alston 2015: 185). Basically BCCSAP was established for the implementation of NAPA. Two trust funds, the Bangladesh Climate Change Trust Fund (BCCTF) and the Bangladesh Climate Change Resilience Fund (BCCRF) have been established to implement the BCCSAP (Ayers et al. 2014: 299). The BCCTF is funded by the government to the value of almost 100 million US dollars, whereas, the BCCRF is funded by nongovernment institutions including some development partners and the World Bank to the value of over 170 million US dollars (Ayers et al. 2014: 299; Alston 2015: 185). Under BCCSAP there are almost 39 activities which focus on food security, social protection, and health but of this number only one directly addresses women and climate change (The Asia Foundation 2012: 39). With so much funding available this constitutes an absence of gender justice and a failure to directly support those most responsible for food security, social protection, and health women.

The BCCTF appears to have secured their political interests rather than considering marginalized people's needs with respect to climate change (Rai et al. 2014: 535). Funding is not allocated on the basis of vulnerability. Two-thirds of the total budget goes to water 'infrastructure' whereas, the 'food security, social protection and health' sector receives only 8.05% of the total budget (Rai et al. 2014: 535). Moreover, the BCCRF is required to prioritize donor agencies interests rather than the needs of vulnerable people such as, women (Rai et al. 2014: 538). Thus, women's inclusion in the budget allocation is not ensured by either type of fund provision within BCCSAP.

A report by Asia Foundation in 2012 on climate change perception in Bangladesh argued that explicit guidelines for addressing the needs of women in the implementation of climate change initiatives are not provided in BCCSAP. Moreover, although initiatives that do address the impact of climate change on women and girls exist they fail to be gender inclusive. In the report respondents in flood zones confirmed that women were treated exclusively as beneficiaries of interventions rather than active members having input into initiatives and participation in the decision-making process. As Asia Foundation shows:

> When the respondents were asked about any intervention in the area to address issues of climate change with specific focus on women and girls, only 10% of the respondents mentioned the existence of such interventions. This was mentioned by 21% of the respondents from flood zones and only 1.5% from drought zones. Of the respondents who knew about any women and/or girl specific intervention….45% said that the women and girls participated only as beneficiaries, while 36% said women and girls participated only in the training sessions. (2012: 45)

A more inclusive approach to program development and implementation that encouraged full participation from those social groups it targeted would be considered an important move to reduce existing vulnerability and prepare for future risk as a result of changing climate (The Asia Foundation 2012: 46). Furthermore, a report on the BCCSAP by Von Ritter in 2012 was highly critical of its failure to implement its own 'commitment' to gender mainstreaming in its programs whereby of 44 BCCASP programs women were specifically mentioned in only four (Cited in MoEF 2013: 19–20). All the more alarming when BCCSAP mentions gender mainstreaming in every strategy and action plan, yet offers no specific guidelines for the implementation process to ensure gender mainstreaming occurs (MoEF 2013: 20).

However, to reduce the adverse effect of climate change on women and to ensure gender inclusive policy, women's participation in local and national politics is inevitable. Since 1991, the heads of the government of Bangladesh and the opposition party have been women (except from 2006–2008 when the government was run by an unelected caretaker government with the support of military), yet women still face many political obstacles in politics due to a highly conservative patriarchal social system. In Bangladesh, some steps are taken for ensuring women's participation in politics, for example: reserved seats for women are ensured both in local level and national level. In the national parliament of Bangladesh, 30 seats out of 330 were allocated for women until 2001 but in 2004, the reserved seats for women were increased to 45 out of 350 seats (Zaman 2012: 86). By 2014 women occupied 70 seats out of 350 (Women in National Parliaments 2016). The Inter-parliamentary Union found that in 2001 Bangladesh had only 2% of women members in the national parliament, whereas by 2016, women constituted 20% of the total parliamentary representatives and ranked 89 out of 189 countries (Women in National Parliaments 2016).[2] In the pressure for gender inclusivity at the highest policy-making levels the increase in the number of female political representatives at national level is both important and significant. Consequently, there is a reasonable expectation that the inclusion of women in decision making will be enhanced.

There is also important visible change at local level with the number of women becoming candidates for local government positions increasing (Khan and Ara 2006: 88). Women's participation in the local government is a reflection of their familiarity with problems at the community level (Huq 2016: 177, Rahman and Siddika 2011). According to the Administrative hierarchy of local government of

[2]Figures refer to the national elections of 2014.

Bangladesh the Union Parishad, the local council division, is the lowest tier of government (Begum 2007:5). Union Parishad consists of 12 sitting members, 3 seats are reserved for women candidates and the ratio of male and female members is about 3:1, where women candidates were directly elected into the reserved seats (Begum 2007: 262; Panday 2008, p-494). By selecting a direct election procedure, women members of the Union Parishad are able to be more vocal with respect to their experiences and about their rights (Nazneen and Tasneem 2010: 37). Union Parishad has a range of local administrative functions including public welfare, tax collection, maintenance of law and order and economic, social and community development activities (Khan and Ara 2006: 79, Nazneen and Tasneem 2010: 36). In this way women can perform an effective role in climate related policy formulations and its implementation. Consequently increasing women's political representation at local and national level offers the possibility of improved outcomes for women in both the policy making process and its implementation.

## Pathways to a Gender Inclusive Climate Change Mitigation Policy

Clearly, climate change is not gender neutral and in rural Bangladesh, women's responsibility for food security, fresh water supply, and the provision of energy for cooking and heating are hampered due to climate change, creating greater workloads for women and increased health hazards. The socioeconomic conditions, patriarchal social system, poverty, women's nutritional status, the gender division of labor and unequal power relations between men and women represent increased vulnerability for women due to climate change. Furthermore, although Bangladeshi women play a vital role in climate change mitigation strategies the effective participation of women in climate change policy and its implementation is not guaranteed. Climate-related policies, strategies and action plans do not pay enough attention to women's needs, now or looking to the future. In Bangladesh government initiated policies and strategies, such as NAPA and BCCSAP, are important to ameliorate the impact of climate change but gender inclusivity is not central to this. Furthermore, a lack of transparency in climate related budget allocation affects women disproportionately.

Aguilar argues that if gender equality is not ensured in climate-related negotiations then it impedes sustainable development (2009: 59). Gender mainstreaming climate change practices can build adaptive capacity and reduce vulnerability at both household and community level (Demetriades and Esplen 2008: 25; Denton 2002: 12). Gender-specific approaches need to focus on both socioeconomic vulnerability and adaptation strategies (Dankelman et al. 2008: 61). Clearly, in the absence of such strategies, women are using their traditional knowledge regarding resource management to initiate local disaster risk management and participation in community-based adaptation strategies in order to confront the challenge of climate change events. As we have seen here, women's adaptation and mitigation action could be an exemplar for the development of awareness building programs to be delivered by women from the community to the national level. Moreover, to facilitate long-term planning it is essential to study adaptive strategies taken by women in order to underpin their role in adjusting to changing climate patterns and the perennial climate change events (Dankelman et al. 2008: 54). In Bangladesh, the relationship between women and climate change is persistent and pervasive and this has repercussions not only locally but nationally as human security in general and food security in particular are increasingly threatened. As long as food production and household subsistence strategies remain in the hands of women then the pivotal focus of climate change mitigation strategies should be on them. In the quotidian of rural life women utilize and manage natural resources. As Rojas et al. (2012: 86–7) points out: 'Women often lead the way in adapting to climate change impacts, but they also play a key role in mitigating climate change by optimizing energy efficiency, using low-footprint energy sources and techniques, and influencing household's and community's consumption patterns' . Thus they have unique experiences and knowledge with respect to the ecosystem and can offer important insights into how we might better engage with the environment. Empowering women in developing countries, such as Bangladesh, and including them in national and international policy formulation, implementation, resource management, and disaster risk management processes as active and valuable members to the process rather than beneficiaries or trainees, increases the possibility of mitigating the negative impacts of climate change in Bangladesh and contributes to the possibility of sustainable development and human security now and in the future.

## References


Agarwal S, Ota T, Ahmed AU, Smith J, Vanaalst M (2003) Development and climate change in Bangladesh: focus on coastal flooding and the Sundarbans. OECOD, France, pp 1–70

Aguilar L (2009) Women and climate change: vulnerabilities and adaptive capacities. In: State of the world: Into a warming world. A World watch institute report on progress towards a sustainable society, pp 59–62

Akhter S, Alamgir M, Sohel MSI, Rana MP, Ahmed SJM, Chowdhury MSH (2010) The role of women in traditional farming systems as practiced in home gardens: a case study in Sylhet SadarUpazila, Bangladesh. Trop Conserv. Sci. 3(1):17–30

Alston M (2015) Women and climate change in Bangladesh, Routledge, pp 1–188

Amin MR, Zhang J, Yang M (2015) Effects of climate change on the yield and cropping area of major food crops: a case of Bangladesh. Sustainability 7:898–915

Ayers J, Huq S, Wright H, Faisal AM, Hussain ST (2014) Mainstreaming climate change mitigation into development in Bangladesh. Climate Dev 6(4):293–305

Begum A (2007) Local Governance in Bangladesh: towards a "Critical Mass" to combat discrimination against women with special reference to India. J Soc Sci 14(3): 261–272

Cannon T (2002) Gender and climate hazards in Bangladesh. Gend Dev 10(2):45–50

CCC (2009) Climate change, gender and vulnerable groups in Bangladesh, DoE, MoEF, Component 4b. CDMP, MoFDM, Dhaka, pp 1–82

Dankelman I (2002) Climate change: learning from gender analysis and women's experiences of organising for sustainable development. Gend Dev 10(2):21–29

Dankelman I, Alam K, Ahmed WB, Gueye YD, Fatema N, Kutin RM (2008) Gender, climate change and human security: lessons from Bangladesh, Ghana and Senegal, ELIAMEP:WEDO pp 1–71

Demetriades J, Esplen E (2008) The gender dimensions of poverty and climate change mitigation. IDS Bull 39(4):24–31

Denton F (2002) Climate change vulnerability, impacts and adaptation: why does gender matters? Gend Dev 10(2):10–20

FAO (Food and Agricultural Organization) (2011) The role of women in agriculture. ESA Working Paper No. 11-02, viewed 1 August 2015. www.fao.org/docrep/013/am307e/am307e00.pdf

Frisby W, Maguire P, Reid C (2009) The 'f' word has everything to do with it. Action Res 7(1): 13–29

Gaard G (2015) Ecoffeminism and climate change. In: Women Studies International Forum, vol 49, pp 20-33

Huq SMS (2016) Women's participation in local Government: a tool for sustainable development of Bangladesh. Eur J Bus Soc Sci 4(11):169–183

Huq S, Reid H, Konate M, Rahman A, Sokona Y, Crick F (2004) Mainstreaming adaptation to climate change in Least Developed Countries (LDCs). Clim Policy 4:25–43

IPCC (2007) Climate change 2007 Synthesis Report, viewed 1 Sept 2015. https://www.ipcc.ch/pdf/assessment-report/ar4/syr/ar4_syr_full_report.pdf

Islam MR (2010/11) Vulnerability and coping strategies of women in disaster: a case study on coastal areas of Bangladesh. Arts Fac J 4:147–169. (University of Dhaka)

Khan MMR, Ara F (2006) Women, participation and empowerment in local Government: Bangladesh union parishad perspective. Asian Aff 29(1):73–92

Lambrou Y, Piana G (2006) Gender: the missing component of the response to climate change. Food and Agriculture Organization of the United Nations (FAO)

Mallick D, Rahman A (2010) National policy and programs for adaptation to climate change in Bangladesh. CEEDIN 35:35–38

Mignaquy J (2014) Gender perspectives on climate change, pp 1–32, viewed 3 August 2015. https://www.sprc.unsw.edu.au/media/SPRCFile/1_Gender_perspectives_on_climate_change__Jazmin_Mignaquy.pdf

MoEF (Ministry of Environment and Forest) (2013) Bangladesh climate change and gender action plan. Government of the People's Republic of Bangladesh, pp 1–122, viewed 7 Sept 2015. https://cmsdata.iucn.org/.../iucn__bangladesh_climate_change___gender

Nazneen S, Tasneem S (2010) A silver lining: women in reserved seats in local Government in Bangladesh. IDS Bull 41(5): pp 35–42

Panday PK (2008) Representation without Participation: Quotas for Women in Bangladesh. Int Polit Sci Rev 29(4):489–512

PRB (Population Reference Bureau) (2012) Women more vulnerable to men than climate change, viewed 4 Sept 2015. http://www.prb.org/Publications/Articles/2012/women-vulnerable-climate-change.aspx

Rai N, Huq S, Huq MJ (2014) Climate resilient planning in Bangladesh: a review of progress and early experiences of moving from planning to implementation. Dev Pract 24(4):527–543

Rahman MM, Siddika A (2011) Women's participation in Local Government (Union Parishad), viewed 20 May 2014. http://www.engenderingdemocracy.net/articles/women%E2%80%99s-participation-local-government-from-bangladesh/

Rahman MS (2013) Climate change, disaster and gender vulnerability: a study on two divisions of Bangladesh. Am J Hum Ecol 2(2):72–82

Rasul M, Chowdhury AJU (2010) Equity and social justice in water resource management in Bangladesh. IIED, 1–20

Resurrección BP (2013) Persistent women and environment linkages in climate change and sustainable development agendas. Women's Stud Int Forum 40:33–43

Rojas AV et al. (2012) Guidelines on Renewable Energy Technologies for Women in Rural and Informal Urban Areas. SanJose, Costa Rica: IUCN and ENERGIA http://genderand environment.org/resource/guidelines-on-renewable-energy-technologies-for-women-in-rural-and-informal-urban-areas/
Shiva V (1995) Staying alive: women, ecology, and survival in India. Kali for Women, New Delhi
Shiva V (2009) Women and the gendered politics of food. Philos Top 37(2):17–32
Stern N (2006) What is the Economics of Climate Change? World Econ 7(2):1–10
Sandilands CM (2008) Eco/Feminism on the Edge. Int Fem J Polit 10(3):305–313
Sharmin Z, Islam MS (2013) Consequences of climate change and gender vulnerability: Bangladesh perspectives. SSRN 2200116:1–14
Swapan MSH, Gavin M (2011) A desert in the delta: Participatory assessment of changing livelihoods induced by commercial shrimp farming in Southwest Bangladesh. Ocean Coast Manag 54:45–54
The Asia Foundation (2012) A situation analysis of climate change mitigation initiatives in Bangladesh, pp 1–68, viewed 31 Aug 2015. https://asiafoundation.org/resources/pdfs/Situation AnalysisofCCinitiatives.pdf
UNDP (2010) Gender, climate change and community-based adaptation, pp. 1–69, viewed 15 Sept 2015. www.undp.org/…/climate-change/gender-climate-change-and-communit
UNFCC (United Nations Framework Convention on Climate Change) (2014) Climate change adaptation and disaster risk reduction in Bangladesh, viewed 2 Aug 2015. http://unfccc.int/secretariat/momentum_for_change/items/7841.php
UNDP (United Nations Development Programme) (2015) A new sustainable development agenda, viewed 29 Sept 2015http://www.undp.org/content/undp/en/home/mdgoverview.html
UNFPA (2009) Common ground: in Bangladesh, Ghana, Nepal, Senegal and Trinidad and Tobago, viewed 17 Sept 2015. http://www.unfpa.org/publications/common-ground-bangladesh-ghana-nepal-senegal-and-trinidad-and-tobago
Wanjiru L (2012) Gender, climate change and sustainable development. Fordham Environ Law Rev 23(2):1–6
Wisner B, Fordham M, Kelman I, Johnston BR, Simon D, Lavell A, Brauch HG, Spring UO, Wilches-Chaux G, Moench M, Weiner D (2007) Climate change and human security 1, 1–15
Women in National Parliaments (2016) World Classification [table], viewed 1st May 2016 http://www.ipu.org/wmn-e/classif.htm
WEDO (2008) Case study: gender human security and climate change in Bangladesh, viewed 19 Sept 2015. www.wedo.org/wp-content/uploads/bangladesh-case-study.pdf
WEDO (Women's Environment & Development Organization) (2015) Biodiversity, viewed 22 Aug 2015. http://www.wedo.org/category/themes/sustainable-development-themes/biodiversity
WEDO (Women's Environment & Development Organization) (2015) Sustainable development, viewed 22 Aug 2015. http://www.wedo.org/category/themes/sustainable-development-themes
Women Watch (2014) Women, gender equality and climate change, The UN internet gateway on gender equality and empowerment of women, viewed 29 March 2015. www.un.org/womenwatch
Zaman F (2012) Bangladeshi Women's Political Empowerment in Urban Local Governance. South Asia Res 32(2):81–101

## Author Biographies

**Dr. Yvonne Corcoran-Nantes** is widely known in the field of Gender Studies, regularly being interviewed on gender and political issues by the media in Australia and overseas. She has worked with women in such diverse locations as Central Asia, Mongolia, Indonesia, East Timor and Brazil in many research and development projects to improve the rights and status of women in their respective countries. At the present time she is undertaking research on women ex combatants in contemporary Vietnam. While Dr Corcoran-Nantes currently teaches in the areas of international studies and women's studies, her main research interests are: Gender and International Politics, Gender and International Development and Women and Armed Conflict. Dr Corcoran-Nantes is Head of Women's Studies and an Associate Professor in the School of Social and Policy Studies at Flinders University.

**Snigdha Roy** a civil servant in Bangladesh, works for the Department of Agricultural Extension under the Ministry of Agriculture. As an Australia Awards Scholarship scholar she completed her Master of Arts (Women's Studies) from Flinders University, South Australia in 2015 and she received her Bachelor of Science in Agriculture from Bangladesh Agricultural University, Bangladesh in 2005. She is an active member of BCS (Bangladesh Civil Service) Women's Network Forum and Krishibid (Agriculturist) Institution of Bangladesh (KIB). She is deeply involved in formulating gender strategy plan for the Department of Agricultural Extension. In her post graduate research, she focused on disproportionate impact of climate change on women which impedes sustainable development in Bangladesh. Her research interests include climate change, gender, agriculture, food security, gender inclusion policy and women's empowerment.

# Chapter 9
# Statistical Variation Versus Nation Cohesion—Contesting Truth Tests in Competing Socio-Ecological Realities

**Susan Goff**

**Abstract** The Aboriginal Sociocultural Survey into the value of environmental water to Aboriginal populations living in Australia's Murray–Darling Basin is an example of a research tool that both accurately analyses cultural values while also communicating the same values to decision-makers whose cultures—including research cultures—are very different from those whose values are being communicated. Using a participatory post-positivist methodology the survey produced results that demonstrated a direct link between environmental water and Aboriginal socioeconomic well-being in Aboriginal terms. It created results that strengthen Aboriginal voices in natural resource management and Aboriginal socioeconomic development. Some mainstream observers queried its validity on the grounds of bias as the results lacked statistical variation. The paper looks into the validity of the challenge. It raises the ethical risk of non-Aboriginal interventions un-self-critically creating community fragmentation and approaches to sampling that weaken the authority of Traditional Owners. Non-Aboriginal researchers at the Murray–Darling Basin Authority agreed that if asked about the value of water, other interest groups would be likely to produce a similarly unified result. In so doing and in the context of an emerging social contract regarding relationships between Aboriginal and non-Aboriginal populations in Australia, the collective Aboriginal understanding that "water is life" has been positioned in the Northern Basin Review's decision-making framework to reach a sustainable balance of water uses for the health and well-being of all life in the Basin.

> "This is not just about me, about my own struggle; it speaks of something much deeper among my people" Stan Grant, 2016, p.156.

S. Goff (✉)
Murray-Darling Basin Authority, Canberra, Australia
e-mail: susan.goff@bigpond.com; Susan.goff@mdba.gov.au



J. McIntyre-Mills et al. (eds.), *Balancing Individualism and Collectivism*,
Contemporary Systems Thinking, DOI 10.1007/978-3-319-58014-2_9

## The Story

> "We need a different kind of survey tool".[1] My heart leapt and sank at the same time—different—good, survey tool—bad. "Tell me more" I said, totally intrigued, knowing my client from many previous project contracts to be a person who had very big, and very clever ideas about how to work with water issues in partnerships with Aboriginal Nations (Nations) in the Murray-Darling Basin (the Basin) in Australia.
>
> "We know there have been problems with surveying Aboriginal populations so we don't want to repeat those issues." Why are we doing a survey then? - I thought. "That's good," I said. "We need a literature review done as a background to a tool that can quantify the value of environmental water to Aboriginal Nations in the north of the Basin."

Now my heart was beating fast. I am not a statistician—a word I can't even say without getting my teeth tangled in professional settings. I am a participatory action research facilitator rarely involving myself with surveys, and even less with numbers.

Where I have involved myself with numbers I have reasoned that numbers are value systems in disguise, each number reflecting a quantity of like values drawn from living experience and translated into a language that people who do not work with experiential knowledge can understand. Then they become inhabited by their own mysterious mathematical powers, which I am never sure have much to do with humanity or reality in general, and risk becoming a belief system imposed on an otherwise wild and wonderful world. Too often the value and means of counting (or valuing) it are assumed at a surface level, resulting in brittle knowledge carrying unquestioned assumptions with little relevance to peoples' actual life experience. Many times in conversation with Aboriginal colleagues they have reminded me that every number in a statistical analysis of Aboriginal conditions of life is a person's actual life experience.

Participatory approaches do not have to be qualitative though, and it was an interesting opportunity to consider how to design and implement a quantitative method in a participatory manner. Here was an opportunity to design something different, which could protect Aboriginal values for water while also communicating their values into western policy and administration systems in a way that had meaning to those systems too. Perhaps.

"Ok" I said, "when do you want it by and how many pages do I have?" "Six weeks and 20 max".

---

[1]Neil Ward, Director of Aboriginal Partnerships for the Murray-Darling Basin Authority, commissioned the project that is the case study for this chapter.

## The Literature

Twenty-one pages and five and a half weeks later, it was clear that conventional—or the usual Western—approaches to socioeconomic surveying do not serve Indigenous populations. This insight was making itself evident in published international and Australian literature (Dockery 2011; Gray 2011; Prout 2012).[2] "Conventional surveying", in the authors' terms, includes Australian Census data and surveys originating from administrative institutions such as National Health Surveys and the National Aboriginal and Torres Strait Islander Social Survey (NATSISS) (Gray 2011, p. 309). The following problems are areas of concern in the literature:

The tendency for socioeconomic surveys to be too broad in scope, fails to deliver information that is precise or relevant to the specifics of very different local Nation realities (Gray 2011).

Failing to include Traditional Owner participation in the design, implementation and use of results diminishes relevance and ownership of results (Dockery 2011; Gray 2011; Izurieta et al. 2011; Prout 2012; Osborne et al. 2013)

Failing to provide information about Aboriginal peoples' own subjective assessment of their circumstances and relationships in the survey design and interpretation limits reporting of people's socioeconomic conditions to non-indigenous interpretations (Dockery 2009, 2011)

However—there is also a difficulty of self-assessments producing high assessments of quality of life conditions, which when compared with non-indigenous populations would rate at a much lower level (Gray 2011)

Western socioeconomic measures of well-being, which make assumptions that solely economic wealth correlates with the notion of well-being, do not necessarily align with Aboriginal or Traditional Owner perspectives on well-being (Prout 2012)

The difficulty for longitudinal surveys to actually measure change in Aboriginal communities, a difficulty due to changes in data gathering practices in institutions, population movements, changes in demographic characteristics of Aboriginal populations, and the problems of identifying causality in complex, interrelated and dynamic social issues (Gray 2011)

Incongruence between the amount of surveying of Aboriginal socioeconomic inequity taking place, and the ability of governments to produce improved socioeconomic conditions with Aboriginal populations (Prout 2012).

The literature also makes useful comments about ways to redress these matters so fundamentally located in presumptions about a people in general, but carrying both the same and very different meanings and consequences for people surviving historical and contemporary colonization.

Prout (2012) makes the point that socioeconomic surveys should enable Aboriginal populations not to react to government process but to actively shape it,

---

[2]The information in this section of the paper discussing current literature is drawn from Goff (2015).

holding government accountable for its actions and strengthening partnerships in and with government (p. 322). Prout finds that the assumptions underpinning concepts of well-being fail to recognize the resilience factors associated with Aboriginal ways of life (Alderete 2004 cited in Prout 2012). The census data presumes western nuclear family aspirations regarding housing arrangements, for example, which for many Aboriginal populations do not apply (Morphy 2007, cited in Prout 2012). Conventional economic indicators assume that wealth accumulation and participation in western workforces is a positive objective, failing to recognize that participation in mining, for example, can contradict cultural obligations to Country for some. The values of subsistence and cultural economies, and the reality for many Aboriginal people that income is at best sporadic and derived from multiple sources including cash loans, gambling and sales of cultural products is largely missed (Taylor 2004, cited in Prout 2012).

This is not to say that western notions of housing and employment are unimportant to Aboriginal or Traditional Owner peoples; it is to say that socioeconomic surveys that fail to recognise the broader diversity of preferences related to cultural values or the ways cultural values are being expressed by a particular people in a particular place do not accurately reflect a specific Nation's ways of living in specific places, nor adequately serve non-assimilationist approaches to improving Aboriginal lives (Dockery 2009, 2011).

Gray (2011) proposes that social surveys for Aboriginal people in Australia should monitor progress with closing the gaps in outcomes rather than the gaps in characteristics between Aboriginal and non-indigenous populations. Surveying should provide information to enable the culturally distinctive lives Aboriginal Australians wish to lead, and empower Aboriginal communities to improve their own lives their ways (p. 317). They should not simply describe symptoms of problems over and over with nothing to say other than the symptoms keep on deteriorating.

The indicators for well-being that may be acceptable to Aboriginal populations are sometimes difficult to measure statistically: they may be more associated with webs of inter-dependent relationships than singular variables (Panelli and Tipa 2009). For example, we know that when there are healthy and seasonal flows in the waterways in the Basin are taking place, Nation populations are happier. There is more for people to do in small rural locations. Healthy fish, viable supplies of medicine plants and good populations of varieties of food sources enable customary economies to flourish and drive related physical, social, cultural and psychological health and well-being.

In reference to designing indicators for managing Indigenous Protected Areas, Aboriginal and non-indigenous scholars Izurieta et al. (2011) recommend never losing monitoring governance arrangements and the outcomes they produce. Where relevant, they recommend that surveys can combine global criteria and measures with a "capital assets" framework (Sayer et al. 2007). The Capitals Framework is made up of five elements: natural capital (biodiversity, ecosystems), human capital (health, education, skills), social capital (institutional arrangements), physical capital (infrastructure and built assets), and financial capital (money and funds)

(Izurieta et al. 2011, p. 8). This framework was developed for African rural communities and if used, needed to be adapted to fit Aboriginal experiences.

An important cautionary note is that measures may involve contradictions that are unique to Aboriginal peoples' experiences of living with colonial legacies. For example, strengthening participation in culture may be good for mental health at one level, but in some situations, may increase a person's exposure to racism, known to have significantly negative impacts on mental health (Gray 2011; Priest et al. (2011); Durey and Thompson 2012; AIHW 2015). It may involve "trespassing" privately owned properties to access ceremonial grounds or food sources, which while arguably a recognized right also puts people at risk of incarceration.

Rather than use global criteria to overcome some of the issues of lack of attention to local specificity, there would also be a case for using more local criteria as indicators: signifiers that local people could recognize in their everyday lives as being true to them and still related to a capital assets framework. Indeed, with the original Sayer et al. approach, the determination of the indicators was done participatively, by local community members.

Osborne et al. (2013) recommend that health and well-being outcomes must always keep sight of the relative degrees of cultural competency being exercised by governing bodies, participating for example, in reflexivity or ongoing questioning of assumptions in how they do what they do with regard to cultural safety. In my experience the term "cultural safety" is still unfamiliar in cross-cultural environmental management practices, requiring some explanation and judicious coaching with regard to correcting culturally unsafe practices.

These authors also recommend Aboriginal ownership and community support of initiatives, and include continuous address over time of the impacts of intergenerational traumas, racism, poverty, and homelessness. They refer to the social determinants of health that underpin either disease risk or well-being, now used globally in understanding health and well-being as a function of society rather than a purely biomedical problem (e.g. Williams 2003). Aboriginal social determinants of health are distinct from those used for western health, and need to be localized to some extent (Osborne et al. 2013). This aligns with our thinking about indicators, though understanding about the realities of intergenerational trauma like that of cultural safety are limited as is the patience and emotional strength of professionals from both Aboriginal and non-Aboriginal backgrounds to deal with the multiple faces such trauma presents.

Aboriginal psychologists Dudgeon and Walker (2015) propose a framework for determinants that measure health and well-being with the impacts of colonization in full view, not only with regard to Aboriginal experience but also in regard to the assumptions underpinning the disciplinary field that is producing the survey (in the authors' case psychology—in ours, water management). They identify Aboriginal social and historical determinants of health as: connection to spirit, spirituality and ancestors; connection to body; connection to mind and emotions; connection to family and kinship; connection to community; connection to culture; and connection to country (p. 279).

Life is understood in holistic terms with the health and well-being of individuals and communities linked to their "control over their physical environment, of dignity, of community self-esteem, and of justice (National Aboriginal Health Strategy Working Party, 1989, p. ix.) (Dudgeon and Walker 2015, p. 278).

The literature was clear: a very different survey tool was needed if we were to avoid repeating old mistakes. But knowledge tools serve existing thinking: the project was not just about a survey tool.

## The Knot of Social and Ecological Injustice

Rigby et al. (2011) identify six ways in which Aboriginal rural communities in locations associated with the Murray–Darling Basin (and elsewhere) are affected by prolonged drought associated with climate change. They include

Damaging traditional culture
Skewing the population profile in smaller centers
Exacerbating underlying grief and trauma
Undermining livelihoods and participation
Aggravating socioeconomic disadvantage; and
Creating a context for behavior that brings shame to culture.

In the context of Australia, it is clear that the legacies of colonialism on the country's fragile if not resilient ecologies, and their strength of intimacy with their Aboriginal peoples, continue to meet forms of resistance as captured in the list above, which remain distinctive from the non-Aboriginal populations residing in their lands. Droughts bring hardships to everyone whose livelihoods depend on a direct relationship with ecology. But where the aim of existence continues to be to limit or even harness nature's powers as a mark of civilisation, and where refusal to agree to this aim is seen as failure of a person or indeed a people, Aboriginal peoples' responses to seeing their Country destroyed remain as incomprehensible to the non-Aboriginal mind today as they were when Cook landed in Botany Bay. One can quote many informed and articulate authors who have now made clear the social and ecological impacts of colonization in Australia on Aboriginal peoples (Jackson 2008; Birckhead et al. 2011; Gubhaju et al. 2013). The Basin is a particular case, being the second line of frontier expansion by Europeans following initial landings. Less than 1% of the Basin is held in Aboriginal hands—and mostly purchased through the Indigenous Land Corporation (Murray-Darling Basin Authority 2012, p. 16) whereas the national figure is closer to 30%—this is even though the Basin supports 15% of the country's total Aboriginal population (Taylor and Biddle 2004, p. 4). It should be noted that population projections predicted a significant out migration of non-indigenous residents, increasing the Aboriginal population to over 4% by 2016 (Ibid, p.19).

Familiar public discourses that challenge the notion of injustice and can be found in many newspapers or dinner conversations include

Why do they consider themselves entitled?
Why don't they just get over it?
Would they really prefer to live without the wheel?
They bring it on themselves
The best of them make it and do well just like anyone else
Why aren't they grateful for what we do for them?
There are winners and losers in any population and we have charity and welfare to catch the losers.

These are individual responses we frequently hear reflective of a non-Aboriginal collectivism that does not see itself as racist and perhaps even less so, as dependent on a functioning ecosystem. Risking criticisms of essentialism, the Aboriginal people I have met see both the racism and the interdependence with a healthy river system. They shake their heads in disbelief at our stupidity and learned ability to dehumanize. The matter of injustice we are addressing is at an exhausted edge between both stances: Aboriginal people working their lives as best they can at the edges of systemic assimilation, and non-Aboriginal people slowly opening our eyes to ourselves and what we do. Together we are realizing our distinctive places in an emerging social contract between Aboriginal and non-Aboriginal peoples in Australia, arriving of its own accord as some critical mass of the tireless efforts of so many who have gone before us in both our camps. Nowhere is this emergent contract more obvious and potent than in the matter of Aboriginal rights and cultural obligations to water—or as Aboriginal people see it, life.

Thus it is that an elder in one of the communities we surveyed could say that if we recognized and realized Aboriginal interests in environmental watering, then the mental health issues of his people would be addressed. He, like his community, saw a direct link between environmental watering and culture, social organization, the viability of nature, daily life, health and well-being, and economic flourishing in terms that strengthened his people's culture. It is perhaps the most exciting, hopeful and creative work that we can do together.

## *Individual and Collective Ways of Knowing*

A methodological challenge that western approaches to research through surveys often face is that data is about individual points of view, collected from individual respondents. The assumption is that knowledge is created by seeking individual descriptors and judgements which researchers synthesize into generalized findings—either through mathematical and/or conceptual manipulations. Culturally, the problem for Aboriginal people with this approach is (at least) twofold.

Knowledge about Country is not always held as individual knowledge in Aboriginal communities that are connected to their cultures. The extent of attenuation of the way knowledge is held depends on local histories, surviving traditions and current conditions. Individualistic survey data does not adequately reflect collectively held knowledge or collectively experienced issues such as the impacts of the Stolen Generation or the witnessing of the deterioration of Country. Moreover the outputs of such survey data could reflect divisions in a community that may not have the internal capacity to deal with them.

Maintaining the power of interpretation of results in the hands of professional and mostly non-indigenous researchers, removes localized ownership of findings from Aboriginal people, and also enables the processes of synthesizing results to be inscrutable to Aboriginal peoples. They have to be taken on trust—or not taken at all. Moreover they mostly misrepresent the actual realities of the people as the researcher's assumptions and intentions inform both the direction of the inquiry and the interpretation of results. Such assumptions and intentions cannot possibly know a local reality that is as damaged and resilient, as isolated and neglected as regional Aboriginal communities. Additionally, finding local leadership that has the organizational and financial capacity to participate in developing such research, interpret and work with the outcomes with adequate local community support is equally difficult.

These two problems were clearly knotted into the research focus of the survey—environmental flows and how surveys account for their impacts on Aboriginal people's well-being. In their discussion about approaches to customary economies and landscape at an international Indigenous level of comparative analysis, Panelli and Tipa note

> Cattell et al. (2008) and Panelli and Tipa (2007) each highlight the diversity of definitions of well-being relevant for both individuals and collective groups. Taken most broadly (after WHO 1948), Cattell et al. emphasize well-being as a multi-dimensional manifestation of positive health which can take physical, mental and social forms (Pannelli and Tipa 2009, p. 457).

The dimensions of collective knowing are specific recognitions of cultural knowledge in the literature and include: collective efficacy, values, livelihoods, well-being, cultural identity and status (Panelli and Tipa 2007); collective rights, responsibilities and ownership (Williams et al. 2007); collective trauma, spirit and activities (King et al. 2009); collective burden (Redding and Wein 2009); collective experience and memory (Durey and Thompson 2012); collective effort (Osborne et al. 2013); collective understanding (King and Furgal 2014); collective responsibility (MacDonald et al. 2013); and collective esteem (Trzepacz et al. 2014).

This matter of collective knowing intrigued me. I was familiar with the practices of collaborative inquiry which enabled a group of people to co-construct frameworks, interpretations of various forms of data, and resulting practices to generate systemic change. However these experiences were based on relatively well-funded research and evaluation strategies, and not with Aboriginal communities trying to address the multiple and traumatizing impacts of consumptive uses of their lands without their law. There is no existing research into collective knowledge in this setting or indeed, how such ways of knowing can contribute to contemporary research methodologies appropriate to the redress of the social and ecological damage that continues. These communities are exposed to endless roundabouts of government programming, some of which includes research and evaluation, little of which is collaborative, even less of which is returned or kept within the community for its own use. Given this reality, what chance have Nations had to actually think about collective knowledge as it is for them? This survey was an opportunity to open the lid on this question without distracting the focus away from the primary matter of the value of environmental water to the respondents and their communities. To aim for a different way of knowing for all of us

> Collectivist, reciprocal ways of being and living in respectful and honest relations are of utmost importance as we have increasingly denounced our connectedness, spiritualities, and possibilities in the name of competition, efficiency, individualism, measurement, and profitability. (Gaile et al. 2008, p. 54)

It is not new science that knowledge cannot be generalized—that is, aggregated and applied across diversities of people and ecologies as if there were no differences between them:

> Practicing and mobilising Indigenous knowledge for various purposes is a matter of people being in place where ways of knowing and being in the world are continually performed through the relationship between people and their custodial estates or country (Ayre and Mackenzie 2013, p. 754)

Water planning, according to the Ayre and Mackenzie, must recognise specific localities of place, collective ownership, and/or use of Country and their interconnections with the indicators for well-being. Aboriginal and non-indigenous knowledge systems need to work together without privileging one kind over the other (p. 764). A survey inquiring into the value of environmental water that produces knowledge relevant to Aboriginal decision-makers in the Basin, as well as being culturally safe for non-indigenous decision-makers to use, needs to attend to these matters respectfully and competently. But who was I to embark on such a pathway, and who was in any way interested in what really was at stake in designing such an intervention?

> This is not just about me, about my own struggle; it speaks of something much deeper among my people (Grant 2016, p. 156).

Wiradjuri Man and journalist, Stan Grant's observation is as true for non-Aboriginal individuals and their "people" as it is for Aboriginal populations as we come to face each other in anything we do. When things get heated and the fury of history turns conversations into crises it is explained as "This isn't personal". Whoever we are, whatever researchers do in this situation is both about us and also our people. How we think about and use knowledge is foundational to our cultures. As a western researcher my holy grail is to create new knowledge; for Indigenist researchers (Rigney 2001) this idea dismisses the cultural authority of heritage. Additionally, my authority to create new knowledge I earn through education and employment. Such opportunities cannot escape their nesting in white privilege, and it takes a life of learning to find a way of being in such work that accepts this ongoing impact of colonization while attempting to intervene at its root level in the interests of socioecological justice.

## In Practice

In the north of the Murray–Darling Basin, we work in partnership with an Aboriginal Nation alliance: Northern Basin Aboriginal Nations (NBAN) which is made up of two Traditional Owners each (delegates) from the 24 Aboriginal Nations currently recognized in the north of the Basin. The Board of this group agreed that I would design the survey prototype, which they would review and test in the field. We would also seek independent academic review. I would make modifications from the feedback to produce a final version. I would then train two groups of Aboriginal survey collectors from two of the three communities we would survey. The survey collectors would use their networks to find people and sit with them to answer the survey. We had target figures of 15–20% of the Aboriginal population in each community to be surveyed to pass the test of representative findings as recognized in mainstream surveying traditions. We would then enter the handwritten results made by the survey collectors into a computerized survey program and produce results which would be reported back to NBAN's Board, as well as the MDBA. The draft report would also be given the benefit of independent academic review. We worked according to this agreement.

The survey itself incorporated some important departures from conventional survey design:

The indicators that were developed were drawn from an extensive database of Aboriginal narratives about the value of the Basin's waterways to them: they were immediately recognizable as local ways of living and each one was water-dependent to trace the effect of environmental water on the capital asset

They also related to Sayer et al's (2007) capital assets framework which was made up of five interrelated categories of a community's asset base: financial, human, social, natural, and physical (or infrastructure). We also added a sixth—"cultural capital"—knowing from previous research that the Sayer et al. framework inadequately reflected Aboriginal ways of living and surviving without this asset

We included questions that identified specific waterways that the participants would bear in mind when considering the value of environmental water to their capital assets so that the responses, expressed as Likert Scale options, would as much as possible be grounded in true local knowledge of a familiar waterway (river, lake, or billabong, for example)

We also included questions to enable a respondent to identify with one or more Nations so that the results could be coded to reflect the extent of Traditional Owner identification with the waterways being considered as an expression of cultural authority or otherwise to make the survey findings. This was a truth test specific to NBAN's requirements

We asked respondents to consider if the indicator question was true to their life experience to test the validity of the measure, and then use it to test its relevance to each of the capitals. In this way we demonstrated an immediate—or otherwise—relationship between environmental water and each of the six capital assets so that the overall valuing of environmental water also reflected this direct relationship

We asked if respondents' families shared their views to see if such issues were being discussed and were causing division or otherwise within local communities. If the latter, the survey would be a strong warning regarding how to proceed with identifying the outcomes of allocating environmental water in communities. This question was intended to enable the respondent to make a judgment about collective knowledge and provide a check for external interpretation of findings—amalgamated results ought to reflect the extent of cohesion or otherwise that the respondents measured

We asked if their local Aboriginal and non-Aboriginal community members whom they knew in their community respected the respondent's views. This question tested cultural safety with regard to a person's considerations regarding Aboriginal valuing of environmental water. If the results showed low respect this too would be important warning regarding greater exposure towards racism or internal conflict; if there were moderate or high degrees of respect however this would suggest a community had degrees of readiness to engage in and benefit from environmental watering. This question also enabled respondents to make a judgment call regarding collective thinking, this time in the very diverse and complex mixes of remote, small rural communities

Last, but not least, throughout the survey at three different places we asked the respondent to think critically about the survey questions themselves. This approach was intended to interrupt survey exhaustion and empower the respondent to determine the validity of the results it produced.

When the results were in, they were both unsurprising and deeply informative. Just over 200 responses were gathered reflecting between 15–20% of each community's Aboriginal populations. Gender balance and age representation was good enough. For the first time, a number could be put to the extent to which Aboriginal populations valued environmental water—collectively that number was 92%. The number was not about money, but what is referred to as "non-consumptive value". When broken down to the three individual communities, the number showed variation: from 84–98%. NBAN explained the variation by the ratio of Aboriginal populations in small communities—the stronger the balance tipped towards Aboriginal populations the higher the valuing of environmental water for capital assets. It was in those communities that Aboriginal cultural life was strongest (Murray-Darling Basin Authority 2016).

The next challenge was that while we had spoken in the language of western decision-makers to the decision-makers, now they did not know what to do with the message. The numbers so redolent with value were disturbing a system that had never had to account for what its numerical values meant as they rubbed up against their like kind and mostly limited to money or quantities of material items (like water). The decision-makers are now integrating the findings into a decision-making model to decide on the metrics of allocating water to environmental, social, and economic interests. The echoing meaning of that 92% figure in such company is not a dissonance that can be rushed over, pointing as it does to the deep heart of knowledge, power, cultural hubris, and transformation.

Ontologically, the methodology could be described as belonging to a participatory post positivist standpoint. "Post positivist" in that while producing generalisable results with which to inform instrumental planning and strategic decision-making, the survey asked participants to critically reflect on their answers from their individual, familial and their larger community points of view. "Participatory" because of its overall project development and delivery, including the participants' own critical review of the survey tool itself, enabling a validity judgment to be made by them with regard to the relationship between the instrument of inquiry and the knowledge it produced. The respondents judged the instrument to rate at 92% with regard to its overall ethical performance. (Murray-Darling Basin Authority 2016).

While these matters are of interest to decision-makers who need to have some faith in the survey tool, they are largely regarded as mystifying or over detailed for institutional decision-makers. Little interest was shown regarding the extent to which the respondents' views were shared by their families or respected in their communities. One independent academic review initially challenged the survey and its results for their lack of statistical variation. There were concerns that the results were "biased" which if so would constitute a serious threat to the whole endeavor. It is here, over and above the matters of participants commenting on their families' and communities' standpoints that the questions of individual as compared to collective knowledge came significantly into view. And they did so within the complexity of cross-cultural research methodology in the colonized settings of Aboriginal Australia.

## Contesting Truths in the Knot of Injustice

It is doubtful, within the limitations of a survey and the politic of Aboriginal interests in Australia that a survey about the importance of environmental water to peoples' well-being would have produced much variation from that which the survey did. All our qualitative data, our everyday interactions with Aboriginal community members and their representatives, and the little amount of research that has been done on the matter in the Basin, all point to the same reality that there is still a firm hold on the connection to Country and thus the value of water for the environment. There is also a firm hold on the importance of connection to Country as the basis of recognition of sovereignty, health and well-being and any future—socioeconomic and otherwise. Through the positivist methodology of an instrumental research tool, the survey generalized the result to a number that was created through analysis of the capital assets which in themselves are also collective measures, considering as they do, collective interests.

The Likert Scales allowed for individual variation, but as the survey required respondents to identify as Aboriginal, and sought their Nation identifiers as an indication of Traditional Ownership, the results were inevitably skewed if they are to be compared to a survey that would also include non-Aboriginal respondents. However, to carry out such an inquiry would undermine Traditional Owner authority. The problem was twofold

Once in the hands of our Aboriginal teams, a survey sampling strategy was not worked out other than that of the survey collectors using their community networks to get to survey participants;

While the survey collectors were trained and coached to maintain participants' focus on the questions, as they acted without external observation, it is not known the extent to which they maintained focus and were able to intervene if respondents grew tired or bored and simply produced unthought responses. This is a risk with all surveys.

On considering the risk of bias, the point was also made by MDBA researchers that had a different interest group been surveyed—say the irrigators or non-Aboriginal town dwellers on the rivers—they also would have shown little variation in their responses though their standpoint would likely have been very different with regard to environmental water. While western instrumental knowledge systems have a truth test that seeks variation: in the context of such displacement, intergenerational disfigurement of Aboriginal cultures in Australia including the wholesale destruction of their landscapes that hold the spirit and story of Country, what impact would a varied result have on a community? Stan Grant explains this state of affairs with striking insight

> Doctors talk about epigenetic inheritance: the experiences of parents and grandparents passed directly to their offspring. Some families carry genetic illness, passed down through the generations. My people inherit the loss of our country. It has proven as incurable and potentially lethal as any cancer (Grant 2016, p. 177).

Would it be helpful for people to know community fracturing existed about specific issues, and to broadcast this state of affairs to decision-makers about their sacred socioeconomic resources and futures? While every community has its differences, is it ethical for a mainstream survey instrument to throw light on such a situation when the results are returned to the community? The survey was responded to by Traditional Owners with cultural obligations to Country. In a manner of thinking, the tool was a means by which they could exercise their cultural authority as key players in the contests of water interests that to date have crippled the Basin's rivers, floodplains, and related ecologies. Is it not a wiser thing to produce a coherent result, reflective of community-wide characteristics where each community can be different to another, but not internally divided?

As a white researcher, I need to acknowledge my inheritance of white man's long history in Aboriginal communities of dividing to conquer his subjects, creating opportunity to insert his control tactics at the expense of his subjects reaching their own sense of coherence and direction. The evidence is overwhelming, but one indicative illustration is the description of Naming Days at Ramahyuck Mission Station in Gipplsand, Victoria (Carter 2010, p. 63) where the Wergaia peoples, were forced to adopt white names for themselves, the names often being those of the white settlers for whom they "worked". This practice is thought to have been commonplace mission management: the names are still in use.

In this historical reality, it is right that the survey collectors sought their own networks to begin participation in the project, being guided by Elders about how to engage in the activity, including how to work with other members of the community in answering the questions. Is this collusion or culturally strong engagement and responsibility?

When we reported back the results to NBAN, they were received with the nods that indicate familiarity with the truth: they sounded right, recognizable to their lives and the way in which they wished their lives to be known by outsiders. When we reported the results back to the policy makers, to some degree they were received as motherhood statements, although the need to rectify any sense of "bias" or "lack of statistical variation" was put to one side for the reasons already discussed in this paper. The recognition that other water users would have a similarly collective voice and position depending on the indicators used was a significant step towards realizing that water is indeed life, and that all people have a right to not only remind those with the responsibility of finding the "balance" between taking and giving back that this is so, but to also argue for water to be given back to nature for life to continue. Quietly, this recognition offered by individuals gathered around an executive mainstream policy table, was a manifestation of justice in the binding knot of that social contract for the well-being of everyone. As a white researcher redressing the ills of previous administrative surveying it was clear to me that there is a readiness in the cross-cultural managerial dialogues for change to be tried, and the results to be encouraged.

As non-Aboriginals we are a researching, policy making, socio-ecologically intervening people, using public moneys to look into a long future of human intervention to keep nature, such as river systems, functioning, as the longer future of rectifying human systems catches up. As the colleague who initiated this project has argued for years, Aboriginal understandings of life—be they traditional or those that reconstruct themselves uniquely in the messiness of today's world—do not wedge conservation in opposition to consumption, but reach into both. They bring about a relationship of obvious wisdom: human beings can and indeed must use our ecologies to live but not at the expense of those ecologies. In that restraint is wisdom, humility, and reverence.

> Our Law, we keeping our law.
>
> We telling you little bit Law, not much.
>
> Looking after one, looking after country.
>
> Looking after water, plain. (Neidjie and Lang 2015, p. 62)

Our collective project is to hold that understanding valid in the contemporary massifs of populations, pollutions, and failing systems of control. In that measure of restraint that the Murray–Darling Basin Authority is instructed to find, lays the metric for a new way of living with justice in our dealings with each other and the astounding Country of Australia. It may be that when cross-cultural participation takes place in the actual crafting of the metric, individual numbers can be poetic in the meanings that they hold, speaking for all of us, imbuing large systems with the Law and enabling eons of intergenerational collectivism to continue to influence our lives.

## References


Alderete E (2004) The importance of statistics on Indigenous Peoples for policy formulation at national and international levels. United Nations Workshop on data collection and disaggregation for Indigenous Peoples. PF11/2004/WS.1/4, New York

Australian Institute of Health and Welfare (2015) The health and welfare of Australia's Aboriginal and Torres Strait Islander peoples, 2015. Cat. No. IHW 147. AIHW: Canberra

Ayre M, Mackenzie J (2013) Unwritten, unsaid, just known: the role of Indigenous knowledge(s) in water planning in Australia. Local Environ Int J Justice Sustain 18(7):753–768

Birkhead J, Greiner R, Hemming S, Rigney D, Rigney M, Trevorrow G, Treverrow T (2011) Economic and cultural values of water to the Ngarrindjeri People of the Lower Lakes, Coorong and Murray Mouth. Report to the Commonwealth Scientific and Industrial Research Organisation (CSIRO). River Consulting, Townsville

Cattell V, Dines N, Gesler W, Curtis S (2008) Mingling, observing and lingering: everyday public spaces and their implications for wellbeing and social relations. Health and Place 14: 544-561

Carter P (2010) Ground truthing: explorations in a creative region. UWA Publishing, W.A

Dockery M (2009) Culture and wellbeing: the case of Indigenous Australians. CMLR Discussion Paper Series, 09/01. The Centre for Labour Market Research, Curtin Business School, Perth

Dockery M (2011) Do traditional culture and identity promote the wellbeing of Indigenous Australians? Evidence from the 2008 NATSISS. In: Hunter Boyd, Biddle Nicholas (eds) Survey analysis for Indigenous policy in Australia: social science perspectives. ANU Press, Canberra

Dudgeon P, Walker R (2015) Decolonising psychology: discourses, strategies and practices. J Soc Polit. Psychol 3(1):276–297

Durey A, Thompson S (2012) Reducing the health disparities of Indigenous Australians: Time to change focus. BMC Health Serv Res 12:151–162

Gaile S, Manuelito C, Manuelito KD (2008) Feminisms from unthought locations: Indigenous worldviews, marginalized feminisms and revisioning and anticolonial social science. In: Denzin N, Lincoln Y, Smith LT (eds) Handbook of critical and Indigenous methodologies. SAGE, Thousand Oaks, LA

Goff S (2015) The rationale for the design of a survey for identifying indicators to monitor the benefits or impacts of the Murray-Darling Basin Plan on Aboriginal peoples. (Unpublished) Cultureshift Pty Ltd, Bungendore, NSW Australia

Grant S (2016) Talking to my Country. Harper Collins, Sydney

Gray M (2011) A mile wide, inch deep: the future for Indigenous social surveys? In: Hunter Boyd, Biddle Nicholas (eds) Survey analysis for Indigenous policy in Australia: social science perspectives. ANU Press, Canberra

Gubhaju L, McNamarra BJ, Banks E, Joshy G, Raphael BM, Williamson A, Eades SJ (2013) The overall health and risk factor profile of Australian Aboriginal and Torres Strait Islander participants from the 45 and up study. BMC Public Health 13:661–675
Izurieta A, Sithole B, Stacey N, Hunter-Xenie H, Campbell B, Donohoe P, Brown J, Wilson L (2011) Developing indicators in monitoring and evaluating joint management effectiveness in protected areas in the Northern Territory, Australia. Ecol Soc 16(3):9–27
Jackson S (2008) Recognition of Indigenous interests in Australian water resource management, with particular reference to environmental flow assessment. Geogr Compass 2(3):874–898
King M, Smith A, Gracey M (2009) Indigenous health part 2: the underlying causes of the health gap. The Lancet 374(9793):76–85
King U, Furgal C (2014) Is hunting still healthy? Understanding the interrelationships between Indigenous participation in land-based practices and human-environmental health. Int J Environ Res Public Health 11:5751–5782
MacDonald JP, Ford JD, Willox AC, Ross NA (2013) A review of protective factors and causal mechanisms that enhance the mental health of Indigenous Circumpola youth. Int J Circumpola Health 72:21775
Morphy F (2007) Uncontained subjects: "population" and "household" in remote Aboriginal Australia. J Popul Res 24(2):165–184
Murray-Darling Basin Authority (2012) The Murray-Darling Basin regional and Basin plans: Indigenous water and land data (June 2010). Prepared by W.S. (Bill) Arthur on behalf of the Murray-Darling Basin Authority: Commonwealth of Australia
Murray-Darling Basin Authority (2016) The value of environmental water to Aboriginal Peoples in the north of the Basin. Prepared by Goff S on behalf of the Northern Basin Review, Commonwealth of Australia
Neidje B, Lang M (2015) Old man's story: The last thoughts of Kakadu Elder Bill Neidjie. Aboriginal Studies Press, AIATSIS, Canberra
Osborne K, Baum F, Brown L (2013) What works? a review of actions addressing the social and economic determinants of Indigenous health. Issue Paper no 7. The Closing the Gap Clearinghouse, Australian Institute of Health and Welfare, Australian Institute of Family Studies, Commonwealth of Australia
Panelli R, Tipa G (2007) Placing wellbeing: a Maori case study of cultural and environmental specificity. Ecohealth 4:445–460
Panelli R, Tipa G (2009) Beyond foodscapes: considering the geographies of Indigenous wellbeing. Health and Place 15: 455–465
Priest N, Paradies Y, Stewart P, Luke J (2011) Racism and health among urban Aboriginal young people. BMC Public Health 11:568–579
Prout S (2012) Indigenous wellbeing frameworks in Australia and the quest for quantification. Soc Indic Res 109:317–336
Redding LC, Wien F (2009) Health inequalities and social determinants of Aboriginal peoples' health. National Collaborating Centre for Aboriginal Health, BC
Rigby CW, Rosen A, Berry HL, Hart CR (2011) If the land is sick, we're sick: the impact of prolonged drought on the social and emotional well-being of Aboriginal communities in rural New South Wales. Aust J Rural Health 19:249–254
Rigby L-I (2001) A first perspective of Indigenous Australian participation in science: framing Indigeous research towards Indigenous Australian intellectual sovereignty. LIR, 1–13 Sept
Sayer JA, Campbell B, Petheram L, Aldrich M, Perez M, Endamana D, Dongmo Z-L, Defo L, Mariki S, Doggart N, Burgess N (2007) Assessing environment and development outcomes in conservation landscapes. Biodivers Conserv. doi:10.1007/s10531-006-9079-9
Taylor J (2004) Social indicators for Aboriginal governance: Insights from the Thamarrurr region, Northern Territory. CAEPR research monograph no 24. CAEPR, ANU, Canberra

Taylor J, Biddle N (2004) Indigenous people in the Murray-Darling Basin: a statistical profile. Discussion Paper no. 264/2004. Centre for Aboriginal Economic Policy Research, ANU, Canberra

Trzepacz D, Guerin B, Thomas J (2014) Indigenous Country as a context for mental and physical health: Yarning with the Nukunu community. Aust Community Psychol 26(2):38–53

Williams G (2003) The determinants of health: structure, context and agency. In: Sociology of Health and Illness, 25, Silver Anniversary Issue, pp 131–154

Williams N, Wearne G, Wearne J, Morrison J (2007) Guidelines and protocols for the conduct of research. North Australian Indigenous Land and Sea Management Alliance, Darwin

## Author Biography

**Dr. Susan Goff** is a specialist in cross-cultural participatory research. She has a Graduate Diploma in Social Ecology (UWS, 1993), a Masters in Applied Science, Social Ecology (UWS 1996) and a PhD in Cultural Research (UWS 2007). These qualifications are in participatory knowledge generation that addresses culturally informed social change. Building on 25 years applied scholarship as an Action Research methodologist, Susan is currently engaged as Senior Researcher with the Aboriginal Partnerships team at the Murray-Darling Basin Authority, Canberra, Australia.

# Chapter 10
# Balancing Individualism and Collectivism in an Australian Aboriginal Context

**Keith Miller**

**Abstract** Epochs have occurred throughout the history of the earth. A move from one epoch to the next can be considered to occur when there is a major transition which has a geological impact on all of life. A transition from the Holocene to the Anthropocene is now considered to have occurred in about the year 1800 with the Industrial Revolution. Dramatic changes to global conditions have occurred in a little over 200 years since then, with the consequent impact on the environment and all living things. Along with a geological change, a cultural transition has occurred. An individualistically oriented style of thinking has come to prominence with an objectification and exploitation of the environment. Yet, among Indigenous cultures, this change has not taken place. They retain a collectivist style of thinking and behavior and a deep respect for the land and all it contains. One of the values we can gain as participants in the Anthropocene is a recognition of these different types of knowledge existing in cohabitation, a comfortableness with an individualistic and relational identity occurring alongside each other. How much more valuable for this epoch to become an inclusive era when the collectivist perspectives from Indigenous cultures are appreciated alongside individualistic perspectives of developed nations?

## Introduction

In *A Short History of Nearly Everything* (2005), Bill Bryson provides a potted and entertaining version of the history of the universe as perceived by humanity. He refers to the mystery of the cosmos, the vastness and intricacy of the universe as we understand it. Bryson mentions the "dangerous planet" and the development of "life itself". He provides a quick glimpse of the wonders of this earth and its changing nature through geological time. And he touches briefly on what are now considered the different eras or epochs.

---

K. Miller (✉)
School of Social and Policy Studies, Flinders University, Adelaide, Australia
e-mail: keith.miller@flinders.edu.au



J. McIntyre-Mills et al. (eds.), *Balancing Individualism and Collectivism*,
Contemporary Systems Thinking, DOI 10.1007/978-3-319-58014-2_10

As indicated by Steffen et al. (2011a), consideration of the defining of a new geological epoch takes place over time. There has never been a neat transition between what are now considered different ages in the earth's development. It is only in retrospect that scientists can look back and determine the different eras of time. Eugene Stoermer began using the term "Anthropocene" in the 1980s following interaction around this theme with Paul Crutzen (Crutzen and Stoermer 2000). As recently as 1992, Revkin referred to "this new post-Holocene period" as the "Anthropocene" (Revkin 1992, p. 55; Steffen et al. 2011a, p. 843). The commencement of the Industrial Revolution around the late 1700s (or 1800, if one wants to be precise, for example Steffen et al. 2011b, p. 741) can now be considered the commencement of what one day may be determined officially as the Anthropocene, some form of geological step-on from the Holocene. In a similar way, the previous transformation from Pleistocene to Holocene is now placed at the end of the Ice Age, about 12,000 years ago—but it may not have been so clear cut to a resident at the time.

These transition periods mark a transformation so profound that all of life is affected. With the dramatic changes to global conditions which have occurred in a little over 200 years since 1800, and its impact on the environment and all living things, it makes sense to recognise that a change in epochs has occurred. The transition from Holocene to Anthropocene marks the commencement of the "human imprint on the global environment" (Romm 2015, p. 2) which "rivals some of the great forces of Nature in its impact on the functioning of the Earth's system" (Steffen et al. 2011a, p. 843).

## Cultural Transition

It is important to recognize that these scientific determinations occur in retrospect. As we look back, we realize that a major transformation has occurred. All of us have a history. There is a geological footprint left behind in the material universe which is noticeable. But there is also a cultural footprint left behind by our ancestors. When we consider an Indigenous group, such as the Australian Aboriginal communities, their cultural history continues in the same developmental way as the different geological time periods. Their dreaming is more than a historically delineated period of myth or legend. The dreaming continues into the present day. What then is their place in the Anthropocene and how have they transitioned from the Holocene? And what does this say about other cultural groups? Would it be true to say that a cultural characteristic of the Holocene period was a collectivist way of thinking among human population groups? What of the transition of these groups into the Anthropocene?

There is a generally held understanding that a more individualistically oriented style of thinking has developed among Western and economically developed cultures in what may now be considered the Anthropocene. It is considered that this style of thinking can be traced back to the Renaissance era in Europe and the development of a more rational perspective which culminated in the Industrial Revolution. Masses of people flooded into metropolitan areas, resulting in the enormous dislocation of family structures and the breakdown of collectivist traditions. In contrast to this, among economically developing cultures, a more community based and collectivist style of thinking is still evident. This appears to remain true among Indigenous cultures and this is certainly the case among Aboriginal Australians.

Among economically developed and individualistically oriented cultures, there is also a disconnection with the land. There is a sense that the land and its material provisions are there to be exploited and raped rather than to be nurtured. Only beginning in the 1960 and 1970s did there even commence an awareness in Western nations that the raping of the land and its contents could have detrimental impacts on the continuation of life (Nordhaus and Shellenberger 2007). Even today, many in the developed and individualistic nations continue with the same mindset that the land and its contents are for the benefit of humanity so the current environmental concern on the part of many is one of sustainability merely in order that the planet will remain in existence for the sake of humankind—rather than for the sake of the environment itself. This is so different to Indigenous ways of thinking.

Romm (2015, p. 1) discusses the Indigenous styles of collectively oriented knowing. Her understanding is that "selves are understood as 'selves-in-relation' to one another and to all living and non-living things, as part of the web of life" (2015, p. 1). This style of relational thinking and knowing has become foreign to the vast majority of members of individualistically oriented cultures. They have lost an understanding of what it means to be a citizen, with reciprocal rights and responsibilities to those with whom they share this planet (Rawls 1971, p. 214). Indigenous groups, on the other hand, have a strong awareness of community and the recognition of involvement with other participants in this community (Miller 2013).

For members of an individualistically oriented society, the new epoch of Anthropocene has indeed become a new era where the accoutrements of daily life are considered as chattels and there is a disjunction between the individual and the other often competing members of society around that person. Compare this with members of a collectively oriented culture who see themselves as at one with other human beings but more importantly with the essence of life.

## *Aboriginal Relationality*

As mentioned before, the dreaming for Aboriginal Australians is present-day. They interpret life in terms of the dreaming and this includes the relational context in which they live. So, when they continue to live in community, Aboriginal Australians understand their lives in terms of their particular world view. Their transition from the Holocene into the Anthropocene has not meant a severing from collectivism into individualism nor a break from relationality and connection into objectifying their surroundings. Never was this more evident to me than when participating in groups with Aboriginal community members who were discussing aspects of loss and grief.

## *Example: Seasons for Healing Project*

Let me first provide a brief description of the *Seasons for Healing* Project and then I will draw out the implications in terms of what I understand to be a collective understanding of community and culture.

The *Seasons for Healing* Program is an educational loss and grief program, "to support Aboriginal and Torres Strait Islander adults" (Grief 2012, p. 2). Two members of a community are selected and trained as "companions", their role being to facilitate a small group of between four and seven people within that community. These co-companions lead the group through a program of four sessions, each session lasting approximately two and a half hours. Through participating in a range of activities, companions enable group members to appreciate the impact of change, loss, and grief on their lives and to gain the language to better articulate experiences of change, loss, and grief. Over a period of four sessions, participants "acknowledge the reality of their loss", "explore the range of feelings and reactions that come with loss", "adjust to their changed circumstances" and "explore the choices that enable participants to let go and move forward" (Grief 2012, pp. 24, 46, 68, 88). Each session incorporates time for discussion, listening, contemplation, activities, and opportunities for writing and self-expression.

Through interaction, the construction of a group understanding of change, loss and grief was developed. The group setting meant that participants shared their views and, by this means, constructed a group understanding of how they could interpret and safely express their new understanding. "Focus groups are used to gather data which is generated in a discussion between focus group members with the help of the focus group facilitator" (Matthews and Ross 2010, p. 235). The very nature of focus group interaction is relational. This interaction between participants in the program enabled a richer understanding for each participant of the issues which were both discussed verbally and communicated in other ways. The group context allowed participants to provide their perspectives and ideas on change, loss and grief and these built upon what others were saying. The role of the researcher was that of "walking with" the participants on their journey of discovery rather than imposing an outside expert perspective as to how they should understand change, loss, and grief. Hence, realities of both participants and researchers were "socially and experientially based" (Guba and Lincoln 1994, p. 110).

Listening to participants describe their understanding and share their experiences was an enriching time for me as an outside researcher. Grief holds a significant place in the lives of Aboriginal people. Any form of loss a person experiences can lead to grief, and this was recognized by participants in the focus groups.

In Aboriginal culture, lots of people die. Sometimes we bury one next month, sometimes ten in a month. Grief takes over our whole lives (B, northern Adelaide).

There are other kinds of loss - identity, land, belongings, where we fit in with all this (M, southern Adelaide).

I came to recognize that grief is not an unfortunate addition to life, because it is often viewed from a western perspective. For Indigenous people, it is an intimate and enduring part of who they are. From my perspective as a non-Indigenous person, this spoke to me of relational identity, so different from the individualism of western cultures.

"Yarning" is an important part of Aboriginal culture. It refers to sharing one's life story or personal journey. It was recognized as a means of individuals sharing parts of who they were for the benefit of the group. So this was incorporated more fully into the program.

When you are sharing a story - you need more time to yarn. Obviously there are things people want to say… We are story tellers (P, northern Adelaide).

Several of the groups commented on the need to keep the group together throughout the program. This was linked to the recognition of the importance of yarning and the relational nature of engagement. A relational way of thinking and knowing leads to a "communication without words" within the groups which indicated an unspoken understanding and awareness of other participants. It was my observation that Indigenous focus groups operated at a different level to non-Indigenous groups and was a reflection of the collectivist way of thinking.

## Example: Dadirri

A distinct aspect of collectivist awareness among Aboriginal communities is *dadirri*. Atkinson refers to *dadirri* as "a deep contemplative process of listening to one another in reciprocal relationships" (2000, p. 1). She speaks of consciousness-raising

The relationship between the inner life—deeply ingrained cultural traditions—and the outer conditions of the social and natural environment that has helped shape the inner world, becomes explicit (2000, pp. 4–5).

And this is done in a community setting.

A big part of *dadirri* is listening…Listening invites responsibility to get the story – the information – right and to be in right relationship. However, listening over extended periods of time also brings the knowledge that the story changes over time as healing occurs when people experience being listened to and having their pain acknowledged (Atkinson 2000, p. 8).

According to Atkinson,

*Dadirri*… at its deepest level is the search for understanding and meaning. It is listening and learning with more than the ear, but also from the heart…*Dadirri* is the process of listening, reflecting, observing the feelings and actions, reflecting and learning, and in the

> cyclic process, re-listening at deeper and deeper levels of understanding and knowledge-building (2000, pp. 8–9).

The process of listening and learning with the ear but also from the heart is important to capture. And then reflecting and re-listening, using more than one's ear but also one's spirit. What appears to be important is to remove one's judgmental and negative or suspicious attitude. Rather, one should sit quietly, observe and listen, and then reflect. Ungunmerr speaks of *dadirri* as "inner deep listening and quiet, still awareness" (1995 p. 179). *Dadirri* is relational and collectivist. One needs to move from the individualistic to a relational perspective to be able to appreciate *dadirri*.

## Balancing Individual and Collective Interests

One of the concerns which comes with an anthropocentric way of thinking is the hegemonic promulgation of individualism. Just as humankind has had a profound "impact on the functioning of the Earth's system" (Steffen et al. 2011a, p. 843), so the powerful voices of western nations have had a profound impact on Earth's cultural understanding. Ritzer suggested that a McDonaldization has taken place, a homogenisation of cultural perspectives. As Ritzer commented, bureaucracy in the western world means that people have become "dehumanized", "rational systems are dehumanizing" (2004, pp. 27, 134). Indeed, Pieterse suggested that one view of cultural difference is that "global interconnectedness leads to increasing cultural convergence" (2009, p. 4). There has been a "worldwide homogenization of societies" (2009, p. 51) and a "homogenization of consumption patterns" (Ritzer 1993, p. 154). This has tended to bury Indigenous perspectives of collectivism under the weight of individualism and the objectification of the relationship between humankind and its surroundings. In contrast to this, McIntyre-Mills refers to "the benefits of balancing individual and collective interests through sociocultural solidarity and collective action for this generation of life and the next" (2014, p. 46). It would appear that, as a generalization, Indigenous societies have largely retained their relational cultures and their collectivist perspectives in the balance of life. It would also appear that, as a generalization, western societies have developed an objective culture and an individualistic perspective which diminishes the life chances of the current and future generations. On current balance, the individualistic perspective far outweighs the collectivist perspective. If we are indeed to develop a "social contract which protects citizens", and particularly "those who are voiceless", then "the balance between individual and collective concerns needs to be redressed" (McIntyre-Mills 2014, p. 48–49).

Within the way of thinking of Aboriginal Australians, there continues a strong connection to land and community, and this is even more the case as one travels from metropolitan areas to more rural and remote communities. An attitude pervades these communities that they share this land with all its inhabitants, including animals, rocks, plants and trees, water and earth. The land is regarded as precious and there is a spiritual connection to the land. So the collectivist attitude among Aboriginal Australians differs markedly from the attitude of non-Indigenous Australians.

Thus a balance needs to be struck between an individualistic perspective and a relational perspective. Cultural difference means that one needs to be reflexive in one's understanding and interpretation of the one culture as interpreted by another (Kovach 2009). What are "the methods of knowledge production" within cultures and how do "particular knowledges achieve legitimacy and authority at the expense of other knowledge" (Nakata 2007, p. 195)?

## *Converging Two Divergent Views*

During the Anthropocene, we have witnessed the development of a hegemonic western perspective imposed on a variety of cultures and a homogenisation of the individualistic and objective perspective brought by western imperialism. This has begun to change in recent decades. There has come a recognition of the validity of world views other than a rational western worldview. Indigenous authors are promoting the recognition of their worldviews, not to replace the western perspective but to sit alongside with equal credibility (Tuhiwai Smith 2012).

To redress the balance between individual and collective concerns, there needs to be a recognition of the equal value of these different world views. One type of knowledge is not wrong and the other right, they are not mutually exclusive. Nakata uses an interpretive approach to speak of the cultural interface, which recognizes that Indigenous knowledge is "positioned within a contested terrain of competing knowledge relations" (2007, p. 199). What is important to Aboriginal people is not categorizing the different approaches used to gain knowledge. What is important is the recognition of the value of different types of knowledge. According to Nakata (2010), Indigenous knowledge and western scientific knowledge are different but both are important. The end result of these types of knowledge is important and this is that the interests of Indigenous people are preserved. Someone with an individual approach to knowledge should not approach an Aboriginal community with a collectivist approach and disregard that community's worldview with the understanding that her/his approach to research cannot be challenged (Hollinsworth 2012). The days when this occurred should be long past. But it may still be the case that some westerners come with an assumed/unchallenged knowledge base and impose this on others, including people from Aboriginal communities. Researchers need to critically assess their own worldview before inflicting themselves on others. The focus has changed from "knowing about" to "learning from" the community with whom one deals (Hollinsworth 2012, p. 5).

Entering the research sphere from an Indigenous paradigm, Martin speaks positively of the relational nature of Indigenous research, and says, "I am often confounded by the levels of trust that have been established, and I attribute this to using a research framework of which relational ontology, epistemology and methodology are a necessary condition" (2003, p. 16). It is also important that a researcher recognizes participants as people who relate in a relational way. According to Gunaratnam, "Relationality (refers) to the epistemological break with thinking of 'race' and ethnicity as unitary, hermetically sealed, homogeneous categories of difference" (2003, p. 20). This means that individuals within a people group are not identical. What this also should mean is that respect is accorded to participants and that a researcher from outside the community genuinely hears what the community is saying and the different perspectives among community members. When a researcher works with a group of people from a different cultural or subcultural background, including an Indigenous background, the researcher should not assume knowledge and should be comfortable with difference.

Romm expresses an important truth: "The (re)credentializing of Indigenous knowledge systems and styles of knowing does not imply that all 'knowledge' (and ways of acting) as proffered within Indigenous systems has to be accepted" (2015, p. 10). As McIntyre-Mills comments, it is only as research "strives to foster and manage diverse forms of knowledge", that we can hope to "address complex socio-environmental challenges" (2014, p. 8).

Researchers have traditionally been powerful people of privilege and belonged to "a given race". They have belonged to the dominant rather than the subservient culture. As Tuhiwai Smith states: "(Researchers) have the power to distort, to overlook, to make invisible, to exaggerate and to draw conclusions based…on assumptions, hidden value judgements, and often downright misunderstandings" (2012, p. 178). So there is a responsibility on the part of researchers to recognize the power imbalance and consequently to accord a rightful sense of power to those being interviewed. As Tuhiwai Smith also says, these researchers are "in receipt of privileged information" from participants (2012, p. 178). Too often, researchers have "come into Indigenous communities to collect their stories to disappear without a word coming back or any benefit returning to the community" (Brydon-Miller et al. 2011, p. 390). In terms of Indigenous communities, Tuhiwai Smith makes a strong comment: "The way in which research is implicated in the worst excesses of colonialism remains a powerful remembered history for many of the world's colonized peoples" (1999, p. 1).

To redress the balance between an individualistic and a collectivist cultural perspective, between a western world view and an Indigenous world view, what is important is to recognize the validity of both. Indigenous groups are not seeking compensation but equal recognition to enable a convergence of these two divergent views. In this way, the Anthropocene will be characterized by a mutual respect and a harmonious recognition of the value of different world views so that the interests of Indigenous peoples are preserved.

## Conclusion

Epochs have occurred throughout the history of the earth. A move from one epoch to the next can be considered to occur when there is a major transition which has a geological impact on all of life. The transition from the Pleistocene to the Holocene is regarded as having taken place about 12,000 years ago. A transition from the Holocene to what has been designated the Anthropocene is now considered to have occurred with the commencement of the Industrial Revolution and is conveniently placed at the turn of the nineteenth-century BCE. Dramatic changes to global conditions have occurred in a little over 200 years since 1800, with the consequent impact on the environment and all living things.

Along with a geological change, a cultural transition has occurred, particularly among western or developed nations. An individualistically oriented style of thinking has come to prominence with an objectification and exploitation of the environment. Yet, among Indigenous cultures, such a profound change has not taken place. They retain a collectivist style of thinking and behavior and a deep respect for the land and all it contains.

One of the values we can gain as participants in the Anthropocene is a recognition of the different types of knowledge existing in cohabitation, a comfortableness with an individualistic and relational identity occurring alongside each other. During the early stages of the Anthropocene, there was a hegemonic bombardment from early industrializing nations which attempted to consume and even ridicule the cultural perspectives of developing nations. How much more valuable for this epoch to become an inclusive era when the collectivist perspectives from Indigenous cultures are appreciated alongside individualistic perspectives of developed nations?

## References

Atkinson J (2000) Privileging Indigenous research methodologies. Paper presented at Cultural Research Centre, James Cook University, Cairns, Queensland, Australia

Brydon-Miller M, Kral M, Maguire P, Noffke S, Sabhlok A (2011) Jazz and the Banyan Tree: roots and riffs on participatory action research. In: Denzin NK, Lincoln YS (eds) The Sage handbook of qualitative research, 4th edn. Sage Publications, Thousand Oaks, CA, pp 387–400

Bryson B (2005) A short history of nearly everything. Broadway Books, New York

Crutzen PJ, Stoermer EF (2000) The anthropocene. Glob Chang Newsl 41:17–18

Grief G (2012) Seasons for healing companion manual. Good Grief Ltd, North Sydney

Guba EG, Lincoln YS (1994) Competing paradigms in qualitative research. In: Denzin NK, Lincoln YS (eds) Handbook of qualitative research. Sage Publications, Thousand Oaks, CA, pp 105–117

Gunaratnam Y (2003) Researching race and ethnicity: methods, knowledge and power. Sage Publications, London

Hollinsworth D. (2012) Forget cultural competence; ask for an autobiography, Soc Work Educ Int J. Epub ahead of print 12 Dec 2012. doi:10.1080/02615479.2012.730513

Kovach M (2009) Indigenous methodologies: characteristics, conversations and contexts. University of Toronto Press, Toronto

Martin KL (2003) Ways of Knowing, Ways of Being and Ways of Doing: a theoretical framework and methods for Indigenous re-search and Indigenist research. In: McWilliam K, Stephenson P, Thompson G (eds) Voicing Dissent, New Talents 21C: Next Generation Australian Studies, vol 76, pp 203–214

Matthews B, Ross L (2010) Research methods: a practical guide for the social sciences. Pearson Education, Harlow

McIntyre-Mills J (2014) Systemic ethics and non-anthropocentric stewardship: implications for transdisciplinarity and cosmopolitan politics. Springer International Publishing, Switzerland

Miller K (2013) Respectful listening and reflective communication from the heart and with the spirit. Qualitative Social Work 13:828–841

Nakata M (2007) Disciplining the savages—Savaging the disciplines. Aboriginal Studies Press, Canberra

Nakata M (2010) The cultural interface of islander and scientific knowledge. Aust J Indig Educ 39 (Supplement):53–57

Nordhaus T, Shellenberger M (2007) Break through: from the death of environmentalism to the politics of possibility. Houghton Mifflin, Boston

Pieterse JN (2009) Globalization and culture: global melange, 2nd edn. Rowman and Littlefield Publishers, Plymouth

Rawls J (1971) A theory of justice. Belknap Press, Cambridge, Mass

Revkin A (1992) Global warming: understanding the forecast. Abbeville Press, New York

Ritzer G (1993) The McDonaldization of society: an Investigation into the changing character of contemporary social life. Pine Forge Press, Thousand Oaks, CA

Ritzer G (2004) The McDonaldization of society, revised new century edition. Pine Forge Press, Thousand Oaks, CA

Romm NRA (2015) Foregrounding critical systemic and Indigenous ways of collective knowing towards (Re)directing the anthropocene. In: Presented at 59th Annual Conference Proceedings of International Systems Sciences Symposium

Steffen W, Grinevald J, Crutzen P, McNeill J (2011a) The anthropocene: conceptual and historical perspectives. Philoso Trans R Soc A 369:842–867

Steffen W, Persson A, Deutsch L, Zalasiewicz J, Williams M, Richardson K et al (2011b) The anthropocene: from global change to planetary stewardship. Ambio 40:739–761

Tuhiwai Smith L (1999) Decolonizing methodologies: research and Indigenous peoples. Zed Books, London

Tuhiwai Smith L (2012) Decolonizing methodologies: research and Indigenous peoples, 2nd edn. Zed Books, London

Ungunmerr M-R (1995) Dadirri. In: Stockton E (ed) The aboriginal gift: spirituality for a nation. Millennium Books, Sydney, pp 179–184 Appendix One

## Author Biography

**Dr. Keith Miller** is a Senior Lecturer in the School of Social and Policy Studies, Flinders University. Miller's adult life has been involved in the human services' field in varying capacities. Immediately prior to commencing at Flinders University, he was employed in the health sector in South Australia in the planning and provision of mental health services. Miller commenced as a lecturer in mid-2006 and continues to be deeply committed to the wellbeing of citizens. Miller's areas of interest include mental health and suicide, Indigenous issues, rural men, and working with practitioners to develop their capacity for research. Governance, participation and democracy are issues of significance which are both challenging and rewarding in enabling capacity development and social inclusion amongst population groups which have not previously experienced social justice.

# Chapter 11
# A Systemic View of the Value of Environmental Conservation: The Case of Bono Takyiman, Ghana

**Kofi P. Quan-Baffour**

**Abstract** From a systemic point of view, it can be understood that the physical environment is important to every living being because it supports and protects life. The physical environment contains the ecosystem in which humans, animals and trees interact. All living organisms depend on the physical environment for survival which is why the environment must be protected. With the increase in world population, pollution, and climate change, environmental conservation has become the dominant concern of everyone: individuals, communities, nations, governments and international organisations. From time immemorial the indigenous people of Bono Takyiman in Ghana have depended on their cultural beliefs and practices to conserve the physical environment. Although the indigenous conservation approach of the Bono is based on traditions, the practice is in tandem with modern scientific methods of environmental protection. In fact the indigenous people seem to be ahead of others in environmental awareness and the general concerns of environmental degradation. Using the relevant literature and the author's lived experience of environmental conservation, this chapter discusses two major approaches which the indigenous people of Bono Takyiman employ in protection of the physical environment. In this chapter, I set out to share with others from so-called developed and developing countries alike this indigenous orientation to saving the environment. I discuss the worthiness of the approach and I consider lessons that can be learned from it for our way of addressing the Anthropocene.

## Introduction

The physical environment is important to every living being—humans, animals and plants alike—because it supports and protects life. The physical environment contains the ecosystem in which living and non-living things, e.g. humans, animals, plants, mountains, rivers, rock and soil interact. The mutual and natural relation-

K.P. Quan-Baffour (✉)
University of South Africa, Pretoria, South Africa
e-mail: quanbkp@unisa.ac.za

 
J. McIntyre-Mills et al. (eds.), *Balancing Individualism and Collectivism*,
Contemporary Systems Thinking, DOI 10.1007/978-3-319-58014-2_11

ships for survival among humans, animals and plants occur in and depend on the physical environment, the natural habitat. Burns (2011) is more than apt when he intimates that individuals are inseparable part of a system and that dysfunctions are the result of a mismatch between individual's skills, knowledge and environmental demands. As inseparable part of the environment all humans have a stake in it and therefore the responsibility to use the environment and its resources judiciously to ensure that its caring capacity is sustainable. The rapid increase in population in the various countries of the world does not only put too much pressure on the physical environment and causes degradation but also brings about drastic climate change with its concomitant calamities, i.e. ***the anthropocene***. The concept *anthropocene* is clearly described by the Cambridge Advanced Learners' Dictionary (2008) as the time from the eighteenth century until now when humans can see or experience the effect that people have had on the environment and climate. Crumley et al. (2015) affirm the need for the concept *Anthropocene* because it can focus the attention of scientists and the public on critical debates about how to shape the future of our planet. The human and environmental relationship has led to the rise of the *Anthropocene* through the examination of geographically and culturally diverse sites and case studies from a deep-time perspective. Roston (2016) affirms that human industry and population have created the *Anthropocene* or human epoch. Humans therefore must understand the complex issue regarding the relationship between themselves and their physical environment, how they arrived in the present environmental situation and how they can chart the way forward into a more sustainable future (Crumley et al. 2015). As Bonneuil (2013) appropriately suggests, the way we tell the 'story' influences the way the future will unfold.

The current human population at the beginning of this millennium stands at 6.055049 billion people (World population prospects 1998), a figure that has serious ramifications for the caring capacity, protection and conservation of the physical environment. With the increase in world population, pollution, and climate change, environmental protection and conservation must be the dominant concern of everyone, i.e. individual human beings, communities, nations, governments and the international community at large. The competition for space as the result of increased population and the concomitant human activities, some of which are harmful, degrade the physical environment and therefore negatively affect life. I agree with Gemeda and Sima (2015) and Roston (2016) that due to various anthropogenic activities, greenhouse gases are increasing in the atmosphere at an alarming rate which leads to extreme temperature, flooding, loss of soil fertility, low agricultural productions, biodiversity loss, risk of water stress and prevalence of various diseases. The activities of humans are leaving pervasive and persistent signature on earth. The shocking change on the physical environment as the result of population growth, industrial resource use, fossil-fuel burning and agriculture is detectable everywhere people live. The evidence of global change caused by human speaks for itself (Roston 2016). The ever-increasing activities of humans on the earth surface such as settlements, cities, farming, lumbering and mining have transformed the earth surface, exposing it to the scorching sun. The changing taking place on the earth has even been extended to the ocean bed through fishing activities and dumping of waste into the sea. In most parts of the so-called third world due to unmanaged human activities, the biodiversity has been under threat from environmental catastrophes ranging from erosion, wildfire, deforestation to hunting. In Ghana, in general, very large expanse of the land used to be deciduous forests but over population and its concomitant crop farming, lumbering and other human activities have caused pollution and environmental degradation. Bonneuil (2013) reports that Economists blame capitalism, globalisation and the struggle to control energy and markets for the destruction of the environment. Indeed human activities expand and accelerate as population increases and the correlation between the two has tremendous disastrous effects on the physical environment and the earth's caring capacity. A mix of circumstances together threatens the stability of the environment and there seems to be no particular identified approach to minimise the negative effect of anthropogenic effects on the environment and its concomitant climate change. Butler (2015) opens that we need many voices and different ways of doing things, if we are to appreciate that covering diagnoses cannot be expected to emerge from a single project. In seeking solutions to the *Anthropocene* one size cannot fit all. The main rationale for putting emphasis on the cultural role in landscape change, more particularly the protection of the environment therefore, is the need to draw more attention to multiple area specific divergencies and discontinuities. Therefore as humans struggle to address the *Anthropocen*e, it may be more prudent to approach it holistically from all fronts—politics, culture, religion, economic, science and technology domains—if we are to succeed in our efforts to make the environment sustainable. Crumley et al. (2015) attest that all these strands of history, politics, landscape, and culture as they relate to the physical world have been tied together. I agree with the authors' strong emphasis on the important role of an interdisciplinary approach to the interactions of humans and the environment on local and global scales, the critical importance of weaving the social science perspectives together with the natural sciences and the key role of viewing these issues within the framework of a deep-time perspective hence they use the unifying concept of the *Anthropcene in the Longue Duree*. We thrive by creating and modifying our environments as we continually inherit new and changed ecologies, constructed environments that are bequeathed to us successively by earlier generations (Crumley et al. 2015). Perhaps we need also to conduct some more research environmental and sociocultural resilience, adaptation and interplay of buffering feedbacks with systemic micro-evolution (Butler 2015).

In spite of the importance of the physical environment to life there are some individuals and organisations among the Bono ethnic group in Ghana and indeed all over the world who in pursuit of profit pay little or no attention to the conservation of the environment. In modern day Ghana lumbermen do not plant trees after felling the matured ones. In the same way, people engaged in surface mining cut deep into the earth, heap soil and neglect their responsibility to level the place and thus causing environmental destruction. As a matter of fact, human or anthropogenic activities increase atmospheric carbon dioxide which in part causes global warming, drought, floods and other environmental disasters. Touching on the urgent need to protect the environment Brown (2015) challenged COP21 which met in France in

December 2015 to seriously negotiate for the drastic reduction in the level of greenhouse gas emissions because as he puts it ‘time is not on our side’.

Tapping from my experiences as someone who grew up in a culturally bound rural area and the relevant literature on environmental conservation, I set out to discuss in this chapter the major approaches which the indigenous people of Bono Takyiman employ overtly or covertly in protecting the physical environment. The chapter shares with readers from both the developed and developing countries the indigenous orientation to saving the environment. The worthiness of the indigenous approach is discussed for other developing countries to consider and learn lessons from it as humans seek ways of addressing the *Anthropocene*.

## Theoretical Framework

This chapter is grounded in the General Systems Evolutionary theory of which Laszlo et al. (1993) are the chief proponents. The theory is an action oriented systems approach that has emerged from evolutionary processes in nature and society. Laszlo and Krippner (1998) describe a system as a complex of interacting components together with the relationships among them that permit identification of a boundary-maintaining entity or process. What is acknowledged here is that the physical environment is a system of integration of various subsystems. In such a system humans make meaning of their physical environment and how its structures function in relation to each other. Von Bertalanffy (1968) attests that the interaction and relationship can lead to a much-needed integration in scientific education.

The concept, evolution, may be described as a gradual development usually from a simple to a more complex form. Evolution is therefore a process of development, change or transformation to a better or improved desirable state or situation. The general system evolutionary theory posits that human societies evolve or change through convergence to progressively higher organisational levels (Laszlo et al. 1993). As a group of people live in an area they naturally interact with the natural environment. The line that separates the aspects of a system from those of its environment tends to blur as the unit of observation moves from natural and designed physical systems to human and conceptual social systems (Laszlo and Krippers 1998). The theory postulates that the description of evolutionary trajectory of dynamic systems as irreversible, periodically chaotic and strongly nonlinear fits certain features of the historical development of human societies. This description of the evolutionary processes has some elements which increase the exploitation by the systems for free energy in their environment. Marten (2001) puts it succinctly that the people make sense of the complexity that surrounds them by carrying hundreds of images and ‘stories’ in their minds about themselves, their society and their bio-environment—how each of these is structured, how each functions and the interrelationships among them. In reality what evolves in peoples’ environment constitutes their world view—i.e. the perception of themselves and the world around them.

The evolutionary systems theory is based on the integration of the relevant principles of the general systems theory which provides people with the knowledge and understanding of how human beings and their societies act in a constantly changing environment. The theory provides a conceptual foundation for theories and principles of evolutionary consciousness, evolutionary action and evolutionary ethics. It suggests that human destiny can be placed in human hands since it advocates a move toward conscious evolution strategies by which to guide the sustainable development of human communities (Laszlo et al. 1993).

## Some Indigenous Environmental Conservation Practices Among the Bono

The Bono are very religious and based on their traditional religious beliefs they have accumulated wisdom to organise their values, perceptions and behaviour. The belief in and practice of African religion provides them with a sense of awe and respect for things larger than themselves, e.g. God, earth, and the universe. As Marten (2001) intimates, religious beliefs are a source of meaning; they tell us what is important in our lives. Religion also offers moral codes or guidelines about rights and wrong and rules of behaviour. The importance of moral codes for human–environment interaction is the balance they promote not only between the desires of each individual and the needs of others but also between short-term desires and long-term considerations such as a concern for future generations (Marten 2001). Religion is a very powerful tool for ethnic groups to organise their perception of the world. The Bono for example are integral part of their physical environment and believe that negative actions against the environment come with divine sanctions; hence they treat nature with care and respect in order to avoid punishment from the spirits of the land.

The Bono are traditional and predominantly peasant farmers who till the land grow and produce foodstuffs for their livelihoods. The religious beliefs and the values of the Bono and their cultural practices permeate all their activities. These include the activities in the physical environment, i.e. the interaction of the people with the physical environment for hunting, farming, lumbering, human settlement, harvesting of medicinal plants or firewood. The Bono rural women interact with the physical environment on daily basis through fetching of water, firewood, medicine, cultivating the land and harvesting food stuff. As Mosala-Wright and Mokotong (2000) observe, they therefore know it better because they collect fire wood for fuel which is essential for survival. In view of their frequent interaction with the physical environment the rural women, particularly, play active role in the context of socio-economic development and environmental conservation. As people who till the land for livelihood or engage in peasant farming activities, animal rearing, hunting and harvesting plants for traditional healing of all sorts of ailments they interact with the physical environment—land, soil and forest farming—on regular basis. The constant interaction with the environment does not only overtly or covertly make the Bono close to nature but also enables them to use their cultural and religious beliefs to protect and conserve the physical environment on which they survive. Butler (2015) intimates that whereas cultural intervention had played no more than an incidental role in pleistocene change, human action now began to redefine, interupt or even control the shaping of landforms, as well as the efficacy and direction of survival processes. Therefore holocene investigation of a landscape with a history of cultural intervention is likely to require adjusted methods, priorities, temporal scales and assumptions. The Bono traditional farmers have designed their agricultural ecosystems to take advantage of natural processes instead of fighting nature. For example, the Bono peasant farmers practice shifting cultivation where they allow a piece of land to fallow for one to two (1–2) years before cultivating it again. In this way the fertility of the soil is assured because of vegetation growth. Marten (2001) aptly affirms that the component species in an ecosystem survive because they fit together in a way that enables the whole system to provide the necessary resources for each species.

Among the Bono, the chiefs use cultural practices, traditional and religious beliefs to stop people from encroaching on some specific pieces of land as a strategy to preserve and conserve the environment. From time immemorial the Bono indigenes have depended on cultural beliefs and practices to conserve the physical environment but the practice seems to be under threat because of the ever increasing population and scientific knowledge. Although their indigenous conservation approach is based on traditions, the practice is in tandem with the objectives of modern scientific methods of environmental protection. The Bono indigenes thus rely on their traditional cultural beliefs to practice their socio-economic activities be it animal rearing or crop production. Hindle et al. (2005) attest that around the world indigenous peoples are struggling to build their 'nations' and improve the socio-economic circumstances of their people. The Bono is a conservative ethnic group which preserves and strengthens traditional values and apply these to socio-economic activities for their livelihoods. The Bono people engage in subsistence agriculture where they use traditional methods to produce food to feed their families. They blend their agricultural practices and cultural heritage to secure the physical environment. The indigenous protection of the environment from degradation increases vegetation and rainfall for food production in the area. Although very much an illiterate group the Bono indigenes seem to be ahead of others in environmental awareness and the general concerns of environmental degradation.

There are many ways the Bono practically do things to protect the environment. One practice relates to their veneration of the River God *Tano.* The River *Tano* (small god) takes its source from the hills around the traditional capital- *Takyiman.* Tano is a state god venerated from time immemorial because of the belief that the spirit of the river protects the Bono state. Geographically the river surrounds the traditional Bono state capital—Takyiman—and one cannot enter the town by road (except from the eastern part) without crossing the river. Tradition has it that in the ancient times the River Tano protected the Bono Kingdom from being conquered by warring kings and nations. The Bono believe that their defeat by the Asante

Empire around the seventieth to eighteenth century (Adu Boahen 1975) was because they were taken unaware from the East when a trusted align, the Nkoranza chief, betrayed them.

The belief in River Tono's spiritual protection makes the Bono venerate the god —*Tano*—to the extent that they do not to kill or eat any fish from the river. Being an important protector the Bono do not like to expose the River to the scorching sun. The belief is that the spirit of the river thrives under shades of trees hence the people's livelihood activities should not encroach on the River basin. This resulted in the growth of forest along the Tano basin within the Bono-Takyiman area. The traditional belief is that any one who offends the River Tano would receive divine punishment from the god, *Tano*. In line with this the Bono do not farm or cut trees at least 500 m to the river Tano. Obedience to this divine or religious decree means that human activities, particularly farming, must not encroach on the river basin. The belief is that those who disobey this would receive punishment on him/herself and family. The fear of spiritual punishment and the respect for the river god has saved the river from drying up because there is a forest around its basin throughout the Bono Takyiman area, which is the catchment area for the River. Most of the rivers which are not protected shrink or dry up but the Tano River is always full of water. Although in recent years Christianity and Western education seem to erode the strong fear and veneration for the Tano god the typical Bono does not take the Tano god for granted despite the profession of the Christian faith. When many deaths occurred in a particular village where some farmers encroached on the Tano basin to grow tomatoes the incident was regarded by many as the direct punishment from the god and the chiefs had to pacify Tano through the slaughtering of a number of sheep.

Tradition has it that the ancient Bono kings were buried in a special place called *amanfo mu* (place of the ancestors). The Bono burry their kings and chiefs with gold ornaments and people are banned from entering the place of the ancestors. Since time immemorial the area was demarcated and preserved as a sacred place for the spirit of the ancestors. The area which is about 3 hectares of land has become a thick forest where no one is allowed to enter or farm. The traditional authority has imposed very strict rules to govern the community forest and any trespassing is regarded as disturbing the tranquillity of the spirits of the ancestors and culprits could be punished. Through the cultural practice of keeping the spirits of the departed kings in the forest the physical environment comprising a land of about 3 hectares have been conserved and protected for centuries. Only the king accompanied by the traditional priest (okomfo) is allowed to enter the place during the annual yam festival to pour libation to the spirits of the ancestors on behalf of the chiefs and the people of the Bono-Takyiman state. The worthiness of these indigenous approaches assist the Bono to seek ways of systematically addressing the *Anthropocene*.

## Lessons for Developing Countries

The physical environment constitutes an ecosystem where humans, animals, plants and non-living things live, interact and depend on each other. In the contemporary modern world, dramatic increase in population has led to competition for space and utilization of the physical environment. Human activities-farming, housing and infrastructure construction—wittingly and unwittingly destroy the environment. For example overgrazing, cultivation, lumbering and pollution can obviously lead to environmental degradation and destruction. These human social and economic activities covertly or overtly cause environmental destruction and very often most humans do not make efforts to protect the land when they engage in various socio-economic activities. In recent times the natural upheavals such as flooding, extreme drought, epidemic and their concomitant loss of life are blamed on environmental neglect and destruction by humans.

Individual countries, international organisations and world leaders meet in various forums to discuss and map out ways of protecting the environment in which life thrives. The recent COP21 in France is a case in point. There can be no specific way of protecting or conserving the environment. It can be scientific or cultural because in my view the end justifies the means. Whatever peaceful approach that can secure the judicious and sustainable use of the environment should be encouraged. It is against this stance that developing countries with limited resources should take a lesson from the Bono ethnic group of Ghana and use their culture, traditions, indigenous beliefs and practices to protect the physical environment. Putting culture at the fore of human activities and interaction with the environment as portrayed in this chapter could be the best way of utilizing the physical environment–land, forest and other organisms-sustainably. The worthiness of the Bono cultural approach to environmental protection and conservation offers lessons to other developing communities, ethnic groups and nations who are grappling with the problems of environmental degradation.

## Conclusion

Culture encompasses the beliefs, traditions, values and the way a particular ethnic or group of people lead their lives. It permeates all the activities and practices of the people such as language, speech, farming, rituals, ceremonies and what the people wear or eat. The value of culture and traditions of the Bono permeate their interaction and engagement with the physical environment. The discussion has so far outlined and analysed the worthiness of the Bono indigenous approaches to systematically seek ways of addressing the *Anthropocene*. The chapter therefore concludes that since culture is the way of life of people any effort or intervention to conserve and protect the physical environment in the developing countries that does not take cognisance of or focus on the cultural practices of the people would be a futile exercise. To be able to systematically address the problem of environmental degradation sustainably developing communities should look back to their culture for guidance. Developing countries need to use every possible approach to stem the tide of environmental destruction because as Brown (2015) asserts the impact of climate change has no respect for borders. Its consequences span generations and it is distinctively irreversible because once a threshold is breached there is no going back.

## References


Adu Boahen A (1975) Ghana: evolutionary and change in the nineteenth and twentieth centuries. Longman Group Ltd, London

Bonneuil C (2013) A time for stories: anthropocene, the earth, history and Us. Paper presented at Thinking the Anthropocene. In: An international conference of science. Paris 14–15 Nov

Burns M (2011) School psychology research: combining ecological theory and prevention science. Sch Psychol Rev 4(1):132–139

Brown M (2015) Either we change or The climate does. Business leaders need to tackle Global Warming with courage. The Sunday Times News Paper June 14 Issue, pp 12

Butler K (2015) Anthropoce as an evolving paradigm. The Holocene 25(10):1539–1549

Combridge Advanced Learners' English Dictionary 2008 edition

Crumley C, Laparidou S, Ramsey M, Rosen AM (2015) A view from the past to the future: concluding remarks on the Anthropocene in the Longue Duree. The Holocene 25:1721–1723

Gemeda DO, Sima AD (2015) The impacts of climate change on african continent and the way forward. J Ecol Nat Environ 7(10): 256–262

Hindle K, Anderson RB, Gibson RJ, Kayseas K (2005) Relating practice to theory in Indigenous entrepreneurship portfolio. Am Indian Q 29(1&2):1–23

Marten GG (2001) Human ecology: basic concepts for sustainable development. Earthscan Publishers Ltd, London

Laszlo A, Krippner S (1998) Systems theories: their origins, foundations and development. In: Jordan JS (ed) Systems theories and a poriori aspects of perception. Elsevier Science, Amsterdam, pp 44–74

Laszlo E, Masulli I, Artigiani R, Csanyi V (1993) The evolution of cognitive maps: new paradigms for the twenty–first century. Gordon & Breach Publishers Ltd, Amsterdam

Mosala-Wright F, Mokotong E (2000) The role of women in sustainable development. In: McKay VI (ed) Development studies for adult basic education practitioners. UNISA Press

Roston R (2016) Greet the '*Anthropocene*': Five Signs Earth's Geology has entered a Man-made Epoch. Sunday Times Newspaper, January 10 Issue, pp 7

Von Bertalanffy L (1968) General systems theory: essays on its foundation and development. George Braziller Publishers Ltd, New York

World Population Prospects (1998) Revision, vol 1. United Nations Department of Economic and Social Affairs

## Author Biography

**Dr. Kofi Quan-Baffour** is a chair and professor in the Department of Adult Basic Education and Youth Development, College of Education, at the University of South Africa. His doctoral degree focused on the evaluation of adult learning (basic education) programs. His research interests include an exploration of ways in which the African philosophy of Ubuntu can be practiced in Open and Distance Learning contexts. He has published more than 35 articles in accredited journals as well as contributed chapters to a number of books. He has also co-authored a book on Indigenous Knowledge Systems (2011), titled*Sankofaism: ReinventingAfrica from its Indigenous Philosophies*(Lambert Academic Publications Ltd). He is the author of over 40 published papers in international peer reviewed journals, 3 book chapters and 1 book. Prof Quan-Baffour believes in development through education and has strong passion for African indigenous knowledge system. He holds a D.Ed. and three masters' degrees in adult/distance education, development studies and education management.

# Chapter 12
# Customary Land Tenure and Ecological Sustainability in Acholi Land, Northern Uganda

**Francis A. Akena**

**Abstract** The Acholi customary land tenure system is one of the most ecologically sustainable forms of land resource utilization in the arable and semi-arid parts of northern Uganda. It is regulated by a complex regime of rights under the authority of traditional leaders, and informed by traditional ecological knowledge of the environment, to manage the diversity of land utilization by farmers and pastoralist communities. The traditional leaders would exclude pastoralists from open access to land resources to give farmers the opportunity to grow crops and after the harvest period, pastoralists can access the vast open rangeland for grazing cattle. This suggests that regulating land access to different occupational groups can prevent land conflict, ensure maximum land resource utilization and sustain the natural cycle of ecological health for communal benefit through prevention of land conflicts. The chapter uses this example to argue that Hardin's agenda regarding the universal "tragedy of the commons" is flawed without solid substantive basis.

## Introduction

Land tenure in its simplest and general understanding, refers to a system in which land is owned (the right to possess land) either by an individual or the collective in any particular society/community. According to the philosophy of most African societies as well as other indigenous communities of the world, land ownership right was vested in the hands of the collective. Bromley and Cernea (1989) state that access or usage of the collective land by an individual or group was regulated by a set of laws. Such laws or bylaws were either developed by contemporary members of that community or passed down generationally from their forefathers. Hanslungule and Jegede (2014) state that lands that are collectively owned within the context of African society includes hunting grounds, forests and grasslands, mixed savannah, fruits gathering areas, water bodies such as rivers, swamps and

F.A. Akena (✉)
University of South Africa, Pretoria, South Africa
e-mail: adyanga1@gmail.com

 
J. McIntyre-Mills et al. (eds.), *Balancing Individualism and Collectivism*,
Contemporary Systems Thinking, DOI 10.1007/978-3-319-58014-2_12

lakes, coastal areas, fishing grounds, mountainous and hilly lands among others. Throughout Ugandan traditional society, the land tenure system was defined, regulated, and managed for social, economic, and political wellbeing of the collective. Different land laws existed from one community to another but with the central pillar anchored on collective ownership. Among the Acholi of northern Uganda for example, land was hereditary according to customary arrangement. What this means is that rights/ownership over land is passed on from one generation to another. In patriarchal systems the male is traditionally the head of the family and according to this system, land rights are vested in his authority. Even under the freehold[1] or leasehold[2] system, a man with more than one wife distributes land to his wives based on the number of children each wife had. Upon death, custody and authority over land is passed on to his eldest son. In the event that all the children are still young or the family has no male child, land is given to the widow (Amone and Lakwo 2014). Therefore, most land ownership in Acholi traditional society was based on a freehold arrangement at the family level. Above the family level, communally owned land includes hunting grounds, swamp areas, fishing grounds, grazing lands among others. These were collectively owned under the authority of a chief and council of elders.

With the advent of colonialism in Uganda, the British protectorate administration declared most land in the territory Crown under the *Crown Lands Ordinance of 1903* (Mugambwa 2007). With the new declaration however, the customary land tenure system was recognized but with some limits. Under the new Ordinance, indigenous Ugandans had the right to take possession of any land outside Buganda Kingdom and urban areas in accordance with their customary land tenure laws (Mugambwa 2007). This is because the colonial authority had earmarked Buganda kingdom land under the *mialo* land and free hold or leasehold system. The term *mailo* system is used in Uganda to describe a land tenure arrangement that came into effect after the kingdom of Buganda signed an agreement with the British Protectorate administration in 1900, commonly known as the 1900 Buganda Agreement. The basic unit of the *mailo* system is a square mile. It is a derivation of *mailo* and equivalent to 640 acres. The *mailo* system offers freehold of land to the natives by the colonial government in exchange for political alliance under the 1900 Buganda Agreement. Under this arrangement, the holder of land title has absolute ownership of that land. However, when such land is required by government for national development programs, ownership is revoked after compensation is paid in full (West 1964). Accordingly, Okuku (1998) states that three sets of land laws existed in colonial Uganda during that period:

[1]Freehold refers to a tenure system with outright ownership of land and any property on it for an unlimited period of time. This means the land belongs to the individual owner.

[2]Leasehold refers to property ownership for a fixed term but not the land on which the property stands. Possession of the property is subject to the payment of an annual ground rent. Usually, ownership of the property reverts back to the freeholder at the expiration of the lease agreement.

> First, in 1903, the Crown Lands Ordinance as a forerunner of public land policies was enacted to provide for the manner in which Crown Land holding emerged. This included freehold and leasehold. Second, in 1908 a Land Law was passed by the Buganda parliament, *Lukiiko*, defining the system of tenure introduced by the 1900 Agreement. It also saw the implementation of rent requirements by tenants and peasants, *bitsiilii* and *envujjo*. The tenants and peasants had to pay dues every year, busulu and a tithe, envujjo in respect of each acre. The 1920s saw agitation by the Bataaka who were dissatisfied with the Agreement, which had not specified the precise rights peasants had. At the same time, there were increased demands by landlords for cash and commodity rents as peasants expanded the cultivation of cash crops (p. 9).

The policy of *busulu* and *envujjo* reduced agricultural production because landlords took advantage of it to impose high rents (*envujjo* and *busulu*) on tenants and peasants.[3] This forced the colonial regime to enact the 1928 *envujjo* and *busulu* laws that put a ceiling on the amount landlords could levy while guaranteeing the tenant complete and hereditary security of tenure so long as he/she continued cultivating the land (Okuku 1998). With the exception of Buganda region therefore, the onslaught of colonization left the status of the customary land tenure system in most parts of Uganda unaltered. The colonial authority must have recognized that the focus of African customary land tenure system was on community self-reliance and sustainability. This self-sustainability arrangement under the customary land tenure system was succinctly applauded by the East African Royal Commission (EARC) report of 1955, thus:

> The absence of a modern system of distribution, the long distances separating populated or cultivable areas, and the inability of the subsistence economy to produce regular marketable surpluses by specialized production without risking a food shortage at critical periods of the year, have led the indigenous populations to seek security by clinging to their customary methods of production. These customary methods of production are based essentially upon the notion of self-sufficiency in food supplies (p.65).

Much as the EARC report recognized the significance of the traditional land tenure system, it placed no commercial value on the practice because under such arrangement, land could not be treated as commodity to be leased, sold, or mortgaged due to collective ownership. Therefore, the EARC report became the catalyst for reform of customary land tenure in British colonies in East Africa (Mugambwa 2007) through championing land privatization as will be seen in the proceeding discussions. In a closely similar argument that relates to factors which influenced the British colonial policy toward customary land tenure system, Sjaatad and Bromley (1997) posit that the lack of legal title of land reduces its value as collateral thereby increasing the price of capital and reducing the value of investments. They further state that high transaction cost in establishing ownership would reduce the value of investment and the absence of a land market means that farmers cannot convert fixed land assets into capital for business ventures. This, they argued reduces value of investment to farmers. However, this argument is flawed and

[3]A Tenant refers to a person who occupies land or property rented from a landlord. Peasant refers to a poor smallholder and or agricultural laborer mainly subsistence farmers.

negates the fact that in most African societies, mutual trust was the guiding principle for social, economic, and political interaction. Among the Acholi for instance, one could borrow other moveable properties such as cattle, goats or tools and verbally place land, immovable property as a collateral security. This would be done in the presence of prominent and respectable members of the community such as elders or council of chiefs. In the event that the borrower failed to meet his/her obligation, the collateral (immovable property) would be taken without hesitation. The execution of this process required no paper work since all transactions were done orally. Affirming this position, Hansungule and Jegede (2014) convincingly state that another important aspect of indigenous people's land tenure is the oral proof of title because the vast majority of laws and customs relating to land in Africa are passed orally from one generation to another.

In terms of population settlement, Sjaatad and Bromley (1997) erroneously argued within the context of traditional Africa that dispersed population, lack of material possessions coupled with an emphasis on self-reliance was a major barrier to the fruitful exchange of commodities. To counter this position, Atkinson (1989) offered a well-organized and condensed description of the Acholi people of northern Uganda which leaves a dent on the temptation of making broad generalization by academics. Atkinson states that by as far back as 1860 according to written [and of course oral traditions], the Acholi people were organized into small polities or chiefdoms which were made up of numerous fenced villages numbering about 80 by the middle of the nineteen century. The chiefdoms ranged in size from about 500–20,000 people with most in the 2000–4000 range. Certainly, these chiefdoms traded among themselves and also beyond their borders with other ethnic groups.

After the publication of the EARC report in 1975, debates about the traditional land tenure system in Uganda took a different and more aggressive channel both by native Ugandans and the colonial authorities who were determined to change the system. On their part as noted in the report, the EARC believed that the best way for African to gain value for land and contribute to economic development was to have the communal land ownership changed to individual. It also felt that land transfer process should be made much easier through individualization of ownership (EARC report 1975). Many native Africans resisted the EARC report and the efforts by colonial authorities to change customary land tenure system arguing that it was a ploy to confiscate and give their land to foreign investors. Others argued that this was a strategy by the colonial administration to purge African of their traditional ways of life, social and economic organization (Mugambwa 2007). In Uganda, protests by the natives however, did not alter the determination of the colonial administration to change the customary land tenure system. The administration proceeded with individualization of land in the heavily populated districts of Kigezi, Ankole and Bugisu. With land in these districts registered under individual ownership, customary law was automatically expunged in these areas.

The attainment of political independence by Uganda in 1962 stagnated the policy of land individualization originally engineered by the colonial regime. African authority that took over power discontinued the policy citing ignorance and misunderstanding of the African land tenure system by the colonial administration.

Besides, African intellectuals also criticized the EARC report as being biased towards the very foundation of African cultures. To them, the customary land tenure system was the foundational social fabric that held African society in peace and harmony (Mugambwa 2007). The step taken by the immediate postcolonial government therefore reasserted the position and popularity of customary land tenure system. The 1962 *Public Land Act* [Cap 21] prohibited the government to grant in freehold or leasehold any land that was lawfully occupied under customary tenure arrangement without the consent of the occupants (Republic of Uganda 1962). The implication here is that land in Uganda with the exception of those in the three districts of Kigezi, Ankole, and Bugisu which had before independence been individualized by the colonial authority, enjoyed the protective laws of customary land tenure system and could not be easily sold or transferred. It also means that applicants for land occupied under customary arrangement had to provide the government with sufficient "evidence that the occupants have consented to the application and the compensation payable to them" (Mugambwa, p. 43). Failure to comply would result in automatic denial of the application. Interestingly, the same Act also granted customary occupants of land the right to apply for individual ownership. Essentially, the Act simply emboldened the already existing arrangement under the customary law of collective ownership and decision making regarding transfer.

By making the provision and flexibility for land holders under the customary tenure arrangement to privatize land ownership, the government by then opened up space for farmers and business entrepreneurs to acquire titles for using their land as security for loans. This however, was left to the discretion of land owners. Arguably, very few applied and even those who applied were only interested in demarcating and protecting their boundaries from encroachment (Mugambwa 2007) since most did not complete the paper work. It can therefore convincingly be argued that most Africans believed the sacred values of land for community development, adaptation, and ecological sustainability to be vested in the collective ownership. Besides, to most indigenous people, customary land tenure systems have the flexibility and adaptation to address the increasing pressure on land due to population explosion as seen earlier with the Acholi example, where land distribution depended on the number of people in a family.

Central to the debate concerning the Uganda land tenure system is that for 8 years from 1971, there were massive political upheavals due to the reign of terror brought by the government of Dictator Idi Amin. Amin overthrew an elected government of Milton Obote through a military coup. Amin's regime nearly brought all government programs to stagnation with massive disruption in the country infrastructures. His government dealt a huge blow to land tenure and the leasehold system in Uganda. In 1975, Amin is reported to have enacted a *Land Reform Decree* that focused on changing the existing land tenure as well as the free/leasehold systems. According to Mugambwa (2007), all land in Uganda under Amin's decree was declared to be public land. Land owned in freehold was converted to leases held from the government subject to development conditions. The *Public Land Act* of 1969 was repealed and the protection that customary land tenure system previously enjoyed under this act was stripped. Under the Decree, the government was authorized to lease any land occupied by customary tenants to any person without the tenants' consent. The government of the day also put in place several unrealistic stringent and punitive laws for the enforcement of the Decree. But interestingly, the military government land reform policy only remained on paper and the customary land tenure system continued to evolve organically throughout Idi Amin's reign of terror.

After the fall of the military regime in 1979, the new government that assumed power in the 1980s prioritized land reform. Mugambwa (2007) further states that several studies were conducted by the post Amin government supported by the World Bank to ascertain the best land reform policy for agricultural promotion. And for more than 10 years, the controversy over the best land policy dragged on. Again the traditional land tenure system was left to evolve organically. It was not until 1995 when a new constitution, *The 1995 Constitution* eventually took clear a position on land. *The 1995 Constitution* vested land ownership in the hands of Ugandan citizens through the recognition of four types of land tenure systems: "freehold; *mailo* (quasi freehold); leasehold; and customary land tenure system" (Mugambwa p. 52). *The 1995 Constitution* also encourages all Ugandan citizens owning land under the customary tenure arrangement to acquire a certificate of customary ownership for their land. Once acquired, the certificate became the official and permanent evidence of land ownership by an individual. The rationale is to make land usage flexible and easy, since certificate holders can apply for loans or mortgage their customary land (Hansungle and Jegede 2014). The changing of customary land tenure laws governing ownership in Uganda allows for easy access to land and use of its resources such as water and trees, by indigenous people.

Having established the operationalization of customary land tenure system and the historical reforms that were brought by colonial and postcolonial governments in Uganda, the rest of the chapter is structured into four parts. The first part examines the literature of our common future and sustainability issues (privatization versus customary land tenure systems, based on traditional ecological knowledge). Part two discusses the theoretical framework. It is anchored on a critique of Garrett Hardin's 1968 thesis *The Tragedy of the Commons* and argues that Hardin's theory championing privatization of land over the communal is flawed without a solid substantive basis within the context of Africa. In trying to diffuse Hardin's theory, part three examines the philosophy of Acholi traditional customary tenure system and its impact on regulating land use, guaranteeing access to diverse uses and maintaining equitable practices for environmental sustainability. It also examines briefly the changing dimension of Acholi customary land tenure system. The last part provides a conclusion.

## Privatization Versus Customary Land Tenure Systems

Many scholarly and professional debates in the present era have examined the efficacy of the traditional land tenure system for economic development in societies like Africa where land is mostly owned collectively (EARC 1955; World Bank

1974; Ault and Rutman 1979; Sjaastad and Bromley 1997; Mugambwa 2007). The controversies arising from these scholars over the extent to which a customary land tenure system provides the stimulus for development demonstrates the complexities and flexibility of this generational tenure arrangement. Such controversies mostly fueled by scholars and economists situated outside of Africa arise due to a lack of detailed understanding of the African land tenure system. For example, there are two major differences in the land tenure system in Africa which exist in the scope of an individual's rights to land use, occupation, and disposition. Individual rights to land can either be under the customary tenure or the proprietary land tenure arrangement. To dispel the general euphoria of the land tenure system in Africa, Ault and Rutman (1979) articulates that in Africa:

> It was and is not unusual to find tribes that have proprietary land tenure systems while other tribes have communal systems. The principal difference between the proprietary system and the communal land tenure system is the extent of the individual's control over the disposition and transfer of specific plots of land. A communal land tenure system is simply a system of undefined individual property rights [the right to individually own or transfer a property is undefined]. Under a proprietary system, the individual [or family] obtains exclusive control over the disposition of specific plots including the right to transfer the land to another person at his [their] own discretion. In a communal system, individual rights to a specific plot are limited regardless of the demand for land (p. 170).

Both the proprietary and communal systems were practiced in Africa prior to colonial contacts and stood the test of time by adopting and mitigating threats arising from changes in local environment. For example, the supposedly "expert" arguments that the African land tenure system limits investment value of land (World Bank 1974; Hardin 1968) is hence flawed and greatly negates the fact that under the proprietary system, the individual reserves the right to use a specified piece of land as he/she wishes including transferring it orally. Under this arrangement, the individual land owner also reserves the right of admission and can exclude anyone from using such land without any penalty (Ault and Rutman 1979). Advocating for the individualization of land under such an arrangement would only require a formalization through paper work of an already orally preexisting process.

Moreover, a study conducted by Mugambwa (2007) reported that by 2003, the World Bank, the main champion for individualization of communal ownership, had concluded that there was no substantive evidence to directly hold the customary land tenure system accountable for lack of economic development. Much as the report did not vindicate customary land tenure system, it shows that the system needs detailed study to understand its complex axiological dimension rather than overturning it in the name of globalization. With globalization, transformations in the structure and circumstances of social life get intertwined with alterations in the kinds of meanings that make sense to people's living standards. The trend, however, comes with injustice against the peasant community as it turns their ways of life into new forms completely alien to them. Similarly, Macrine (2009) pointed out that globalization literally and figuratively uproots people, throwing them out of occupations that gave meaning to their lives and disrupting communities and cultures. Imposed on community, privatization of land leads to the creation of class, the "haves and have not" which in turn destabilizes a hitherto harmonious society.

There is a rebuttal argument against traditional land tenure arrangement that this system creates inequality in society because it reserves the rights of land in the hands of men. Because of this, women have to rely on the goodwill of men to determine land use. This restrains their rights as women to make social, economic, and environmental decisions and it will also impact on their entrepreneurial capacity (Merab 2008) since women have to rely on men on land matters. This policy leads to underutilization of arable land resource because acquisition of modern farming methods by women becomes restricted due to authority being squarely vested in the hands of the men. In contrast, accredited anthropologists (Richard 1939; Mackenzie 1991) have argued that women in traditional African society under the customary land tenure system were the main cultivators of farm land. The implication is that they had the power alongside men to decide which farmland to use for different crops. Women were central in the management of ecological sustainability through the close observation of the different seasons to determine crops to be farmed.

The contemporary ecological sustainability approach that dispossesses African indigenous people from following their customary land tenure rights have boomeranged in Central Africa, Democratic Republic of Congo. For instance, Barume (2006) states that all the reasons for the expulsion of the Twa from Kahuzi-Biega Park in DRC beginning from 1967 were never achieved. Problems such as poaching continued unabated after the expulsion, ecological damage, settlement, agriculture, and illegal mining increased. The park also became a habitat for criminals, armed gangs and refugees. Twa's expulsion from the park was executed under legal regime that handed control of forest resource to the government. The allegation against the Twa leading to their eviction from the park was that as "natural" inhabitants of the forest, they are the "traditional" enemy of the wildlife of the forest (Albert 2000). Therefore, along with their generational customary practices, they were seen as presenting a great danger to ecological sustainability.

However, Hansungule and Jegede (2014) criticized the policy of taking control and use of land away from indigenous people in the name of conservation as a driver for climate change. They argued that the policy compels the disposed indigenous people into practices such as increased cutting down of trees and illegal hunting in search of shelter and a new livelihood. What is viewed as a gain in one area may promote deforestation and depletion of animal population in another, which directly contributes to climate change. The changes in climate bring other adverse effects like droughts flooding, crop failures, and starvation as has been experienced in parts of Africa among the indigenous pastoralist groups like the Karimajong in Uganda, Batwa in Rwanda, Burundi and Uganda among others. Land individualization is a threat to food security for indigenous communities who rely on collective ownership to cultivate, hunt, and gather food. Food gathering and the collection process in Africa was centered on the sparing use of natural surroundings for sustainability. Africans believed that humans have close links to the land and everything it offers. Maturity accorded to the proper and respectful use of land is paramount for peaceful future society because it leads to ecological suitability hence balancing natural resource use with human activities/consumptions. Balancing natural resource use implies meeting basic human needs while upholding the environmental cycle in a constantly changing society. Wangoola (2000) elaborates that such belief also challenged locals to make peace with plants, animals, stone, living and nonliving things. In this way, good consideration was extended to the earth. The soil was synonymous to a bank account from which the account holders withdrew only part of the accrued interests without depleting the principal.

Besides stripping people of their generational practices, privatization of indigenous land and resources offers fertile ground for insecurity. When people are dispossessed of their land and left with no option, it can lead to violent uprising and resistance. The case of the Mau Mau rebellion of 1952 underscores a fitting illustration of how imposed land policy is a dragnet for insecurity. Furedi (1989) argued that the most convincing reason for the Mau Mau uprising against the British colonial rule in Kenya was economic discontent caused by white settlers claiming Kikuyu land. Fertile arable land, traditionally owned under the communal arrangement, was coercively privatized and handed over to white settlers in colonial Kenya. To exacerbate the already volatile situation, land privatization was enforced through restrictive economic and social policy placed upon the native Kikuyu (Presley 1988; Lonsdale 1990; Kennedy 1992). By stripping them of their land and traditional way of life, indigenous Kikuyu felt insulted, dehumanized and isolated from their own ancestral society. Therefore, the resolve to pick up arms became not just a protest against oppressive colonial policy but a strategy for reclaiming and preserving African dignity in its totality.

Other researchers (Merab 2008; Amone and Lakwo 2014) have however presented sets of research findings in support of reforming the customary land tenure system, hence falling into the same trap of colonial misconception of this policy with the claim that it is an obstacle to development. Much as their work has managed to penetrate the academic repository, they fail to provide convincing research-based evidence to support the claim that the customary land tenure system is a hindrance to development. Moreover, their studies were conducted in very restricted localities of Manafwa and Lamwo districts with a limited number of respondents, mostly local leaders who champion of free/leasehold land policy for personal gain. Certainly, their methodology of study lacked transparent rationality regarding the voices of respondents and falls within the old fashioned colonial canons of subjective universal imposition. Besides, their arguments failed to consider the 2003 World Bank report (cited in Mugambwa 2007) which concluded that there was no substantive evidence to link the customary land tenure system to a lack of development. Much as the report does not also vindicate customary land tenure system in as far as economic development is concerned, it played a significant role in the continuation of the system in most part of East Africa.

## Theoretical Premise

The theoretical framework proffered here is anchored in a critique of Garrett Hardin's "*The Tragedy of the Commons*" thesis of 1968. Hardin, a professor of genetic biology at the University of California, Santa Barbara argues that privatization of land is the best way to manage land resources for ecological sustainability and economic development. His argument persuaded the World Bank and International Monetary Fund to influence many developing countries to privatize communal resources for economic development. In depicting what he calls *the tragedy of the commons* to argue against collective land ownership, Hardin provides an illustration of an open grazing land, a common practice among most indigenous societies. He states:

> Picture a pasture open to all. It is to be expected that each herds-man will try to keep as many cattle as possible on the commons. Such an arrangement may work reasonably satisfactorily for centuries because tribal wars, poaching, and disease keep number of both man and beast well below the carrying capacity of the land. Finally, however, comes the day of reckoning, that is, the day when the long desired goal of social stability becomes a reality. At this point, the inherent logic of the commons remorselessly generates tragedy.... For each man is locked on a system that compels him to increase his herd without limit-in a world that is limited. Ruin is the destination toward which all men rush, each pursuing his own best interest in a society that believe in the freedom of the commons. Freedom in common brings ruins to all. (p. 1244)

In the first place, Hardin situates communal land ownership within a misdiagnosed and generalized context by failing to delve deeper into the practice by different communities such as pastoralist, hunters, fruit gatherers, and subsistence farmers. His theory negates the fact that every indigenous society has laws governing the use/consumption of collective resources such as grazing land, hunting grounds, forests and water points. Such laws were meant to ensure resource preservation and ecological sustainability. Among the pastoral communities in East Africa for example, rotational grazing of animals was practiced to ensure regeneration of the soil and pastures.

Also, cattle raids regulate animal population and it is a common occurrence among most pastoral communities. For example, a study conducted by Meier et al. (2007) found that livestock raids among pastoral communities of East Africa were worsened by violent provocative behaviors, reduction in peace efforts, poor reciprocal exchanges and an increase in vegetation that provide cover for organized raids. The existence of conditions for raids, therefore, dents a hole in Hardin's argument that domesticated animal population would explode in excess of the static graze land in times of stability. It is worthy of note that among pastoral groups where land is collectively owned, family status is determined by the number of cattle it had. Livestock raids and counter raids to increase animal population were, therefore, based on traditional norms and principles. For example, elders from the attacking group would often notify their enemy of the impending raids. Of course, pastoral groups sometimes wage war against each other for different reasons, and disputes are common both within and across pastoral lines (Meier et al. 2007).

Realistically, the time of perfect peace and stability that Hardin envisions in which everything functions relationally in harmony is implausible among such groups. Finally, Hardin failed to acknowledge the fact that animal diseases in societies that practice either communal or individual land ownership is a common occurrence that the advancement in veterinary medicine and pharmacology has failed to contain. Coupled with drought in some parts of the world, it leads to a reduction in animal population below the number that a herdsman could dream of, and naturally regulates pressure on land resource.

## Traditional Acholi Land Tenure System and Ecological Sustainability

The Acholi landscape is a typical characteristic of the East African scenery with expansive grassland, scattered trees, valleys, and seasonal rivers. The region has two seasons: wet and dry season. For over 2000 years, this region was known for its agricultural activity with a variety of farmed food crops such as millet, simsim (sesame), and sorghum as the main staple foods. To supplement subsistence agriculture, hunting and herding of livestock was also practiced. In terms of social–economic and political settings, the village lineage was the central pillar of the Acholi people. The villages were usually under the leadership of a recognized lineage head deputized by a council of elders. These councils of elders and the lineage heads had control over hunting, herding, and agricultural lands (Atkinson 1989). They were also charged with managing renewable land use and environmental resources for ecological sustainability.

Beyond the villages, existed the larger sociopolitical structure called the chiefdom. The chiefdom was headed by a Chief (*Rwot* in Acholi language), whose office was hereditary. This means, at death, the eldest son would be crowned as the new chief. According to Atkinson (1989), the *Rwot* was the central social and political figure in the chiefdom. "He enjoyed great prestige and respect; he was surrounded by royal regalia (most importantly royal drums); and he was given tribute by his subjects (most of which was redistributed rather than accumulated in recognition of his authority" (p. 21). To demonstrate the *Rwot*'s authority and generosity, there are oral traditions today that narrate how the *Rwodi* (plural) gave refuge to needy non-Acholi who fled their homeland due to different reasons such as famine, civil war, epidemic outbreak, etc. Such were offered food, security and land for resettlement and cultivation. Traders, travelers, and explorers such as Sir Samuel Baker and his entourage from distant lands were treated with utmost respect as guests. They were gradually integrated into the community. Land in traditional Acholi society was owned under the customary tenure arrangement. There were demarcated lands for hunting, farming, water points, domesticated animal grazing zones, forests, foot path, and human settlement.

Among the Acholi people, a large portion of land is occupied by peasant subsistence farmers under the customary tenure arrangement. Traditionally under the customary tenure system, land was owned by a family and/or clan, hence the phrase *ngom kwaro* meaning ancestral land. During the drier seasons usually from around early November to mid-April, clansmen gather, earmark, and demarcate large land for farming in the next rainy season. This practice, called *koyo aker,* is being threatened to extinction today due to land privatization. The *aker* is demarcated to prevent wild bush fire, a common occurrence in dry seasons due to hunting activities. The demarcated *aker* is then split into small pieces and divided among families based on their ability and needs for the field. To avoid conflict, the process of land demarcation is overseen by *Rwot kweri*. Literally translated as "Chief of hoes", *Rwot Kweri* is a leader elected by the community to coordinate subsistence farming activities in the community. A candidate for this office must be of good reputations, integrity, and competence with detailed understanding of the community land boundaries in order to mediate land-related disputes. Un-hereditary by virtue of being elected, *Rwot kweri* office holder directly oversees land matters. The bearer of this office reports to the council of elders who are collectively headed by the Chief. At the beginning of each rainy season, the demarcated *aker* are cleared and the dry grass left to rot into manure before seedlings are planted. This ensured maximum productivity. To correspond with the collective nature of landownership, Acholi people practiced collective rotational tilling/ploughing of gardens. What this means is that clearing of gardens/farm lands are done by able bodied men in turn beginning from one household until all households in the clan or community get their turn. The cycle then starts again and progresses throughout the rainy season. Men plough/till the farmland while the women prepare meals and local brews for the gardeners. The ontological implication of rotational ploughing is that it ensured fairly equitable distribution of harvested food crops since female-headed households, widows, and the elderly would have their farmland cultivated by the collective. In the demarcation and distribution of gardens during dry seasons, that of widows, orphans, elderly, and those with disability were given priority. In this way, the gap between the rich and poor, the haves and have-not, the strong and the weak, was greatly minimized. Everyone owned land and produced enough food for self-sustenance of their family and the entire community without disrupting the natural ecological cycle.

Contrary to Hardin whose argument suggests that laws of our society are anchored on the pattern of ancient ethics and therefore are poorly suited to govern a complex changeable world, the Acholi customary land tenure system proved otherwise. It was vested on flexible and changing laws that regulate land use for ecological sustainability. After harvest for example, access to graze land was required by law to be opened for all. The herdsmen would graze their cattle freely on the open farm land. The droppings from the animals during grazing secure the richness of the soil with nutrients for farming in the next rainy season. Opening access to grazing land in the postharvest period has a unique epistemological dimension because the herder/famers' conviction is that animal hooves breaks and loosen the soil for the proper circulation of air which further enriches its fertility.

Coupled with droppings and breakages resulting from wild animal hooves as they graze, it ensured proper growth/vegetation coverage, an essential component for a reliable rainfall cycle. The Acholi use of a soil blanket such as trees and grass for house construction was premised on regulatory bylaws focused on ecological sustainability. Certain areas/part of the forests would be reserved where poles, bamboos and grass for house construction and other activities were acquired. In the next season, such areas were left fallow to regenerate.

Soil conservation is another important epistemological aspect of Acholi traditional land tenure system. Acholi subsistence farmers place significant emphasis on selection of risk-resistant crops that withstand environmental adversity and produce not only enough yield, but ensure soil fertility. Mixed cropping was highly practiced to not only guard against crop failure in the event of drought, but also for the crops to add different nutrients into the soil within any given farming season. For instance, millet was intercropped with pigeon peas, a rich source of legumes to the soil. The knowledge of leguminous plants and its efficacy in soil conservation was emphasized to the young generation during planting seasons. This permeated a complex learning dimension nurtured orally and practically from one generation to the other. Rotational grazing of animals practiced by the Acholi people under the customary land tenure system was an important element of ecological sustainability. It allows for regeneration of the soil and natural vegetation.

Further, under the communal arrangement, everyone had the responsibility to maintain and watch over the collective properties. Therefore, fishing and hunting were regulated by the complex regime of laws passed by council of elders. Every clan had their hunting grounds, knew the boundaries and bylaws governing hunting and were not permitted to cross over to a different clan/community's hunting zones. It was the obligation of every hunter to ensure that young animals were preserved. Sparing hunting was conducted to allow for the animal population to multiply. This is also true of fishing communities settled around water bodies. They knew that trapping premature fish was unethical and not accepted. It is because of this that traditional Acholi fishing baskets commonly known as *ugwa rec* were made of reeds with ample room to allow for premature fish to slide back in the water. The aim was to preserve fish species. The preservation of species during hunting, fishing, food and fruits gathering, land use was premised on the collective and agreed upon laws. Such laws were oral and passed on generationally. The laws evolve with the natural changes in society. Citing McHugh (2011) *The Modern Jurisprudence of Tribal Land Rights*, Hansungule and Jegede (2014) state that:

> It is a system of law that was known to the community, practiced and passed on from generation to generation. It is a system of law that has its own values and norms. Throughout its history it has evolved and developed to meet the changing needs of the community. And it will continue to evolve within the context of its values and norms. (p. 263)

The Acholi customary land tenure system and its governing laws were flexibly designed to adapt to climate change for ecological sustainability. The laws ensured that land use remain in the possession of the collective; and egocentric members of community found it hard to claim the collective resources for individual benefit. It was structured in such a way that every generation would blend in. However, the rise of globalization piloted adverse forces such as the negative impacts of advancement of scientific and technological innovations leading to increased climate change, new state laws, and civil wars among others. The new forces have directly threatened and in some cases altered customary land tenure system across the world. The 1998 *Land Act* which ratified the right to convert customary land tenure into free or leasehold (Mugambwa 2007) has witnessed a surge by crafty individuals to amass large swathes of land originally owned under the collective arrangement leaving many people landless. This is a testament that Hardin's theory championing land privatization is the real threat to the collective existence and ecological sustainability in societies where customary land tenure is the norm.

## Armed Conflict and Acholi Land Tenure System

Acholi Land tenure system has been significantly compromised by civil wars beginning from the 1970s. As seen earlier, the insecurity in the early 1970s, 1980s, and 1990s disrupted traditional tenure and other land reform policies in Uganda. The turbulent period of the military regime in the 1970s reigned by decrees directly targeted the obliteration of customary land tenure arrangement. Those closely aligned to the regime and in position of power used their wealth and influence to convert large pieces of customary land to private ownership. Additionally, the violent two-decade civil war fought in northern Uganda from 1986 between the Lord Resistance Army (LRA) rebels and the national army, the Uganda People Defense Force (UPDF) dealt a final blow to Acholi customary land tenure system. The war led to the massive relocation of people by the government from their homes to protected villages named Internally Displaced People (IDPs) camps by the early 1990s. After the IDPs were dismantled in 2005 due to relative peace and stability in the region, the locals who returned to their original homesteads embarked on land fragmentation and privatization. In some cases, the old boundaries were either forgotten, due to prolonged absence, or were deliberately violated by wily powerful political clan leaders and business people. There are also increased cases of forceful land grabbing and dispossession of locals using bribery, perverting justice, threats and intimidations by those in a position of authority. Consequently, cases of land disputes have skyrocketed in the region leading to violent confrontations among the locals. Traditional leaders that used to settle such conflicts in ancient societies have been stripped of their political powers by the government. What is left of them are only ceremonial supremacy mainly cultural and social authority. Coupled with the above, climate change has unleashed adverse impacts on traditional land tenure system. Climate change affects the pattern of rainfall distribution making farming unproductive. This has forced many young people to fragment and sell off lands that were collectively owned and move to urban areas or cities for small/petty businesses and other odd jobs.

The disruption of customary land tenure system has resulted in an increased wave of insecurity in Acholi land from 2005 onwards. Many lives have been lost and causalities reported due to violent land disputes. It has led to extensive destruction of property and disruption of settlement and agricultural productivity with a profound impact on ecological sustainability. Many hitherto communally owned land such as hunting grounds, rivers, graze land, forests and national parks are being encroached upon for individual gain. In the process, violent confrontations often erupt over competition for accumulation leaving death and destruction in its path. The traditional customary laws that regulate land use for a harmonious society is being negated in favor of the 1998 *Land Act* for the latter promotes the interest of the individual at the expense of the collective. Despite the above and the broad based support that customary tenure has enjoyed for centuries, it is unlikely that the practice will be acquitted of the charge that it is a constraint to economic development (Mugambwa 2007). The government of Uganda seems resolute that reforming this generational land tenure system is the only way to achieve economic development. This is despite the fact that the same government has failed to offer a lasting solution to the massive insecurity, famine and increasing cycle of ecological destruction resulting from land individualization. Land fragmentation emanating from privatization has also resulted in lower agricultural production. This primarily is due to the fact that those with money buy large chunks of land for cash crop productions and/or hording in anticipation for land value to heighten for profit maximization.

## Conclusion

In most African societies that rely on subsistence farming, land is the most important resource for the survival of families, clans, and the community. In such societies, land is collectively owned under a prescribed set of traditional laws and authority. Among the Acholi people, the laws and institutions of traditional leadership offered protection over land and ensured that its use was for the collective benefit and ecological sustainability. Any disputes related to land was amicably settled before *Rwot Kweri* without resorting to violence. Rare complex cases that were above the capacity of *Rwot Kweri* were settled by the council of elders. The case of the Acholi suggest that customary land tenure remains the most effective land management system for ecological and community preservation. Best environmental management is based on traditional customary knowledge that government need to acknowledge, tap into and blend in a national development agenda. Total overhaul of the traditional policy is counterproductive. With the preceding discussions, it is apparent that the traditional Acholi land tenure system has powerful implications for socioeconomic development without jeopardizing the potential of future generations to live a decent and healthy life with their needs met maximally. As the historical experience from Africa and other societies indicates, land tenure can either impede or facilitate positive socioeconomic change in a given economy (Okuku 2006). The 1998 *Land Act*, a creation of the Ugandan government, has failed to achieve its objective of boosting agricultural productivity through establishing security of tenure. Instead, it has created a class of haves and have-nots, increased insecurity, starvation, destitution and mistrust among the locals, many of whom are accusing the same government of harboring a sinister agenda to steal their land under the pretext of foreign investment.

This chapter has therefore attempted to rebut Hardin's (1968) account of the Universal Tragedy of the Commons and to suggest that his theory in practice, which favors individualization, does not necessarily have the consequence that he envisaged. I identified some of the fallacies of this theory with reference to the case of the Acholi community in Uganda. I am hoping via this case to offer a different understanding of the potential and actual value of the customary/communal land tenure system which can contribute to local and global discourses, so that narratives that run counter to Hardin's interpretation can become further juxtaposed in this and other contexts.

**Ethical Statement** In contributing to this chapter, I hereby confirm that all ethical standards regarding a theoretical piece have been complied with.

## References


Albert KB (2000) Heading towards extinction? indigenous rights in Africa: the case of the Twa of the Kahuzi-Biega National Park, Democratic Republic of Congo. International Work Group for Indigenous Affairs, Copenhagen, IGWIA Document No. 101, 142

Amone C, Lakwo C (2014) Customary land ownership and underdevelopment in Northern Uganda. Int J Soc Sci Hum Res 2(3):117–125

Atkinson RR (1989) The evolution of ethnicity among the acholi of Uganda: the precolonial Phase. Ethnohistory 36(1):19–43

Ault DE, Rutman GL (1979) The development of individual rights to property in Tribal Africa. J Law Econ 22(1):163–182

Bromley DW, Cernea MM (1989) The management of common property natural resources: some conception and operational fallacies. World Bank, Washington D.C

East Africa Royal Commission 1953–1955 Report (1955) Presented by the Secretary of State for the Colonies to Parliament by Command of Her Majesty

Furedi F (1989) The Mau Mau war in perspective. James Currey Publisers

Hardin G (1968) The tragedy of the commons. Science, New Series 162(3859):1243–1248

Hansungule M, Jegede AO (2014) The impact of climate change on indigenous peoples' land tenure and use. Int J Minor Group Rights 21(2):256–291

Kennedy D (1992) Constructing the colonial myth of Mau Mau. Int J Afr Hist Stud 25(2):241–260

Lonsdale J (1990) Mau Maus of the mind: making Mau Mau and remaking Kenya. J Afr Hist 31 (03):393–421

MacKenzie F (1991) Political economy of the environment, gender and resistance under colonialism: Murang'a District, Kenya. Can J Afr Stud 25(2) (Land, Ecology and Resistance)

Macrine S (2009) Critical pedagogy in uncertain times: Hope and possibilities. Palgrave Macmillan

Meier P, Bond D, Bond J (2007) Environmental influences on pastoral conflict in the Horn of Africa. Polit Geogr 26(6):716–735

Mugambwa J (2007) A comparative analysis of land tenure law reform in Uganda and Papua New Guinea. J South Pacific Law 11(1):39–55
Merab A (2008) The effect of land tenure system on women's knowledge-base and resource management in Manjiya County, Uganda. Educ Res Rev 3(12):365
Okuku JA (2006) The Land Act (1998) and land tenure reform in Uganda. Afr Dev 31(1):1–26
Presley CA (1988) The Mau Mau rebellion, Kikuyu women, and social change. Can J Afr Stud 22 (3):502–527
Republic of Uganda (1962) Public Lands Act 1962. Section 22 (1)
Richards A (1939) Land, labour and diet in Northern Rhodesia: an economic study of the Bemba Tribe (International African Institute, London
Sjaatad E, Bromley DW (1997) Indigenous land rights in Sub-Saharan Africa: appropriation. Security and investment demand. World Dev 25(4):549–562
Wangoola P (2000) Mpambo, the African multiversity: a philosophy to Rekindle the African Spirit. In: Dei G, Hall B, Goldin Rosenberg D (eds) Indigenous knowledges in global contexts: multiple readings of our world. University of Toronto Press
West HW (1964) The *Mailo* system in Buganda. Uganda Government
World Bank (1974) "Land reform," Mimeo. World Bank Development Series, Washington DC

## Author Biography

**Dr. Francis Akena** is a postdoctoral fellow at the Department of Adult Basic Education and Youth Development at the College of Education, University of South Africa (UNISA). Dr Akena is a committed educator with a keen interest in African Indigenous Science, Indigenous Knowledge, Social/Environmental Justice Education, Education in Emergencies and Post Emergencies Contexts. His skills, experiences and passion have been manifested in different publications in journals such as *Journal of Black Studies, Journal of the Society for Socialist Studies, Journal of Family Medicine and Community Health* and in the co-editing of the book with Wane and Ilmi (2014) entitled *Spiritual Discourse in The Academy* (in which he also wrote a chapter and contributed to the conclusion).

# Chapter 13 The Role of Participatory and Inclusive Governance in Sustainable Urban Development of Nairobi, Kenya: A Participatory Approach

**Stanley Machuki and Janet McIntyre-Mills**

**Abstract** This paper is based on a PhD project seeking to develop a unique participatory and inclusive urban governance of model of Nairobi city in Kenya. This paper, therefore sets to address the gap in the life chances between the haves and have nots in the city of Nairobi by using a participatory action research (PAR) approach in the course of rapid untamed urbanization. The paper moves to discuss contemporary challenges associated with such development and how they can be mitigated for a sustainable future. The paper is based on the hypothesis that the more an urban governance scheme is participatory and inclusive; a. the greater the life chances of citizens and b. the more sustainable the urban development process.

## Introduction

Development must be sustainable and just. However, in our times— the age of Anthropocene, and in a highly urbanizing world this is not happening, particularly so in the developing countries. In 2014, 54% of the world population was urban and by the end of the century 80% of the world population will be urban. Good urban governance mechanisms must therefore be put in place to ensure that cities remain liveable and sustainable during and after the implementation of development processes.

---

S. Machuki (✉) · J. McIntyre-Mills
Flinders University, Bedford Park, SA, Australia
e-mail: stanley.machuki@flinders.edu.au

J. McIntyre-Mills
University of Nairobi and UN Habitat, Nairobi, Kenya
e-mail: janet.mcintyre@flinders.edu.au

S. Machuki
UN Habitat, Nairobi, Kenya



J. McIntyre-Mills et al. (eds.), *Balancing Individualism and Collectivism*,
Contemporary Systems Thinking, DOI 10.1007/978-3-319-58014-2_13

Over a long period of time long neoliberalism theories have informed urban planning and governing polices where profit has been exploited from the people and the environment in a bid to maintain the status quo (Davidson et al. 2012; McIntyre-Mills 2016). The result is widening the income inequality gap, social exclusion, prostitution, terrorism, environmental degradation and the rise of slums. For instance, in Nairobi, Kenya's capital city over 2.4 M (approximately 65% of the total city population) people live in slums. Such statistics indicates negative impacts of rapid urbanization that adversely affect the life chances of the urban poor. As such this research is going to address the gap in the life chances between the haves and have nots in Nairobi as the city continues to undergo rapid urbanization process. A participatory action research (PAR) approach will be employed to develop a unique participatory and inclusive urban governance model which will aim to: 1. Enhance the participation and inclusion of all citizens in urban development process. 2. Operationalise justice and equity that needs to be upheld in order to translate the constitutional norms into practice as rule of law and 3. Ensure the needs of both present and future generations are met sustainably in the course of urban development.

The city of Nairobi (capital of Kenya and a key city in Africa) exhibits all the world dynamics of development and is home to Africa's largest slum is the selected area of policy research. The paper is based on the hypothesis that the more an urban governance scheme is participatory and inclusive: a) the better the life chances of the citizens and b) the more sustainable the urban development process. Therefore, this paper foregrounds a case to investigate the role participatory and inclusive governance can play in enhancing the life chances of the citizens in pursuit of sustainable urbanization. It establishes the platform for participatory action research (PAR) to be conducted in later phases of the PhD project with a community of practice from Nairobi. The researcher aims to co-work with UN-Habitat to engage the community in the research process. The goal of this study is to make a practical contribution to the governance system and urbanization process through policy research to ensure development is sustainable and just.

## Kenya/ Nairobi Development Process

Since independence, Kenya has pursued various ways to address issues of both development and popular participation (Omiya 2000). However, for a long time decisions regarding effective participation have seemed to follow the general pattern of British colonies which was based on administration, rather than development thus making the process of participation ineffective (Omiya 2000). Effective local and national citizen participation must specifically relate to effective devolution of power.

Nairobi is probably one of the best-known African capital cities, but surprisingly, it has been the subject of few comprehensive studies. It is indeed the subject of a pioneer analysis of the labour market by the ILO team in the early 1970s (Agwanda et al. 2004).

The challenge is that most forms of governments have, for a long time, remained highly centralized in developing countries, hindering efficiency in public services delivery and slowing development process in these countries (Ontita and Misati 2011). The unfortunate truth is that past efforts and initiatives based on centralized governments to enhance economic growth and reduce poverty have not produced desired outcomes, particularly in Kenya (Kibua 2008).

Widespread dissatisfaction with over-centralized planning and administration began to be noted in late 1970s to early 1980s by governments in developing countries prompting the countries to seek more equitable distribution of benefits of economic growth to increase productivity and improve the living conditions of the poor (Rondinelli and Nellis 1986). In other instances changes were triggered by the need to respond to changes in international development strategies as well as in the funding priorities of the aid agencies (Rondinelli and Nellis 1986).

Centralized form of government in Kenya has had it headquarters' in the country's capital, Nairobi. This made the city of Nairobi become a centre of interest due to its numerous functions, among them those of commercial centre, regional hub in East and Central Africa and a headquarter for many regional and international organizations (Owuor 2009).

First established as a transportation centre by the Kenya-Uganda Railway constructors in 1989 Nairobi later grew to become an administrative centre (Owuor 2009). This was facilitated by the transfer of provincial offices from Machakos to Nairobi and later the protectorate headquarter from Mombasa to Nairobi (Owuor and Mbatia c. 2012).

Like other African cities after independence Nairobi experienced rapid population growth, 12.2% was the population growth rate between 1962 and 1969, resulting from massive rural–urban migration following relaxation of colonial rules that had always restricted Africans access to the city (Agwanda et al. 2004). The resulting impacts of this influx was unserviced and unauthorized housing, proliferation of small-scale trade and petty commodity production (Owuor 2009).

Poor housing that resulted in slums with a big population of unemployed people began filling up the city. This was the beginning of current crisis that faces Nairobi city today, among others like those of congestion and poor transport network.

Also Nairobi is a city with its suburbs socially segregated mainly on basis of income an indicator of inequity. This segregation can be traced back from colonial era, where areas north and the west of the railway line were resided by the Europeans due to their favourable topographic and climatic conditions while eastern and southern areas were occupied by Indians and Africans. These areas were unhealthy due to frequent flooding, high incidence of malaria and neglect of municipal services (Achola 2001). Racial segregation created in the city early stages of development has resulted to the organizational structure of the city to have social patchwork with very high territorial segregation Rodriguez-Tores 1998 (cited in Owuor and Mbatia c 2012).

Unfortunately, Kenya's economic growth like other developing nations has been associated with environmental degradation and pollution, including declining forest area; decreased wetlands; falling wildlife numbers; water and land shortage; rapid depletion of renewable and non-renewable natural resources; increased use of toxic chemicals; and discharge of waste and effluent into water, soil and air. Other significant threats to the environment arise from poverty, overpopulation, climate change, political insecurity, pollution and unregulated bioprospecting (Amman and Duraiappah 2004; Mwenda and Kibutu 2012). A governance scheme that takes into account environmental management should be a central part of the constitutional order (Juma and Ojwang 1996).

Recognizing the need to achieve high economic growth and reduce poverty related inequalities for a sustainable development Kenyans pushed for a decentralized form of government. Kenya's New Constitution advocating for devolution is one of the major reforms the country has embarked on to strengthen institutional capacities which is a central part for sustainable development even in the Rio + 20 (Abbott 2012; Ontita and Misati 2011).

Devolution is a multidimensional approach that seeks to organize governance while managing states power along multiple lines (Bigambo 2015). Essentially, it forms the foundation for federal systems and structures of government founded in the concept of decentralization and devolution of power.

Kenya as a nation went into a referendum to pass a new constitution which was promulgated in August 2010 by Mwai Kibaki who was the then president. The Kenyan approach to devolution can be argued to be explicitly integrated as it incorporates strong administrative, fiscal and political elements. The new constitution seeks to reverse the centralized non-participatory governance paradigm by institutionalizing and embracing governance and leadership based on the integrity (Bigambo 2015).

## Governance and Development

Good governance and citizen participation are an integral part of development agenda (Omiya 2000). The role that a good governance scheme and its constituents can play and how it can be operationalized needs to be clearly understood by the citizens and policy makers to enhance a creation of a pragmatic regulatory mechanism and logical framework in the development process. This is fundamental in understanding the urban economy and its decision-making process (de Oliveira et al. 2013) considering the apparent increase in urbanization that has emerged as a dominant global trend, especially in the developing countries (Chaudhuri 2015; Sivam 2012). Apparent challenge remains inhibiting efforts to scale efforts for adapting alternative forms of democracy and governance that would address present economic, social and environmental challenges (McIntyre-Mills 2016). This can be attributed to the failure to take advantage of systems thinking which results in decision-making processes being less effective than they could be (Davidson and Venning 2011).

Democratic and participatory governance established in the twentieth century came as a preeminent model of political organization (Sen 2001) hence implying that the role of participatory and inclusive governance is crucial in contemporary paradigm shift of urban development and transformations (de Oliveira et al. 2013; Jiboye 2011; MTANI 2004).

In the twenty-first century, the age of Anthropocene and neoliberal dominance (Marshall and Glasson 2007; Rockström et al. 2014) profit is extracted from the people and environment as objectives and nature of planning remaining contested in a bid to maintain the status quo (Marshall and Glasson 2007; McIntyre-Mills 2016). This is mainly so in the urban environment as it is always faced by unprecedented challenges from climate change, population pressures, growing ecological footprints and widening social inequity (Davidson et al. 2012).

Urban development is increasingly becoming an aspect of focus as nations continue to fight sustainability challenges (Mutisya and Yarime 2014). The development must be sustainable to ensure emerging cities and urban environs are just, ideal and resilient as Paul Mees' idealized an urban ideal (Gleeson and Beza 2014). Thus from Paul's idea, the sustainable ideal urban needs to count on a watchful, confident and well-informed citizenry to work collaboratively for fair and just cities. In pursuit of a sustainable urban development arising from participatory and inclusive governance of citizens, this research examines the development process of Nairobi under the new Kenyan constitution, from the perspectives of urban habitats.

This will help identify the underlying causes of prevalence of poverty in Nairobi and the associated health, environmental, social, institutional and economic problems. Nairobi is one of the best-known African capital cities which surprisingly has been a subject of few comprehensive studies (Agwanda et al. 2004). The city has a population of approximately3.5 million of whom 60–70% are slum dwellers (Population and Center 2002). Projections casted in 2009 suggested that by 2015 Nairobi would have three hundred thousand new slum dwellers a figure that would increase to over a million by 2030 (Brugmann 2010). The rise and growth of slums in cities is a product of poor governance, where wealth and power is inequitably distributed. This indicates apparent poverty associated with food insecurity, unhygienic water and sanitation system, crime, diseases, prostitution, environmental degradation, poor housing and transport. Indeed, Nairobi, at present is a classic example of a world where though democracy and participation has been established by the new constitution, there still remains remarkable deprivation, oppression and destitution (Sen 2001).

New and old problems continue to prevail, such as persistent poverty, unfulfilled elementary needs, occurrence of famine and widespread hunger, violation of political freedom and basic liberties, extensive neglect of interests and agency of women, worsening threats to the environment and sustainability of our economic and social lives (Sen 2001).

While the phenomenon of rapid urbanization across the world has become a topic of increased scholarly inquiry there still remains gaps to be filled that could address the above problems as the world continues to get more urbanized (Szabo 2016). For instance, little attention has been paid to how urbanization affects countries' food security together with that of other basic needs and whether this association is affected by a country's level of development (Szabo 2016). In light of this concern what are the underlying causes that would be causing prevalence of poverty in the context of urban development? The widening of the income inequality gap, social exclusion environmental degradation and the rise of slums in Nairobi is an indicator of unsustainable development where the vicious cycle of poverty is perpetuated. Rapidly urbanizing countries especially in Africa where urban growth is highest with the low levels of human development are most at risk of food insecurity and other basic needs (Szabo 2016). The main cause of this is the prioritization of economic prosperity as for so long the urban development process have been majorly informed by neoliberalism theories, where profit is exploited from the people and the environment. To put humans well-being as a central concern over the economic growth and profit, new theoretical paradigm in the development and policy world emerged—like the 'Human Development' approach or 'Capability Approach' or 'Capabilities Approach' (Nussbaum 2012). It is important to have good systems of governance to ensure that human well— being remain a central concern in the urbanization process which is an irreversible trend (Wang and Prominski 2016). Urbanization, which brings a change in the social and economic development of humankind is an important index of prosperity and social progress in the country and the region (Wang and Prominski 2016). However, in Nairobi and other developing countries this important index is not evenly distributed as it mainly works for the good of the few political elites in power at the expenses of the urban poor. Therefore, this research seeks to address this gap in the life chances between the haves and have not in the city of Nairobi by developing an urban governance model that puts human well-being as the central concern. This model will be developed from perspectives of urban habitats and the country's devolution process with an aim to increase citizen participation and inclusion in the development process. The research aims to:

- Examine whether participatory and inclusive governance has been successful in the jurisdictions of other countries.
- Establish success factors, criteria and conditions for participatory and inclusive governance compared with centralized forms.
- Ascertain the role that participatory and inclusive governance can play in empowering citizens to their live chances, including increased employment, improved living conditions, health, education and reduction in crime and environmental degradation in the development process.
    - Develop a governance model that can be used as a tool to operationalise participatory and inclusive governance in urban development processes. The aim of the model is to: a) Enhance the participation and inclusion of all citizens in urban development process. b) Operationalise justice and equity that needs to be upheld in order to translate the constitutional norms into practice as rule of law and c) Ensure the needs of both present and future generations are met sustainably in the course of urban development

The research questions are as follows:

How can participatory and inclusive governance be operationalized in Nairobi to enhance justice and equity in order to translate constitutional norms into practice as rule of law? In the context of Nairobi, will the country's new constitution enhance participatory and inclusive governance in the urban development process when compared to more centralized forms of government? Most populations of Nairobi are slum dwellers; will participatory and inclusive governance reduce prevalence of slums by raising living standards and reducing income and social inequalities?

## Participatory Action Research

The approach is to analyse the present structure and characteristics of governance in Nairobi and the urbanization process. It examines how participatory and inclusive forms of governance have been developed and executed in other countries' jurisdiction systems and as certain whether such mechanisms can benefit the present and future development of Nairobi while upholding justice, equity and sustainable principles.

The literature review identifies theories, models and approaches that can inform this study and develops a governance model that can enhance citizenry participation and inclusiveness in the urban development process by using primary and secondary data while building on existing knowledge. The next step is to apply and test the model by using a community of practice. Urban development is a complex process and so is its governance. This complexity stems from the many activities and interactions happening in the urban environment as influenced by urban populations. This research aims to use a participatory action research as a powerful strategy to advance knowledge and practice (Whyte 1991). The evolution of PAR from the streams of intellectual development and action in social research methodology, participation in decision-making by low-ranking people in organizations and communities and socio-technical systems thinking regarding organizational behaviour (Whyte 1991) puts a case why it is a suitable approach for this particular research on participatory and inclusive urban governance. In fact, participatory research focuses on sequential reflection and action carried out with and by local people rather than on actions imposed the local people as in conventional research (Cornwall and Jewkes 1995).

The urban poor have remained voiceless, oppressed and marginalized in the development process in not only in Nairobi but in all cities around the world. In Nairobi, this poses a big threat to the overall development as the population of the urban poor constitutes more than half the total urban population. These urban poor people lives on survival means and predominantly reside in slums. To enhance citizen engagement and participation in the urban development process is a fundamental requirement to ensure the sustainability of the development.

With community-based participatory research has emerged as an alternative research paradigm which integrates education and social action (Wallerstein and

Duran 2006), there is need to increase the use of such paradigm in social and policy research and studies to empower the community sustainably.

More than often the interests of the poor are not well represented in development processes nor are the governance practices and patterns aligned to address such situations. However, this is a challenge that can be mitigated by antecedent of PAR as it reflects questioning about the nature of knowledge and the extent to which knowledge can represent the interests of the powerful and serve to reinforce their positions in society (Baum et al. 2006). Since representation is a major challenge in enhancing democracy (McIntyre-Mills et al. 2008), understanding such power relations and dynamics would help to develop models that enhance equality and democracy with minimal power distances. This would be a result of increase in citizen participation and inclusion in diverse democracies by basing representation on engagement rather than just voting (McIntyre-Mills et al. 2008).

Community empowerment should be a central concern for policy research. As such traditional research approaches in which the researchers generate the ideas for projects, define the methods and interpret the outcomes do not adequately address this concern as participatory research which empowers community populations to shape the research agenda (Jason et al. 2004). Participation of the community in research results in generating greater sociopolitical awareness and effecting systemic change in the community (Jason et al. 2004). In Nairobi, a participatory research seeking to improve the urban governance is critical as it would not only determine the role of participation and inclusion but also help in operationalizing the ways in which participation and inclusion in daily governance operations.

According to (McIntyre 2007), PAR is a method ideal for researchers who are committed to co-developing research programs with people rather than for people. As such, this research seeks to develop urban governance model with the people of Nairobi and not a model for the people of Nairobi. The argument is to ensure the decision arrived at the end is a consequence of the parties involved in the decision-making process. This will in turn ensure that power, knowledge, lived experiences, creativity and skills are shared in all the stages of the democratic process (McIntyre-Mills 2006a, b). Participation is an end in itself as it enables people to have greater understanding of one another and a better match of service to needs (McIntyre-Mills 2010a, b).

## Literature Review

### *Neoliberalism*

The public city is largely a critique of neoliberalism and its arguably negative influence on urban development (Gleeson and Beza 2014). As such Mees' described neoliberal urbanism worse than a political aberration which was a threat that imposed many costly failures in an age overshadowed by grave ecological challenges (Gleeson and Beza 2014). This implies a future with disaster in waiting if urban development continues to operate under the influence of neoliberalism. Thus assessment of urban development needs to shift from a neoliberal ontology to a social democratic foundation with relational themes of amenity, accessibility, equity and environmental performance in relative to resource conservation (Davidson et al. 2012).

## *Sustainable Development and Gender Mainstreaming in Developing Countries*

Sustainable development became a common in the 1990s meriting attention not only to environmental scientists and activists but also to economists, social scientists and policy makers in the mainstream development agenda (Mudacumura and Morçöl 2014). In 1992, sustainable development became of particular interest at the United Nations Conference on Environment and Development in Rio de Janeiro. The world leaders concluded that the development of nation could not occur sustainably while others remained underdeveloped (Mudacumura and Morçöl 2014). Since then, large amounts of human and financial resources have been invested in developing nations to promote sustainable development. However, due to insufficient socioeconomic policies and poor governance in the developing countries, these efforts have not achieved the desired success (Mudacumura and Morçöl 2014).

Sustainable development must have principles of justice and equality. A particular focus should be on empowering women and protecting children rights and those of the environment. To empower women gender mainstreaming must be an integral part in the development process. A concern for gender equality in development has well been identified as a paramount thing in two policy perspectives: WID (Women in Development) and GAD (Gender and Development) (March et al. 1999). In African development or rather civilization, women have been always marginalized in the mainstream development process assuming primary roles as domestic workers. A nation that segregates women in production activities will face inherent development challenges that will eventually contribute to low economic growth and lower human development index. To counter such difficulties (Moser 1993) welfare approach which prioritizes equity, then efficiency and finally espouses women's empowerment could be adopted. In light of this paper will analyse Moser's Welfare approach in relation to the first fundamental theorem of welfare economics to determine the contribution and welfare of women in urbanization process.

## *Governance*

Governance can be seen in various forms and means. For instance (Smith 2007) describes governance as an end in its own rights especially when it's about protection and advancement of human rights. He further claims that governance can be viewed as a means to development and poverty reduction. To support these views it is a means to development when the rule of law is a requirement for economic development and a means to poverty reduction when reduction in corruption is regarded as a strategy to fro increasing assets and thus wealth of the poor (Smith 2007). (Gamble 2000) argues to govern means to influence, shape, regulate or determine outcomes implying there are many agencies and institutions that are involved. He further moves to denote governance as the steering capacities of a political systems.

Twentieth Century saw the establishment of democratic and participatory governance as preeminent models of political organizations (Sen 2001). This establishment enhanced the concepts of human rights and political liberty become part of the prevailing rhetoric in the fields of trade, commerce, communication and more so in human ideas and ideals (Sen 2001).

## *Economic Governance and Political Systems*

Interactions between the economic and political domains are crucial for development (Dervis 2006). There is a common understanding that in many ways the economic and political system have failed and that both are fundamentally unfair (Stiglitz 2012). Application of the idea of governance to the economy raises crucial issues about the nature of governance and the economy (Gamble 2000). The presumed notion that the economy belongs to the private sector while governance belong s to the public sector is a source of major difficulty in economic governance discourse (Gamble 2000). This makes appear that the discussion of economic governance seeks to understand the relationship between the economy and the state. Precisely, this would be make one to explain economic governance as how the state governs the economy. However, this is not the case since there is a clear distinction between governing as a process and government as a particular agent. In essence governance is not the exclusive preserve of government (Gamble 2000)

## *Governance in Africa*

Empirical evidence point inappropriate governing strategies which are precarious and problematic are the main obstacles to development in Africa, especially in Cameroon (Fonchingong and Gemandze 2009).To improve governance in development process, an understanding of the links between communication, governance and development must be identified as communication plays a pivotal role in improving governance especially in developing countries (Servaes 2009). At a global level, governance has the capacity to change the global economy. In the past few decades, significant changes have occurred in the global economy emanating from the way in which the economy is organized and governed (Gereffi 2005).

## *Modernization Theory*

Modernization theory, pioneered by Seymour Martin Lipset, holds that as a country grows richer and its citizens more prosperous, they demand more freedom and a larger say in how they are governed (Dervis 2006). In his book, *Development as Freedom,* Amartya Sen views expansion of freedom as the primary end and principal means of development (Sen 2001). In this view, he moves to argue that the removal of substantial unfreedoms, which leave people with little choice and opportunity of exercising their reasoned agency, is constitutive development. However, a greater understanding of the connection between freedom and development is crucial. Such an understanding must go beyond the basic recognition of intrinsic importance of human freedom in general to advanced understanding of linkages between various types of freedom as empirical and casual rather than constitutive and compositional (Sen 2001). Thus from this theory, development leads to higher income, social change and then into democracy (Dervis 2006).

Other modernization theorists like Samuel Huntington argue that social mobilization and economic development are the driving forces of modernization (Winston 2016). Increased social mobilization implies that individual and societal groups change their aspirations while increased economic development means capabilities of newly modern society will change (Winston 2016). In a civil society democratic government and market economy must operate together (Bruyn 2009). A careful planning for a developed future need to examine the civil underpinnings of capitalism in light of how a civil economy evolves in the course of development (Bruyn 2009). Government officials needs to organize markets to reduce government costs, local leaders need to have strategies to deal with global corporations that would unfairly exploit their community resources and employees become co-participants in the development of human values in the market (Bruyn 2009).

Governments, businesses, non-profits and civil groups should jointly work to develop a civil economy by developing an accountable, self-regulating, profitable, humane and competitive system of market (Dervis 2006).

Development in all sectors is an inherently political process necessitating aid providers to think and act politically (Carothers and De Gramont 2013). Developing countries can shift to lower carbon paths while promoting development and reducing poverty (The World Bank 2010). However the World Bank report on World Development Reports (2013) claims that such achievement is dependent on financial and technical assistance from high-income countries. Both developed and developing countries need to act together to keep the costs down and to effectively tackle adaptation and mitigation of climate change (World Bank 2013). To enable a sustainable future in a changing world, in the next few decades, agricultural productivity and efficiency of water use must improve to feed three more billion without further threatening already stressed ecosystems (World Bank 2013).

## *Political and Economic Institutions*

Human empowerment and well-being should be the ultimate objective of political and economic institutions which in turn requires both democratic institutions and economic prosperity (Dervis 2006). Strong democratic political institutions that promote fairness and equity should be embedded in a vibrant market economy. This would ensure that in the course of development political and economic empowerment play equal and complementary roles in improving the lives of citizens across the world (Dervis 2006).

To operationalise participation and inclusiveness practical theories must inform the process. For instance theory of justice, can serve as a practical reasoning basis which must include ways of judging how to reduce injustice and advance justice rather than aiming at the characterization of complete just societies (Sen 2011). This implies that to operationalise an idea practical mechanisms with logic must be enacted to the society which is subject to such governance system. Markets, even when they are stable continue to yield and perpetuate high levels of inequality outcomes which are widely viewed as unfair (Stiglitz 2012). As a result more, more than anything else, a sense and perception that the economic and political systems are unfair is what motivates protests around the world (Stiglitz 2012). Kenya political unrest and violence of 2007/08 which famously came to be known as Post-Election Violence (PEV) was purely caused by a long-term cumulative effect of unfairness in the economic and political systems (Brugmann 2010).

## *Citizen/Human Development and Empowerment*

Citizen empowerment is necessary for the democracy process to be effective. In essence (Nussbaum 2012) claims that a democracy filled with citizens who lack empathy will inevitably breed more marginalization and stigmatization, thus exacerbating rather than solving its problems. This is mainly the case for developing economies where low income and education levels result to compounded poverty and thus less social inclusion and participation in the development process. The outcome of this is underdevelopment, marginalization and stigmatization of some members of the community.

Economic growth is sought by all nations with rush to profitability in the global market risking the loss of values and precious of future democracy in an age of religious and economic anxiety (Nussbaum 2012).

**Urbanization**

Apparent increase in urbanization has emerged as a dominant trend all over the world, particularly in developing countries (Chaudhuri 2015; Sivam 2012). The world is in the middle of an urbanization process predicted to rise from low double digit rates to 40% by 2050 and more than 80% by the end of the century (Sivam 2012) Organization for Economic Co-operation and Development, OECD, 2015). This being both a great opportunity and a challenge, it calls for sound decisions to be taken as they will affect the lives of the people for a very long time (OECD 2015). Evidently, conflicts exist in the urbanization process (Wang and Prominski 2016).

In the twenty-first century, an age of neoliberal dominance, the objectives and nature of planning are contested (Marshall and Glasson 2007). This can be emphasized by the fact that while latest planning strategies appear clearer in focus and purpose than some of their predecessors, arrangements for their implementation are not quite so clear (Hamnett and Hutchings 2009).

Contemporary urban settlement is defining people's lives across the planet as a new human ecosystem (Spencer 2014). This settlement is in turn influenced by the urbanization process which is occurring rapidly across the globe raising concerns in nutrition, health and safety among other challenges facing urban dwellers (Ahn et al. 2015). The onset of industrialization triggered rapid urbanization which came along with numerous social, economic, political and environmental implications (Chaudhuri 2015). With societies in cities being heterogeneous and pluralistic as a result of several ethnic communities, the process of urbanization becomes more complicated thus demanding good governance especially if development is to be sustainable (Chaudhuri 2015). In essence, to understand the working of world's ecosystem, we need to understand cities; and to create better cities we need to understand the ecosystems they depend on (Elmqvist et al. 2013). However, most governments, markets, policies and even studies have failed to take into account these relations and thus positioning and the whole world in a difficult position (Elmqvist et al. 2013).

Population of cities around the world is growing at alarming rates resulting to tremendous changes in most landscapes of the city (Dordrecht 2014). Fertile agricultural lands at the periphery of cities are being developed without consideration of holistic planning. This in turn is resulting to peri-urban areas being transformed from rural to urban land uses causing loss of agricultural land, increased runoff and water quality degradation. Consequently, the demands for water, food and energy are increased beyond the supply (Dordrecht 2014). Rural interventions influence urbanization and its associated problems and solutions (Sridhar and Wan 2013).

Rapid urbanization has the ability to alleviate poverty by providing abundant labour, cheap land and good infrastructure resulting to overall economic growth and development (The World Bank, TWB, and Development Research Center of the State Council, DRCSC 2014). More so, cities can reconcile human society and biodiversity by creating environments that are ecologically sustainable, economically productive, socially just, politically participatory and culturally vibrant if the relationships in which cities operate are understood and well placed in the urban planning and development (Elmqvist et al. 2013). Nonetheless, urbanization accompanied by inefficient land development leads to urban sprawl, ghost towns, pollution and scarcity of basic resources such as water (TWB and DRCSC 2014). At current urbanization rates especially in developing countries, there is a concern whether cities will be able to provide housing to the urban poor (Sivam 2012). Informal housing has been the dominant provider of housing to the urban poor in form of slums and squatters implying unsustainable and low index of quality of life. As research indicate that informal housing is the not the answer to accommodate the growing population of the urban poor, there is thus a pressing need for the respective government to look for alternatives strategies to possible solutions to housing and overall well-being of the urban poor in pursuit of sustainable urban development (Ahn et al. 2015; Sivam 2012).

A more human approach should be pursued in city development (Tanghe 2013). Contact between city dweller should be encouraged to reduce isolation marginalized city dwellers and dispersion of urban functions (Tanghe 2013). This would in turn result to increased citizen inclusion and participation in urban activities. Comprehensive, integrated and standardized measures of health must be in place for healthy urbanization to occur (Ahn et al. 2015).

Countries respond to public rankings which are based on Gross Domestic Product (GDP) per capita that affect their international reputation (Nussbaum 2012). While responding to the rankings, the countries work for economic growth alone neglecting the living standards of the poorer inhabitants, and also not addressing issues such as health and education which typically do not improve the economic growth (Nussbaum 2012).

## *Mitigation of Social Policy and Governance Challenges*

To adequately address social policy and governance challenges new approaches must be adopted in research, policy and practice. Such approaches will need to be timely, inclusive and responsive to citizens (McIntyre-Mills 2010a, b). Participation of citizens in development process must be considered paramount by researchers seeking to improve or change the systems thinking for increased democracy, justice and equity. In urbanization processes, the concept of participation must seek to integrate all the stakeholders involved with an emphasis to giving a voice to the destitute urban poor and women who are always marginalize and marginalized from mainstream society.

It is important to consider who is making the argument and what the argument means to individuals and interest group (McIntyre-Mills et al. 2008). This would then imply the need to consider why the argument matters in different ways to individuals and interest groups and also why and how it matters differently depending on whose is raising the argument. Legal measures needs to be embedded in the constitution to ensure complex decisions are made representing the needs of the majority whilst not overlooking the needs of the minority (McIntyre-Mills et al. 2008).

## *Addressing Diversity in Urban Governance*

There is need to re-consider structures and processes of governance to address diversity (McIntyre-Mills 2006a, b). In essence, this should be a point of focus in developing models of governance for cities like Nairobi which have high degrees of diversity ranging from culture, socioeconomic, political and environmental aspects. As such policy makers and urban governors need to work with theoretical and methodological frameworks by using conceptual tools to achieve multidimensional and multilayered policy decisions and enhance systemic governance in the diverse and complex process of urban development (McIntyre-Mills 2006a, b). The conceptual tools need to incorporate transcultural thinking tools in order to solve the problems and facilitate the understanding of the nature of the problems at hand be it social, economic or environmental (McIntyre-Mills 2003).

Sustainable governance must be democratic and be embedded in citizen participation and inclusion. Informed citizenry then becomes a critical aspect if sound and sustainable decisions are to be made. As such capacity building of citizens is necessary to develop an ability to think about ontology and epistemology of development (McIntyre-Mills 2006a, b).

Poor governance and corruption should be highlighted as the most important systemic factors contributing to poverty in developing countries (Mudacumura and Morçöl 2014). This then results to weakened institutional foundations, misappropriation of public funds and undermining of policies and programs which are aimed to reduce poverty by fostering sustainable economic growth.

Systemic governance should take ontological and epistemological stance (Altavilla and Meglio 2009);

- Ontological: Work in whole not in parts. Develop organizational structure in public and proactive approaches to be pursued.
- Epistemological: Link knowledge across individuals, local groups, national and international levels. Contextual knowledge (meaning and relevance). Human being and scientist are ends and thus need to be addressed with respect and compassion.

The scope of democracy and governance comprise local and national boundaries and hence the need to think in many dimensions (McIntyre-Mills 2010a, b). A democratic government must consider the participation of citizens as a critical ingredient in the development process for its sustainability. Peoples' associations, either past or current, shape their identity (McIntyre-Mills 2010). Thus people must be engaged in the governance process and be allowed to associate freely to achieve a common identity and goal.

## *Systemic Approaches to Governance and Democracy*

In modern our politics and times we are faced by the challenge of enabling people to think in terms of whole by going beyond compartmentalized thinking at the state level in pursuit of achieving cosmopolitan politics McIntyre-Mills et al. 2011a). In most developing countries, centralized forms of government have prevailed. The result of this is reduced democracy with minimal citizen participation and inclusion. However, in recent times these countries have come to realization that centralized forms of governments have not been very efficient and effective and have for so long retained the countries in low levels of overall development, particularly economic. A more holistic approach in understanding the politics and policies must be pursued for increased democracy and citizen participation. To achieve this governance and democracy will need to be underpinned by more systemic approaches (McIntyre-Mills et al. 2011b).

## References

Abbott KW (2012) Engaging the public and the private in global sustainability governance. Int Aff 88(3):543–564

Achola MA (2001) Colonial policy and urban health: The case of colonial Nairobi. AZANIA: J Brit Inst Eastern Africa 36(1):119–137

Agwanda AO, Bocquier P, Khasakhala A, Owuor S (2004) The effect of economic crisis on youth precariousness in Nairobi: an analysis of itinerary to adulthood of three generations of men and women. Développement, Institutions & Analyses de Long terme (DIAL) Working Paper

Ahn R, Burke TF, McGahan AM (2015) Innovating for healthy urbanization. Springer

Altavilla A, Meglio O (2009) Janet McIntyre-mills, systemic governance and accountability: working and re-working the conceptual and spatial boundaries. J Manage Governance 13 (4):365–373

Amman HM, Duraiappah AK (2004) Land tenure and conflict resolution: a game theoretic approach in the Narok district in Kenya. Environ Dev Econ 9(03):383–407

Baum F, MacDougall C, Smith D (2006) Participatory action research. J Epidemiol Community Health 60(10):854–857

Brugmann J (2010) Welcome to the urban revolution: how cities are changing the world. Bloomsbury Publishing USA

Bruyn ST (2009) A civil economy: transforming the marketplace in the twenty-first century. University of Michigan Press

Carothers T, De Gramont D (2013) Development aid confronts politics.Carnegie Endowment for International Peace, Washington DC

Chaudhuri S (2015) The marginal people in the urban context. Facets of urbanisation: views from anthropology, vol 7

Cornwall A, Jewkes R (1995) What is participatory research? Soc Sci Med 41(12):1667–1676

Davidson KM, Venning J (2011) Sustainability decision-making frameworks and the application of systems thinking: an urban context. Local Environ 16(3):213–228

Davidson KM, Kellett J, Wilson L, Pullen S (2012) Assessing urban sustainability from a social democratic perspective: a thematic approach. Local Environ 17(1):57–73

de Oliveira JAP, Doll CN, Balaban O, Jiang P, Dreyfus M, Suwa A, Dirgahayani P (2013) Green economy and governance in cities: assessing good governance in key urban economic processes. J Clean Prod 58:138–152
Dervis K (2006) Governance and development. J Democracy 17(4):153–159
Elmqvist T, Fragkias M, Goodness J, Güneralp B, Marcotullio PJ, McDonald RI, … Seto KC (2013) Urbanization, biodiversity and ecosystem services: challenges and opportunities: a global assessment. Springer
Fonchingong TN, Gemandze JB (2009) Cameroon: the stakes and challenges of governance and development. African Books Collective
Gamble A (2000) Economic governance. Debating governance, pp 110–137
Gereffi G (2005) The global economy: organization, governance, and development. The handbook of economic sociology 2:160–182
Gleeson B, Beza BB (2014) The public city: essays in honour of Paul Mees. Melbourne Univ. Publishing
Hamnett S, Hutchings A (2009) Urban development and planning. Wakefield Press
Jason LA, Keys CB, Suarez-Balcazar YE, Taylor RR, Davis MI (2004) Participatory community research: Theories and methods in action. American Psychological Association
Jiboye AD (2011) Sustainable urbanization: issues and challenges for effective urban governance in Nigeria. J Sustain Dev 4(6):211
Kibua TN (2008) Decentralization and devolution in Kenya: New approaches. University of Nairobi Press
March C, Smyth IA, Mukhopadhyay M (1999) A guide to gender-analysis frameworks. Oxfam
Marshall T, Glasson J (2007) Regional planning. Routledge
McIntyre-Mills J (2003) Global citizenship and social movements: creating transcultural webs of meaning for the new millennium. Routledge
McIntyre A (2007) Participatory action research, vol 52. Sage Publications
McIntyre-Mills J (2006a) Molar and molecular identity and politics. Wisdom, knowledge, and management. Springer, pp 227–268
McIntyre-Mills J (2006b) Rescuing the enlightenment from itself. Springer
McIntyre-Mills J (2010a) Editorial: constructing citizenship and transnational identity. Syst Pract Action Res 23(1):1–19
McIntyre-Mills J (2010b) Wellbeing, mindfulness and the global commons. J Conscious Stud 17 (7–8):47–72
McIntyre-Mills J (2016) Ecological footprint and governing the Anthropocene through balancing individualism and collectivism. In: Proceedings of the 59th annual meeting of the international systems sciences—2015 Berlin, Germany
McIntyre-Mills JJ, de Vries D, Christakis A, Bausch K (2008) How can we break the mould? Democracy, semiotics and regional governance. Syst Res Behav Sci 25(2):305–321
McIntyre-Mills J, Goff S, Hillier D (2011) Systemic action research: a strategy for whole system change. Educ Action Res 19(2):245–251
Moser CO (1993) Gender planning and development: theory practice and training
Mtani A (2004) Governance challenges and coalition building among urban environmental stakeholders in Dar es Salaam, Tanzania. Ann NY Acad Sci 1023(1):300–307
Mudacumura GM, Morçöl G (2014) Challenges to democratic governance in developing countries. Springer
Mutisya E, Yarime M (2014) Moving towards urban sustainability in Kenya: a framework for integration of environmental, economic, social and governance dimensions. Sustain Sci 9 (2):205–215
Mwenda A, Kibutu TN (2012) Implications of the new constitution on environmental management in Kenya. Law Environ Dev J 8:76
Nussbaum MC (2012) Not for profit: why democracy needs the humanities. Princeton University Press
Omiya PJ (2000) Citizen participation for good governance and development at the local level in Kenya. Region Dev Dialogue 21(1):198–212

Ontita E, Misati JA (2011) Revitalising transformational governance for sustainable development: perspectives from Kenya
Owuor SO (2009) Party politics and Governance in Nairobi. Paper presented at the GDRI Governing Cities in Africa Conference Stellenbosch University
Population A, Center HR (2002) Population and health dynamics in Nairobi's informal settlements: report of the Nairobi cross-sectional slums survey (NCSS) 2000. African Population and Health Research Center
Rockström J, Falkenmark M, Allan T, Folke C, Gordon L, Jägerskog A, Molden D (2014) The unfolding water drama in the Anthropocene: towards a resilience-based perspective on water for global sustainability. Ecohydrology 7(5):1249–1261
Rondinelli DA, Nellis JR (1986) Assessing decentralization policies in developing countries: the case for cautious optimism1. Dev Policy Rev 4(1):3–23
Sen A (2001) Development as freedom. Oxford Paperbacks
Sen A (2011) The idea of justice. Harvard University Press
Servaes J (2009) Communication policies, good governance and development journalism. Communication: South Afr J Commun Theory Res 35(1):50–80
Sivam A (2012) Urbanisation and housing for the urban poor: Delhi, India
Smith BC (2007) Good governance and development. Palgrave Macmillan
Sridhar KS, Wan G (2013) Urbanization in Asia: governance, infrastructure and the environment. Springer Science & Business Media, New York
Stiglitz J (2012) The price of inequality. Penguin UK
Szabo S (2016) Urbanisation and food insecurity risks: assessing the role of human development. Oxf Dev Stud 44(1):28–48
Tanghe J (2013) Living cities: a case for urbanism and guidelines for re-urbanization. Elsevier
Wallerstein NB, Duran B (2006) Using community-based participatory research to address health disparities. Health Promot Pract 7(3):312–323
Wang F, Prominski M (2016) Urbanization and locality
Whyte WFE (1991) Participatory action research. Sage Publications, Inc

## Author Biographies

**Stanley Machuki** is a PhD Candidate in the School of Social & Policy Studies at Flinders University of South Australia. His research focuses on sustainable development in particular urbanisation and governance processes. His aim is to develop integrated models and approaches to sustainability. Stanley is also a great proponent of sustainability reporting as means of ensuring growth and development is underpinned by justice, equity, transparency and accountability principles through comprehensive corporate social responsibility and reporting practices. He has a Master's Degree in Environmental Management & Sustainability from University of South Australia and a Bachelor's Degree in Agricultural Economics & Resource Management from Moi University in Kenya.

**Dr. Janet McIntyre-Mills** is an Associate Professor in the School of Social and Policy Studies at Flinders University, Adjunct Professor at the University of Indonesia and Islamic National University in Indonesia, and Honorary Professor at the University of South Africa. Her research focuses on systemic representation, accountability and re-generation applied to social and environmental justice concerns such as health, housing and social inclusion and the mitigation and adaptation to climate change. She addresses complex needs by exploring the meanings and 'what if' questions with diverse stakeholders.

Her recent books include 'From Wall Street to Wellbeing: Joining up the dots through Participatory Democracy and Governance to Mitigate the Causes and Adapt to the Effects of Climate Change'. ISBN 978-1-4899-7465-5 and 'Systemic ethics and Non-anthropocentric Stewardship: Implications for Trans disciplinarity and Cosmopolitan politics', ISBN 978-3-519-07655-3.

# Chapter 14
# Analytical Framework for a Systemic Analysis of Drivers and Dynamics of Historical Land-Use Changes: A Shift Toward Systems Thinking

**Claudia Coral**

**Abstract** Drivers of land-use change processes include but are not limited to agricultural innovation and reforms, demography and policy changes, and external conservation trends. Research on land-use changes has concentrated on developing both spatially focused models and reductionist approaches. However, reductionist science has shown itself to be incapable of providing the complete and accurate information required to successfully address nature situations involving human values. This research proposes a shift towards "systems thinking" to capture the real motives behind land-use decision-making, in addition to understanding the interconnections between a given system's elements and its dynamics in relation to the environment. The objective of this paper is to introduce an analytical framework that will assist in analysing land-use change dynamics, in addition to presenting a discussion as to why a paradigm shift towards systems thinking in land-use research is necessary. In addition, because changes occur not only spatially, but temporally, a historical approach is used to recognize this changing state. Land-use decisions are heavily influenced by drivers such as social constructions and needs, values and emotions, and the personal history of each decision-maker. Those drivers (internal to the human condition) are reflected in the individual landowner and land manager cognitive representations of reality. The framework guide the researcher in understanding individual incentives and motivations and to aggregate it at a collective level, by identifying which of these drivers contributes to the creation of a collective bond. Further efforts are required to understand all motives behind decision-making and the co-evolution of human and natural systems. To this end, the analysis of dynamics of space, time, and human choice play a crucial role.

---

C. Coral (✉)
Humboldt University of Berlin, Berlin, Germany
e-mail: coguerrc@cms.hu-berlin.de

 
J. McIntyre-Mills et al. (eds.), *Balancing Individualism and Collectivism*,
Contemporary Systems Thinking, DOI 10.1007/978-3-319-58014-2_14

## Introduction

Research on land-use changes has concentrated on the development of spatially - focused models. This paper proposes a shift towards systems thinking, specifically a mix of soft systems methodologies. This shift abandons reductionist approaches. Furthermore, such a shift is needed to understand the interconnections between a system's fundamental elements and its dynamics in relation to the environment. This paper's argument concerns the reasons as to why a shift toward systems thinking is needed in land-use research (see Sect. 14.2). In addition, it proposes an analytical framework (see Sect. 14.4), which is grounded in the assumption that social systems are linked to their specific ambient ecological systems, so that both systems jointly form a co-evolutionary, self-organizing unit (Naveh 2000). For this reason, the groundwork is built upon general systems theory, systems thinking approach and some elements of Luhmann's theory of autopoietic social systems. Moreover, a historical approach is necessary as land-use change occurs neither evenly, nor temporally, nor spatially (Goldewijk and Ramankutty 2004). Human history fundamentally informs the present, by allowing us to understand the meanings of human actions and decisions. Furthermore, these decisions, i.e. land-use choices, are heavily influenced by drivers such as social constructions and needs, values and emotions, and the personal history of each decision-maker (Hutchison and Charlesworth 2008: 53). These decisions are reflected in landowner and manager mental models—cognitive representations of external reality. For this reason, the analysis of the decision-making process is the starting point from which to derive different system perceptions.

The objective of this research is, therefore, to clarify the ways in which some drivers have influenced historical land-use changes, with the purpose of—with relevant evidence—contributing to the design of land-use alternatives and policy, which respond to community goals set for the future.

## Discussion: Why Is a Paradigm Shift Towards Systems Thinking in Land-Use Research Necessary?

Drivers of land-use change processes include agricultural innovation and reforms, demography and policy changes, and external conservation trends, among others. However, research on land-use changes has concentrated on developing spatially focused models and reductionist approaches. Nonetheless, reductionist science has shown itself to be incapable of providing the complete and accurate information required to successfully address environmental problems (Huesemann 2001; Bawden et al. 1984). In the area of agriculture, problem-solving in research has been being categorized by Bawden et al. (1984) into four approaches: (A) the reductionist scientific approach, which basically reduces the problem to some testable proportions, for the purpose of experimentally testing the resultant hypothesis.

In this process, the reduction of as many variables as possible will result in a reduced problem explained (Bawden et al. 1984); (B) the reductionist technological approach, which is common in agricultural technology and responsible for technical solutions with the objective of increasing agricultural productivity. Later, as a result of a shift towards systems approaches, (C) a hard system approach emerged, in which the focus is not the reduction of the problem, but its statement in the context of a so-called "descriptive system". This system is then modelled into that of a system, which includes discernible boundaries, inputs, outputs, essential transformation, and some parameters of performance. However, for this purpose, quantifiable objectives are to be clearly set. This kind of systems thinking was understood as the development of a mathematically expressed general theory of systems (Checkland 2000: 13). However, as stated by Bawden et al. (1984), another approach is needed when the goals or purposes of the system are vague and non-quantifiable, usually the case in nature situations involving human values. In response to this need and to the complexity of situations concerning everyday problems, (D) a soft system approach, developed by Peter Checkland and his colleagues at Lancaster University, emerged (Checkland 2000: 13). As a response to the so-called 'wicked' problem, after Professor Horst Rittel's idea, wicked problem is "a class of social problems which are ill-formulated, where the information is confusing, where there are many clients and decision makers with conflicting values, and where the ramifications in the whole system are thoroughly confusing"[1] (in Churchman 1967: 141). These kinds of problems drive important land-use changes, or are caused by land-use changes themselves. For this reason, it is of great importance to develop an approach, which can deal with the complexity created by situations that not only involve the environmental system but that also stem from human nature. In addition, they involve a complex combination of fields, such as social and life sciences. The multifaceted situations that these systems elicit create the need for a holistic approach in solving and understanding these problems. With respect to socio-ecological systems, the debate in this paper centres on how to analyse ecological changes and dynamics without forgetting the links to the people themselves—those, who have historically influenced such changes.

But why is there a need for addressing these socio-ecological problems by taking a systems view?

First and foremost, regarding the motives of decision-making, according to Polanyi, a well-known economic anthropologist of the twentieth century, people are not always forced to make choices on scarce resource allocation between alternative ends, motivated by self-interest alone, and are not always oriented towards utility maximization. In Polanyi's words, "The outstanding discovery of recent historical and anthropological research is that man's economy, as a rule, is submerged in his social relationships. He does not act so as to safeguard his individual interest in the possession of material goods; he acts so as to safeguard his social standing,

[1]In C. West Churchman, "Wicked Problems," Management Science, (December 1967), Vol. 4, No. 14, B-141-B142

his social claims, and his social assets. He values material goods only insofar as they serve this end" (Polanyi 1944/2001: 48). In this regard, traditional economic theories have failed to explain all human motives behind decision-making. Furthermore, how many researchers, policy-makers, or decision-makers take situations into account that do not respond to profit maximization? Why do governments neglect traditional forms of land usage and promote more profitable land-use that, nevertheless, does not take minorities and all other motives behind decision-making into account? What are the real expectations of the rural landscape? What about a small farmer who decides to continue running a small family business based on ancestral farming practices (succession) and what about the forceful power of rural communities? It has become known that the world can no longer be understood as one that is purely human (Moeller 2006: 5), rather humans are a part of a bigger system. Furthermore, indigenous communities around the world think in a systemic way. For instance, mother earth (*Pachamama*), equilibrium, and good living concepts have contributed to different peoples' worldviews for centuries. We just have to recognize these elements. I am arguing, here, that we must take the human behind the studied monetary transactions into account, and that we must recognize the strong linkages and interconnections between human and nature.

Second, regarding historical changes, human decisions affect nature. The impact of our actions is illustrated in the domino theory metaphor, or the so-called "falling domino" principle. If a row of dominoes is arranged, and the first domino is made to knock over the next one in line, it will certainly make the final domino fall very quickly. In other words, what happens today will impact not just our lives but also the environment of tomorrow. By saying tomorrow, we are not referring to the nearest future, but also the future in terms of life on earth. This is especially true when referring to land-use changes, whose externalities are often unpredictable. This framework intends to help track these historical changes, in order to understand particular dynamics that could help decision-makers take more sustainable action in the future. The final question in this regard is as follows: Are these two gaps, empirically speaking (from an observer′s perspective), traceable to the following conditions: 1) that human nature and the motives behind actions are not taken into account, and/or 2) that in the long-term, unintended impacts of our decisions are overlooked, responsible for an increasing erosion of humanity and for increasing environmental degradation?

## Theoretical Considerations

### *"System Thinking" Approach*

As defined in Laszlo and Krippner (1998), the concept of "system" serves to identify manifestations of natural phenomena and processes. The term also connotes "a complex of interacting components together with the relationships among them that permit the identification of a boundary-maintaining entity or process" (Laszlo and Krippner 1998: 7). In addition, Russell Ackoff (1981) states that a system is a set of two or more interrelated elements. Each element has an effect on the functioning of the whole and is affected by at least one other element in the system, and all possible subgroups of elements also exhibit the first two properties (Ackoff 1981: 15–16 in Laszlo and Krippner 1998). Systems thinking stems from the general systems theory or cybernetics and sees the world as dynamically composed of self-organizing systems of human and social nature. The new conceptualization of systems research draws attention to the relationship between elements, rather than to the study of specific elements in isolation. Hence, systems research focuses on entanglements, dependencies, exchange, connections, relationship, and co-evolution (Darnhofer et al. 2012: 6).

Furthermore, as recognized by the systems thinking approach and for this paper's purposes, the farming system can be characterized as open, as it has an environment that affects its state. It is also dynamic, meaning that the state of the system changes over time. Finally, farming systems are purposeful; hence the system itself can produce the same outcome in different ways as farmers exercise choices (Ackoff 1999: 49; Darnhofer et al. 2012: 7).

The systems thinking approach has already been introduced to the agricultural field by Bawden in 1984. The so-called Hawkesbury conceptual model of farming as a human activity system was depicted as a system co-evolving with a changing environment (Bawden 1984). As demonstrated by scholars and practitioners, it has been identified as an important influence in shaping research (Ison 2008).

## *Luhmann's Theory of Autopoietic Social Systems*

It is not the purpose of this paper to exhaustively present all the ideas and philosophy behind Luhmann´s theory of social systems. Rather, the purpose of this paper is to present the components and ideas that have influence the analytical framework summarized below. First and foremost, it is important to make clear that systems theory was understood and adapted by Luhmann to create his theory. The central concept of the theory of autopoiesis, developed by the two Chilean biologists Humberto Maturana and Francisco Varela, was adopted by Niklas Luhmann and applied to social systems. The main idea behind autopoiesis is that the different elements of a given system interact, producing and reproducing the elements of the system (Seidl 2004: 2). A system that produces itself also produces its own boundary between itself and the environment (Moeller 2006: 14). Regarding the openness of the system, Luhmann argues that systems are not open, as stated by the general systems theory, but operationally closed (there are no operations entering the system from outside or vice versa), which gives a makeover to the concept of openness (Luhmann 2013: 28). Autopoietic systems are, nevertheless, open systems at the level of their interactions with the environment. Moreover, a system is structurally coupled to its environment, or other systems in its environment (structural coupling), as their structures might be adjusted to the structures of the environment (Seidl 2004: 4).

Social systems theory establishes three main system types: social systems (systems of communication, such as organizations and interactions), living systems (cells, body, brain, and organisms), and psychic systems or system of consciousness (mind—thoughts).

Each system is within the environment of others (Moeller 2006: 14). According to Luhmann, living systems reproduce themselves on the basis of life, social systems on the basis of communication, and psychic systems on the basis of consciousness or thoughts (Seidl 2004, p. 5). It is important to take into account that, regarding communication (or more specifically, the communicative event), "communication is a genuinely social—and the only genuinely social –operation. It is genuinely social insofar as it presupposes the involvement of a multitude of psychic systems, or *better because of that*, it cannot be attributed as a unit to a single psychic system" (Luhmann 1997: 81 translation of David Seidl). In other words, communication emerges as an interaction between at least two psychic systems.

Finally, as analysed in (Moeller 2006: 10) according to Luhmann's ideas, any system is somehow individual; for example, a mind is a unique psychic system. In this sense, individuality still exists in systems theory, but as a systemic individuality. In other words, a human being is composed of an individual body, an individual mind, and will participate in many individual communication systems. However, what is most important is to clarify that these individualities do not exist in a hierarchical relationship (Moeller 2006: 10). With reference to the relationship between social and psychic systems, it is said that these two systems' structures are adjusted to each other, allowing mutual irritations (structurally coupled).

## *Proposed Analytical Framework for the Analysis of Dynamics Concerning Land-Use Changes*

Figure 14.1 shows a schematic representation of the analytical framework for the analysis of land-use change dynamics proposed in this paper. This framework focuses on landowner choices or decisions, the values they assign to different outcomes, and how these individual choices are reflected in the community and its environment. This research is therefore based on the assumption that these choices are heavily influenced by social constructions, values, and the personal history of each decision-maker (see Fig. 14.1). These internal (to the human condition) drivers are represented by a "funnel" (depicted in Fig. 14.1), which filters all these elements into a purposeful decision. In fact, human activity has been recognized as the primary determinant of land-use. Thus, these choices reflect societal structures and processes of learning and interaction among a broad range of actors (Darnhofer et al. 2012: 10).

In the same "funnel", landowner decisions are influenced by a number of other external factors, such as conservations trends, agricultural reforms, agricultural technology, and formal and informal institutions, such as markets or regulations,

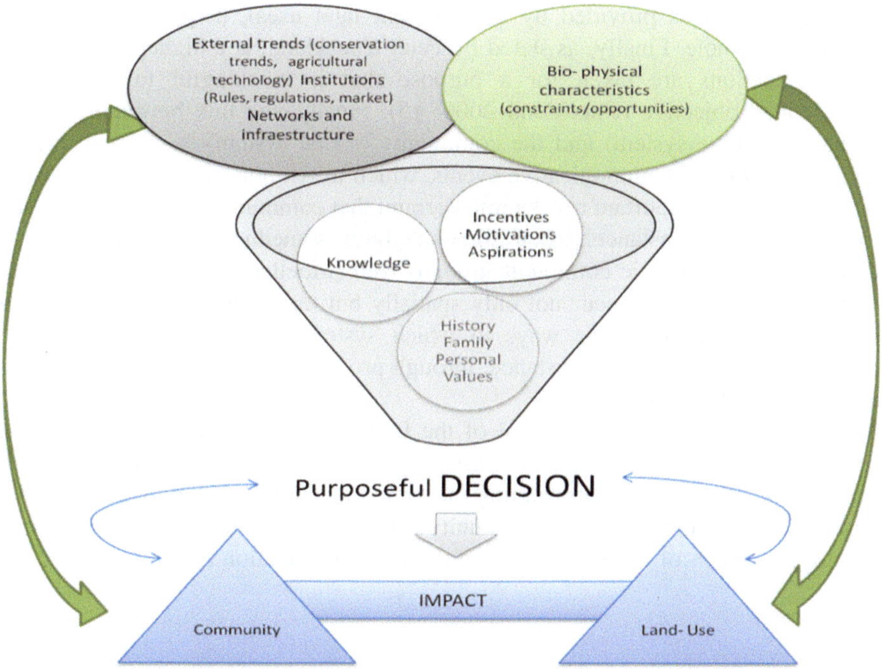


**Fig. 14. 1** Analytical framework for a systemic analysis of drivers and dynamics of historical land-use changes. *Source* Claudia Coral, concept accepted and presented at the ISSS Conference Berlin 2015

which also contribute to the final purposeful decision. These external factors are depicted by a grey circle on the left side (see Fig. 14.1). In this model, we also assume that the bio-physical characteristics of the environment also influence decision-makers. For instance, they provide limitations and requirements for the production of crops and constitute both a constraint and/or opportunities. Present actions and decisions will again affect the ambient and its bio-physical characteristics, which might affect future decisions and system dynamics. This is shown graphically and symbolized by the green arrows in Fig. 14.1. We recognize that ecosystems exist independent of their social structure. However, research on how ecosystems evolve and have evolved requires trade-offs to understand effects in nature and society. Furthermore, "community" symbolizes the relationship of each individual and its social responsibility. Individuals are not isolated; communal values and aspirations also influence decision-makers. We also assume that these decisions and choices impact the community and land-use functions[2] (for instance,

[2]"Land Use Functions (LUFs) are the goods and services provided by the different land uses that summarise the most relevant economic, environmental, and societal issues of a region. The LUFs framework integrates the changes observed in a large set of impact indicators into nine LUFs, which are balanced among the three pillars of sustainability (Perez-Soba et. al. 2008)

goods and services provided by the different land uses), in particular, and the system as a whole. Finally, as stated by Peter Checkland, at a higher level, human action situations are taken for a purpose that is meaningful to them, or a well-defined objective (Checkland 2000: 15). Finally, the link between the individual (cognitive system) and the community (social system) is realized through communication, or communicative events, which is symbolized by the blue arrows in Fig. 14.1. It is important to take into account that communication is not restricted to language. For instance, when someone buys something, this action can be understood as economic communication, as well (Moeller 2006: 6).

Finally, as changes occur not only spatially but temporally, historical land-use changes over time and the ways in which systems have co-evolved with the changing environment—for instance, through processes of social learning—will be analysed (see Fig. 14.2).

In conclusion, the ultimate goal of the framework is to identify people's perceptions of reality and the meaning assigned to their world. This framework is to guide the researcher in understanding individual incentives and motivations and to aggregate it for the purpose of community decision-making at a collective level, by identifying which of these drivers contributes to the creation of a collective bond.

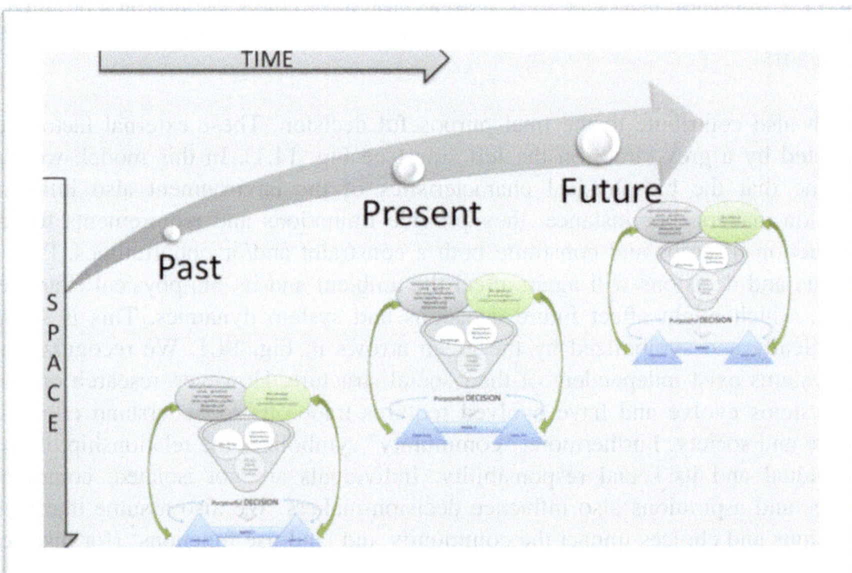


**Fig. 14. 2** Schematic representation of the historical analysis. *Source* Claudia Coral (2015)

## *The Analytical Framework in Practice*

The framework organizes research in such a way that a mix of methods can be used as toolbox for analysis. As already stated, a historical perspective is taken to understand meaningful historical changes. For this purpose, the systematic analysis and historical reconstruction of the past could be done by way of analysing historical traces, such as entire landscapes, satellite images, written documents, orally transmitted stories, and songs. This can be combined with other methods to engage social research and research of landscapes (see Jupp 2006; Cronon 2009).

Rich pictures, for instance, are drawings that indicate many elements and interactions occurring in any given human situation. These pictures are aimed at taking a holistic rather than a reductionist approach to a situation (Checkland 2000: 22). Other options are group model building, cognitive maps, and metal maps or models (cognitive representations of external reality), among others. These methods offer elicitation techniques (process of inquiry to encourage a person to externalize a mental model): for instance, through interviews with individuals or groups of people (shared mental models) (Jones et al. 2011, 2014).

When conducting our systemic inquiry with a historical focus, it is important to focus on following the co-evolutionary trajectory of the different systems with its environment, for example. Talking about co-evolution, specifically adaptation as co-evolution, as stated in Ison (2010) "rather than seeing adaptation as one way, co-evolution is different—the idea of a separate environment is set aside in favour of processes of mutual interaction which in human social systems can be seen as processes of learning and development" (Fairtlough 2007; Ison 2008: 3, 2010: 13). These processes of learning and development are of particular interest for us.

Regarding how to delimit our system, the decision concept world is not seen as a way to reduce the problem, but as a starting point of a systemic inquiry or as a way to frame our boundaries. Furthermore, the traditional notion of the "human being" is a simplification of the actual complexity of the human existence. Thus, in this framework, we recognize that the psychic system and the social system interact and symbolize the aggregation from individual decision-making to a collective process. As Talcott Parsons stated, collectively binding decision-making, referring to politics, generates decisions that are recognized and supported by the community, thus also providing satisfaction (in Luhmann 2013: 20). This framework helps us identify these external drivers of decision-making.

Finally, it is a general framework that focuses on decision-making but does not provide a clear focus on other more specific issues. It is the work of the researcher to identify these issues, while applying the framework: for instance, power relationships or co-evolution between social and ecological systems.

## Conclusion

Reductionist science has proved incapable of successfully addressing the "wicked" problems of nature situations involving human values. For this reason, the issues discussed in this paper address the question of how to analyse land-use changes and dynamics without forgetting the link between nature and the people themselves, who have historically influenced these changes. This comes in addition to including the long-term, unintended impacts of decisions, which are responsible for an increasing erosion of humanity and environmental degradation. The proposed framework is based on the idea of classical systems thinking, combined with select notions of Luhmann's theory of autopoietic social systems. This framework centres on landowner choices or decisions and the values that they assign to different outcomes. These choices are influenced by social constructions, values, and the personal history of each decision-maker. However, the framework helps to draw attention to the relationship between elements, rather than merely to the study of specific elements in isolation. It encourages the researcher to identify entanglements, dependencies, exchange, connections, relationship, and co-evolution (for instance, social learning). The ultimate goal is to identify people´s perception of reality and the meaning and significance of their world. Further efforts are required to understand all the drivers behind decision-making in land-use systems and co-evolution of human and natural systems, but also to raise consciousness about systems thinking in the broader community and among stakeholders. For this purpose, dynamics of space, time, and human choice play a crucial role in designing policies that respond to the people´s aspirations and perceptions.

## References

Ackoff RL (1999) Ackoff's best: His classic writings on management. Wiley, New York

Bawden RJ, Macadam RD, Packham RG, Valentine I (1984) Systems thinking and practices in the education of agriculturalists. Agric Syst 13:205–225

Checkland P (2000) Soft systems methodology: a thirty year retrospective. Syst Res Behav Sci 17:11–58

Churchman CW (1967) "Wicked Problems" management Science, vol 4, no 14, pp B-141–B142

Cronon W (2009) Learning to do historical research: a primer for environmental historians and others. http://www.williamcronon.net/researching/. Accessed 23 March 2009

Darnhofer ID, Gibbon BD (2012) Farming systems research into the 21st century: the new dynamic. Chapter 1 Farming systems research: an approach to inquiry. Springer Science + Business Media, Dordrecht (XIII), pp 3–31

Fairtlough G (2007) The three ways of getting things done. Hierarchy, heterarchy and responsible autonomy in organizations. Axminster, Triarchy

Goldewijk KK, Ramankutty N (2004) Land use changes during the past 300 years. In: Verheye WH (ed) Land use, land cover and soil sciences in encyclopedia of life support systems (EOLSS), vol 1. Developed under the Auspices of the UNESCO, EOLSS Publishers, Oxford, UK

Huesemann M (2001) Can pollution problems be effectively solved by environmental science and technology? An analysis of critical limitations. Ecol Econ 37:271–288
Hutchison ED, Charlesworth LW (2008) Theoretical perspectives on human behavior. In: Hutchison E (ed) Dimensions of human behavior, 3rd edn, pp 37–76
Ison R (2008) Understandings and practices for a complex, coevolutionary systems approach. In: Proceedings of the international symposium: selected topics on complex systems engineering applied to sustainable animal production, 29–31 Oct 2008, Instituto Tecnológico del Valle de Morelia, in Morelia Michoac Mexico
Ison R (2010) Systems practice: how to act in a climate change world. The Open University and Springer, London
Jones NA, Ross H, Lynam T, Perez P, Leitch A (2011) Mental models: an interdisciplinary synthesis of theory and methods. Ecol Soc 16(1):46
Jones NA, Ross H, Lynam T, Perez P (2014) Eliciting mental models: a comparison of interview procedures in the context of natural resource management. Ecol Soc 19(1):13
Laszlo A, Krippner S (1998) Systems theories: their origins, foundations and development. In: Scott Jordan J (eds) Systems theories and a priori aspects of perception. Elsevier, Amsterdam, pp 47–74
Luhmann N (1997) Die Gesellschaft der Gesellschaft. Frankfurt a.M, Suhrkamp
Luhmann N (2013) Introduction to systems theory (trans: Gilgen P, Baecker D, ed). Polity Press
Moeller H (2006) Luhmann explained: from soul to systems, vol 3. Ideas Explained Series, Illinois
Naveh Z (2000) What is holistic landscape ecology? A conceptual introduction. Landscape Urban Plann 50:7–26
Perez-Soba M, Petit S, Jones L, Bertrand N, Briquel V, Omodei-Zorini L, Contini C, Helming K, Farrington J, Mossello T, Wascher D, Kienast F, de Groot RS (2008) Land use functions—a new conceptual approach to assess the impact of land use changes on land use sustainability through multifunctionality. In: Helming K, Tabbush P, Perez-Soba M (eds) Sustainability impact assessment of land use policies. Springer, Berlin
Polanyi K (2001) The great transformation: the political and economic origins of our time, 2nd edn. Beacon Press, Boston
Seidl D (2004) "Luhmann's theory of autopoietic social systems. Munich Business Research Paper 2004-2. Ludwig-Maximilians-Universität München, Munich
Victor Jupp (ed) (2006) The SAGE dictionary of social research methods. SAGE Publications Ltd., London

## Author Biography

**Claudia Coral** is a Ph.D. candidate in Agricultural Sciences at Humboldt University of Berlin, Faculty of Life Sciences, Department of Agricultural Economics. Additionally, she is currently completing the Doctoral Certificate Program in Agricultural Economics conducted jointly by numerous German and Austrian faculties and research institutes. In 2014 she obtained a Master of Science (M.Sc.) degree in the Integrated Natural Resource Management program at Humboldt University of Berlin. Claudia has developed research in Germany (Accounting for Environmental (GHG) Effects in Cattle Production Systems for Securing a Sustainable Value Chain Development), Madagascar (Integration of smallholder farmers into agribusiness value chains under restrictive markets) and currently in Ecuador (Assessment of the drivers and dynamics of historical land-use changes in Protected Forests in Ecuador). In the last years, Claudia has been developing an analytical framework for a systemic analysis of drivers and dynamics of historical land-use changes – a shift toward Systems Thinking. When she is not working in Germany or conducting "systemic inquiries", she spends time gardening and enjoying nature in her home country, Ecuador.

# Chapter 15
# Decentralization, Participatory Planning, and the Anthropocene in Indonesia, with a Case Example of the Berugak Dese, Lombok, Indonesia

**Ida Widianingsih, Helen Jaqueline McLaren and Janet McIntyre-Mills**

**Abstract** Successful government decentralization requires the participation of all levels of government, industry, and civil society, and especially benefits from the traditions, wisdom, and ownership of local communities. However, Indonesia's central government was not assisted by international aid donors to undertake a decentralization process that was participatory in design or application. Nor did donor invest trust in Indonesia's government to achieve decentralization, which is typical of critiques on development. Processes have resulted in the failure of complete decentralization, which has had adverse outcomes for people, their communities, and the environmental justice required to achieve a non-anthropocentric stewardship. In providing the *Berugak Dese*, a locally grown planning institution in Lombok, Indonesia, we present this village level model of participatory planning as an exemplar for participatory planning and distributive governance. We pose that for successful development aimed to enhance the welfare of people, collectives, and planet, that there are lessons to be learned from the engagement of successful and sustained activities at the grassroots.

I. Widianingsih · H.J. McLaren
Public Administration Department, Universitas Padjadjaran,
Bandung, West Java, Indonesia
e-mail: ida.widianingsih@unpad.ac.id

I. Widianingsih · H.J. McLaren (✉) · J. McIntyre-Mills
Flinders University, Adelaide, Australia
e-mail: helen.mclaren@flinders.edu.au

J. McIntyre-Mills
e-mail: janet.mcintyre@flinders.edu.au



J. McIntyre-Mills et al. (eds.), *Balancing Individualism and Collectivism*,
Contemporary Systems Thinking, DOI 10.1007/978-3-319-58014-2_15

## Introduction

As the fourth most populous nation in the world, Indonesia has been one of the largest recipients of international aid for development finance and technical assistance. Donor assistance has proliferated since the 2004 tsunami and also with the rise of global political Islam (Edi and Setianingtias 2007; McCormick and Schmitz 2009; OECD-DAC 2011). At the same time the international aid community has increased its focus on the importance of aid effectiveness in development. However, criticisms exist in relation to the influence of developed over developing countries. On the one hand, there is growing concern about effectiveness of support to recipient countries and communities, their people, and the environment, in this age of the Anthropocene. Donors frequently question the capacity of recipients to deal with poverty, to initiate reforms, achieve change, and advance the Sustainable Development Goals(SDGs) agenda. On the other hand, there are hidden assumptions of cultural hegemony in development projects that imply traditional or local ways have no valuable contribution to make in helping disadvantaged individuals to achieve a better life. As a team of researchers, authors and advocates, we seek in this chapter to make sense of both the problems with development and also opportunities for individual, collective, and environmental progress.

The first author of this paper has long-standing reputation in local governance and participatory planning in Indonesia. In this chapter we draw upon her research expertise in the Paris Declaration Agenda, particularly the efforts and difficulties in establishing distributive governance in Indonesia (Widianingsih 2005, 2006a, b, 2013, 2014, 2015; Widianingsih and Morrell 2007). The second author provides a critical lens that questions international aid and the tendency of those engaged in development to colonize the other (McLaren 2015a, 2016; Nawaz and McLaren 2016; Gatwiri and McLaren 2016a, b), thereby eroding traditional values and environmental qualities of local people (McLaren et al. 2008; McLaren 2015b; McLaren and Kenny 2015). Finally, McIntyre-Mill asserts the need for a non-Anthropocentric stewardship (2004, 2008, 2013, 2014, 2016; McIntyre-Mills et al. 2008) which enables our observation of more recent developments in Lombok focused on environment and habitat; valuing governance and participatory planning methods founded upon traditionally cultivated practices.

Together we argue that development must engage distributive governance that is respectful of individuals, collectives, their traditional cultures, the environment, and Anthropocene. We commence this chapter with an overview of some critiques of development, followed by highlighting key points related to the Paris Declaration Agenda and Indonesia's attempts to decentralize government. We propose that the participation of local planning and decision-making mechanisms, which are culturally relevant for the people, are more likely to achieve sustained change than top-down approaches. This leads to the end of this chapter where we offer, as a case example, an overview of the Berugak Dese[1] on the island of Lombok, Indonesia. The Berugak Dese is a local institution that has adopted traditional practices. It prioritizes collective citizen engagement, culturally relevant practices for planning and development and has achieved some sustainable outcomes for the people of Lombok and their habitat.

## Critiques of Development

Good theoretical and empirical reasons exist for the international aid community to support economic, political, and social development. This includes a focus on helping people to improve their well-being via activities aimed to support complex governance systems, build capacity, and provision of environmental conditions that will sustain improvement. While the underpinning philosophy of development is respectable, there are well-founded critiques that the development activities of the international aid community do not always achieve positive outcomes for people or the planet. While ideally development should be approached with a long-term progress mindset, the problem is that initial investments do not always translate into measurable and sustained improvement. Some authors, as discussed below, suggest this is due to poor regard for community initiative, participation, and ownership.

Arturo Escobar (1984–1985, 1988, 1992, 2012) is well known for his position on development and posed an alternative in favor of traditionally cultivated progress that translates to a collective well-being of humans and non-humans, of human beings and nature, and in harmonious existence with the environment. He critiqued development, likening it to an activity in which traditional communities are observed and clinically treated by aid institutions that spread problematic post-colonial power–knowledge–discourse trilogies. In respect to the people, he asserted that frequently 'What has been traditionally cultivated among indigenous communities, is not even a notion of development' (Escobar, cited in Hopkins 2012). Others such as Wendy Harcourt (1994) agree, adding that the notion of development is inadequate without considering local knowledge and participation, especially when seeking to address extreme forms of human adversity and environmental degradation.

[1]The Berugak (or Berugaq) is a typical building of the Sasak tribe in Lombok that dates back to the 17th century Kingdom of Karangasem. As an open-air structure separate to the house, consisting of a roof held up by four pillars, the Berugak is a place where people gather to meet, engage activities, plan events and respond to problems. Each pillar has a significant philosophical value to inform customary village life: 1. Prioritize truth; 2. Uphold confidence; 3. Communicate virtuously; 4. Contribute positively and smartly (respect) in responding to problems. The open walls allow for others to see. Decisions made in the Berugak must be respected or they will be subject to sanctions/curse. The Berugak continues to play an important role in planning and development in Lombok, which is now the icon of the Berugak Dese—an institution for participatory planning, capacity building and development.

These positions call to question the motives of international development agencies who present themselves as a solution as opposed to realizing they are part of the problem (Peet and Hartwick 2015; Akers 2016). Some development agencies have even claimed ownership over centuries of indigenous knowledge, innovations, and solutions. Such claims deny the expertise and traditionally cultivated progress that indigenous communities already have (Tuana 2006; Anning et al. 2012) and potentially silence them. Together, forces of global capital and political economy that attempt to homogenize the global south are oppressive and not progressive (Escobar 1984–1985, 1988, 1992, 2012; Peet and Hartwick 2015). International aid organizations have likewise been accused of prioritizing their own business interests over those they espouse to help. It is only when the local practices are valued in development, and the traditional structures acknowledged, that local communities will be able to avoid exploitation of their people, systems, and natural surroundings by the broader sociopolitical and economic mechanisms confronting them.

In the shadow of such critiques, many scholars and activists have sought alternatives to development as opposed to searching for development alternatives. For example, Rajni Kothari (1993, 2005) advocated for substantive forms of participatory engagement and a more democratic governance structure that is appreciative of social justice. Peet and Hartwick (2015) favor diverse, innovative, and participatory approaches rather than imposing alternative blueprints for development. Janet McIntyre-Mills and colleagues (2004, 2008, 2013, 2014, 2016; McIntyre-Mills et al. 2008) propose a systemic praxis that engages user-centric participatory approaches, necessary not only for sustained practice aimed at the well-being of people in their communities but also for the environmental justice required to achieve a non-anthropocentric stewardship. What is consistent across arguments, if development is to be sustained, is collective citizen participation, democratic process, and justice. These principles have in more recent times been documented in international aid covenants.

Concerns regarding the effectiveness of international aid activities align with global forums having a view on donor-funded programs; the Rome Aid Effectiveness High Level Forum in 2003, the Paris Declaration Agenda 2005, ACCRA Doha Conference 2008, and the Busan High Level Forum 2011 (Kaufmann 2009). The Paris Declaration Agenda of 2005 is especially significant because it highlights five important principles in development. These are ownership, alignment, harmonization, managing for results, and mutual accountability (Walsh 2005; Hyden 2008; Smoke and Winters 2011). These principles are consistent with long-standing evidence that successful and sustained progress requires observable evidence among host communities that change is worthwhile; individuals and collectives must be convinced of the benefit of something new, then choose to change (Rogers 2003; Crawford 2004; McLaren et al. 2008; McLaren 2015b: McLaren and Kenny 2015). As well, the Paris Declaration Agenda principles reflect the value of participatory engagement in planning, development, and democratic ownership (Widianingsih 2005, 2006a, b, 2013; Widianingsih and Morrell 2007) necessary to achieve sustainable development.

Hyden (2008) in particular states how the Paris Declaration Agenda marks a shift in understanding development assistance and cooperation. He points out that the Paris Declaration Agenda's new approach to international aid embraced the importance of addressing power relations between donor and recipient countries as well as between government and civil society institutions (Hyden 2008, p. 259). Donors are encouraged to increasingly work with partners to implement the five Paris Declaration Agenda's principles of ownership, alignment, harmonization, managing for results, and mutual accountability (Riddell 2007; Hyden 2008). We suggest herewith that aid partnerships, those which are inclusive of grassroots stakeholders, respectful of traditionally cultivated planning and development practices, and consistent with principles of the Paris Declaration Agenda, offers channels to increase both international development aid effectiveness as well as fair governance. Such a practice offers reassurances for the progressive governing of Indonesia's people.

While greater efforts are needed to achieve sustained outcomes, some small shifts towards implementing the five principles of the Paris Declaration agenda are evident in Indonesia's decentralization agenda.

## The Paris Declaration Agenda and Indonesia's Decentralization

Indonesia‘s formal allegiance to international aid development success is documented in the Jakarta Commitment 2007 in which government and donor partners agree to cooperate with international agreements. This includes the Paris Declaration Agenda and its five principles: ownership, alignment, harmonization, managing for results, and mutual accountability (Winters 2012). As a result, the Jakarta Commitment 2007 has propelled efforts to achieve government decentralization, foster partnerships for governing with international aid programs, and seek to avoid overlapping programs through better coordination across government and with key actors. These include international aid partners, industry, and civil society.

Despite good intentions, difficulties have arisen in the decentralization processes due to implied control by foreign powers over the direction of Indonesian development. According to Knack (2012, 2013) there is frequently a lack of donor trust in the ability of recipient countries and their systems to decentralize. This has resulted in donor–push partnerships (Keijzer 2016) as opposed to a collective effort based on social justice principles. Efforts have also been complicated by fragmented development activities already in place, inconsistencies in design across donor programs, policy gaps between donors and beneficiaries, and poor understanding by donors of the existing governing mechanisms (Walsh 2005; DPWG LGD 2007; Eaton et al. 2010; Knack and Smets 2013). As a result, the first evaluation of the implementation of the Paris Declaration Agenda principles in Indonesia (OECD 2008; OECD-DAC 2011) resulted in the effectiveness of all five principles of the Agenda being assessed as moderate to low.

By 2010 decentralization had become an important part of the Indonesian government's agenda. Achievements included devolving key public service provisions and reassigning two and a half million civil servants to the district level, and conducting local government elections (UNDP 2010). Despite a rapid increase in donor involvement and formal government restructure, misunderstandings about the Paris Declaration Agenda on both sides resulted in an incomplete decentralization process (Widianingsih 2014; Bunnell et al. 2013; Holzhacker et al. 2016). This is because successful decentralization requires parallel strengthening across all levels of government (Mietzner 2014), with participation of industry and civil society. This did not happen in Indonesia. Aid organizations supporting decentralization predominantly worked with the central government, which created obstacles that prevented the achievement of complete success.

Difficulties stemmed from the Indonesian central government's perception that it was their responsibility to govern the decentralization process. Donors did not support the central government to develop the capacity of provincial and district governments to contribute to the decentralization processes. Nor were provincial and district governments aided to build capacity to engage participatory planning with their counterparts at the grassroots (Widianingsih 2014). This is a concern frequently raised by researchers and academics who argue that donors fail to achieve capacity building and technical transfer (Unsworth 2009; Widianingsih 2014; Keijzer 2016). For Indonesia, this meant that provincial and district governments had no capacity to facilitate and manage change with local and village level governing bodies (Bräutigam and Knack 2004; De Janvry and Dethier 2012; Christoplos et al. 2014; Widianingsih 2015). Without participation of civil society and the grassroots in Indonesia's decentralization agenda, the Paris Declaration Agenda principles were therefore not achieved.

While the physical structure of government in Indonesia has changed as a result of decentralization, the system of upward accountability has been reinforced. Local government areas have continued to rely on central government (UNDP 2010). Civil servants at the provincial and district level remain answerable to central government, which has little capacity to support them. International aid donors involved in deinstitutionalization have been frustrated by limited coordination between key government actors and levels of government, the contradictory policies, and overlapping programs (Widianingsih 2014). However, donors must also take some responsibility due to their failure support a parallel decentralization process that involved the participation of all government levels, civil society institutions (e.g. the Berugak Dese), and affected individuals.

While decentralization has sought to achieve distributive governance and mutual accountability in a move towards achieving the Paris Declaration Agenda principles, this has been further hampered by a system of fragmented and uncoordinated international aid programs involved in the decentralization agenda and in other development projects. In Indonesia, most development projects have operated as single entity rather than working as part of an overall coordinated structure (Widianingsih 2014). Some examples of different programs engaged in decentralization include the Enterprises for Governance Reform (USAID), the Multi Donor Trust Fund (UNDP), and the multi-donor Support Office for Eastern Indonesia known as SoFEI (Edi and Setianingtias 2007). There have been a number of efforts to identify, map, and coordinate decentralization activities, but it was not until the Decentralization Support

Facility in 2005 was established that some progress was achieved. This included the development of regional government performance indicators via the Governance and Decentralization Survey and the Stocktaking on Decentralization Program (DRSP 2006, p. 45). A challenge, however, is that sustainability of any initiative is threatened by Indonesia's frequent rotation of government leaders and staff.

Few coordination efforts have been sustained due to the fluidity of Indonesia's government (Widianingsih 2014). Senior government employees are on a 3-year employment rotation system through different ministerial portfolios or departments. Each individual brings new knowledge, expertise, and ideology, but the instability threatens establishment of institutional memory and knowledge (Jarvie et al. 2015). At the local level, it is common practice for newly elected members bring in a full complement of new staff. New staff do not have established relationships with donors or knowledge of all the funded programs in their region (Widianingsih 2014). This hinders partnership with development donors who need a counterpart in each of the government levels to achieve success. In terms of the implementation of the Paris Declaration Agenda, this is difficult to achieve without having consistent working relationships across the levels of government, industry, and civil society.

Winters (2012) noted that there is no single central institution with the responsibility for donor-funded decentralization, or other aid programs, and this hampers achievement of the Paris Declaration Agenda principles. As well, each ministry and government department has its own interests in particular policies and programs that are influenced by budget allocations to the implementing institution (Widianingsih 2014, 2015). Without coordination, both decentralization and other development aid efforts will remain haphazard and fragmented. We suggest that a coordinating institution offers the potential for the knowledge and practices of locally grown development and governing institutions to be harnessed and utilized. The Berugak Dese is one such example of a locally grown institution where donor and civil society partnership has been sustained. Its practices align with the five Paris Declaration Agenda principles. Missions and visions extend to the achievement of collective care of people, the environment, and global commons. The origins of the Berugak Dese extend back long before the Paris Declaration Agenda and long before the international aid community's involvement in Indonesia's decentralization agenda.

## The Berugak Dese Making Participatory Governance Real

The Berugak is a traditional building of the Sasak[2] people in Lombok. It has philosophical meaning in its design (each pillar supporting the roof represents truth, confidence, virtuosity, and respect) and this is underpinned by a system of

[2]The Sasak people have been the dominant ethnic group in Lombok since the 1930s (Lawrence et al. 2013) and, based on the latest census available, they represented 87% of Lombok population in 2000 (Badan Pusat Statistik 2013).

customary rules. The Berugak is a traditional meeting place for collective activities that include participatory planning and decision-making in regard to community life; e.g. collective care of the people and of natural resources (Lawrence et al. 2013). The implementation of good local governance in Central Lombok started in 1992–1993.[3] Based on these traditional planning and development practices of the Sasak people, the Berugak Dese institution was established in 2006. It was equipped with the mission to engage traditional, culturally appropriate governance principles in planning, implementation and evaluation processes at village level.

Fieldwork interviews in 2009 (Widianingsih 2014) in six villages in Lombok, in the province of West Nusa Tenggara, Indonesia, revealed the donor community's frustration with the limited coordination between key actors (government, donors, industry and civil society) in Indonesia's decentralization agenda. Local knowledges and success stories, especially evidences of culturally appropriate sustained development achieved in partnership with civil society and local governing institutions, were overlooked. The top-down approach to decentralization, which was poorly supported by aid organizations involved in decentralization, is typical of the problems associated with development as argued by Escobar (1984–1985, 1988, 1992, 2012) and others cited earlier.

In 2007 a good governance award was initiated by an international development company GTZ GLG (now known as GIZ, Deutsche Gesellschaft für Internationale Zusammenarbeit). While the Berugak Dese did not receive an award, recent Internet searching reveals it to be one of the only institutions in the province of West Nusa Tenggara, Indonesia that has sustained its approach to participatory governance, development, and advocacy projects over the last decade. The Berugak Dese has even diffused from Kopang, Central Lombok, to other locations on the island (Widianingsih 2014; Berugak Dese 2016). We suggest that this achievement is partially dependent on village partnerships with the GTZ GLG and other international development organizations, and also on the Berugak Dese's alignment with Paris Declaration Agenda principles on the value of ownership, alignment, harmonization, managing for results, and mutual accountability. Success and sustainability is evidenced by the value of harnessing traditional methods in its participatory approach for planning, development, and democratic ownership (Widianingsih 2005, 2006a, b, 2013, Widianingsih and Morrell 2007). As well the success of the Berugak Dese institution, through working in partnership with international donors and the grass roots, indicates that decentralization outcomes may be achieved by drawing on existing strengths at the local and village levels. As

[3]The Practice of good local governance in Central Lombok was supported by various donors. At the local level, planning and decision-making was dominated by local government and powerful religious institutions. In 2005 the then KKMS (a civil society working group) declared the need to strengthen local community and was supported by YAPIKA, a Jakarta based NGO. Together they developed a vision for Central Lombok future development, which was necessary due to too many methods having been introduced by donors and central government projects since 1992–1993 by programs such as CLAP (Access AusAID), PNPM Mandiri, PPK, and Westlic (UNICEF).

Mietzner (2014) proposed, successful decentralization requires parallel strengthening across all levels.

Some significant achievements observed of the Berugak Dese during field research were improvements to basic public services in the region, development planning for slum areas, and successfully advocating for local laws on the age limit for marriage. The sustainability of the Berugak Dese, when compared to development approaches to Indonesia's decentralization activities, are critical for understanding that successful implementation of the Paris Declaration Agenda must include decentralized processes, equitable governance, and also local knowledge. As stated earlier the weakness of donor-funded decentralization programs in Indonesia is due to two factors. In the first instance, the provision of parallel technical assistance across government levels was not achieved. Second, donors were unable to attract counterparts necessary for Paris Declaration Agenda implementation due to the fluidity of the Indonesian government. We suggest that working from the grassroots and building on the strength of civil society networks offers the potential for better outcomes.

Dominant development discourse favor project sustainability based on market viability, but researchers argue that sustainability is also contingent with the strength of civil society networks (Fortier 1999; Van Rooy 2009; Widianingsih 2014). In the case of the Berugak Dese, fieldwork in Lombok indicated that staff rotation at the village and district levels did not impact on the sustainability of program activities. Discussion with local activists in Lombok indicated that the Berugak Dese drew its development agenda from the local people, local issues, and expressions of need, and partnered with the international aid community when necessary to address identified needs. For this reason, staff rotation at the village and various government levels have not hindered the Berugak Dese activities because the focus on awareness, understanding, and responding to local issues, as well as having donor counterparts, has remained consistent.

However, significant needs continue to exist for the residents of Lombok due to few river systems, unequal distribution of dam water and high reliance on dry land farming and rains (Atwell 2006). The traditional diet primarily exists of kangkung (water spinach), insects, rice, and coconut. There are poor sanitation and high poverty, and the infant mortality rate of Lombok is one of the highest in the world (Baldwin and Sjah 2012). In the last couple decades, tourism and entrepreneurship have taken a key role in poverty alleviation and strengthening Lombok's economy. Tourism is localized in a few seaside areas and habitat has become vulnerable due to increased human activity (Kurniawan et al. 2016), but it does not directly benefit all of Lombok's population. Poverty has served to compel men from non-tourism areas to move away for work and females have become vulnerable to being forced into sex work associated with increased tourism (Dentith et al. 2013). Internal migration reduces agricultural labor available, and there is loss of habitat from climate change and ongoing threats to the environment exist due to increased tourism.

Lawrence et al. (2013, p. 7) wrote "The traditional forest stewards of Lombok have almost disappeared and the ecological and sacred functions of forest guardianship have been lost …" Tourism, climate change, and migration have had catalytic impact on the natural environment and on food security. In responding to these local needs, the Berugak Dese in partnership with local government, industry, and donors have more recently focused the environmental concerns. Specific activities have included advocacy and community capacity building to address the individual and collective needs arising from environmental change, loss of agriculture, and habitat (Berugak Dese 2016), as well as participatory planning and developing of tools and concepts necessary to respond to a changing world and the interdependent structures of Indonesia's broader governance systems.

## Conclusions on the Need for Participatory, Decentralized Governance

In consideration of Indonesia's decentralization agenda, one can suggest there are benefits to be gained from the use of participatory approaches in planning and development. Such approaches are inclusive and have the potential to draw expertise from all levels of government, donors, industry, villages, and individuals. The Paris Declaration Agenda principles of ownership, alignment, harmonization, managing for results, and mutual accountability rely on distributive, participatory governance. However, Indonesia's top-down decentralization attempts have risked increasing inequalities in human rights appropriation, disregarded local leadership and expertise, failed to achieve cooperative changes between cities, districts, and villages, and so forth. The adverse effect is an increasing gap between rich and poor, individualism prospering over collectivism, and growing diversity and competitiveness (Malik 2013). These activities put the environment and global commons at stake. They are side effects of development.

What is then needed to rebalance individual functioning with collective and environmental functioning? We suggest better interaction between individual, community, and nature, achieved through distributive governance, participatory approaches, and empowerment of the local people. Participatory approaches seek to bring the village collective back together to assess need and develop social life according to what is best from the perspective of local inhabitants. The Beruguk Dese, based on local meeting traditions, is an example of an institution that has historically involved systemic thinking about the village and society. It has sustained its approach to participatory planning and development despite the fluidity of the Indonesian government, imposing activities of international aid development and incomplete decentralization agenda. We argue that for successful and sustained development in accordance with the Paris Declaration Agenda principles, that government-donor decentralization has missed achieving the right balance in participatory planning. Humanity, global commons, and a non-anthropocentric stewardship require a 'grassroots surge' in Indonesia's distributive governance.

## References

Akers P (2016) Establishing rule of law through informal justice systems and development programs. Notre Dame J Law Ethics Public Policy 30:115–449
Anning B, Arbon V, Robertson B, Thomas, G (2012) Celebrating and sustaining Indigenous knowledges through higher education. WINHEC J 3(1):27–45
Atwell A (2006) The impact of a leadership training program on school based management and school community action in Praya Barat Daya, Lombok, Indonesia. Doctor of Education Thesis, Faculty of Education, University of Southern Queensland
Badan Pusat Statistik (Statistics Indonesia) (2013) Result of Indonesia population census 2010. Available at http://www.bps.go.id/index.php/publikasi/14
Baldwin C, Sjah T (2012) Water governance in east Lombok: the feasibility of co-management to resolve competing uses. Paper presented at tapping the turn: water's social dimensions conference, Australian National University, Canberra, Australia, 15–16 Nov 2012
Berugak Dese (2016) Kopang Lombok Tengah, Berugak Dese, Berjuk Gagas Kesejahteraan Masyarakat Dese: Konservasi Sumber Mata Air Di Desa Aik Bual. Available at https://kmberugakdese.wordpress.com/
Bräutigam DA, Knack S (2004) Foreign aid, institutions, and governance in sub-Saharan Africa. Econ Dev Cult Change 52(2):255–285
Bunnell T, Miller MA, Phelps NA, Taylor J (2013) Urban development in a decentralized Indonesia: two success stories? Pac Aff 86(4):857–876
Christoplos I, Hedquist AL, Engstrand K (2014) Capacity development literature review. Sida, Sweden. Available at http://www.sida.se/contentassets/a91ee363c301497ea206f48500a93203/literature-review-cd_2014.pdf
Crawford PW (2004) Aiding aid: a monitoring & evaluating framework to enhance international aid effectiveness. University of Technology, Sydney
De Janvry A, Dethier JJ (2012) The world bank and governance: the bank's efforts to help developing countries build state capacity. World Bank Policy Research Working Paper, (6275)
Dentith J, Hong E, Loy I, Mihlar F, Openshaw D, Zalcberg J (2013) Asia and Oceania. In: Walker B (ed) State of the world's minorities and indigenous peoples 2013: events of 2012. London, UK, Minority Rights Group International, pp 117–176
DPWG LGD (2007) Alignment strategies in the field of decentralization and governance: a review of country practices and experiences. Final Main Report on International Development partner harmonization for Enhanced Aid Effectiveness
DRSP (2006) Decentralization 2006: stock taking on Indonesia's recent decentralization reforms, Summary of Findings. AUSAID Democratic Reform Support Program (DRSP) for the Donor Working Group on Decentralization, Jakarta. Available at http://pdf.usaid.gov/pdf_docs/PNADH311.pdf
Eaton K, Kaiser Kai, Smoke P (2010) Political economy of decentralization reforms: implication for aid effectiveness. The World Bank, Washington
Edi J, Setianingtias A (2007) Donor proliferation and donor coordination in Indonesia: the case of governance reform. Centre for the Future State, Institute of Development Studies, University of Sussex
Escobar A (1984–1985) Discourse and power in development: Michel Foucault and the relevance of his work to the third world. Alternatives 10:377–400
Escobar A (1988) Power and visibility: development and the invention and management of the third world. Cult Anthropol 3:428–443
Escobar A (1992) Imagining a post-development era? Critical thought, development and social movements. Soc al Text 31(32):20–56
Escobar A (2012) Encountering development: the making and unmaking of the Third World, 7th edn. Princeton University Press, Princeton, NJ

Fortier F (1999) Virtual communities, real struggles: seeking alternatives for democratic networking. In: Gurstein M (ed) Community informatics: enabling communities with information and communications technologies. Idea Group Publishing, Hershey, USA, pp 446–469

Gatwiri GJ, McLaren HJ (2016a) Discovering my own black feminism: embarking on a journey to explore Kenyan women's oppression. Int J Int Women's Stud 17(1):202–211

Gatwiri GJ, McLaren HJ (2016b) Discovering my own African feminism: embarking on a journey to explore Kenyan women's oppression. J Int Women's Stud 17(4):263–273

Harcourt W (ed) (1994) Introduction. In: Feminist perspectives on sustainable development. Zed Books, London, pp 1–8

Holzhacker RL, Wittek R, Woltjer J (2016) Decentralization and governance for sustainable society in Indonesia. In: Holzhacker RL, Wittek R, Woltjer J (Eds.) Decentralization and governance in Indonesia. Springer, London, UK, pp 3–29

Hopkins, R. (2012). 'Alternatives to development': an interview with Arturo Escobar. In: Transition Culture: an evolving exploration into the head, heart and hands of energy descent. Available at https://www.transitionculture.org/2012/09/28/alternatives-to-development-an-interview-with-arturo-escobar/

Hyden G (2008) After the Paris declaration: taking on the issue of power. Dev Policy Rev 26 (3):259–274

Jarvie J, Sutarto R, Syam D, Jeffery P (2015) Lessons for Africa from urban climate change resilience building in Indonesia. Curr Opin Environ Sustain 13:19–24

Kaufmann D (2009) Aid effectiveness and governance: the good, the bad and the ugly. Dev Outreach 11(1):26–29

Keijzer N (2016) Open data on a closed shop? Assessing the potential of transparency initiatives with a focus on efforts to strengthen capacity development support. Dev Policy Rev 34(1):83–100

Knack S (2012) When do donors trust recipient country systems? World Bank Policy Research Working Paper, (6019)

Knack S (2013) Aid and donor trust in recipient country systems. J Dev Econ 101:316–329

Knack S, Smets L (2013) Aid tying and donor fragmentation. World Dev 44:63–76

Kothari R (1993) Rethinking development and democracy. In: Wignaraja P (ed) New social movements in the south: empowering the people. Vistaar Publications, New Delhi

Kothari R (2005) Rethinking democracy. Orient Longman, New Delhi

Kurniawan F, Adrianto L, Bengen DG, Prasetyo LB (2016) Vulnerability assessment of small islands to tourism: the case of the Marine tourism park of the Gili Matra Islands, Indonesia. Glob Ecol Conserv 6:308–326

Lawrence MD, Filer C, Potter L, Resosudarmo BP (2013) Local management arrangement in Sesaot Forest, Lombok, Indonesia. J Environ Technol Manag 4(1):1–21

Malik K (2013) Human development report 2013. The rise of the south: human progress in a diverse world. In: Human development report 2013. United Nations Development Programme, New York

McCormick D, Schmitz H (2009) Donor proliferation and coordination: experiences of Kenya and Indonesia. Institute for Development Studies, University of Nairobi, and Institute of Development Studies, University of Sussex

McIntyre-Mills J (2004) Critical systemic praxis for social and environmental justice: participatory policy design and governance for a global age. Springer Science & Business Media, Berlin

Mcintyre-Mills J (2008) Systemic ethics: social, economic and environmental implications of eating our yellow cake in South Australia. Syst Res Behav Sci 25(2):225–248

McIntyre-Mills JJ (2013) Anthropocentrism and well-being: a way out of the Lobster pot? Syst Res Behav Sci 30(2):136–155

McIntyre-Mills J (2014) Systemic ethics for social and environmental justice. In: Systemic ethics and non-anthropocentric stewardship. Springer International Publishing, Cham, pp 121–153

McIntyre-Mills JJ (2016) Ecological footprint and governing the Anthropocene through balancing individualism and collectivism. In: Proceedings of the 59th annual meeting of the ISSS-2015 Berlin, Germany, vol 1, no 1
McIntyre-Mills J, De Vries D, Deakin J (2008) Participatory democracy based on user-centric policy design to address complex needs. Citizenship in the 21st Century, 1
McLaren H, Gibson C, Arney F, Scott D, Brown L (2008) Sowing the seeds of innovation: exploring strategies for sustaining the spread of innovative approaches in child and family work. In: The history and future of social innovation. The Hawke Institute, Adelaide http://www.unisa.edu.au/hawkeinstitute/publications/social-innovation
McLaren HJ (2015a) Geographic labour mobility, workers and family in China and Australia. In: Andressen C (ed) China's changing economy: trends, impacts and the future. Routledge, London, pp 22–34
McLaren HJ (2015b) Traversing organisational cultures: building student capacity to lead conversations about child protection policy reform. Particip Educ Res 2015–1:132–144 (Special Issue)
McLaren HJ (2016) Introduction: silence as a power. Soc Altern 35(1):3–5
McLaren HJ, Kenny PL (2015) Motivating change from lecture-tutorial modes to less traditional forms of teaching. Aust Univ Rev 57(1):26
Mietzner M (2014) Indonesia's decentralization: the rise of local identities and the survival of the nation-state. In: Hall H (ed) Regional dynamics in a decentralized Indonesia. Institute of South East Asian Studies, Singapore, pp 45–67
Nawaz F, McLaren HJ (2016) Silencing the hardship: Bangladeshi women, microfinance and reproductive work. Soc Altern 35(1):19–25
OECD (2008) Indonesia' in OECD 2008 Survey on Monitoring the Paris Declaration: making Aid More Effective by 2010, OECD
OECD (2011). Development cooperation report 2011. 50th Anniversary Edition, Development Assistance Committee (DAC), OECD Publishing
Peet R, Hartwick E (2015) Theories of development: contentions, arguments, alternatives, 3rd edn. The Guilford Press, New York
Riddell RC (2007) Effective aid requires new structures: poverty in focus. Brasilia, UNDP. Available at http://www.ipc-undp.org/pub/IPCPovertyInFocus12.pdf
Rogers E (2003) Diffusion of innovations, 5th edn. Free Press, New York
Smoke P, Winters MS (2011) Donor program harmonization, aid effectiveness, and decentralized governance, January 2011, Local Governance and Decentralization. Available at http://www.delog.org/cms/upload/pdf/DLGHarmonization_AidEffectivenessJan2011.pdf
Tuana N (2006) The speculum of ignorance: the women's health movement and epistemologies of ignorance. Hypatia 21(3):1–19
UNDP (2010) Assessment of development results: evaluation of UNDP contribution, Indonesia. United Nations Development fund (UNDP), Indonesia. Available at http://www.oecd.org/derec/undp/47865010.pdf
Unsworth S (2009) What's politics got to do with it?: why donors find it so hard to come to terms with politics, and why this matters. J Int Dev 21(6):883–894
Van Rooy A (2009) The art of strengthening civil society. In: Van Rooy A (ed) Civil society and the aid industry. Earthscan Publishing, London, UK, pp 197–220
Walsh T (2005) Perceptions of development partners and evidence on aid effectiveness in Indonesia, Report Submitted to Department for International Development (DFID), September 14, 2005
Widianingsih I (2005) The practice of participatory planning in Indonesia after the reform era: a case study of Solo municipality. Center for Development Studies, Flinders University, Australia, Discussion Paper
Widianingsih I (2006a) Local governance. In: Achmad R (ed) Decentralisation and participatory planning in Indonesia: seeking a new path to a harmonious society. (The role of public administration in building harmonious society, selected proceedings from the annual conference of the network of Asia-Pacific schools and institutes of public administration and

governance (NAPSIPAG), Asian Development Bank, Network of Asia-Pacific Schools and Institutes of Public Administration and Governance, Philippines, pp 69–89. Available in http://unpan1.un.org/intradoc/groups/public/documents/apcity/unpan026011.pdf)

Widianingsih I (2006b) Decentralization and participation in Indonesia: moving towards more participatory planning? Sosiohumaniora 8(1):39

Widianingsih I (2013) In search of collaborative policy practice at local level: the case of safe school against disaster in West Nusa Tenggara, Indonesia. 한국정책학회 하계학술발표논문집 2013(2):578–596

Widianingsih I (2014) International donor policy and local government in Indonesia: establishing good governance? Ph.D Thesis, School of International Studies, Flinders University, Adelaide

Widianingsih I (2015) International technical assistance for local governance reform in the post-Suharto Indonesia: sustaining aid effectiveness? In: International conference on public administration (ICPA 11th). Available at http://www.icpa-uestc.cn/upimages/1-2-4%20%20Ida%20Widianingsih.pdf

Widianingsih I, Morrell E (2007) Participatory planning in Indonesia: seeking a new path to democracy. Policy Stud 28(1):1–15

Winters M (2012) The obstacles to Foreign aid harmonization: lessons from the decentralization sector in Indonesia (February 1, 2012). Available at SSRN http://ssrn.com/abstract-2009992 or doi:10.2139/ssrn.2009992

## Author Biographies

**Dr. Ida Widianingsih** is Head of Public Administration Department and Associate Professor in the Faculty of Social and Political Sciences, Universitas Padjadjaran (Unpad), Indonesia. She is a PhD graduate of Flinders University. Her focus is on participatory approaches to development and translating the theory of development into practice.

**Dr. Helen McLaren** is a Senior Lecturer in the School of Social & Policy Studies, Flinders University, Australia. Dr. McLaren specializes in research related child and family systems with a focus on gender and development, child welfare, welfare system reform and distributive governance. Having been a visiting research fellow at the Chinese Academy of Social Sciences, Beijing, and at Universitas Padjadjaran, West Java, Indonesia, her research priorities currently traverse nations bordering the Indian and Pacific Oceans, with Australia at the crossroads.

**Dr. Janet McIntyre-Mills** is an Associate Professor in the School of Social and Policy Studies at Flinders University, Adjunct Professor at the University of Indonesia and Islamic National University in Indonesia, and Honorary Professor at the University of South Africa.Her research focuses on systemic representation, accountability and re-generation applied to social and environmental justice concerns such as health, housing and social inclusion and the mitigation and adaptation to climate change. She addresses complex needs by exploring the meanings and 'what if' questions with diverse stakeholders.

Her recent books include 'From Wall Street to Wellbeing: Joining up the dots through Participatory Democracy and Governance to Mitigate the Causes and Adapt to the Effects of Climate Change'. ISBN 978-1-4899-7465-5 and 'Systemic ethics and Non-anthropocentric Stewardship: Implications for Trans disciplinarity and Cosmopolitan politics', ISBN 978-3-519-07655-3.

# Chapter 16
# Critical Systems Thinking Review on the Challenges of Decentralised Drinking Water Management in City of 'Nauli', Indonesia

**Jackwin Simbolon**

**Abstract** This paper is based on a PhD project that strives to assess the performance of decentralised drinking water management in the city of Nauli, Indonesia. The implementation of decentralised government system followed by decentralising some functions including drinking water services is unsatisfactory in providing access to drinking water for all residents in the city of Nauli. Nauli Municipality that has just split up as an autonomous local government under the decentralised government system in Indonesia is facing conflicts in providing water provision to the society, since there are three public water companies in this region: City PDAM, District PDAM, and Provincial BLUD. Furthermore, these governments and their water companies seem to forget the main objective of government in water provision as stated in the Indonesia Constitution: to fully control the water and manage it for meeting the people's needs. The aim of this research is to apply Ulrich's critical systems heuristics (CSH) to address the following research questions: (i) how effective is the current decentralised water management system? and (ii) how the current system can be improved and what ought to be done?

## Introduction

The Indonesian Constitution article 33 states that '*The land, the waters and the natural resources within shall be under the powers of the State and shall be used to the greatest benefit of the people*'. It goes on to say that in Indonesia, government has the responsibility to provide public utilities to the people. In terms of providing water, Indonesia has implemented the decentralised system in water management, meaning that the responsibility of water provision is one of local governments'

J. Simbolon (✉)
Flinders University, Adelaide, Australia
e-mail: simb0006@uni.flinders.edu.au



J. McIntyre-Mills et al. (eds.), *Balancing Individualism and Collectivism*, Contemporary Systems Thinking, DOI 10.1007/978-3-319-58014-2_16

functions. However, the effectiveness of the system is still unsatisfactory compared to some targets that have been established. This paper as part of a PhD project[1] tries to unravel the cause of poor water management in Indonesia, with Nauli Region as a case study. I am currently pursuing my PhD in the School of Social and Policy Studies on improving Water Supply Management in Nauli region, to examine the problems and to find a better model of institutional arrangements of water supply management. The empirical research assesses the extent to which the management approaches support the UN Sustainable Development Goals (SDGs). I will consider the how and why of what works and what does not work.

This research will try to examine the performance of water providers—namely water companies—and local governments in the Nauli region in providing drinking water. However, this is not merely related to political and management per se, but other related aspects that are surrounding it will also be considered, which makes the provision of water problematic or so-called 'a wicked problem' (Churchman 1967) due to competing interests at the different levels of government. This paper will use a critical systemic approach with four aspects, namely, social, economic, environment, health, and politics (Elkington 1999; Gleick 2013; Gorre-Dale 1992; Mcdonnell 2008; McIntyre-Mills 2008; Schelwald-van der Kley and Reijerkerk 2009, p. 8; Zaag and Savenije 2006).[2,3] Moreover, water governance is a part of bigger local, national, and global system, so it will be especially vulnerable to any changes in other sectors (Biswas and Tortajada 2010), and every solution of one aspect has a great connection to or implications for other aspects, and sometimes the issues are overlapping (Churchman 1979, p. 4). This research will apply Werner Ulrich's Critical Systems Heuristics (CSH) analysis to obtain a more detailed picture to answer two research questions: (i) how effective is the current water management system in providing drinking water to the society; and (ii) how can the current system be improved and what ought to be done?

Indeed similar research has been conducted in other countries (developed and developing);[4] however, many aspects and conditions have changed over time, so '…what may have been a viable solution a decade ago or in a particular region may not be so now or in other region. This means that water policies need to be updated periodically so that they reflect the changing requirements' (Biswas 2001, 2007). The paper will be divided into seven parts: first part will discuss decentralisation euphoria in Indonesia and its impact on drinking water management; the second part will discuss about the performance of drinking water provision in Indonesia; the third part will discuss about the background of drinking water management in Nauli; the fourth part will describe a little bit about key concept, approach, and

[1]Ethics approval No. 6861

[2]The first three aspects, social, economic and environment, known as the Triple Bottom Line coined by Elkington (1999) in his book Cannibals with Forks: The Triple Bottom Line of 21st Century Business.

[3]McIntyre-Mills (2008, p. 10) constitutes these aspects as 'The Dimensions of Wellbeing'.

[4]See also (Domènech 2011; Hwang et al. 2014; Kim 2008; Moglia et al. 2011; Reynoso 2000; Wilder and Lankao 2006)

methodology; the fifth part will discuss about field findings of problems that are caused by poor water management system, the sixth part will examine the effectiveness of this system through Werner Ulrich's CSH; and it finally concludes with recommendations for future improvement.

## Decentralisation Euphoria in Indonesia and its Impact on Drinking Water Management

Indonesia under President Sukarno administration had adopted a regional government system since the introduction of Law no. 1/1945 about Regional National-Committee, and then developed by a number of subsequent laws, which later revised former law: Law No. 22/1948, Law no. 1/1957, and Law no. 18/1965. However, the term 'decentralisation' was formally introduced in the President Suharto era, through Law no. 5/1974 about Government in Regions, which is regarded by Sulistiyanto and Erb (2005, p. 6) as 'limited decentralisation while preserving the unitary system' (Purwanto 2005). With this regulation, the President Suharto regime seemed to introduce regional autonomy and implemented decentralisation, but still has the power to appoint the head of regional governments, and to intervene in local administration. In principle, this law did not give power to regional government to manage their affairs (Sulistiyanto and Erb 2005), and with the military behind the regime, it was also very intimidating. In terms of water management, the Ministry of Public Works had strong control through its regional offices (*kantor wilayah*) in each province, which decided on the areas of development as well as proposing funding to Jakarta. The ministry issued Ministerial Decree no.3/PRT/1968 which has been regarded as the starting point of nationally integrated water management. In the First Medium Term Development (Pelita I[5]), Ministry of Public Works acted as the key player in organising water-related investment all over the country, which began in 120 cities funded by foreign loans. In the Second Medium Term Development (Pelita II[6]), the ministry then expanded all local government units in charge to water management units into local-government-owned water companies called PDAM.[7] However, in practice, water management nationally was regulated and controlled by the Ministry of Public Works, and PDAM management must comply with regulations stipulated by the Ministry of Home Affairs.

Since 1999 following the downfall of Suharto, Law no. 22/1999 was introduced and had gradually dismantled the centralistic system in favour of decentralisation (Sulistiyanto and Erb 2005). By this law, local governments heads are not appointed by central government but directly elected by the people, and there is clear separation of functions between central government and local governments

[5]Pelita: Pembangunan Lima Tahun (Medium Term Development). Pelita I was from 1969 to 1973.
[6]Pelita II: 1974–1978.
[7]PDAM: Perusahaan Daerah Air Minum.

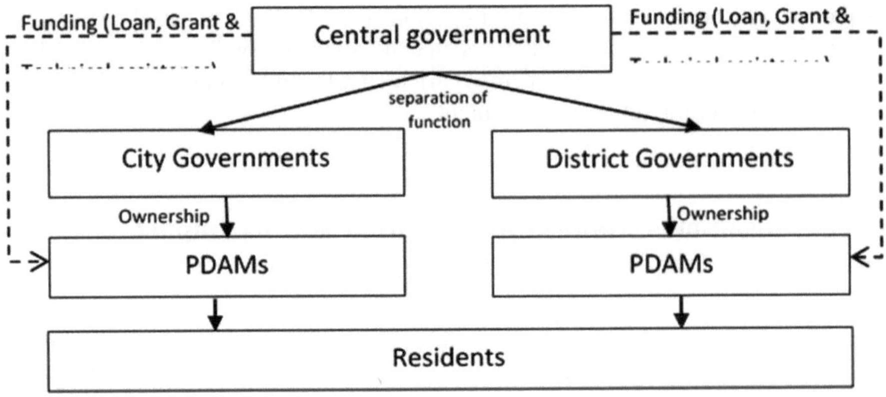


**Fig. 1** Transfer of water service function from central government to local government

(municipal and district government) which means that local governments have the authority to perform the functions without any intervention from central government. Drinking water management is one of the transferred functions and the Department of Public Work regional offices are closed down as shown in Fig. 1.

The government started to assign water supply provision to PDAM since 1970 s, and at the beginning of 1980s there were only 12 PDAMs established in Indonesia[8] with overall service coverage in urban area was only 7% (Simbolon 2007). However, regulatory functions and policies are still shared among several government institutions before the function is really landed into the hands of PDAM. Some of the institutions are the National Development Planning Agency (establishing water blueprint and coordinate all sectors), Ministry of Public Works (execution of the planning), Ministry of Home Affairs (managing local government issues including PDAM management and water tariff), Ministry of Health (establishing healthy water standard), and local governments (responsible for delivering water to residents).

During 16 years of the implementation of decentralisation in Indonesia (from 1999 to 2015), there have been 215 new district and city governments were established.[9] These new local governments then began to create their own PDAM to perform water service in their region, with the aim of accelerating water provision to the people.[10] There are 117 new PDAMs established by those new local governments, and water management has moved towards more local-based rather than partnerships between local governments (OECD 2010, p. 113). However, in

[8]Some of them were not really established by the local government, since they are already existed since the colonial era. Some of the oldest water companies for example: in Medan (1905), in Jakarta (1918), in Makassar (1924), in Semarang (1911).

[9]Data generated from Directorate General of Fiscal Balance, Ministry of Finance,2015.

[10]Until 2015 there have been 117 new PDAMs and it is still counting. (Perpamsi,2015).

many cases,[11] problems arise and in Nauli region, for example, conflicts between old and new local governments and their PDAMs regarding transfer of assets, lack of resources (technology, fund, and human resources) of new PDAMs, and intervention from local governments to new PDAM management, and they have neglected services with the result that people suffer from a shortage of water. This phenomenon of establishing new water company without considering the economies of scale, cultural, and environment detriment has been taken place recently in many regions in Indonesia, due to a proliferation of local governments.

After about 50 years of the existence of PDAMs, PDAMs have been experiencing unsatisfactory performance. First, financial performance, the Water Supply System Development Support Body (BPPSPAM[12]) released the national recapitulation of PDAM performance, and in 2013, only 50 per cent of 350 PDAMs can be categorised as financially healthy, while the rest are less healthy and sick. Second, by the end of 2011 PDAMs could only cover 55.04% of population (13.94% in rural area and 41.88% in urban area),[13] while if the target set by the Millennium Development Goals (MDGs)[14] on water access is implemented in Indonesia, it should be 68,87 per cent coverage in 2015.[15]

In several big cities, residents have increasingly complained about PDAMs services since PDAMs applied very high water rates but still delivered poor services and unreliable access to water. Moreover, PDAM were slow to respond to customers' complaints, and there were cases where new commercial customers should pay unlawful fees for setting up a new connection (Winters et al. 2014).

Overall, poor water management has led to over 100 million people in Indonesia lacking access to safe water and in more than 70% of the country 220 million people rely on water obtained from potentially contaminated sources. This unsafe drinking water is a major cause of diarrhoea, which is the second leading killer of children under five in Indonesia and the major cause of 20% of child deaths each year (Dursin 2006). Sustainable water experts believe that the world is approaching (or maybe now experiencing) a water crisis. Some believe that the rapid growth in population has been the major cause (Biswas 1999; Ehrlich 1970; Gilles 2006; Gleick 1993; Jain and Singh 2010; Magelgaard 2011; Sears 1936; Shiva 2008). Increasing population

[11]From preliminary research, this conflict also occurred at least in 15 cases: Kab Kerinci and Kab Sungai penuh, Kab Ketapang and Kab Kayong Utara, Kab Bengkalis and Kab Meranti, Kab Bekasi and Kota Bekasi, Kab Tangerang and Kota Tangerang Selatan, Kab Minahasa and Kab Minahasa Utara, Kab Bogor and Kota Depok, Kab Sambas to Kab Bengkayang and Kota Singkawang, Kab Buru to Kab Buru Selatan, Kab Minahasa and Kota Tomohon, Kab Bandung and Kota Cimahi, Kab Asahan and Kab Batubara, Kabupaten Kotabaru and Kab Tanah Bumbu, Kabupaten Maluku Tenggara to Kota Tual and Kab. Kepulauan Aru.

[12]BPPSPAM: Badan Pendukung Pengembangan Sistem Penyediaan Air Minum

[13](Pembaruan 2013)

[14]Millennium Development Goals (MDGs): Goal 7: Ensure Environmental Sustainability. Target 7C: Halved, by 2015, the proportion of the population without sustainable access to safe drinking water. Source: http://www.un.org/millenniumgoals/environ.shtml, retrieved 3 October 2014.

[15]DG Human Settlements (2009)

means increasing demand for all human needs, agriculture, industry, and also duplication of waste disposal, which means higher competition for water use. However, Amartya Sen stresses that food crisis would never happen if democracy is functioning (Massing 2003), meaning that the role of the government in providing basic needs is the key. Another argument comes from Hoekstra and Chapagain (2006) and (Wackernagel and Rees 1998), saying that human lifestyle, industry booming, and climate—instead of population—determines food and water consumption, proven by the fact that the ecological footprint and water footprint in developed countries, agricultural countries, and dry countries are much higher.

The UN proclaimed in 2010 that water rights are human rights, then urged its members to ratify the Millennium Development Goals in 2000 which has a specific water issue 'Halve, by 2015, the proportion of people without sustainable access to safe drinking water and basic sanitation'.[16] To continue the MDGs, the UN through Rio+20 Earth Summit 2012 had established post-2015 goals and set a new target in drinking water sector, namely to 'achieve universal and equitable access to safe and affordable drinking water for all by 2030', and this means providing water for all in better quality and use it efficiently, as well as preserving water sources and water-related ecosystems.[17] In some countries, extreme poverty has a strong connection with food scarcity, as a result of not having access to good water (FAO et al. 2013, p. 27). In 2000, approximately 150 million urbanites suffered annual water shortage and 886 million city dwellers experienced seasonal water shortage (McDonald et al. 2011).[18] As the increase in population still going on, in 2050, it is expected that the need for water will rise almost sixfold and the number of people who experience water shortage will increase by almost 50%, and it happens mainly in poor area of developing countries, where women and children have to travel for hours to collect water (Jain and Singh 2010). People in poverty, especially in the Third World countries, are hardly hit due to lack of access to sewers and clean water while having to suffer from overwhelming waste generated by burgeoning populations and unregulated industry (Rees 1992). Furthermore, Rees argues that human beings should maintain a balance between their resource needs and discharge of waste to avoid harming the ecosystem, known as the ecological footprint. By acknowledging the ecological footprint of a population, people will know the carrying capacity or the demand from the nature's ecosystem, or the capacity of land to support its population sustainably (Rees 1992; Wackernagel and Rees 1998).

From the water footprint perspective,[19] one needs water for direct consumption (for home or individual necessities) and indirect consumption (from products and

---

[16]See http://www.un.org/millenniumgoals/environ.shtml Millenium Development Goals, Goal 7, Target 7c.

[17]Sustainable Development Goals, Goal 6, https://sustainabledevelopment.un.org/focussdgs.html, retrieved 31 August 2015

[18]McDonald et al. (2011) define water shortage as a condition where one has less than 100 liter per day.

[19]This concept was introduced by A.Y. Hoekstra in 2002 (Avlonas and Nassos 2014), and the term 'water footprint' is an analogy of the 'ecological footprint' (Hoekstra and Hung 2002).

services) (Avlonas and Nassos 2014). Water footprint is a method to calculate '*water used in relation to consumption of people in a particular region*' (Hoekstra and Chapagain 2006). It is important for people to be aware of the water footprint, likewise to know the ecological footprint, as the water footprint will indicate the amount of water needed to support a population sustainably (Hoekstra and Chapagain 2006), as human demand on water is growing rapidly (Wackernagel 1994). For instance, on average, there are 135 l of water needed when we eat only one egg, or we need 35 litres of water to drink a cup of coffee (Antonelli and Greco 2015). However, water consumption differs between regions, and an arid environment will need more water than those of water-rich areas. In this context, the integrated water resources management concept[20] is vital so water will be managed across sectors, administrative areas, and social systems (Braga et al. 2014).

## Nauli City Profile and Drinking Water Management Problem

The Nauli region consists of two neighbouring autonomous local governments: the District of Nauli and City of Nauli. Overall, the total area of this region is 5478.4 $km^2$, of which 3.3% or 180.27 $km^2$ is City of Nauli jurisdiction and 96.7% or 5298.13 $km^2$ as Nauli District administrative area. Most of the area surface is mountainous and rocky landscape with very little precipitation (raining only between December and March, while from May to November precipitation rate almost zero (BPS 2014)).

The District of Nauli was established on 9 August 1958 with Law No. 69/1958[21] and the subdistrict (kecamatan) of Nauli as the capital city. In year 1978 with Government Regulation Nr. 22/1978, the subdistrict of Nauli was upgraded into the administrative municipality[22] of Nauli. In 1996, the status of administrative city of Nauli was then upgraded to Nauli City, which had all the structure of an autonomous city.[23] According to the Statistical body of Nauli City, Nauli City population in 2013 was 318,425 people, of which 33,800 people or 10.6% lived under poverty line. In terms of level of education, only 13% of the population have graduated high school or above, while 11% of the residents had never finished primary school. As a capital city, the city government itself can be considered as the poorest in Indonesia,

[20]The integrated water resources management is defined as 'a process which promotes the coordinated development and management of water, land and related resources, in order to maximize the resultant economic and social welfare in an equitable manner, without compromising the sustainability of vital

[21]BPS Nauli District (2013)

[22]During the New Order Era under president Suharto administration, administrative city was prepared as a candidate of new city, it had its own structure, led by a mayor, but was still under the parent District jurisdiction (Firman 2013, p. 186).

[23]BPS Nauli City (2014)

as its budget was the second lowest amongst 32 capital cities in Indonesia, and surprisingly this local government was ranked as the most corrupt city government in 2015 according to the Indonesia Corruption Watch.

Water management in the Nauli region has become more organised since 1986 after that the status of District Government local water body was upgraded to a water company or PDAM.[24] After almost 30 years of operation, the PDAM of Nauli District has become one of the largest in Indonesia with more than 30.000 connections, supplied by 25 water sources with a capacity of 575 l/s, and it is financially healthy.

In September 2005, the government of Nauli City established its own PDAM (the PDAM of Nauli City). In 2014, the number of connections reached 6573 served by 16 water sources with 108 production capacity. However, the District PDAM still operates their business in the Nauli City administrative territory. In 2012, 85.8% (22.629 out of 26015 connections) of the district PDAM customers were located in Nauli City, which comprised 56.01% of Nauli City population.[25] Until now its head office and 19 out of 25 of its water sources are located in Nauli City.

This has been a major cause of dispute between the two PDAMs, and more widely, between the mayor and head of district. According to national regulations,[26] the function of delivering water provision belongs to the local governments, the local government as regulator and PDAM as the operator, and water tariff must be authorised by the head of local government (Mayor and Head of District). The regulations mean a policy of delivering water in a particular region is made by the local government. The government of Nauli City has asked the Nauli District government to transfer its water service network from the district PDAM to the city PDAM, but the district government refused.[27] There had been efforts by the governor of Samsoir[28] and also some national parliamentary members[29] to reconcile these two local governments, but they still could not arrive at an agreement.

This condition has triggered poor performance in drinking water provision in the Nauli region. In Nauli City, 38.17% of households had access to PDAM water (piped water), while the others should fulfil their need through other sources like water merchants (32.84%), bore well (24.16%), and other unprotected water sources (4.43%), and sadly there are 0.4% or more than 15,000 people that do not

---

[24]PDAM of Nauli District was formally founded on 15 May 1986.

[25]PDAM Kabupaten Nauli Company Profile 2013.

[26]Government Regulation No. 16/2005 and Ministry of Home Affairs Decree No. 23/2006.

[27]Pos Nauli news: Pemkot akan ambil alih PDAM (City government will take over PDAM), dated 8 September 2013, http://Nauli.tribunnews.com/2013/09/08/pemkot-akan-ambil-alih-pdam

[28]Pos Nauli news: Gubernur Pertemukan Bupati dan Walikota (Governor gathered the Regent and the Mayor), dated 5 February 2014, http://Nauli.tribunnews.com/2014/02/05/gubernur-pertemukan-bupati-dan-walikota-Nauli

[29]Pos Nauli news: Bupati Curhat PDAM ke Komisi V DPR RI (The Regent converse about PDAM to Indonesia Parliament member), dated 14 March 2014, http://Nauli.tribunnews.com/2014/03/14/bupati-curhat-pdam-ke-komisi-v-dpr-ri

**Fig. 2** A well with 70-m deep and still no water in dry season

**Fig. 3** People carry water bucket on from a spring sometimes for hundreds of metre

have access to water sources at all (BPS Nauli City 2014). Meanwhile, in the Nauli District the situation was much worse, with only 1.63% of households served by piped water, while 5.43% of the population had to buy water from water merchants, 92.94% got water from a protected water well, spring, river, or even rain water (BPS Nauli District 2013) (Figs. 2, 3, 4, 5).

To support both PDAMs in obtaining drinking water as well as water for irrigation and other needs, central government had built the Tilong dam with 19.07 million $m^3$ capacity, a dam located in Nauli District, 25 km from the city of Nauli. Samsoir provincial government[30] is assigned to operate the dam. In 2011, the provincial government then established a new department with a semi-private

[30]According to Law 23/2014 article 4: provincial government is representative of central government.

**Fig. 4** Unprotected water source, a small river used for domestic needs

**Fig. 5** Rainwater harvested from roof gutter

financial management system *(Pola Pengelolaan Keuangan Badan Layanan Umum Daerah/PPK BLUD)*, and it is called BLUD SPAM (Sistem Penyediaan Air Minum/Drinking Water Provision System). In terms of drinking water, the main objective of this unit is to provide bulk water to PDAM of Nauli City and PDAM of Nauli District. However, in point of fact, BLUD SPAM is not only selling bulk water to PDAM of Nauli City (because PDAM of Nauli District does not want to buy), but started to sell bulk water direct to user such as the residents of Nauli City and Nauli District, University of Meranti, and the El Loco airport.

It means both PDAMs only concentrate to expand their business in Nauli City region, because this area contains most of profitable customers in Nauli area. Despite the fact that PDAM of Nauli District should serve residents in Nauli District area, this company is still reluctant to discharge their coverage in Nauli City and hand it over to the city PDAM, since it needs the revenue collected from the city to finance their operation in district area. Meanwhile, the quality and quantity of the piped water were also problematic. Supply of water from PDAM is not reliable. Many people in Nauli City area witnessed that buying water from the water retailers sometimes is better than paying for PDAM water, since the water tap is not flowing regularly, and it often releases only foul smelling air—not water.[31] These two PDAMs are also in conflict over acquiring water sources. Most of high debit water sources in Nauli city area are controlled by PDAM of Nauli District,[32] and it has caused PDAM of Nauli City to employ 21 relatively small debit[33] of water sources, where 18 of them are using bore wells which generate high electricity costs (Simanjuntak et al. 2015, pp. 44–5). In fact, both PDAMs have to struggle to find reliable water sources in Nauli city since this area is very arid with an uncertain climate. In the dry season between May and November each year, Nauli city experiences a water crisis. There are three rivers in Nauli city which flow only during rainy season (BPS Nauli City 2014), which makes groundwater sources as very important alternatives for PDAM. The building of reservoirs is not optimal since there had been miscalculated in yields of surface water, and groundwater does not supply enough water.[34] If this deteriorating water crisis is not addressed immediately, it could impact on the sustainable delivery of services to business and tourism in Nauli City, and since most of them rely on ground and surface water withdrawal rather than from PDAM piped water.[35]

## Key Concepts and Approach

It is generally accepted[36] that public utilities (such as electricity, water, transportation, and waste collection) should be provided or at least controlled by the government, and it is part of the development driven by the government. That is also the case in Indonesia. With the purpose of conducting the above-mentioned responsibility, the government established and implemented a great deal of regulations, and often changed repeatedly. Public utilities regulation is very dependent on the political structure and the ruling regime (Gormley Jr 1983). Wilson makes a strong argument that the politics of regulation, especially for intervening in the

---

[31]Institute of Resource Governance and Social Change, http://www.irgsc.org/opinion/Stop-Balakai.html, retrieved 2 August 2015.

[32]PDAM of Nauli District utilize 25 water sources, 19 of which are located in Nauli City area.

[33]A hydrology term for water discharge rate per second.

[34]ADB 2015 Annual Evaluation Review, http://www.adb.org/sites/default/files/linked-documents/F-Lessons-on-WSS-Projects.pdf, retrieved 1 September 2015.

[35]Agriculture only acquires 4.15% of land in Nauli City, and it is shrinking due to swift development and growing service sectors (BPS Nauli City 2014).

[36]See for example da Cruz et al. (2013); Drakakis-Smith (1995); Laffont (2004).

market and providing utilities, does exist (Wilson 1980, p. 357). By and large, one way that government can regulate or control its political power to public service provision is through the government institutions: centralised and decentralised.

The term decentralization was used by Thomas Jefferson as

> by dividing and subdividing these republics from the great national one down through all its subordinations, until it ends in the administration of every man's farm by himself; by placing under everyone what his own eye may superintend, that all will be done for the best... (Thomas Jefferson 1999, quoted in Treisman 2002).

The UNDP defines decentralisation as a restructuring of the power of central government and expanding the responsibilities and capacities of subnational government level, to achieve effectiveness and better quality in the system of governance (UNDP 1997). As Cohen and Peterson (1999) explain, decentralisation is not only based on historical origins or territorial cluster, but can also be based on problem/valued centre and service delivery focuses. Bahl and Martinez-Vazquez (2006, p. 6) stressed that the implementation of decentralization is mainly because of people's disappointment with the existing centralised system. There are several underlying factors behind it: bigger population and central government failed to serve one or some particular areas; worsened public services, poor performance, and poor accountability of government officials; cultural and ethnic egoism that makes people want to have more autonomy to rule their region. However, the UNDP (1999) emphasised that decentralisation is definitely not regarded as an alternative to centralisation since the centralisation of policy is still needed in a national regulating context, and successful decentralisation will greatly depend on coordination and relationships between all stakeholders: the government, private sectors, and the civil society.

According to UNDP (2014, pp. 5, 85), providing access to adequate clean water is one of the *universal provision of social services,*[37] and it is essential in order to strengthen the quality of life of the people especially in early stages of development. Scarce water is now a big problem for some countries, and it has to be addressed to assure that health security is achieved. In formulising the 2013 human development index, UNDP (2014, pp. 212–5) included 'child mortality rate caused by unsafe water supply and unimproved sanitation' as a parameter, and it shows that even countries in the very high human development index group (8 out of 49 countries) still experienced the unsafe water supply.[38] While Indonesia ranked 16 in gross domestic product, it only ranked 108 in human development index (clustered as Medium Human Development) and has abundant of water in the country, it had 130 deaths per 100,000 of children under the age of 5.

[37]UNDP emphasizes that universal provision of social services are: education, health care, water supply and sanitation, and public safety.

[38]It shows that per 100,000 cases of death of children under age 5: Denmark (1 case), Luxembourg (2 cases), Czech Republic (1 case), Cyprus (13 cases), Qatar (6 cases), United Arab Emirates (10 cases), Chile (1 case), and Cuba (1 case).

Mahbub ul Haq said that "*people are the real wealth of a nation*" (UNDP 2010). 'Development means good change' (Chambers 1995). Development constitutes the quality of life of the citizens, and "access to education and health care, employment opportunities, availability of clean air and safe drinking water, the threat of crime, and so on" (World Bank Group 2012). The goal is the development or improvement of the citizen as an individual, not only citizens collectively as a society or as a group (Nussbaum 2011), and these goals are referred to as Capabilities. The Capability Approach emphasises freedom of the individual to make decisions as a basic right, and according to Amartya Sen, development must pay most attention to promote such freedom (Deneulin 2006; Sen 1999). Sen argues that in constructing development, the freedom of individual should be treated as one of the basic building blocks (Sen 1999). Martha Nussbaum (2011, pp. 17–44) emphasises that the government should secure for all citizens the Ten Central Capabilities[39] at a threshold level, and 'healthiness' (the ability to have a healthy living includes access to clean water) is at the second most important. It means that providing water is considered a basic need and it is also important to sustain human life not only for current but also for future generations (Stiglitz et al. 2010, p. 98). Robert Chambers emphasises that when well-being in terms of experiencing a good quality of life is regarded as the objective of development, then a sustainable livelihood is fundamental to support well-being (Chambers 1997, pp. 9–10).

The UNDP introduced the human security approach in the Human Development Report 1994, with central idea: 'the right to live in freedom and dignity, free from poverty and despair… with an equal opportunity to enjoy all their rights and fully develop their human potential' (Gómez and Gasper 2013; UNDP 1994). Whilst the human development approach is talking about freedoms and people's choice, a human security concept is prioritising the choices and assuring the provision and implementation, and water security is one of the human security components (Gómez and Gasper 2013, pp. 3, 14). People, or citizen, should be treated as participants, rather than consumers, because their role and wisdom are vital for democracy and to achieve sustainability in a social and environmental context (McIntyre-Mills 2003, pp. 14, 54). Formulating water policies should regard the reality of life of the poor at the periphery level instead of those in elite groups, and

[39]Ten Central Capabilities: (i) Life: to have the ability to enjoy living until normal age or longevity; (ii) Healthiness: to have the ability to have adequate food, clothing, shelter, and healthy living; (iii) Feeling Secure: have the ability to travel freely, free from crime and also free from domestic violence; (iv) creativity: have the ability to expand their knowledge, free to express their mind in terms of political, religious, artistic, and so forth; (v) Emotions: have the ability to express emotions like to love, to grieve, to feel desire, and also anger; (vi) Practical reason: to have the ability to use reason to decide how to act; (vii) Social interaction: to have the ability to affiliate with other human being, or to form a group, without feeling scared of discrimination of race, sexual orientation, religion, caste, ethnicity, and so forth; (viii) the nature: have the ability to pay attention and give concern to animals, plants, and the nature; (ix) Relax: to have the ability to play, laugh, and have fun; and (x) take control on their environment: have the ability to have political stand, free speech, to hold a property, to have equal treatment in social life, and mutual recognition with other people.

able to reduce poverty by providing broader access for the poor to health service and water provision (Chambers 1995, pp. 175, 82). Therefore, expanding pragmatism in water policy is needed, especially to widen perspectives towards balancing individual versus collective interests and also the environment (McIntyre-Mills 2014, pp. 45–6).

Managing water has moved to be a more political commodity and not merely as public service provision. 'The emergence of water extraction technologies has increased the role of the state in water management' wrote Shiva (2002, p. 20). The increasing role of government in managing water has made 'water management is inherently political' (Mollinga 2008, p. 8). In the context of a nation, water supply management will be very depending on political situation and governmental system in the country. Water sources and water provision are usually controlled by the government and then delegated to be performed by one particular government department, or lower level government, or a water authority, or even a company (Stephenson 1998, p. 295). Biswas (2001, pp. 493–4) explains that in the past, most developing countries water decision was held at central level by a water ministry. However, this approach has changed drastically in recent years since rather than centralised was often regarded inefficient and decentralised system has been viewed as the most appropriate way to water provision (Naddeo et al. 2013).

The Dublin Statement on Water and Sustainable Development in Principle 2 states

> Water development and management should be based on a participatory approach, involving users, planners and policy-makers at all levels.

The participatory approach involves raising awareness of the importance of water among policy-makers and the general public. It means that decisions are taken at the lowest appropriate level, with full public consultation and involvement of users in the planning and implementation of water projects.

This view was then supported by Mcdonnell (2008, p. 132), saying that water management should be more decentralised to accommodate 'local ideas and demand management'. In the process of making water policies, there are negotiations between all levels of government, government apparatus, and even all groups that will be affected by the policies (Mollinga 2008, p. 12). The government uses its power to stipulate law and regulation to intervene water service and water business. Negotiations may occur during formulating and implementing of the policy. Mollinga uses a term 'politics of policy' to describe the national policy processes. Local leaders tend to use the public service provision as a political vehicle to gain votes from constituents, to consolidate only select small-scale alliances, or even worse to feed the predatory business interests who support them during election process (Sulistiyanto et al. 2011).

## Sustainable Water

Water experts believe that the world is approaching (or maybe now experiencing) a water crisis. Some believe that rapid growth in population has been the major cause (Biswas 1999; Ehrlich 1970; Gilles 2006; Gleick 1993; Jain and Singh 2010; Magelgaard 2011; Sears 1936; Shiva 2008). Increasing population means increasing demand for all human needs, agriculture, industry, and also duplication of waste disposal, which means higher competition for water use. However, Amartya Sen stresses that food crisis will never happen if democracy is functioning (Massing 2003), meaning that the role of the government in providing basic needs is the key. Another argument comes from Hoekstra and Chapagain (2006) and (Wackernagel and Rees 1998), saying that human lifestyle, industry booming, and climate—instead of population—determine food and water consumption, proven by the fact that the ecological footprint and water footprint in developed countries, agricultural countries, and dry countries are much higher.

## Methodology

'Systemic thinking helps to explore conceptual and spatial boundaries that address social, cultural, political, economic, and environmental considerations' (McIntyre-Mills 2006, p. 31). Churchman (1979) described that in systems thinking, a problem is part of a system that has several interconnected subsystems, and these subsystems work together to attain the total system objective. According to Midgley (2000, pp. 2–4), systems thinking was introduced in the latter half of the twentieth century to attack the traditional *mechanism* approach—an approach that viewed everything or every problem as if it is a machine, and tends to simplify solutions. Systems thinking will not break down parts of the system separately, but will treat them and their environment holistically, use models rather than experiments, unfolding values and sweeping in the aspects (Jackson 2000; McIntyre-Mills 2006).

The analysis will be focusing on Werner Ulrich's twelve boundary critical heuristic questions (Midgley 2000, p. 141; Ulrich 1989, p. 244; 1996, pp. 24–31; Ulrich and Reynolds 2010), because we need to consider what Ulrich said as the 'context of application', which means wider circumstances and consequences (Ulrich 1996, p. 18). Critical heuristics will not give theoretical justification 'why' and 'how' the solutions are taken, but rather to give stakeholders (decision maker, planners, and affected citizens) understanding about defining problems, design a system and its implications, and evaluate the programs (Ulrich 1989, p. 277). These questions are essential to explore and justify boundaries in understanding an improvement that has been or has to be achieved (Midgley 2000, p. 138), because how we value an improvement will be very depending on the boundaries of the context or the system of concern (Ulrich 2003, p. 5). In examining an improvement,

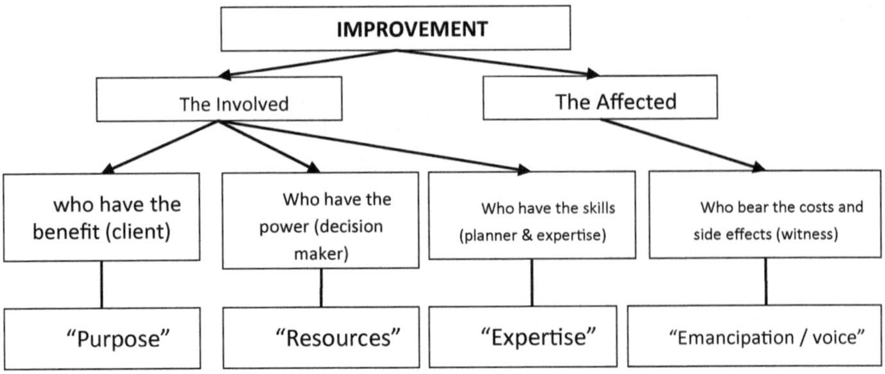


**Fig. 6** Dimensional analysis to determine the meaning of improvement

**Table 1** List of Interviewee

| Nauli district gov't | Nauli city gov't | Central gov't | Water company | Residents |
|---|---|---|---|---|
| Head of district | Local planning agency | Ministry of public works | PDAM of Nauli district | 46 households in Nauli district |
| Local planning agency | Public works dept. | Ministry of home affairs | PDAM of Nauli city | 45 households in Nauli city |
| Public works dept. | Health dept. | Ministry of finance | BLUD SPAM (province) | DAMIU owners |
| Health dept. | Mining dept. | National planning agency | Trucked water merchants | |
| | Environment control body | | | |

people have to have similar lens and perspective or what so-called 'reference system', so we have to make sense the situation and unfolding multiple perspectives by circumscribing our understanding in order to encourage a more holistic awareness (Ulrich and Reynolds 2010).

These questions will set boundaries in further analysis, because by applying boundaries we can sweep in as much relevant information as possible, and in social context, setting up the boundaries will allow us to include relevant stakeholders and most importantly, decision-makers (Churchman 1970). As Cabrera (2006, p. 10) states, boundaries will distinguish what to or not to include for a particular paradigm. This approach then so-called boundary critique, coined by Werner Ulrich,[40] which mainly tries to describe that people's perspectives and judgements have

[40]Ulrich W (1996). Critical systems thinking for citizens: A research proposal. Centre for Systems Studies Research Memorandum #10. Centre for Systems Studies, University of Hull.

interconnections, that different values will yield to different judgements and possible conflicts, and how people can manage their perception and understanding over a particular context and address the problem (Midgley and Pinzón 2011; Ulrich 1983).[41] Ulrich applied a *dimensional analysis*[42] to determine the meaning of improvement, and to describe the role of people in that particular improvement (Fig. 6). Mainly, there will be two groups of people: *the involved* that act as planners, decision-makers, and who get benefit; and *the affected (witness),* that suffer the costs or the expenses from the improvement. Development is meant to increase the prosperity of the people, then the people should have the opportunity to decide what sort of development that they should get (Sen 1999, p. 31).

There are two data gathering techniques used. First, semi-structured interview (in-depth interview) with open-ended questions based on the research topic, that provides opportunities for both researcher and interviewee to discuss the topics in more detail (Hancock et al. 1998). Interviews were conducted in November–December 2015 with relevant officials and residents as described in Table 1.

Second, secondary data is used in this paper namely works and knowledge produced by other people or researchers that were used for other purposes (Vartanian 2010). Secondary data analysis is suitable for this paper since it gives financial and time savings to collect the data (Castle 2003; Heaton 2003), and it also allows opportunity to reshape and further elaborate the research question(s) (Hyman 1972). The data come from various sources: Nauli city in Figures (from Nauli City Statistics Bureau Office), Nauli District in Figures (from Nauli District Statistics Bureau Office), PDAM Financial Report (from Financial and Development Supervisory Agency/BPKP), PDAM Performance Report (from BPPSPAM), PDAM Company Profiles (from PDAM Kota Nauli and PDAM Kabupaten Nauli), BLUD SPAM Company Profile, Audit Report on Water Provision in Nauli and Samsoir Province by the Indonesian Supreme Audit Institution, several regulations from related government institutions, and news articles from various newspapers.

## The Commodification of Water in Nauli

Water provision in most regions in Indonesia (including Nauli City) are conducted by a company. Even though the company is solely owned by the government, but it is still a company which constructs and evaluates performance on a profit and loss statement. Kosar (2006, p. 3) defines privatisation as *the use of private sector in the provision of a good and service, the components of which include financing, operations (supplying, production and delivery) and quality control.* The World

[41]Ulrich (1983; 1996, p. 15) uses the terms *boundary judgements* to define boundaries of planning effort, i.e. facts and values that have to be included and to be left out, or *justification break-offs* because 'they define the point at which justification ends'.

[42]Also called the system of concern or the context of application.

**Fig. 7** A water tank dock

**Fig. 8** A water tank is filling up water to a resident

Bank, IMF, and several regional development banks have also claimed that water privatisation will enhance the effort of providing access to water and sanitation to more (even billions of) people worldwide, since the private sector is more efficient, cost-effective, competitive, and able to provide financing (Public Citizen 2003, p. 1). However, Kurniasih (2008) argues that in many countries water privatisation cannot do much to offer better water provision, but those privatisations always followed by a significant increase in water tariffs and leave the poor with no option but to utilise unsafe water sources.

As explained above, until 2013 only 38.17% of households in the Nauli City area that had access to piped water, while others should fulfil their needs through sources such as water merchants (32.84%), bore well (24.16%), and other unprotected water sources (4.83%) (BPS Nauli City 2014). In fact the scarcity of water in Nauli during the 8 month dry season, and aggravated by the failure of the government(s) to provide reliable water provision, has been exploited as an arena in which to profit by the private sector such as the trucked water merchants and DAMIU. These local private players have entered the market to fill the huge gap in the water supply as a consequence of chaotic water management by the three public water operators: city PDAM, district PDAM, and BLUD SPAM. Here I will compare and contrast how these five perpetrators deliver and sell water to the residents.

## *The Trucked Water*

The trucked water is the most favourable option for the residents (Figs. 7 and 8). Merchants deliver the water using a 5000-litre tank truck for Rp.80,000 to Rp.100,000. In terms of profit, the total cost to fill up the tank and deliver it was only Rp.10,000 depending on the distance. For a tank of water, they could get at least Rp.75,000 of net profit. They just bore into the ground, draw water with a high capacity machine, fill up the tank, and send it off with no further treatment to the water. According to interviews[43] with two merchants, there are currently at least 5 water tank truck merchants in Nauli city. During the dry season (usually between May to August), each dock can sell at least 200 tanks per day on average. In terms of profit, they can generate almost Rp.18 million daily. While during rainy season, each dock can only sell 30 tanks of water daily. Within a year, this practice renders approximately Rp.18 billion in revenue and Rp.13 billion net profit from tanked water.

Based on Law No. 28/2009 concerning Local Tax and Retribution, Chap. 14 concerning Ground Water Tax, it stresses that groundwater taken for commercial use should be taxed by the local government. To implement the law at local level, the government of Nauli municipality has issued Local Regulation (*Peraturan Daerah/Perda*) No. 6 year 2012 concerning Ground Water Tax. However, the Mining and Energy Department *(Dinas Pertambangan dan Energi)* of Nauli municipality has never at any point collected any tax from groundwater exploitation by the water tank business. The head of the department explained [44]

> We have limited funding to buy water metre to be planted in their water sources. We have proposed budget allocation for buying the water metres, but it was removed by the parliament members. The reason is it did not meet the priority. However we have put water metres in district PDAM water sources, and we have taxed them. There are about 20 water metres for PDAM water sources. Indeed, when we proposed to instal water metres for those merchants, the parliament members resisted. Indeed we can control the massive water

[43]Interviews were conducted separately at their stations in Oepura and Koinoni on 6th November 2015.

[44]Interview the Head of Mining and Energy Department (Dinas Pertambangan dan Energi) of Nauli City, 17th November 2015.

**Fig. 9** A DAMIU stall in a resident house

discharge through periodic certification. However it is still difficult since we do not have water metres.

However, on a separate occasion, someone from a non-government organisation[45] in Nauli revealed that

> …some of the parliament members were sponsored by the vendors during their campaign, and even still receive bribes until now. Moreover, one of the DPRD members owns a dock. Nobody knows how much money the vendors can get every year, but it is big enough to secure their business from tax. They feed officers, military, and policemen in town. And even the mayor himself. And if you visit one of their bases where they pump out the water and filled up the tanks, military and police water tanks were also taking water together with them. They share the spring.

## DAMIU (Depot Air Minum Isi Ulang/Refilled Drinkable Water)

DAMIU is a business that offers cheap drinkable water, stored in a 19-litre gallon. It purifies untreated water with reverse osmosis system, as shown in Fig. 9.

DAMIU business has been becoming very popular in Nauli due to the increasing scarcity of water. DAMIU can be an instant solution for people to drink, instead of buying a packaged water like AQUA—the most famous packaged water brand in Indonesia. A 19-litre gallon of DAMIU only costs Rp.4.000, while same size of

[45]He does not want his organisation and his name to be revealed in any report. Interview was conducted during lunch in a canteen, 7th November 2015.

AQUA can cost Rp.12.000. According to Department of Health of Nauli Municipality records, there were 376 DAIMU stalls in Nauli as of 21 November 2015. Based on my interviews with 5 DAMIU stall owners in Nauli,[46] each DAMIU booth can sell up to 40 gallons per day at least. In total that will make up to more than Rp.22 billions of revenue from DAMIU sold throughout Nauli every year. The standard minimum cost for a gallon is Rp.1200, so the net profit per year can reach Rp.14 billions in total. This can be a very lucrative business for companies that supply and instal DAMIU equipment, as well as to tanked water businesses that supply untreated water to DAMIU.

Since DAMIU stalls are selling drinking water—water that it is ready to drink, the government should pay substantial attention to it and as stipulated in Minister of Health Decree No. 736/2010, local government should conduct regular checks of each of the DAMIU stalls. From interviews with DAMIU stall owners I found that their stalls are subject to inspection and they signed an agreement that they would maintain the quality of water. However, the local government had never visited and inspected their stalls, so they do not have any financial incentive to deliver or sell healthy water. As a result, many DAMIU stalls do not treat the water properly lowering the cost of production so they can provide more bonuses to customers.

## PDAM of Nauli City

The city PDAM, established in 2005, has had 7512 connections per Semester I 2015 with a service coverage of 10.22% according to the Head of Human Resources and General Affairs Division.[47] The PDAM sells water with a progressive tariff, the lowest was Rp.3, 200 per cubic metre for social customers and the highest was Rp.40, 000 per cubic metre for big industries. From an audited Financial Report (conducted by a Public Accountant) and Performance Report (conducted by BPKP) year ending 31 December 2014, the total revenue for 2014 was Rp.7.6 billion, and the average tariff was Rp.7, 475 per $m^3$. Thus the total volume of water distributed and sold (billed) during 2014 was 1.2 million cubic metres and 796,997 cubic metres, respectively, which made 32% of water losses, or if we take the minimum tolerance in Indonesia 20% for unaccounted for water, then for 12% water losses the PDAM had lost approximately Rp.9 billion of revenue. Moreover, this percentage of non-revenue raising water (NRW) had increased by 4.25% compared to 27.69% in 2013.

The high water loss is due to two reasons: pipe leakage and broken water metres (technical loss) and fraud by billing staff during metre reading (administrative loss). Consequently, there was no demonstrable effort to maintain the technical aspect of

[46]Interviews were conducted on 19th November 2015 with 5 DAMIU owners that are located in Balgie Township, Angloka Township (3 DAMIU booths), and Mandalingi Township.

[47]Interviewed on 13th November 2015

PDAM, since the PDAM has only 10 years of operation. Furthermore, the increasing rate of non-revenue raising water showed that PDAM did not pay much attention to improving this situation.

## PDAM of Nauli District

According to the Executive Director of PDAM in an interview on 16 November 2015, the PDAM of Nauli District currently has 33,272 connections as of 30 September 2015. Only 3.72% or 1238 connections were buried in district area, while 96.28% or 32,034 connections cover approximately 42% of residents in the city area. In 2013 the district PDAM could only obtain slightly less than Rp.30 billion of revenue and has implemented FCR average tariff of Rp.4,124 per cubic metre. In terms of water losses, this district PDAM had been doing well proven by its NRW percentage was only 22%, only 2% above the tolerable NRW water of 20% (BPPSPAM 2014). However, from interviews with several residents, they said that PDAM service performance decreased from time to time. Water did not flow for 2 weeks or so (62 out of 80 residents admitted this. I asked them to rate PDAM performance with 0 as the worst and 10 as the best score, 52.6% of them gave 5, 22.12% gave 6, and 25.28% gave 7 or above). However, for some residents the bill claimed water usage for almost Rp500, 000 to Rp.1 million, and the customer had to pay regardless, whether the customers wanted to take the issue to court or not, and there was no action from the company to investigate the problem.

## Provincial BLUD SPAM

BLUD SPAM that was originally instituted to operate big dams that are built by central government and intended to supply the needs of bulk water to PDAMs surrounding the dams has started to sell water directly to users. This situation had resulted in greater conflict over water provision. Based on 2013 Financial Report, beside selling bulk water to the city PDAM (district PDAM does not want to buy it), BLUD SPAM has connected its pipes directly to end users like the Nauli airport, Meranti University, the Polytechnic of Nauli, and two master metres to several groups of residents. Their tariff was very low compared to PDAMs tariffs, which was only Rp.2,500 per cubic metre. From the tariff calculation that appeared in its business plan, the FCR tariff of BLUD should be Rp.7,275 per $m^3$. However, BLUD has implemented Lowest Cost Recovery tariff (LCR) which did not include investment cost, depreciation expenses, and profit in the structure, which comes to Rp.3,842 per $m^3$. Furthermore, BLUD only charges bulk water to PDAM and end users with 40% to consider their ability to pay, so it comes to an average of Rp.2.500 per $m^3$.

According to the report, BLUD SPAM sold 226,725 cubic metres of water consisting of 110,025 cubic metres to city PDAM and 116,700 cubic metres to end users in the city of Nauli. This means that the volume of water sold is approximately 15% compared to the city PDAM. From end users only, BLUD had earned Rp.283.4 million of revenue. Not much compared to other two PDAMs because its tariff is very low.

The head of BLUD SPAM clearly stated that[48]

> BLUD SPAM is allowed to fill the gap of water provision that cannot be covered by city and district PDAMs. Additionally, our transmission pipes are going to reach PDAM reservoirs across residential complexes that are not in PDAMs coverage. So we provide service to them, with very low rate even lower than the PDAMs', and the people are very happy with that. However BLUD SPAM does not provide free water to serve the poor because BLUD SPAM needs to run its operation with lowest cost recovery. Every year we have got subsidised by the provincial budget. We do not insist to get profit, but we do not want to suffer losses. Besides, providing water to the people is the responsibility of local government or in this case, Nauli Municipality with its PDAM.

## Health, Environmental, and Social Problems

From a health perspective, the Head of Environment Control Body of Nauli City government revealed that all water sources in Nauli City are highly contaminated by coliform bacteria. They had conducted sampling to 100 water source sites and found Coliform contamination in each of the water sources including PDAMs' reached an index level which varied between 5000 and 80,000, and more specifically the faecal coliform index spanned from 100 to 16,500.[49] According to the Ministry of Health of Indonesia Decree No. 492/2010 and 739/2010, the coliform index in drinking water should be zero. Based on a study conducted by the WHO in 2008, Indonesia had 39,000 incidents of child mortality due to diarrhoea (Boschi-Pinto et al. 2008), and International Vaccine Access Centre released that there were 30,000 cases in 2014 in Indonesia which ranked number 9 in the index on Global Mortality in Children under 5 caused by Diarrhoea. Based on Nauli City Health Profile 2014 (released by the Department of Health of Nauli City) the number of diarrhoeal incidences is only 17,526 and ranked 5 of the most frequent diseases in Nauli City. An official of Health Department of Nauli City in an interview stated that the department had never done regular inspection or conducted

[48]Interviewed on 20th November 2015

[49]Total Coliform bacteria are common in the environment like soil, water, and vegetables. They are harmless. However a high level of contamination indicates that the source of water should be examined and need to solve the problems. On the other hand *Fecal* coliform contamination indicates that there is high risk of illness for water consumers (Washington State Department of Health 2016).

treatment to water sources, whether it is a commercial, communal, or private water source due to the limited budget allocated for it.

Nauli geographical conditions (arid and very little periods of rain) makes water less available from time to time. "*Ten years ago we could get water from a shallow bore well only 15 meters deep. However today we have dug until 70 m, and still in dry season it has no water*", said a resident. The water table is decreasing, and the government has never paid attention to this deteriorating condition. The Head of Nauli City Environment Control Body stated

If the government, particularly the Department of Mining does not take immediate action regarding water discharge by commercial water sellers, then we will not be able to preserve the environment and in the next 25 years Nauli City will run out of ground water. Moreover, people should be educated to not waste the water.

Central government had tried to overcome water crisis in Nauli City by introducing a community-based water management system (PAMSIMAS). Under this system, central government and local government encourage communities to form a small body to build a public hydrant or other water sources under the supervision of the government, and to operate them independently. Based on Ministry of Public Works data, as of 2014 there had been 52 public hydrant and 8 open water sources built to support water provision in Nauli City, but almost all of them do not operate properly. During my visit to 15 public hydrants that were built under this system, there is only one that operates and the people were thinking of ceasing the operation since it always provoked disputes between members. I mentioned the situation to related officials in-charge at the Department of Public Works of Nauli City and at national level, but they merely shifted the responsibility for the situation to the local people: "…they should responsible for that. We have built the infrastructure and set up a managing body. Perhaps the failure is due to their low level of education that made them selfish", said the local level official. While Jakarta official said "We have transferred them to the local governments. So it should be their responsibility".

## Assessment of Water Service Performance

Ulrich distinguished the twelve questions into 'is' mode and 'ought' mode. The two modes are closely related, as the 'ought' mode will come first to give us a standard for evaluating the 'is' mode (Ulrich 1996). The twelve questions are then grouped into 4 (McIntyre-Mills 2006; Midgley 2000; Ulrich 1983, 1989; Ulrich and Reynolds 2010): the sources of motivation (as the value basis of the design), the sources of control (or sources of power that needed or available in order to attain the objectives of the programs), the sources of expertise (to know the information, experiences, and skills that are relevant), and the sources of legitimation (to identify the ethical assumptions and possible deficiencies, and justification from the people vis-a-vis, the involved and the affected).

The assessment of water service performance in Nauli is summarised in Table 2.

**Table 2** Assessment of the water performance in Nauli using the CSH

| Question | "is" condition | Problems | "ought to" be done |
|---|---|---|---|
| *The source of motivation* | | | |
| 1 **Beneficiary**: 'who' is the actual client of the system? | Customers: people who can pay connection fee and water charge | Connection charge and water tariff have prohibited the poor to get piped water | All residents in terms of individual including marginal and poor people, in urban and remote areas |
| 2 **Purpose**: 'what' is the purpose of the system? | Providing water in good quantity and quality to all residents | • Customers still complain as water does not flow constantly<br>• No chemical treatment on water (water contains very high *e-coli)*<br>• No prevention on water exploitation | • Production and distribution capacity should be expanded to reach all residents<br>• Water should be chemically treated before distributed to residents<br>• Need regulation and real action to balance needs for water and environment preservation |
| 3 **Measure**: 'what' is the actual (built-in) performance measurement of the system? | • Coverage ratio: MDGs target: 68.87% in 2015. National target: 100% in 2019<br>• Water loss below 20% | • Nauli City coverage: 38.17%, water loss: 33.7%<br>• Nauli District coverage: 1.63%, water loss: 32% | • Need to accelerate expansion of coverage<br>• Not only need to repair old and broken installation, but more urgently need to increase compliance in water metering |
| *The source of power* | | | |
| 4 **Decision maker**: 'who' is the decision maker? | • National regulation by central government<br>• Local design and regulation by local government<br>• Water operator by PDAMs | • There are many overlapping regulations at national level<br>• In local level, water tends to be used as political issue and compelled to contribute to local revenue<br>• PDAMs difficult to grow business and do service | Water should be managed more regionally; local governments and provincial governments through their water company should not compete against each other to sell water |

(continued)

**Table 2** (continued)

| Question | "is" condition | Problems | "ought to" be done |
|---|---|---|---|
| 5 **Resources**: 'what' recourses and conditions are really controlled by the decision maker? | • Central, provincial and local government: financial resources, inter-border power, legal power<br>• Water companies: technical aspects | The governments never really coordinate to build up grand design in water provision in Nauli, so there are very often conflicts of overlapping programs | Since water is the responsibility of the state, then all level of governments should coordinate and use their legal power to ensure water is well provided |
| 6 **Environment**: 'what' are conditions that cannot be controlled? | Water sources, population and demography | • Groundwater discharge has sporadically happened by all water suppliers without thinking of controlling it<br>• Population dispersed made it difficult to cover remote area | • The three water companies need to coordinate in organising the use of water sources to save water and reduce production cost<br>• The local governments need to provide financial and technical assistance for PDAM to expansion |
| *The source of knowledge* | | | |
| 7 **Expert**: 'who' are the planners? | Local governments and water companies | Local governments only rely on water companies' planning on piped water | Need to clarify the role of local governments in water sector |
| 8 **Expertise**: what skills and knowledge are relevant or needed? | Planners and key persons need to acquire skills in managing issues of water, corporate, financial, environment and social issues | Planners and key persons lack of experience, multidisciplinary understanding and attention in water provision related aspects | Planners and key persons need to be aware of many relevant aspects that should be considered, so involving more relevant experienced people like the academia and the community is needed |
| 9 **Guarantor**: where do the designers seek guarantee that their planning will be successful? | Central government; local governments, and local parliaments | • Uncoordinated programs between governments made the implementation and maintenance not optimal<br>• Executives and legislatives often cannot reach political agreement in managing water | • Local, provincial and central governments should actively synchronise programs<br>• Service users should be involved in designing water development plan to obtain insight and setting priorities |

(continued)

**Table 2** (continued)

| Question | "is" condition | Problems | "ought to" be done |
|---|---|---|---|
| *The source of legitimation* | | | |
| 10 **Witness**: 'who' will be the affected people? | Poor people; children and those who unable to raise their voice | Water management design only involves top level decision-makers | The system needs to accommodate the interest of marginal people (All water users; those who are excluded) |
| 11 **Emancipation**: are the affected people allowed to involve in the system? | No | Water companies only serve customers, not all residents Local governments only rely on water companies | The system has to provide equal opportunities to all people |
| 12 **Worldview**: on what worldview the system should be based? | Water development planning is included in the local governments' medium-term planning | Designing the system is based on technical and financial aspect, and not considering social aspect. Water development is still not in high priority in the medium-term planning | As stipulated by the constitution, the system should be able to provide water for the maximum benefit of the people |

## Recommendation

Based on the aforementioned assessments, this research offers some suggestions to be taken to address the problems in water service provision in Nauli City: (i) Both local governments in Nauli region and the provincial government need to find a better model to manage drinking water in order to attain better cooperation and coordination in water provision. Nauli City and District leaders admitted that they have failed to provide adequate water service to the people (Indonesian Supreme Audit 2014), and it means current practice needs to be revisited. In a decentralised system, where PDAM can only cover residents in the local government area, this could be adjusted and a more regional mindset needs to be formulated. Drinking water-related regulations at national level need to be re-examined so there will not be a 'one size fits all' regulation, but instead one able to accommodate local aspirations; (ii) Governments should not just sell the water to the residents, but instead have to provide water for all especially the poor who cannot afford to pay. Tariff structure has accommodated cross-subsidy from the rich to the poor, but still a real subsidy from the local budget is still needed for the poor; (iii) improving financial and technical performance of PDAMs is crucially needed. PDAMs audit report described how PDAMs operated inefficiently, proven by the high water losses—technical and administrative losses, low water bill collection rate by 62% and inefficient operational expenses; (iv) Water development planning needs to be supported and included in the local government medium-term planning (5 years span), to avoid further debate and political disagreement between executives and legislatives when enacting the annual program; (v) water development planning needs to be pictured as a grand design and not partial, bringing together all relevant planners from central, provincial, and local governments. The planning process needs to involve people from universities and communities not only to obtain wider social–cultural and environmental perspectives, but also to arrange prioritisation in water development. Building communication through engagement (doing things together with other relevant people and engage with the world), imagination (construct an image of what we will do and how we will do it), and alignment (to assure that related programs and activities are aligned) (Wenger 2000) can be implemented towards better outcomes. More frequent meeting with the communities is needed to hear their voices, complaints, and demands regarding water service performance. Conducting a community of practice (a community which members come from different backgrounds but have common interest and same goal) can be implemented to give the members the sense of bounding, mutuality, and sharing repertoire (Wenger 1999); (viii) any planning that is made for water expansion should be based on the triple bottom line analysis: economic, social, and environmental (Elkington 1999), to ensure that all current water development program is still preserving balance for future generation.

## Conclusion

It has to be admitted water provision is a significantly large to be addressed by the government. Indonesia is still trying to pursue the global in water provision, and it has been adopted as the government's medium-term target: to reach 100% of coverage in 2019. However, national data has shown significant growth in water service, some areas like Nauli region for instance, and is still struggling to find the best way to manage drinking water, especially when the trend of the local autonomous system is emerging and where local ego sometimes disregards the main objective of the development: the people. Developing the people should be the main goal of every kind of development, physical and non-physical, as it is the people—as an individual—who will enjoy and continue the development (UNDP 1994).

Using a CSH approach to assess drinking water management in Nauli, it can be seen that there is still much to be done to improve the current situation. First, as the source of motivation, a change in mindset that all people with no exception are the real beneficiaries of water service. Second, as the source of power, water providers and all level of governments have to integrate all water programs and water policies, and coordination whether in planning and institutional arrangement needs to be improved. Third, as the source of knowledge, water management planning should be viewed from broader aspect to consider social and environment perspectives, so people from different backgrounds of expertise should be involved. And finally as the source of legitimation, planning in water system should give equal opportunities to all, since the basic standpoint for starting any kind of public services is the constitution: to employ all services for the maximum benefit of the people.

## References


Agarwal A, Bhatia R, Chéret I, Davila-Poblete S, Falkenmark M, Jønch-Clausen T, Kindler J (2000) Integrated water resources management, Global Water Partnerships

Antonelli M and Greco F (2015) The water we eat: combining virtual water and water footprints. Springer, Berlin

Avlonas N and Nassos GP (2014) Water footprint. In: Practical sustainability strategies: how to gain a competitive advantage, pp 227–234

Bahl RW and Martinez-Vazquez J (2006) Sequencing fiscal decentralization, vol 3914. World Bank Publications, Washington DC

Bakker K, Kooy M, Shofiani NE, Martijn E-J (2008) Governance failure: rethinking the institutional dimensions of urban water supply to poor households. World Dev 36(10): 1891–1915

Braga B, Chartres C, Cosgrove WJ, da Cunha LV, Chartres C, Cosgrove WJ, da Cunha LV, Gleick PH, Kabat P, Kadi MA, Loucks DP, Lundqvist J, Narain S, Xia J (2014) Water and the future of humanity revisiting water security, water and the future of humanity. Springer International Publishing, Imprint, Springer, Cham

Biswas AK (1999) Water crisis: current perceptions and future realities. Water Int 24(4):363–367

Biswas AK (2001) Water policies in the developing world. Int J Water Resour Dev 17(4):11

Biswas AK (2007) Fundamental changes needed in water governance. Viewed 5 Oct 2012. http://www.thirdworldcentre.org/epubli.html

Biswas AK, Tortajada C (2010) Future water governance: problems and perspectives. Water Resour Dev 26(2):129–139

BPPSPAM (2014) Kinerja PDAM 2013—Wilayah II Pulau Jawa/ PDAM Performance in 2013—Region II Java, Badan Pendukung Sistem Penyediaan Air Minum/Water Supply System Development Support Body Jakarta

BPS Nauli District (2013) Nauli regency in figures 2013. BPS-Statistics of Nauli Regency, Nauli

BPS Nauli City (2014) Nauli city in figures 2014. BPS Nauli City, Nauli

Cabrera D (2006) Boundary critique: a minimal concept theory of systems thinking. In Proceedings of the 50th annual meeting of the international society for the systems sciences, North America. Retrieved from http://journals.isss.org/index.php/proceedings50th/article/view/403/161

Castle JE (2003) Maximizing research opportunities: secondary data analysis. J Neurosci Nurs 35(5):287–290

Churchman CW (1967) Guest editorial: wicked problems. Manag Sci 14(4)

Churchman CW (1970) Operations research as a profession. Manag Sci 17(2):B-37–B-53

Churchman CW (1979) The systems approach. In: Rev. and updated. Dell Publishing Co., New York

Chambers R (1995) Poverty and livelihoods: whose reality counts? Environ Urban 7(1):173–204

Chambers R (1997) Whose reality counts?: putting the first last. Intermediate Technology Publications Ltd (ITP)

Cohen JM, Peterson SB (1999) Administrative decentralization: strategies for developing countries. Kumarian Press, West Hartford

da Cruz NF, Berg S, Marques RC (2013) Managing public utilities: lessons from Florida. Lex Localis-J Local Self-Govern 11(2)
Deneulin S (2006) The capability approach and the praxis of development. Palgrave Macmillan, Basingstoke
DG Human Settlements (2009) Banyak Jalan Menuju 10 Juta Sambungan (many ways to reach 10 million connections). Viewed 10 Oct 2014. http://ciptakarya.pu.go.id/dok/bulletin/bulletinCK_mei09.pdf
Domènech L (2011) Rethinking water management: from centralised to decentralised water supply and sanitation models. Documents d'anàlisi geogràfica 57(2):293–310
Drakakis-Smith D (1995) Third world cities: sustainable urban development 1. Urban Stud 32(4–5):659–677
Dursin R (2006) Country water action: Indonesia simple solution for drinking water makes big difference, Asian development bank. In: Water for All. Viewed 6 Mar 2010
Ehrlich P (1970) The population bomb. In: New York times, p 47
Elkington J (1999) Cannibals with forks: the triple bottom line of 21st century business, Pbk. ed. edn. Capstone, Oxford, U. K
FAO, IFAD, WFP (2013) The state of food insecurity in the world 2013. The multiple dimensions of food security. FAO, Rome
Firman T (2013) Territorial splits (pemekaran daerah) in decentralising Indonesia, 2000–2012: local development drivers or hindrance? Space Polity 17(2):180–196
Gilles J (2006) Water crisis happening now. Nat Int Wkly J Sci
Gleick PH (1993) Water in crisis, vol 9. Pacific Institute for Studies in Developement, Environment & Security. Stockholm Environment Institute, Oxford University Press, 473p
Gleick PH (2013) A drop in the bucket: successful management of water must balance development needs and economic considerations. Financ Dev 50(3):12
Gómez O, Gasper D (2013) Human security: a thematic guidance note for regional and national human development report teams
Gormley WT Jr (1983) Policy, politics, and public utility regulation. Am J Polit Sci 86–105
Gorre-Dale E (1992) The Dublin statement on water and sustainable development. Environ Conserv 19(02):181
Hadipuro W (2010) Indonesia's water supply regulatory framework: between commercialisation and public service. Water Altern 3(3):475–491
Hancock B, Ockleford E, Windridge K (1998) An introduction to qualitative research. Trent focus group, Nottingham
Heaton J (2003) Secondary data analysis. In: The AZ of Social Research. Sage, London, pp. 285-8
Hoekstra AY, Hung P (2002) Virtual water trade. In: A quantification of virtual water flows between nations in relation to international crop trade. Value of water research report series, vol 11, p 166
Hoekstra AY, Chapagain AK (2006) Water footprints of nations: water use by people as a function of their consumption pattern. Water Resour Manag 21(1):35–48
Hwang H, Forrester A, Lansey K (2014) Decentralized water reuse: regional water supply system resilience benefits. Procedia Eng 70:853–856
Hyman HH (1972) Secondary analysis of sample surveys: principles, procedures, and potentialities. Wiley, New York
Indonesia Infrastructure Initiatives (2013) Commitment of local governments still constrains efforts to improve PDAM health. Investor Daily, 23 Aug 2013
Indonesian Supreme Audit (2014) Audit report on water provision in Nauli. The Indonesian Supreme Audit Institution, Nauli
Jackson MC (2000) Systems approaches to management Springer Science & Business Media, New York
Jain SK, Singh VP (2010) Water crisis. J Comp Soc Welf 26(2–3):215–237
Kim A (2008) Decentralization and the provision of public services, vol 4503. World Bank Publications, Washington DC

Laffont J-J (2004) Management of public utilities in China. Ann Econ Financ 5(2):185–210
Magelgaard K (2011) Why population matters to water resources. Viewed 27 Jan 2015. http://populationaction.org/wp-content/uploads/2012/04/PAI-1293-WATER-4PG.pdf
Massing M (2003) Does democracy avert famine. In: New York times, vol 1
McDonald RI, Green P, Balk D, Fekete BM, Revenga C, Todd M, Montgomery M (2011) Urban growth, climate change, and freshwater availability. Proc Natl Acad Sci USA 108(15):6312–6317
Mcdonnell RA (2008) Challenges for integrated water resources management: how do we provide the knowledge to support truly integrated thinking? Water Resour Dev 24(1):131–143
McIntyre-Mills J (2003) Critical systemic praxis for social and environmental justice: participatory policy design and governance for a global age. Springer Science & Business Media, New York
McIntyre-Mills J (2006) Systemic governance and accountability working and re-working the conceptual and spatial boundaries. Springer Science+Business Media, New York
McIntyre-Mills J (2008) New directions for social wellbeing through extending deliberative democracy to enhance participation. In: International systems sciences conference, Madison, Wisconsin. ISBN, pp 978–981
McIntyre-Mills J (2014) Systemic ethics and non-anthropocentric stewardship: implications for transdisciplinarity and cosmopolitan politics. Springer, Berlin
Midgley G (2000) Systemic intervention philosophy, methodology, and practice. Springer, US, Imprint, Springer, Boston
Midgley G, Pinzón LA (2011) Boundary critique and its implications for conflict prevention. J Oper Res Soc 62(8):1543–1554
Moglia M, Cook S, Sharma AK, Burn S (2011) Assessing decentralised water solutions: towards a framework for adaptive learning. Water Resour Manage 25(1):217–238
Mollinga PP (2008) Water, politics and development: framing a political sociology of water resources management. Water Altern 1(1):7–23
Naddeo V, Scannapieco D, Belgiorno V (2013) Enhanced drinking water supply through harvested rainwater treatment. J Hydrol 498:287–291
Nussbaum MC (2011) Creating capabilities: the human development approach. Harvard University Press, Cambridge
OECD (2010) OECD economic surveys: Indonesia 2010, vol. 2010. OECD Publishing
Pembaruan S (2013) Cakupan Pelayanan Air Minum di Indonesia Masih Rendah. Suara Pembaruan, 2 Mar 2013
Purwanto SA (2005) Forest resource management and self-governance in regional autonomy Indonesia. In: Regionalism in post-Suharto Indonesia, vol 4, p 211
Rees WE (1992) Ecological footprints and appropriated carrying capacity: what urban economics leaves out. Environ Urban 4(2):121–130
Reynoso LAEVG (2000) Towards a new water management practice: experiences and proposals from Guanajuato State for a participatory and decentralized water management structure in Mexico. Int J Water Resour Dev 16(4):571–588
Schelwald-van der Kley AL, Reijerkerk L (2009) Water: a way of life: sustainable water management in a cultural context. CRC Press, Boca Raton
Sears P (1936) Crisis under water. Science 83(2143):81
Sen A (1999) Development as freedom. Oxford University Press, Oxford
Shiva V (2002) Water wars: privatization, pollution and profit. India Research Press, Delhi
Shiva V (2008) From water crisis to water culture. Cult Stud 22(3–4):498–509
Simanjuntak E, Baskoro LS, Aulia M, Argiono I, Wahyuningsih M (2015) Pemantauan Pelaksanaan Investasi Infrastruktur Bidang Pekerjaan Umum. Kasus Studi Lima Provinsi di Indonesia, Pusat Kajian Strategis Kementerian Pekerjaan Umum

Simbolon J (2007) Optimalisasi Penyertaan Modal Pemerintah (PMP) Pada Perusahaan Daerah Air Minum (PDAM) Sebagai Solusi Upaya Penyehatan PDAM dan Penyelesaian Pinjaman PDAM Pada Pemerintah/Optimization of Government share on PDAM to PDAM recovery. Financ Econ J Minist Financ Repub Indones 11(4):17

Stephenson D (1998) Water supply management, vol 29. Water Science and Technology Library, Kluwer Academic Publishers, The Netherlands

Stiglitz JE, Sen A, Fitoussi J-P (2010) Mismeasuring our lives why GDP doesn't add up. New Press, Distributed by Perseus Distribution, New York

Sulistiyanto P, Erb M (2005) Introduction: entangled politics in post-Suharto Indonesia. In: Regionalism in post-Suharto Indonesia, pp 1–17

Sulistiyanto P, Rosser A, Wilson I (2011) Leaders, elites and coalitions: the politics of free public services in decentralised Indonesia

Treisman D (2002) Defining and measuring decentralization: a global perspective (Unpublished manuscript)

Ulrich W (1983) Critical heuristics of social planning: a new approach to practical philosophy

Ulrich W (1989) Critical heuristics of social systems design. In: Operational research and the social sciences. Springer, Berlin, pp 79–87

Ulrich W (1996) A primer to critical systems heuristics for action researchers, University of Hull, Centre for Systems Studies Hull, UK

Ulrich W (2003) A brief introduction to critical systems thinking for professionals and citizens. Werner Ulrich. Viewed 21-03-2015. http://www.wulrich.com/cst_brief.html

Ulrich W and Reynolds M (2010) Critical systems heuristics. In Systems approaches to managing change: a practical guide. Springer, Berlin, pp 243–292

UNDP (1994) Human development report 2014, United Nations, New York

UNDP (1997) Decentralized governance programme: strengthening capacity for people-centered development. Management Development and Governance Division, Bureau for Development Policy, Sept 1997

UNDP (1999) Decentralization: a sampling of definitions

UNDP (2010) Human development report 2010. United Nations, New York

UNDP (2014) Human development report 2014 United Nations New York

Vartanian TP (2010) Secondary data analysis. Oxford University Press, Oxford

Wackernagel M (1994) Ecological footprint and appropriated carrying capacity : a tool for planning toward sustainability. The University of British, Columbia

Wackernagel M, Rees W (1998) Our ecological footprint: reducing human impact on the earth. New Society Publishers, Philadelphia

Wenger E (1999) Communities of practice: learning, meaning, and identity. Cambridge university press, Cambridge

Wenger E (2000) Communities of practice and social learning systems. Organization 7(2): 225–246

Wilder M, Lankao PR (2006) Paradoxes of decentralization: water reform and social implications in Mexico. World Dev 34(11):1977–1995

Wilson JQ (1980) The politics of regulation. Basic Books Inc, New York

Winters MS, Karim AG, Martawardaya B (2014) Public service provision under conditions of insufficient citizen demand: Insights from the urban sanitation sector in Indonesia. World Dev 60:31–42

World Bank Group (2012) World development indicators 2012. World Bank Publications, Washington DC

Zaag PVD, Savenije HHG (2006) Water as economic good: the value of pricing and the failure of markets

## Author Biography

**Jackwin Simbolon** is currently pursuing his PhD program at Flinders University, Adelaide, School of Social and Policy Studies, started in August 2014 until August 2018. He works in the Ministry of Finance where he was Head of Regional Borrowing, and worked with local governments and local water companies (PDAM) as well as for instances assessing new loans to PDAM Tirtanadi Medan (Asian Development Bank) and the Local Government Loan Restructuring Program to formulate policies to Water and Sanitation Financing Initiatives (from World Bank 2008-2009 and from Australia Aid. He has given plenary presentations for the National Planning and Development Agency of Indonesia and the World Bank. He presented the research published in this volume at the 60th Annual Conference of the International Society for the Systems Sciences in Colorado, 2016 and won the Margaret Mead Award.

# Chapter 17
# Empowering Indigenous People: Voice, Choice and Agency in Rural Development Planning in Mindanao

**Mervin Gascon and Janet McIntyre-Mills**

**Abstract** The chapter explores the disempowered role of women in rural development planning in Mindanao, Philippines. It argues that women are excluded from opportunities to participate actively in making development decisions as a result of the rise in multinationals who take over small farms and combine them into plantations growing only one crop. These monocultural growing techniques exclude the knowledge that women have about the role of diverse crops and the diverse (including wild) fauna and flora on which many Indigenous people depend for their food security. The repression and 'weeding out' of women's knowledge by multinationals builds upon the patriarchal domination of decision-making. The result is that the knowledge of women about seed diversity, wild fauna and flora is being lost. Following Shiva, a case is made for the representation of women in public decision-making at the community and regional level so that women's policy suggestions (based on their experience as farmers) is listened to, respected and acted upon, in order to preserve diversity. It is argued that active participation at the community, local government and state government levels should be encouraged to preserve diverse living systems as well as the life chances of the most disadvantaged women and their children. Moser's framework is used to analyse inequality in the existing gender division of labour while Kabeer's social relations approach is used as a lens to critique the existing gender inequality in various institutions spanning the household, community, state and market level. This qualitative research was conducted in the rural and Indigenous communities of Mindanao in 2013. A total of 105 participants were interviewed through theoretical sampling. This study used participant observation, interviews and focus group discussions. The Human Ethics clearance is 6046.

M. Gascon (✉) · J. McIntyre-Mills
Flinders University, Adelaide, Australia
e-mail: gasc0018@uni.flinders.edu.au

J. McIntyre-Mills
e-mail: janet.mcintyre@flinders.edu.au



J. McIntyre-Mills et al. (eds.), *Balancing Individualism and Collectivism*,
Contemporary Systems Thinking, DOI 10.1007/978-3-319-58014-2_17

## Introduction

This paper analyses the existing governance and development frameworks based on user-centric approaches to support the wellbeing of rural and Indigenous people in Mindanao (see McIntyre-Mills 2008, 2014a). Drawing on the five axial themes highlighted, namely: 'Home safety, Health, Purpose, Connection/belonging (people and place), Self-respect and confidence' which form the basis of this paper. The sample comprised of men and women in the rural and Indigenous communities in Mindanao who are subsistence farmers (44), contractual workers in banana and pineapple plantations (15), heads of tribal councils (26), local government officials (5), academics/researchers (5) businessmen (5) and NGO workers (5).

Community-based rural development planning should encourage participation among the local people so that they are able to help shape the services in ways that enhance their relevance. The paper addresses the following services: agriculture, health and education using Naila Kabeer's Social Relations Approach (SRA) and John Gaventa's power cube. The two sociological theories address power and control dynamics of the people and institutions bargaining for voice, choice, rights and agency. It is argued that the poorest and most marginalised groups, comprised of women, young people, elderly, sick and differently abled are being left out in the decision-making processes in policymaking. Their participation in the decision-making process is hindered primarily by gender-blindness (Kabeer 1999, 2005) and gender-blinkeredness (Cornwall 2003) of the prevailing practices headed by the elite and powerful people and organisations. This paper adds another dimension of the development issues in Mindanao, namely the capabilities of non-human animals as sentient beings. It is argued that nonhuman animals have inherent rights to survive and furthermore constitute a vital part of the biodiversity and agro-ecological food system. Without biodiversity, a human community is less resilient. Plants and animals are critically linked to the survival of the rural and Indigenous people in Mindanao. Nonhuman animals have 'agency or striving accompanied by sentience' that demands protection through an appropriate political theory of justice (Nussbaum 2011, p. 88). Ethically it requires a systemic stewardship response to sentient others and the environment (McIntyre-Mills 2014b).

## Research Design and Process

Engaging with the local people to discuss issues relating to their wellbeing needs 'walk through' using 'if-then' scenarios (McIntyre-Mills and de Vries 2013, pp. 447–450). Doing 'if-then scenarios' enables the research participants to reflect on the current practices or ways of dealing with development and disaster issues in Mindanao. Thinking about the wellbeing of self and others through a respectful dialogue allows the poor and powerless members of the community to be heard to ensure representation and accountability in democracies (Dobson 2014). If-then scenarios enable the participants to imagine the possible consequences of their ideas and plans relating to rural development and disaster planning in such a way that benefits, as well as risks, are co-learned and shared. For McIntyre-Mills and de Vries (2013, p. 452), 'scenarios can enhance our capability to join up the dots' in dealing with complex social problems.

The research combines qualitative and quantitative approaches in a complementary manner to achieve the study objectives. Primarily, this is a systemic action research that strives to identify practical solutions and interventions (Midgley 2001 cited in McIntyre 2005, p. 217) to address the development challenges in Mindanao. The approach enabled the different stakeholders, both experts and ordinary local people who are smallholder farmers, to engage in 'respectful dialogue' to get to truth (McIntyre 2005). The goal of the study is to improve the life chances and wellbeing of the poorest and most marginalised rural people by affecting and reframing the existing governance system through 'sweeping in' as many voices and choices in the decision-making process. McIntyre (2005), in relation to encouraging people to act and address social issues, argues that: 'the only hope is to ask questions, to listen to many people, to unfold meanings and 'to sweep in', to use Churchman's phrase, the social, cultural, political, economic, and environmental considerations and hope that right decisions are made in context. This is surely what democracy is about'.

Qualitative research strategies were used to reflect on the lives of the participants and the lens was also turned upon the researcher. (Besra 2014). The methods used were direct observation, interview, and focus group discussion. The overall research approach thereby combined a range of methods, including critical auto-ethnography and case studies with participant groups, by doing so, it was well placed to identify the challenges that impinge quality of life and wellbeing in the local communities where the development project paradigm mediates thoughts, worldviews, and practices of the people and institutions in Mindanao. Critical ethnography, in particular is the more popular type of its kind as it is emancipatory (Thomas 1993) in nature through its 'critical' approaches (Carspecken 1995; Creswell 2007; Madison 2005; Thomas 1993) to the issues pertaining to local peoples' rights and needs. It creates an active 'advocacy' (Creswell 2007, p. 70) to affect and change the systems that hinder the capabilities and violates the basic human rights of the people in Mindanao.

Direct observation was initially undertaken in the communities involved after the granting of full consent of the authorities and community people concerned. Consent was first sought from the regional offices of the National Commission for Indigenous Peoples and the Department of Interior and Local Government. Community leaders and the target participants were invited to engage in the study in fully voluntary manner. Those who indicated they wished to participate were asked to make a specific time and location for the interview. From those who were initially interviewed, many names were referred to and sought for an opportunity to take part in the in-depth interviews.

Semi-structured key informant interviews were carried out with interview guides that listed topics and issues discussed in an individual session. At this stage, the criteria for selection of participants were as follows: (a) knowledge and experience on the topic under study; (b) must be a bona fide resident/member/official of any of the groups; (c) must be trustworthy and credible; and (d) must be willing to participate. Focus group discussions were conducted in parallel to address the informants' interview results. The focus group members were carefully selected in a similar manner to the one used in the key informant interview. The criteria for selection were as follows: (a) groups may be heterogeneous or homogeneous in composition; (b) group members should be able to participate in discussion; (c) group members have knowledge on the subject of discussion; and (d) they have similar background or knowledge.

## Reconstructing the Power Cube

This paper argues that participatory approaches used in rural development planning in the Philippines are limited in their scope and intention to harness the real and personal voices, choices, agency and rights of the poorest and most marginalised Indigenous people, which in this study, comprised of women, young people, elderly, sick and differently abled persons. Participation and development discourses point out that the poor and powerless individuals are made invisible at the planning stage. The surveys conducted that serve as basis for the rural development planning skipped and misrepresented the voice and choice of the poor and powerless individuals by making them passive participants (Agarwal 2001; Cornwall 2003, 2004) in various decision-making opportunities made at the household and community level. The case is made that women and other household dependents are in fact being excluded in the actual making of 'democratic spaces' created and controlled by the different state and non-state actors and organisations.

The prevailing governance and development architectures are proud to promote 'full participation' and 'participation of all stakeholders' (Gaventa 2006) and yet, as evidences would show, poor and powerless women and their dependents are being left out in the decision-making process. Their voices and choices are parroted by the able men, in partnership with other powerful and elite men in the society (Bacchi 2010).

What is wrong with the current emphasis on 'full participation' and 'participation of all stakeholders'? Cornwall argues that most of the time, when these generalised rhetoric is used, the actual voice and representation of the weak, the less powerful and the most marginalised are not heard and often overlooked (2003, p. 1325). The full participation clauses found in legal and administrative instruments of governments and international aid organisations are in actual fact, voiced out by the powerful and elite members of the society, especially those who hold elective and administrative positions. The voice of the rural and Indigenous people, especially the poorest and most marginalised women are constituted in the discourse of development favouring the interests of the educated and influential elite and leaders in state and non-state organisations (Bacchi 2010).

Women in Development (WID) and 'participatory development' scaffold neoliberal development programmes while Gender and Development (GAD) and 'participation in development' support the need to address social inequalities by promoting gender-aware and participatory development interventions in order to provide transformation rights, agency, voice and choice to local people (Cornwall 2003, p. 1326). GAD has enhanced WID with its commitment to analyse and reduce the counter-effects of power inequalities among all stakeholders at various levels by listening, planning and acting based on the voice and choice of women and other disadvantaged groups in the society. The distinct voice and representation of women in particular, as Cornwall argues, are being factored in the social planning processes at the community level. Women's issues at the personal and household are therefore not being listened to in the actual social planning processes (2003, p. 1327). Based on the review of the literature on the area of gender and participation, women and other household dependents are constituted in the discourse of development planning (Bacchi 2000, 2004, 2010; Dobson 2014; Eveline and Bacchi 2005) by limiting the boundaries of the decision-making processes to privileged men and more influential people in the society, to hold more power leverage and decide for the silenced others. Making women and other disadvantaged groups in the society instrumental and passive participants in the decision-making platforms destroys their enthusiasm and aspiration to step up and exercise their freedom (Agarwal 1994, 2001, 2010). Women and other disadvantaged groups in the rural areas have unique local, complex, diverse, dynamic, and unstable realities (Chambers 1997), which needs to be dealt with locally by providing women the chance to develop ample participation capabilities to exercise their rights to enter into critical community dialogues especially those pertaining to land, food, livelihood, health and education. Improving participation as fertile functioning among Indigenous women in Mindanao is ideal not only in improving their wellbeing but also in developing their resilience as individuals against man-made and natural hazards.

GAD and 'participation in development' concepts coincide with Bacchi's idea on the need to emphasise gender as an action-oriented construct, rather than as a problem that needs tools to be solved. The importance of participation of women in development discourse is undermined by the existing governance and development paradigms that focus on generalised participation of all regardless of whether women are actively involved or not. Participation has become the 'development orthodoxy' (Chambers 1997) and it has systematic loopholes being generic rather than disaggregated and being tool- rather than action-oriented (Cornwall 2003, p. 1325).

Gaventa's (2006) power cube comprises of three factors, namely: (a) places/levels (local, national, global); (b) spaces (visible, hidden, invisible); and (c) forms of power (closed, invited, claimed/created). He identified the levels of power—from local to global, which are all part of the 'traded' or 'formal' sector in Kabeer's 'iceberg' view of the economy (2003, p. 28). Kabeer argues that below the local or community level, which comprised the majority in the developing countries such as the Philippines, are the invisible informal sectors struggling to claim their rights to land, food, livelihood, health and education. The invisible informal sectors, in this study, I argue are the households, peers, and individuals, especially the poorest and most marginalised women and their dependents.

According to Chambers (1983), these invisible groups and individuals are the victims of the development biases, namely spatial bias (tendency of the outsiders to visit and work only in the conspicuous locations); person bias (preference of male over female participants, also known as male bias); project bias (preference of outsiders on model and successful projects, season bias (absence of the outsiders in the rural area during rainy seasons), and diplomatic bias (tendency of the outsiders to deal closely with the popular and powerful local individuals).

The reconstructed power cube (Fig. 17.1) retains in the analysis, Gaventa's spaces and forms of power as bases in examining the issues confronted by the invisible and informal sectors lobbying for their voice, choice and agency in promoting wellbeing and life chances as individuals with equal rights or entitlements as men. The main purpose of this analytical framework is not to lock Kabeer's social relations approach and Gaventa's power cube as a fixed representation of the issue of marginalisation of the invisible and informal sectors, but to provide a fluid guide for analysing and understanding the power dynamics of people situated below the formal and market-oriented economy.

Kabeer points out that social institutions have distinct characteristics; their form and significance depend on the unique cultural contexts. However unique, Kabeer argues that there are at least five common aspects of social relationships to be considered for effective institutional analysis, namely: rules, resources, people, activities and power (cited in March et al. 2005, p. 104). Rules pertain to 'how things get done'. Rules cover institutional formal and informal 'norms, values, laws, traditions, and customs'. Informal rules include the assumptions and implied meanings of unwritten rules adopted by the institutions. Activities refer to 'what is done' in institutions. Broadly, activities comprise of the practices being done to achieve the goals. Resources pertain to 'what is used' and 'what is produced'. Production and distribution of resources depend on 'who produced what?'. According to Kabeer, if a woman helps in the actual production of any resource, she gets some sort of agency and entitlement to use the resource under her control (cited in March et al. 2005, p. 104). The analysis addresses who actually does what, who is included and who is left out? The purpose of this aspect of the analysis is to show that despite improved rate of generalised participation of the local people in the decision-making, it is paramount to re-examine who in actual fact carries out what particular roles in what type of responsibilities. Women have, to a greater extent, been left out performing their 'triple-roles', namely, reproductive, productive and community responsibilities underneath the purview of the formal economy (Moser 1989, 2003). The last aspect in the analysis is power; it asks the questions: Who decides what? Who gains, who loses? Social relationships are ruled by power dynamics. It is important to know the extent to which the elite and more powerful rule the poor and the powerless in the actual decision-making process.

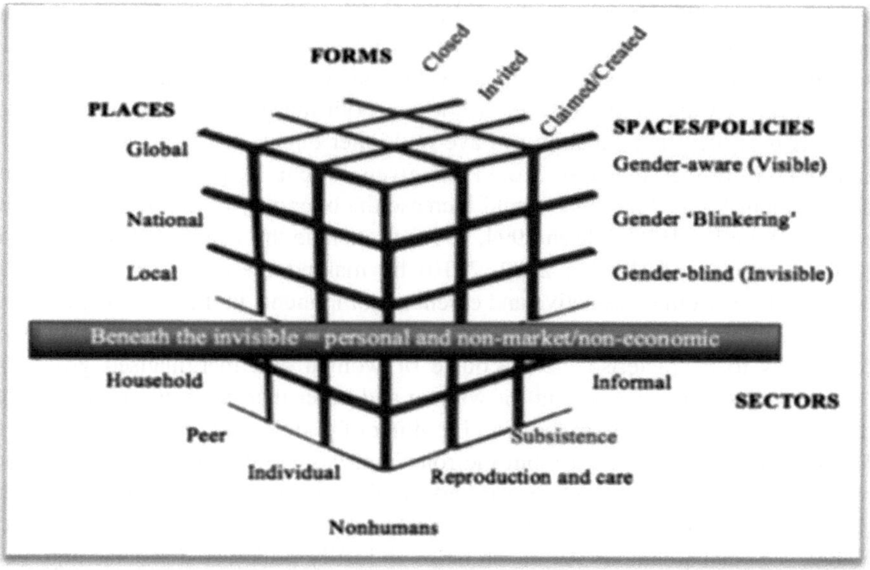


**Fig. 17.1** Reconstructed Power Cube: Basis for the proposed empowerment framework for rural and Indigenous farmers in Mindanao, Philippines. Adapted from Cornwall (2003), Nussbaum (2011), and Gaventa (2006, p. 25). Adapted from Cornwall (2003), Nussbaum (2011), and Gaventa (2006, p. 25)

## The Nexus of Capabilities Approach, Moser's and Kabeer's Gender Mainstreaming Theories

This chapter highlights the critical ways in which rural and Indigenous women in Mindanao are able to transform their disadvantaged status by being able to move along with men in rural development planning and improve their wellbeing and resilience.

Nussbaum (2011) and Kabeer (2003) share the same view about development. The former argues that 'development is an a priori guide and the latter also provides a means to assess the extent to which norms are implemented in context increasing human wellbeing' (cited in March et al. 2005, p. 101). Kabeer's social relations approach theory argues that wellbeing is not only measured in terms of 'economic growth or improved productivity'. It is covers more than just quantitative parameters of human growth and improvement such as income and wealth, and covers important social anthropological constructs such as 'survival, security, and autonomy'. Autonomy, according to Kabeer, refers to the individual's capability to decide and participate independently in the personal, familial, and community affairs that are deemed necessary to promote one's wellbeing and life chances. Simple forms of autonomy include woman's ability to make decisions about her own body as well as her capability to achieve strategic goals within the public sphere.

This current study tries to extend Nussbaum's Capabilities Approach by theorising and justifying sets of capabilities for women triggers the cycle or web of opportunities that in turn, encourage and support the development of capabilities of other persons directly under the care of women in both the household and community level. It is argued that capabilities have multiplier effect, just like functionings, if and only if proper attention would be given to put in place governance and development frameworks that would increase the boundary of the decision-making process (Midgley 1997; Ulrich 1994, 1996) to include the voice and representation of the marginalised (Bacchi 2000, 2010) by making the discourse of the poor, particularly of women, as active and essential components in the 'meaning making' involved in the social planning. Eveline and Bacchi (2005) argue that the way forward is to characterise the discourse of women and marginalised groups as 'action words'. Social planning for women and other marginalised groups call for the use of forceful 'verbs' in the actual framing of policies to emphasise the need to focus not only on the process but the roles that women can play strategically not merely as unpaid reproductive workers at the household or volunteers at the community level—but as active agents within the state, market and civil society, Kabeer's Social Relations Approach helps to justify policy-as-discourse argument in framing the interests of the poor or the 'peripheral rural people' (Chambers 1983, 1997) by understanding that the duty of the state to provide decent and justifiable social minimum based on Nussbaum's 10 Central Capabilities Kabeer's thesis goes to prove that Kabeer's concept of 'institutional analysis' provides the framework in which Nussbaum's Capabilities Approach will be further expanded in this study. Kabeer defines institution as 'a framework of rules for achieving certain social and economic goals' and organisation as the structure created by institutions cited in March et al. 2005, p. 104). In this regard, Kabeer addresses the points where inequality is being produced, reinforced, and reproduced. She makes the point that one needs to consider the 'institutional realms—the state, the market, the community, and the family/kinship' (pp. 104–105). The state constitutes the government, legal and security frameworks governing the state and the lower government bodies and line agencies. The market includes such institutions as private businesses both local and foreign, operating and/or affecting primarily the state's financial and economic affairs. The community comprises of all organisations directly and indirectly outside the realms of family/kinship. They may be formal and informal groups where families and individuals interact, depend and take leadership roles, when afforded the chance. Lastly, the family/kinship level includes couples/partners, siblings, and extended families related both by consanguinity and affinity.

Kabeer does more than just offering explanation about the dynamics of institutional domains in the production, reinforcement and reproduction of social inequalities as presented previously. There are 'official ideologies' heavily established in the basic institutional domains that have been adversely affecting the design of social actions. These assumptions are said to be the obstacles in the meaning making to emancipate the poorest and most marginalised people through social deconstruction. These myths or so-called assumptions are comprised of and controlled by the discourse of the elite (Bacchi 2010) expressed in the texts and speeches controlled by the dominant, influential and powerful groups. Kabeer argues that the common assumptions being predominantly attributed to the state is that it always 'pursues the national interest and national welfare'; to the market, that it 'pursues about profit maximisation'; the community, that is 'about service provision; and the family/kinship is 'about altruism' and that it is always 'cooperative, not conflictual institutions (March et al. p. 103). Policy-as-discourse as a form of systemic social action, must therefore proceed to analyse through 'open dialogue' (Christakis 2004, Christakis and Bausch 2006, Christakis and Harris 2004) and minimise the impact of power in the actual planning process. For Kabeer, reflecting on these sets of neutrality denies the entire effort to include the voice and representation of the poor and the marginalised in the social action. The challenge for the policy-as-discourse analysts would be to carry out systemic analysis taking off from Churchman's 'sweeping in' as many interrelated issues as possible (cited in Midgley 2000, p. 291) and by expanding the sphere of the decision-making boundary to include the 'involved and affected' (Ulrich 1994, 1996) in the actual planning or social designing process.

These institutional levels or domains, are the sources of either fertile functioning and capability (Nussbaum 2011, p. 44) or 'corrosive disadvantage' Wolff and De Shalit 2013). Fertile capabilities are produced, reinforced and reproduced in Kabeer's 'four key institutional realms' or domains much in the same way corrosive disadvantages are created. Fertile capabilities open up opportunities for other more or less complex capabilities. For example, giving women the proper skills, through training them how to safely and creatively process fruit preserves locally, will open up other windows for women to improve other life skills such as but not limited to networking, selling, and gaining higher analytical and creative thinking required in managing small family business. The flip side of this positive story, however, is the challenge imposed by so-called corrosive disadvantages. When women are forced to focus only on their reproductive and productive roles, and are inhibited, by virtue of customs and traditions to perform such other important and meaningful roles—spanning productive and community roles (Moser 1989, 2003) Crehan (1992b, p. 113) further classifies Moser's (1989, 2003) idea of reproductive burden of women into at least three categories, namely: 'biological reproduction' or child-bearing, 'generational reproduction' or childrearing, and 'daily reproduction or maintenance' or the household rigmaroles such as cleaning, feeding, foraging, gardening/farming and many other countless and hitherto unaccounted time and efforts spent by women to raise their families.

Corrosive disadvantages or the institutional barriers are as important as the fertile capabilities in the analysis of this study. They constitute the active processes involved in carrying out policy-as-discourse for 'social deconstruction'. Social deconstruction is the twin sister of policy-as-discourse. The theory is developed through the scholarly work of Foucault (1975) and supports the need to emphasise the process of generating truths through looking at the processes in which social actions have become relevant or irrelevant to the needs of the poor and the marginalised (cited in Bacchi 2010, p. 46). Examining and identifying the institutional barriers confronting women as well as their dependants require reifying the actual processes through the vivid narratives of the local people caught up in marginalised and pauperized status. Knowing what these barriers are, straight from the holders and/or guardians of LCDDU (local, complex, diverse, dynamic, and unstable) realities (Chambers 1997) assures that more ethical social action could take place to help emancipate women and other marginalised groups from the structural barriers created by dissonant versions of inequalities and injustices perpetrated simultaneously or independently within and outside all the institutional frames identified by Kabeer. Another advantage of looking closely at these corrosive disadvantages is to identify ways in which provision by the state of minimum social capabilities, and allocating corresponding resources could be easily directed to the institutional barriers that have adversely affected other supporting structures. There are institutional barriers, by their very nature, lump together closely and annihilate the structures belonging to a specific institution and spread across others. Such is the case involved when a woman is restricted to control land and other resources transferred through patrilineal arrangements to her family. Patrilineal transfer of property denies women the actual chance of ownership and control of land and other wealth bestowed through the father or male side (Crehan 1992a, p. 92 and 114). This family/kinship level barrier is produced, reinforced and reproduced both at the community and state levels. Therefore, giving women an increased access and control over conjugal or partnership properties, regardless of the manner they are acquired, helps to address women's vulnerability to be dragged further down the quicksand of marginalisation and pauperisation. These corrosive disadvantages correspond to Chambers' interlocking 'deprivation trap' (1983, p. 112) comprises of 'poverty, physical weakness, powerlessness, vulnerability, and isolation'. Chamber's thesis does not build on causality and correlation of these disadvantages but instead offers a conceptual and practical way of using self-critical awareness to understand the dynamics or the process involved in policy-as-discourse and empowerment the poor and voiceless local people. Nussbaum's ideas of giving each person rather than the protracted aggregate of family or community units, and of focusing on dignity rather than satisfaction, reinforce each person's agency to do and to be.

## Listening as the Missing Key in Empowerment

Sensory democracy provides the impetus for focusing on 'speaking' and 'watching' as critical aspects of political and democratic process nowadays. The conventional emphasis on speaking provides a limited chance for ordinary people to be genuinely heard because speaking is a privilege role of the patriarchy and dominant discourse holders in the society (Jenson 1997). Dobson (2014) argues that sensory democracy must consider not just speaking and watching as aspects to minimise power barriers and empower people. It should also focus on the role of listening in dialogic process of democracy where people engage in political and democratic actions with the capabilities to enter and enjoy the dynamics of the whole range of communication process—speaking, watching, feeling, and listening. In the West Churchman Series, Wisdom, Knowledge and Management (McIntyre-Mills 2006), McIntyre-Mills stresses that listening is a priority if we are to build in the 'requisite variety' (Ashby 1956) when we design responses to complex needs. Dobson (2014) in 'Democratic Deficits' stresses that the powerful dominate and block the political discourse of those who are marginalised. Listening has 'active and agentic role to play' in protecting the interests of the disadvantaged groups to claim decent democratic space where they can negotiate for their wellbeing (Dobson 2014, p. 20). Listening is a form of exercising power over those who will be listened to and those who will be refused and marginalised in the political process.

Dobson (2014, p. 22) argues that the 'sensory approach to politics and democracy can entail empowerment' by emphasising the need to listen and see the actual outcomes of the dialogic type of democracy. Entering into dialogic, rather than political monologues, encourages political and democratic actions to focus on the need to consider the whole range of processes involved in the communication system. If Aristotle argues that man is a political animal because he has the capacity to speak, Dobson tries to extend the idea by arguing that sensory democracy includes, apart from capacities for speaking and seeing—listening (2014, p. 18). Dobson stresses the need to implore the power of listening to break the barriers created by power itself. He argues that listening is a form of power. The listener has the power not to listen, to twist and misunderstand the meaning of verbal and nonverbal messages and to hijack the communication process to favour his/her own self-interests (p. 21).

Dobson's theorising of listening as a missing key in dialogic democracy is used as a lens to critique the existing participatory development framework that supports 'participation of all' and 'stakeholders participation' (Cornwall 2003) in rural development planning. It is argued that the existing rural development planning processes in Mindanao subjugate and disempower Indigenous women. Indigenous women and their dependents are made passive and silent participants in the decision-making opportunities for rural development planning that privilege leaders, experts, and men. Their voice, choice and agency as individuals are repressed and underrepresented by undermining their capabilities to enter into the decision-making processes. It is argued that active participation is a fertile capability that must be supported by the state and local governments to allow women and other disadvantaged groups to become part of the whole process of rural development. Moser's framework was used as a tool to analyse gender inequality while Kabeer's social relations approach was used as lens to critique the existing gender inequality in various institutions—household, community, state and market level.

This chapter addresses the critical role of Indigenous women in helping themselves reverse their disempowered status in the decision-making processes involved in rural development planning in Mindanao. It is argued that giving Indigenous women agentic voice and choice in the policy-making arenas, namely, household, community, state and market (Kabeer 2003) must include not just speaking but also listening (Dobson 2014). This is to ensure that power bases are equally shared and preconceptions of the local people ‘involved and affected’ (Ulrich 1994) are managed in order to co-create understanding of and solution to local issues. Providing the Indigenous women the chance to actually speak, see and listen to their individual and collective voice and choice will improve the legitimacy of the policies targeted for their wellbeing and life chances as individuals. Legitimacy is a democratic credo that demands government to be ‘responsive’ by ‘listening’ (Ulrich 1994) to as many people as possible. Engaging with the local people especially women and other disadvantaged group is a way of expanding the boundaries of decision-making (Ulrich 1994) by believing that the rural and Indigenous women have unique stories, different sets of needs, and complex aspirations that must be listened to and regarded as critically important in improving their wellbeing and life chances.

The aim of this chapter is to characterise and understand the LCDDU (local, complex, diverse, dynamic and unstable) realities (Chambers 1997) of the rural and Indigenous women in Mindanao. The case is made that the government and non-government officials and experts must work closely with the local women in respectful dialogues to get to truth (McIntyre-Mills 2006, p. 10). Entering into respectful dialogue requires improved auditory capacity of the officials and experts to not just hear but listen to the Indigenous women’s voice and choice on how their wellbeing should be planned for the current and future generation. The proposed women empowerment framework is anchored on sensory and dialogic form of democracy that must become the major platform where gender inequality is strategically addressed.

## Socio-Economic Typology of Participants

One-third or 31% of the farmer-participants declared, in terms of land ownership, that they are marginal to landless. Even those who still have considerable sizes of land under leasing and growership agreements say they have never gone out of poverty as yet. Using the current state of land ownership, household income, unpaid loan balance, level of education, health and employment status, Table 17.1 presents the typology of participants in terms of the deprivation they experience. In the survey, each participant is categorised under the status (e.g. level of education) and each category is assigned a score starting with zero (0) as the absence or the lowest state, such that a participant who declared that he/she has never been to any formal school is categorised, under level of education, as 0. To establish the range in each category, for example in land ownership status, the difference between the lowest and highest value in terms of hectares of land was divided into 3, corresponding the typologies.

In terms of household income per month, majority of the participants have income below Php500 per month (roughly USD12). All of them have average monthly income below the poverty threshold set by the Philippine government of Php8,022 per month for a family of five to sustain its food and non-food needs (Philippine Statistics Authority 2014). Financially, what makes income deprivation worst is the state of indebtedness the participants have experienced as shown in

**Table 17.1** Typology of farmer-participants according to socio-economic indicators

| Socio-economic indicators | Category | | | | | |
|---|---|---|---|---|---|---|
| (a) Land ownership (in hectares) | ≥4 | | 1–3 | | 0 | |
| | N | % | N | % | N | % |
| | 14 | 13 | 58 | 55 | 33 | 31 |
| | **Landed** | | **Marginal** | | **Landless** | |
| (b) Household income (in Php per month) | 2001 and above | | 501–2,000 | | ≤500 | |
| | N | % | N | % | N | % |
| | 15 | 15 | 20 | 19 | 70 | 67 |
| (c) Unpaid loan balance (aggregated in Php) | ≤500 | | 501–10,000 | | 10,001 and above | |
| | N | % | N | % | N | % |
| | 2 | 2 | 30 | 29 | 73 | 70 |
| (d) Level of education | Secondary to college | | Primary | | No formal education | |
| | N | % | N | % | N | % |
| | 30 | 29 | 31 | 30 | 44 | 41 |
| (e) Employment status | Employed | | Under-employed | | Unemployed | |
| | N | % | N | % | N | % |
| | 32 | 30 | 37 | 35 | 36 | 34 |
| (f) Health status (number of sick family member) | 0 | | 1 | | ≥2 | |
| | N | % | N | % | N | % |
| | 32 | 30 | 31 | 30 | 42 | 40 |

*Source* Face-to-face interview with the Indigenous farmers in Mindanao and validated during FGD conducted from 28 September 2013 to 10 May 2014

Table 17.1. Majority or 79% of them have existing unpaid loans ranging from Php10.000 and above. These loans were accessed mostly from the "loan sharks" who offer farmers fast and easy access to cash for their household and farm needs. Mrs. ST shared her story as follows:

> We have no choice. We cannot go to the cooperative we already owed with money. We are paying a loan through another loan. We are forced to do so to get by.

In the rural Philippines, loan sharks are those who provide fast and easy loans to farmers in exchange of a hefty interest rate of 20% per month. The local people called this popular practice as "5–6" (read as five–six; a loan of Php5.000 will gain an interest of 20%, making it Php6,000 at the end of the month, hence the term "5–6"). In terms of education, 44 or 41% of the participants have not attended any formal education. Thirty-one or 30% have been to primary school while 30 or 29% attended secondary school to college.

Marginal and landless farmers have reported to have 1–2 family member/s who is/are sick and old dependent/s. This data shows that since most of the marginal and landless participants are women, and being women means directly responsible for the reproductive task, particularly on 'maintenance role' (Crehan 1992a, b). Women are socially and culturally expected to concentrate primarily on domestic duties—

childrearing, foraging, cooking, feeding, caring for the sick and elderly in the family. Caring for the sick and the elderly, if not shared with any able member in the family makes women's role even more burdensome and complicated.

Table 17.1 also shows the basic food items rural and Indigenous people in Mindanao eat on a regular basis. The landed people (10 or 10%) have the capability to eat three square meals a day usually comprised of seafood, at least once a week, meat, poultry and vegetables, more than three times a week, and rice or corn, seven times a week. The marginal landholding farmers are capable of eating at least once a week of any type of seafood—fish and seashell. They can also afford to feed themselves and their families with meat and poultry two times a week; vegetables, four times; and rice or corn, 5–6 times a week. The landless farmers on the other hand, are not capable of feeding themselves with any type of seafood in a week's time. They barely even eat meat and poultry on a regular weekly basis. Their diet relies primarily on the fruits and vegetables grown in their farms and backyard gardens. In terms of rice or corn diet, they are only capable of eating either type of grain 3–4 times a week. The landless and the poorest in the continuum experience hunger 7 times and more in the last 4 weeks. In terms of the most staple food—rice or corn meal, the landless people have a deficit of 3–4 meals of this kind. When this happens, especially during the rainy season months of June to August, focus group discussion participants reveal that they turn to their local banana for source of carbohydrates and fibre.

## Analysing Social Vulnerability Using the Interlocking Deprivation Trap

This section will provide a further analysis on the nature and scope of the interlocking deprivation experienced by the rural and Indigenous people in Mindanao. To describe deprivation among the rural farmer-participants, I used Robert Chambers' deprivation trap shown in Fig. 17.2. This representation of poverty and deprivation entanglement can aid in explaining the complex interconnections of rural poverty and vulnerability of the Indigenous people in Mindanao. According to Chambers, rural people who are materially and food poor suffer from the multiple effects of pauperisation. The poorest and the most marginalised are physically weak due to income and food insecurity. The participants acknowledged the fact that their experience of poverty leads them to poor health and nutrition as narrated by Mrs. OP below:

> The midwives working at the health centre found all my 4 kids malnourished and underweight. I really know the reason why they are suffering from ill health. We are experiencing "seasonal" hunger. When our corn harvest is low and our loan is high.

A state that is a combination of poor health and poverty leads people to a more vulnerable condition. The absence of substantial social protection such as provision of more opportunities for the poorest Indigenous farmers to earn a living other than

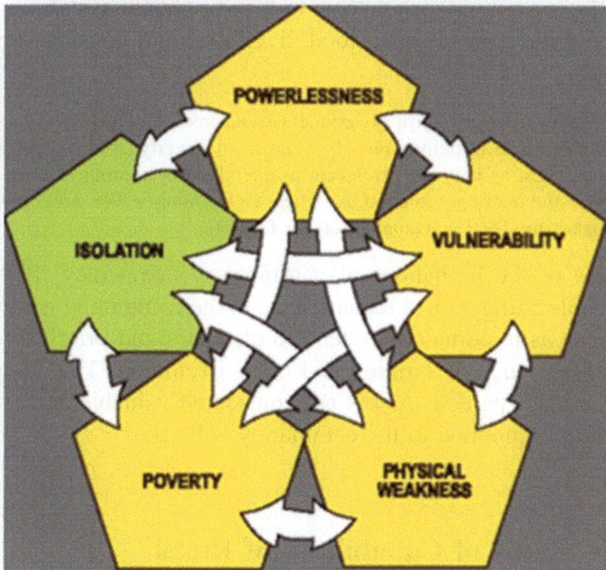


**Fig. 17.2** Deprivation trap: Source: Chambers (1983, p. 112)

farming like being able to earn money or food stuff in exchange of communal manual labour, makes them prone to natural and manmade calamities. The poorest Indigenous farmers, if they choose to remain in the rural areas, have to contend with the poor state of housing and poor health due to low to zero farm productivity. If they wish to leave their farmland and relocate in other rural areas where their extended families can support them, the uncertainty can further worsen the vulnerability of the internally migrated families. Mrs. UV described her family's experience moving away from the civil conflict only to end up hungry in their new location in the plantation community in the following quote:

> We came from the hinterlands of Bukidnon. We transferred here in Davao del Norte near our families in 1990. We experienced war, flood and hunger in our previous community. Now, there is no war here but we still fight against hunger and our lives are still threatened by natural calamities.

The interlocking of poverty, poor health and vulnerability amongst rural Indigenous people in the plantation communities in Mindanao leads to critical state of powerlessness. Powerlessness of rural people, in terms of not being able to do and to be and to live life with dignity (Nussbaum 2011), escalates into people's acceptance of their dire living conditions. They tend to isolate themselves away from the vital processes of democratisation, which are supposed to emancipate them from poverty and all other social inequalities. Isolation can be a way to express apathy towards the prevailing social, economic and political system that does not protect the rights of the poor for land, food, livelihood and housing security. Mrs. WX shared her story as follows:

> We tend to hide away from any local government-sponsored activity because we believe that we have not been able to deliver ourselves out from poverty. It is useless to discuss local government issues, as it is also irrelevant to attend skills training that we have not been able to master and really put to good use when we are hungry. We would rather go to our farms and make sure food is available for our families.

Isolation is one of the limitations of participatory democracy (Pieterse 2001, p. 410). When people being invited to participate in the community activities do not value their presence as important, they tend to disregard and prioritise other more important undertaking such as farming and other livelihood. This happens when people believe that their participation is not considered valuable enough to justify their time and effort committed to the community activity.

## Exploring the Status of Capabilities of Rural and Indigenous Farmers in Mindanao

This section explores in further details the extent to which each of Nussbaum's 10 Central Capabilities indicators are being practiced or not practiced in the rural and Indigenous communities in Mindanao. I argue that the voice and representation of the poorest and most marginalised rural and Indigenous farmers in rural development planning should be enhanced to improve their wellbeing and life chances. As can be seen in Table 17.3, even the Coping participants in the typology, being in the middle, a step higher the Poorest and Most Marginalised, and a notch lower the Better-off, has higher vulnerability to be dragged further to the bottom—one with the lowest typology, due to any sudden risk and shock. A sudden death of the head of the family or of any member can cause the whole family's miserable state of deprivation. The same type of undesirable outcome is expected when a farmer gives up his/her control and/or ownership of land due to distress sale, lease and other arrangements that decapitate farmer to till and manage his/her own land. This issue on land is strongly connected to the financialisation of land and other resources in the Philippines, which is part of the globalisation strategies enforced under the Agreement on Agriculture (AoA). AoA is one of the trade liberalisation policies established by the World Trade Organisation (WTO), which according to Panhwar (2001), has encouraged countries to open up their markets by allowing freer importation of products and services. In the Philippines, Mindanao serves as the monoculture plantation hub planting primarily high-value crops such as bananas and pineapples (Gutierrez and Borras 2004).

Nussbaum's list of capabilities starts with life. Nussbaum defines life as 'being able to live to the end of a human life of normal length; not dying prematurely, or before one's life is so reduced as to be not worth living'. Living a decent and dignified life is one of basic entitlements or rights protected by the state and international laws. The Universal Declaration of Human Rights for example (UDHR) of 1948 declares under Article 3, that 'everyone has the right to life, liberty and security of person'. Other vital international laws and legal instruments include among others the UN Convention of the Rights of the Child (UNCRC), which specifically protects the rights of every child to life (Articles 6, 23, and 29) and the International Covenant on Civil and Political Rights (Article 6). The 1987 Philippine Constitution enshrines right to life in Article 2, Sect. 17.5 and Article 3, Sect. 17.1. According to Sison (2014), right to life is considered a moral and legal principle in the Philippine Constitution. It guarantees protection of life of each Filipino as 'essential for the enjoyment by all the people of the blessings of democracy'.

In the rural and Indigenous communities in Mindanao where this study was conducted deprivation is continuously challenging the quality and normal length of life of the local people especially the poorest and the most marginalised who are comprised of women, young people, sick, elderly and different-abled, who by virtue of culture and traditions are left under the direct care of women themselves. According to Moser (1989, 2003), reproductive roles of a woman eat up most of her time and energy. For Crehan (1992a, b), woman's burgeoning reproductive tasks include not just childbearing and childrearing. It also includes all other household and farm workloads not ably performed by the husband such as caring for the sick and looking after the welfare of the elderly and differently abled members in the household. These maintenance tasks are part of the subordinated role of women which are produced, reinforced and reproduced in various institutional domains, namely: family, community, market, and state (Kabeer 2003). According to Kabeer, our society has edified various institutional assumptions, which make efforts to address this form of social inequality extremely difficult if not impossible to address. For example, family is always considered 'cooperative, not conflictual institution' and that the community is always 'about service provision' (March et al. 2005, p. 103). These assumptions prevail and developed into rigid political and development discourses. For Bacchi (2010), the voice and representation of the powerless and the poor people are constituted in discourse of the elite and powerful state and non-state actors. For example, gender mainstreaming as a strategy to address gender inequality suffers from lack of legitimacy in many of the planning platforms because the concept itself is made passive. Eveline and Bacchi (2005) suggested that the concept gender mainstreaming must be made 'active', a forceful action- and therefore process-oriented evolving construct whose development must be well participated by the local people, especially the poor and marginalised women. Dispelling the myths and common assumptions require focus on action or process rather than on the passive state of issue at hand such as gender mainstreaming. It requires policy-as-discourse (Bacchi 2010) to socially deconstruct the rigid and passive realities imposed by empiricism in order to hear the voice and gather the representation of the powerless and the poor. The goal is to provide process-oriented frameworks of development and governance for the improvement of wellbeing and life chances of the people affected and marginalised by development bias and their effects.

Just how quality of life varies across the different typologies of participants in this study, namely: the Better-off, the Coping, and the Poorest and Most Marginalised? I make the case that quality of life varies across different typologies. The Better-off have the control and the privileged access to resources to support a choice to live well and longer. As the gatekeepers of the resources and power being distributed by the government and non-government organisations, they enjoy the privilege of managing, taking advantage of their ranks, whatever social goods or services falling under their jurisdiction and control. Being predominantly male, the Better-off group possesses relative financial and leadership capabilities necessary to maintain their post, being influential leaders in their tribe. The *datus* (male tribal chieftains) have the cultural, political and economic mandate to head their tribes to achieve common welfare and protect their members at all times. The disadvantage of *datuism,* however, is more serious than the issue of just maintaining leadership and communal welfare of the tribal leaders and of the landed and the moneyed members of the tribes in rural Mindanao. The Coping group have limited chance to protect one's life in order to live longer but are still better-off than the Poorest and the Most Marginalised group. Being in the middle of the continuum, the Coping group struggles to adapt to the practices of the Better-off in order to gain attention and get favoured access to the social goods and services for distribution. The Poorest and the Most Marginalised group have highly limited and extremely vulnerable state of life to live longer; these rural people rely primarily on their Indigenous knowledge systems and practices (IKSP) to survive as evidences would show.

The World Health Organization (2015) data shows that the average life expectancy at birth, in 2012 in the Philippines, is 69. This is 7 years lower compared to the life expectancy in the Western Pacific region in the same year. Healthy life expectancy in the country starting at birth is 60. This means that on the average, Filipinos remain healthy at the age of 60. Through focus group discussion, and on the basis of secondary data collected from the Ancestral Domain Sustainable Development and Protection Plan (ADSDPP) of the Matigsalug-Manobo Tribal People Council of Elders in Davao City or MAMATRIPCEDI, Table 17.4 presents the population distribution in one of the Indigenous communities covered by this study in Davao City area in 2013. The Indigenous area is under Certificate of Ancestral Domain Title (CADT) No. R10-KIT-0703-0011. It is covering 26,632 hectares of forestland, which is at present faces the danger of being converted to commercial monoculture farms. At present, the community has just signed the land deal for the conversion of ancestral land into cacao plantation. The whole business operation is under the management of a multi-national company named Kennemer Foods Corporation.

The Participatory Rural Appraisal (PRA) conducted for this study estimates the population distribution in terms of gender in the five Indigenous communities. The participants' responses as well as the notebooks kept by the tribal council secretaries were used to come up with the communally produced figures. This means to

**Table 17.2** Population distribution and average life expectancy based on PRA 2013 and National Statistics Office Survey in 2006

| Village | Population | | | | | % Differ-ence in total | No. of households | Ave. household size | Life expectancy | | | |
|---|---|---|---|---|---|---|---|---|---|---|---|---|
| | PRA 2013 | | | NSO 2006[8] | | | | | PRA | | NSO | |
| | M | F | Total | M | F | | | | M | F | M | F |
| Buda | 731 | 685 | 1,416 | 1,612 | | 196 (14%) | 309 | 5 | 72 | 60 | No data | |
| Baganihan | 683 | 740 | 1,423 | 246 | | 1,177 (83%) | 238 | 6 | | | No data | |
| Tapak | 1,172 | 1,267 | 2,439 | 1,509 | | 930 (38%) | 406 | 6 | | | No data | |
| Marilog | 7,283 | 6,707 | 13,990 | 13,071 | | 919 (7%) | 2,798 | 5 | | | No data | |
| Gumitan | 473 | 557 | 1,030 | 843 | | 187 (18%) | 147 | 7 | | | No data | |
| Total | 10,342 | 9,956 | 20,298 | 17,468 | | 2,830 (14%) | 3,898 | 5 | | | No data | |

*Source* Face-to-face interview with the Indigenous farmers in Mindanao and validated during FGD conducted from 28 September 2013 to 10 May 2014

say that the actual reckoning of population in each community was based on the local ability of the rural and Indigenous people to count their members of the tribe with better precision compared to the national census conducted every 2–3 years by the National Statistics Office (NSO). NSO population data in the same year do not jibe with the PRA data on population. As can be seen in Table 17.2, PRA data are disaggregated according to gender while NSO is not. More importantly, PRA data on population in these 5 specific Indigenous communities in Davao City reveal that NSO data differs from PRA by at least 14%. Sad to say, it means that 2,830 people living in these communities are not counted in the census, and are thus being excluded in the actual rural development planning in Mindanao and in the entire Philippines. PRA and other types of agricultural census and surveys conducted with the rural and Indigenous people highlight the importance of disaggregating data into gender and other relevant categories to make rural development planning more inclusive and responsive to the local needs of the people (Quisumbing et al. 2014). Chambers (1983, 1995, 1997) describes PRA as a tool to ensure that the realities of the local and poor people prevail.

The average life expectancy, as shown, is based on the estimates of the participants. The data were validated in reference to the notes kept by the tribal councils and through the confirmation of the FGD participants. NSO, which is the official statistical body for local and national development planning in the Philippines, do not have data on life expectancy at the local level. The life expectancy estimates of 72 for male and 60 for female were derived from the responses given by some participants and validated during the focus group discussion.

Based on the narrations of some participants, poorest and remotest Indigenous people die much earlier than those who are better-off—who have access to basic and emergency medical facilities located in the town centre. The participants confirmed that poor women tend to die younger due to fatigue doing all sorts of reproductive and productive roles specifically household chores, foraging, and farming. These poor women's tasks demand a great deal of time and effort; unlike men, who after farm work are culturally allowed to rest and go to bed early, women need to do menial tasks in preparation for the next day. Studies comparing time use in reproductive, productive and community roles of men and women show that women work longer hours than men (Juster and Stafford 1991; Ruth Meinzen-Dick et al. 2014; World Bank 2001).

Another reason that is believed to compromise women's lives is the poor state of prenatal and maternal care in the rural and remote communities. Indigenous women are burdened by childbearing and childrearing responsibilities. As shown in Table 17.2, on the average, Indigenous families have 5–6 children primarily under the direct care and responsibility of women. The reproductive burden of childbearing and childrearing, as well as doing other more time-consuming and strength-draining household rigmaroles such as cleaning, washing clothes, gardening, feeding animals, etc. places women in a higher health risk compared to men (Harris 2014, p. 267). Women are more exposed to infections while they are pregnant (United Nations Standing Committee on Nutrition 1990). Poor rural women who do not have the control on the use of resources at home end up seriously ill before they are brought to the nearest health facility (Okwa 2007).

Adding more burden to this big reproductive responsibility is the fact that poor Indigenous women cannot afford to leave their children and other dependants behind to go to the town centre where the nearest health facility is located. It is typical for a pregnant woman from the remote rural area to postpone and worst, cancel her appointment at the health centre to avoid the long walk or get away from unsafe travel by horse or *habal-habal*. *Habal-habal* is the major means of transport in rural Mindanao. It is basically a motorcycle with extended wooden seats on both sides that can carry a load of 6–8 persons including the driver. Riding on it makes it dangerous for pregnant women as well as sick and the elderly to travel 30–60 min along off-road terrain.

Another type of gendered shock confronting the poorest and the most marginalised women in rural Mindanao is marriage separation and death of the husband. According to Peterman (2010, cited in Ruth Meinzen-Dick, Nancy Johnson et al. 2014, p. 102), divorcees and widows suffer from loss of loved one but women suffer even more from the lasting effects of loss of rights over their husbands' property as commanded by customary laws.

Women in the Better-off typology are the wives of the *datus* or tribal chieftains. They perform reproductive and productive roles in the household, farm and community, doing the diligence of being good wives and supporters of their husbands who are leaders in their tribe. Their main responsibilities still revolve around reproductive duties, but unlike the poor women, better-off women, being members of the royalty, enjoy such privilege of seeking assistance from other members in the tribe for their domestic responsibilities such as cooking, gathering of firewood, foraging, gardening and including childrearing. Being the *bae* (first wife of the *datu*), she is expected to fulfil administrative and cultural duties that may be required of her by her *datu* and the tribe. These responsibilities include but not limited to attending meetings and public functions together with the *datu*, gathering other women for talking, and many others.

Working closely as ally of the 'Better-off' are the 'Coping' men and women. As the ones who live closer to the town centre where the tribal heads live, the Coping group is the easy target participants for administrative and tribal activities of the Better-off such as meetings and caucuses to talk about the plans of the local officials in line with the coming elections, livelihood, and other community development matters. The Coping group is usually part of the active voting population in the rural area. Even if most of them are illiterate, not able to read and write, they are easily dragged by any political organisers in meetings and election rallies to make it appear that the local candidate is popular and would be able to garner votes during the election proper. These middling responsibilities commonly expected of the Coping group enable them to take advantage of the communal blessings received by the Better-off. For example, whenever the government allocates fund to help farmers improve their farm productivity, farm technicians from the urban area locate the *datus* and their families living along the highway and near the town centre. The outsiders conduct trainings and distribute seedlings and sample fertilisers to the people most accessible and familiar. This scenario, according to Chambers (1983), is flagrant display of the outsiders of their biases, namely in this case are spatial, person, and project biases. When the social goods and services are distributed in bulk at the premises of the Better-off, the immediate people that would come to mind are the Coping group. They are the ones to be called for meetings and forced adoption of the technologies being introduced by the outsider farm technician to the Better-off. This somehow temporarily alleviates the dire socio-economic condition of the Coping group. Being able to ease up the burden caused by poor knowledge to improve productivity and by high price of farm inputs.

## The Analytical Typology of Participants and Capabilities Characteristics

The experiences of the rural and Indigenous people are examined by applying the 'Overlapping Consensus' of Nussbaum's Capabilities Approach and gender mainstreaming theories and approaches of Moser (1989) and Kabeer (2003). The overlapping consensus of these development approaches are presented and analysed using the analytical typology—which classifies participants in the study according to their social, economic, political, and cultural circumstances. Specifically, the typology demarcates major classification of participants and the extent to which capabilities have been provided by state and non-state actors in the Philippines, particularly in rural Mindanao. The analytical typology is done by plotting in rows (X axis), Nussbaum's 10 Central Capabilities indicators and in columns (Y axis), the classification of people along the continuum. For the purpose of this study, the continuum is presented in three classifications, namely: (A) The Better-off, (B) The Coping, and (C) The Poorest and Most Marginalised. These analytical typologies are based on the typical narratives and socio-economic circumstances of the participants in the study.

Developing a typology is one way of presenting the interrelated and unique variations of participants' circumstances and narratives into categories or classifications. Besra (2014), in his study on the life chances of Indigenous people in Bangladesh, used typology to classify his participants' land ownership, health, employment, and education status. For example, he classified participants' landholding status into three as: landless, marginal, and medium.

In this study, I classified the participants into three, namely: (A) the Better-off, (B) the Coping, and (C) the Poorest and Most Marginalised. The upper part of Table 17.3 (grey) presents the summary of socio-economic typology presented in Table 17.1. In terms of land ownership and other socio-economic indicators, typology of participants is identified in the continuum as landless, marginal (sliding to landlessness) and landed. These two sets of typologies, namely, (1) the analytical typology presented in Table 17.3, and (2) the typology of farmer-participants according to land ownership and other socio-economic indicators shown in Table 17.1, are complementary to each other. Please note that the issue of land ownership presented in Table 17.1—analytical typology of participants, are classified as medium to landed, marginal to medium, and landless to marginal for the Better-off, the Coping, and the Poorest and Most Marginalised, respectively. This means that the 'Poorest and Most Marginalised' participants include not just the landless but also some farmers with marginal ownership of lands. The domains in the typology overlap. They are not rigid and linear constructs (McIntyre-Mills 2008, pp. 291–292), which means that the characteristics of persons and their narratives can be classified under specific domain and can be shared across the typology in the continuum. Such is the case for stories of women pertaining to their power to access and control land in the Indigenous communities. Evidently, landed women who are immediate members of the family of the tribal chieftains still struggle to assert their rights and raise their agentic voice and choice in the decision-making pertaining to land use, particularly the land being allocated for commercial monoculture plantations. The 'better-off' women enjoy some level of comfort and enhanced wellbeing as members of the royal family or clan. The coping women as well as the poorest and the most marginalised, are placed in the rather inconvenient social standing being unaccounted and unable to elevate their voice for matters that directly impact the use of land, their livelihoods and their wellbeing as a whole. Table 17.3 presents the summary of the typologies based on the narratives of the participants.

The narratives of the rural and Indigenous people in Mindanao along the 10 domains of Nussbaum's Central Capabilities can be narrowed down into at least four major domains based on the commonality of themes, such that capabilities 1 to 3 are altogether named as Life. Capabilities 4 to 7, Affiliation; 8 to 9, Concern for Nonhuman Animals and Recreation; and 10 as Political and Material Control. Summarising the 10 Central Capabilities gives leeway in analysing the interlocking

**Table 17.3** Characteristics of capabilities across typology of participants

| Capabilities | Typology of participants | | | | | |
|---|---|---|---|---|---|---|
| | Better-off | | Coping | | Poorest and most marginalised | |
| | 15 (14%) | | 20 (19%) | | 70 (67%) | |
| | Male | Female | Male | Female | Male | Female |
| | 14 (93%) | 1 (7%) | 18 (90%) | 2 (10%) | 20 (29%) | 50 (71%) |
| | ***Who***: comprised of individuals, mostly male tribal chieftains, elected local government leaders, landed farmers, and small store owners<br>***Where***: These people live along the main roads and/or town centres<br>***Land ownership:*** Medium to Landed (14 or 13%)<br>***Household income (in Php per month):*** PhP2001 and above (16 or 14%)<br>***Unpaid loan balance (aggregated in Php):*** ≤ 500 (2 or 2%)<br>***Average level of education:*** Secondary | | ***Who***: comprised of active, healthy male household heads who have limited access to resources such as land and with sparse livelihood opportunities<br>***Where***: They live in outer communities (1–2 km away from the town centre)<br>***Land ownership:*** Medium to Marginal (58 or 55%)<br>***Household income (in Php per month):*** PhP501–2,000 (20 or 19%)<br>***Unpaid loan balance (aggregated in Php):*** 501–10,000 (30 or 29%)<br>***Average level of education:*** Primary | | ***Who***: comprised of mostly women, elderly, sick and differently- abled<br>***Where***: They live in the remotest part of the rural communities (more than 3 km away from the town centre)<br>***Land ownership:*** Marginal to Landless (33 or 31%)<br>***Household income (in Php per month):*** < PhP 500 (70 or 67%)<br>***Unpaid loan balance (aggregated in Php):*** 10,001 and above (73 or 69%)<br>***Average level of education:*** Nil | |
| (1) Life | • Have control and privileged access to resources to support a choice to live well and longer | | • Have limited chance to protect one's life in order to live longer | | • Have highly limited and extremely vulnerable state of life to live longer; these rural people rely primarily on their indigenous knowledge systems and practices (IKSP) to survive | |
| (2) Health | • Are able to use and access both IKSP and modern medicine for basic health needs such as maternal care, childcare, vaccinations, etc.<br>• 52% has visited the nearest hospitals and community health centres in the past 12 months | | • Are able to use and access both IKSP and modern medicine for basic health needs much in the same way the better-off do. In extreme cases such as life threatening emergencies, this group depends on the resources and power of the better-off to seek assistance including loaning money<br>• 41% have visited the nearest hospitals and community health centres in the past 12 months | | • Are able to use and access primarily IKSP for basic health needs. Have become fatalistic and rely heavily much on prayers for the fate of sick and disabled state of some members in the family<br>• 7% have visited the nearest hospitals and community health centres in the past 12 months | |
| (3) Bodily integrity | • Are active and able to move to and fro rural and urban areas. The tribal and community leaders are called regularly by city officials to travel to the urban centres for meetings and for all other official functions<br>• These active tribal and influential men have the widest and freest choice in selecting partners. Some of the *datus* (male tribal chieftains) have multiple—2–3 wives at the same time with children of up to 15 | | • Are active and able to move to and fro rural and urban centres but on limited instances only as their main focus is working in their own farm or working for the farms of the better-off<br>• Active men in this typology, unlike the *datu*, preferred to practice monogamy. In the tribal communities under study, only the *datu* is allowed to be polygamous | | • Are isolated, remote and almost obscure even in the small rural communities. They prefer to stay most of the time within the limits of their house, their small farm and in the farms of better-off working for wage or kind goods<br>• This group, mostly women, do not have much choice to roam around and socialise with others. In terms of selecting life partners, their tendency is to pair with their kind—poor and remote | |
| (4) Senses, imagination and thought | • People in this group are able to access free primary and secondary education offered in schools located within their easy reach. Some of their youth are given the privilege access to scholarships in the state university<br>• 32% of the people in this group are literate and numerate<br>• In terms of freedom of expression, the better-off have the capability to voice sentiments, interests and motives for personal and community matters. Their eloquence reflects their confidence and power to influence the decisions of other members in the community | | • People in this group have limited access to free primary and secondary education due to their distance from schools<br>• only 9% of the participants in this typology are literate and numerate<br>• In terms of freedom of expression, this group know that such freedom exists but opted not to exercise or harness such freedom to improve and protect their social and economic status as they see less meaning in it in relation to the amount of power and influence the better-off | | • These people have never been to any formal schools for education. They refuse to go to school due to distance (again, more than 3 kilometres or a total of 6 kilometres to and fro the town centre<br>• only 2% are literate and numerate<br>• In terms of capability to express one's idea and exercise one's freedom of expression, these group barely even know that such freedom or entitlement exists. They decide based on the whim and interest of the male household heads and of the better-off leaders | |

(continued)

**Table 17.3** (continued)

| Capabilities | Typology of participants | | | | | |
|---|---|---|---|---|---|---|
| | Better-off | | Coping | | Poorest and most marginalised | |
| | 15 (14%) | | 20 (19%) | | 70 (67%) | |
| | Male | Female | Male | Female | Male | Female |
| | 14 (93%) | 1 (7%) | 18 (90%) | 2 (10%) | 20 (29%) | 50 (71%) |
| | ***Who***: comprised of individuals, mostly male tribal chieftains, elected local government leaders, landed farmers, and small store owners<br>***Where***: These people live along the main roads and/or town centres<br>***Land ownership:*** Medium to Landed (14 or 13%)<br>***Household income (in Php per month):*** PhP2001 and above (16 or 14%)<br>***Unpaid loan balance (aggregated in Php):*** ≤ 500 (2 or 2%)<br>***Average level of education:*** Secondary | | ***Who***: comprised of active, healthy male household heads who have limited access to resources such as land and with sparse livelihood opportunities<br>***Where***: They live in outer communities (1–2 km away from the town centre)<br>***Land ownership:*** Medium to Marginal (58 or 55%)<br>***Household income (in Php per month):*** PhP501–2,000 (20 or 19%)<br>***Unpaid loan balance (aggregated in Php):*** 501–10,000 (30 or 29%)<br>***Average level of education:*** Primary | | ***Who***: comprised of mostly women, elderly, sick and differently- abled<br>***Where***: They live in the remotest part of the rural communities (more than 3 km away from the town centre)<br>***Land ownership:*** Marginal to Landless (33 or 31%)<br>***Household income (in Php per month):*** ≤ PhP 500 (70 or 67%)<br>***Unpaid loan balance (aggregated in Php):*** 10,001 and above (73 or 69%)<br>***Average level of education:*** Nil | |
| (5) Emotions | • This group can have the better chance to associate by forming or joining in clubs and organisations that help protect their interests, advocacies, and passions in life. Human organisations are usually active and are attracting members within the rural centre only | | • On some occasions, this group of people joins in organisations upon strong influence and/or endorsement of the better-off. This is mostly happening to beef up attendance sheets and to produce attractive documentation for the community development workers and officials representing the government and NGOs | | • This isolated group ceased to associate themselves with other members in their communities for reasons of distance and absence of leverage such as power and influence over one's interests, advocacies, and passions in life. Fatalism and isolation have brought them to accept the way of life in the remotest rural areas | |
| (6) Practical reason | • People in this group use their social and political leverages to shape the local policies, practices, and traditions | | • People under this typology depend on the institutionalised and dominant laws, practices, and traditions controlled and exercised by the better-off | | • People under this typology depend on the institutionalised and dominant laws, practices, and traditions controlled and exercised by the better-off | |
| (7) Affiliation | • Better-off participants enjoy the privilege of joining in political organisations to express their ideas and interest at the community and state level without fear of humiliation and discrimination<br>• Active first person "I" in political and development discussions | | • People in this group have delegated their entitlement for free political expression or by joining in political organisation to the better-off. If the need arises, coping participants are the ones called upon by the better-off to rally behind or show support, again, by beefing up human presence or signatures in attendance sheets to make political gatherings and agenda look official and attractive. Signature campaigns needed to back up rural development project petition permeate from the better-off to the coping group levels<br>• Dependent second person "YOU" in political and development discussions | | • People in this typology are usually invisible in the community's political arena. They choose or are prevented to join in political activities in the community to perform such menial roles confined in the household and farm. Due to the spatial bias of the outsider rural development workers, they are not being talked to and listened of their political interests and views critical to their wellbeing. The dominant discourse treats them as part of collateral damage and sacrificial lambs of development issues confronting the whole community. People in this typology find political affiliation humiliating and discriminatory. The prevailing system remains blind and mute to advance their interests as persons<br>• Passive third person "THEY" in political and development discussions | |

(continued)

**Table 17.3** (continued)

| Capabilities | Typology of participants | | | | | |
|---|---|---|---|---|---|---|
| | Better-off | | Coping | | Poorest and most marginalised | |
| | 15 (14%) | | 20 (19%) | | 70 (67%) | |
| | Male | Female | Male | Female | Male | Female |
| | 14 (93%) | 1 (7%) | 18 (90%) | 2 (10%) | 20 (29%) | 50 (71%) |
| | ***Who***: comprised of individuals, mostly male tribal chieftains, elected local government leaders, landed farmers, and small store owners<br>***Where***: These people live along the main roads and/or town centres<br>***Land ownership:*** Medium to Landed (14 or 13%)<br>***Household income (in Php per month):*** PhP2001 and above (16 or 14%)<br>***Unpaid loan balance (aggregated in Php):*** ≤ 500 (2 or 2%)<br>***Average level of education:*** Secondary | | ***Who***: comprised of active, healthy male household heads who have limited access to resources such as land and with sparse livelihood opportunities<br>***Where***: They live in outer communities (1–2 km away from the town centre)<br>***Land ownership:*** Medium to Marginal (58 or 55%)<br>***Household income (in Php per month):*** PhP501–2,000 (20 or 19%)<br>***Unpaid loan balance (aggregated in Php):*** 501–10,000 (30 or 29%)<br>***Average level of education:*** Primary | | ***Who***: comprised of mostly women, elderly, sick and differently- abled<br>***Where***: They live in the remotest part of the rural communities (more than 3 km away from the town centre)<br>***Land ownership:*** Marginal to Landless (33 or 31%)<br>***Household income (in Php per month):*** < PhP 500 (70 or 67%)<br>***Unpaid loan balance (aggregated in Php):*** 10,001 and above (73 or 69%)<br>***Average level of education:*** Nil | |
| (8) Other Species | • Low involvement and concern for nonhuman animals, plants and the world of nature<br>• Reason: high preoccupation doing productive and community roles including but not limited to 'market pricing' (Fiske 1992) | | • Medium<br>• Reason: medium preoccupation doing reproductive, productive and community roles; depend on 'communal sharing' and 'authority ranking' to survive (Fiske 1992) | | • High<br>• Reason: high preoccupation doing primarily, reproductive role; depend on 'communal sharing' to survive (Fiske 1992) | |
| (9) Play | • People in this typology have time to play and enjoy using the basic sports and recreation infrastructures built by the local governments. They have access to electricity, mobile phones and internet. They can watch movies, connect with loved ones through email, Facebook and Skype | | • Coping participants struggle in accessing the basic sports facilities located at the town centre. The common sport that people in this group play in their outer communities is basketball. Their makeshift basketball court is unpaved ground with the metal ring attached to the coconut tree. People in this typology also struggle to possess mobile phones and other communication and entertainment facilities. Some of them use generator sets for 2–3 h in the evening | | • The poorest and most marginalised people have practically no modern communication and entertainment implements. Common forms of sports and recreation enjoyed by this group are the traditional games both young and old people play such as *tagu-anay* (hide-and-seek), *biros* (a group game played with two teams standing opposite each other, approximately 10 feet away. The rule is to catch each member in the team in order to win)<br>• As an outsider, I enjoyed the most the forms of play and recreation I have participated in these communities | |
| (10) Control over one's environment | • People in this typology, mostly men, have the privilege access and control over property such as land, house, livestock and all other farm goods. They are the royal *datu*, and some are elected local government leaders in their community. They can shape or can help directly in shaping policies for the entire community as influential and powerful leaders in the tribe | | • Coping participants depend in large part on the wealth and power of their leaders. Their control of land is subsumed under the direct management of the tribal *datu*. In short, they follow the communal decision bestowed by the *datu* regarding the use of land for farming, selling, and leasing. People in this typology have the slim chance to reach positive social mobility, they have more tendency to slide down the poorest and most marginalised group | | • People in this typology are prevented by tribal customs and traditions to control, manage, and own property such as land, house, livestock and all other farm goods. These are comprised of women who are subordinated by institutions—family, community, market, and state. This group of people is the most vulnerable to natural and manmade disasters | |

*Source* Face-to-face interview with the Indigenous farmers in Mindanao and validated during FGD conducted from 28 September 2013 to 10 May 2014 dimensions of health, life and bodily integrity that altogether share the common idea or theme which is life, summarised as being able to live a healthy and generative life.

## Maregyew Ne Peg Egpe[1]: *Exploring the Capabilities of the 'Better-Off'*

The following case studies are derived from selected participants who belong to the 'better-off' group. Participants in this group comprised of tribal council and local government officials and their families in the Indigenous and rural communities of Mindanao. At least two sets of typical narratives are presented each to represent men and women.

Case 1 is about *Datu* Umpay. *Datu* Umpay represents the 'better-off' group; he is the richest and the most powerful man in the tribe and he enjoys such privileges afforded to him by the local government and his tribesmen. His decision-making power is considered to be the strongest and most influential amongst all tribal elders/leaders. Being male, powerful and influential, he is the gatekeeper—the main contact point for any development projects 'planned for' (VeneKlasen and Miller 2002) them by the local government leaders and experts in the government, NGO and business organisations (Chambers 1997). The existing governance and development paradigms that require 'participation for all' and stakeholders participation' (Agarwal 2001) largely depends on him. He has the direct access and control of the basic institutions—family, clan, and community as well as other small peoples' organisations initiated by some NGOs operating in the area. He can call upon his members in the tribe, mostly those who belong to the 'coping group' of people, those whose livelihood and survival depends on his communal leadership and resources, to gather in the community centre whenever 'outsiders' or visitors from the government, NGOs and other groups require their consent, signature and picture documentation. Chambers (1983, 1997) argued that 'rural development tourists'—the experts and leaders who are fixated in their urban biases are 'pervasively ignorant, out-of-touch and out-of-date' of the local, complex, diverse, dynamic and unpredictable realities of the rural people especially those whose voices and choices are not being listened to. *Datu* Umpay is the direct representative of his tribe, he voiced out his choices for his people. He decides for them in a wide range of activities including land use and livelihood.

Case 2 is about the life and capabilities of *Kapitan* Tinong and his wife Mitring. The couple owns a medium-size grocery store in the community centre. *Kapitan* Tinong is highly respected in the community being the barangay captain (community chieftain). The couple also operates a sizable land banana plantation. The lands they

[1]Matigsalug term for the better-off, living a comfortable and convenient life even if materially poor.

use are leased to them by their poor neighbours, those who are 'coping' and 'poorest and most marginalised'. For 20 years now, the couple depends on cheap manual labours of the poor rural Indigenous people to operate their farm. In an interview, being a small-scale banana operator in the area, the couple pays PhP150 (USD3.50) per day. They employ women, men and young people below 18 years old, especially those who are out-of-school. Mitring, being a storeowner and wife of the political leader, she enjoys such privileges that have been denied to other Indigenous women in her tribe. She is able to socialise and join in women's group. She is able to freely go to the city alone or accompanied unlike other women in her neighbourhood. However, Mitring depends on her husband for almost all decisions especially pertaining to finance and land use. Mitring does not own any land. She claims to co-own the store but not the building and the land where it is established. Kiriti and Tisdell (2002) reported that rural women struggle to claim their rights over landownership and access thereby compromising their wellbeing and life chances.

Case 3 is about the life of *Bai* Nelia, *Bai* Nelia is a wife of a *datu* (male tribal chieftain). She comes from a non-Indigenous family living in the nearby town. Cram et al. (2013) confirmed that Indigenous status can also be acquired through marriage to an Indigenous person. *Bai* Nelia enjoys such privileges as living in the biggest house in the tribe and being able to lead and gain the respect of other women in the community. *Bai* Nelia advocates for her tribe's reliance of their indigenous knowledge systems and practices to support their livelihood and identity as people. However, just like Mitring, *Bai* Nelia has a limited leverage over decisions pertaining to finance and land use. In her story, *Bai* Nelia describes her leadership as instrumental and attached to the power and influence of her husband who is the most powerful man in the community. Cornwall (2003) argued that voice and choice of women become instrumental when their presence and not their decisions are being counted. *Bai* Nelia is required by her husband *datu* to accompany him in social gatherings and meetings.

Case 4 is about *Bai* Petra, a *babaylan* (medicine woman), is a close friend of *Bai* Nelia. *Bai* Petra is the health and wellness advocate in her tribe. She depends on her traditional and spiritual healing skills and ethnobotanical resources available in her garden and the forest. Her idea of wellbeing is attached to her capability to maintain a good relationship with other people and the environment. She cares for the medicinal plants that she, and the rest of her tribe, believes can cure any form of illness. She has a spiritual relationship with the forest or the environment. Walker (2013) argued that Indigenous people live in dialogue and relationship with the place. Place represents 'country', a 'nourishing terrain' for Indigenous people to openly communicate with their land and all its natural components (Bird Rose and Australian Heritage Commission 1996). Walker (2013) argued that existing researches that failed to capture and balance the interdependent relationship of mind, body, spirit, and the natural world suffer from epistemic violence that treats Indigenous knowledge systems and practices as traditional, backward and unscientific (Shiva 1988, 1993). *Bai* Petra plays a very important role in keeping her family and neighbours safe from any form 'structural violence' (Galtung 1969 cited in Shepherd 2011) brought by 'state simplification' (Scott 1998) and the establishment of monocultural commercial farms that alter the agroecological system of the poorest and most vulnerable Indigenous people in Mindanao.

**Case 1: *Datu* Umpay, the rich and the most powerful man in the tribe**

*Datu* Umpay is the head of the Matigsalug tribe in Marilog District bordering Davao and Bukidnon regions in the Northern part of Mindanao. He is 72 years old and has been the head of his tribe for 30 years now. He has a wife and six children who are now married and have their own families. Two of his married sons and their families live with him in his house thereby making his family size and house the biggest in his community. His house is made of wood with galvanised iron roofing. It has five bedrooms, two living rooms and three toilets and baths. *Datu* Umpay's residence is called the 'grand house' in his tribal community. It does not only house the royal family, it is also serves as a place of worship of a Christian group where *Datu* Umpay is also serving as the pastor.

Being the **head of his tribe for political, economic, environmental, and religious affairs,** *Datu* Umpay is considered as the **most powerful** person in his immediate tribal community. His people accord him high regard and respect for his leadership. All his family members are also proud of being part of the tribal hierarchical structure. People in the tribe extend the *datu's* family with the same respect and honour they give him. This high respect and trust to the leadership of the *datu* becomes more evident during decision-making activities in the tribe. Decisions on land and agriculture development in the tribe rest first of all on the decision of *Datu* Umpay, in close coordination with the advisory group, the tribal council of elders. The tribal council of elders is comprised of male household heads who are themselves *datus* in their small communities under the headship of the supreme *datu*. They are not necessarily elders; some of them are in fact, within the age range of 30–40 years old. The younger members of the tribal council of elders have inherited their positions upon the death and/or physical incapacities of the elder *datu* in the family.

*Datu* Umpay, being the supreme *datu* of his tribe, enjoys the privilege of **leading his people in the local negotiations pertaining to land** and development. All rural development projects earmarked for his community **comes through him. *Datu* Umpay and the rest of the members of the tribal** council of elders enter into contract of agreement before any development project can start to operate in the area. *Datu* Umpay and his tribal council are the guardians of the vast tract of ancestral lands measuring 102,324 hectares. The land is under a lumped Certificate of Ancestral Domain Title (CADT) and is being subdivided to the members of the Matigsalug tribe. The tribal household **heads, mostly men, hold the individual titles attached to the lumped CADT.**

Recently, *Datu* Umpay and his comrades in the tribal council of elders entered into an agreement for the **operation of the "agro-forestry plantation"**, which in fact is a form of monoculture **planting of cacao**, a raw ingredient for making chocolate. The current Memorandum of Agreement (MOA) covers at least 200 hectares of land for its initial operation and it is expected to expand even more in the coming years. *Datu* Umpay is tasked by the tribal council to submit, transact, negotiate, follow-up and sign the MOA that is entered by and between parties involved, namely the Kennemer Foods Corporation (KFC), a multinational company engaged in contract-farming of various high-end agricultural crops such as cacao. In the MOA, KFC is described as a company that has the "technology, management, and marketing capability required to plant, cultivate, harvest, market and export agricultural crops".

***Life and health capabilities***:

*Datu* **Umpay is able to balance work and life** being surrounded by devoted supporters both at the household and the wider community. His vegetable **farm is known as the biggest in the community**. His sons and other close family relatives are tending the 6-hectare farm that produces mainly cabbage and tomatoes for the Bankerohan Public Market, the largest public market in Davao City. *Datu* Umpay and his family rely on the proceeds of their farm for food and other needs. *Datu* Umpay describes his life and health as generally fair. He is proud that his family **never experienced involuntary hunger** due to absence or lack of food. He said that food for his family could easily be accessed from the neighbourhood. *Datu* Umpay rec**eives gifts from his supporters in the form of rice, corn, vegetables, chicken, goat and even cow especially during the town fiesta.**

> When someone in my family is sick and needs medicine and health checkup, I can send them to the nearest health centre or hospital. I have good friends in these hospitals and some of them are not charging me for the consultation. These doctors who know me even give free medicines and vitamins for me and my grandchildren.

***Affiliation capabilities***:

Being the supreme *datu*, *Datu* Umpay is **able to join all the organisations** and clubs he wishes to be part of. He has travelled around the country to represent his tribe in various meetings and conferences. He is always present in decision-making meetings in his immediate and outer communities. He used to be one of the **consultants of the city mayor of Davao for cultural affairs**. Until now, he is still **invited in major conferences and gatherings to represent his tribe.**

***Concern for nonhuman and recreational capabilities***:

At 72, *Datu* Umpay is still healthy and active. His secret is his love for horses and basketball. He has five horses that he uses to take him to remote places in his community to visit his tribe members and family. During the interview, *Datu* Umpay was asked the question: What role do you play in sealing the MOA for the cacao plantation in your community? What do you see are its benefits and risks?

*Datu* Umpay in reply, says:

> I head the entire tribe in finalising the deal or contract between parties involved being the head tribal chieftain. Being the head, I am being given the power to decide for my people who are just like me, poorly educated. Most of us do not know how to read and write. We only communicate orally using either Visayan dialect or our tribal language. I sign for and in behalf of all members of the tribal council elders as you can see on the final MOA.
>
> I believe this project will benefit the people. We will be able to get revenue share for allowing them to use our land. The project will initially occupy 200 hectares for 25 years renewable for another term. I think the revenue sharing scheme is nice. Our tribe gets 4% of the gross revenue of cacao beans. Ninety percent of this share goes to tenurial holders while 10% will be allocated for small community projects. The contract provides that revenue

sharing is made semi-annually. It will start beginning of the third year after the signing of MOA. For the initial years (at least 3–5 years), we are given the projected revenue of PhP5,000 per producing hectare. Another thing that attracts us to enter into MOA is the signing bonus of PhP2,000 per hectare or a total of PhP400,000 to be divided according to land allocated by tenurial holders.

I believe this project is helping us to alleviate our state of poverty. Most of us have given up to our fight against poor education, poor harvest, hunger, and poor health. My main concern about this project is that we have to demand our people to relocate their farms and other forms of livelihoods to other places. Some even have to move their houses to give way to the project area. I also fear that our rivers, forest and spring water will be adversely affected by the project. I also have heard complains from my people regarding their possible problems with herding their cows, carabaos and goats. They are in fact prohibited to enter the enclosure with or without their animals.

**Case 2: *Kapitan* Tinong and his wife Mitring, the entrepreneurial duo**

*Kapitan* Tinong, as his constituents in the community fondly call him, is the **barangay captain** in one of the remote communities in Davao del Norte. He is of Christian descent and is married to Mitring, an Indigenous woman. *Kapitan* Tinong's family owns the largest *sari-sari* (variety) store that sells all the basic home supplies—foods, soft drinks, toiletries, animal feeds and a lot more. Mitring manages the family's store operation while *Kapitan* Tinong is focusing mostly on his duties as head of his community.

The family's business started small in the 1990s. All the five children of *Kapitan* Tinong and Mitring are able to graduate from college using the income derived by the couple from their store and other means. *Kapitan* Tinong also **operates a 21-hectare banana farm**. **Ten hectares are titled under his name while the rest are currently under lease agreement with smaller land tenurial holders who are members of the Indigenous tribe**. *Kapitan* Tinong **hires, as part-time contractual employees**, 11 men and 3 women from among those whose land are being leased to him.

***Life and health capabilities***:

*Kapitan* Tinong and Mitring **looks healthy**. Both 60 years old, the couple feels fortunate to **afford annual medical and dental services at the private hospital** in the nearest city. All the **children have grown healthy being provided with good food and nutrition since childhood**.

In the community, the family's house is known to be the **biggest and most beautiful being made of concrete**. The house is fully painted, well designed and furnished with good quality of furniture and fixture.

***Affiliation capabilities***:

As the barangay captain, Tinong is able to **join as many organisations as he like. Mitring** is also being given the **chance to go out and participate in any social and political activities especially the ones for women**. Mitring is now a grandmother. She is proud of what her family has achieved. And she gives full support to the political career of her husband. Mitring is able to spend most of her spare time outside the store management doing community projects for women. She is the elected p**resident of the Mother's Club** in her community. Mitring explains,

I am now able to do whatever I want. I have free time being a grandmother and now that my children have their own families. Before, it was difficult for me to go out and meet other people outside our home and store premise. Raising kids and maintaining store before kept me away from joining groups that I like.

*Kapitan* Tinong has been in the office for 6 years now. He believes that he has the mandate of his people to lead his community and he sees himself to be reelected for the last term during the election in 2016. When asked what is his next step when his term of office ends, *Kapitan* Tinong proudly says,

I would like to try higher office. My comrades, and the Municipal Mayor himself, encourage me to seek higher position. Maybe I would run for municipal councilor. I think I will win because of my good influence and relationship with people I meet and work with in the banana industry. As you can see, the mayor needs me to support the banana industry where he and other family members and relatives are currently the bigwigs.

***Concern for nonhuman and recreational capabilities***:

*Kapitan* Tinong is a **proud medium-scale banana plantation operator**. He believes that the banana industry is able to deliver people out from poverty by giving them the chance to earn money from operating, leasing and selling of lands. Indigenous members in my community hold tenurial rights over their lands for as long as they are not leasing and selling it. The main reason why they lease or sell their lands is that they lack the capital and the expertise to operate the farm. They seek the help of those who have the money capital. Most of them enter into lease agreement for the period of 20–25 years renewable for another term depending on the outcome of the operation and if both parties involved agreed.

When asked to describe how the banana plantation has altered the natural landscape in his community, he replied:

Yes, there is a huge difference between before and now as far as the environment is concerned. **We have converted our mountainside into banana farms only.** In the 1990s, there were only few rich families who have operated the business. They use their families' acquired land assets for the operation. As each year passes, many were attracted to join the bandwagon and that is why we are expanding. Local businessmen engage with leasing agreements with small Indigenous and rural farmers. And for this reason, many of the Indigenous farmers have become part-time contractual employees of these banana farms.

When *Kapitan* Tinong was asked whom he thinks loses and wins in the banana industry, he says,

The Indigenous tenurial land holders, especially those who practically do not have any sizeable land to farm and produce basic foods are the losers in this game. They lack social support after losing control and access to their lands for farming and grazing. I pity them for being so poor and dependent on the minimal support derived from the local governments and NGOs. I know, they have become hungry and many of them as a matter of fact have left their homelands and relocate in the city slums relying on the slim chance of surviving city life.

**Case 3: *Bai* Nelia, the 'controlled' leader**

Nelia is a wife of *datu* (tribal chieftain). She comes from non-indigenous family in Davao City and moved into the Indigenous community immediately after her marriage with the *datu* in 1971. Her Christian family lives in the suburban area.

Her father was a fishmonger while her mother is a laundry woman. She said that life before her marriage to the *datu* was worse. At present, her Indigenous community calls her *bai* (wife of *datu*). Being a *bai,* she is **respected and highly regarded by her community**. She is expected to perform community leadership and social roles, apart from her domestic responsibilities being the mother to her seven children and a wife.

> I am **able to help others** in the community being their *bai.* I am keen of helping other women learn our traditional skills and practices like planting or gardening, cooking, crafts making and many others. I am doing communal activities during my spare time. I am capable of spending more hours for community duties because my children are all grown up now and we have my *datu's* nephew and his family of 4 living with us in the house. Our nephew and his wife take charge of most of the household chores in exchange of house to live in, food and other basic needs.

***Life and health capabilities***:

In terms of life and health capabilities, Nelia is **able to take advantage of the resources poured in directly and indirectly to her family by the government and non-government organisations**. These resources include free seedlings, fertilisers and pesticides of the Department of Agriculture and other NGOs. Other forms of goods being channelled to her family are food hampers being distributed by the city government to indigent families. Social services such as free health clinics are also usually conducted in the community centre located next to her house. Even the cemented basketball court with standard provision of bleachers is located just few steps away from her kitchen.

> My boys love to play basketball". The basketball games every weekend makes me happy seeing my family and other members in the tribe gather and cheer around for their respective teams.

> Being a *bai* comes with heavy responsibilities to my *datu*, family, clan, and the whole community. Everyone expects me to help the *datu* in his official and tribal duties. I am more like a personal secretary for the *datu.* I take that credit of being the right hand. Sad to say, I am not independent. I act only based on the decision of my *datu*; I mean, in everything—personal to communal matters I refer to him for his decision. Decisions such as providing weekly budget for our food and other needs depend much to our *datu.* I can't decide on what to buy and how much should I spend for food and non-food items.

***Affiliation capabilities***:

Nelia is **limited in her choice on the type of organisations** she can join into help her express her ideas, creativity and intellect. The types of organisations her *datu* and the community expect her to be around are limited to those that have already existed in her community. She is not allowed to join conferences or meetings of women leaders in the city area without the *datu.*

> Being a woman is considered a weakness even in my tribe. I hate this feeling of being unable to move around and join in clubs and organisations that I think could help me expand my horizon. This issue, I usually keep it to myself. I don't want to appear bold enough to change the customs and traditions of my community. I still feel fortunate however being in this stature now even if I have limited rights to affiliate myself into other

> bigger organisations. I feel sad for most of the women of my tribe who are poor and are locked in their household responsibilities in their entire life.

***Concern for nonhuman and recreational capabilities***:

Being the *bai*, Nelia enjoys the privilege of leading and advocating for her tribe's adherence to their Indigenous knowledge systems and practices (IKSP). She heads other members of the tribe especially women in learning and rediscovering the bountiful floras and faunas left under their care in the forest. They face existential risks and shocks brought about by modern agriculture that advocated monoculture planting of bananas and pineapples.

> We are afraid our ancestral land will be under the concession of these private plantation companies like Stanfilco and Dole Philippines. Our way of staging protest against the further proliferation of these plantations to our communities is by showing them we are truly passionate about protecting our land and all its inhabitants including plants and animals.

Nelia is able to show her aversion to the ongoing massive land conversion for commercial agriculture in her area. With the help of some NGO workers whose advocacy is focused on sustainable rural agriculture, Nelia and other women in her tribe are conducting informal conversations to discuss their role in protecting their lands and environment as women. The NGO workers and this research have given Nelia and her group another chance to sit together and narrate their stories mostly reeling around their limited roles in entering into the discussion forums and participating in the decision-making for their community's common welfare. Nelia gives her group the assurance that they will continue their efforts to assert their rights as women to discuss any development issues that pertain to their wellbeing as Indigenous people. She said:

> Indigenous women must be given the rights to enter into decision-making platforms in our tribe. We should be allowed to express critical ideas for our welfare as women. We should be part of the actual and formal decision-makers for any rural land development project. We care for our future, they (referring to government and business capitalist) care for their profit at the expense of our environment, food and water system, livelihood and freedom to plan and direct our lives as Indigenous people.

***Political and material control***:

> Being a woman, I technically and practically don't own any piece of land. My *datu* owns it being the head of the family and of our tribe. He is going to transfer his power and property to his sons. Our sons will soon inherent the land and I am hoping that my two girls will have their fair share too.

Nelia shared her experience being *bai* who belong to the landed family of the *datu*.

> I still feel fortunate being part of this royal family in the entire community. Even if I don't have a say on anything pertaining to decision on the use and disposal of our lands, I am still able to take advantage of other benefits such as being able to buy new clothes and mobile phones for my own personal use from the money the *datu* has given me—usually in exchange of a favour or a reward of a good deed. He keeps all our money. That's the way it

> is since he owns the property—the land, the livestock, the farm, and the two houses we built.

**Case 4: Petra, the caring and nourishing *babaylan* (medicine woman)**

Petra is the Matigsalug tribe's *babaylan* (traditional medicine woman). Like Nelia, she is also a *bai* (tribal chieftain's wife). Petra and Nelia are close friends being part of the most powerful women in their Indigenous community. They meet whenever their *datus* require them to be around during official and cultural gatherings in the other tribal communities and in city meetings and conferences where they are invited as guests or participants. Petra hails from another royal family of the neighbouring and close ally Bagobo tribe. She has 4 sons and 3 daughters. She takes care of the *datu's* bedridden mother for almost 10 years now. Petra inherited her skills in traditional medicine from the *datu's* mother and she believes her devotion to the old *babaylan* continues as long as the mother is alive. Until now, she still gets a lot of insights from the old woman. She has been taught and directed what, where, when and how medicinal plants can be derived and used. She also learns the traditional crafts making particularly weaving rattan baskets and tikug bracelets. She teaches how to make these handicrafts to her own children and others in the community so that they too will learn and make money out of it.

> I can buy rice out from the proceeds after selling my crafts". Petra is also teaching younger generations how to find, prepare and use safely the ethnobotanicals she said her community is very proud of using since time immemorial. When asked about the efficacy and safety of using these traditional medicines, confidently she replied, "We have learned about the power of these herbal and plant medicines from our ancestors. They must have proven these safe and effective after generations of use. We still find our traditional cure system effective and spiritual. It connects us to our ancestors and bridges us to the future generations.

***Life and health capabilities***

Petra believes in the strong connection between her faith in God and the healing wonders of her medicinal plants. She is in fact happy that the Department of Health (DOH) studies have confirmed the efficacy of the herbal plants her community has been relying on. The DOH has in fact endorsed the use of some traditional and herbal plants such as mayana, cogon, hilbas and lagundi for cure of common illnesses. Being a *bai* and at the same time *babaylan*, she is able to use her time freely to practice indigenous knowledge systems and practices (IKSP) to promote better health in her neighbourhood. She said she has enough time to rest and take care of herself. She is able to watch television using their family's generator set and is able to communicate with her relatives abroad using her Facebook account. Petra owns a Samsung tablet and a mobile phone. These gadgets are just some of the products of her hard work, weaving baskets and bracelets for selling at the town centre and in the city. When asked if she is happy with her life in general, she replied:

> Yes I am. I find happiness in my limited power as a woman for others. I find satisfaction in what I do as a *babaylan*, being an instrument of our tribe to enrich our cultural and spiritual heritage. I ask Manama, our God to help me in my goal to keep our traditions alive for the

> next generations. What will happen to them if all of our lands are converted to modern farms? How will they live without our traditions, our identity as Indigenous people?

***Affiliation capabilities***:

> Because I have free time for myself and to do things for other people, I am able to gain lots of friends and supporters in my community. I am active in most organisations such as Mother's club where I am elected as president in the whole barangay. I am also a barangay health worker. Our neighbourhood gathers around when I call them for traditional skills training. I do this under the National Commission for Culture and the Arts (NCCA). NCCA allocates some seed money three years ago to start our weaving project to help develop our traditional skills and also to augment our income.

When asked if she thinks supply of raw and organic materials will dwindle eventually in the future because of their local crafts making, she said:

> Yes, it will come if we are the ones controlling these resources. We need to adapt certain measures to ensure that harvesting of rattan and other plant materials from the forest will not impact negatively on other species relying on them on the food web. We have a team, mostly of men who are skilled and trained in gathering these materials to make sure we don't disturb the balance. We are willing to stop our handicrafts making if we face depletion issues in the future.

Establishing these affiliations in her community with other Indigenous peoples, Petra was awarded as the outstanding farmer in the province in 2011. Petra promised to dedicate her life for the preservation of her rich culture and the promotion of health and wellness in her tribe.

***Concern for nonhuman and recreational capabilities***

> Being a *bai* means being responsible for the environment. I love plants and animals. I love nature—forest, mountains, rivers and spring waters. We do our best to protect these natural resources.

When asked if she has a voice in decision-making pertaining to the use of land and its resources, she replied: I can only advice the *datu*. I can't impose upon him what I truly want because that is not what a woman is expected to do to her *datu*. She only supports him in his decisions. Sometimes my suggestions are heard but oftentimes when they are out there, all of them *datus*, on a meeting they decide based on their own interests not wive's or women's.

Petra says that she is happy to take care of her two dogs and a cat. She is able to feed them sardines and rice. She loves her animals because they entertain her and they relieve her stress from daily activities.

***Political and material control***

Important decision on selling or leasing of our lands is not part of being an Indigenous woman. Petra says she can only suggest but not impose upon her *datu* her personal decision. The main reason is culture and tradition. Indigenous women are inhibited to participate in the decision-making platforms. Decision pertaining to disposal and use of land is left to the full power and discretion of men or *datus* in the tribe.

> I wish time will come when our decisions as women regarding the use and disposal of our lands will be heard before it is really too late. Men are good decision-makers but I argue that women's input in the whole decision-making process would yield best outcomes.

**Summary of the characteristics of the 'better-off' group**

*Datu* Umpay, the rich and the most powerful man in the tribe; *Kapitan* Tinong and his wife Mitring, the entrepreneurial duo; and *Bai* Nelia, the 'controlled' leader described above are typical representations of powerful men and women in the Indigenous tribes I met during my fieldwork in Mindanao. *Datu* Umpay is the supreme tribal chieftain of his tribe. All the other *datus* (male tribal chieftains) are under his control and power. *Kapitan* Tinong is the elective local political leader in his barangay (community). He is rich, as he possesses political power as well as wealth being a medium-scale banana plantation operator. He accumulates cash to acquire lease of sizable Indigenous lands to plant with bananas mainly from their income in the store he co-own with his wife Mitring. The couple owns the biggest retail store in the Indigenous community. *Bai* Nelia, the wife of a *datu* is relatively powerful and is able to socialise but only in proximity to her husband. Other women in her tribe are looking up to *Bai* Nelia but she is not allowed, just like any other women in the tribe, to decide and participate in any tribal decision-making process. *Bai* Nelia only performs such roles that may be assigned to her by her husband like meeting the wives of other *datus* and visitors from the local government and other organisations.

Male tribal leaders constitute the better-off group. They are able to control and lead their lives by taking advantage of the 'rules, resources, people, activities and power' (Kabeer 2003 cited in March et al. 2005, p. 104) which they have a privileged access to being leaders. They partner with the 'outsiders' (Chambers 1983) who are expert planners, engineers, and agriculturists of the government and non-government agencies to 'plan for' (VeneKlasen and Miller 2002) for the 'passive and instrumental' (Cornwall 2003; Gaventa and Cornwall 2001) participation of the poorest and most vulnerable women, children, elderly and differently abled. Women and their dependents being the poorest and most vulnerable even in the 'better-off' group are not able to lead their lives socially, economically, and politically as the stories above show. *Bai* Nelia, even if she is considered to be the most powerful woman in the tribe, being a *bai* or wife of as *datu*, she is struggling to make independent decision for her own wellbeing. She is not allowed to socialise and participate in the tribe's decision-making meetings or gatherings. Her husband mostly needs her presence when visitors arrive. *Bai* Nelia, even if she enjoys the good house, good food and good name being provided by the *datu*, she still feels empty, as she is unable to own land and other movable property and unable to participate socio-politically to enter into 'open dialogue' (Christakis and Bausch 2006), to listen and be listened to (Dobson 2014) in the rural development planning. Her strategic gender needs (SGN) to actualize her voice, choice and agency and emancipate herself, and the other persons closely dependent on her from their disadvantage status, are not being addressed under the current 'participation for all' (Agarwal 2001) framework. Hence, in this particular typology comprised of the 'better-off' group, women and their disadvantage status have high tendency to become 'coping' or to become one of the 'poorest and most vulnerable' amongst the 'better-off'.

**Eleg eleg de ne peg egpe[2]: In constant danger of sliding down to the bottom (Coping)**

This section presents the two case studies about two women whose lives are typical representations of people of their kind who are 'coping' or those whose lives are continuously being threatened by sudden risks and shocks such as ill health and death of a member in the family, dispossession of land, poor harvest, indebtedness, and natural disasters. The coping group comprised of Indigenous people living along outer area, away from the town centre (some 1–2 kilometres away). The 'coping group' is the close ally of the 'better-off', they live in close proximity to the latter. The 'coping' group is composed of poor Indigenous people who have medium to marginal land-holding. In this study, they make up the majority, 55 out of 105 participants or 55% of the total. The 'coping' group is in constant danger of being dragged back to extreme poverty once they lose their land and livelihood. They constantly depend on or claim the limited chances or opportunities held and controlled by the 'outsiders' (Chambers 1997) and experts/leaders who dominate the discourse (Bacchi 2010) of rural development planning, those who 'plan for' them (VeneKlasen and Miller 2002). Eveline and Bacchi (2005) argued that the poor and marginalised people in the society have become victims of development by being excluded in the decision-making arenas tackling social and political issues. Ulrich (1994) has the similar view and argued that the existing social planning frameworks fail to engage the 'involved' and the 'affected' to expand the boundaries of decision-making and include those who are made 'passive and instrumental' participants (Agarwal 2001) paradoxically in the "participatory development" framework.

Presented as Case 5 is the story of the couple, Juan and Nelly. Juan is the political coordinator working locally for the barangay captain but being paid by the city government. During election season, he is the campaign coordinator for the administration or ruling party. Being one in the 'coping' group means that Juan and his family's survival depends largely on the power and influence of his boss, the barangay captain and the higher city administration officials who paid his salary. If by chance the ruling or administration candidates lose in the election, Juan and his family will become poorer. The couple narrated that before, for 6 years, when their mayoralty candidate lost in the election, Juan became jobless and all the family experienced extreme poverty and hunger.

Case 6 is about Bonie. Bonie is uncertain about the latest development project craze, the cacao plantation. He is left with 0.8 hectare of land and is about to be leased for planting cacao under the lease agreement with a multinational company. Bonie has 5 children who are all honour students and ambitious. They would like to finish college degrees. But the main problem is whether the cacao land deal Bonie

[2]Matigsalug term for the coping group, those whose living conditions are easily threatened by sudden risks and shocks such as disease or loss of a family member, poor cropping and indebtedness.

has already signed up to would become successful. In case, the cacao land deal fails and he already gave up his traditional and mixed farming, his family will be at risk of becoming one of the poorest people in the community who suffer more than them from being landless, jobless and voiceless in the local planning.

Case 7 is about the life of Leoning. She is a mother of six and takes care of two elderly parents of her husband. Her husband works in the banana plantation as contractual worker. The family's farmland left under their care is less than 600 square metres that they have planted with vegetables and corn. But their produce is not sufficient for the food requirement of her big family. Leoning's children and parents depend on her for food and other basic needs. At one point, her teenage daughter tried working as a domestic helper in the city, to help the family sustain its basic needs. But after the male house owner sexually molested her daughter, Leoning swore not to allow any of her children to work as domestic helper ever again. Leoning confirmed that it is a lot harder to feed her family this time that she is not able to depend on her daughter and that they almost ran out of land space too to plant their food crops. Leoning's family were slowly dispossessed of their lands through selling their land rights to.

**Case 5: Juan and Nelly, the coordinating couple**

Juan is a father of three kids aged 15, 14 and 11 years old. His wife, Nelly is 3 months pregnant during the interview. All the kids are studying in the public school, which is **5 kilometres away from their house**. Juan **uses a motorcycle lent to him by the barangay council**, as a service vehicle used in patrolling around the community. Juan is appointed as a barangay police because he is a passionate supporter of the incumbent barangay captain. Juan is works as the election **campaign coordinator** for a political party holding currently holding the majority seats in the city government. Juan shares that giving all his time and efforts for the party pays him the privileges of being able to get casual and co-terminus government jobs from time to time.

Juan works for the barangay **captain as a special adviser on security**. Being so, he heads the barangay police task force in the community and receives meagre allowance performing his duty of patrolling the community especially at nighttime. Apart from this, he also receives a salary for being a "ghost" employee of the city. When asked about the reason why he calls himself a "ghost" employee, he explains that he receives PhP5,000 monthly salary from the city government payroll because he is endorsed by his barangay captain as one of the five "quota" personnel that each barangay captain, who is supporting the mayor, can get as a form of reward for the successful election campaigning.

> I am not doing any official duty in the city government offices being appointed as casual employee. I only take errands from the barangay captain. I am not required to report to work every day. Most of the time I am in the barangay council office when the captain is there, usually on Mondays. We would be there for meetings lasting about 3–5 h each time. I love it being there because I feel I am one of the powerful leaders in our community. I get to talk to every barangay official and get to enjoy the comfort of their office amenities and services. I am also served with snacks and lunches whenever I am around with my community leaders.

***Life and health capabilities***:

Juan is proud about his interpersonal skills. He is able to gain good network of friends because of his friendly and supportive attitude. He thinks that what helps him become likeable and popular to peers is his being close to the city mayor and the barangay captain.

> It is easier for me to access free medical goods and services in my barangay. I know everyone in the medical team. They are my friends too. They give me free vitamins and non-prescription medicine whenever I need for my family and myself. When any member in my family is sick, I know where to go for help. I usually use my Philhealth (Philippine Health) card, which gives me the benefit of paying only the gap of about 20–30% of the total hospital bill.

***Affiliation capabilities***:

Juan is an experienced election coordinator of the dominant political party that is also closely affiliated with the national administration party (the political party of the current president, the Liberal Party). Being a trusted coordinator, he is being sought of his service to carry the names of individual party candidates in his house-to-house "talks" in the community. Political party and Individual candidate's campaign are conducted only in the town centre where basic physical infrastructures are present such as the town hall, stage, bleachers/chairs, electricity and sound system. Town centres are the favourite locations of the political wannabes because they are assured that many rural and Indigenous people could gather around during their campaign talk. The political candidates are not reaching people who live in the remotest area, and that is why they rely on the services of people like Juan. Juan brings sample ballots and asks the household heads to vote only the candidates listed as their barangay captain also endorses them. Poor households in the remotest areas in Mindanao rely on their male heads decision who to vote. Usually the decision is based on the endorsement of the incumbent local government officials.

> You know how it operates, right?" Juan laughs shyly. Apparently, he pretends not to care about what he is going to say next. He believes that I am not ignorant of the issue of vote buying. I assured him that I know and have already researched and published articles in my university's journal about the topic. He seems satisfied and goes on to say, "Maybe this time is another case. Vote buying here in the rural and remote areas is different and even worse than your case in the city. Here I am part of the deal of "buying" the whole clan or family. We can even set up "buying" the whole *purok* (a group of clans; the political unit below the barangay level). As a coordinator, I negotiate with the local leaders of the tribal clans and families. It is vote buying really because it involves giving of money in exchange for the "solid" or "block" voting. Solid or block voting means that individuals, families and clans only vote for those on the list. We pay PhP500 per voting individual. And the male household heads are the entry points of these transactions. To simplify the process and to avoid legal and electoral complications, we give the money not to individuals but to the purok leaders who in turn will distribute the payout to the household heads. We can easily monitor whether clans and families complied with solid and block voting. We check on the number of votes per voting precinct (location). Families and clans living together closely in one place constitute voting precinct. See? In the city it is hard to monitor whether paid voters comply with their promise to vote in a candidate because your voting precincts are comprised of individuals from different families and locations. Here in the rural areas, it is very easy.

He awkwardly laughs and begs me to understand him for what he is doing. I assured him that nothing from what he has shared would be identified as coming from him.

> I am not happy as you see doing this. I am not proud of this. I am only proud of the influence I get but on the things that I have to do get this influence and power.

**Case 6: Bonie's uncertain about the latest development project craze, the cacao plantation**

Bonie is a father aged 42 whose livelihood and food for his family are largely dependent on his farm produce. Currently, he has **0.8 hectare of land that is about to be given up for planting cacao under the lease agreement with a multinational company**. Bonie has 5 children who are all honour students, are ambitious, and would like to finish college degrees. Bonie is unsure whether the cacao land deal he has already signed up to would become successful. He is persuaded by his friend, *datu* to follow his other mates who would be trying their luck under the current land deal with the whole tribe. The cacao plantation project in Marilog District, Davao City initially covers at least 200 hectares of ancestral land, which have already been subdivided to individual landholders under the name of the male household heads. The project will operate for the next 25 years and the local people believe that the area will eventually be expanded just like the case of banana plantations in nearby district of Paquibato and in many areas in Bukidnon.

***Life and health capabilities***:

Being the patriarch of his big family with promising and ambitious kids, Bonie finds it hard to settle for anything less than what he needs, to support his dear family. He is afraid that the last parcel of land he is giving up for the cacao plantation might not be enough for food, education and health needs of his family. He has been working closely with the *datus* around his village, which means he has a good connection and relationship with them. Bonie is designated by the barangay captain as the purok leader[3] because of his active engagement with the tribe's and local government's activities. He is an outgoing person who gained lots of friends outside his immediate surrounding. **He is able to access free medical checkup easily. He is actually health conscious. He plays basketball with his friends almost every weekend.**

***Affiliation capabilities***:

As an extrovert person, Bonie is well connected with other people. He gains lots of friends because of his pleasant personality. He smiles and takes life's difficulty as lightly as possible. He finds time giving other farmers advices on how to deal with life in general. He is a skilled swine breeder. He used to have 2 boars for hire but he lost them to diarrhoea a year ago. He intends to restart his small community livelihood if the cacao venture would turn out to be good.

[3]Purok leader is a designated community leader by the barangay captain to oversee and represent the whole community, usually made up of clans, in the local governance. In some cases, the community constituents elect a purok leader at large.

> I miss my frequent visits to houses everywhere for the boar service. That's how I gained lots of friends in my community.

As head of his family, he decides for his wife and children. He represents them in community meetings. As a matter of fact, he is proud that attendance sheet of government workers visiting his community for short trainings have already encoded his name for him to sign just like what his tribal chieftains do.

> I am the man in the house, I represent my family and I believe they respect my decision.

***Concern for nonhuman and recreational capabilities***:

If the new cacao venture would be able to help alleviate Bonie's state of deprivation, he is positive that one of the first things he is going to purchase is a boar to bring him back to business. He is hoping that things will be a lot better in the coming 2–3 years so that he can send all his children to college. There are scholarships available for Indigenous people's youth offered in the state university in the city but it only convers tuition and matriculation fees. According to him, board and lodging is very costly these days. He believes he cannot afford the expense considering he has 5 children and he has no means of producing funds for the purpose. When asked if he still finds time to play, he gladly said:

> Yes, I do. I love to play basketball despite many problems. I can release my stress through playing basketball.

When asked about his concerns regarding farming as his main livelihood, he shared that:

> Farming these days is really worst. I lost the courage to take seriously planting vegetables for selling in the nearby public market. Prices of fertilisers and pesticides have gone up and we cannot afford to purchase these unless through loans. For the past three years, I forced myself to engage in farming because I didn't have any choice. I do not have formal education, no employable skills and no capital to start up a small business. I needed to get money from "loan sharks" in the community. They are those who offer you money for loan for an interest of 20% at the end of each month. Until now, I'm still paying the debt I owe from different people and the cooperative. When asked how much his outstanding loan balance in total is, he said,

> The total amount of my loan is almost the same as the estimated price of our piece of land when it is sold at current prices.

He looked sad and shy after revealing his debt to different people and the cooperative. When asked why, he continued:

> I'm not ashamed being poor and powerless in our community but I am very ashamed when these people chase me in my house to force me to pay the money I owed them. I have thumb-marked the promissory notes they have given before because they required me to. And when the promise is due, they get in my house and harass me in front my family to compel me to pay. Several times before, my wife and I have given them instant relief by allowing them to take our pigs and goats. We have never talked about collaterals in the loans we have gotten from them. Suddenly, these people out of desperation change their minds and try to put value, usually negligible and unfair price to our livestock just so they can get something from us when they come to our house.

***Political and material control***:

Bonie, just like other male household heads, enjoys his privileged access to public and private resources made available for everyone. The last piece of land is under his name. He inherited the land from his Indigenous father. It used to be 5.4 hectares, but in less than 10 years he lost most part of his land to banana plantation. Christians or non-indigenous people rented his parcels in different timing and prices, primarily for them to plant banana under growership agreement. Growership agreement gives farmers the chance to enter into business tie up with big banana companies. The growers who have medium-sized capital, finance for renting or buying of lands, purchase of seedlings, human labour and other costs.

**Case 7: Leoning, the struggling mother**

Leoning is a mother of six and takes care of two elderly who are the parents of her husband. Her husband works in the banana plantation as contractual worker. The family's farmland left under their care is **less than 600 square metres** that they have planted with **vegetables and corn** that is not enough for the food requirement of her family. Only two of her children are able to graduate from high school. The four older children did not because they help her husband's work in the farm. The two elder brothers also take part-time farm work from the pineapple plantations, 2–6 days in a month. Leoning describes her family as poor and is always at risk of becoming ultra-poor—not being able to feed, clothe, give decent house and treat sick family members. She describes her life prior to the coming of plantation companies in her community. She says that life was better before even if they were poor. They were lesser times they have experienced hunger. She laughs at the fact that before, her family only experienced foodlessness during the rainy season when they are least able to forage or cultivate their farm to produce sustainable food supply. After her husband decided to give up 80% of his landholding initially for leasing and then 5 years later for selling. She remembers how her family was robbed of its rights to control their farmland in exchange of a selling price of PhP 8,000 per hectare (USD190). She says that the only thing her family is able to acquire to start life anew after selling most of his husband's land is a carabao.

***Life and health capabilities***:

Having a big family size but with only a small piece of land to depend on for livelihood and food is extremely difficult according to Leoning. Ever since her life is solely dedicated to performing reproductive roles to save her family from intermittent hunger. She remembers how her poor kids had survived being malnourished 10 years ago.

Leoning describes her everyday life as a continuous fight against deprivation. The farm produce is not enough for her big family. She tried her best to help her husband build stable vegetable and roots crops garden but since they only have limited land left, they are forced to resort to other means of livelihood to survive. Her elder daughter used to work for a family in the city as housemaid even when she was just 15 years old. Leoning cried almost all night feeling sorry for her daughter's miserable working condition. The husband, whom her daughter worked for 6 months, molested her. She filed a case but they ended up settled prior to court hearing after the perpetrator's family paid PhP10,000 (USD238).

> They took advantage of my daughter's weakness being uneducated and young. I promise to family not to allow any of my two daughters to work as housemaids again. I would rather that we live poor as poor as life gets but I can't give away my kids to sexual predators again.

***Affiliation capabilities***:

Being a mother whose life is spent performing purely reproductive tasks such as childbearing, childrearing, foraging, gardening, cooking, and a lot more, denies her the chance of being associated with the other people outside her immediate family or clan. She doesn't find time to be part of the wider community activities. She only waits for the time when she is obligated by her tribal leaders to participate in cultural activities and in local elections. Leoning shares that she used to be the lead tribal dancer but everything has stopped after her marriage when all she cares about is her family and how they can survive.

> Being a wife and mother is really hard especially when everyone in the community expects me to be able to give good life and care for my family. When something happens to my family just like when my neighbours knew about my daughter's case, they ridicule me. They blame me, not anyone else in the family for the ill fate of my kid. I believe it was unfair of them to judge my choice of letting my daughter work as a housemaid at a young age. But you know, it already happened.

***Concern for nonhuman and recreational capabilities***:

Leoning is in a difficult situation trying to make both ends meet for her family to survive. She cannot rely only on husband to provide them food and medicines whenever someone is ill. She has to focus all her time and effort looking for ways in which her family can gather food to eat. She is spending at least 4 h daily in her vegetable garden. She sells and barters some of her good produce to her immediate neighbours in order to buy corn feeds for her four hens and a rooster. Her family depends on her chicken for protein requirement. They eat fish at 1–2 times a month. Fish is a lot expensive in the rural area of Mindanao where fishcars have to travel 60–80 km to vend.

> I love my chickens and I want to raise more so that my family would have a steady supply of meat for our meals. I also want to raise goats and cows but the problem is we can't afford to buy them. I used to raise goats before. It was fun and lucrative because we were able to produce milk and meat once in a while. Our only carabao, the one we bought after selling our land is now sickly. We are afraid to lose him. He is very close to my husband and sons. We wanted some help from the veterinarian but sad to say that the doctor comes to our town centre only once a year. If only a sick carabao can be treated with our medicinal plants we would give him some but the problem is the abscess in his right hind leg has really grown big now. We need the right animal medicine to give our carabao the second chance in life.

***Political and material control***:

After some deep reflections on the things Leoning has narrated so far to me, she exclaims:

> I am really poor! God, please help me help my family!

After a pause for about one minute, she continues by saying,

> The only possession I can truly call my own is my family. I don't have land title under my name, no house, no carabao, no farm. I only have these little things that have great help and significance to the survival of my big family. The chickens and the vegetable patch I nurtured and maintained are my last hope to ensure that we have food on our table.

## Summary of the Characteristics of the 'Coping' Group

The stories of Juan and Nelly, Bonie and Leoning as described above illustrate how the wellbeing and life chances of the 'coping' Indigenous people depend on the 'better-off' people—the male leaders who have the privilege ownership, access and control of the 'rules, resources, people, activities and power' (Kabeer 2003 cited in March et al. 2005, p. 104) in rural Mindanao. Their survival just like the story of the life of Juan and Nelly is intimately linked to the reigning power of their political leaders in the local government. Juan and Nelly's family experienced severe and prolonged hunger during the time their local government politician lost in the mayoralty election. Leoning on the other hand relied on her daughter to help her get of poverty. She gambled by sending her daughter to the city to work as domestic helper but she was terrified knowing the male house owner sexually molested her daughter. Leoning is transitioning from being 'coping' to becoming one of the 'poorest and most marginalised' when her family decided not to allow any one of the daughters to work as domestic helper in the city. Her family has been left with a small parcel of land due to distress sale and Leoning's small vegetable garden's produce is not enough for big family.

The 'coping' group of Indigenous people is the close ally of the 'better-off'. They live in inner communities next to the town centre where the 'better-off' Indigenous people live. They can readily take advantage of the resources being poured by the government and non-government organisations at the town centre. They are also the easiest ones to grab by their leaders to gather as audience in any seminar or project of the outsiders in their area.

They are in the 'coping' group because their survival and life chances are intimately linked to their limited landholding and capabilities to claim their rights over the resources centrally controlled by the 'better-off'. Their wellbeing and life chances as poor people are continuously at risk of becoming 'poorest and most marginalised' as their voice, choice, and agency as individuals are constituted in the discourse of the powerful leaders who are male and expert outsiders (Bacchi 2010; Chambers 1983). The nature of their participation in rural development planning, as the stories suggest, is 'nominal' (Agarwal 2001, pp. 1624–1625). Agarwal described nominal participation as being 'a member of a group'. It means that when someone's participation is nominal, one is not able to exercise her/his social and political capabilities to enter into decision-making opportunities. On the hand, Cornwall (2003, p. 1327) argued that the least important mode of participation is called functional participation where participants are needed only to show up and be counted in the documentation of the project management team. Participants in this mode of activity are viewed as objects of the project. For Nussbaum (2011), this is an instance where people are considered as means not ends of development.

## *Malisen Ne Peg Egpe*[4]*: Living a Life of Destitution in Rural Mindanao*

This section presents the three case studies illustrating the living conditions of the poorest and most marginalised groups of participants in this study. These persons are the ones classified as worst off in terms of being the least supported and protected to maintain life and to possess material and political control over property and livelihood necessary for their wellbeing. This group of participants is comprised mostly of rural Indigenous women who have limited rights and negligible capabilities towards improvement of their wellbeing and life chances as citizens. Women who belong to this category in the typology are wives in the marginal and poorest rural families who perform subordinated roles mainly associated with their reproductive responsibilities at home. These poorest Indigenous people are those who are living in the remotest areas in rural Mindanao. They practically have poor access to basic services as government and other state actors pour most of their resources only to the town centre and to people they are usually in contact with—the *datus* (male tribal leaders). Chambers (1983) argued that leaders and expert planners who are 'outsiders', use their urban ideologies in rural development planning. The outsiders carry with them spatial, project, person, dry season, diplomatic and professional biases. Spatial bias happens when the outsiders prefer to visit only the town centre and leave the remote areas behind. Project bias is the tendency of the outsiders to frequently focus on model projects for ease of documentation and to "guarantee success". Person or male bias is the preference of the outsiders to deal mostly with local leaders or the *datus* (male tribal chieftains). Dry season bias refers to the outsiders' tendency of visiting the rural area during non-rainy season only. Diplomatic bias refers to the tendency of according unnecessary amount of politeness to senior staff by the junior staff assigned in the field. This diplomacy is also happening between the relationship of junior outsiders and the local people. Lastly, professional bias refers to the propensity of the outsiders who are trained in universities to adhere to their specialisation bias. The engagement of outsiders who belong to the same field, for example, agricultural science fields such as animal husbandry, crop protection, plant pathology, etc. leaves other dimensions of rural poverty unaddressed.

---

[4]Matigsalug term for the Poorest and Most Marginalised group, those whose living conditions are considered in the worst off cases due to loss of control and access to farm land, disease or loss of a family member, poor cropping and indebtedness. In this study, they comprised mostly of women whose lives are subordinated by household, community, market and state systems and rules (Kabeer 2003).

Spatial bias, as well as the other biases described above, are considered to be 'corrosive disadvantages' (Wolff and De Shalit 2013) that hamper rural people, especially women, children and differently abled in Mindanao to become active partners of men and elite groups in development. Being missed out in the actual social action, even in a simple meeting or community gathering neglects a woman the chance to listen and be listened to (Dobson 2014) of her realities reflected through her 'self-critical awareness' (Chambers 1997, p. 32).

Case 8 is about the life of the widower Jun-jun. He lost his wife after giving birth to their daughter. Jun-jun takes care of his four young children all by himself. He struggles to find work because he cannot leave his kids to his mother who is already old and sick. He depends from time to time to anyone in his neighbourhood who is available to take care of his baby while he goes to *bayanihan* (communal work) with his other young children.

Case 9 is about Besing, a woman with 6 children, has a goitre, and pregnant during the time of interview. She lives in a makeshift thatched house provided by the landlord who is the owner of the pineapple farm her whole family has worked for 8 years now. Her husband is sickly and she wanted him checked by a health professional as soon as possible. She is terrified about the diagnosis as she has just lost a son to pneumonia last year. At least two of her six kids have chronic bronchial asthma and are at risk of tuberculosis. Being poor, isolated, and physically weak, Besing has a very poor chance of improving her capabilities in terms of associating herself with other people. Inasmuch as she dreams of a life being closely surrounded and supported by peers, she cannot materialise whatever she aspires as she is locked into her deprivations. Her family's survival depends on her time and efforts. She depends heavily on her small vegetable patch for food.

Case 10 describes the life of Nida, a mother of 5 who lost her husband and subsequently her land through distress sale is now managing her depression. Her anxiety caused her to lock herself inside her house sleeping for most of the day and crying from time to time. She depends on her two under aged sons who are taking any manual labour available in the community. The young boys work and find food to eat for their mother and other siblings. Her neighbours, who are also poor, help her family in many different ways. They help provide food and occasional care to children being left to wander and play around by Nida. Amongst all participants, Nida is probably one of the poorest and most marginalised rural people who are left to fend for themselves despite extreme poverty, hunger and depression.

**Case 8: Jun-jun, the poorest widower**

Jun-jun is an Indigenous father of four kids aged 8 months, 1, 2 and 4 years old. His wife Teling was sick and left undiagnosed until her death in 2013. According to Jun-jun, Teling suffered from *bughat* (relapse). The *comadrona* (traditional midwife) during the separate interview, says that Teling was suffering from eclampsia. She reportedly had high fever some few weeks before her scheduled child delivery. The *comadrona* confirmed that Teling was severely malnourished. She did not have any prenatal checkup done at the health centre. The nearest **health centre is 10.5 kilometres away** from the remote tribal village where Jun-jun's family lives. Jun-jun looks so sad and flimsy just like his kids who are walking around the bamboo house without sandals. The three kids move around the village without short pants and are wearing tattered Sandoz that look like they have never been washed for weeks. The family lives in a very small bamboo house that has no toilet and water facilities. The kids have been trained to find their places in the bushes to pass their wastes. Even Jun-jun does the same.

Jun-jun feels sorry for losing his wife. He regrets being poor and unable to give his wife and children decent and comfortable lives. Jun-jun has never attended any formal school just like his wife Teling. When Teling was still alive, the couple helps other Indigenous farmers in the community in either *bayanihan* (community harvesting based on reciprocity) or paid casual work in the banana farm. They usually take their kids with them whenever they can find occasional farm work. They leave their kids playing usually under the fruits trees while they work. Now that Jun-jun is a widower and being left with 4 lonely and malnourished kids, he feels like giving up. **He shares his desire to find a better job for his kids but he does not know how since he cannot leave his kids with his mother who is sickly and old.**

***Life and health capabilities***:

Jun-jun has never bought or received any free clothes for himself for 3 years now. When Teling was alive, Jun-jun loves to buy his wife new duster or blouse every Christmas time. During the same time, he also buys his kids some pairs of sando and short pants from the town's public market. Jun-jun relies from pre-loved clothes shared to him by his aunt who lives in the city. But for several years now, his aunt never came back to visit their village. Jun-jun says he does not care whether he only has 2 pairs of pants and 3 t-shirts for as long his kids are alive.

Doing the same casual work, Jun-jun has to take his kids to the farm except the baby. He has to ask his good neighbours who are willing and available to look after the baby while he is out for work.

> I am just blessed to have neighbours who truly care and understand my need. As long as they are available, they would take my baby girl for a day's care. Some neighbours would even like me to leave all the kids with them while I am away without asking anything in return. But because my three older kids would now **cry when left to my neighbours, I take them to work.** I think they like it there because we can eat snacks and lunch offered by the host farmer who invited us for *bayanihan*.
>
> I don't want to lose anyone of my kids.

**Case 9: Besing,**

Besing is pregnant and a mother of 6 kids. She lives in the innermost part of the pineapple plantation in the Bukidnon area. She is diagnosed of goitre (otherwise known as Grave's disease) 5 years ago and her **husband is sickly** and she fears that if something happens to him, her family would be in a total wreck. Her husband works in the pineapple plantation as labourer. Lately, because of **chest pain, her husband is unable to work**. She wants to take him to the nearest hospital for medical check up but is unable to do it, as she doesn't have money for the transportation, snacks, and payment for doctor's fee. She said that she has been **borrowing money from almost all people she knows** in her neighbourhood. Her family also has an outstanding loan from the "5–6"[5] being offered by some moneyed locals. Her family's total amount of loan is close to **PhP60,000 (USD1,428).** Besing and her husband are members of the Indigenous tribe in Bukidnon. They used to have a farmland measuring at least 1.5 hectares but they sold it to local pineapple businessman. They thought selling their land is a good strategy to overcome poverty. They intended to start up a small business, particularly a *sari-sari*[6] store. They did not realise their plan. They spent most of their money saving the life of their **son who they have lost to pneumonia** last year.

***Life and health capabilities***:

Having been physically weak, food poor and isolated, Besing finds it really hard to meet her family's daily basic needs. Her house made of **plastic tarpaulin wall and roofing**, is probably one of the worst in the community. She says, "We don't own the lot where this house is built. The owner of the farm allows us to live here while my husband is still working in this farm. These materials we used to build this house—the **tarpaulin are from the election banners** used by politicians". Her children whose ages range from below 1 to 9 years old look physically weak and malnourished just like their parents. The kids were happy to receive my presents for them, a bag of bread, peanut butter and cookies. In one sitting, all the food I offered them was gone. Besing tearfully recalls her departed son. She says that the only hope left for her to hold on to life is her other kids. Besing describes how hard it is to see her children cry because they are hungry. When her husband is not working, they won't be able to buy rice. Even the daily wage from the farm work of her husband amounting to **PhP150 (USD3)** is barely enough for their daily food requirement. She said that her big family consumes at least 2 kilos of rice for about PhP100 (USD2) and her husband, for his cigarette, keeps the PhP50 (USD1). When asked how she feels about her husband's smoking habit, she said:

> Cigarette smoking is the cause I know why my husband is ill nowadays. We are not certain yet about his medical condition but his chest pain and frequent cough indicate that something really is wrong. I ask him to stop smoking because we need to spend more money for food but he refused to take heed of my advice.

Besing forgets her responsibility to herself and the child in her womb. She is on the last trimester of her pregnancy but she said that she never gotten herself to the nearest clinic for prenatal and vitamin supplement needs yet. She cannot leave her small children unattended. Besing appears sickly with her protruding thyroid gland. She speaks and walks slowly during the time of the first interview. I requested her to give me another chance to see her in the following week so that I can coordinate with the nearest health centre for her immediate health needs. I was successful to get her and her husband's approval to meet them again in their house.

---

[5]Otherwise known as "loan sharks" or those who provide easy loan and charge hefty interest rate of 20 percent per month on top of the principal loan amount.

[6]A Filipino term for variety store selling all sorts of basic commodities such as rice, canned goods, dried fish, toiletries, etc.

The weeks after, Besing was happy to inform me that she went to the clinic with a neighbour. Her husband did not go to work that day to take care of the kids.

> The nurse told me I'm at risk for this pregnancy because of my goiter and low hemoglobin count. They have given me vitamins and a dose of tetanus toxoid. I hope me and my baby would be fine.

***Affiliation capabilities***:

Being poor, isolated, and physically weak, Besing has been given a very poor chance to improve her capabilities in terms of associating herself with other people. Inasmuch as she dreams of a life being closely surrounded and supported by peers, she cannot materialise whatever she aspires as she is locked into her deprivations. Her family's survival depends on her time and efforts, however flimsy and difficult it is for her to make both ends meet. She depends heavily on her small vegetable patch for food.

> We learn to eat these pineapples in various ways. We cook it with other vegetables mixed with coconut milk, just to survive. I cry every time my kids complain hunger. I pity them.

**Concern for nonhuman and recreational capabilities:**

Poor Besing is highly dependent on the scanty produce of her small vegetable garden.

> I am very close nature because it gives me hope and assurance that when something grows from the bowel of the earth, it will become our food.

She used to have more than 10 matured chickens but she lost them after a virus outbreak on chickens plagued hers and others in the neighbourhood. She longs for someone to help her start raising chickens again. She told me, each hen costs PhP200 (USD4). I refused to grant her right there and then her wish. Instead, I coordinated with a local government official to help her to start raising chickens in her backyard. After two weeks, a neighbour has offered Besing a chance to grow her own chickens in the backyard through *batun*[7] system. The arrangement expects her to return the pair of chicken on the second time the hen weans its juvenile chicks. In this case, the good neighbour does not expect more than a pair to be given back to his family. The usual arrangement when neighbours enter into *batun* agreement involves the receiver's responsibility of returning the full value (ratio of 1:1) plus 1/3 of the total value of the first progeny.

***Political and material control***:

Besing is desperate to help family at least achieve food sufficiency. Her family does not own land and any material things. Their survival is continuously being challenged by the interlocking deprivations they experience. Besing's family is a perfect example of Robert Chamber's explanation about how the poorest become and will stay poor without changing from the bottom, meaning from the local people to define and construct their ideas and plans based on their local issues

[7]A local arrangement of entering into shepherding cows, carabaos, goats, chicken, geese, etc., for other families.

reflecting their lcddu (local, complex, diverse, dynamic, and unstable) realities Chambers (1983). The family cannot overcome the interlocking deprivations caused by poverty, physical weakness, powerlessness, vulnerability, and isolation. Besing is completely trapped and in unable to move up the social mobility ladder unless and until rural development planning is change to focus on the rural and Indigenous people's needs. The family has lost their land through stealthy land deals. Their ignorance leads them to the hands of treacherous and unscrupulous local businessmen who support modern monoculture plantation. Losing their land, house and livelihood to monoculture pineapple plantation does not give them any social and economic benefit. Besing and her husband did not have any formal education. The couple is illiterate and innumerate just like their children.

In terms of Besing's participation in community affairs such as meetings, elections and festivals, she said,

> I don't attend in any activities in our town centre. I can't leave my kids behind. I would rather find some staple food in my neighbourhood rather than attending in any activities outside our home. My husband is active in almost all community affairs. He can go out from the house anytime he wishes being the head of the family. He spends a lot of time chatting and drinking with his friends while I'm attending to the needs of my children. During elections, he is the only one able to participate. I have not been able to vote since.

**Case 10: Nida, the miserable mother and depressed widow**

Nida is a mother of **five doting kids** whose ages range from 6 to 16. She lost her husband 3 years ago to heart attack. With almost nothing to call her own except her kids, Nida feels like giving up her fight against extreme poverty. For food, she is depending on whatever her kids would give her after a long day of playing and collecting fruits and vegetables from the neighbourhood. Nida looks messy and acts disorderly but she can at least keep her composure during the interview. Her neighbours are helping her cope from the depression she is experiencing. Lately, her neighbours observed Nida's melt down. She could cry all day regardless of reason. But when Nida is in a good mood, her neighbours describe her as pleasant, helpful and friendly. This interview with her happened only after one of her neighbours introduced me to her. Nida likes the idea of being interviewed.

All her school-age kids are out-of-school. The children, two girls and three boys look flimsy and weak and yet their faces are beaming, reflecting their innocence. During the interview the kids were playing and I have in fact witnessed that after being gone for 3 h, the eldest son came back with a basket full of corn and coconuts. The son said, he got them from helping a neighbour harvest his corn. His son participated in the *bayanihan* (communal work) harvesting of corn. Nida is very proud of her children especially his elder sons. Her 16 and 14 year-old sons are accepting manual labour jobs wanted by the banana growers in the community.

The family used to own at least 500 $m^2$ of land planted to bananas. They sold their land distressfully to save the life of her husband who was in comatose for 2 months in the hospital. The only land left for the family now is the one where their house stands. The house is built in 1991. It is made of bamboo stilts and nipa leaves for roofing. Nida shows the interior part of her house. There is no flooring but the earth. It is muddy because it rained the night before the interview. She shows how they slept and got wet the previous night with the severely damaged roofing above them.

***Life and health capabilities***:

Nida is in a state of depression. She needs mental health support apart from other needs but she has never been to the hospital or the clinic to help her with her anxiety. She is not mothering quite well her children because she sleeps and cries a lot. She is worried about her children's future. She is thinking that they are going to die after all. The neighbours who are also impoverished, tried their best to support the poor family. Nida's depression locked her inside the house while her children roam around the community to survive. When any of the kids is sick, the neighbours offer their help wholeheartedly to the family. No one in the neighbourhood thinks that Nida needs medical treatment to help her get well and be back to her feet again for her poor little kids. I thought she needs mental health support first so that she can at least stand up and support herself and her children.

The problem is, mental health care in the rural Mindanao is totally unheard of. The local people would be able to identify one who is mentally sick when someone manifests overt signs of severe mental illness usually associated with violent behaviour, obscenity, and talking to oneself. Depression among rural Indigenous people is hard to detect. I stood up using my basic social skills and knowledge to coordinate with the good friend who is a practicing psychologist to address the anxiety issues confronted by Nida. I accompanied Nida to the city while I asked the neighbours to look after the kids. After the first visit, the psychologist confirmed that Nida is in a state of depression. She needs anti-depressant medicines to help her get well. She needs good nutrition too. We were able to manage the first treatment as well as the first two weeks medication. The regional hospital in southern Mindanao, with the help of a politician, has continued the treatment of Nida while her kids are still being looked after her good neighbours.

***Affiliation capabilities***:

Due to her poor mental state, Nida has isolated herself by staying inside the house sleeping and crying almost always. She forgets to associate herself with her neighbours to get social support. Her incapability has forced her children to wander for food in the neighbourhood for almost a year now. When asked if she has opened up her emotional distress to anyone including any local official, she said:

> No, I am fine. I just need to be alone most of the time. I am losing hope but I know I'll be fine soon.

***Concern for nonhuman and recreational capabilities***:

> I can't afford to go out and play and have a chat with my neighbours. I can't see myself enjoying while in fact I'm hurting. I can't be who they want me to be because I lost hope. I lost my husband and our land. And all I want to do now is wait until we are all gone.

It is hopelessness that leads Nida to isolation and depression. Her neighbours, who are obviously unfamiliar of depression and anxiety, think that someday soon she is going to get up. Even Nida is in a state of denial of her own experience of pain exacerbated by extreme deprivations. She needs help but the government and non-government actors are nowhere to be found in the remote rural community she is being hidden. She needs mental support to help her claim her full right to live and save her children. When asked about what are the most important needs of her family at present, she said:

> Food and roofing for our house.

Nida did not think about addressing her mental condition as important. She thought only of the immediate needs of her hungry children.

***Political and material control***:

Nida, being a poor widow and a mother of 5 physically weak children is severely impoverished and is completely hopeless after losing her husband and their only piece of land. Losing her land through distressful sale just to save her husband's life was the only choice she was left with being unable to access reliable medical and other social services in rural Mindanao.

> I did not know what else to do when I lost my husband. I am not prepared to take his responsibilities for our family. I am just trained and skilled doing domestic duties.

## *Summary of the Characteristics of the 'Poorest and Most Marginalised' Group*

The stories of Jun-jun, Besing and Nida represent the characteristics of the 'poorest and most vulnerable' people in the plantation communities of rural Mindanao. Their destitution is a result of their being deprived systematically—poor social services and poor capabilities to lead their lives out of extreme poverty and hunger. They live in the remotest rural area and they have been left out in the rural development planning. Their wellbeing and life chances depend delicately on their poor agroecological resources and *bayanihan* (communal work and sharing). The resources being poured at the town centre do not reach them simply because they are expected to go out from their remote communities and walk long kilometres to claim their rights over scanty social services available at the centre. Nida represents the poorest Indigenous mothers/women in the community. Her poor mental health is left unaddressed as her community leaders think she only represents a minority and hence, no voice and choice to assert for her rights to be helped by any means to save her and her poor little children. The life of Nida is a life not worthy of living at all. Nussbaum (2011) argued that everyone in a democratic state should be afforded a decent social minimum provision of support to build up ones capabilities to do and to be. Nida, and the rest of the poorest and most marganalised Indigenous people who are mostly women, children, elderly and differently abled, are the victims of the structural and positivist 'development project' (McMichael 2008) promoting modern monoculture plantation.

The prevailing 'monocultures of the mind' (Shiva 1993) marginalised the poorest rural Indigenous people and dispossessed them of their land rights. The lcddu (local, complex, diverse, dynamic, and unstable) realities Chambers (1983) of the poorest and most marginalised rural people are not being listened to (Dobson 2014) and included in the existing framework for open dialogue. Christakis and Bausch (2006) argued that what we need in order to reinvent democracy to work for the poorest and most marginalised is to take their collective wisdom as part of the whole human development efforts through open dialogue. For Girardet (2015), giving the poorest rural people their chance to improve locally their food and livelihood system means giving them the chance to regenerate the rural communities under the so-called regenerative development framework. Regenerative development framework is more than just sustainable development. It is a form of critique of the existing practices surrounding the global sustainability development agenda. The idea support Dobson's (2007, p. 2) ecologism' principle which holds that 'a sustainable and fulfilling existence presupposes radical changes in our relationship with the non-human natural world and in our mode of social and political life'. It is a form of critique on the prevailing 'environmentalism' movement that is usually managerial in its approach. Environmentalism is anthropocentric in nature. It supports the idea that nature is just an object of development for humans to use. This idea according to Schneider and McMichael (2010) is form of metabolic rift, a serious threat to our survival and this happens when there is a huge discrepancy in the relationship between human production and nature. The monoculture plantations in Mindanao causes major metabolic rifts as the case studies illustrate. The Indigenous women have lost their seeds, they clamour for poor soil fertility due to heavy reliance of the plantation communities on commercial petrochemical fertilisers and pesticides. These forms of metabolic rifts are evidenced in the works of Gonzales (2006) and Shiva (2001). They reported that modern agro-industrial mode of production that exploited Indigenous soils in the South to support the food security agenda favouring the market and business interests of the North has caused the rural communities too much ecological and human stress. Soil fertility has depleted and diverse crop seeds have disappeared as the monoculture system favour only the crops/seeds they have prepared in their laboratories.

## They Hold Not Just Half but Most of the Power and the Resources

Community, market and state level platforms, with legal and administrative regimes, dominate the visible, formal and powerful structure of decision-making in the Philippines. Participation in development undertakings is often limited to people who are active, educated, men, landed, moneyed and influential. Negotiations made in public sphere related to health, food, land, livelihood and education in the rural areas in Mindanao are perceived as directly influenced by the interests of the more powerful individuals and institutions in the island. The Venn diagram shown in

Fig. 17.3 illustrates how the participants perceived the extent to which rural development planning has proceeded mostly in the absence of individual and household participation in rural and Indigenous communities in Mindanao. The diagram came out as a result of the consensus of the participants during the focus group discussions.

The Venn diagram as a participatory rural appraisal (PRA) tool is an effective graphic representation of nominal resource/wealth, power, and influence distribution in a given community. The size of the circles indicates magnitude of power or status of individuals and groups in the negotiated space, in this case participation in rural development planning. As shown, the participants of this study describe rural development planning as a social action that is predominantly entered and negotiated by their community leaders and experts of the various state and non-state organisations. In this study, community leaders are comprised of men as the head of their tribal councils. They are called *datus* (male tribal chieftains). Some of them are elected and appointed leaders in the various local government units and agencies. This finding coincides with Chambers' (1997) idea that rural development tourism of the outsiders manipulates and coerces the lcddu (local, complex, diverse, dynamic, and unstable) realities by being negligent and disinterested in their approaches to ensure local people's participation in development. The local people, as shown in the diagram, believe that the voice and choice of their leaders dominate in the whole decision-making process to come up with a local development plan.

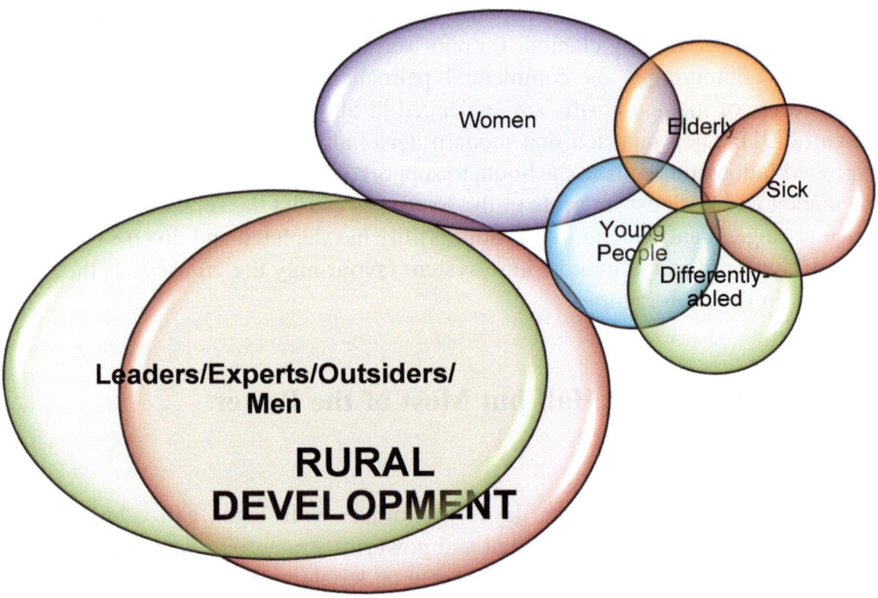


**Fig. 17.3** Venn diagram illustrating the extent of participation of men, women and their dependents in rural development planning in Mindanao. *Source* Face-to-face interview with the Indigenous farmers in Mindanao and validated during FGD conducted from 28 September 2013 to 10 May 2014

Figure 17.3 shows the participants' perception on the extent of their participation in rural development planning in Mindanao. As indicated, the participants see women as partners of men in most of the household and community activities. However, women's bargaining power in the decision-making at the community level is but a marginal claimed space in the rural development planning that is provoked by women themselves to be part of the wider discussion for various personal, household and community concerns. This 'claimed space' (Gaventa 2006), is also known as the facilitated social and political space initiated by the civil society groups that have begun to change the mindsets of the local people pertaining to promoting women's voice and choice in the local policymaking. As shown, the claimed space of women (indicated by the common point created between red and green circles) is a marginal space in the whole process of rural development planning. Joining the impoverished and powerless rank of women are their dependents—young people, elderly, sick and differently abled persons. The physical weaknesses of these vulnerable groups place them as passive recipients of the decisions of the state and local leaders. Being poor, physically and mentally weak considers them insignificant in the existing decision-making platforms. Therefore, the outsiders have the 'power-over' (VeneKlasen and Miller 2002) the weak and the powerless rural people to plan for them (Bacchi 2004, 2010; Eveline and Bacchi 2005) and constitute them in the development discourse as passive objects and problems in the policy-making (Bacchi 2004, 2010; Eveline and Bacchi 2005) rather than as persons with voice, choice and agency (Cornwall 2003; Gaventa and Cornwall 2001; Nussbaum 2011). Mr. WX described below how he is being excluded from any sort of socio-economic planning in rural Mindanao.

> As I'm handicapped, I have not been able to participate in the local planning. I feel that I am not needed. They give some sort of social and medical support for my maintenance medicine but there never was a time when I am asked of my idea about the services they provide and of ways to improve them.

During the focus group discussion, specifically on the deliberation on Venn diagram, participants say that women and their dependents are just 'decorations' on the 'hat' made-up predominantly of leaders, experts and men who partake in rural development tourism. One of the women participants, Mrs. YZ, narrated as follows:

> We are asked to participate sometimes in community-wide projects as women. They call us to join meetings, mainly to thumbmark and/or sign in their attendance sheets. They ask us to prepare the town hall before everyone arrives. They even asked us to prepare an intermission number. We feel that our presence is valued but honestly, I feel disgusted being unable to sustain my participation in community activities. Men are the preferred and expected attendees of community meetings in our tribe. Men are being listened to.

The narrative depicts a glaring weakness of participatory development approaches in rural Mindanao that proceeded under the idea of 'stakeholder's participation' or 'participation for all'. Agarwal (2001, p. 1623) argued that participatory development projects espoused 'participatory exclusion' by putting up seemingly participatory activities that in fact quell women's voice and choice in the actual decision-making platforms promoting their wellbeing. Women become incidental

**Table 17.4** Typical sequences of activities performed by men and women during community meeting and/or gathering

| Activities by time | Man | Woman |
|---|---|---|
| Before | At home:<br>wakes up<br>eats<br>feeds animals<br>grooms self<br>walks to meeting hall | At home:<br>wakes up ahead of her husband<br>cooks<br>feeds children<br>washes dishes<br>prepares clothes for husband and herself<br>walks to meeting hall<br>*(Pending and continuing tasks)*<br>washes clothes<br>feeds children<br>feeds animals<br>forage food/gardening |
| During | At the meeting hall:<br>meets/greets other men<br>signs/thumbmarks attendance sheet<br>sits in front and middle rows<br>participates in discussion<br>signs/thumbmarks official documents such as contracts<br>leaves the meeting hall | At the meeting hall:<br>arrives usually late; early to arrive prepare the meeting hall<br>signs/thumbmarks attendance sheet<br>sits in last rows<br>timid and shy; does not participate in discussion<br>serves refreshment<br>renders dance/song number with other women<br>does not sign/thumbmark official documents |
| After | At the community centre:<br>hangs around with other men for chatting, drinking and playing basketball<br>goes home at nighttime | Still at the meeting hall:<br>helps in restoration of the meeting hall<br>goes home directly to perform pending and continuing tasks at home |

*Source: Face-to-face interview with the Indigenous farmers in Mindanao and validated during FGD conducted from 28 September 2013 to 10 May 2014*

and worst, accidental participants in various community projects when they are being limited to perform only such mundane roles like signing or thumbmarking the attendance sheets, seating in the last rows, rendering dance and song number, and preparing refreshments and venue. Table 17.4 shows the typical sequence of activities performed by men and women during community meeting and/or gathering. Men at the community level decision-making platforms enjoy the privilege of being served by women starting from the house, some few hours before the community meeting. In terms of number and time required to finish various activities before the meeting, women run out both time and stamina to prepare and assert their views and ideas during the meeting after they perform multitude of reproductive tasks at home. In this study, women are found to wake up at least one hour before their husbands, primarily to cook and feed their families. They typically do not arrive at the meeting hall at the exact time for the meeting. They are either late or way advance to arrive. Latecomers have been over burdened by household chores. The early birds take some key responsibilities for cleaning, arranging the seats and tables, fixing the sound system and stage or backdrop, etc.

During the meeting, women are seated in the last rows while men are usually being allotted seats next to other men especially the *datus* (male tribal chieftains). The tribal council comprised of *datus* is seated at the presidential table facing other participants. During the meeting, women perform another round of subordinated duties to men by serving refreshments and offering some special production number to entertain other participants.

Women do not talk and participate in the discussions as they expect their men to do the talking for them. Men doing the talk for women repressed latter's capability to express their ideas and concerns, which have not been heard and addressed collectively at the community level. This passive form of participation in rural development activities, prevent women's concerns to be elevated and discussed at the community and higher policy arenas. This study found that women either arrive late or come prior to meetings and spend more time and physical efforts than their men counterpart. This form of multiple burdens of women at the household resonates at the community level decision-making platforms where women play losers in the process of being physically exhausted before, during and after the community meeting or gathering.

Figure 17.4 shows a sample of attendance sheet in a seminar conducted by a government agency. The figure shows that only 2 or 9% are women (both named Catalina) who joined in the activity together with 22 other men. This shows that

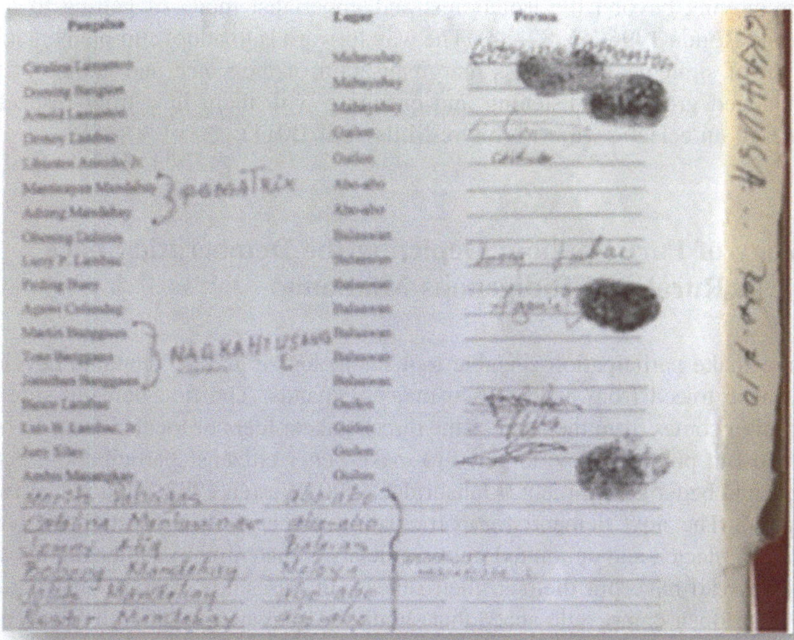

**Fig. 17.4** Sample attendance sheet in a training conducted by a government agency. *Source* Secretary of the Matigsalug-Manobo Tribal People Council of Elders in Davao City (MAMATRIPCEDI)

women as minority in the planning platform feel overwhelmed and intimidated to actively speak if they are given the chance to partake in the discussion. As shared by one of the women leaders, Mrs. ABC as follows:

> I feel shy being surrounded by active male leaders in our community. I stammer because of shyness whenever I'm asked to introduce myself. I don't have the confidence to speak and express my opinion on the issue or topic we are called to discuss.

While there is no agreement across studies conducted worldwide to date on gender and participation, Agarwal (2001, pp. 170–171) reported that at least one-third proportion of women in a single committee work constitutes the 'critical mass' and has been proven to significantly improve the effectiveness of women's participation. More than this suggested proportion is indeed ethical. Providing more diversity in a respectful dialogue (McIntyre-Mills 2014a) to discuss diverse issues pertaining to rural development expands the boundaries (Midgley 1997; Ulrich 1994, 1996) in which the local people can actively and interactively participate (Agarwal 2001) and be able to see their diverse ideas and collective consensus moving progressively with them. This is also about sharing responsibilities for the inevitable risks and failures brought about by the collective social action. Promoting diversity on the aspect of participation of men and women, as well as the other members in the society who are constituted in the discourses of development, requires moving beyond the isolationist and imperialist mode of getting to truth (Flood and Romm 1996, pp. 82–84). The way forward is to adopt complementarism in the set of strategies to address marginalisation of the voice and choice of the disadvantaged groups by listening and engaging with them in a truly respectful dialogue, in an eclectic way (McIntyre-Mills et al. 2011).

## Typology of Participation: Depicting the Democratic Space Deficit in Rural and Indigenous Mindanao

Efforts to make participation a viable tool for inclusive and accountable development can be traced from at least two major demands. The first demand side for participation comes from the need of the direct stakeholders or local citizens to help shape relevant public policy, targeted to make better citizens' participation, better decision, and better government (Mansbridge 1990; Warren 1992, cited in Cornwall 2004 p. 1). The next demand for participation comes from opportunities being provided by elected and appointed public officials by listening to and engaging with the people who have put them in their offices. In this study, I argue that participation is an open democratic space that should be activated at the individual, peer and family levels; treating each individual person as an end itself and not as means for the welfare of others (Nussbaum 2011; Sen 1999). Participation as a process of earning and claiming the negotiated democratic space is crucial to analysing the role of power relations amongst participants in the creation of knowledge and truth (Cornwall 2003; Gaventa and Cornwall 2001).

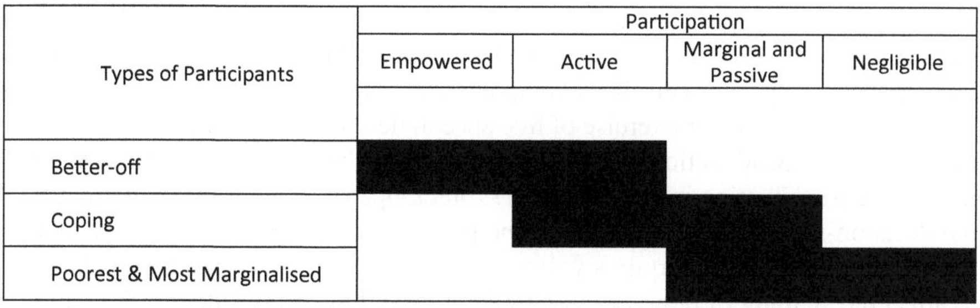


**Fig. 17.5** Typology of participation across types of participants. *Source* Face-to-face interview with the Indigenous farmers in Mindanao and validated during FGD conducted from 28 September 2013 to 10 May 2014

This section presents the typical narratives of the rural and Indigenous people participants on the nature, types and extent to which they are able/not able to participate in various community, city, provincial and national gatherings tackling rural Mindanao development. The case studies provided here include the actual stories of men, women, young people, elderly and sick, and differently abled persons. The purpose of this analysis is to describe the issues confronted by the rural and Indigenous people in Mindanao as they negotiate for the ideal democratic spaces that will support their land rights, livelihood, food and water system, health and education. The case is made that those who are at the bottom of the socio-economic and political hierarchy—the poorest and the most marginalised, are neglected and deprived of their rights to participate in various decision-making platforms at the community, market and state level. The typology of participation as shown in Fig. 17.5 illustrates that across types of participants, namely the better-off, coping and the poorest and most marginalised, nature and extent of participation vary.

## *The Passive to Negligible Participation of the Better-Off*

Agarwal describes participation in a typology—nominal, passive, consultative, activity-specific, active and interactive participation (2001, p. 1624). Nominal participation takes place when men and women are being grouped and called members of the various community organisations such as mother's club, farmers' organisation, etc. Passive participation happens when farmers, especially women are called to participate in community meetings to simply sit and listen. Consultative participation happens when the participants are asked of their ideas and opinions on the issues at hand. Usually, this sort of community activity requires the male local leaders and elders' participation. In this study, women are prevented by the existing norms, customs and traditions to partake openly in the discussions at the community level. Women can, however, find their place in activity-specific projects. These are projects developed by the outsiders comprised of leaders and technical experts of the local government and national government agencies. Active participation happens when the participants are able to express their opinions and ideas unhampered. Their exercise of free speech denotes power and agency to affect the proposed social action. In this instance, just like the next typology called interactive participation inhibits women's direct, open and definitive participation in the decision-making processes that shape policies and programme implementation. Interactive participation requires voice, choice and agency of the actual participants to affect the shaping of policies through their critical ideas considering the rural and Indigenous people's local, complex, diverse, dynamic, and unstable realities (Chambers 1997).

Gaventa and Valderrama (2001, cited in Cornwall 2006) offer vital explanation about the modes of participation and the reasons and treatment of participants in each mode by the sponsoring institution. First is the ***functional mode of participation***. People are being invited and enlisted as passive participants in the development projects (for example in trainings). The community organisers who are targeting compliance and agreement to the proposed intervention usually seek their participation. Participants in this mode are being treated as objects of the project. Next is ***instrumental mode of participation.*** This mode requires people to participate and take some hands-on responsibilities in the project. The participants are being treated as instruments to make the project become successful. ***Consultative mode of participation*** invites the participants to express their views and opinions about the proposed social action. The participants are being viewed as actors and/or direct stakeholders of the project. Lastly, the ***transformative mode of participation*** enhances people's capabilities and enforces them to exercise their rights and claim their basic entitlements as individuals to help transform social inequalities and improve their wellbeing. The participants are being viewed in this mode as agents of development. They are being given the chance, as individuals rather than just mere representatives of their households and/or communities. In this mode, participants being the agents are considered as ends rather than means of development. It is apparent that the first three modes have become the norm of the prevailing participatory development approaches. The local people are being treated as means to development.

When development projects require only representatives of each basic unit, the household, women and their dependents such as young people, elderly, sick and differently abled persons are extremely limited in their chance to participate and be heard of their voice and choice to promote their agency as individuals with dignity. Focusing on dignity rather than mere satisfaction, according to Nussbaum (2011), supports wellbeing and life chances for the disadvantaged members of the household and the wider community to be represented, heard and included in the decision-making process pertaining to issues of life, land, food, livelihood, education and health. Extending the notion of human dignity 'to do to be' (Nussbaum 2011; Sen 1999) in participatory development approaches for the rural development planning requires women and their household dependents to be given the chance to enter into 'respectful dialogues' (McIntyre 2002, p. 30; McIntyre-Mills et al. 2011).

**Table 17.5** Participants' perception on the extent of their participation in some aspects of rural development planning

| My level of participation in rural development planning for… | Men | | Women | |
|---|---|---|---|---|
| | Mean | Description | Mean | Description |
| Land development | 4.56 | Very high | 1.20 | Very low |
| Farming/Agriculture | 4.67 | Very high | 1.89 | Very low |
| Livelihood | 4.51 | Very high | 2.11 | Low |
| Food and water | 4.54 | Very high | 1.23 | Very low |
| Health and nutrition | 4.52 | Very high | 2.32 | Low |
| Education | 4.54 | Very high | 1.22 | Very low |
| Family planning | 4.58 | Very high | 1.54 | Low |
| Disaster planning | 4.57 | Very high | 1.19 | Very low |
| Overall Mean | 4.56 | Very high | 1.59 | Low |

*Source* Face-to-face interview with the Indigenous farmers in Mindanao and validated during FGD conducted from 28 September 2013 to 10 May 2014

This study finds that rural development planning in Mindanao as a whole, which zooms in households and not individuals, gives extremely limited participation chances to women and other disadvantaged groups. Their participation is just limited to nominal, passive and consultative levels of participation, where according to the study conducted by Ruth Meinzen-Dick, Behrman, Pandolfelli et al. (2014), is due largely to women's burden of performing their reproductive roles such as child bearing, child rearing, gardening, foraging and other household rigmaroles.

Participation of the rural and Indigenous people in rural development planning, in this study, includes some aspects such as land development, farming or agriculture, livelihood, food and water security, health and nutrition, education, and family planning (Table 17.5). In terms of gender, men have generally high participation in all aspects. The overall mean of 4.56 indicates that men have very high participation in rural development planning in Mindanao. Comparatively, women perceived their participation in the decision-making as very low in land development, farming/agriculture, food and water security, education planning components. The overall mean of 1.59 indicates that women participants in this study perceived their participation in the rural development planning in Mindanao as low or marginal.

*Legend*:

| Scale | Range | Description |
|---|---|---|
| 5 | 4.50–5.00 | Very high |
| 4 | 3.50–4.49 | High |
| 3 | 2.50–3.49 | Moderate |
| 2 | 1.50–2.49 | Low |
| 1 | 1.00–1.49 | Very low |

## Summary and Conclusion

The existing participatory development discourses that focus on 'participation for all' and 'stakeholder's participation' (Cornwall 2003) in rural development planning, privilege men and experts in the actual democratic and political platforms. Gender and development (GAD) approaches in the developing countries like the Philippines still regard 'gender' as a passive problem to be solved rather than as a discourse to be actively participated by both men and women (Eveline and Bacchi 2005) in order to help transform the disadvantaged and disempowered status of women and their dependents.

Giving women voice, choice and agency in the decision-making process in rural development must consider the 'strategic gender needs' of women (Moser 2003) to help them become active partners of men in all political and democratic arenas ranging from personal, household, community, market and state (Kabeer 2003). This means that women must be empowered to perform their agentic role in rural development planning as individuals rather than as a passive cluster of interests and voice that are hitherto constituted in the discourse of men and powerful elite in the society (Bacchi 2000). Women have distinct sets of needs and aspirations that must be decently supported and protected by appropriate policies. The role of the state and the local governments must be to help provide a just social minimum provision of resources that will help build the basic human capabilities of women in order for them to do and to be (Nussbaum 2011; Sen 1999). Providing Indigenous women the chance to be heard of their voice in the decision-making platforms also requires changing the way we provide democratic spaces for them to be part of. By expanding the boundaries of decision-making means that policy-makers (involved) should acknowledge the critical role of women and other disadvantaged groups (affected) (Ulrich 1994) in learning and problem solving together as a human community. The role of listening as an agentic tool to strengthen the capabilities of Indigenous women requires that state and non-state actors, working as outsiders or 'rural development tourists' (Chambers 1997) in Mindanao, must co-learn with the women and other people in the rural communities. By adding listening in the 'sensory democracy' (Dobson 2014), it means that political and democratic projects in rural Mindanao are meant to be dialogic—that the Indigenous women's agentic voice is delivered and heard; and their presence is actually seen.

This chapter makes the case that existing rural development planning processes in Mindanao subjugate and disempower Indigenous women. It presents and analyses the evidence gathered from the fieldwork, namely, that women are made passive and silent participants in the decision-making opportunities for rural development planning that privilege leaders, experts, and men. Their voice, choice and agency as individuals are repressed and underrepresented by undermining their capabilities to enter into the decision-making processes. It is argued that active participation is a fertile capability that must be supported by the state and local governments to allow women and other disadvantaged groups to become part of the whole process of rural development. Moser's framework was used as a tool to analyse gender inequality while Kabeer's social relations approach was used as lens to critique the existing gender inequality in various institutions—household, community, state and market level. This study used qualitative research data collected from the fieldwork in the rural and Indigenous communities of Mindanao in 2013. A total of 105 participants were interviewed through theoretical sampling. This study used participant's observation, key informants interview, and focus group discussions as data gathering tools.

The approach needs to address prevention planning through enhancing opportunities to prepare and voice concerns about safety at home as well as rapid response measures that encompass both technocratic and institutional preparations informed by user-centric approaches to support 'Home safety, Health, Purpose, Connection/belonging (people and place), Self-respect and confidence'. This is undertaken through considering what resources people have, what they need, what they are prepared to add or discard from their lives, turning points for the better and worse in social, economic and environmental terms (see McIntyre-Mills and de Vries 2013; McIntyre-Mills et al. 2008) these are the a posteriori consequences of change and also need to address socio-cultural and political barriers to change and to develop information and resources that are readily accessible to the community. In times of crisis, according to Professor Paul Arbon of the Torrens Resilience Institute at Flinders University, the first people to respond are members of the community. So, developing ways to respond to disaster needs to start with the community by 'expanding the boundaries' (Ulrich 1994, 1996) of participation platforms to include the poorest and the most marginalised members of the local communities. Women must work in close partnership with men to discuss, plan and act on critical issues pertaining to social, economic and environmental vulnerabilities to stress the importance of addressing strategic gender needs (Moser 1989, 2003) of men and women. Social vulnerabilities, characterised in this study as extreme poverty, landlessness, involuntary hunger, physical weakness and isolation confronted by the rural and Indigenous people in Mindanao, particularly women, are worsening as evidences would show in the preceding discussion. These vulnerabilities are complex and interconnected and require reversal by 'putting people first' or by 'putting the last first' (Chambers 1983, 1997) in rural development planning. Gender and Development (GAD) constructs and processes, which rely primarily on 'participation of all' (Cornwall 2003) must be challenged by empowering women and their dependents to actually 'hold half of the sky' (Doss 2014). Women need to be empowered—to be seen and be able to speak, and be listened to 'apophatically' (Waks 2010 cited in Dobson 2014 p. 69). Apopathic listening gives both the listeners (experts and officials) and the speakers (women) the opportunity to share power by setting their biases or preconceived categories aside in order for the voice of both listeners and speakers to come through in its 'authentic' form. For Dobson (2014), this is the essence of sensory and dialogic democracy where power is shared by the appreciation of the viewpoints of people 'involved' in and 'affected' by the area of concern (Ulrich 1994).

Another way to ensure empowered participation of women in rural development planning is to put in place a gender quota for participation in democratic and political decision-making platforms. Agarwal (2010) stresses that at least one-third of women in a political decision-making platform constitute a critical mass for them to gain confidence to engage with men in active dialogue where both speaking and listening can be present. The current participation framework mainly emphasised voice or the speaking aspect. It does not guarantee that the limited voice and choice are indeed being included in the actual policy decisions as rural development experts and local government officials are trapped in their urban/rural biases being 'rural development tourists' (Chambers 1997). In the same vein, women have to be empowered by strengthening their capabilities 'to do and to be' (Nussbaum 2011; Sen 1999) and to engage in democratic and political dialogues dealing with issues regarding their wellbeing. Rural development planning is a social action that requires women's voice, choice and agency. Women must be allocated just and decent social minimum provision of policy support to overcome their current state of passive and instrumental participation (Cornwall 2003; Gaventa and Cornwall 2001) in the political decision-making to help improve their wellbeing and life chances. The Indigenous women, with the rest of other disadvantaged members of the rural and Indigenous households or communities such as young people, elderly, sick, and differently abled persons must be given the chance to represent themselves in higher decision-making platforms, should they find their local governments' and/or tribal councils' decision unsatisfactory and derogatory to their interests as people with full sets of rights and entitlements.

## References

Agarwal B (1994) A field of one's own: gender and land rights in South Asia. Cambridge University Press, Cambridge [England]; New York, NY, USA: Cambridge England; New York, NY, USA

Agarwal B (2001) Participatory exclusions, community forestry, and gender: an analysis for South Asia and a conceptual framework. World Dev 29(10):1623–1648

Agarwal B (2010) Gender and green governance: the political economy of women's presence within and beyond community forestry. Oxford University Press, New Delhi

Ashby WR (1956) Introduction to cybernetics. Chapman & Hall

Bacchi C (2000) Policy as Discourse: what does it mean? where does it get us? Discourse: Stud Cult Polit Educ 21(1):45–57. http://www.tandfonline.com.ezproxy.flinders.edu.au/doi/pdf/10.1080/01596300050005493

Bacchi C (2004) Policy and discourse: challenging the construction of affirmative action as preferential treatment. J Eur Public Policy 11(1):128–146

Bacchi C (2010) Policy and discourse: challenging the construction of affirmative action as preferential treatment. J Eur Public Policy 11(1):128–146. doi:10.1080/1350176042000164334

Besra L (2014) A critical review of democracy and governance challenges in Bangladesh with special reference to a human rights-based approach for the development of marginalised communities including indigenous people, women and children. PhD Social Sciences, Flinders University, Adelaide, South Australia

Bird Rose D, Commission Australian Heritage (1996) Nourishing terrains: Australian Aboriginal views of landscape and wilderness. Australian Heritage Commission, Caberra

Carspecken, P. F. (1995). Critical ethnography in educational research: a theoretical and practical guide. New York: New York: Routledge

Chambers R (1983) Rural development: putting the last first. Longman, New York

Chambers R (1995) Poverty and livelihoods: whose reality counts? Environ Urban 7(1):173–204

Chambers R (1997) Whose reality counts? Putting the first last. Intermediate Technology Publications, London

Christakis A (2004) Wisdom of the people. Syst Res Behav Sci 21(5):479–488

Christakis A, Bausch K (2006) How people harness their collective wisdom and power to construct the future in co-laboratories of democracy. USA Information Age Publishing, Inc

Christakis A, Harris L (2004) Designing a transnational indigenous leaders interaction in the context of globalization: a wisdom of the people forum. Syst Res Behav Sci 21(3):251–259. doi:10.1002/sres.619

Cornwall A (2003) Whose voices? Whose choices? Reflections on gender and participatory development. World Dev 31(8):1325–1342. doi:10.1016/S0305-750X(03)00086-X

Cornwall A (2004) Introduction: new democratic spaces? The Politics and Dynamics of Institutionalised Participation. Retrieved from London

Cram F, Chilisa B, Mertens D (2013) The journey begins. In Mertens D, Cram F, Chilisa B (eds) Indigenous pathways into social research. Left Coast Press, pp 11–40

Crehan K (1992a) Rural households: making a living. In Bernstein H, Crow B, Jonhson H (eds) Rural livelihoods: crises and responses. Oxford University Press, pp 87–112

Crehan K (1992b) Rural Households: Survival and Change. In: Bernstein H, Crow B, Jonhson H (eds) Rural livelihoods: crises and responses. Oxford University Press, United Kingdom, pp 113–135

Creswell JW (2007) Qualitative inquiry and research design: choosing among five approaches, 2nd edn. Sage Publications, Inc, US

Dobson A (2014) Listening for democracy: Recognition, representation, reconciliation

Doss C (2014) If women hold up half the sky, how much of the world's food do they produce? In: Quisumbing AR, Meinzen-Dick R, Raney TL, Croppenstedt A, Behrman JA, Peterman A (eds) Gender in agriculture: closing the knowledge gap. The Food and Agriculture Organization of the United Nations and Springer Science + Business Media B.V, Dordrecht, pp 69–90

Eveline J, Bacchi C (2005) What are we mainstreaming when we mainstream gender? Int Feminist J Polit 7(4):496–512. doi:10.1080/14616740500284417

Fiske AP (1992) The four elementary forms of sociality: framework for a unified theory of social relations. Psychol Rev 99(4):689–723

Flood R, Romm N (1996) Diversity Management. In: Flood R, Romm N (eds) Critical Systems thinking. Springer, US, pp 81–92

Foucault M (1975) Discipline and Punish: the birth of the prison. Vintage Books, New York

Gaventa J (2006) Finding the spaces for change: a power analysis. IDS Bull 37(6):23–33. http://www.powercube.net/wp-content/uploads/2009/12/finding_spaces_for_change.pdf

Gaventa J, Cornwall A (2001) Power and knowledge. Sage Publications Ltd, London

Girardet H (2015) Sustainability is unhelpful: we need to think about regeneration. Retrieved from http://www.theguardian.com/sustainable-business/blog/sustainability-unhelpful-think-regeneration

Gonzales C (2006) Markets, monocultures, and malnutrition: agricultural trade policy through and environmental justice lens. J Int Law 14(2–3):345–382

Gutierrez E, Borras S (2004) The Moro conflict: landlessness and misdirected state policies

Harris J (2014) Gender implications of poor nutrition and health in agricultural households. In: Quisumbing AR, Meinzen-Dick R, Raney TL, Croppenstedt A, Behrman JA, Peterman A (eds) The gender asset gap and its implications for agricultural and rural development. The Food and Agriculture Organization of the United Nations and Springer Science + Business Media B.V, Dordrecht

Jenson J (1997) Competing representations: the politics of abortion in Canada. In: ndrew C, Rodgers S (eds) Women and the Canadian State. McGill–Queen's University Press, Montreal
Juster FT, Stafford FP (1991) The allocation of time: empirical findings, behavioral models, and problems of measurement. J Econ Lit 29(4):471–522
Kabeer N (1999) The conditions and consequences of choice: reflections on the measurement of womenís empowerment. http://www.unrisd.org/80256B3C005BCCF9/(httpAuxPages)/31EEF181BEC398A380256B67005B720A/$file/dp108.pdf
Kabeer N (2003) Gender mainstreaming in poverty eradication and the millennium development goals: a handbook for policy-makers and other stakeholders. Commonwealth Secretariat: International Development Research Centre, London
Kabeer N (2005) Gender equality and women's empowerment: A critical analysis of the third millennium development goal 1. Gend Dev 13(1):13–24. doi:10.1080/13552070512331332273
Kiriti T, Tisdell C (2002) Gender, marital status, farm size and other factors influencing the extent of cash cropping in Kenya: a case study. Retrieved from Australia: http://www.uq.edu.au/rsmg/docs/ClemWPapers/SEPD/WP 26.pdf
Madison, D. S. (2005). Critical ethnography: method, ethics, and performance. Thousand Oaks, Calif.: Thousand Oaks, Calif.: Sage
March C, Smyth I, Mukhopadhyay M (2005) A guide to gender analysis frameworks. Oxfam, UK
McIntyre J (2002) Critical systemic praxis for social and environmental justice: a case study of management, governance, and policy. Syst Pract Action Res 15(1):3–35. doi:10.1023/A:1014237603948
McIntyre J (2005) Part 1: working and re-working the conceptual and geographical boundaries of governance and international relations. Syst Pract Action Res 18(2):173–220. doi:10.1007/s11213-005-4157-6
McIntyre-Mills J (2006) Systemic governance and accountability working and re-working the conceptual and spatial boundaries, vol 3. Springer, Dordrecht
McIntyre-Mills J (2008) User-centric policy design to address complex needs. Nova Science Publishers, Inc, New York
McIntyre-Mills J (2014a) From wall street to wellbeing: joining up the dots through participatory democracy and governance to mitigate the causes and adapt to the effects of climate change. Springer, Boston
McIntyre-Mills J (2014b) Systemic ethics and non-anthropocentric stewardship: implications for transdisciplinarity and cosmopolitan politics. Springer, Cham
McIntyre-Mills J, de Vries D (2013) Part 2: transformation from wall street to well-being. Syst Res Behav Sci 30(4):444–469. doi:10.1002/sres.2133
McIntyre-Mills J, De Vries D, Deakin J (2008) Participatory democracy based on user-centric policy design to address complex needs. In: Kane L, Poweller M (eds) Citizenship in the 21st century. Nova Science, New York, pp 1–54
McIntyre-Mills J, Goff S, Hillier D (2011) Systemic action research: a strategy for whole system change. Educ Action Res 19(2):245–251. doi:10.1080/09650792.2011.569137
McMichael P (2008) Development and social change: a global perspective, 4th edn. Pine Forge Press, Los Angeles
Meinzen-Dick R, Behrman JA, Pandolfelli L, Peterman A, Quisumbing AR (2014a) Gender and social capital for agricultural development. In: Quisumbing AR, Meinzen-Dick R, Raney TL, Croppenstedt A, Behrman JA, Peterman A (eds) Closing the knowledge gap on gender in agriculture. The Food and Agriculture Organization of the United Nations and Springer Science + Business Media B.V, Dordrecht, pp 235–266
Meinzen-Dick R, Johnson N, Quisumbing AR, Njuki J, Behrman JA, Rubin D, Waithanji E (2014b) The gender asset gap and its implications for agricultural and rural development. In: Quisumbing AR, Meinzen-Dick R, Raney TL, Croppenstedt A, Behrman JA, Peterman A (eds) Gender in agriculture: closing the knowledge gap. The Food and Agriculture Organization of the United Nations and Springer Science + Business Media B.V, Dordrecht, pp 91–116

Meinzen-Dick R, Quisumbing AR, Behrman JA (2014c) A system that delivers: integrating gender into agricultural research, development, and extension. In: Quisumbing AR, Meinzen-Dick R, Raney TL, Croppenstedt A, Behrman JA, Peterman A (eds) The gender asset gap and its implications for agricultural and rural development. The Food and Agriculture Organization of the United Nations and Springer Science + Business Media B.V, Dordrecht

Midgley G (1997) Dealing with coercion: critical systems heuristics and beyond. Systems Practice 10(1):37–57

Midgley G (2000) Systemic intervention: philosophy, methodology, and practice. Kluwer Academic/Plenum, New York

Moser C (1989) Gender planning in the third world: meeting practical and strategic gender needs. World Dev 17(11):1799–1825. doi:10.1016/0305-750X(89)90201-5

Moser, C. (2003). Gender Planning and Development: Theory, Practice and Training. Retrieved from http://www.eblib.com

Nussbaum MC (2011) Creating capabilities: the human development approach. The Belknap Press of Harvard University Press, London

Okwa O (2007) Tropical parasitic diseases and women. Ann Afr Med 6(4):157–163

Panhwar F (2001) Trade and hunger: the impact of trade liberalisation on small farmers. Leisa Magazine

Philippine Statistics Authority (2014) PSA: poverty incidence among Filipinos registered at 24.9% as of first semester of 2013. Official Gazette. http://www.gov.ph/2014/04/29/psa-poverty-incidence-among-filipinos-registered-at-24-9-as-of-first-semester-of-2013/

Pieterse JN (2001) Participatory democratization reconceived. Futures 33(5):407–422. http://www.sciencedirect.com.ezproxy.flinders.edu.au/science/article/pii/S0016328700000835

Quisumbing AR, Meinzen-Dick R, Raney TL, Croppenstedt A, Behrman JA, Peterman A (2014) Closing the knowledge gap on gender in agriculture. In Quisumbing AR, Meinzen-Dick R, Raney TL, Croppenstedt A, Behrman JA, Peterman A (eds) The gender asset gap and its implications for agricultural and rural development. The Food and Agriculture Organization of the United Nations and Springer Science + Business Media B.V, Dordrecht, pp 3–30

Schneider M, McMichael P (2010) Deepening, and repairing, the metabolic rift. J Peasant Stud 37 (3):461–484. doi:10.1080/03066150.2010.494371

Scott JC (1998) Seeing like a state: how certain schemes to improve the human condition have failed. Yale University Press, New Haven and London

Sen A (1999) Development as freedom. Knopf, New York

Shepherd B (2011) Redefining food security in the face of foreign land investors: The Philippine Case, NTS-Asia Research Paper No. 6. http://www.rsis.edu.sg/wp-content/uploads/rsis-pubs/NTS/HTML-Newsletter/Report/pdf/NTS-Asia_Ben_Shepherd.pdf, http://www.rsis.edu.sg/wp-content/uploads/rsis-pubs/NTS/HTML-Newsletter/Report/pdf/NTS-Asia_Ben_Shepherd.pdf

Shiva V (1988) Staying alive: women, ecology, and development. Zed Books, London

Shiva V (1993) Monocultures of the mind: perspectives on biodiversity and biotechnology. Zed Books, London

Shiva V (2001) The real reasons for hunger

Sison JC (2014) Right to life. The Philippine Star. http://www.philstar.com/opinion/2014/01/31/1284979/right-life

Thomas J (1993) Doing critical ethnography. Sage Publications, Newbury Park, CA

Ulrich W (1994) Critical heuristics of social planning: a new approach to practical philosophy. Wiley, Chichester; New York

Ulrich W (1996) Critical systems thinking for citizens. In: Flood R, Romm NA (eds) Critical Systems thinking. Springer, US, pp 165–178

United Nations Standing Committee on Nutrition (1990) Women and nutrition. Nutrition policy discussion paper no. 6

VeneKlasen L, Miller V (2002) Power and empowerment. PLA Notes 43:39–41

Walker P (2013) Research relationship with humans, the spirit world, and the natural world. In Mertens D, Cram F, Chilisa B (eds) Indigenous pathways into social research. Left Coast Press, pp 299–316

Wolff J, De-Shalit A (2013) On fertile functionings: a response to Martha Nussbaum. J Hum Dev Capabil: Multi-Discipl J People-Center Dev 14(1):161–165. doi:10.1080/19452829.2013.762177

World Bank (2001) Engendering development through gender equality in rights, resources, and voice, Washington, DC

World Health Organization (2015) Philippines: WHO statistical profile. http://www.who.int/gho/countries/phl.pdf

## Author Biographies

**Dr. Mervin Gascon** is an Associate Professor at the College of Development Management and concurrently the University Director of the Extension Division of the University of Southeastern Philippines. Dr. Gascon holds a PhD from Flinders University of South Australia under the Australia Development Awards. His research and publication focus on the application of critical systemic thinking and participatory action planning in democracy, governance and development studies.

**Janet McIntyre-Mills** is an Associate Professor in the School of Social and Policy Studies at Flinders University, Adjunct Professor at the University of Indonesia and Islamic National University in Indonesia, and Honorary Professor at the University of South Africa. Her research focuses on systemic representation, accountability and re-generation applied to social and environmental justice concerns such as health, housing and social inclusion and the mitigation and adaptation to climate change. She addresses complex needs by exploring the meanings and 'what if' questions with diverse stakeholders.

Her recent books include 'From Wall Street to Wellbeing: Joining up the dots through Participatory Democracy and Governance to Mitigate the Causes and Adapt to the Effects of Climate Change'. ISBN 978-1-4899-7465-5 and 'Systemic ethics and Non-anthropocentric Stewardship: Implications for Trans disciplinarity and Cosmopolitan politics', ISBN 978-3-519-07655-3.

# Chapter 18
# Supporting Indigenous Environmental Health Action: A Vignette

**Jeff Foote, Maria Hepi, M. Rogers-Koroheke and Hone Taimona**

**Abstract** While most New Zealanders take safe drinking water for granted, rural communities can lack access to safe drinking water placing them at increased risk of waterborne illnesses. Many these rural communities lack the finance or technical expertise needed to improve drinking water quality. This vignette details the findings from a cross-cultural collaborative evaluation of a central government pilot to improve drinking quality in a Māori (indigenous people of New Zealand) community.

## Introduction

The evaluation was based in the Hokianga, an isolated region in New Zealand which suffers from 'multiple disadvantage' including high levels of unemployment and substandard housing. The evaluation was done in partnership between the Institute of Environmental Science and Research, Hokianga Health Enterprise Trust (HHET) and the Whirinaki Māori Committee (WMC). Our evaluation focuses on Whirinaki community water supply and highlights the ways in which the WMC leveraged the pilot to develop solutions to pressing problems beyond the provision of safe drinking water.

J. Foote (✉) · M. Hepi
Institute of Environmental Science and Research, Christchurch, New Zealand
e-mail: Jeff.Foote@esr.cri.nz

J. Foote
School of Health Sciences, University of Canterbury, Christchurch, New Zealand

M. Rogers-Koroheke · H. Taimona
Hokianga Health Enterprise Trust, Rawene, New Zealand
e-mail: marara.rogers@hokiangahealth.org.nz

H. Taimona
e-mail: hone.taimona@hokiangahealth.org.nz



J. McIntyre-Mills et al. (eds.), *Balancing Individualism and Collectivism*,
Contemporary Systems Thinking, DOI 10.1007/978-3-319-58014-2_18

## *Ngā Puna Wai (Safe Drinking Water) o Hokianga Pilot*

The pilot is Ngā Puna Wai o Hokianga (safe drinking water) which was developed by the Ministry of Health (MoH) following the 1999 Hokianga floods and ongoing concerns about marae[1] drinking water safety. The pilot has focused on improving marae drinking water supplies given the central role that marae play in community life and also the potential for tangi (funerals), weddings and hui (meetings) to expose a large number of people to waterborne illnesses. Key aspects of the pilot included a multi-agency approach, devolution of central government funding ($\sim$NZ $1.5 million) and active participation of the community. The pilot ran from 2000 to 2002 resulting in improvements to 36 marae and two community drinking water supplies.

Given that the community was likely to be suspicious of MoH interest in their drinking water supplies, central government funding was devolved to Hokianga Health Enterprise Trust (HHET) (a community owned and governed health service) given its established relationships with hapū (sub-tribes). HHET recruited two local kaiwhakakōkiri (negotiators) with knowledge about tikanga (Māori customs), te reo Māori (Māori language), and whakapapa (history/relationships) to consult with hapū. The kaiwhakakōkiri utilised a kaupapa Māori consultation process (following cultural protocols) and worked with two engineering companies responsible for designing appropriate water treatment solutions. The Northland District Health Board (a regional public health service) provided technical assistance to HHET given the local health service had little experience dealing with drinking water quality issues and clinical staff were sceptical about the promised health gain from clean drinking water.

In recognition that concerns about microbiological contamination of drinking water was a central government priority, the kaiwhakakōkiri facilitated two major hui to introduce the pilot and determine which hapū would be interested in participating. Further consultation hui were held to determine what form of treatment would be culturally appropriate.

## Collaborative Cross Cultural Evaluation

Our evaluation followed a cross-cultural collaborative model and is reported in detail elsewhere by Foote et al. (2005) and Hepi et al. (2007). The evaluation design drew on kaupapa Māori and systems thinking methods including undertaking data collection and analysis kanohi ki te kanohi (face-to-face) and using rich pictures (Checkland 1981) to develop evaluation questions (Fig. 18.1). In total, 26 in-depth

---

[1]A marae is the focal area of a Māori village and consists of a large meeting house, dining area and ablution block.

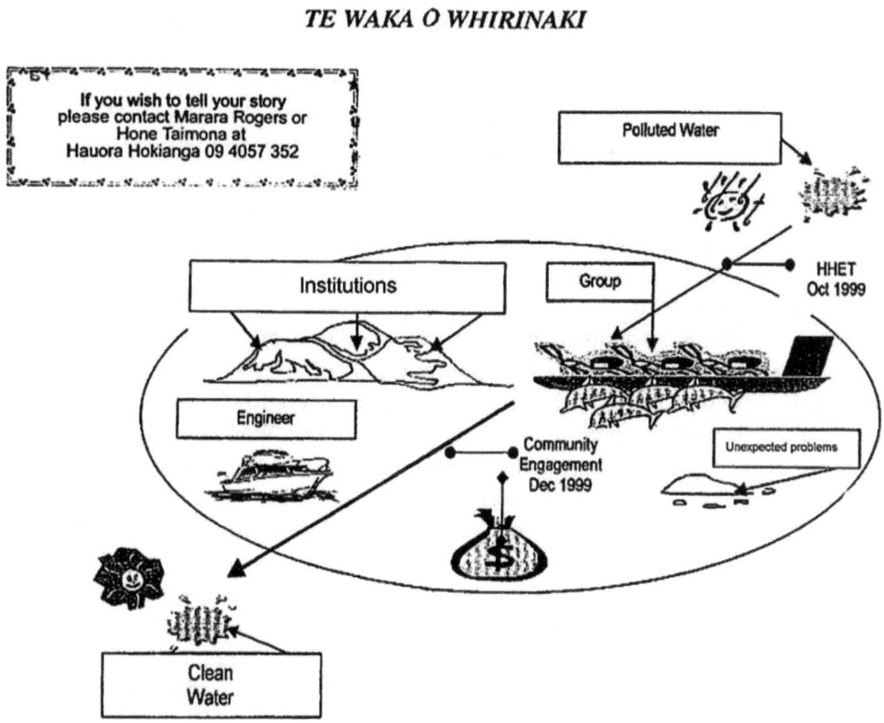


**Fig. 18.1** 'Te Waka o Whirinaki', a visual representation of the journey undertaken by the WMC from a state of polluted water to clean water, and how the community had negotiated various icebergs (unexpected problems) and identified taniwha (supportive individuals and organisations)

interviews were undertaken with key individuals and organisational representatives from local government, the health sector, engineering companies, hapū and marae committees (between 2002 and 2003). Interviews lasted between 45 min to three hours, were audio recorded for later transcription and thematic analysis.

## Evaluation Findings

A key aim of Ngā Puna Wai o Hokianga was to determine how isolated rural communities might be involved in improving drinking water supplies, and whether it was possible for the MoH to extend the pilot to other parts of New Zealand. The 1999 Hokianga floods drew attention to the failure of existing institutional arrangements under the Health Act, 1956 and Local Government Act, 1974 to ensure safe drinking water exacerbated by the 'hollowing out' effects of the public sector reforms from the 1980s. The pilot was conceived by the MoH and developed in consultation with the Northland District Health Board, and HHET. Despite a legislative responsibility to provide safe drinking water, the Far North District Council was not involved given its then poor relationship with Hokianga hapū.

HHET was tasked with implementing the pilot and consulted with Hokianga hapū about their participation in the pilot.

Initially the Whirinaki community[2] was unsure about its participation in Ngā Puna Wai o Hokianga. Some kaumātua (elders) felt insulted by the MoH claim that the community's drinking water was contaminated. However, after much discussion, the Whirinaki community agreed to participate in the pilot for those who might lack immunity to any pathogens in the drinking water. The community was undecided on whether the water supply should be marae or community-based. While other hapū had tentatively agreed to proceed with the community water supply option, the WMC instead engaged in planning, examined the implications of different water supply options, and learnt from other hapū experiences.

A decision to proceed with a community water supply was seen by the WMC as an opportunity to generate work for community members who would be involved in the construction of the community water supply. The WMC asked the HHET's Chief Executive Officer whether the community could become the main contractor and undertake the construction work for the community drinking water supply. MoH funding was then 'devolved' to the WMC and also brokered additional funding to supplement the MoH funding. HHET's decision to allow the WMC to be the main contractor was consistent with its guiding principle of subsidiarity where authority and self-determination belongs to the community, rested on an explicit recognition of the community's competence to manage a complex project.

The WMC involvement as the main contractor resulted in design improvements, enabled engineering specifications to be tailored to local conditions and outcomes that went beyond the provision of safe drinking water. A notable design improvement was a hydropower system that eliminates the need for mains power and considerably reduces operational costs. The WMC also developed a track record as a contractor which has allowed it to undertake future projects as a way to bring work into the community where employment opportunities are sparse.

While the WMC was confident in its ability to complete the drinking water supply construction, this supplementary funding was 'frozen' until certain conditions could be met. These included gaining appropriate resource consents and property easements as well as proving to the funder that sufficient funds existed to complete the project. Other obstacles included a requirement from Transit New Zealand that the community pay a substantial bond before pipe laying could commerce on the State Highway, inaccurate costing provided by the engineering companies, a time limit on when the MoH funding would have to be used by all placed the community project at risk. Unlike other contractors, the WMC could run

---

[2]Whirinaki is a small settlement of approximately 200 people on the southern side of the Hokianga harbour near Opononi, and is home to Te Hikutu hapū. At time of Ngā Puna Wai o Hokianga, the community consisted of over 60 houses, a kohanga reo, a kura kaupapa Māori school, a sports complex and three marae. Whirinaki was badly affected by the 1999 Hokianga floods with 13 houses damaged. Prior to Ngā Puna Wai o Hokianga, the community was serviced by untreated individual water systems. Whirinaki is notable for the extent to which the community was involved in the design and construction of its community water supply.

the project on a ‘smell of an oily rag’ thereby keeping the project solvent. The WMC showed considerable initiative ringing around suppliers to get the best deals, borrowing material and equipment, ‘jiggling’ project budgets to minimise the impact of funding shortfall, and ensuring that the community would not be left with debt if the project failed.

These external obstacles highlight two issues associated with community involvement and control. First, without a track record in completing complex projects the community faced a credibility issue when negotiating with external organisations which had then to be addressed somehow. Credibility issues were managed through negotiation with external organisations kanohi ki te kanohi (face-to-face) and HHET’s continued involvement until the WMC had fully established relationships with external organisations. For example, Transit New Zealand allowed the WMC to lay pipes on the state highway subject to paying a $10,000 bond, but then had difficulties in processing the required bond because this was the first time a community organisation had applied to undertake work on a state highway. Second, while an obstacle such as the Transit New Zealand bond created delays and stressed the project budget, it was seen as an unnecessary government imposition on the community especially since the state highway passed through land traditionally owned by the local hapū.

The success of the Whirinaki community water supply demonstrates benefits of community involvement and control, but also importance of strong community identify, dedicated group of skilled individuals who with the support from kaumātua were prepared to work through problems with external organisations.

## Key Lessons for Indigenous Environmental Health Action

*Community control*: Since the signing of the Treaty of Waitangi in 1840, Māori mistrust of the Crown and central government agencies has resulted from numerous breaches of the Treaty. The MoH recognised early on that the pilot would not be successful if central government drove the pilot. HHET who had a positive relationship with local Māori were tasked with implementation giving the pilot a locally trusted face.

*Local knowledge*: HHET has an established relationship with their community and understood hapū interests, values and needs. A ‘top down’ approach based on government regulation and professional expertise was unlikely to be successful. Two kaiwhakakōkiri, who were respected members from the marae areas acted as a broker between HHET, hapū and the engineering companies. HHET also subcontracted engineers who could demonstrate that they were able to work constructively with hapū. The engineering companies understood they would be working in a different cultural context and different processes not utilised in other engineering projects such as extensive consultation would be involved.

*Papakāinga (Māori village or communal land) autonomy*: Local knowledge enabled HHET's CEO to say 'yes' when WMC requested that they take on the contract to design and build their community water supply. HHET's CEO held that for the pilot to be successful the work had to be completed, for this reason, if the WMC wanted to undertake the management contract for their own community water supply then they should be able to, this acknowledged their autonomy over their papakāinga. If their autonomy had not been acknowledged, there would have been a chance the community would not cooperate fully with outside contractors and hence the work would not be completed and the community water supply would not have been successful. The acknowledgement of self-determination for Māori by hapū participating in the design and the control in the consultation process of pilot was an overall critical factor to the pilot being a success.

*Culturally reframing public health interventions*: Hokianga hapū were initially unsure about the pilot. They did not agree that water treatment was needed, and some community leaders felt that the claim their water was polluted was a slight on their mana (status). However, the kaiwhakakōkiri drew on the cultural practice of manaakitanga (looking after each other, especially guests) to highlight the responsibility that hapū had to ensure that manuhiri (guests) and whānau (extended family) and mokopuna (grandchildren) visiting from the cities would not fall ill. Kaiwhakakōkiri reframed the pilot by asking 'why is the river polluted?' drawing attention to the importance of kaitiakitanga (stewardship over the environment). As access to a clean and healthy environment is critical to hapū well-being, this framing better resonated with hapū and was instrumental in securing their ongoing participation in the pilot.

**Acknowledgements** We would like to acknowledge our Whirinaki Māori Committee co-researchers, and the Whirinaki community for allowing us to undertake this evaluation. We also thank everyone who agreed to be interviewed and generously shared their insights. Finally, we acknowledge the financial support provided by the Foundation for Research, Science and Technology.

## References

Checkland P (1981) Systems thinking, systems practice. Wiley, Chichester 1981

Foote J, Hepi M, Rogers-Koroheke M, Taimona H (2005) Urban water decision making project: learning from the Stories of Ngā Puna Wai o Hokianga. Institute of Environmental Science and Research, Christchurch

Hepi M, Foote J, Marino M, Rogers M, Taimona H (2007) Koe wai hoki koe?! Or who are you?! Issues of trust in cross-cultural collaborative research. Kotuitui. New Zealand J Soc Sci 2 (2):37–53

## Author Biographies

**Jeff Foote** is a Science Leader, Institute of Environmental Science and Research. His research centres on applying systems approaches to complex public policy issues including freshwater management, family violence prevention and non-communicable diseases. His research interests include systems methodology, complex change and involving the 'hard to reach' in service design and delivery. Jeff holds postgraduate qualifications in management systems and public health.

**Maria Hepi** holds a Masters in Māori and is a social scientist for the Social Systems group at the Institute of Environmental Science and Research. She specialises in bi-cultural research and applies social science methods to expand the understanding of representatives from mainstream organizations past their own worldview to include an understanding of how Māori may address the same issue. She undertakes research with communities, hapū, industry, local and central government, and other agencies to address challenging or intractable problems that involve high levels of complexity and uncertainty.

**Rogers-Koroheke, M.** is a project manager at Hokianga Health Enterprise Trust. Experienced in participatory action and kaupapa Māori research, Marara has developed a Māori community model of engagement to improve marae-based assets including sewage treatment and disposal, and community water lines. Marara holds a Postgraduate Diploma in Māori Health.

**Taimona, H.** is a project manager at Hokianga Health Enterprise Trust. He is experienced in culturally appropriate research processes, and has been instrumental in assisting marae and hapū to further their aspirations for safe drinking water and sanitation. Hone is a strong advocate for the health of the Hokianga people.

# Chapter 19
# Precarious Liaisons: Gender, Moral Authority and Marriage in Colonial Kenya

**Clare Buswell and Yvonne Corcoran-Nantes**

**Abstract** The concept of moral authority facilitates a deeper understanding of the fluid interconnections that exist between what are seemingly separate spheres of women's lives. Moral authority highlights the way in which agency, power, culture and meaning impact on the daily experience of life. This article examines the gendered notions of moral authority that protect women's political spaces and identity within the context of marriage in Colonial Kenya. For women under colonial rule in Kenya, the use of moral authority provided not only a sense of personal power but a method of confronting powerful menfolk and undermining the colonial regime. In exploiting the implied power of moral authority that came from being a wife, or a mother, or via links with the spirit world, women confronted those who encroached on their rights and livelihoods. The colonial experience tested women's survival instincts and the capacity to challenge the injustice that would serve to undermine their socio-economic status in a colonised nation, and most importantly, reshape personal and social relations within their ethnic community.

## Introduction

Clearly, it is important to examine the history of gender relations in Kenya's colonial era in view of the fact that the lived experience of women and men differ widely. Here we unpack the gender division of labour enshrined within agricultural practice of culturally distinct Kenyan farming systems. This article will focus on the Kikuyu, Kenya's largest ethnic group, in view of the precipitous socio-economic change that they experienced under colonial rule with regards to land ownership, agricultural practices and incorporation into the wage labour economy. Moreover, it

C. Buswell (✉) · Y. Corcoran-Nantes
Flinders University, Bedford Park, Australia
e-mail: Clare.Buswell@flinders.edu.au

Y. Corcoran-Nantes
e-mail: Yvonne.Corcoran-Nantes@flinders.edu.au



J. McIntyre-Mills et al. (eds.), *Balancing Individualism and Collectivism*,
Contemporary Systems Thinking, DOI 10.1007/978-3-319-58014-2_19

was the men and women of the Kikuyu, the most politically organised ethnic group, which offered the greatest threat to the colonial authority and as such suffered an unprecedented, targeted assault on its social organisation and culture (See Anderson 2005; Elkins 2005).

A focus on gender relations is pivotal to an understanding of change in this context. They define male and female behaviour and highlight how access to resources such as food, crops and land, and social class is contingent upon being male or female, married, or revered as an important female or male elder. By examining the historical context of gender relations we are able to analyse a gendered moral authority which acts as an empowering agent interconnecting relational positions, social standing and place. Moral authority, as an effective power, is directly related to an individual's legal status and position within the family, the workplace and the community. Its fluidity is relational, continuously renegotiated and linked to reputation, which, over time, can be reaffirmed, destroyed and rebuilt (Moore 1992: 38). Moreover, moral authority acts as an empowering agent; it empowers those who dispense justice within communities.

In this article we will examine how the power which arises from one's identity is exercised and maintained. Can moral authority and its connections with identity politics promote women's ability to provide a livelihood, enhance security and exercise agency? Or does the use of moral authority further entrench cultural norms, which may work to the detriment of women? These two positions, of course, are not mutually exclusive but serve to influence the expressions of women's power in both the colonial period and present day Kenya. This article examines how women utilised the gendered expressions of moral authority to directly locate their experience of colonial rule in the public domain. An experience that emanated from the politics of everyday life, the essence of women's instincts of survival and the capacity to challenge the injustice that would serve to undermine their socio-economic status in a colonised nation and, most importantly, within the personal and social relations of their community.

Women's resistance to the colonial regimes that ruled over different parts of the African continent often found a direct outlet within the constructs and responsibilities of marriage. In Kenya, as elsewhere in colonial Africa, when Kikuyu men went away to labour on European farms and plantations or were recruited into administrative positions, it was women who were left to undertake two sets of responsibilities: their own and those of their husbands. This is the context in which the reciprocal rights and obligations required within marriage broke down. These changing circumstances within the household economy provided women with opportunities to engage in activities through which they would establish lives largely independent of male control. Moreover, this brought into sharp relief the issue of what constituted marriage, the expectations associated with it and, in particular, the complexity of women's status in relation to that of men. Whilst men became the negotiating agents with colonial administrators as they dealt with the pressures of the colonial administration, they depended on their womenfolk to hold households and farms together. Daughters, widows and wives emerged as the link between the machinations of land entitlements of the past, based on marriage alliances, usufruct and patronage (and the concomitant understandings of male status, lineage and clan stability) and their now de facto position as household heads without male control. The colonial regime engaged in a process of collusion with chiefs, headmen and important indigenous political players in order to keep the peace and help establish British control and rule of law (Coplan 2001: 188). Meanwhile, women, in taking charge of households and their husband's land, began challenging the moral authority which underpinned accepted constructions of gender and gender relations that had effectively disempowered them socially, economically and politically.

## A Gendered Pathway to Moral Authority

The perspective from which this article is developed derives from E P Thompson's notion of a moral economy originating from the pursuit or realisations of justice through sociopolitical action. Thompson writes about the 'power and complexity' of this form of popular politics, just as the reciprocal relations and the notion of rights and obligations between the empowered elites and a disempowered working poor broke down at the height of the industrial revolution in the nineteenth century (Thompson 1971: 136). Here we employ the basic ethics of a moral economy to inform the development of a notion of moral authority among a disempowered sector of society, in this case women, and more specifically in the cultural context of Kikuyu society. Here moral authority is manifested within heterogeneous, social contexts and in complex cultural practices. The exercise of moral authority is not a given, nor in many cases recognised, thus the claim to moral authority by women through political means, such as forms of resistance and individual and collective 'imposition', becomes an act of empowerment via public acts winning recognition for claims that are gender specific and that not only call for but enact, gender justice.

Moral authority is, above all things, a sociocultural right that comes from experience rather than from a 'claim to know'. Understandings of moral authority within communities arise from a sense of solidarity brought about by common experiences: sharing resources, or experiences of war, or by rituals: initiation ceremonies, storytelling and by building alliances: within and across families via marriage for example. Stoll argues

> Any social group with a distinct sense of morality… produces ritual exchange… [In that]… ritual produces… solidarity, credibility and in a political context, political capital (2013, 35).

The power of moral authority is found in a seemingly unspoken consensus about its origins and use. For example, for Kikuyu women the use of sexual cursing was a most powerful tool, used to gain what was rightfully theirs, to bring men into line and express moral outrage. Sexual cursing has a long history in eastern Africa and was most especially feared by men because it exposed women's real power as each symbolic act of defiance could remove his acquired rights, status and respect as a man (Ardener 1973: 422–440). This example highlights that notions of right and power were clearly understood by all in a patriarchal society, within which power was controlled by male age-grade structures and between male elders of families and ethnic groups.

In this context, the concept of moral authority goes further than that of Thompson, in that it encompasses more than justice: that is, of right and wrong with associated retribution and restoration.[1] It is a statement about power. In colonial Kenya, women using moral authority as a basis for action brought into stark relief the relationship between the power of women's livelihoods over community survival and men's patriarchal power as experienced in their making and enforcing customary law. Both types of authority were seriously challenged by the newly forming political economy of British imperialism. Despite this, both women and men knew that the origins of women's resistance and actions lay not only in notions of right and wrong, but also in the need to maintain the domination of a moral high ground that ensured fertility in all its forms.

Understandings and experiences of what constituted marriage in particular highlighted the gendered power of moral authority. Allman (1996) in examining colonial Asante marriage disputes that appeared before the courts, found that it was the women that had very strong notions of what constitutes a marriage:

> [women] maintained that a husband's exclusive sexual rights [with] his wife were contingent upon his provision of subsistence support' (202–4).

Thus, when husbands were able to guarantee a wife's basic maintenance, that is the first clearing of new land, a hut and personal clothing, then a marriage was viewed by women to have some value. However, during the colonial period Kenyan men were increasingly absent for extended periods of time, labouring on plantations and settler farms for low wages unable to meet their obligations. Meanwhile, rural Kikuyu women faced increasingly burdensome agricultural workloads and personal abandonment in marriages as absent husbands failed to provide what was expected of them (Clayton and Savage 1974: 148, Fearn 1961: 52).

In an effort to deal with these pressures, both married and unmarried women took up trading, joined Christian churches or left their homes. Consequently, women were routinely rounded up by the colonial authorities, arrested, sentenced to prison, or sent back to their villages because their actions threatened male notions of what constituted acceptable female behaviour. According to Peterson, Kenyan men, for their part, 'worried that wives maddened with money would sap a husband's virility with sorcery' (Peterson 2001: 476). Therefore, it 'made sense to be careful of women who traded with cash because such women were known as harlots'.[2]

---

[1]We would like to thank the research librarians at Rhodes House, Oxford and the Seerley library, Cambridge University for their generous help and invaluable knowledge of the colonial record collections which form the basis of this paper. We would also like to thank the Centre for Development Studies at Flinders University, South Australia for providing a grant to undertake this research.

[2]Peterson 2001 p. 476. He cites the case of Duncan Thinji who in 1940 complained to the church that his wife, a trader, had caused him to become sexually impotent. He called a witch doctor who determined that his wife was not at fault. (See Heyer 2005)

(Peterson 2001: 476). Conversely, women condemned wage-earning men that were unable to fulfil marital duties, and those who wasted household resources on cigarettes and beer, as impotent (Peterson 2001: 483). Salvation came through Christianity which offered a way out of a life of impotency and marital strife by providing discipline, salvation and god. Moreover, women and men who joined the Missions sought a climate of certainty to ameliorate the moral and social chaos created by land loss, wage employment and the 'evils of urban life' (Peterson 2001: 470–2).

Since independence in both Kenya and the wider African context, with men working in cities and women involved with trade and other agricultural pursuits, marriage remained a site of contest regarding 'rebellious' wives. Women who spent most of the week working on their farms to earn the majority of the household income were labelled, according to Abbott, "weekend wives" (Abbott: 1976). Or, in the case of the women who worked in the horticultural sectors of the Gambian economy, as 'going to their second husbands' (Schroeder 1996: 76), because their gardens provided food and an income. Thus, these 'second husbands' were viewed by women as nurturing and providing a degree of protection from physical, financial and social ruin, something that their actual husbands failed to do. Similarly, Lovett (1996), in her work on marriage in Western Tanzania, finds that the husband's views of their wives illustrate the relational tensions that occur:

> Today women are argumentative and fight with their husbands. … a wife will talk back to her husband. She thinks she's like a man. (52)

Such outspoken women were criticised by the community because they were not respectful of their menfolk, challenged the decisions of their husbands, controlled and directed labour and other resources, and in particular, would wield power and authority within both the household and the community (Lovett 1996: 53). Furthermore, such behaviours indicate that their lives operated outside the norms of accepted gender behaviour, most especially in rural areas, and thus women were blamed for the social and economic breakdown of their family and lineages (Hodgson 1996: 107).

Similarly, Cornwall's work on gender relations in South West Nigeria has revealed that when men's financial support for their wives and families is sporadic, women regard men as 'useless' (Cornwall 2001: 67). This is a common theme in the experience of women in Kenya, who do the bulk of the farming work without the physical and financial support of men and yet they are obliged to deal with their increasing interference. The work of Heyer (2006: 71) highlights this in relation to coffee crop returns and men's attempts to control those female cash crops, in particular bananas, which generate high returns. Heyer found that the downturn of coffee crop yields, coupled with the decreasing value of wages, led to an intensification of male control over household outputs, in particular crops grown by women as food, or saleable crops such as bananas or French beans (Heyer 2006: 73). In an effort to regain control over money and their trading wives, men initiated a direct move into the banana market, in order to re-situate bananas as a cash crop, thereby gaining access to its returns. However, bananas are traditionally regarded as women's crops and have long been grown by them. Bananas are considered a major source of nourishment for weaning babies and they are involved in bridewealth payments, given to the mother of the bride as an acknowledgement of the bride's virginity (Heyer 2005: 45). As such, women control the crop and its returns, which is paid in cash and not into a joint bank account. This cash is considered hers alone (Heyer 2006: 78). The tensions within marriages in which wives had higher incomes than their husbands were further fuelled by the vicissitudes of market fluctuations and social attitudes concerning marital expectations and gender relations.

An examination of the marriage contract in the literature reveals its relational multilayering and contradictions. On scrutinising risk sharing within households, Jackson has challenged the notion that the joint ownership of assets, or joint decision-making, is necessarily detrimental for women (Jackson 2007: 129). She argues that 'disaggregating decisions within households can distort the conjugality of the husband and wife, setting up assumptions that shared outcomes would maintain women's subordination' (Jackson 2007: 122). Rather, Jackson maintains that women are able to 'manoeuvre resources for their own advantage by using the moral expectations that come from being a wife' (Jackson 2007: 124). This, of course, challenges the long-held feminist position that marriage as a patriarchal institution necessarily panders to male advantage, controlling women's reproduction and labour power (See Young et al. 1988, Rogers 1980). Guyer (1988) in her work on the Beti women, looked at the position of married women in relation to unmarried women and found that, generally, 'unmarried women were not able to utilise kin relationships to help gain access to finances to pay for children's school fees, or other significant expenses, because their status was not as important as that of married women' (Guyer 1988: 160). Here we see the power of moral authority vested within marriage and its contradictions. On the one hand, it can play an important role in maintaining women's social and political security insomuch as it can, and does, give women a base from which to negotiate the entitlements due to them as wives, something that is not available to unmarried daughters or widows. On the other hand, within the volatile economic climate experienced in Kenya over the last three decades—GDP has dropped by half, going from 4.2% in 1980–90 to 2.0% in 2008, declining incomes and reduced government expenditure on social goods[3]—it created a scenario whereby marriage is, as the literature shows, the site for major confrontation over social responsibilities and expectations (See Cooper 2012: 648–9).

Thus, personal negotiations that occur between husband and wives, brothers and sons, elders and the other members of a rural family compound are multilayered and not necessarily transferable across other sections of the wider community. These negotiations, and subsequent decisions, reflect both a market economy and a moral

[3]Thompson used the term moral economy to describe the disconnect between morality and economics so that economics—wages, markets and prices, production and exchange—became the arbiter of understandings of right and wrong.

economy, which are not always based on values of justice or fairness, but on the relations of power stemming from the ability to accumulate assets and, in the case of the moral economy, on an implied power based on perceptions concerning symbols of fertility or abundance, relationships and mythologies relating to the spirit world. Throughout Kenya the gendered nature of resource allocation and dispute resolution practices is multifaceted with origins in myths and constructed traditions which enable men, via the use of patronage, to maintain positions of power both as individuals and as members of age sets, elders or politicians (Stamp 1995: 90).

## Familial Obligation Under Colonial Occupation

For Kikuyu women in precolonial and colonial Kenya, marriage conferred security, social relations, status and class. Women were affiliated with their husband's patrilineage through the payment of bridewealth on marriage. This secured a woman's land use rights and, importantly, established lineage membership for her children (O'Laughlin 1995: 71–73). Within those contexts, a marriage demarcated the rights and obligations of both parties. For women, marriage ensured sexual exclusivity and personal protection by her husband from the sexual advances of others. Marriage gave men exclusive rights over his wife's fertility while he, in turn, had obligations towards her well-being. Any failure to meet his obligations risked a woman's wrath which, by exercising her reproductive rights, could purportedly unleash barrenness, childlessness and the inevitable demise of one's lineage (Stamp 1995: 74, Shadle 2003: 245). Women's farming roles, in particular the production of food for family subsistence, carried with it responsibilities, obligations and a degree of independence. Kikuyu women had control over what they produced on the land allocated to them and they were responsible for the planting, harvesting, storage and distribution of its produce.[4] Marriage required that men provide wives not only with certain goods and resources such as land, but most importantly, a personal connection to his clan, social status and protection from the spirit world. Moreover, bridewealth payments bound both the husband's and wife's families together, supporting each other in times of difficulty and forging new opportunities in times of good fortune (Kershaw 1997: 24).

Married women and their mothers needed marriages to work. The mothers of newly married daughters were proud of them and expected them to uphold the family name and status by being an obedient, deferential, hardworking wife, who

[4]Annual average growth of GDP has gone from 4.2% in 1980–90 to 2.0% in 1990–2001, to 5.8% in 2005 and returned 2.0% in 2008. The age of population who completed primary school has dropped from 87% in 1990 to 63% in 2001. In 2009 42.8% of the population was under 14yrs. World Development Indicators 2003. World Bank. p. 185. The 2008 figures are from Summary Statistics Region Eastern Africa. http://data.un.org/CountryProfile.aspx?crName=KENYA. accessed March 15 2010

bore many children. Furthermore, mothers needed the marriages of their daughters to last because it reflected her status as the provider of labour, influencing fertility and lineage. Wives wanted their marriages to endure because they gained the respect and protection that came from being a first wife or a second wife. They understood clan knowledge and lore: that the children they bore, the access to land and the food that their farming produced, gave them status and security within their communities. Importantly, they understood the destitution that arose when marriage failed (Tabet 1991: 8–10).

Marital obligations for men and women changed during the colonial period. This was principally due to the advent of male out-migration, the introduction and production for sale of maize, the sale of surplus food crops and the commercialisation of land. In the precolonial period, food produced by either party was for consumption or barter. Although both women and men were involved in the market place, trading cereals, animal skins, pots and tools, the remuneration from this barter system was the property of the individual seller to use how they saw fit (Muriuki 1974: 101–108). In the Kikuyu areas maize was initially grown on men's land and sold by them to the government-controlled market.[5] Over time women became increasingly involved in the production of maize, as their allocated land began to be utilised to grow it. This practice expanded as male out-migration from the family farm pushed women into working on men's land to grow maize and other cash crops, the returns from which became increasingly valued. For example, the sale of maize and any surplus food crops, paid the hut and poll taxes, something that benefited both men and women, in that neither could go to prison for non-payment of these taxes. In 1940, 201 women out of 770 people were prosecuted for Hut and Poll tax avoidance and committed to prison and detention camps (Mackenzie 1998: 137). However, in the context of both public and private obligations owed by husbands and wives to each other, the production of maize not only exemplified a changing gender division of labour but reflected the transformation of the personal expectations of both men and women of marriage (Hay 1976: 100–103).

Maize production changed women's production from one aimed at consumption, to that of production for the market. In the precolonial period, Kikuyu women were engaged in production for use which included food not just for the immediate family but for the fulfilment of family social obligations including some of those of her husband.[6] Kikuyu women kept any income from sales of any surplus produced, often using it to buy goats which acted as part of a son's inheritance, as Kikuyu males could only inherit property associated with their mother and her house

[5]Kenya National Archives Micro film. Miscellaneous Correspondence /File Number: 363 District Commissioner/Fort Hall/3/1 Fisher, J. Report on the Kikuyu. 1950–1951. 91. Herein after cited as KNA MC. DC/FH

[6]Maize was sold to the State controlled Maize Marketing Board, which sold it to settler farmers and plantation owners as food for labourers. This aimed to control the quality of the maize sold and to prevent African grown maize from being exported and therefore competing with Settler grown maize. (Fearn 1961).

(Middleton and Kershaw 1972: 46–48). Kikuyu women were also known to supply the caravan traders that passed through from Mombasa to Mt Kenya with grain and beans (Robertson 1995: 100). Women's gardens were not only planted with the dietary staples of sorghum, millet, maize, beans, peas and root vegetables such as sweet potatoes and cassava, but with foods considered to be women's food crops. Taro and *njahe*, lablab beans, were associated with women's fertility and were only cultivated by women (Kershaw 1975: 180). They were also consumed by women at important events associated with fertility: circumcision, pregnancy, birth and menopause.[7] Moreover, the increasing use of women's food crops to pay hut and poll taxes meant that women enjoyed little to no financial return for their labour. Consequently, the implicated obligations of husbands and wives in marriage radically changed. In the case of hut and poll taxes, women became indirectly responsible for men's traditional debt obligations, recognised as such by the men of the colonial administration, but ultimately paid for by women's labour. Cash cropping therefore broke the nexus between mutual obligations concerning labour and reciprocal care that indigenous marriage contracts assured. Similarly, male out-migration to labour on settler farms, plantations and in the towns, had the effect of absenting men from immediate responsibilities to provide for their wives' security, for example, male labour for hut construction or for clearing new areas for crop production (Driberg 1932: 407).

The production of cash crops of maize, wattle bark and, later, coffee, had yet another impact. It caused an inflationary rise in bridewealth costs. Maize prices more than doubled during the 1950s, going from 'Shs 13/- to Shs 28/- per bag by 1954' (Fearn 1961: 161). At the end of the 1950s wealth flowed to those men who had appropriated their wives' land and labour from crops for family consumption, into the production of cash crops such as maize, potatoes and coffee. Women's labour became more valuable than ever and bridewealth rose accordingly (Shadle 2003: 246). The colonial records showed that

> [In the past] Bridewealth was less than at present. 1 cow, few sheep and goats instead of the modern average of 6 cattle, 10 sheep, 10 goats. If no sheep or goats, a man had to pay Sh/-1000. In the old days a little beer and food were used at weddings but now there is a great expense of church, [registration] at the District commissioner's office and native ceremony … which takes another Sh/-1000 for food.[8]

The demand for women's labour in the production of cash crops, coupled with the inflationary rise in bridewealth over the colonial period, tied women definitively into their marriages. For men, an inflated bridewealth gave them the respect and standing of wealthy men, whether or not that was the case. As Mutongi (2007) points out, men claimed

> You paid a lot of money because you had to act like a man. You had to show you could take care of a wife, and this responsibility began with paying a good bridewealth. As long

[7]KNA MC/363 DC/FH/3/1 Fisher, J. Report on the Kikuyu. 1950–1951. p. 83

[8]KNA Fall Hall Annual Report 1939. pp. 18–19

> as a man understood that he was getting a good, well-mannered, educated wife, he did not hesitate to pay (212).

Thus, via the payment of bridewealth, men demonstrated that they 'acted' like men, securing the reproductive and productive labour of a wife for clan and household, and they therefore wanted their wives to act like wives. But how were wives supposed to behave? What were women actually agreeing to when they married, in view of the production transformations caused by a newly emerging market economy that brought major changes to women's labour arrangements with the family?

We know from the colonial record in Kenya that there are numerous examples of women who, in order to protect their interests, openly challenged the power of both the colonial regime and their menfolk via the use of public protest.[9] Presley (1986: 262) shows that, from 1920 onwards, women who worked in the coffee plantations organised strikes and harvesting boycotts in an effort to drive up wages and improve working conditions. Within the purely agricultural labour force, women and children accounted for as much as 35–40% of total employees in the peak coffee harvesting seasons. Such boycotts would have put pressure on plantation owners' returns if the State had not intervened and ended the strikes (Wolf 1974: 128, Presley 1986: 263). After the passage of Ordinance No. 40 in 1934, women became responsible for their own hut taxes.[10] By 1937, 550 women had been prosecuted for non-payment of taxes, and, in 1938, a strike was called by women to stop paying the tax in Muranga sub-location.[11]

Furthermore, in the 1940s three riots occurred in which women were again the main instigators. In 1940 some 500 women revolted against the use of their labour to build terraces and grass areas of eroded land.[12] Once again in 1948 and 1949 Kikuyu women in the Central Province stopped soil conservation work altogether and held demonstrations outside of the District Commissioner's office. For example, in 1948, 2000 women engaged in a street protest with some of the women arrested but, as the Commissioner reported; 'were quickly released by a large crowd of their own sex brandishing sticks and shouting Amazonian war-cries'[13] For their actions in refusing to obey their Chief, some of these women were later fined by the Native Tribunal at Fort Hall.[14] What is important here is the fact women were willing to risk fines and imprisonment in order to bring their grievances concerning

---

[9]KNA/99 Annual Report. Central Province. Windley E.H. 1948 p.1

[10]KNA MC/363 DC/FH/3/1 Fisher, J. Report on the Kikuyu. 1950–1951. p. 92

[11]Mss. Afr. s. 1792. Matson. 16/3/41:24. Matson Papers. Manuscripts. Africa. (Rhodes House. Oxford.) Series Nr. 1792. Box 16. File 3. Item 41:24. Herein after cited as: Mss. Afr. s. followed by series numbers

[12]See KNA AR/369 Fort Hall/27.1947 Coutts W. F. (1947):1–2. KNA/99 Annual Report. Central Province. Windley. E.H. (1948):1.

[13]KNA Fort Hall Annual Report. 1937. p. 4. Kikuyu women lived on their shambas with their children, with the husband visiting. Mss. Afr. s. 1672/4

[14]KNA Fall Hall Annual Report 1939. pp. 18–19

the demands on their labour, loss of land and security of livelihoods, into the public space.[15]

The majority of women, however, negotiated spaces of power by utilising the moral authority that existed within positional relationships such as being a mother, widow, or first or second wife. In establishing and/or demanding rights, women, during the colonial period, like their menfolk, forged strategic alliances with significant people and made use of institutions in their communities: fathers, their married sons, co-wives, administrative officers, churches and women's councils. They relied on the importance of reputation and utilised accepted behavioural practices to make their case. For example, the power and prestige that came from being a married woman gave her, implied or otherwise, certain entitlements which arose from the obligations and responsibilities of the husband to provide land, clothes and a house in which to live.[16] If a husband failed to meet his obligations and these things were not supplied, then 'she was reputed to be a *mukoma thi*, someone who sleeps on the ground—a concubine' (Peterson 2001: 474). This was as ruinous to her reputation as that of her husband's family. Women did not fail to make such shortcomings public by informing uncles, sons or their husband's brothers of their plight. In this way, men would be publicly shamed for their failure to meet their responsibilities and it was hoped that this would lead to a change in attitude, forcing wayward husbands or fathers to care for, and respect, their wives or mothers and daughters (Mutongi 2007: 131–2).

By speaking out and engaging in sociopolitical action against the colonial authorities and a compliant indigenous male community, perceptions of women changed. They were no longer viewed as deferential and obedient wives but potential and actual radical outcasts who would no longer automatically conform to the expectations of fathers and husbands (See Hodgson and McCurdy 2001). Without doubt, the willingness of women to publicly voice their discontent demonstrates that women made use of the moral authority imbued within customary gender relations when rights and obligations within personal and public relationships broke down. Faced with less than fortuitous changes in their lives, married women insisted that their recalcitrant husbands respect them. If they failed to do so, these men risked female censure and the possible loss of respect from important male individuals within their communities. Kikuyu women's councils, for example, had the power to enforce female condemnation such as imposing fines on men who abused their wives and banning co-wives from cooking for troublesome husbands.[17] This could have a devastating effect on a man's reputation and deny him a place in the ranks of important men whose role it was to settle disputes within the community, or to negotiate with colonial administrators. Such a man would remain, as Peterson notes 'an *atereki,* a silent, timid man, sitting on the wood heap listening to the deliberations of his peers' (Peterson 2001: 473). In this context, women using

[15]KNA AR/369 Fort Hall/27. 1947. Coutts W. F. pp. 1–2

[16]KNA/99 Annual Report. Central Province. Windley E.H. (1948):1

[17]KNA/99 Annual Report. Central Province. Windley E.H. (1948):1.

their moral authority to make their menfolk 'lose face' in public were both effective and powerful.

Nevertheless, the strategies which women used to negotiate their rights and entitlements with husbands, brothers and sons were often contradictory. Mothers stood by their daughters and utilised the British legal system to take abusive or negligent husbands to court, despite the fact that these same courts often ruled against them (Mutongi 2007: 150). They formed alliances with colonial officials to gain compensation from men who had abandoned their wives, leaving them to single-handedly support the children of failed relationships (Thomas 2003: 103–134). Mutongi cites the case of a mother who successfully initiated a divorce case against her son-in-law because he had beaten her daughter so badly that she had gone blind in one eye (2007, 156–7). By taking such men to court women, once again, utilised public space to shame men. The fact that the public space in this case was a court room made little difference to the act; it was men losing face that gave power and resonance to moral authority.

Similarly, strategies to obtain marital rights were used by both men and women, but for different reasons. Women would try to arrange their own choice of marriage partner—something that was quite rare and avoiding a forced marriage—because parents chose the marital partners of their sons and daughters[18] Men, for example, would argue with their elders over inflated bridewealth costs because often their meagre wages failed to provide enough savings to be able to pay bridewealth for a future wife. These men then faced the options of either stealing stock to pay the bridewealth or to elope or abduct a wife. In the latter two situations no bridewealth payments would be forthcoming to the fathers of the women concerned. Such actions threatened the power of male elders to control avenues of wealth creation, and it meant that the labour of the woman involved was not under the control of her husband or his family because the payment of bridewealth secured the labour power of a wife for her husband's family (Kanogo 2005: 123). On the other hand, runaway wives and girls who received a mission education and who may have been forced out of parental households went to the towns and mission stations as places of refuge.[19] Here they established for themselves a new sense of security and identity, which was beyond the control of their immediate kin. We see yet again, in these examples, the use by women of public spaces to claim their voice and power. By taking advantage of the social changes such as access to a mission education and a modernity that challenged customary law, women's views began to gain far more influence than that of her kin.[20]

[18]KNA. MC 363 DC/FH Report on the Kikuyu. 1950–52. Fisher. J. p. 91.

[19]KNA AR/493 Meru District Annual Report 1934. District Commissioner Lambert H E. p. 77-80. In Kikuyu society, there were both women and men's councils which had their own duties and rules that decided on such as when initiation would occur, took care of internal disputes, and educated women and men about proper social behaviour.

[20]Phillips Arthur, Report on Native Tribunals. Colony and Protectorate of Kenya. Nairobi. 1944. p. 294.

These changes influenced the inherent moral authority and obligations that informed the important social conventions involved in negotiating marriage and familial relationships. All of these actions challenged generational politics, gender politics and class relations, as well as dealing with the pressures of a new social order brought about by colonial rule. Significantly, underlying these social relations was an attempt to carve out a social moral order from which a new moral authority could exercise political influence and social respect. Such actions were fraught with risk. Women who sustained a living through sex work in the cities could find themselves fined Sh/- 200 or given 2 months imprisonment.[21] Such punishments were considered 'just' according to the Registrar of the Supreme Court in Kenya:

> Those concerned [Wairimu d/o Njoroge and four others] where in an area without the correct permit… the residence of the accused in the area was considered undesirable, and rightly so, … they had shown their contempt of the previous convictions and sentences by returning to the prohibited area not only without permission, but within full knowledge that no permission would be granted.[22]

Or, if a woman ran away to a town to escape a violent husband or crippling workload, she could be forcibly removed back to the marital home and ostracised for her behaviour. As Mutongi (2007) states, that, if a suspicious woman was spotted in town, village elders assisted by strong men

> …would grab her, pull her aside into some out-of-the-way corner or alleyway, and begin interrogating her about her business in town. Almost always, the intimidated young woman would surrender without a struggle; if she resisted the "strong young men" would body-punch her until she relented. If she did not give what they felt was a satisfactory answer or if the men remained suspicious of her motives they would strip her and roughly drape a coarse burlap bag over her naked body. She would then be dragged by her accusers onto a crowded bus and forced to sit silent, sullen and sore until she was deposited in the village to be paraded around for all the villagers to ogle and insult her. (142)

Should familial misfortune arise after her foolhardy actions, she could face accusations of witchcraft for which the punishment was exile or perhaps death. Today rural-to-urban and rural-to-rural migration remains a major source of complaint concerning witchcraft, with people using it to demand possessions, land, or political patronage from those in positions of power (Geschiere and Nyamnjoh 1998: 71). Witchcraft, once a common explanation of a sudden unexpected event, such as a death, or an adverse natural event, such as drought or flood, now can be used as an explanation for the sudden accumulation of wealth, be that money, land or power (See Dolan 2002; Blunt 2013).

In an effort to create an economic and political space of their own, women contested the domain of familial obligation. They reinvented or demanded that the reciprocal and implied obligations owed by husbands to wives, by in-laws to in-laws, married sons to their mothers and unmarred sisters, or daughters to their

---

[21]CO 847/6/11. Archdeacon Owen. Letters and Articles Concerning the Forced Marriage of Girls in Kenya. No page numbers given.

[22]Mss. Afr. s 1672/6. Minutes of the Law Panel Committee. 29-30th November 1954. p. 4.

fathers and brothers, be upheld. Women insisted on the interdependence and reciprocity of marital relations and a reaffirmation of the communal good over the importance of individual gain. Women demanded that husbands, brothers and uncles respect their womenfolk who held together families, food supplies and households under the increasing agricultural disparities and mounting political pressure from the colonial regime itself. Women, through the use of collective public protest, individual forms of everyday resistance and public declaration, accused men of a dereliction of duty. Moreover, men, because of their collusion with the colonial regime, had failed to respect the moral order and, in the case of the Kikuyu, wrought cultural destruction. By the mid-1930s, this was visible to all as clans lost land to settler occupation, bans were placed on cattle raiding, initiation rites were sporadic and female circumcision was banned.[23] Husbands had failed their wives. To all intents and purposes, Kenyan civil society had not only imploded, it had fallen apart. The challenge of the use of moral authority by women, instituted a process of socio-economic change in a colonial context of repression and colonial political mendacity. The ability of women to draw on the same processes of empowerment to negotiate and maintain their well-being and economic security in the climate of political uncertainty and economic downturn in a contemporary Kenya was to be sorely tested.

## Agency, Opportunity and Moral Authority Today

For the majority of women in Kenya, agriculture remains the basis of their economic security. After fifty years of independence, Kenya remains a predominantly agricultural country, with women constituting 70% of the agricultural workforce, providing 80% of the labour for food production and 50% of the labour for cash crop production (World Bank 2007: 10, Africa Research Bulletin 2010: 18695A). Agriculture accounts for the largest percentage of Kenya's Gross Domestic Product at 26% (Word Bank 2010: 13). Women's wages are, on average, 58% lower than men's, and women's literacy rate, at 76%, is also lower than men's at 89% (World Bank 2007: 76). Despite such an important contribution to Kenya's economic output, women's property rights with respect to land they cultivate and its control, remains insecure. Women only hold 1% of registered land titles, with around 5–6% of titles held in joint, that is husband's and wife's, names (World Bank 2007: 21). Land in Kenya is subject to approximately 75 different laws, some of which contradict each other or are subject to particular clan arrangements.[24] For women, however, their access to land has not been advanced by the existence of statutory

[23]Colony and Protectorate of Kenya. Law Reports Vol 20 Part 1. 1942. Supreme Court. Criminal Revision Case: No. 80. of 1942. Rex vs Wairimu d/o Njoroge and others. 23, June. 1942. Nairobi.
[24]Colony and Protectorate of Kenya. Law Reports Vol 20 Part 1. 1942. Supreme Court. Criminal Revision Case: No. 80. of 1942. Rex vs Wairimu d/o Njoroge and others. 23, June. 1942. Nairobi.

land law or land titling, not only due to the corruption prevalent in the Ministry of Lands and Settlements, but because customary practice remains entrenched. (Manji 2012: 477). Thus civil status—being married, single or divorced—always determines women's land access and limits women's opportunities to purchase land outright (Whitehead and Dzodzi 2003: 79). Land ownership and access across Sub-Saharan Africa is predicated on the belief that women's property allocations are only available to them either through marriage or inheritance (Razavi 2007: 1489). The development of land markets which, some argue, could circumvent customary practices in relation to women's land access (Agarwal 1994, Tripp 2004: 4), has merely added another layer of disadvantage for the majority of women who are poor, cash-strapped and rely on land for their livelihoods (Lastarria-Cornhiel 1997: 1323). Given this situation, women's use of the moral authority inherent in the marriage contract may well be a useful strategy available to women in pursuing their livelihoods (Hardee 2007: 748/9).

In Kenya marriage remains central to the distribution of resources within the household. Thus the effect of women generating more income than their spouses, coupled with a decline in income-generating opportunities for men in a contracting formal economy, presents its own challenges. Without doubt the retreat of state involvement in the agricultural sector has sharpened perceptions of appropriate gender behaviour, intensifying the connections between identity, lineage, wealth and livelihoods (Turner and Brownhill 2004: 27–30). Heyer's (2005) examination of the position of single mothers, for example, offers an insight to the resulting cultural and social resistance to change:

> Single mothers are referred to as 'housebreakers'. As girlfriends they break up men's marriages, syphoning off men's wealth for their own *nyumbas* (households) rather than those of the men themselves. Furthermore, as sisters they not only fail to bring in bride-wealth which their brothers may then use to get married, they are also now in competition with their brothers over the resources of the clan (50).

Here conflicts, attributed to women who do not marry, deny men the stability of legitimacy and wealth brought to them solely through marriage. Unmarried women, who are involved in trade and are able to bring an income into the households of their parents, assert a new kind of claim for control over the wealth of that household. Independent single women, or married women who are the main breadwinners with absent husbands, unlike their mothers and grandmothers, are not under the control of the father, husband or clan. Their labour contributes to the wealth of their own households and not necessarily to male lineages or the wider clan. Thus these women are weakening the kin-wealth nexus and perhaps are creating alliances with women in similar circumstances in which class interests supersede those of kinship (See Gordon 1995: 891). These women, then, violate male constructions of the household, defy accepted understandings of behavioural norms and question cultural understandings of what constitutes marriage, a wife, or family, or indeed womanhood itself (Heyer 2006: 77, Oyewuni 2000: 1093–8). Indeed, the 2004 Noble Peace Prize winner, Wangari Maathai's actions and outspoken views on the environment, government corruption and political oppression saw her beaten and imprisoned many times. When she became an assistant minister in the Kibaki government, her continued outspokenness saw her politically sidelined, losing her seat after one term of office (See Maathai 2007; Nixon 2006: 7). Maathai's rage can be seen as a continuation of women's use of moral authority to bring male politician's misuse of power to account.

Methods used by the colonial administration to co-opt men into the colonial economy through labour migration, cash cropping and, in particular maize production changed the nature of mutual obligation and moral authority between men and women. The gendered division of labour existing in colonial Kenya was not simply a way of organising labour for family food production or commercial cropping. It was integral to the exercise of power within ethnic communities. Familial position, social status and class all confer a sense of personal identity, security, solidarity and moral authority. Notably, such societal positions absolve one from certain expectations and give rise to others, which are seen as innate to a particular gendered role, position or status. As the colonial period progressed, the Kikuyu questioned who they were: men sowing and digging on settler farms or carrying head-loads were becoming like women. Women demanding a choice of husband or leaving husbands to live in the towns, or earning money for themselves, who were they? What threat were these new identities to the stability of family life and the moral authority that underpinned the identity of a woman or a man?

Kikuyu women's resistance to their loss of land and production processes, a loss of security within marriage, abandonment and restrictions placed on their movements by both colonial men and chiefs, was completely understandable. Women were not simply engaged in political action because newly formed political groups, such as the Kikuyu Central Association, asked them to; or because disgruntled men put them up to it as the colonial record likes to claim. Nor were women's actions sporadic, only coming to the notice of officials when women rioted. Kikuyu women's actions were deeply nuanced as they drew on long accepted understandings of the gendered nature of moral authority.

Women in colonial Kenya not only made use of accepted social dispute mechanisms, such as women's councils, or by complaining to brothers, uncles and in-laws, but combined them with new opportunities, particularly the establishment of English law, to voice their opinions and call their menfolk to account. By actions such as public shaming, women proffered a political mirror, showing husbands, male elders, brothers and sons that male co-option into the colonial enterprise was culturally destructive and they, in turn, were cast adrift by the power that women's moral authority bestowed.

In modern-day Kenya, marriage and agriculture remain central to the majority of women's lives and, similar to the colonial period, economic uncertainty and social change influence expressions of moral right and authority. In a household, being a mother or husband, for example, grants one more entitlements than being an unmarried son or daughter. Moreover, such positions deliver the power to decide such things as marriage privileges or inheritance entitlements. Today, whether or not a woman in Kenya obtains access to land depends not only on statutory laws that give her that right, but on being a wife, and on the relationships she utilises which help reinforce her moral authority. For women in modern Kenya, land security and economic stability, then, are linked to the identities bound up in familial relationships as well as their ability to negotiate the political spaces found within them. When identities change, so too does the accompanying power of moral authority. By utilising expectations associated with a particular identity, women challenge legal impediments to their right to land, demand that husbands fulfil conjugal obligations while instituting a cultural shift that sees women imbued with a sociocultural agency in which their moral authority is not only recognised but enforced.

## References


Abbott S (1976) Full-Time Farmers and Week-End Wives: an Analysis of Altering Conjugal Roles. Journal of Marriage and Family 38(1):165–174

Africa Research Bulletin: Economic, Financial, and Technical Series (2010) 47(5):18695A–18696A

Agarwal B (1994) A field of one's own: gender and land rights in South Asia. Cambridge University Press, Cambridge

Allman J (1996) Rounding up spinsters: gender chaos and unmarried women in colonial Asante. J Afr Hist. 37(2):195–214

Anderson D (2005) A history of the hanged: the dirty war in Kenya and the end of empire. W.W. Norton, New York

Ardener S (1973) Sexual insult and female militancy. Man 8(3):422–440

Blunt R (2013) Oracles, trauma, and the limits of contextualization: naming the witch in contemporary Kenya. J Relig Afr 43:329–349

Bryceson D (ed) (1995) Women wielding the hoe: lessons from rural Africa for feminist theory and development practice. Berg Publishers, Oxford

Clayton A, Savage D (1974) Government and labour in Kenya. Frank Cass, London

Coplan D (2001) You have left me wondering about: basotho women and the culture of mobility. In: Hodgson D, McCurdy S (eds) "Wicked women" and the reconfiguration of gender in Africa. James Currey, Oxford, pp 188–211

Cooper E (2012) Women and inheritance in sub-saharan Africa: what can change? Dev Policy Rev 30(5):641–657

Cornwall A (2001) Wayward women and useless men: contest and change in gender relations in Ado-Odo, S.W. Nigeria. In: Hodgson D, McCurdy S (eds) "Wicked women" and the reconfiguration of gender in Africa. James Currey, Oxford, pp. 67–84

Dolan C (2002) Gender and witchcraft in agrarian transition: the case of kenyan horticulture. Dev Change 33(4):659–681

Driberg JH (1932) The status of women among the nilotics and nilo-hamitics. Africa 5(4):404–421

Elkins C (2005) Imperial reckoning: the untold story of Britain's gulag in Kenya. Holt, New York

Fearn H (1961) An African economy: a study of the economic development of the Nyanza province of Kenya. Oxford University Press, London

Gordon A (1995) Gender, ethnicity, and class in Kenya: "Burying Otieno" revisited. Signs J Women Cult Soc 20(4):883–912

Geschiere P, Nyamnjoh F (1998) Witchcraft as an issue in the "politics of belonging": democratization and urban migrant's involvement with the home village. Afr Stud Rev 41 (3):69–91

Guyer J (1988) Dynamic approaches to domestic budgeting: class and methods for Africa. In: Dwyer D, Bruce J (eds) A home divided. Women and income in the third world. Stanford University Press, Stanford, pp 115–172

Hardee C (2007) Balancing Acts: The Rights of Women and Cultural Minorities in Kenyan Martial Law. New York University Law Review 79:712–749

Hay M (1976) Luo women and economic change during the colonial period. In: Hafkin N, Bay E (eds) Women in Africa: studies in social and economic change. Stanford University Press, Stanford, pp 87–109

Heyer, A. (2005) "Nowadays they can even kill you for that which they feel is theirs": gender and the production of ethnic identity in kikuyu-speaking central Kenya. In: Broch-Due V (ed) Violence and belonging: the quest for identity in post-colonial Africa. Routledge, London, pp 41–59

Heyer A (2006) The gender of wealth: markets and power in central Kenya. Rev Afr Polit Econ 107:66–80

Hodgson D, McCurdy S (eds) (2001) "Wicked women" and the reconfiguration of gender in Africa. James Currey, Oxford

Hodgson D (1996) "My daughter belongs to the government now": marriage, maasai and the Tanzanian state. Can J Afr Stud 30(1):106–123

Jackson C (2007) Resolving risk, marriage and creative conjugality. Dev Change 38(1):107–129

Kanogo T (2005) African womanhood in colonial Kenya, 1900–1950. James Currey, Oxford

Kenya National Archives, [KNA] (1968) Microfilm. The Provincial and District Annual Reports, Political Record Books and Handing Over Reports, Syracuse: Syracuse University

Kershaw G (1975) The changing roles of women and men in the kikuyu family by socioeconomic strata. Rural Africana 29:173–194

Kershaw G (1997) Mau Mau from below. James Currey, Oxford

Lastarria-Cornhiel S (1997) Impact of privatization on gender and property rights in Africa. World Dev 25(8):1317–1333

Lovett M (1996) "She thinks she's like a man": marriage and (de)constructing gender identity in colonial buha, western Tanzania, 1943–60. Can J Afr Stud 30(1):52–68

Maathai W (2007) Unbowed: a memoir. William Heinemann, London

Mackenzie A, Fiona D (1998) Land, Ecology and Resistance in Kenya, 1880–1952. Edinburgh University Press, Edinburgh

Manji A (2012) The grabbed state: lawyers, politics and public land in Kenya. J Mod Afr Stud 50 (3):467–492

Manuscripts [Mss. Afr. s.] Series Nr, Author, Box/file/item Nr. Rhodes House, Oxford

Middleton J, Kershaw G (1972) The Kikuyu and Kamba of Kenya. International African Institute, London

Moore SF (1992) Treating law as knowledge: telling colonial officers what to say to Africans about running "their own" native courts. Law Soc Rev 26(1):11–46

Muriuki G (1974) A history of the kikuyu 1500–1900. Oxford University Press, London

Mutongi K (2007) Worries of the heart. University of Chicago, Chicago

Mweseli T (2000) Women and the law of succession. In: Kibwana K, Lawrence M (eds) Law and the quest for gender equality in Kenya. Claripress, Nairobi, pp 141–160

Nixon R (2006–7) Slow Violence, Gender and Environmentalism of the Poor. J Commonwealth Postcolonial Stud, 13:2–14:1

O'Laughlin B (1995) Myth of the African family. In: Bryceson D (ed) Women wielding the hoe. Berg Press, Oxford

Oyewuni O (2000) Family bonds/conceptual binds: African notes on feminist epistemologies. Signs 25(4):1093–1098

Peterson D (2001) Wordy women: gender trouble and the oral politics of the East African revival in northern Gikuyuland. J Afr Hist 42(3):469–489

Presley C (1986) Labor unrest among Kikuyu women in colonial Kenya. In: Robertson C, Berger I (eds) Women and class in Africa. Africana Publishing Company, New York, pp 255–273

Public Records Office, Colonial Office Records, [CO] 840 Series. London

Razavi S (2007) Liberalisation and the debates on women's access to land. Third World Q 28 (8):1479–1500
Robertson C (1995) Comparative advantage: women in trade in Accra, Ghana, and Nairobi, Kenya. In: House-Midamba B, Ekechi F (eds) African market women and economic power: the role of women in African economic development. Greenwood Press, Westport, pp 99–119
Rogers B (1980) The domestication of women. Kegan Paul, London
Schroeder R (1996) 'Gone to their second husbands': marital metaphors and conjugal contracts in The Gambia's female garden sector. Can J Afr Stud 30(1):69–88
Shadle B (2003) Bridewealth and female consent: marriage disputes in African courts, Gusiiland, Kenya. J Afr Hist 44(2):241–262
Stamp P (1995) Mothers of invention: women's agency in the Kenyan state. In: Gardiner J (ed) Provoking agents: gender and agency in theory and practice. University of Illinois Press, Urbana, pp 69–92
Stoll D (2013) Strategic essentialism, scholarly Inflation, and political litmus tests: the moral economy of hyping the contemporary Mayas. In: Vargas-Cetina G (ed) Anthropology and the politics of representation. University of Alabama Press, Tuscaloosa, pp 33–48
Tabet P (1991) "I'm the meat, i'm the knife": sexual service migration, and repression in some African societies. Feminist Issues 11(1):3–21
Thomas L (2003) Politics of the womb: women, reproduction, and the state in Kenya. University of California, Berkeley
Thompson E (1971) The moral economy of the english crowd in the eighteenth century. Past Present 50:76–136
Tripp A (2004) Women's movements, customary law, and land rights in Africa: the case of Uganda. Afr Stud Q, 7(4) http://www.africa.ufl.edu/asq/v7/v7i4a1.htm. Accessed 20 August 2010
Tsikata D (2003) Securing women's interests within land tenure reforms: recent debates in tanzania. J Agrarian Change 3(1&2):149–183
Turner TE, Brownhill LS (2004) We want our land back: gendered class analysis, the second contradiction of capitalism and social movement theory. Capitalism Nature Socialism 15 (4):21–40
Walsh J (2003) Double Standards: Women's Property Rights Violations in Kenya. Hum Rights Watch, 15(5) http://www.hrw.org/reports/2003/kenya0303/kenya0303.pdf. Accessed 20 July 2010
Whitehead A, Dzodzi D (2003) Policy Discourses on women's land rights in sub-saharan Africa: the implications of the re-turn to the customary. J Agrarian Change 3(1&2):67–112
Wolff R (1974) The economics of colonialism: Britain and Kenya, 1870–1930. Yale University Press, New Haven
World development indicators (2003) world bank. http://data.un.org/CountryProfile.aspx?crName=KENYA. Accessed 15 March 2010
World Bank (2007) Gender and Economic Growth in Kenya: Unleashing the Power of Women. World Bank, Washington DC
World Bank (2010) Kenya Economic Update. 2nd edn. World Bank, Washington DC
Young K, Wolkowitz C, McCullagh R (eds) (1988) Of marriage and the market: women's subordination internationally and its lessons, 2nd edn. Routledge and Kegan Paul, London

## Author Biographies

**Dr. Clare Buswell** is an adjunct academic staff member in the School of Social and Policy Studies. Her research is in Gender and the Colonial History of East Africa. Dr Buswell's research and writing focuses on Women's Experiences of Colonial Occupation in Eastern Africa and the Philippines, Women, Witchcraft and Social Ostracism in Africa, Gender and International Development, Customary Lore and Law in Kenya.

**Dr. Yvonne Corcoran-Nantes** is widely known in the field of Gender Studies, regularly being interviewed on gender and political issues by the media in Australia and overseas. She has worked with women in such diverse locations as Central Asia, Mongolia, Indonesia, East Timor and Brazil in many research and development projects to improve the rights and status of women in their respective countries. At the present time she is undertaking research on women ex-combatants in contemporary Vietnam. While Dr Corcoran-Nantes currently teaches in the areas of international studies and women's studies, her main research interests are: Gender and International Politics, Gender and International Development and Women and Armed Conflict. Dr Corcoran-Nantes is Head of Women's Studies and an Associate Professor in the School of Social and Policy Studies at Flinders University

# Chapter 20
# Rumour and Innuendo Witchcraft and Women's Power in the 'Colonised' State

**Yvonne Corcoran-Nantes and Clare Buswell**

**Abstract** Women's voices and actions resonate throughout the African colonial archives, on which this research is based, ever evolving, articulating and resonating in contemporary manifestations of spirituality. This article applies the inside/outsider analogy employed by Trinh Minh Ha in the analysis of both colonial and postcolonial gender relations and demonstrate that irrespective of the 'location' of women as the 'native other' they were able to have a voice and command respect (Minh Ha 1997). The marginalization of women first by the colonial western outsiders and second by the, usually, male insiders of their ethnic group and cultural communities leaves them as Minh Ha would say 'not quite insiders and not quite outsiders'(Minh Ha 1997: p. 418). Not voiceless, not powerless but located outside of hub of institutional power women were able to subvert, challenge and resist.

> [Kenyan] women's experience of social, political, and economic inequality has inspired them to create ways to reshape the social forces around them and to redefine some of the dominant conceptualizations that disadvantage them.(Ciekawy 1999: p. 232),

Explanations given for the modern day re-emergence of witchcraft or occult practices within African countries, south of the Sahel, range from the increasing inequality arising from the hegemonic effects of global capitalism to the failure of state institutions and the state itself, to combat the proliferation of war and the rising death tolls caused by AIDS and other epidemics (Smith 2001). Others have argued

We would like to thank the research librarians at Rhodes House, Oxford and the Seerley library, Cambridge University for their generous help and invaluable knowledge of the colonial record collections which form the basis of this paper.

Y. Corcoran-Nantes (✉) · C. Buswell
Flinders University, Bedford Park, Australia
e-mail: Yvonne.Corcoran-Nantes@flinders.edu.au

C. Buswell
e-mail: Clare.Buswell@flinders.edu.au



J. McIntyre-Mills et al. (eds.), *Balancing Individualism and Collectivism*, Contemporary Systems Thinking, DOI 10.1007/978-3-319-58014-2_20

that the involvement of evangelical church movements has also contributed to the resurgent power of the occult (Behrend 2007). The gender specific focus of naming and retribution involved in identifying and destroying women's cultural and spiritual power positions throughout the colonial period and beyond failed to silence or annihilate 'subversive women'. As in the past 'naming the witch' is an outsider interpretation of cultural practice and a gender division of labour that excludes insider voices, experiences and sense of justice (See Blunt 2013). Women's voices and actions resonate throughout the African colonial archives, on which this research is based, ever evolving, articulating and resonating in contemporary twenty-first-century manifestations of spirituality.[1]

This chapter applies the inside/outsider analogy employed by Trinh Minh Ha in the analysis of both colonial and postcolonial gender relations and demonstrate that irrespective of the 'location' of women as the 'native other' they were able to have a voice and command respect (Minh Ha 1997). The marginalization of women first by the colonial western outsiders and second by the, usually, male insiders of their ethnic group and cultural communities leaves them as Minh Ha would say 'not quite insiders and not quite outsiders'(Minh Ha Minh Ha 1997: 418). Not voiceless, not powerless but located outside of hub of institutional power women were able to subvert, challenge and resist.

In the chapter, we wish to argue that an assumed resurgence of belief and interaction with the spirit world in Kenya is not akin to a phoenix arising from the ashes of the postcolonial experience but rather one from which spiritualism and magic has found the ability to adapt, finding expressions that resonate within a modernist discourse. In the contemporary period, as in the past, witchcraft remains a 'manifestation of Africa's magic worldview' and an integral part of all aspects of people's lives (Leistner 2014: p. 54). Moreover, economic development and urbanization in contemporary Africa has presented more incisive challenges to traditional belief systems in which socio-economic inequality, political pecuniary advantage and contemporary challenges to traditional gender relations underwrite the difficulties confronting African development. Wherein, the use of 'witchcraft', has re-voiced differing expressions of cultural and gendered power, juxtaposed against those that the Kenyan State has come to represent.

## Unsettling the Colonial Narrative

The global colonial project has often been perceived as reading from the same political script but in Africa there was a particular focus on strong independent women, the antithesis of the European ideal woman, unacceptable in a colonial

[1]Research of the colonial records relating to east Africa and Kenya in particular was undertaken at Rhodes House, Oxford and the Seerley library, Cambridge University and the Public Records Office, London.

society in which women became the ultimate subaltern. The European colonial project on the African continent focussed on the indigenous assimilation of western culture and was driven by Eurocentric interpretations of difference. For the colonial government 'proud and cheeky' women had no place in a Europeanised Africa and from West to East Africa women found themselves divested of property rights, independent sources of income, and their monopoly of overland trading routes as well as rural and urban markets. In a radical recalibration of gender relations African men, in some ethnic groups, became the beneficiaries of women's loss of status and economic independence, as colonial intermediaries or collaborators they were given increased control over women of their community (Parpart 1989: pp. 3–5). Thus European colonial interpretations of customary law led to a reconstitution of 'tradition' and 'traditional practice that reflected a specific colonial view of African society. Within this scenario colonial policy and law specifically privileged men over women influencing women's status and influence in many communities as they were side-lined in the patriarchal politics of the colonial project.

Under colonialism, women were the subalterns due to gender difference and the prioritization of male prerogative. Women were less able to speak and as such, the subaltern voice is lost in history (Spivak 1988: pp. 83–91). But is it? Even in Spivak's seminal work on western interpretations of history with respect to India she ultimately demonstrates that often what is not said is more important than what is. Using the suicide of Bhuraeswari Bhaduri, a female activist of the colonial resistance, she demonstrates how the 'voiceless' are able to speak through actions rather than words. Whereby Bhaduri, in order that her suicide not be attributed to an 'illegitimate passion' she waited until she was menstruating to take her own life.[2] Could this be seen as the 'subaltern rewriting the social text'? (Spivak 1988: 103–4). For Stoler, this would depend on who was interpreting the actions of the colonial subjects. Colonial archives as the site of contested knowledge offer an insight into the political and social conditions of the colonial period, as such the context in which actions are interpreted and decisions are made. Thus it allows us 'to identify the conditions of possibility that shaped what could be written, what warranted repetition, what competencies were rewarded in archival writing, what stories could not be told and what could not be said' (Stoler 2002: 91). When studying the past or the present what we seek is pathways through patriarchal knowledge production to a sensitive understanding of human agency ever present albeit through silence, non-conformity or active resistance.

In the colonial context, interpretations of tradition or cultural mores can lead to the mystification of cultural practice as norm. Mani's work on the practice of sati in colonial India identifies a colonial project of the authentication of cultural practice eventuating in a reconstitution of tradition. This was achieved through a 'convergence of understanding' arrived at by colonial officials, missionaries and indigenous elites, it was one in which women were clearly disadvantaged in an alliance secured

[2]In a trusted position in the resistance, she was given the task of taking someone's life unable to do that she chose to take her own.

by religious precedent and material gain (Mani 1987: 122–4). These were the kind of alliances which underwrote the global colonial project in Africa by which women's words and actions are consistently interpreted for them rather than by them in both the past and the present. The work of Trinh Minh Ha, which strongly informs the analysis in this chapter, offers a pertinent focus on the question of authenticity and the way that difference undermines identity. One in which the indigenous colonial insider and the 'native other' can be one and the same depending on their location to the colonial project at any point in time. Complicit in the redefining of 'authentic' cultural practice by the colonial state 'often situated within a process of elimination of all that is considered other, superfluous, fake, corrupted, or Westernized' (Minh Ha 1997: 415).

So it was in the 'othering' of Africa, whereby the indigenous male collaborators and informants engaged in political connivance to challenge and undermine the cultural practices of magic, witchcraft and spirituality in which women had a central role. While it certainly served the interest of the colonial state it clearly benefitted indigenous men by directly attacking the women who exercised social and political power through magic, spirit possession and healing. Magic became the antithesis of the 'modern' and a political obstacle to the colonial project—a competitor for the 'hearts and minds' of the indigenous colonial outsider. In East Africa, colonial officials were well aware that irrespective of the status or position of the indigenous population that magic and witchcraft formed part of their traditional belief systems in which women as spirit mediums would be called upon when hardship or difficulty arose to open the pathways to good fortune, pacify deities and ancestors or heal the sick (See Berger 2005: 148–155).

The Eurocentric term witchcraft was employed to 'name' the belief systems and spiritual practice of the 'native other' and for the colonial project it was the means by which women could escape government control and most of all male domination. As such it was malevolent, no longer a force for good but one inordinately associated with evil (Ciekawy 1999). This was to remain the 'authentic' interpretation of indigenous spirituality and practice throughout the colonial period passing seamlessly into the postcolonial project of economic and political development. The Colonial archives open a window that offers insights into how women dealt with the colonial state and its collaborators through the use of myth, ritual, song and witchcraft, and the informal institutions that supported them, to voice not only their concerns but to challenge those who threatened to take away their rights and livelihoods.

## Colonial Encounters: Women Agency and Witchcraft

In precolonial Kenya, the spirit world strongly influenced daily life and underwrote the traditional belief systems of clans, families, elders, social structures and accepted understandings of gender relations themselves. This world was used to interpret the incidence of wrongdoing, misfortune, familial disputes, sickness and natural disasters (Richards 1935: 456). Ritual associated with fertility, marriage, rain ceremonies, or against epidemics, droughts, and enmity, was imbued within the cultural mores of each ethnic community and social group.[3] Thus, the living had to be careful not to antagonise the spirit world of ancestors, of spirits that cause sickness, influence natural events or form part of the environment (Hoehler-Fatton 1996: 215). Ceremonies made use of charms and spirit mediums, to cure illness, or to make threats and oaths to maintain agreements between disaffected parties. Appeals were made to those skilled in dealing with the spirits to help settle serious disputes such as accusations of adultery, theft, murder or indeed the practice of evil itself (Lambert 1965: 124, 141–144). Among the Meru, for example, distinctions were made between a Morogi 'a poisoner who collects medicines secretly at night', a Muga, a healer who has a power for good/healing, and a Muroria, a soothsayer who foretells the length of famine, or war, as revealed in dreams (Fadiman 1993: p. 272). Recourse to the spirit world was a method of social control, in that behaviour outside of what was considered socially acceptable would be dealt with by invoking the powers of malevolent spirits. The authority of female and male elders relied on councils, kin loyalty, the placement of fines and the use of oaths to bring about social order (Peristiany 1964: 188).

Nevertheless, this authority could be challenged through magic and spiritual intervention. Women became most adept at invoking a politics of confrontation particularly during colonial rule when their rights were infringed upon and justice was denied. It was the colonial rulers and missionaries that turned the beliefs of the majority of the Kenyan population into something maleficent using the European terms of 'witchcraft' and the 'occult' to describe inexplicable acts of spirit intervention and possession invoked and witnessed in public space. For example, female Christian converts who on the loss of family members returned to their villages to carry out mourning, cleansing rituals and sacrifices to appease spiritual ancestors were often expelled from missionary stations (Mutongi 2007: 49). Such practices were seen by both missionaries and the administration alike as evil.

Witchcraft made use of rumour, hints, suspicion and insinuations in all Kenyan ethnic groups and was commented on at length in Colonial Papers. Thus for the Nandi, 'witches' bewitch from pure hatred, jealousy, revenge or manipulation, for example, to settle debts such as bridewealth payments (Huntingford 1963: 180). Unexplained sickness was principally attributed to female spiritual practices in Nandi communities in view of women's role in traditional healing and the well-being of the community.[4] The use of the 'evil eye' *Sihoho* in Luo communities was also attributed to women.[5] The Luo live in compounds, (*Keyo*) with co-wives

[3]For examples of healing rituals see: Manuscripts. Africa. (Rhodes House. Oxford.) Series Nr. 1153. Box 1. File b. Item 1. p. 5. Herein after cited as: Mss. Afr. s. followed by series numbers. Mss. Afr. s. 1153 1/b/1 Fazan Papers, and Peristiany J.G., The Social Institutions of the Kipsigis. 1964. Routledge and Kegan Paul. London. p. 221–2.

[4]Mss. Afr. s. 1792. 4/4–6/4. Hamstead C. S. Notes on Nandi. Kisumu Provincial Annual Report. 1907–8. p. 35.

[5]Mss. Afr. s. 1792. 45/7/15. Whisson M. G. p. 11.

sharing a courtyard.[6] This living arrangement, according to Levine, made the Luo women'quarrelsome, litigious and susceptible to accusations of sorcery and witchcraft' (Levine 1962: 43). Yet the threat of its use could keep the peace between co-wives, because a person who practised it, not only brought trouble and quarrelling into the home but they also risked ostracism and banishment. Thus the fear of being accused of being a witch by, for example, brothers in law, served as a low-level sanction against the use of sorcery and witchcraft.[7]

At the same time however, in Luo mythology spirits (*Juogi*) exist in everything and they possess both the ability to do good and inflict harm (Ocholla-Ayayo 1976: 187). For example, offerings are made adjacent to trees and rocks because they are thought to house ancestral spirits.[8] Within the Luo belief systems, there was a clear gender division of labour, men dealt with ancestor spirits and their impact on lineage while women were inclined to dominate spirit possession, or ecstatic experiences of spirit encounters. Here a woman could publicly name the disquiet or disruptive entity in the hope of re-establishing social harmony. In this way, women made use of socially accepted behaviours, spirit possession and naming, to air grievances while claiming protection from sorcery or trouble because their actions emanated from the spirit's power. A political skill women used to their benefit throughout the colonial period to highlight men's responsibilities and their weaknesses (Mutongi 2007: p. 8).

In contrast, the Kipsigis, according to Peristiany, have four purveyors, of magic. The *laibon*, of the Massai clans who exercised their power through spirit possession, dreams, and magic amulets; the *orgoyot,* male members of specific clans attributed with a variety of supernatural powers; the *ponindet,* someone able to use the 'evil eye' and the *chebsogeyot*, a female healer with only curative powers.[9] Each possessed important powers, the *laibon* for example would use dreams to bring about successful cattle raids, to predict droughts or successful harvests. The *ponindet,* who could be male or female, was considered the most dangerous type of sorcerer, always jealous and casting curses, (*chubisiet),* that could only be removed by the *chebsogeyot*. This type of 'evil' practice, Peristiany claims, has a recognized gender specific lineage passed from female to female or male to male (Peristiany 1964: p. 94) For example, he cites the trial of a woman accused of sorcery whose acquittal was based on the fact that no such lineage existed—neither her mother, grandmother or great-grandmother were known witches (Peristiany 1964: p. 201).

In the ethnic groups cited here, recourse to the spirit world and the punishment of 'named' witches was considered essential for keeping the peace and the

---

[6]Kenya National Archives Micro film. The Provincial and District Annual Reports, (AR), Political Record Books, (PRB), and Handing Over Reports, (HOR) Miscellaneous Correspondence, (MC). Syracuse: Syracuse University. NA PRB file No: 22/EN/10. ELGON Nyanza Political Record Book. Luo Law and Custom Regarding Land. 1953. p. 4.

[7]Mss. Afr. s. 1792. 45/7/15. Whisson M. G. p. 10.

[8]Mss. Afr. s. 1792. 45/7/15. Whisson M. G. p. 14.

[9]The Laibon were deported out of the Kipsigis land unit shortly after the arrival of the British. Peristiany J. G., Op. cit. pp. 225–227.

maintenance of social harmony. The punishment of witches in Kikuyu communities, as amongst the Kipsigis, Luo and Nandi peoples, was a community affair whereby accepted punishment consisted of banishment, public purging or flogging and execution. (Waller 2001: 270). The family of the accused was usually consulted and would often be the first to institute the execution process.[10] This symbolized the breaking of familial bonds. The whole process of conviction and punishment was long and deeply disruptive to the community and carried out only after rituals of cleansing and oaths had failed to get the offender to mend their ways, (Fadiman 1993: 268). Such community actions, exposed the extensive linkages between the spirit world and familial relationships which could bind as well as destroy marriages, families and communities with its emphasis on appropriate gender behaviours, sacrifices and rituals.

In colonial, as in precolonial, society the spirit world continued to influence attitudes and behaviour when the indigenous 'insider' communities were confronted with the moralizing discourses of missionary societies and the changes demanded by the colonial government of local cultural mores and customary law. Indeed, how could this 'intimate circle of the family', when faced with the challenges of colonial rule, not pursue the power of the spirit world, and call upon the spirits of the ancestors to deal with these problems. (Ciekawy and Geschiere 1998: p. 5) The advent of migrant labour, for example, changed the community's ability to control sorcerers and the 'occult', to seek out person's accused of such actions and to keep the peace. Nowhere was this more prevalent than the concerted efforts by indigenous elders and the successive colonial administrations to control women (White 1990: 194). Disabused of the rights to land they voted with their feet and moved in large number into urban areas. Women who were traders and engaged in independent economic activity or who lived in the city out of the control of their families were under suspicion from their husbands and communities. Spiritual power was seen to be translating into economic power as members of the indigenous insider community claimed such women were harbouring harmful charms and medicines to be used on those who did not share in their new-found wealth (Mutongi 2007: 140). Thus a woman of independent means, it was believed, could lead 'Kenyan men [to be] worried that wives maddened with money would sap a husbands' virility with sorcery' (Peterson 2001: 473). One such case was that of Duncan Thinji who in 1940, complained to the church that his wife, a trader, had caused him to become sexually impotent. A claim refuted by a local witch doctor.[11] These allegations might also be interpreted as an act of self defence instituted by men that women accused of impotence because they failed to fulfil marital duties, and wasted household resources on cigarettes and beer.[12]

[10]Mss. Afr. s. 742/2 Punishment of a Witchdoctor by Death in Meru—1933. Cites a case in Machakos, where 60 people were convicted in the High Court of Kenya for beating to death a witch. These 60 people constituted the members of her family, and her neighbours. p. 1.

[11]Ibid. p. 476.

[12]Ibid. p. 483.

The fact remains that the impact of colonial rule created new behaviours and situations that were not controlled by accepted sets of rituals or recourse to advice obtained from the *laibon* or ancestors. Women who traded or sold parts of the crops that they planted were often accused of being 'out of control', immoral women trading away the life of the family and causing starvation within their homes. Women's economic activities frequently brought claims of bewitchment into the home particularly if the woman in question purchased 'medicinal' items. One such claim, cited in the East Africa Law Reports, involved a man who killed his wife when she failed to tell him from where she had obtained her medicine. His defence was that her silence was an indication of witchcraft and believed the medicine was to be used to harm him. The presiding judge, however, stated that the accusation of witchcraft was unreasonable and difficult to believe and found the husband guilty of murder.[13]

Kenyan women, the antithesis of their European counterparts, were forced to resist their social and legal disempowerment throughout the colonial period. Many women who faced land loss, removal of trading rights, destruction of property, heavy taxation and separation from their husbands and families due to migration were more than determined to survive. Survival often meant confronting and living outside of accepted social behaviours and norms. They became outsiders, the 'other', bereft of male control and therefore posed the possibility of harm and discord within their families and communities. Yet, women in colonial Kenya had recourse to powerful acts and relationships that gave legitimacy to their condemnation and exposure of corruption in their communities by male kin and the colonial administration itself.[14] These women held up the proverbial mirrors, which revealed the nature of betrayal and the power of corruption that Kenyan men were involved in under colonial rule. Women challenged the interlopers and indigenous mediators who benefitted extensively from colonial rule, neither insiders nor outsiders, socially rejected by colonial society and resented by a large part of their community and kin. Such actions could only result in the full force of both customary and colonial law being used to protect a new nation. Women often 'seen as signifiers of the nation, both old and new—through motherhood and the reproduction of future generations' bore the strokes of that violence with all the power they could muster (Smith 2008: 47). The postcolonial period, rather than delivering new beginnings saw the tools of colonial society, accusations of sorcery and witchcraft, used once again against women in the struggle for economic empowerment and benefit.

[13]Petero Wabwire s/o Malemo, the appellant. East Africa Law Reports, Vol. 16. 1949. p. 131.

[14]KNA/370. Annual Report Fort Hall/28. Jan. 1949. Coutts W. F. pp. 1–2. Women's actions included rioting and making use of sexual insults, over the use of their labour to work on soil conservation projects. Women deeply resented as it took their labour away from their own sources of income and power. These conservation projects were viewed by women as a collaboration between the male elders of their communities and the administration to undermine women's influence.

## Postcolonial Endeavours: Reframing 'Tradition' and Renaming Cultural Mores in the Context of Economic Development and Social Change

Recent tales from Africa with respect to witch-hunts, witch burning and the evolution of witch camps raises the question of whether spiritualism and magic is indeed the antithesis of the modern. Indeed indigenous spiritual beliefs and practices have been strengthened by the negative influences of modernization such as adversity, marginalization and oppression and have become part of the individual and collective struggle against economic exclusion in the face of economic development and social change (Kohnert 1996: 1347–8). In Kenya as in the rest of Africa, structural adjustment policies introduced from the 1980 s onwards led to growing social inequality, high unemployment and imbued political corruption. Just like the idea of development itself this was believed to be a result of the intervention of outsiders such as the IMF, The World Bank, and NGOs and as such viewed with suspicion (Geschiere and Nyamnjoh 1998: 71). Added to this the relative tsunami of Pentecostalism and its attempt to colonize if not usurp traditional belief systems from West to East Africa in the same period created a formidable challenge to indigenous spiritualism and magic, ancestral tradition and deity worship (Deacon and Lynch 2013 p. 108). In the battle for hearts and minds in the process of socio-cultural renovation through economic development and a commitment to the Holy Spirit once again women found themselves at the centre of disputed territory in both the acquisition of land and the esoteric terrain of spiritual belief.

Women's experiences of both the colonised state and the postcolonial state of Kenya varied markedly from those of men. Post-independence women's education, employment opportunities, control over the land they cultivate (usufruct rights) and life choices were, once again constrained. Women's efforts to arrest these disadvantages range, as they did in the colonial period, from utilizing familial support networks, migrating to urban areas, trading, joining women's organizations and churches to seeking legal redress through the court system, activism, public protest and 'witchcraft' (Stamp 1995; Nelson 2001; Hodgson and McCurdy 2001; Kameri-Mbote 2006). More often than not women's complaints revolve around access to resources, land rights, income, all of which are tied to marital obligations[15] Within most east African countries there exists a delineation between the gender division of labour and its associated gender division of income (Heyer 2006). That is, women and men farm separate crops and the income, harvest and use values, derived therefrom is divided along gender lines which reinforce accepted notions of male and female virtue and social harmony. The impact of capitalist development and its emphasis on male employment and male commercial farming enterprises in particular, has eroded these divisions leaving women's production and incomes severely stressed and precarious. In both rural and urban areas women have turned to

[15]See Buswell & Corcoran-Nantes Chapter 11 in this volume

income generating activities using resources and skills available to them to maintain their independence and strengthen their economic status.

The increasing incidence of witchcraft accusations against women in Eastern Africa in the contemporary period is found often in situations where they stand outside of expected norms or in the way of male 'right' and privilege in the process of economic development. The work of James Smith in Northern Kenya illustrates the growing confrontation between traditional gender relations and the household facing the austerity politics of economic development. Households may have maintained the veneer of patriarchal authority but in reality this was being subverted by circumstance. Women were becoming the 'primary producers and 'owners' of household wealth. For example, wealthy Kikuyu women monopolized the trading of gems. They brought benefit to the family through the relationship between NGOs and women's groups as male salaries were increasingly insufficient to meet household needs. Smith demonstrates the impact of all of this on households and male control as the number of matricentric households increased (Smith 2008: 119–124). The work of Erich Leistner demonstrates how, in the face of economic adversity, witchcraft and magic become the conduit for rationalization of the fortunes and misfortunes emanating from contemporary African capitalist development. In the zero sum economy of traditional thinking, a belief in finite resources, believed those 'doing well' accessed the benefits of development through the use of magic and witchcraft. As suspicion and resentment increased so did accusations of witchcraft, sorcery and possession (2014: 55–57).

It is no coincidence that there is a direct link between witch-hunts and land. In Kenya witch-hunts against, principally, elderly women who maintain rights over land they continue to cultivate have come from members of the local community as well members of the accused's own family. All of whom see such elders as 'dead weight' benefiting in the battle for survival while the dispossessed suffer (Ogembo 2006: 125). As both Ciekawy and Geshiere have remarked 'witchcraft of the house' is the most dangerous revealing the 'dark side of kinship' (Ciekawy 1998: 5). In the breakdown of the village economy the rights of widowed or divorced women to land for cultivation fly in the face of the incapacity of male members of the community to provide for their families (Walsh 2003: 42). Federici argues that witch-hunting is in fact a war on women and the cache of beliefs of what constitutes womanhood in a changing environment. Thus women who claim their rights, or choose to fight for them, stand in the way of economic development:

> There can be little doubt that the abuses inflicted on 'witches' served to discipline all women thereby preventing them from asserting their rights (Federici 2010: 22).

Similarly in urban areas where, traditionally, women monopolize the trade of certain goods they are being accused of witchcraft by male traders who wish to move into once 'female' dominated areas of trade. In the prevailing culture of neoliberalism a recalibration of gender relations is coerced by defining once acceptable female activities as inherently malevolent (Federici 2008: p. 27),

Perhaps the greatest threat to women's status within the sphere of spiritualism, healing and magic came from Pentecostalism and the spiritual entrenchment of a 'faith' that essentially appropriated the practices of traditional beliefs and made them its own. Christianity deemed that there was only one spiritual deity, the Holy Spirit, and any claims to others were maleficent. The success of Pentecostalism across Africa was its capacity to incorporate indigenous practices and cultural mores into charismatic religiosity and with a deft sleight of hand attempt to restore the patriarchal imbalance. Thus, while women formed the large proportion of the Pentecostalist congregation, it was male spiritualists that moved into the field of Christian faith healing under the training and guidance of male church leaders 'channeling the Holy Spirit'. Women were rarely if ever recruited to the same levels as men (Hoehler-Fatton 1996: p. 118). Yet, under the traditional belief system faith healing was considered to be a calling and female spiritual healers would train under a divine mentor. This role also required spiritual channeling as well as bestowing the capacity to protect against the 'malevolence of witches' (Anyinam 1997: p. 104). The two were in contradistinction to one another a friction that fuelled the Pentecostalist fear mongering with its cult of the devil and as such members of its congregation in continuing to engage in traditional belief systems parallel to Christian worship were accused of 'allowing Satan in'. Such teachings were believed to be directly associated with the upsurge in accusations of witchcraft and magic and the witch-hunts which ensued (Deacon and Lynch 2013: p. 111). This was a curious war waged by an outside religious force on behalf of its predominantly female congregation against indigenous female spiritualists who also act for and on behalf of women in the community.

Female spiritualists, 'priestesses' and natural healers are most prevalent in rural areas where the opportunities for income generation in contemporary Kenya especially for women has declined considerably this is above all else a profession, a traditional livelihood. One that women could not afford to lose. Women who were classed as sacred healers, with inherited powers maintained a special status among both women and men in indigenous communities. The female spiritual healer was used as a conduit by women to deal with a patriarchal society and emit its own form of justice and comfort in a challenging world.

> It is the spiritual healer who provides charms and prescribes the rituals to neutralize the effect of the enemy's charms, wards off evil spirits, and intercedes between the community and the gods and spirits of deceased ancestors (Anyinam 1997: 106)

No outside religious force could combat such spiritual beliefs which remain deeply rooted within Kenyan society irrespective of the class, ethnicity or religion of the individual. While both men and women are spiritualists and healers, in equal measure, women have traditionally exercised a political role as social mediators with the means of defying male domination. Conceivably, that is the key to understanding the targeting of women a politics unrecognized by the antipathy of male journalists and academics who write about witch-hunting (Federici 2008: 24–5). Across the literature it is acknowledged that without doubt women were primarily the target of seething discontent at the less than successful trajectory of economic development right the way across Africa. A recent sermon by a Catholic priest in Uganda stating that it was easy to avoid being accused of witchcraft perhaps offers the best indictment of the previous statements when advising his congregation; ‘to make sure you are not a migrant, an unprotected woman, poor, use farm land that someone else wants or be someone whose relatives have died’ (Allen and Reid 2015: p. 119). Those who best fit these categories would be, without question, predominantly women. Women’s actions rise above this and as such it is not surprising to increasingly see ‘witchcraft’ being used by women in public spaces as an empowering agent calling attention to male avarice and their complicity in the political economy of development. (Chonghaile 2012).

As outsiders to the colonial project and usurpers in the contemporary one, in all its genres, female spiritualists have demonstrated their capacity to adapt to social and economic change, tout power and influence and rise above challenges which question the veritability of their social status. In neoliberal Kenya witchcraft and development coexist as the former remains part of the established order and a belief system that underwrites the latter. Nevertheless, women as spiritual mediums remain a force to be reckoned with and the site of gendered resistance in contemporary East African society.

## References

Allen T, Reid K (2015) Justice at the margins: witches, poisoners and social accountability in Northern Uganda. Medial Anthropol 34(2):106–123

Anyinam C (1997) The role of female spiritualists in Africa: persistence with change. Can Women Stud 17(1):103–106

Behrend H (2007) The rise of occult powers, AIDS and the Roman Catholic Church in Western Uganda. J Relig Afr 37(1):41–58

Berger I (2005) ‘Rebels or status seekers? : women as spirit mediums in east Africa’. In: Andrea C (ed) Readings in Gender and Africa. Indiana University Press, Bloomington, pp 148–155

Blunt R (2013) Oracles, trauma, and the limits of contextualization: naming the witch in contemporary Kenya. J Relig Afr 43:329–349

Chonghaile CN (2012) Kenyan graffiti artists target ‘Vulture’ politicians. The Guardian Weekly, p 8. (30/3/2012)

Ciekawy D (1998) Witchcraft in statecraft: five technologies of power in colonial and postcolonial coastal Kenya. Afr Stud Rev 41(3):119–141

Ciekawy D, Geschiere P (1998) Witchcraft: conflicting scenarios in postcolonial Africa. Afr Stud Rev 41(3):1–14

Ciekawy D (1999) Women’s “work” and the construction of witchcraft accusations in coastal Kenya. Women’s Stud Int Forum 22(2):225–235

Deacon G, Lynch G (2013) Allowing Satan in? Moving toward a political economy of Neo Pentecostalism in Kenya. J Relig Afr 43:108–130

Fadiman JA (1993) When we began there were witchmen. An oral history from Mount Kenya. University of California Press, Berkeley

Federici S (2008) Witch-Hunting, globalization, and feminist solidarity in Africa today. J Int Women’s Stud 10(1):21–35

Federici S (2010) Women, witch-hunting and enclosures in Africa today Sozial.Geschichte Online 3, pp 10–27. http://www.stiftung-sozialgeschichte.de

Geschiere P, Nyamnjoh F (1998) Witchcraft as an issue in the "politics of belonging": democratization and urban migrant's involvement with the home village. Afr Stud Rev 41(3):69–91

Heyer A (2006) The gender of wealth: markets and power in central Kenya. Rev Afr Polit Econ 33(107):67–80

Hoehler-Fatton C (1996) Women of fire and spirit: history, faith, and gender in Roho religion in western Kenya. Oxford University Press, Oxford

Hodgson DL, McCurdy Sheryl A (2001) "Wicked women" and the reconfiguration of gender in Africa. James Currey, Oxford

Huntingford GWB (1963) Nandi witchcraft. In: Middleton J, Winter EH (eds) Witchcraft and sorcery in east Africa. Routledge & Kegan Paul, London, pp 175–186

Kameri-Mbote P (2006) Women, land rights and the environment: the Kenyan experience. Development 49(3):43–48

Kohnert D (1996) Magic and witchcraft: implications for democratization and poverty alleviating aid in Africa. World Dev 24(8):1347–1355

Lambert H (1965) Kikuyu social and political institutions. Oxford University Press, London

Leistner E (2014) Witchcraft and African development. Afr Secur Rev 23(1): 53–77

LeVine R (1962) Witchcraft and co-wife proximity in south-western Kenya. Ethnology 1(1):39–45

Mani L (1987) Contentious traditions: The debate on Sati in colonial India. Cult. Critique 7: 119–156

Minh Ha T (1997) Not you/like you: post-colonial women and the interlocking questions of identity and difference In Mclintock A, Mufti A, Shohat E (eds) Dangerous liaisons: gender nation and postcolonial perspectives. University of Minnesota Press, Minneapolis, pp 415–419

Mutongi K (2007) Worries of the heart: widows, family and community in Kenya. University of Chicago Press, Chicago

Nelson N (ed) (2001) African women in the development process. Frank Cass, London

Ocholla-Ayayo ABC (1976) Traditional ideology and ethics among the southern Luo. Africana Publishing, Uppsala

Ogembo JM (2006) Contemporary witch-hunting in Gusii, southwestern Kenya. Edward Mellen Press, New York

Parpart JL (ed) (1989) Women and development in Africa: comparative perspectives. University Press of America, Lanham, Maryland

Peristiany JG (1964) The social institutions of the Kipsigis. Routledge and Kegan Paul, London

Peterson D (2001) Wordy women: gender trouble and the oral politics of the east African revival in northern Gikuyuland. J Afr His 42(3): 469–489

Richards A (1935) A modern movement of witch-finders. Africa 8(4):448–461

Smith JH (2001) Of spirit possession and structural adjustment programs: government downsizing education and the enchantments in Neo-liberal Kenya. J Relig Afr 31(4):427–456

Smith JH (2008) Bewitching development: witchcraft and the reinvention of development in Neoliberal Kenya. University of Chicago Press, Chicago

Spivak GC (1988) Can the Subaltern speak? In: Nelson C, Grossberg L (eds) Marxism and the interpretation of culture. Macmillan Education, Basingstoke, pp 271–313

Stamp P (1995) Mothers of invention: women's agency in the Kenyan state. In: G JK (ed) Provoking agents: gender and agency in theory and practice. University of Illinois Press, Urbana, pp 69–92

Stoler AL (2002) Colonial archives and the arts of governance. Arch Sci 2:87–109

Waller R (2001) Witchcraft and colonial law in Kenya. Past Present 180:241–275

Walsh J (2003) Double standards: women's property rights violations in Kenya. Hum Rights Watch 15(5). http://www.hrw.org/reports/2003/kenya0303/kenya0303.pdf

White L (1990) The comforts of home: prostitution in colonial Nairobi. University of Chicago Press, Chicago

## Author Biographies

**Dr. Yvonne Corcoran-Nantes** is widely known in the field of Gender Studies, regularly being interviewed on gender and political issues by the media in Australia and overseas. She has worked with women in such diverse locations as Central Asia, Mongolia, Indonesia, East Timor and Brazil in many research and development projects to improve the rights and status of women in their respective countries. At the present time she is undertaking research on women ex combatants in contemporary Vietnam. While Dr Corcoran-Nantes currently teaches in the areas of international studies and women's studies, her main research interests are: Gender and International Politics, Gender and International Development and Women and Armed Conflict. Dr Corcoran-Nantes is Head of Women's Studies and an Associate Professor in the School of Social and Policy Studies at Flinders University.

**Dr. Clare Buswell** is an adjunct academic staff member in the School of Social and Policy Studies. Her research is in Gender and the Colonial History of East Africa. Dr Buswell's research and writing focuses on Women's Experiences of Colonial Occupation in Eastern Africa and the Philippines, Women, Witchcraft and Social Ostracism in Africa, Gender and International Development, Customary Lore and Law in Kenya.

# Chapter 21
# Demoscopio: The Demosensual [R] evolutionary Eutopia

**Maria Kakoulaki and Alexander N. Christakis**

**Abstract** For the emergence of a Demosensual [R]evolutionary Eutopia in the twenty-first century, we ought to transcend the totalitarian, elitist approaches of political, financial, and societal policies and the obsolete social design methods, with innovative democratic practices, that will enable citizens from all walks of life, in participating in meaningful, authentic, demosensual dialogue. This chapter is inspired by the foundation for a locally based, but globally connected capability that transcends the conventional approach of Systems Science and marks the emergence of a new epoch for engaging stakeholders in social design practices. Demoscopio Center of the Science of Dialogic Design, Innovation and Entrepreneurship has been officially approved and adopted by the City Council of the Municipality of Heraklion, which is the capital of the Greek island of Crete, and a historical and culturally sensitive center, since the Minoan era. It is the culmination of 50 years of work of visionary systems thinkers, such as Harold Lasswell, Hasan Ozbekhan, John N. Warfield, and Alexander N. Christakis. Demoscopio is the contemporary reenactment of the Ancient Athenian Agora of the fifth-century B.C, with advanced technological and methodological means. It represents an innovative way to talk the

---

Demosensus: the term has been created and used by Dr. Alexander N. Christakis as an "acronym" for the proposal, "Global Systems Science for Human-centered Policy Making in Complex Environments" GSS H2020-FETPROACT-2014. The proposal was submitted by professor Gerald Midgley, Director of the Center for Systems Research, University of Hull. In this chapter, the word "demosensual" is defined to mean the emergence of a linguistic, and cognitive emotional, consensual domain, by engaging a community of stakeholders in the methodology of Structured Democratic Dialogue (SDD).

Eutopia: is a term proposed by Maria Kakoulaki, (inspired by the terms utopia, dystopia, entopia, protopia), and is defined as the normative visualization of an ideal future state of a social system, which is profoundly different from the present and the extrapolated future, and requires intellectual and emotional qualities of creativity, synthesis, and empathy. Eutopia emerges from the demosensual engagement of stakeholders.

---

M. Kakoulaki (✉) · A.N. Christakis
Institute for 21Century Agoras, Lavyrinthou 6, Archanes, 70100 Heraklion, Crete, Greece
e-mail: MariaKakoulaki@hotmail.com

A.N. Christakis
e-mail: alexander.n.christakis@gmail.com



J. McIntyre-Mills et al. (eds.), *Balancing Individualism and Collectivism*,
Contemporary Systems Thinking, DOI 10.1007/978-3-319-58014-2_21

walk, and walk the talk! It is the [r]evolutionary scientific implementation of the complementarity among the "Three Phases of Science" for fostering cooperation, enhancing communication, and activating social networking among citizens, innovators, and entrepreneurs. It offers the opportunity for co-designing resolutions for complex issues, through evolutionary learning and applications of the Science of Dialogic Design. It is the innovation for innovations, entrepreneurial development, democratic eutopia, for thinking globally, [inter]acting locally and making an impact glocally.

# Introduction

## *Philosophical Context and Contemporary Needs*

> We are living though a crisis; and because we have failed to respond properly, we are heading towards disaster. Our settlements are lagging behind the worlds' overall progress, our ideas are confused, we are moving without coordination and adjustment, and we have not even defined our role. However, we do have a historic responsibility, and that is to understand the crisis and develop a new approach in order to face it
>
> Constantinos A. Doxiadis 1968

Democracy in the twenty-first century refers almost exclusively to the right to vote and sometimes revolt against those in power. Meanwhile many utopias dystopias, entopias, protopias are entrapping our democratic consciousness and jeopardize our engagement, by imposing invisible limitations, disruptive forces and short-term improvements. This observation comes into contrast with the tremendous possibilities of technological progress and raises a whole new series of questions: How can we as human beings design our own future? Why so many well-educated and trained "experts", all around the world, with excellent skills and experiences, are continuously failing in anticipating, addressing, and resolving contemporary challenges, such as poverty, hunger, lack of drinking water, climate change, terrorism, armed conflict and war, nuclear weapons, humanitarian and financial crises, and the availability of energy resources? Does voting every four or five years fulfill our democratic consciousness, rights and obligations as citizens? How can [be]come part of what is being decided for us, often without us, i.e., without the inclusion or our opinions, understandings, consent, and commitment? Can we talk authentically, can we listen effectively, and can we collaborate with each other? Can we really design new common "grounds" for dealing with contemporary complexities? And if the answer is "yes", then which methodological procedures can we employ for developing long-term visions and policy-designs for our own life worlds?

Modern societies have been challenged by the way technology is changing, not only in our ways of thinking and acting, but in the evolution of our bodies, of our feelings, and our democratic consciousness as citizens. Nowadays, we experience the enormous power and possibilities of our digital and technical systems. Yet we do not appear to be closer to processes of democratization and reforms but rather authoritarian governance that is often elitist and exclusive. Furthermore, we ought to make progress on the democratic evolution of our technologies and on technological evolution of our democratic practices. This is a current requirement, since opinion pollsters, analysts, and policy-makers tend to emphasize and value exclusively quantitative metrics for monitoring democratic practices, many of which are designed by technocrats, "experts", and elites. These metrics are reproduced and applied in a variety of situations; as a result the statistical data and "expert" models very often fail to capture any qualitative aspects of citizen's political opinions and subjective observations. The question is: how can we design innovative and customized democratic practices, which are technologically advanced and concurrently capable in supporting citizen's democratic participation, innovation and entrepreneurship?

The lack of common understanding and shared vision has already shadowed modernity as the ongoing sameness of the unchanging. Post-modernism brought new ways for accessibility and interactivity. Meta-modernism comes with a series of new questions: How can we really create conscious evolution? How can we redesign our local communities in sharing authentic, participative experiences, promoting transparency and minimizing secrecy and undiscussability?

Experiences of the past, new ideas of the present, and visions of an ideal future, can be designed collectively and demosensually as a bottom-up, value-driven planning, and policy-making. This approach requires that we develop skills and qualities, visions and values that we did not even know we had before. We ought educate ourselves to perceive the present, from the space and time of an eutopian future, instead as an extrapolated prediction and "certainty" of a dystopian past (Ozbekhan 1968). Demoscopio is defined as a culture capable of inventing and engaging networks of citizens, from all walks of life, in applying the methodology of the Science of Dialogue for designing social systems. It is the community wisdom (demosophia) and collective consciousness in conjunction with technological advances compatible with humanistic value base.

## Demoscopio: Origin, Influences, and Inspirations

### *The Athenian Agora of Direct Democracy*

The vision for Demoscopio begins from the Ancient Athenian Democracy of the sixth-Century B.C., where citizenship could be practiced on a daily basis in the public arena of the Agora, with the shortcoming of the exclusion of women and slaves. The Agora was not simply a public dialogic space, but also a commercial, political, administrative, religious, and cultural center. It was a space where thoughts and actions were conceptualized, designed, and implemented. Athenians were also using the space of the theater for interacting, which it was considered as the ideal space sustaining the attention required for group decision-making; Furthermore, in the space of Pnyx, the Athenians were standing high on a stone platform called "bema" from where they could deliver speeches. This unique combination of an aesthetically stimulating space, just above the rest of the city, across the acropolis and the Odeon of Herodes Atticus, under the Athenian sky, enlightened the soul and spirit and emancipated their capacity to become deliberative. The coexistence of these important components in the Ancient Athenian Democracy, are evident to the visitors until today, not simply as testimonials of great ideals and practices of direct democracy, but also as proves of the framework in which democratic consciousness was immersed. The allocation of a space in a city dedicated to dialogue and direct interaction among the citizens, and their communication with the leadership of the city represented a foundational prerequisite of democratic practice (Sennet 1999).

## *Harold D. Lasswell's "Social Planetarium"*

The vision and the steps toward the conceptualization for Demoscopio, have rather a long history and some recent milestone events. Beyond the model of direct democracy, applied in the Ancient Athenian Agora, the creative innovator and sociologist Harold Lasswell captured the idea of a methodological structure that could inspire public engagement. Lasswell articulated in the decade of 1960, the equivalent of an astronomical type of planetarium, which he defined as "social planetarium", for the purpose of informing and engaging the citizens of a city in decision-making, by the process of decision-seminars. Lasswell's social planetarium like its astronomical counterpart, would serve to collect and display graphical data, but in this case the data would be drawn from a city or region, for the purpose of citizens' education and participation in policy-making. When he became a member of the Board of the Academy for Contemporary Problems in 1970 (an Institution funded by Battelle Memorial Institute in Columbus, Ohio), he collaborated with John N. Warfield and Alexander N. Christakis, who were fellows of the Academy, in promoting the implementation of this idea, that involves an interactive public space (Lasswell 1959; Lasswell 1963). Warfield and Christakis continued the work initiated at the Academy of the Contemporary Problems by developing consensus methods, promoting the implementation of the idea of the Social Planetarium and initiated the practice of Interactive Management (CIM), through the establishment of the Center of Interactive Management in 1981, first at the University of Virginia and later in 1984 at George Mason University. The first "Demosophia Facility" for engaging stakeholders in structured dialogue was founded at CIM of George Mason University (Fig. 21.1).

**Fig. 21.1** DEMOSOPHIA (at CIM)-a specially designed room for practicing Interactive Management. The room provides display space supporting a sense of a problem resolution and development of an audit trial

## *A.N. Christakis and J.N. Warfield "CIM" in Crete*

In 1983, Alexander N. Christakis and J. N. Warfield wrote a proposal for establishing a Center for Interactive Management (C.I.M.) on the island of Crete which had three objectives: (a) assisting to resolve ongoing or emerging conflicts among nations or groups in the general vicinity of the Middle East, (b) providing a source of consulting assistance for management and organizational development, and long-range planning to organizations and nations, and (c) providing training opportunities for interactive planning and management for professionals and managers in the Middle East region. The island of Crete was selected among alternatives as a location of geopolitical importance in the Mediterranean and its advantage for preserving neutrality for the participants in the deliberations. Even though this proposal obtained sponsorship and funding, the government of Greece at the time did not adopt it because it could not accept responsibility for the security of visitors from different nations at the Center (Christakis and Warfield 1983).

## *John N. Warfield "Corporate Observatorium"*

In 1996 J. N. Warfield revisited Lasswell's Social Planetarium idea, and he produced a paper titled "The Corporate Observatorium: Sustaining Management Communication and Continuity in the Age of Complexity". In this paper he advocates that a space, which is specially designed and very different from a museum, will contribute in minimizing complexity and would allow for deeper understanding of the issues, obstacles, and visions that a corporate or even an educational institution might have. Based on Lasswell's concept vision (Lasswell 1960; 1963), Warfield envisioned facilities for people dealing with complexity, developing high quality designs, and exhibits presented, so that it could offer an experiential and educational impact to the visitors. Warfield claimed that "no one would expect that Observatorium would be brought into place unless the "art" required to fill it were available, and that all topics discussed were of vital social importance (Warfield 1996).

## *Mathew Shapiro "Boise of Commons"*

In 2000, a colleague of Alexander N. Christakis, Matthew Shapiro, initiated a project of implementing the concept of Social Planetarium in Boise, Idaho, which in 2003, in collaboration with Mary Parker Follett Foundation, it was named Social Planetarium Initiative. Ten years later, Shapiro realized how his idea could work effectively in "building community capacity and affecting deep-rooted change" In the fall of 2014, the Social Planetarium of Boise/Treasure Valley was organized as an Idaho non-profit corporation. In September of 2015 and as the vision and the objectives were evolving, it was renamed "The Boise Commons". The Boise Commons was conceived by Matthew Shapiro and formed in collaboration with Jerome Mapp (a planning consultant and former city council member), and Dean Gunderson (an urban design expert), and it is a nonprofit, nonpartisan organization, whose mission is to foster an empowering and inclusive civic life among the citizenry of Boise and the greater Treasure Valley. Boise Commons mission is to operate community-building, civic development, and participatory governance through a variety of projects, events, spaces, processes, tools, and campaigns; in this ways it attempts to address the critical need for a locally based catalyst having a focus on civic capacity-building and the restoration of a healthy public sphere (Shapiro 2013, 2016).

## *Institute for 21st Century Agoras "Re-inventing Democracy": The Meta-Science Co-laboratory*

On 10 March 2012, the Board of the Institute for 21st Centuries Agoras, and its president, Dr. Thomas Flanagan, conceived and proposed to the Stavros S. Niarchos Foundation in Greece an initiative for reinventing democracy in the country. The title of that project was "Re-inventing democracy: A 2-year project with massive bottom-up, authentic participation of thousands of people from all walks of life, jointly developing a new vision for important concepts, such as those of accountability, ethics, the world of business, recharging the entrepreneurial spirit of the Greek people, and contribute towards a paradigm shift that could offer direction and purpose. The project would be designed in such a way as to facilitate a nationwide internalization and conceptualization of the problematique, starting from a major municipality of the country This proposal of socio-technological intervention was suggesting that "*the crisis in Greece is not merely economic but involves all spheres of life, including crises of institutions and ethics accompanied with severe lost of trust towards practical all systems of management and governance weather corporate or public*" (Flanagan et al. 2013).

## *Tom Flanagan's "Blueprint for Digital Observatorium"*

In 2013 Dr. Thomas Flanagan, inspired by Lasswell's concept, presented a paper called "Blueprint for a Digital Observatorium" in the World Future Forum Conference, in Montreal. Flanagan introduces the idea of a nonlinear dynamic digital space that will interact with the visitors and create aesthetic and experiential understandings in a rapidly changing technological environment. He also talks about the idea of expanding social learning and closing the existing learning gaps by an ongoing dialogue civic process, where those engaged could extract meaning through a scientific, as well as an aesthetic experiential exhibit; such a goal, according to the author, is only possible with means of unbiased curation and apolitical facilitation, when it comes to dialogue. Flanagan connects the effectiveness of such interactive space with data-intensive digital displays, digital dashboards, digital portals, digital and live curators, informal civic and deliberations. Finally, he defines his Observatorium vision as the coexistence of artistic inquiry and democratic practice.

## *"Local Agoras for Dialogue and Citizens' Participation"*

> The science of dialogic design is truly a science that enables people from all walks of life to become 'systems thinkers.' This is the sole rationale for its invention and evolution.
>
> -Aleco Christakis

The first author of this chapter, Maria Kakoulaki, since her early childhood was envisioning a way and a space of interdisciplinary collaboration, where people could discuss about their own visions and problems, and help each other to regain their commitment and enthusiasm towards their community life. A coalition for change, where great ideas will not fade away, because someone or many will take charge and responsibility, and proposals will be viable and people will learn how to be proactive. An interdisciplinary think tank that will work before, during, and beyond any crises, against any well-established stereotypes, obstacles, and constrains. Such a think tank could also design and launch the mobilization of the people around their own ideas, increase their competence, enhance the implementation of their decisions, and sustain the momentum of an evolving culture.

In 2011 an interview and a public presentation in Heraklion by Professor Nicholas A. Christakis, on wonk on Social Networks (Christakis 2009) and the coincidence of meeting the father of Professor Christakis, Dr. Alexander N. Christakis, was the trigger and the inspiration to begin her journey in the world of Systems Thinking. From this time onwards, she became almost obsessed with research in the connections and relations between social network theory and social systems design. The question that remains with her all these years is: how social network theory and practice could be utilized in a normative way for designing social systems? Further more how can improve our society while considering all relevant scientific evidence for human behavior, including cooperation, collaboration and solidarity (Christakis 2011)?

On 19 September 19 2012, Maria Kakoulaki, participated in a co-laboratory of Structured Democratic Dialogue (SDD), organized in Nicosia, Cyprus, by the Future Worlds Center, and the Digital Futures Task Force of the European Commission. This co-laboratory was influenced by the proposal to the Stavros' Niarchos foundation, discussed before, and it had a similar title: Reinventing Democracy in the Digital Era. The overall objective of the project was the engagement of stakeholders in envisioning new models of democratic governance that utilizes the advantages deriving from contemporary as well as emerging digital technologies.

During this SDD co-laboratory, she conceptualized and introduced to the group of participants the idea that became the foundation for Demoscopio. The SDD triggering question was *"What are the features of an ideal future system of governance that fully utilizes innovative emerging technologies?"* The idea, described during the process as "Feature 54", was titled: Local Agoras for Dialogue and Citizens' Participation. The clarification was: the creation of public spaces, where dialogue and plurality will be promoted and cultivated with scientific means and citizens could develop an oral culture. Spaces where systemic reasoning and dialogic design will allow developing a whole new paradigm shift of values, and democratic qualities. The concept was about empowering and emancipating the linguistic potential of the citizens, while providing them with means to externalize their life experiences, and personal opinions on social issues, so that they would create new commonly owned, and shared collective wisdom (demosophia). The goal for Local Agoras, would be to promote ethics, political learning, and competence, and sensitize citizens for taking action, by knowing how to map the political terrain, identify stakeholders, and create new collaborative networks.

## *The European "Parliamentarium" in Brussels*

On March 2016, the two authors visited the Parlamentarium, which is the European Parliament's visitor center in Brussels. The objective was to familiarize themselves with the exhibitions and the technological advances of an interactive space that portrays the unique features of the European Parliament, the history of the European integration, and the different key stakeholders (individual members, political groups, the President, and political group leaders). It is a space that has been designed to cultivate the Europeanism feeling and spirit to those who are visiting it. Concurrently, it is a multimedia experience, smartly designed. Parliamentarium has attracted more than 900.000 visitors, since its opening in 2011, won 16 national and international awards in the field of design, communication, and tourism, is the most visited indoor tourist attraction in Brussels, and visitors' satisfaction is being rated at 90% (during their first visit).

However, the Parliamentarium lacks the capacity to engage visitors in experiential learning about the power of participative democracy. The experience of visitors is primarily focused on interactive computer-based displays of information, which are smartly designed and presented, but they do not allow for input or ideas regarding policy-making, as Lasswell proposed it in his "Social Planetarium" idea, by means of decision seminars. The Parliamentarium setting and technological competence have significant common elements with Flanagan's "Digital Observatorium" proposal. Moreover, they offered the experiential atmosphere and some artistic influences on the design, with main difference that this design does not include dialogic engagements and it is missing evolutionary ephemerality.[1]

Parliamentarium is a technological "miracle" of a futuristic type of "museum", which represents the closest analog of the type of technological exhibits the authors have envisioned as appropriate for Demoscopio capability. Though the technological requirements for Demoscopio, would not be predetermined, but will evolve with the input and participation of the community of users. The innovation of Demoscopio should be perceived and understood as a continuous evolution and dynamic balance between technology and society. Therefore, it should be culturally sensitive and customized to the specific requirements of the people, space, and time for which it is being developed. This implies that development and installation of Demoscopio capabilities, in different locations of the world, must address thoughtfully the balancing of the forces between "technology push" and "societal pull" (Boroush et al. 1980).

[1]Evolutionary ephemerality, although it appears to be an oxymoron, describes the blending of continuous progress with flexibility of thought and structure. Individualism can be perceived as expressed forms or art, but in collectivism as the demosensual outcome of collective wisdom.

## Demoscopio: A Meta-scientific Approach

### *Philosophical Thoughts on Technology and Democracy*

> There are, no doubt, many ways of judging what the advent of the technological age has done to as well as for–mankind. It has changed and is changing, under our very eyes, the face of the physical environment both in the technologically advanced and the technologically backward countries, al- though the advanced countries are more visibly affected by the direct application of science and engineering to the environment. Probably more important by far is what the age of technology has done to the geography of human outlook and expectation.
>
> Ozbekhan 1968

Reflecting on philosophical contributions from Heraclitus' representation of change as the continuously flowing river, considering the Hegelian dialectic of change based on synthesis of the opposing forces (thesis vs. antithesis), the Marxist perspective on humankind's fundamental struggle between social classes the Kuhnian idea of scientific revolution (Kuhn 1970) and Adorno's negative dialectic, (that any meaning does not fit into its context without leaving a remainder (Adorno 1966) one can make the inference that the notion of change is embedded in the concept of a evolutionary balance, defined in this chapter as a "groundless ground".[2] So the title of this book, namely "Balancing Individualism and Collectivism to Support Social and Environmental Justice", should be conceived and interpreted as an ongoing evolutionary process.

Continuing the philosophical reflections, considering Max Weber's famous reference on dystopian modernity theory (Weber 1958), Heidegger's formulation of "the question about technology (Heidegger 1977), Ellul's theory of "the technical phenomenon" and Marshall McLuhan's perception that, the humans have been incorporated into the mechanisms they created, one discovers that there are many different approaches regarding the role and the relationship between technology and society.

Technological determinism and the belief that modern technologies have their own autonomous, nonlinear logic, and the belief that social institutions evolve according to the technological evolution (Marx 1906), created the misconception that implies that technology has a "universal" scope of thinking and practicing, which evolves independently of societal progress. The approach of constructivism implied that theories and technologies encompass scientific and technical characteristics, which suggest specific solutions to any problems; only those who are technically educated can offer these (Fig. 21.2).

On the other hand, indeterminism claims that there is tremendous flexibility of the technical system and its adaptability to a variety of social demand, therefore

---

[2]Groundless ground: not frozen-stereotypical ways of understanding and designing.

**Fig. 21.2** Snapshot from the visit of the authors at the European Parliamentarium. Photography: Maria Kakoulaki 2016

technology can be redefined and adapted according to the various social circumstances as a social factor which is not a panacea in every case. Heidegger claims that technological form is not much different to the religious form that existed during the medieval years and he perceives technology as a process of revelation unfolding, (Heidegger 1971; 1977).

These brief philosophical reflections inspire a whole new series of questions: how technology is connected to our society? How it interacts with it? How can it affect the evolution of one or many social systems? How technology, can inspire or contribute to the evolution of new societal value bases? Can technology change our culture, not simply by contributing in collecting or predicting on the basis of existing data but also on the basis of anticipated future data? How can technology be guided and enhanced through societal evolution? How can we synthesize our democratic and technological practices with new methodological procedures and experiences so that we can synthesize and embody new visions for balancing individualism and collectivism to support societal and environmental justice? (Ozbekhan 1968, 1970; Arnstein and Christakis 1976).

## *Demoscopio and the Three Phases of Science*

Forty-five years ago, the Executive Committed of The Club of Rome (CoR) failed to adopt the original prospectus on "The Predicament of Mankind," as conceptualized by Hasan Ozbekhan. This failure corresponded to a triumph of technocratic approaches to the definition and resolution of the Global Problematique, which was identified for the first time in the prospectus as the complex system resulting from the strong interactions among a set of 49 Continuous Critical Problems (CCPs). The original CoR prospectus espoused an innovative systems approach of a democratic/participative engagement of a variety of citizens/stakeholders in the definition and resolution of the Problematique. Today, the development of the DEMOSCOPIO capability in the City of Heraklion, Crete, as well as other cities around the world, corresponds to the original intent and vision of the CoR prospectus.

Although science for many people means theory supported with evidence, it can also be characterized as a form of collective learning that concentrates on observation as its main vehicle (de Zeeuw 1996). The scientific revolution (Kuhn 1970) for the science of dialogue started in the 1970s (Christakis 1973); it was a consequence of the failure of the Executive Committee of the Club of Rome to appreciate two fundamental concepts: (a) the complexity of the Global Problematique, and (b) the necessity for a new value-base in creating alternative and sustainable futures. The new paradigm has been called DEMOSOPHIA, "wisdom of the people" (Christakis 1993). Dialogue is the infrastructure—a word that means 'beneath the structure' for all of our collective learning. Dialogue science is a science for learning how to learn together. It is a very deep and inclusive science and it has come to an age with the recognition of three major phases in the way that we construct observations and consensual linguistic domains.

A. **First Phase Science** considered learning as a matter of observing phenomena, which are understood to be independent of the observer. In other words, an observer seeing an apple falling from a tree in ancient Athens, in 500 BC, will report the same phenomenon as an observer seeing an apple falling from a tree in New York, today. It is a science deliberately focused on "objectivity," as opposed to "subjectivity." Classical Newtonian physics represents objectivity and the capacity to collect observer-independent data or facts. **It does not include the actions necessary for improving the situation of a social system**. For example, an astronaut landing on the moon in 1969.
B. **Second Phase Science** considers learning to be shaped by the interaction between an observer and the entity being observed. Anthropologists understand this, as do business managers. The quality of observation is impacted by the presence of an observer within a community; in medicine, interactions with clinical staff in clinical environments can impact patient responses, including blood pressure. This is called the "white coat phenomenon."
C. **Third Phase Science**: It appreciated the interdependence and the inter-subjectivity of observations. It promotes the creation of new future data and fully includes the actions necessary for the improvement of a situation of a

| Data-Dependency | 1st Phase of Science | 2nd Phase of Science | 3rd Phase of Science |
|---|---|---|---|
| Observer-Independent | Apples falling from trees, at different times in different places e.g., New York, Athens | | |
| Observer-Dependent | | A doctor measuring blood pressure | |
| Observer Independent | | | A witness of a murder talking to the court, A journalist covering a road accident |

**Fig. 21.3** Drawing distinctions among the three types of observations and the corresponding relationships to the three phases of science

social system. The implications of the distinction, between First Phase Science, in which the actions are not included, and Third Phase, in which the actions are included, is liberating in the context of envisioning new future data. For example, changing the behavior of American citizens regarding racialism and sexism required the passage of legislation that prohibited the use of political incorrect language (Fig. 21.3).

## *Three Process Models of Consultation in Demoscopio*

There are distinct process models of consultations in Demoscopio. These three models graphically displayed and discussed in the figure below (Fig. 21.4)

## *Three Key Concept Distinctions in the SDD Process Model*

(a) **The Context—Design Management Team**
(b) **The Content—Stakeholder as Designers**
(c) **The Process—SDD Facilitation Team**

Understanding one's involvement in a problem-solving situation is critical for its success. The Structured Dialogic Design (SDD) practitioner is an expert in the theory and practice of the Dialogic Design Science. However, he/she is not to be the problem definition and solutions' content expert, or the designer of the solutions. For the practitioner to better understand the role distinctions and their necessity, he/she should learn precisely and practice effectively the dimensions of context, content, and process.

(a) **The Context**

The term context, in design situations, describes all potential causes for a problem and all surrounding aspects of it; for instance, who are the key-players, the stakeholders, the owner of the problem, and whose accountability it is. The context is what will drive the problem resolution. It is a broad picture of an issue, which will eventually will be defined as a "system of problems" or problematique. The SDD practitioner, originally, might have has some knowledge about the type of problem being discussed, but he/she remains out of any content analysis or explanation as he/she perceives it as "open" to be redefined and redesigned by the stakeholders involved. The facilitator works with the client in formulating a problem-solving question (triggering question). This question is extremely important, because it will guide all the activities prescribed by the SDD process. The triggering question will help the client select who are the stakeholders. The facilitator, understands very well the complexity, and will contribute in creating an atmosphere of trust and respect among all stakeholders, so that they can visualize the problem in its contextual perspectives.

(b) **The Content**

If the problem has been described as a complex, wicked problem, then it is a stakeholder-dependent situation. The content for resolving the problem is a stakeholder prerogative. A SDD practitioner, in his/her facilitator role is never to interfere or interject with stakeholder's perspectives. This is the exclusive domain of the client and the client's stakeholders. The SDD practitioner will only facilitate the content dialogue, by employing the Science of Dialogic Design.

(c) **The Process**

This is where the SDD practioner exhibits his/her expertise; it is truly the exclusive domain where a successful SDD practioner who knows the process very well, can apply it appropriately, by protecting the authenticity and autonomy of all stakeholders. He/she knows that during the process of dialogue, there are some non-negotiable aspects. Also he/she knows why these aspects are non-negotiable for the process to be successful. It is a parallel situation as the taking off of a plane, the pilot could never negotiate the technical situation of the plane with the passengers, while he/she is flying the plane and trying to keep them safe.

**The Expert Model.**

The consultant collects information from the stakeholders and formulates an expert opinion of what needs to be done. This opinion is summarized into a report. Management evaluates the report and makes decisions for improvements. Although this model utilizes observer's perspectives, it does not allow for the observer to be part of the decision-making process. Their perspectives are utilized to validate the consultant's analysis of a situation. Management, stakeholders, and consultant work from isolated domains.

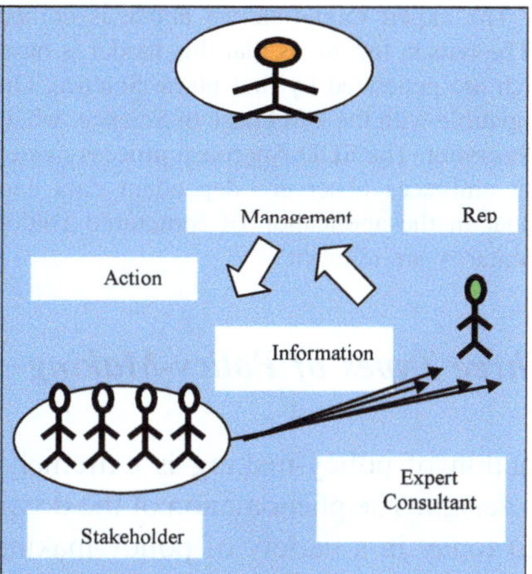


**The Empowerment Model.**

The consultant interacts with the stakeholders and engages them to gather information. Although stakeholders have an increase in their degrees of freedom, and work on the same domain as the consultant, the consultant still operates as the knowledge expert. The consultant's report is still the basis for the decision making process, and the design of the improvement plan (or action plan). The stakeholders' participation validates the consultant's work and recommendation.

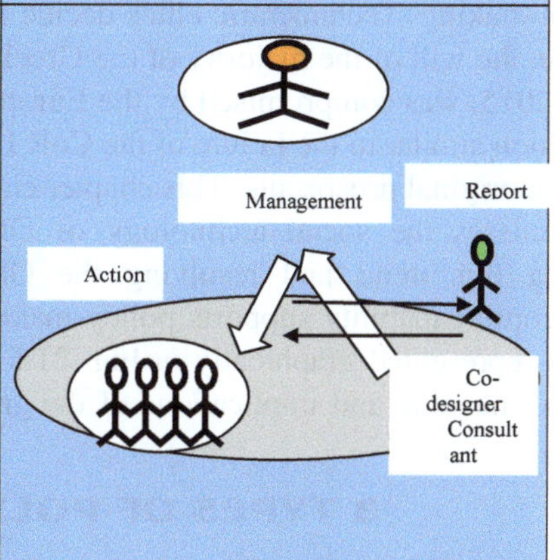


**The SDD Approach (Demoscopio)**

**In the SDD approach, the consultant does not contribute with content expertise to the problem definition and design of solutions. This is solely the role of the management and of the stakeholders. The consultant interacts with management and stakeholders to guide them during discovery of the situation (Discovery) and co-design of process. During the Diagnosis and Design phases the SDD practitioner operates as process implementer and facilitator (no content expertise contributions during the Diagnosis).**

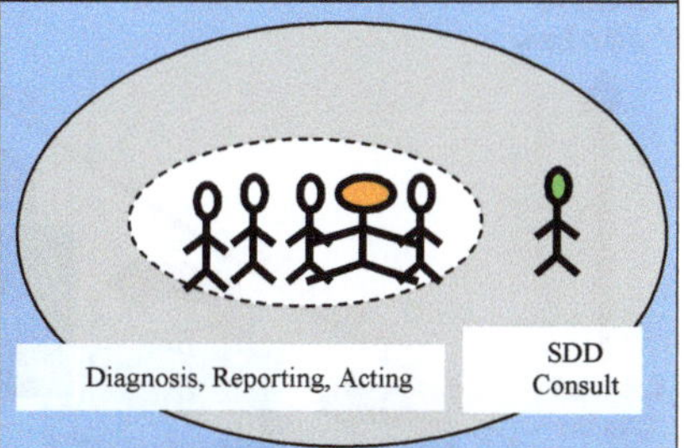

◂**Fig. 21.4** The expert model shown above is compatible and corresponds to the first phase of science. The reason for this is that this model is based on the utilization of observer independent data, which are generated by first phase Science. On the other hand the empowerment model is more compatible with the 2nd Phase of Science, where there is an interaction between the observer and the observant. The SDD Approach process model is compatible with the first phase of science because it embraces observer—dependent data and inter-subjectivity. It should be, however, realized that in the application of Structured Dialogic Design, all phases of science and their complementarity are relevant

## *The Three Types of Policy-Making*

The function of policy-making is extremely challenging in the context of social systems design. The phenomenon of the dominance of the technocratic rationality is observed today in a variety of policy-making situations at all scales and levels of decision-making. Technocratic elites decide for the people without the people. For example, the will of the majority of the Greek people, as expressed in a referendum in July 2015, was compromised by the European Commission's technocratic elites, in a fashion similar to the failure of the CoR Executive Committee to appreciate and adopt the original prospectus. This chapter elaborates on this dominant global trend, and discusses the social technology of DEMOSCOPIO as the innovation for reversing this trend and resolving the Global and local Problematique. The Demoscopio capability supports policy-making by drawing three types of distinctions as represented graphically in Fig. 21.5. In the following paragraph we elaborate the meaning and implications of the graphic.

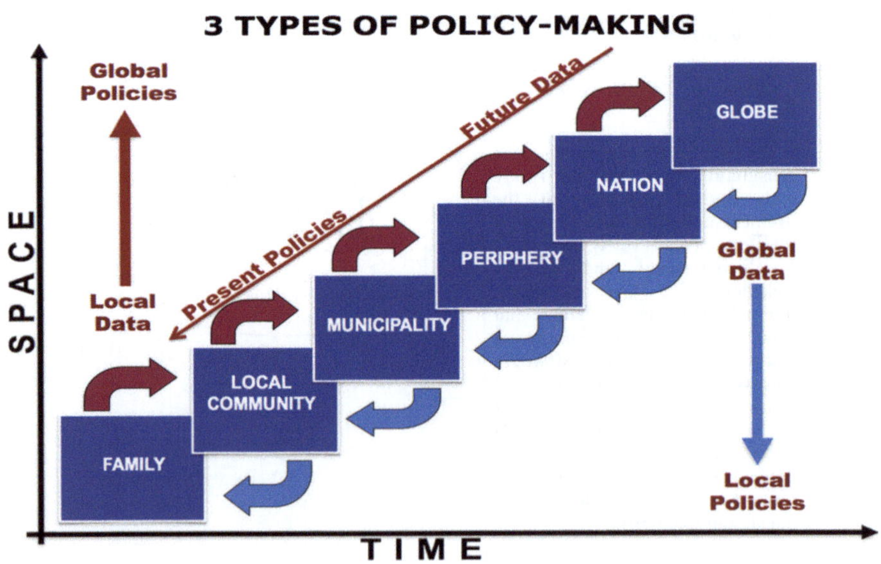


**Fig. 21.5** Policy making supported the Demoscopio capability through the methodology of Structured Democratic Dialogue

The two axes display the dimensions of time (x) and space (y). The diagonal line from global to local geographical units displays the requirements for feed upwards and feed downwards for knowledge information and data among the units. The three arrows in the diagram represent three distinct but complementary types of inferences: (a) The bottom-up from local data to global policies, (b) the top-down from global data to local policies, (c) the future-to-present arrow represents how new visionary data influence present policies and actions on the present. This bottom-up arrow is similar to inductive logic in science; the top-down to deductive logic, and the future-to-present represents retrodructive logic as conceptualized by Charles Saunders Pierce (Apel 1981)

## Demoscopio of the Municipality of Heraklion

### *A Democratic Innovation for a Smart City*

"While a new idea is a thought about something new or unique,
and making that idea real is an invention,
innovation is an invention that has a socioeconomic effect.
Innovation changes the way people live."
Wiebe Bijker

The Municipality of Heraklion is the largest urban and economic center, the administrative capital of the island of Crete and one of the Mediterranean region's most vibrant and lively cities. With 140,730 inhabitants in the city and 173,993 in the rest of the Municipality area, Heraklion today, has a population of 225,574 (Demographics 2011). It is a very dynamic, and cosmopolitan area, and is located extremely close to Minoan Palace of Knossos, where the first European civilization, the Minoan civilization, flourished 5000 years ago and it lasted about 600 years, following 2000 BC.

Today the Municipality of Heraklion has a deep and continuous motive in transforming this region into a sustainable "Smart City". For this reason, the City Council has worked toward establishing specific plans for making the city a place for economic growth, development, and sustainability. There some questions that need to be taken into consideration here: How can we turn a city, any city in the world, into a smart city? Which are the characteristics, visions, scientific practices, and cultural attributes that can contribute in "smart" ways of thinking and acting as citizens? It is common knowledge that information technology offers opportunities for the citizens to be informed and engaged into their political practices. However, can technology alone create a culture of participative democratic practice and the right conditions for consensual dialogue? Demoscopio as the innovative center for dialogue, collaboration, innovation, social planning, and entrepreneurship, has been

**Fig. 21.6** The building designated and dedicated by the Municipality of Heraklion to become "Heraklion Demoscopio"

envisioned as the capability for closing this very gap. The intent of Demoscopio is to explicate the wisdom of the people as a bottom-up and top-down process of learning and planning, including the visions and the aspirations, the experiences and the expertise of all citizens (Fig. 21.6).

> What we need is a place where the dream can meet with reality, the place which can satisfy the dreamer, be accepted by the scientist and someday be built by the builder, the city which will be in place-the entopia (Doxiadis 1966).

At the moment, the Municipality of Heraklion is a member of the networks "Eurocities" and "Balkan cities", aiming at the exchange of information and good practices, facilitating the organization of joint events and the implementation of joint projects. Also, it is goal to collaborate with very profound partners, next to the City Council, to educational and research organizations, (the University of Crete, the Technological Educational Institute, and the Hellenic Center for Marine Research), the Chamber of Commerce of Heraklion, the Urban Transportation Organization, etc. This collaboration is structured around six priority domains: (Fig. 21.7)

In the twenty-first century the problems are now inverted. The world is not only flat but also ephemeral. Consumers and entrepreneurs are interconnected, through social networks. The necessity to include the voices new stakeholders, users, and

| | |
|---|---|
| **Energy & Environment** | Smart buildings, smart resources, management and viable urban planning |
| **Mobility** | Efficient transportation, multimodal access and technological infrastructure |
| **e-Governance** | Online services and smart infrastructures |
| **Economy** | Entrepreneurship and innovation, productivity, local and global connections |
| **Citizens** | Digital, social inclusion and participation, education and creativity |
| **Living** | Culture, safety and health |

**Fig. 21.7** The six priority domains of collaboration of the Municipality of Heraklion with prominent partners in the context of the "Smart City" program

customers is growing exponentially. Competition comes not only from companies in local, regional, or national markets; innovation now comes from local to global context. The Internet accessibility to a wired planet means most markets are being reimagined as part of a connected world. The democratization of entrepreneurship from Silicon Valley and from startup ecosystems (such Air-bnb, Uber, Up works, etc.) all over the world is creating new strategies and structures for innovative entrepreneurship. We have to realize that we were just beginning the economic revolution of a connected world. And the amazing challenge is to discover who we are, where is our position as human beings, and how can we [re]design or influence the topology of our connections (Christakis 2009).

The municipality has invested in promoting and supporting innovation, entrepreneurship, improved quality of life, and participatory e-governance. The challenges that the municipality aims to address span a variety of areas, for example improving the quality of the environment in urban areas, minimizing traffic in the main road arteries of the city, improving the water management for minimizing the consumption, contributing to local economic growth, and supporting disabled citizens and those in need of monetary support. Other challenges are related to improving the air quality in urban areas, minimizing the energy consumption and increasing the city's energy efficiency, and encouraging the participation of the citizens in the decision-making processes. In light of these contemporary urgent challenges, the City Council has passed a resolution for the establishment of the Heraklion Demoscopio capability in a very challenging time for the city and the Greece.

## *Demoscopio Scope of Work*

The vision of Demoscopio applies to the challenge of utilization and promotion, in terms of dialogue and consensus, of all competitive advantages of the Municipality of Heraklion, by creating new narratives for the local communities for innovation and business growth. Demoscopio facility addresses the policy statements and the long-lasting efforts of the municipality to achieve the conscious engagement and participation of the citizens, in resolving problems consciously and consensually. The uniqueness of this innovation and its competitive advantage, as compared to similar initiatives and business and development proposals, is that from the outset is designed to foster a spirit of cooperation, communication and networking of local communities with an appreciation to the cultural character of the island and the country. For example, the combination of conventional models of entrepreneurship with the Science of Dialogic Design, would overcome a major weakness of Greek entrepreneurship, namely the lack of networking, the absence of consensual collaborative vision, and overcome the barriers of implementing interdisciplinarity where it is needed. Concurrently, as a space for Structured Dialogue, Innovation and Entrepreneurship, it will ensure participation by citizens, researchers, production and business entities, and will directly and efficiently produce social and business resolutions. It will also provide expertise and support-advisory services to all citizens, including the training for dealing with complex social issues and resolving conflicts of interest and disagreements.

The economic crisis, with all austerity measures, spending cuts and tax raises, influenced dramatically all Greek metropolitan areas including Heraklion, reducing the available financial resources, increasing the unemployment rates and the social protection needs. This crisis has had a tremendous impact among the youth with unemployment's rates approaching 50%. In this context, the Municipality of Heraklion makes a conscious effort in addressing the situation, by initiating a space and a method, where a new culture of social dialogue and collaboration can be created, as a hub of networking for new ideas. The smart city policy adopted by Heraklion, as mentioned before, highlights the meaning and role of the "Smart Citizen" as well, as co-designer and stakeholder of policy-making affecting him/her life. The ideas of the Smart Citizen, which will be produced through the Demoscopio process, would contribute to the renewal of the city and municipal policies and they will increase entrepreneurship and growth. Cooperation with civil associations, collective bodies and with the research and academic community, is a key success factor. That is why it is essential, for the Smart Citizen to have all the necessary infrastructure and methodological support to unfold his/her potential and develop new skills and values.

Moreover, recently there has been an emergence of entrepreneurial and innovative talents, mainly by young people, who are able to develop new mechanical or digital devices, smart online services, and applications. Also, there is a large set of new and creative graduates who have innovative ideas and need support to transform those ideas into viable businesses, services, and products. For all these reasons the city of Heraklion, has become a prototype model of innovative ideas, product development, communications applications and services and has contributed to the transformation of the traditional models of development.

## *The Process of Demoscopio*

Demoscopio is designed[3] It will also develop a interactive online platform website where all information and communication with the citizens will establish a permanent physical and digital hub of navigating the completed or ongoing work and dialogues, raise an issue of discussion, report problems, inform other citizens. This application will based on the Cogniscope algorithms for information convergence and consensus building, it can be describe as a digital platform, where ideas will come together to create the greater "image", of the issues discussed, along with discovery of roadmaps for issue-resolution. and intends to produce new knowledge through innovative ideas and the possibility of connecting young people or any citizen interested to innovators, academic departments, and successful entrepreneurs. Stakeholders not only discuss their municipality's problems and concerns, but also they can come up with new business ideas. Demoscopio promotes an oral culture and enhances feelings of inclusion, participation, and liberation from stereotypes and oppressing limitations. It allows for stakeholders to have a clear, common vision and produces deep consensus, even in divisive situations. Stakeholders with a wide variety of perspectives generate a list of challenges or goals and clarify their meanings. Dozens, even scores, of discrete statements are made, and participants discover together which challenges or goals matter most. Next, aided by computer programs, (Cogniscope, Logosofia) workgroup members organize their statements into categories to better understand how they are similar or different. Participants then map challenges or goals to see the "pattern of influence" among them. The resulting diagram or shows how statements interrelate. In this way a handful of deep-rooted challenges or goals—those that exert great leverage, or influence, over the entire system, are being revealed. By the end of that stage, there has been a fundamental shift; what individuals originally thought as the most important is not at the crux of the matter. The group then has to agree (through voting processes) on a collective definition of the complex problem.

A structured dialogue design (SDD) team will be organized to manage the tasks of focusing, tracking, and reporting citizen deliberations and presenting the result of those deliberations to large public audiences. Each community of stakeholders addressing an issue of their concern will identify 30-40 representatives who collectively will span the full diversity of the community—in income, age, education, wealth, gender, race, and religious or political persuasion. The citizens will convene

[3]In the operation of Demoscopio space will create an operational an information system, through which resource management and content management will be offered.

in a co-laboratory of democracy that it will last according to the level of complexity and the needs of the problem-situation. The ideas of the people, will result in demosensual wisdom and will be will be shared with policy-makers to support the implementation of action plans. Co-laboratories will support citizen summits in venue most appropriate for specific communities—schools, libraries, meeting halls, etc. The consensus from the citizen summits will be presented in narrative and graphic form through displays in the Demoscopio facilities for visitors to review and discuss. Depending on the situation and the need it is anticipated the presentation of all Demoscopio findings and recommendations to be disseminated widely through social media and alternative form of representation such as art exhibits, documentaries etc.

## *Demoscopio as a Culture of Innovation*

In light of the above, that new economic, technological, scientific, political, and cultural models are emerging and most political, academic and educational systems are failing, to [re]design an up-to-date paradigm culture, a new generation of change makers is required for progressing with conscious evolution, balancing individualism and collectivism and work consensually and proactively for the sustainability of our planet. The necessity for innovation in such an environment is more of a new set of intents, values and principles, rather than any kind of theoretical or empirical experiment. Innovation as expression of the evolution is not a linear process; it unfolds, as a rhizome, and it is as complex, as complex our contemporary societal systems are:

> Innovation is more complex than ever. Complexity, chaos and non-linearity have been seen since the 1970s as the defining features of our age (Ozbekhan 1970).

Demoscopio is/brings a new culture of innovation for dialogue, and entrepreneurship and it aims in building capacities for common understandings, for redefining and redesigning new values, priorities and goals for the future. In the Municipality of Heraklion, the main objective today is to integrate, harness and exploit the city's potential in ways that create new ecosystems, by bringing together stakeholders across policies, sectors and scientific disciplines. It is a effort for creating contemporary social technologies, designed by the people and for the people, which will create a whole new series of groundless grounds The Science of Dialogic Design, which is a third0phase scientific approach, enables stakeholders to be engaged in the process of problem defining, in solution designing and action implementation (Christakis 2006).

Demoscopio ought to be used as a new collaboration platform for public and private organizations and affairs, and its main objective is not only to bring people closer together, but also to shorten the gap between policy-maker and public authority and between end-user and innovator. It is to go beyond simple integration of resources but also to address and design larger scale social challenges and drive systemic changes. The generation of systemic thinkers of Demoscopio will envision and finally change the governmental systems that do not fit in the current requirements, with peaceful means Sect. 4.5

## Demoscopio Objectives and Follow-up

Demoscopio will help people in the Municipality of Heraklion and any other potential Municipality or arena of practice in developing consensual action plans and products and services such as roadmaps for overcoming barriers and making decisions. It uses scientific tools with which stakeholders can engage in authentic and open dialogues, by connecting thoughts, ideas, and perspectives with greater insights and understandings. The process leads to wider perception, appreciation of dissonances and acceptance of individual differences, through the application of SDD, which creates conditions of equality, humility, and empathy among the stakeholders. Furthermore, the process broadens the knowledge base and establishes co-ownership of problem definition and plans for resolution. A preliminary set of objectives has been identified for the Heraklion Demoscopio; contacting stakeholder's engagements during the implementation of the capability will enhance these objectives. The available set of objectives has been assigned to the three categories of the process model as discussed in the previous section of this chapter Fig. 21.8.

All the aforementioned will be part of the application(s) designed and along with all publicized outcomes, achievements, news or invitations to social and mainstream media (always in agreement and respect to the stakeholders involved). Also face-to-face activities, events and opportunities with volunteers, members or supporters will gradually contribute in the scaling up of Demoscopio's new culture. In any case all outcomes and contributions will be monitored and should reflect the Demoscopio's intent, values, and aesthetics. The impact of the co-laboratories and the communication campaigns associated with each co-laboratory will be assessed by follow-up interviews with participants to determine the strength of bonds which were constructed during co-laboratories and the activity that has resulted from information, connections, and energy mobilized in the co-laboratories. A second tier of influence will include a randomized assessment of awareness of the co-laboratories and their findings through interviews with citizens who were not participants. And a third tier of influence will include interviews with political decision makers to assess if and how findings from co-laboratories have impacted decisions that they have made. Impact assessments will be independently reported, in order that citizens of Heraklion can improve the quality and enthusiasm in the process of Demoscopio.

| a) The Expert Model Objectives |
|---|
| ➢ To support the development of community capacity and networking possibilities<br>➢ To create new socio-technological innovations (such as digital apps.) for observer-dependent data and training possibilities<br>➢ To operate as a new medium of communication and information exchange between citizens and politicians<br>➢ To create new opportunities for employment and economic growth (organize innovative entrepreneurs' activities, career days, mentoring workshops, business acceleration, exhibitions etc.)<br>➢ To offer knowledge to young people / students who have creative ideas and want to turn them into viable businesses or products or to improve the social environment and the City. |
| **b) The Empowerment Model Objectives** |
| ➢ To enhance community participation and engagement of all citizen, so that they realize their rights and responsibilities<br>➢ To serve as a design-hub and innovative laboratory for inter-disciplinary research and dialogue<br>➢ To create and organize new social capital among citizens, Municipality of Heraklion, institutions, the academic community and external business entitles<br>➢ To guide business groups and innovators in all stages of converting an idea into a product or a business.<br>➢ To act and an innovative lab and alternative medium of communication with citizens, through transparent displays and exhibits of information relevant to the city |
| **c) The SDD Approach Objectives** |
| ➢ To support the building of communities and new networks of stakeholders<br>➢ To foster citizen's individual and collective understanding and knowledge (demosophia) for civil council's decisions and policy-design making<br>➢ To minimize pessimism and political polarization through dialogue<br>➢ To deal with societal complexity as a bottom-up process, by using local knowledge and global data, to produce glocal resolutions<br>➢ To boost up a new model of civic-oriented leadership and social policy design by offering interdisciplinary knowledge and new linguistic skills |

**Fig. 21.8** An illustrative set of Demoscopioobjectives assigned to the three types of process models discussed in Subsect. 3.3 (Fig. 21.4)

## *Designing for Balancing "Technology-Push" with Societal Pull"*

Today, even though we have so many opportunities to connect and interact with each other, in our environment, in our communities, we are often silenced by our own technologies. On the other hand we struggle to pay attention to each other and that suffers our ability to know ourselves. Though, real people need real responses to what they think and to what they feel and without real conversation, we are loosing our humanism and so that we become less empathic, less connected, less creative and less fulfilled. So how can we reclaim conversation? It can begin with the acknowledgment that speaking and listening are skills, which can be taught (Turkle 2005).

Demoscopio as physical and virtual space of information, interconnectivity, and a new dialogic practicing culture, can adapt to a demanding new era as a democratic "museum" of/for the people's thoughts, ideas, decisions, and visions. Its exhibits will not be static or "frozen" but will evolve according to the ways people will change their plans, dialogues and interests. People will think and reflect on their social identity and learn how they can develop their democratic participation in implementing local policies. The purpose is not to become another futuristic museum, following the trend of digitization or Futurization, which is a fag-oriented culture, often led by market trends and subconscious fears and needs, based on power-games of changing the world all at once, or expanding new type of fads, often through social and mainstream media. Demoscopio is not about preserving the past, nor transcending the future; is about creating opportunities for the discussions of tomorrow for visitors and communities of practice.

Conventional museums offer people a sense of history, a source of inspiration and a place for learning about the past so that we can chart a course forwards. But the question is: How can we make a museum today the place that you want to visit everyday? How can we create meaningful inspirations and reasons for attraction for audiences, so that they can feel welcome and represented all times? The landmark for Demoscopio is the new value-base of connecting with each other and to those who are taking the decisions for our lives; it is the artistic dialogue and dialogic art of spreading the word and connecting to the world. It is a physical place to explore the self and the other, for a new type of experience that is friction-free and brings back the possibility for feeling empathy, real life experiences and face-to-face interactions, for redesigning technology and changing how it is introduced into our lives.

Furthermore, principles such as the sustainability of our planet, the natural environment, and human rights will be the cornerstones for any enterprise management types and marketing tactics. In this way will work more as a "dialogic-artistic-gallery" between citizen-media-political sphere. It will be the safe space of free expression for diverse audiences that will reflect the communities they serve, by sharing perspectives and by embracing stories and thoughts that tie us together, regardless all our differences. It will be the community resource that is engaged to move people forward from being reactive to being proactive and interactive. It will be committed through its people and partnerships, to extend and expand the experience of participating by gathering multiple perspectives and by offering unique-competent outcomes. In this manner there are challenges such as: How to make the losses of people's truthfulness to the minimum scale in the process of digitalization of Demoscopio dialogues and data? How to create the "win-win" situation between "virtual" and "real" by well adopting the advantages of digitalization?

When our lives gradually surrounded by high-tech products like mobile phones and Internet, more and more people will be eager to find their ways to feel their human nature possibilities. New technologies do not guarantee necessarily good exhibitions. Under the constantly changing environment, any contemporary attempt in exhibiting and engaging people must be carefully examine itself in the context of its targeting, missions, demands of audience, etc.

## Discussion: Tomorrow Is Designed Today

> Wisdom in only found in truth…
> and truth is only found in consensus.
> Maria Kakoulaki 2011

There are some good reasons for suggesting that the modern age has ended. Today, many things indicate that we are going through a transitional period, when it seems that something is on the way out and something else is painfully being born. Resolutions of complex societal problems of the contemporary cities require a [r] evolutionary systems approach for balancing individualism and collectivism for supporting social and environmental justice. Designing, educating, and acting with a normative, collaborative, open engagement of citizens, scientists, innovators, entrepreneurs, and policy-makers is the main purpose for Demoscopio. The Agora of Athens was the place for the citizens to congregate and deliberate in making policies and designing for the future of their city. We need the contemporary equivalent of the Athenian Agora to manage the complexity of social system designing and discover an evolutionary balance between democracy and technocracy. Demoscopio strategically employs a variety of methods, activities, and process models, to encourage the reframing of complex problems and visions in a “whole systems view”, by deepening feelings of community through collaborative policy designing and acting.

A new era of Demosophia, enhanced by the knowledge and experiences of the people, and affected by the velocity and penetrability of all new technological possibilities of the information age and social networks, has already started. The vibrations of the phenomenon that many definitions are outdated and unsuitable, and that meaning does not quit fit within preconceived concepts, without people grasping evolutionary ephemerality, challenges traditional norms and stereotypes. How change in society can be[come] and remain meaningful? How, inspite of any societal and technological change, a system remains open and flexible? Which are the ways to design and sustain new commonly understood discourses on complex social–political issues? Can we create, learn, and evolve new “geometries” of languaging and understanding that address our dissonances as integral parts of individualism and collectivism?

While many existing initiatives focus simply on increasing levels of engagement, or improving the quality of deliberation, or reducing conflict, Demoscopio is the comprehensive systemic response to the questions above. It is harnessing the

**Fig. 21.9** 1986–2016, Thirty years of technological advances in the services of Demoscopio and public engagement. Dr Alexander N. Christakis with his portable computer in "DEMOSOPHIA" of George Mason University (1986, September, Business Magazine, Northern Virginia), and 30 years later in the Parliamentarium in Brussels, 2016 (photography: Maria Kakoulaki)

momentum of an evolving epoch and it is reclaiming conversation in a public space, offering the opportunity to the citizens, for example in the Municipality of Heraklion, to talk the walk towards new democratic practices of engagement, innovative ideas, and entrepreneurship and walk the talk of contemporary, collective, demosensual design narratives. Demoscopio culture is the ability to will and own an eutopian future and consciously design it by being emancipated from current dystopian narratives and beliefs.

Difficult truths which are agreed to be essential to the future of the economic and political systems of the communities of Crete will be forged through the strong individual will of the participating Cretans, and the success of the democratic dialogues on Heraklion will provide a stepping stone for additional Structured Democratic Dialogues throughout Greece. As theses community dialogues unfold, they will be woven into an emerging fabric of a new epoch, where the ancient aspirations of democracy will take hold for the new millennium. The findings from the dialogues will be captured and held for all to see in the Demoscopio facility. The collective stories will not be the stories that will be stored quietly in bookshelves in individual communities, but they will be disseminated and exhibited as the defining collective saga for the generations to come. Thus, Demoscopio is not the destination, but the pathway to a dynamic-evolving, contemporary Agora of direct democracy for the 21st Century's demosensual, [r]evolutionary eutopia (Fig. 21.9).

**Instead of an Epilogue**
**"With Reason & Vision"**

And YES, we choose to remain the visionaries of the "Ought to be"
nowadays, that societies invent infinite masks of "Can be".
Our authentic opinions and ideas create
our conscious [r]evolutionary pathways ahead
for ideal futures to be attained,
by those whose life world is painfully affected
and their choices, perpetually neglected.

Words without meaning have condemned meaning without words!
For the individual's distinct knowledge and experience
for the suppressed and repressed human voice
for the unheard and ignored individual perception
for the construction of sustainable realities,
for the protection and preservation of our planet,
for the emancipation with peace and justice
for all these reasons I am speaking…

And I am looking for a world by us, with us, for us
where "democracy" will be democracy and "freedom", freedom,
where no matter the differences and dissonances
collaboration and participation *with reason and vision*
will transcend any predictions of the current situation;
for a new value base, that empowers flexibility of thought and structure
and flows as crystal clear water in the river of Heraclitus.

And yes, I reject "science" and every "science"
when they fail to include variety and authenticity
of an individual or of a culture,
when they restrain possibilities yet to be born,
within theories, hypotheses, observations, generalizations;
and I reject anyone who is self-defined as "specialist", "savior" or"expert"
who proposes generic "solutions",
instead of co-designing customized [re]solutions.

In the desert of [meta]modern "markets"
I discovered the real meaning of Agora
where the Anthropolis of all beings is being designed,
not only with roots but also with wings,
not only with facts but also with dreams
by the New Citizen, who espouses inquiry and doubt as the groundless
ground for dialogue and collective wisdom
*Maria Kakoulaki (2014)*

## References

Adorno TW (1966) Negative dialektik. English Edition: Adorno, T.W. 11973. Suhrkamp, Frankfurt. Negative Dialectics (trans: Ashton, E.B.)
Apel K (1981) Charles S from pragmatism to pragmaticism. University of Massachusetts Press, Amherst, Peirce
Arnstein S, Christakis AN (1976) Perspectives on technology assessment. Science and Technology Publishers, Jerusalem, Israel
Bausch K (2000) The practice and ethics of design. Syst Res Behav Sci, 17(1): 23–51
Bausch K (2001) The emerging consensus in social system theory. Plenum, New York
Bausch K, Christakis AN (2003) Technology to liberate rather than imprison consciousness. In: Loye D (ed) The great adventure: toward a fully human theory of evolution, SUNY Press
Bausch K, Christakis AN (2015). With reason and vision: structured dialogic design. Emergence Publications
Christakis AN (1973) A new policy science paradigm. Futures 5(6):543–558
Christakis A, Warfield NJ (1983) Proposal for the establishment of interactive management of Crete. Submitted to the Ministry of Coordination, Government of Greece
Christakis AN, Warfield JN (1987). NSF DTM, Ohio
Christakis AN (1987) High technology participative design: the space- based laser, in general systems. In: Dillon JA, Jr (ed) International society for the systems sciences, vol XXX, pp 69–75
Christakis AN (1988) The club of rome revisited in: general systems. In: Reckmeyer WJ (ed) International society for the systems sciences, vol XXXI, pp 35–38, New York
Christakis AN, Warfield JN, Keever D (1988) Systems design: generic design theory and methodology. In: Decleris M (ed) Systems governance. Publisher Ant N. Sakkoylas, Athens-Komotini, Greece, pp 143–210
Christakis AN (1993) The inevitability of demosophia. In: Tsivacou I (ed) A challenge for systems thinking: the aegean seminar. University of the Aegean Press, Athens, Greece, pp 187–197
Christakis AN, Christakis NA, Conaway D, Feudtner C, Geranmayeh A, Whitehouse RJ (1994) Designing the good review practices, CWA
Christakis AN (1996) A people science: the cogniscope system approach. Syst J Trans-disciplinary Syst Sci, 1(1)
Christakis AN, Dye KM (1999) Collaboration through communicative action: resolving the systems dilemma through the cogniscope. Syst J Trans-disciplinary Syst Sci, 4(1)
Christakis AN, Bausch K (2002) Technologue: technology- supported disciplined dialogue. In: Nancy, R (ed) Transformative power of dialogue. Elsevier Publishing Co
Christakis AN, Brahms S (2003) Boundary-spanning dialogue for 21st -century agoras. Syst Res Behav Sci 20:371–382
Christakis AN, Harris L (2004) Designing a Transnational Indigenous Leaders Interaction in the Context of Globalization: Wisdom of the People Forum, Systems Research and Behavioral Sciences
Christakis AN, Bausch KC (2006) Co-laboratories of democracy: how people harness their collective wisdom to create the future. Information Age Publishing
Christakis AN, Bausch K (2006) How people harness their collective wisdom and power to construct the future in co-laboratories of democracy. Information Age Publishing, Inc
Christakis AN (2014) An epic learning journey: from the club of rome to dialogic design science and demosophia. In: Metcalf G (ed) Social systems and design. Springer Press, New York
Christakis A, Nicholas A, Fowler JH (2009) Connected: the surprising power of our social networks and how they shape our lives—how your friends' friends' friends affect everything you feel, think, and do, New York
Christakis AN (2011) Dynamic social networks promote cooperation in experiments with humans. In: Douglas SM (ed) Princeton University, Princeton, NJ, and approved October 18, 2011, Boston, MA

Doxiadis CA (1968) Ekistics: An introduction to the science of human settlements. Oxford University Press, London, pp 27–31
Doxiadis CA (1969) The future of human settlements, speech, delivered at the 14th Nobel Symposium, Stockholm, Sweden, September. Wiley, New York (in press)
de Zeeuw G (1996) Second order organizational research, working papers in systems and information sciences, University of Humberside, Hull, England
Doxiadis CA (1968) Ekistics: an introduction to the science of human settlements, Hutchinson of London
Doxiadis CA (1966) Between Dystopia and Utopia. Trinity College Press, Hartford, Conn; Dye KM (1997) Collaborative Design Process Science, Working Papers at MIT, Boston
Dye KM, Feudtner C, Post D, Vogt EM (1999) Developing collaborative leadership to reframe the safe use of pharmaceuticals as a national health priority, final report. CWA Ltd., Paoli, PA
Dye KM, Conaway DS (1999) Lessons learned from five years of application of the cogniscope approach to the food and drug administration. CWA Ltd. Report, Paoli, PA
Ellul J (1964) The technological society. Vintage, New York. J. Wilkinson, trans.
European Parliamentarium, Brussels (2016). (http://www.europarl.europa.eu/visiting/en/parlamentarium)
Flanagan TR (2008) Scripting a collaborative narrative: an approach for spanning boundaries. Desig Manag Rev 19(3):80–86
Flanagan T, Christakis A (2010) The talking point: creating an environment for exploring complex meaning. Information Age Publishing, Charlotte
Flanagan T, Bausch K (2010) A democratic approach to sustainable futures. Emergence Press
Flanagan T (2013) Blueprint for a digital observatorium. Worlds Futures Forum, Montreal, Canada
Future Worlds Center Publication (2102) Reinventing Democracy in the Digital Era v.1, Elia Petridou, Eleni Michail, Maria Georgiou, Danae Psilla, Jurrien Stutterheim Yiannis Laouris, Afonso Ferreira, Nicosia, Cyprus. www.reinventdemocracyindigitalera.wikispaces.com
Heidegger M (1977) The question concerning technology (Lovitt W trans). Harper and Row, New York
Kakoulaki M (2011–2016) Futu[R]evolution blog. www.leregardcretois.blogspot.com
Kakoulaki M (2012) The wine villages of cyprus: from the visionary anticipation to the sustainable development. Cyprus Academy of Public Administration & Nicosia Town Planning Department
Kakoulaki M (2015) Dialogue beyond borders documentary based on interviews Israel, Palestine, Cyprus. https://www.youtube.com/watch?v=SKwXw6hFpAA
Kuhn T (1970) The structure of scientific revolutions, (2nd edn). University of Chicago Press, Chicago. Institute for 21$^{st}$ Century Agoras. www.globalagoras.org
Lasswell HD (1960) The techniques of decision seminars. Midwest J Polit Sci 4:213–236
Lasswell H (1963) Strategies of inquiry: the rational use of observation in Lasswell HD. Atherton Press, New York. The Future of Political Science
Lasswell H (1962) The future of political science, p 242
Lasswell HD (1971) A pre-view of the policy sciences. In: Learner D (ed) The human meaning of the social sciences. American Elsevier, New York. 1959
Lyotard JF (1979) La Condition Postmoderne. Editions de Minuit, Paris, p 34
The texts by Heidegger discussed here are, in order, "The Question Concerning Technology," op. cit.; "The Thing," and "Building Dwelling Thinking" in Poetry, Language, Thought, A. Hofstadter, trans. (New York: Harper & Row, 1971)
Marx K (1906) Capital modern library, New York, p 13
McIntyre JJ (2003) Participatory democracy: drawing on C. West Churchman's thinking when making public policy. Syst Res Behav Sci, 20(6): 489–499
Richard MW (1984) Analyzing marx: morality, power and history. Princeton University Press, Princeton, pp 188–195
Mochianakis K, Tragos ZE, Fotakis M. Heraklion-roadmap towards becoming a smart city. https://www.eurescom.eu/news-and-events/eurescommessage/eurescom-message-winter-2015/heraklion-roadmap-towards-becoming-a-smart-city.html

Ozbekhan H (1968) The triumph of technology: "can implies ought." King Resources, Los AngeZes, CaZif., U.S.A. http://redesignresearch.com/docs/Ozbekhan%20%20The%20Triumph%20Of%20Technology%20-%20_Can%20Implies%20Ought_.pdf
Ozbekhan H (1970) The predicament of mankind. quest for structured responses to growing world-wide complexities and uncertainties. http://quergeist.net/Christakis/predicament.pdf
Ozbekhan H (1977) Pertinent excerpts on "Futures Creation" from Part 3; Ozbekhan H Toward A General Theory of Planning, pp 47–155. In Jantsch (ed) (1968) OEDC Report; explained in Christakis AN (1977) A new policy science paradigm, FUTURES, Dec 1973; applied in Ozbekhan, The future of Paris. R Soc Lond Philos Trans Ser A 287:523
Pinch T, Bijker W (1984) The social construction of facts and artifacts: or how the sociology of science and the sociology of technology might benefit each other, Soc Stud Sci, 14(3)
Turkle S (2005) reclaiming conversation-the power of talk in the digital age. Penguin Press, pp 4–16
Sennet R (1999) The spaces of democracy. Harvard Desig Mag 8:68–72
Schreibman V, Christakis AN (2007) New Agora: new geometry of languaging and new technology of democracy: the structured dialogue process. Int. J. Appl Syst Stud 1(1):2007
Shapiro MA (2002) Facilitating a global conversation through the universal demosophia facility. In: Banathy B, Jenlick P (eds) Dialogue as a means of collective communication. Kluwer Academic/Plenum Publishers
Shapiro MA (2013) Report: the boise commons
Shapiro MA (2016) Report: the state of boise's neighborhood association, results of a survey contacted the boise commons
Warfield JN (1976) Societal systems: planning, policy, and complexity. Wiley, New York
Warfield JN (1994) A science of generic design, 2nd edn. The Iowa State University Press, Ames, IA
Warfield JN, Cárdenas A Roxana (1994) A handbook of interactive management. The Iowa State University Press, Ames, IA
Weber M (1958) The protestant ethic and the spirit of capitalism.. Scribners, New York, pp. 181–82. Parsons T trans
Weigand K, Flanagan TR, Dye KMC, Jones, PH (2013). Collaborative foresight in long-horizon planning: contrasting dialogic and rational planning traditions in R&D strategy. Technological Forecasting & Social Change. (Accepted article, in revision)

## Author Biographies

**Maria Kakoulaki** is a journalist who works with social and environmental justice organisations to address the big issues of the day, namely poverty and climate change. As an active journalist, reporter in political and financial affairs for Greece and Europe, she undertakes interviews globally in a range of media. She is a Systemic Design Facilitator with the Science of Dialogic Design (SDD) and works with Emeritus Professor Dr Alexander Christakis on peace- building and conflict resolution across the world. Her academic background includes inter-disciplinary studies, in Psychology, Media Culture & Communications,Creative Entrepreneurship and Media Arts and Philosophy, in London. She is a Board member of the Institute for 21st CenturyAgoras, an organisation which focuses on the expansion of Democratic Dialogue and the Design of Sustainable Futures. As a practitioner, she has applied SDD in Cyprus, Greece (http://clinical-trialsdialogue.eplo.eu), Bosnia & Herzegovina and in United States. She was the principal director and producer of the documentary, 'Dialogue Beyond Borders' (https://www.youtube.com/watch?v=SKwXw6hFpAA), focusing on people's voices and peace building among Israelis, Palestinians, and Turkish and Greek Cypriots. Recently, she was invited as keynote speaker in Toronto RSD5 Symposium (www.rsd5.com), where she presented the concept of Demoscopio of Heraklion.

**Emeritus Professor Dr. Alexander N. Christakis** has a PhD in Theoretical Nuclear Physics from Yale University (1964), and a Bachelor in Theoretical Physics from Princeton University (1959). He has over 40 years of experience in developing and testing methods for engaging stakeholders in authentic Structured Democratic Dialogue (SDD). He has applied the Science of Dialogic Design (www.dialogicdesignscience.wikispaces.com) in a variety of government agencies (US Food and Drug Administration, World Health Organization, the US Departments of Agriculture, Defense, and Commerce, among others), as well as private companies in the pharmaceutical, health, and chemical industries.He is a past President of the International Society for the Systems Sciences, member of the Board of the Americans for Indian Opportunity (www.AIO.org), Advisor to the AIO Ambassador's leadership program for engaging tribal leaders from the USA and internationally, and the founder of the Institute for 21st Century Agoras (www.globalagoras.org). From 1965 till 1970, he was an advisor to the Urban Design Firm of Konstantinos Doxiadis Associates, and to the Athens Center for Ekistics (the Science of Human Settlements). In the 1970s, he collaborated with Hasan Ozbekhan in developing the prospectus of the Club of Rome titled 'The Predicament of Mankind'. From 1979 till 1989 he served in the faculties of the University of Virginia and George Mason University as the Director of the Center for Interactive Management. In 1989 he establishes a dialogic design consultancy dedicated to the application and evolution of the Science of Dialogue.

# Epilogue
# Natural Inclusion

**Alan Rayner**

## *A New Understanding of the Evolutionary Kinship of All Life on Earth*

## Entrance

Imagine yourself standing petrified on the concrete edge of a swimming pool, while being jostled by those next to you. Someone splashing about in the water shouts to you. 'Come on in, the water's lovely!' But you've never experienced full immersion in water before and you've never been taught how to swim. How do you feel? Do you believe them, and take the plunge? Or do you err on the side of caution and stay put, digging in your heels? How can you appreciate the possibilities of what you are missing, and how you could escape from being hemmed in, when you have no knowledge, no actual experience of it?

Your understandable edginess in this situation is like what I encounter as an experienced 'swimmer', when trying to help people become aware of the limitless pool in which we can appreciate our self-identities as fluidly dynamic 'natural inclusions' of our neighbourhood, not stand-alone objects set apart from it. How can I entice you to leap through the mental barrier—the invisible wall—between the concrete surface where you feel secure, yet are immobilized and jostled upon, into the depth in which you can become alive and kicking, but could also drown if you or I are not careful enough?

Before I get any further, I need to point out that the limitless pool I have now just slipped into talking about is in a crucial way very different from but utterly vital to the very existence of a pool of water! By its very nature, it is uncontainable, an endless, frictionless source of freedom for movement that in itself is utterly still. It is an endless pool of space.



J. McIntyre-Mills et al. (eds.), *Balancing Individualism and Collectivism*,
Contemporary Systems Thinking, DOI 10.1007/978-3-319-58014-2

## Movement

Now, let me say a bit more about myself. As far as I can recall, I have always felt a close kinship with Nature. I have recognized that what is all around me cannot be isolated from, and is just as vital to who and how I am as what is inside me. It is also continually changing. Correspondingly, you are all included in my world just as much as I am included in yours—I think Bob Dylan once said something like that. We live inescapably within each other's natural neighbourhood.

Having long perceived myself and all other natural forms as inhabiting each other's neighbourhood, I have been dismayed by the fact that most people nowadays don't feel quite the same way. Instead, our cultural and educational institutions teach us, from a young age, to *perceive* ourselves and others as if we were hermetically sealed units, that is as isolated objects, both set apart from one another and boxed in by *rigid boundaries* and gaps of space, like the solid-looking coloured balls in this abstract three-dimensional diagram: and unlike the *dynamically bounded* flow-form I made below, which I made for my grandson in a beach, by moving sand around *in* space.

Over 40 years ago, I illustrated my feelings about the terrible damage caused by this alienating perception in a painting called 'Arid Confrontation'.

In order to feel secure, we mentally sever ourselves from each other and the creative wildness of the natural world by setting in place an imaginary barricade—what I call 'the space barrier'—that enforces profound social and psychological conflict and environmental destruction. Instead of loving our neighbourhood as a source of sustenance for our self-identity to come into being and be included within, like my sand-whirl, we make an enemy of whatever we perceive and label to be on the 'other' side of a rigidly defined boundary. That is, we mentally exclude from 'me' or 'us' whatever we define to be 'outside' of 'me' or 'us', and then seek to control or eliminate it in acts of exploitation and war.

Recall Hamlet's famous soliloquy and where it led him: 'To be or not to be, that is the question: whether 'tis nobler in the mind to suffer the slings and arrows of outrageous fortune, OR, to take arms *against* a sea of troubles and, by *opposing*, end them'.

Nowhere has this *abstract* sense of *severance* of 'each *from* the other' by rigid boundaries been more prevalent than in modern science. It is embedded in Darwin's view of 'natural selection' as 'the preservation of favoured races in the struggle for life', and is associated with the idea that evolutionary success is dependent on the competitive elimination of others. Even Albert Einstein declared that 'the environment is everything that isn't me'. His paradoxical isolation of 'self' from 'other' is evident in his following statement concerning what he called 'the problem of space':-

"When a smaller box $s$ is situated, relatively at rest, inside the hollow space of a larger box $S$, then the hollow space of $s$ is a part of the hollow space of $S$, and the same 'space', which contains both of them, belongs to each of the boxes. When $s$ is in motion with respect to $S$, however, the concept is less simple. One is then inclined to think that *s* encloses always the same space, but a variable part of the space *S*. It then becomes necessary to apportion to each box its particular space, *not thought of as bounded*, and to assume that these *two spaces* are in motion with respect to each other."

How, you might ask, can an unbounded box of space be distinguished from its environment, yet alone move around in and relative to it?

If you stop to think carefully about why we impose these definitive limits on ourselves and Nature, it becomes clear that to do so simply cannot make sense. Ask yourself what kind of a boundary could *actually* separate the space within you from the space around you *without itself including space*? That's right: it would have to have no thickness and hence be nowhere! The intangible, frictionless, space within you and without you is continuous throughout you! As I move around, space is slipping through me—I am not moving space aside from me. Space is an intangible presence. My body, like all bodies, is a tangible, permeable and variably cohesive presence that includes and is included in space.

When I breathe *in*, my *body* expands as my *outside* simultaneously contracts and breathes *out* into me. The situation is reversed when I breathe out. There is *no delay* between what happens *inwardly* and what happens *outwardly*. My *bodily* boundary *distinguishes* my *inner space* from my *outer space* and mediates their *reciprocal correspondence*. It does not isolate them.

Space gives material form somewhere to exist and move around in—it is not a material in itself. So what the Devil have we been doing, for millennia, by not only pretending that zero-thickness boundaries exist, but actually incorporating this pretence into our systems of abstract logic, conventional mathematics, objectivist science, hierarchical governance and elitist education? Here, according to C.S. Lewis is what the Devil himself liked about it:

> The Whole Philosophy of Hell…rests on a recognition of the axiom that one thing is not another thing, and, specifically, that one self is not another self. My good is my good and your good is yours…'To be' means to be in competition (C.S. Lewis "The Screwtape Letters")

So, how can we liberate ourselves from this hellish mental isolation of one self from another self by definitive boundaries and gaps of space?

Quite simply, I think we can liberate ourselves by recognizing how natural space and boundaries actually are and must be *as distinct but mutually inclusive presences*. We can do this by appreciating:

> Natural space as a presence that is not a substance but makes the existence of substance possible i.e. limitless, motionless, frictionless and hence **receptive** and **infinite** omnipresence **everywhere** that provides possibility and freedom for movement energy as continuous motion or flux i.e. a presence that is packaged into local substance as 'matter', and dispersed as 'radiation' (known as 'light', when visible)

When we think about it, everything is necessarily 100 % space PLUS energy, not *part* space and *part* energy. That's how Nature is, including human nature.

Now I think a vital principle of *life* and *love* as mutually inclusive presences begins to emerge.

My painting, 'Holding Openness', below, expresses how all natural form is the co-creation of continuously mobile, informative presence (energetic flux) and continuous immobile receptive presence (space). Light cannot *Live* without Darkness (i.e. space), Darkness is *Void* without light. Each necessarily includes and is included in the other.

As William Wordsworth once declared:

'In nature, everything is distinct, yet nothing is defined into absolute, independent singleness'.

And so it is that when all is in the flowing mutuality of energy and space, any kind of mathematics or science that either excludes space from matter as a dimensionless point of mass, or conflates space with matter as One and the same self-contained 'Whole', entire of it self—cannot make natural sense. Truly natural numbers and geometric figures both include and are included in space: they are never 'alone' or 'All One'.

Now I'd like to introduce some observations that helped to reveal this radically different perception of individual and collective identity to me, through showing how fungi are capable of sustainable growth in circumstances where their supplies of energy vary.

The 'mushrooms and toadstools', like the 'magpie ink cap', below, which our superficial view of things might deceive us into thinking is 'the whole fungus' is, in reality, no more 'all there is' to a fungus than an apple is all of an apple tree!

As with a 'star' of film or stage, behind the scenes of that outward appearance is an extraordinary, hidden production team that does all the hard work of gathering in the energy required to make it possible. This is what is known as the 'mycelium' of the fungus, a collective organization of microscopic, branching tubes called 'hyphae', which grow from their tips in a radiating pattern. Here is a view of the pattern formed when the mycelium of the magpie ink cap is cultured in an array of alternating, energy-rich and energy-scarce localities:-

What we are witnessing here is the ability of a *dynamic* living organization to change its pattern of growth in direct response to its neighbourhood. In conditions of abundance it multiplies; in conditions of scarcity it conserves and redistributes what it already has in the process of preparing and exploring for more to come its way. Unlike our current, divisive social and economic systems that are based on abstract perceptions of space and boundaries, *it does not borrow what it hasn't got from a future that hasn't come in order to gain a competitive advantage over its rivals!*

Isn't there a very simple lesson in this for human organizations? That is:

## *In Naturally Sustainable Organizations, Life is a Gift of Energy to be Received, Sustained and Passed on in Natural Relay*

If we look a little closer, at the microscopic, branching hyphal tubes themselves, we can see how their ability literally to 'club together' and 'pool resources' in order to produce a 'mushroom' depends on the capacity of their dynamic boundaries to grow towards one another, make contact and then dissolve to open up internal spatial communication channels. Flow within and between these channels is then regulated by valve-like partitions, known as septa, with central holes that can be blocked or unblocked. As illustrated in the following time-lapse sequence, shown clockwise from top left:-

But there is yet another ability that is vital to the ability of the mycelium sustainably to locate, gather in, conserve and redistribute sources of energy. This is their ability to degenerate and die in the process of 'passing on' the gift of life to others, as illustrated in the next time-lapse sequence of the mycelium of the sulphur tuft fungus growing out through the 'desert' of intervening soil between one source of nutrients (a small block of wood, in this case) to another small block of wood:

The vitality of death and decay to the opening up of new possibilities for life is illustrated in the painting below of a dying elm tree and the multitude of life forms that inhabit and supersede it.

Without death, life as a manifestation of natural energy flow stalls. In Nature, death feeds life, not the other way round. And where energy is the currency of life, the abstract economic notion of growth in excess of available resources by borrowing from the future is unsustainable.

This brings me to consider how evolutionary diversification arises through a dynamic transformational process of natural inclusion of each in the other, NOT, as envisaged by Darwinian selection theory, through the competitive elimination of one by another falsely perceived as an opponent of self:

I call the painting below, 'Future Present', and it is indeed intended to convey a 'Perception of the Future' in which the 'Present' is not a definitive line or 'cut', drawn between Past and Future, but a continual 'bringing of past into the coming of future in the process of natural energy flow.

The evolutionary diversification of life is here perceived as a fluid dynamic process of cumulative energetic transformation of each in others' co-creative influence, over vastly differing scales from microcosm to macrocosm. It cannot be prescribed or contained in a rigidly defined box of genetic information alone, frozen in discontinuous time and space.

The ancient idea of a Great Chain of Being or Hierarchy, reaching down via the utter perfection of God as a Judgmental Figure to the dominion of Superior Man over Inferior Man over Inferior Nature still holds a powerful sway over our human attitudes towards one another and our natural neighbourhood. It even persists in the Darwinian notion of 'selection' as the preservation of favoured races in the struggle for life: an external judgmental agency views Nature as a set of discrete objects and decides which ones are good or not good enough to survive. Almighty Authority sits atop of a pyramid of numbers and views the pitiful masses beneath in a pitiless way that takes no account of what it is actually like to live amongst them, within their natural neighbourhood.

My following poem describes this situation:

**The Humility of the Valley**

Life doesn't strive

To secure its foundation

Upon the rocky serrations of the High-minded

Where Men build castles in the air

To furnish that false sense of superiority

Which comes from the pretence

Of overlooking all around

To the edge of infinity

Life thrives

In the seclusion of the valleys

Where dampness accumulates

In the earthy humidity

Of humility

Warmly tucked in

To the bed of sea and land

Rich with variety

Exuding

Intruding

Out and into the cosiness

Of each lovingly enveloped

In the other's influence

Wisdom cannot be found

On peaks of adaptive fitness

Running with Red Queens

But only in that radiant depth

That reaches everywhere

Through the heart of somewhere

Alan Rayner, 2009

Symbolically, the story of the New Testament is that of an Authority Figure come down to Earth as a Lover amidst the flow of life instead of an independent and manipulative arbiter. In this new-found situation, a radical shift in attitude takes place, from one of judgemental condescension to one of tender care for the needs of self and others in the natural companionship of their natural neighbourhood, not a singular figure alone. Hierarchy of increasing independent perfection is subsumed by 'lowerarchy' of mutual needfulness. Self becomes receptive and attentive to what is needed to sustain life, by way of attuning with the availability and flow of sources of energy. Such attentive receptivity is also known as 'Gorm', which is associated with lively passion, compassion and responsiveness, the lack of which, 'Gormlessness', is associated with insolence, compliance, inconsideration and talking non-sense! The quest for hierarchical power leads not only to corruption but to gormlessness—not a desirable state of affairs by which to be governed, but which continues to dominate the aspirations and expirations of human leaders and followers alike!

To return to the abstract, definitive logic of Darwinian selection, what is ultimately envisaged is an incoherent universe of *virgin* territory (void) populated instantaneously by a random set of pre-existing independent occurrences perceived numerically and geometrically as atomistic whole objects, i.e. dimensionless 'point masses', devoid of space. For this original and ultimate 'chaos' to be called into *motion* and coherent *order* requires the intervention of external 'Force', which imposes the 'Laws of Nature' that, Sherlock Holmes-like, determine what is and is not permissible *and eliminate the latter*. Notice here the tautological conundrum that what is being eliminated is what is impossible in the first place! This gives rise to the 'Just So' stories of Darwinan Selection Theory, which explain away all the attributes of living creatures as the product of competitive adaptation to a pre-existing set of environmental specifications (a so-called 'niche' or 'box of limited space'). Tales of selfish genes as randomly generated tyrannical units of selection, monkeys randomly generating the works of Shakespeare on a typewriter given infinite time, blind watchmakers assembling bits and pieces into coherent order and the like are works of objectivistic science fiction, founded in fallacy. An insult to our natural intelligence, couched in digital machine code of one or none. It is these damaging impossibilities that really need to be eliminated from our understanding of human and natural evolution, not the rich variety of possibilities that arise through natural companionship.

So how, then, can an appreciative understanding and awareness of natural companionship help to transform the way we have become prone to think about the evolution of natural diversity and our human place in it? How can we live co-creatively, sustainably and compassionately without feeling forced to compete or co-operate with or against one another? How can we recognize the enormous variety of life-sustaining relationships that can develop between different neighbouring identities besides unity or division?

Essentially I think this understanding becomes possible as soon as we STOP thinking of ourselves and others as autonomous, free-willed objects subjected to external administration and judgement, and START thinking of ourselves and others as dynamic inhabitants and expressions of our natural neighbourhood, living within each other's mutual influence. We may then understand evolution as a cumulative, fluid process of mutual transformation within each other's company, not a selective sorting mechanism that judges goodness of fit to a preconceived ideal.

In other words, we need to move on from viewing evolution in terms of abstract selection by an extrinsic arbiter, to understanding evolution as an intrinsic process of *natural inclusion*, i.e. the fluid dynamics, co-creative transformation of all through all in receptive spatial neighbourhood. Underlying this move is a simple but fundamental shift in the way we perceive all natural, tangible phenomena, including ourselves, as local expressions of a mutually inclusive relationship between energy and space as distinctive informative and receptive presences. Once we make that move and embrace it in our minds, hearts and guts, the restrictive way of life that has been blighting our humanity for millennia radically transforms into one that makes a lot more natural sense. Instead of denigrating our natural companions as inferior, we recognize their vital place in the natural scheme of life, where it truly does take all kinds to co-create a viable, sustainable world.

As I once expressed it in the following poem and painting:

**The Hole in the Mole**

**I AM** the hole

That lives in a mole

That induces the mole

To dig the hole

That moves the mole

Through the earth

That forms a hill

That becomes a mountain

That reaches to sky

That pools in stars

And brings the rain

That the mountain collects

Into streams and rivers

That moisten the earth

That grows the grass

That freshens the air

That condenses to rain

That carries the water

That brings the mole

To Life

And as this appeal for the conservation of hedgehogs calls to us:

**Respite**

Finally, I want to offer some thought about how this new, natural perception of space and boundaries could allay our deeply entrenched fear of 'what's on the other side' through appreciating 'uncertainty' as 'the imagination of Nature' expressed in natural flow-form as an energetic inclusion of space.

Here are two quotes from famous naturalistic poets:

> The tree which moves some to tears of joy is in the eyes of others only a green thing which stands in the way. Some see nature as all ridicule and deformity…and some scarce see nature at all. But by the eyes of a man of imagination, nature is imagination itself
>
> William Blake

> Nature does not complete things. She is chaotic. Man must finish, and he does so by making a garden and building a wall
>
> Robert Frost

Perhaps by cherishing the uncertainty of the fathomless pool as a vital ingredient of life and love, instead of seeking to remove or wall off uncertainty, we can let go of our hankering to define things into an abstract, unnatural order. We can then learn to perceive and live in a more naturally attuned, passionate, compassionate and sustainable way than we currently do.

## Author Biography

**Alan Rayner** was born in Nairobi, Kenya in 1950. He obtained BA and PhD degrees in Natural Sciences at King's College, Cambridge and has been a Reader in Biology at the University of Bath.

Dr. Rayner is an enthusiastic natural scientist, artist and writer. He has published around 160 scientific articles, over 80 internet-downloadable essays, 7 formal academic books (including Degrees of Freedom – Living in Dynamic Boundaries, Imperial College Press, 1997 and NaturesScope – Unlocking Our Natural Empathy and Creativity, O Books, 2011), a 3 volume multi-author e-book and seven Internet-downloadable books. He has contributed to a variety of science- and art-based TV and radio broadcasts and presented many seminars and conference papers as well as co-convening several international conferences and symposia. Since spring 2000, he has been pioneering a fluid new way of understanding self-identity and ecological and evolutionary diversity and sustainability, based on 'natural inclusion' – the mutual inclusion of space and energy as receptive and informative presences in all distinguishable natural occurrences.

Alan was President of the British Mycological Society in 1998 and has been a BP Venture Research Fellow and a Miller Visiting Research Professor at the University of California, Berkeley. He became a Fellow of the Royal Society of Arts in 2010, and President of Bath Natural History Society in 2012. Further information and downloadable publications can be found via http://www.naturalinclusion.org and http://www.bestthinking.com.

# Index





J. McIntyre-Mills et al. (eds.), *Balancing Individualism and Collectivism*,
Contemporary Systems Thinking, DOI 10.1007/978-3-319-58014-2

MIX
Papier aus verantwortungsvollen Quellen
Paper from responsible sources
FSC® C105338

If you have any concerns about our products,
you can contact us on
**ProductSafety@springernature.com**

In case Publisher is established outside the EU,
the EU authorized representative is:
**Springer Nature Customer Service Center GmbH**
**Europaplatz 3, 69115 Heidelberg, Germany**

Printed by Libri Plureos GmbH
in Hamburg, Germany